The Editor

GORDON TESKEY is Francis Lee Higginson Professor of English Literature at Harvard University, where he teaches Renaissance poetry. He is the author of *Allegory and Violence*, *Delirious Milton*, *Spenserian Moments*, and *The Poetry of John Milton*, which was awarded the Christian Gauss Award for literary criticism. He has been a Guggenheim fellow and is an Honored Scholar of the Milton Society of America.

For a complete list of Norton Critical Editions, visit
wwnorton.com/nortoncriticals

A NORTON CRITICAL EDITION

John Milton
PARADISE LOST

AUTHORITATIVE TEXT
SOURCES AND BACKGROUNDS
CRITICISM

SECOND EDITION

Edited by

GORDON TESKEY
HARVARD UNIVERSITY

W. W. NORTON & COMPANY
Independent Publishers Since 1923

W. W. Norton & Company has been independent since its founding in 1923, when William Warder Norton and Mary D. Herter Norton first published lectures delivered at the People's Institute, the adult education division of New York City's Cooper Union. The Nortons soon expanded their program beyond the Institute, publishing books by celebrated academics from America and abroad. By mid-century, the two major pillars of Norton's publishing program—trade books and college texts—were firmly established. In the 1950s, the Norton family transferred control of the company to its employees, and today—with a staff of four hundred and a comparable number of trade, college, and professional titles published each year—W. W. Norton & Company stands as the largest and oldest publishing house owned wholly by its employees.

This title is printed on permanent paper containing 30 percent post-consumer waste recycled fiber.

Library of Congress Cataloging-in-Publication Data

Names: Milton, John, 1608-1674, author. | Teskey, Gordon, 1953- editor.
Title: Paradise lost : authoritative text, sources and backgrounds, criticism /
    John Milton ; edited by Gordon Teskey.
Description: Second edition. | New York, N.Y. : W. W. Norton & Company,
    [2020] | Series: A Norton critical edition
Identifiers: LCCN 2020010647 | **ISBN 9780393617085** (paperback ; alk.
    paper)
Subjects: LCSH: Bible. Genesis—History of Biblical events—Poetry. | Milton,
    John, 1608–1674. Paradise lost. | Adam (Biblical figure)—Poetry. | Eve
    (Biblical figure)—Poetry. | Fall of man in literature. | Fall of man—Poetry.
Classification: LCC PR3560.A2 T47 2020 | DDC 821/.4—dc23
LC record available at https://lccn.loc.gov/2020010647

W. W. Norton & Company, Inc., 500 Fifth Avenue, New York, N.Y. 10110
            www.wwnorton.com

W. W. Norton & Company Ltd., Castle House,
75/76 Wells Street, London W1T 3QT

1 2 3 4 5 6 7 8 9 0

This second edition of the Norton *Paradise Lost*
is dedicated to my mother,
Ann Camilla Teskey

Contents

Preface to the Second Edition

In this second edition of the Norton *Paradise Lost* the annotations and the Glossary have been revised. Notes have been added to the selection from Milton's *Reason of Church Government* and to *Areopagitica*, which is reproduced here in full. I have made some changes in the textual notes for which I am grateful to my late colleague Barbara Lewalski.

In the present edition half the selections of modern criticism are by women, whereas before the proportion was about one to three. More work has been included by scholars with non-Eurocentric, non-Christian, non-white, and non-hetero-normative perspectives— again, to the great enrichment of the field. I have used shorter selections to give students the widest possible view of Milton studies at the present time, hoping that some of these will entice students to look up the original works in their entirety. Specialized, scholarly notes in the original sources, except for notes essential to understanding the argument, have been removed.

My editorial principles remain the same, as explained in the preface to the first edition: modernized spelling; punctuation that is as light as possible, to preserve Milton's rapidity; and, in the notes, attention to syntax—that is, to the meaning and structure of Milton's complex, periodic sentences. This last is surprisingly absent from editions of *Paradise Lost* as far back as the eighteenth century. I hope the example will prompt future and better editors to take up questions of syntax and improve on my efforts. Proper nouns—that is, place-names, characters, and figures from classical and Near Eastern mythology—are explained in the Glossary. In general, the notes to the text of the poem address difficulties arising from the *combinations* of words, the Glossary difficulties arising from the *referents* of words. (See Roman Jakobson, "Two Aspects of Language and Two Types of Linguistic Aphasia," in *On Language*, ed. Linda R. Waugh and Monique Monville-Burston [Cambridge, Mass.: Harvard University Press, 1990], pp. 115–33.)

For many, the most striking changes in this edition will appear in the selection of contemporary criticism. From the beginning of the twenty-first century, Milton studies has seen an upsurge in challenges to his views and to those of more traditional critics devoted to explaining the poet's intentions. This development has had a most salutary effect on the perspectives of scholars in the field, including those of the traditional critics. More important in the long run, this widening inclusiveness is winning for the poet an increasingly global audience beyond the English-speaking world. Many of these readers of Milton are attracted by an emerging view of him not as the untroubled high priest of Christian humanist ideology but rather as a poet struggling with and against that ideology in the face of a rapidly changing world. It is from the conflict between these incompatible viewpoints, and not from the simple desire to represent one or the other, that the energy of Milton's poetry is generated. He stands midway between Dante and Goethe. That is because, as I have had occasion to say in the past, Milton is the last major poet in the European cultural tradition for whom the act of creation is centered in God and the first in whom the act of creation begins to find its center in the human.

In a field as rich as Milton studies it is impossible to include every important scholar or even every distinct point of view. I am painfully aware of omissions. But my purpose has been to capture the widest possible range of views as the field exists now, not to provide an anthology, in Matthew Arnold's phrase, of the best that has been thought and said in the world regarding Milton.

For advice on critical selections and annotations I thank Professors Jennifer Lewin, Jennifer A. Newton, and Melissa E. Sanchez. For Hebrew and Aramaic expertise I thank Professor Jason P. Rosenblatt, editor of the Norton Critical Edition of *Milton's Selected Poetry and Prose*, also from Norton, and David Schwerdt, my former student and gifted teacher of elementary Hebrew, now a Ph.D. candidate in physics. I give special thanks to my doctoral student Elizabeth Weckhurst, whose wise assistance with the selection of criticism was indispensable. I am grateful to my colleagues in the Harvard Department of English for fellowship and high example. Shortcomings of this edition will not be due to any of these generous people and should be laid at my door.

It is a pleasure once again to express my admiration for and thanks to Carol Bemis, Rachel Goodman, and the staff of W. W. Norton & Company, including the most conscientious and erudite copyeditor, Alice Falk. The Milton Society of America has sustained scholarly work on the poet for the past seventy years, during half of which I have been a proud member. I would also thank the members, past and present, of the Northeast Milton Seminar. I have never come away from its gatherings without having learned more than I could have imagined from scholars whose passion for truth reflects that of the poet himself. My greatest debt is to my wife, Anna, for loving help and wise advice.

A day seldom goes by without my reflecting with gratitude on the students it has been my privilege to teach, now over almost four decades. Their enthusiasm and interest has been a source of inspiration and pleasure in the study of poetry, which is always a shared and collaborative enterprise. I feel the same toward students in the future, most of whom I shall never see; and also toward students today who are far from my classroom but with whom I hope to connect through this edition of *Paradise Lost*. It has been prepared with all of you constantly in mind.

Gordon Teskey
Cambridge, Massachusetts

Preface and Acknowledgments
to the First Edition

This edition of Milton's *Paradise Lost* is intended for the general reader and for students encountering the poem for the first time. Spelling and punctuation have been modernized, the latter, however, as I shall explain in a moment, within limits imposed by Milton's syntax. The few words whose spelling probably reflects how Milton pronounced them, for example, *contemned, sovran,* and *hunderd,* are not, in my view, different enough to warrant retaining. But I have retained *heighth* (which is spelled *highth* in the early editions), *stupendious,* and *amarantine.* Speeches are introduced with a colon but are not enclosed in quotation marks, which are used only at a second remove—that is, when a speaker in the poem is quoting someone else. In a few places I have indented to make extra verse paragraphs.

I have capitalized outright personifications such as *Death* and, when appropriate, rhetorical personifications such as *Shame* (9.1058). What I would term *vestigial personifications* are frequent in *Paradise Lost,* especially before the Fall, when created beings such as the Sun and the Ocean seem to oscillate between the states of being an object and being a person: "The Sun that light imparts to all receives / From all his alimental recompense / In humid exhalations and at ev'n / Sups with the Ocean" (5.423–26). The most celebrated moment in which vestigial personifications appear is when Eve eats the forbidden fruit: "she plucked, she eat: / Earth felt the wound, and Nature from her seat / Sighing through all her works gave signs of woe / That all was lost" (9.781–84). See 3.710–13 and note.

Place-names such as *Heaven, Hell,* and *Earth* are capitalized; but the *heavens* within the created universe are not; nor is the *earth* when it is named as a thing and not as a person or place. Especially important terms, such as *Man* (but not *mankind*) and *Adversary* (a more literal rendering of the Hebrew meaning of Satan's name), have been capitalized. The somewhat old-fashioned practice of capitalizing terms referring to God—*the Father, the Son, the Spirit, th' Almighty, Anointed King, Messiah*—as well as pronouns referring to God (*Thou, Thee, Him*) is useful in a poem in which God is on a different level of being from other characters. But for the sake of clarity I have often put in lowercase pronouns referring to the Son. And when the capitalization of pronouns of God becomes obtrusive, for example, when He is speaking of Himself, I have reverted to lowercase.

The syntax of *Paradise Lost* is looser and more complex, and the clauses more subtly blended with one another, than fully modern punctuation allows. The stricter logic of modern punctuation can have a flattening effect on Milton's verse at some moments, forcing the sense in one direction alone when two possibilities should be held in suspense for a time.

The punctuation of the two editions of *Paradise Lost* to appear in Milton's lifetime has, in my judgment, no authority. The supposition that the original punctuation reflects the poet's intentions has caused a fashion for centaur-like editions of *Paradise Lost* in which the spelling is modernized and the heavy, often misleading seventeenth-century punctuation retained. In Milton's day punctuation was more the concern of copyists and printers than of poets, still less of blind poets. In a letter to a European correspondent (Peter Heimbach, August 15, 1666) Milton mentions as exceptional that the person taking dictation does not know how to spell or to punctuate, forcing him to do so himself. Clearly, specifying punctuation was not something Milton usually did. In the only sample we have of unrhymed narrative verse in Milton's hand—the Trinity manuscript *Comus*—the punctuation is extremely light: commas are infrequent and in many places even periods are omitted. Milton was formed as a poet by the discipline of composing Latin verse. He would have believed that all significant relationships between the words in a poem should inhere in those words and their syntactical arrangement. I have therefore punctuated as lightly as possible, that is, only where for lack of a comma the reader would take a wrong turn and be forced to go back.

Light punctuation is also crucial for hearing the rhythm. Milton's poems are not so much works on the page, meant to be interpreted as texts, as they are structures of sound meant to be heard, to be listened to, even when one is silently reading. *Paradise Lost* is modeled on the epic poems of Homer and Virgil, which were intended for memorization and oral recitation, and Milton's verse is strongly influenced by Greek and Latin oratory, which was written to be publicly declaimed. (There is as much Cicero as Virgil in the fabric of *Paradise Lost*.) It is this declamatory character of *Paradise Lost* that prompted Samuel Johnson to call it "that wonderful performance," and that is what *Paradise Lost* is: a wonderful performance, which the reader recaptures by listening to the poem as physical effort and physical sound. The one piece of advice I would offer the first-time reader of *Paradise Lost* is to take the poem in as a performance, not as a riddle.

The poetic line in *Paradise Lost* is generally (though not without exception; see 2.27 n.) ten syllables long. But a considerable amount of elision and contraction is needed, especially for North American speakers of English, to recapture the rhythm intended. I have given in the notes some help with pronunciation, but the reader will soon become accustomed to such things as *the* being contracted when it appears before nouns beginning with a vowel (*th' Almighty*), *Heaven* being pronounced in one syllable (*Heav'n*), the letters *ie*, as in *disobedience*, being pronounced like a *j* (dis-o-bee-jence), and so on. All such indications and helps are approximate. Sometimes (although not as often as might be supposed) there is more than one way to say a line. In such cases I have indicated the way that to my ear sounds best. There are no hard and fast rules for the scansion of Milton's verse, but the general pattern, to the reader who cares about such things, soon becomes clear.

Growing to understand *Paradise Lost* is a lifelong adventure. The same may be said of the rhythms of *Paradise Lost:* appreciating them fully is an ongoing project, not a question of getting everything right the first time. Nor is the rhythm of *Paradise Lost* confined to the single verse line, as it most often is, for example, in the poetry of Pope and even of Chaucer. Like Shakespeare's later verse, Milton's lines are heavily enjambed (running on without a pause at the end of the line), opening them to the longer and more complex rhythms of the glorious sentences of *Paradise Lost*. (The verse paragraph has no prosodic significance.) Developing longer rhythms, like ocean swells, than are possible in the single verse line is Milton's most important technical contribution to later verse in English, notably that of the English Romantics, especially Wordsworth and Keats, but also that of American poets from Walt Whitman to A. R. Ammons.

The notes in this edition are intended to elucidate difficulty, not to interpret the poem. As a rule, I have given biblical and classical sources only when they are important enough to be quoted. For these quotations I have used the Authorized (King James) Version of the Bible and have translated the classical sources myself. Latin and Greek verbs referred to in the notes are given in the first-person singular. The texture of Milton's verse is thickened by an extraordinary number of exotic place-names (Milton is the first truly global poet of the modern world), not all of which need to be looked up immediately. A glossary has been added to make it possible to keep the notes within compass and to separate, so far as is possible, the semantic and syntactic axes of difficulty. Semantic difficulties are dealt with mostly in the glossary, and problems of syntax, the heart of Milton's verse, are explained in the notes. I have also used the glossary to give fuller accounts of such things as Eden, Angels, Chaos, Typhon, Sin, Death, and the Son. References to Milton's prose are from *The Complete*

Prose Works of John Milton, 7 vols., ed. Don M. Wolfe et al. (New Haven, Conn.: Yale University Press, 1953–80), abbreviated as *YP*.

It is a pleasure to acknowledge the support of the Department of English at Cornell University, the Harvard Department of English and American Literature and Language, and the Harvard College Faculty of Arts and Sciences. It is also a pleasure to acknowledge the enthusiasm and patience (hard virtues to reconcile) of the staff of W. W. Norton & Company, especially Carol Bemis. I am indebted, as all editors of Milton are, to a tradition of scholarship and editorial work on the poet that goes back three hundred years. The spirit of that tradition is very much alive today in the community of Miltonists. For valuable discussion on textual matters relating to seventeenth-century poetry I thank Roy Flannagan, John Leonard, Jennifer Lewin, Charles Mahoney, Arthur Marotti, and John T. Shawcross. I have benefited from the editions of Flannagan, Leonard, and Shawcross as well as those of Douglas Bush, Gordon Campbell, Alastair Fowler, and Christopher Ricks. I should like particularly to acknowledge my Milton teacher in graduate school, H. R. MacCallum, and two distinguished Miltonists at Cornell whom it was my privilege to have as colleagues, Mary Ann Radzinowicz, who has taught us so much about the scope and power of Milton's mind, and the late Scott Elledge, the editor of the first Norton Critical Edition of *Paradise Lost*. As always in matters concerning English poetry, my greatest debt is to William Blissett.

Four former students and one present student have assisted me with this edition: my former doctoral student at Cornell, Professor Joseph Campana; Elise Cavaney, who studied Milton with me at Cornell and has worked with me ever since on this edition; Michael Zacchilli, who studied seventeenth-century poetry with me at Harvard; and my present student at Harvard, Yulia Ryzhik, without whose dedication and accuracy this project would still be far from complete. Work on this project began in discussions of the text of *Paradise Lost* in a reading course I did at Cornell with Ellen Devine. I wish to thank also the many students who have read Milton with me over the past twenty years. Although I am responsible for any errors and misjudgments, it may be said of this edition that students, to use the words of the publisher of Shakespeare's sonnets, are its "only begetters."

GORDON TESKEY
Cambridge, Massachusetts

Introduction

The Life of John Milton

John Milton was born on December 9, 1608, in London, into an upper-middle-class, deeply religious Puritan family. The family home, and the father's place of business, was in Bread Street, Cheapside, where the well-to-do lived, in the westerly part of the old city, on Ludgate Hill. Just steps away, dominating the neighborhood and indeed the entire city, stood the huge cathedral of Saint Paul's, one of the largest in Europe. To the east, downstream on the Thames, was London Bridge, which backed up the river to form a broad expanse of water. Below the bridge, farther downstream, lay the massive fortress of the Tower. To the west were the Inns of Court, Charing Cross, and, around the bend in the Thames, the City of Westminster, with Westminster Abbey, the Court, and the Houses of Parliament. In Milton's day London was still a walled, medieval city of narrow lanes, muddy streets, and mostly wooden buildings. But it was already becoming one of the most important trading centers in the world, and what was once open country between it and Westminster was rapidly filling up. One could still walk out of the city into the countryside to the north. At a dramatic moment in *Paradise Lost*, when Satan first catches sight of Eve alone, Milton briefly diverts our attention from the action at hand, comparing Satan's taking pleasure in Paradise, and especially in the sight of Eve, to the pleasure of walking out of the city on a summer morning:

> As one who long in populous city pent
> Where houses thick and sewers annoy the air
> Forth issuing on a summer's morn to breathe
> Among the pleasant villages and farms
> Adjoined, from each thing met conceives delight—
> The smell of grain or tedded grass, or kine
> Or dairy, each rural sight, each rural sound—
> If chance with nymph-like step fair virgin pass
> What pleasing seemed, for her now pleases more,
> She most, and in her look sums all delight.
>
> (9.445–54)

Queen Elizabeth I had died in 1603 and James I was on the throne. The tensions between the king and Parliament, and between the Anglican Church and the Puritans, which would lead to civil war and the execution of James's son, Charles I, were already great. As always in times of trouble, literature flourished. The Authorized (King James) Version of the Bible would appear in 1611, Shakespeare was writing his last plays, John Donne's poems were circulating in manuscript, and Ben Jonson and his literary entourage were still gathering at the Mermaid Tavern on Bread Street to drink its superior (and more expensive) wine.

Milton was educated at home and at Saint Paul's school, beside the cathedral, and later at Christ's College, Cambridge. Saint Paul's was perhaps the best school in England at the time and excelled in humanistic studies, especially the teaching of Latin and Greek. By the time he went to Cambridge, at age seventeen, Milton had read an impressive range of ancient authors and was accomplished at Latin composition in prose and verse. Milton's father, John, a successful scrivener (a profession that combined money lending, investing, and drawing up contracts), was a musician and a composer of some repute. In most middle-class homes before the age of radio and television, music was a regular part of family life, but it was exceptionally so in Milton's home. The poet played the organ and the viola da gamba, and even in old age he sang.[1] The many descriptions of music in *Paradise Lost* betray deep passion for it as well as exceptional knowledge.

In addition to sending his son to an expensive and challenging school, Milton's father hired tutors to instruct the boy in subjects not taught at Saint Paul's, among which were modern languages, especially French and Italian. Hebrew was taught to the senior boys at Saint Paul's, but Milton might have been tutored in it earlier, at home. By the time he went to Cambridge he was proficient in at least three languages other than English and expert in two, Latin and Greek. So avid was the boy for his studies that from the age of twelve his father arranged for a servant to sit up with him (no doubt keeping the candles trimmed) while he studied until midnight.

While at Cambridge Milton wrote much Latin poetry and, at age twenty-one, his first undoubted masterpiece in English, "Ode on the Morning of Christ's Nativity." In this poem we see already formed, though in brief outline, the human and cosmic concerns of Milton's mature poems, including a complete Christian vision of history. The Nativity Ode also shows Milton's lifelong preoccupation with using classical poetic forms to express Christian events and ideas. This artistic success confirmed Milton in his ambition to rival the Greek

---

1. The biographer John Aubrey said, "He would be cheerful even in his gout fits, and sing."

and Latin poets of antiquity by applying what he had learned from them to the Christian vision of history. He could not have known then that this ambition would not be fulfilled until he was in his mid-fifties. He did know that it would take him some time. In a sonnet written for his twenty-fourth birthday (that is, upon completing his "three-and-twentieth year"), Milton expresses his concern that at that advanced age he had as yet achieved very little: "my late spring no bud or blossom show'th." But he concludes with a remarkably mature statement of confidence in himself and in God's will:

> Yet be it less or more, or soon or slow,
> It shall be still in strictest measure even
> To that same lot, however mean or high,
> Toward which Time leads me, and the will of Heav'n.
> All is, if I have grace to use it so,
> As ever in my great Task-Master's eye.

After taking his B.A. in March 1630, Milton remained at Cambridge two more years, took his M.A. in July 1632, and then embarked on another six years of arduous private study in the country, to which his parents had retired, first at Hammersmith, upstream from London on the Thames, and then at Horton, in Buckinghamshire. Both places were near London, which the poet visited often to buy books and to see friends. The beautiful poems "L'Allegro" (the cheerful man) and "Il Penseroso" (the thoughtful, melancholy man) were likely written at this time.

Milton's parents intended him (and he had shared the intention) to enter the priesthood in the Anglican Church. But disillusionment with the conservatism, worldliness, and increasing authoritarianism of the church caused him to abandon that course and to devote himself exclusively to poetry and learning—not without causing his father some anxiety. In addition to acquiring immense erudition and making the by no means easy transition from brilliant student to serious scholar, Milton composed two major poetical works: the court drama, or masque, subsequently called *Comus* and the funeral elegy "Lycidas," the most intellectually intense and emotionally powerful short poem (or shorter poem: 193 lines) in the English language. He was not yet thirty years old.

To round out his education (still at his father's expense) Milton departed, with a manservant, for what would prove to be a fifteen-month tour of the European continent, passing almost all of that time in Italy, the faded home of the Renaissance. (It was in Paris, however, a city with a brilliant future rather than a brilliant past, that Milton met the great jurist and theorist of international law Hugo Grotius, who was also a poet.) Milton made intellectual and literary friends in Florence, Rome, and Naples; and while in Florence he visited (in nearby Arcetri) the most important man in Europe at the time, Galileo, whom Milton recalls in *Areopagitica* and mentions on more than one occasion in *Paradise Lost*. (Indeed, it can be said that Galileo is implicitly mentioned in *Paradise Lost* every time the order of the cosmos is seen or discussed, as so often it is.)

When he arrived in Naples Milton was befriended by a person who, although they knew each other for only several weeks, had a decisive influence on him. This was the seventy-eight-year-old Giovanni Manso, the marquis of Villa, who recognized the quality of Milton's genius and cultivated the poet's friendship with many marks of respect. Manso was venerable in Milton's eyes because he had been the patron and biographer of the famous Italian epic poet Torquato Tasso, whom Manso cared for at the end of that poet's life. In his *Jerusalem Liberated* (*Gerusalemme liberata*, 1581), Tasso demonstrated two things that would prove crucially important to Milton: that an epic poem in the tradition of Homer and Virgil could be written in the modern age and that the specific conventions of the epic poem—set battles and single combats, noble speeches and debates, elaborate descriptions and similes, supernatural interventions and omens, and, not the least of these, invocations of the muse—could be adapted to a Christian subject.

In a Latin poem addressed to Manso, Milton discloses his ambition to write an epic poem. Although uncertain as to subject, Milton was considering a patriotic work on King Arthur, following the example of Spenser's *Faerie Queene*. As Manso conducted Milton to places of interest in the area around Naples, it is inconceivable they would not have visited the spectacular site of ancient Cumae, with its temple of Apollo and its mysterious underground passages of pre-Roman Samnite construction—the haunt, in antiquity, of the Cumaean Sibyl. It is there that Virgil has his hero Aeneas descend to the underworld to receive a prophetic vision of the future of Rome. That episode would be transformed into the mountaintop vision of history that the angel Michael accords Adam in the final two books of *Paradise Lost*. Of perhaps still greater significance to the future author of *Paradise Lost* is the visible presence, southeast of Naples, of Mount Vesuvius, which with Mount Etna, in Sicily, is one of two active volcanoes in Europe. In this region of intense geologic activity there had been two major earthquakes, and an eruption of Vesuvius, in the previous decade. Milton knew the ancient legend that Zeus pinned the monster Typhon beneath Etna (and, Pindar adds, the "sea-enclosed cliffs above Cuma"), where he now heaves in his torment, vomiting lava and fire. (See Glossary, TYPHON.) Milton would situate his Hell away from the earth, far off in chaos, but his explosive, sublime description of it (and chaos) would be inspired by the ancient authors' accounts of this region between Naples and Sicily.

Milton's plans to visit Sicily, rich in Greek antiquities, and to sail to Greece itself were cut short by the news of dangerously escalating religious and political tensions at home. The political left (as we would now call it), the English Puritans and Scottish Presbyterians, was, with growing effectiveness, challenging the legitimacy of the Anglican Church, which became, with the support of King Charles I, more uncompromisingly hierarchical and dogmatic in response to that challenge. When Parliament was recalled after an absence of a decade, it shook the authority of King Charles I, who had been attempting throughout that period to rule, and to collect taxes, without it. This "Short Parliament," as it was called, was soon dismissed. But political circumstances and desperation for money made it impossible for the king's personal rule to continue any longer. The momentous "Long Parliament," which would soon be in arms against the king, was summoned.

Milton's love of liberty, his English patriotism, his hatred of tyranny and especially of political control over spiritual matters, made him the ally of the Presbyterians, who dominated the Long Parliament. But he would eventually find them, as successful revolutionaries often are, more rigidly authoritarian than what they overthrew. Their hypocrisy would inspire the sonnet "On the New Forcers of Conscience Under the Long Parliament" with its hard-hitting final line: "New Presbyter is but old Priest writ large."

Some years later Milton would say, when explaining his early return from Italy, that he thought it wrong for him to be traveling for his personal improvement while his countrymen were fighting for liberty at home. Still, he was in Italy, and his return was unhurried. Traveling north, he passed several months in Rome and Florence to consult works in the Vatican and Laurentian libraries and to confer with learned men.

After crossing the Apennine Mountains, which run down the spine of the Italian peninsula, and traveling northeast through Bologna and Ferrara, Milton passed a month in Venice, where he added musical scores (Venetian music was the most advanced in Europe at that time) to the many books he had already collected. He then traveled west on the rich Lombardy plain to Verona (with its huge Roman amphitheater) and the great city of Milan before heading north on the arduous journey across the Alps to Switzerland and along Lake Leman to Geneva. The journey across the Alps, which was no easy undertaking in those days, and along the beautiful Lake Leman must have been thrilling to Milton, who had a passion for geography, for the complex, physical reality of the earth, which is everywhere apparent in *Paradise Lost* and is equaled by no other great poet. The mountains and plateaus of central Asia, the torrid sands of the Sahara, the icebergs and violent winds of the Arctic, and the dangerous sea route around Africa into the Indian Ocean are all vividly imagined.

Geneva was then the center of the Protestant Reformation in Europe. It was there Milton met and spent much time with the Protestant theologian Giovanni Diodati, the uncle of his boyhood friend Charles Diodati. Milton had probably already learned by letter of the death of his friend, for whom he would write a moving Latin elegy. In that elegy he again reflects on his ambition to write an epic poem on an English theme. Although he enjoyed Italy immensely, Milton must have felt relieved to be again among people whose religious views were close to his own. In the autograph book of the humanist scholar Camillo Cerdogni (it was fashionable in those days to collect samples of the handwriting of eminent and potentially eminent persons), Milton modified a verse from Horace, wittily altering its original meaning. Criticizing travel, Horace said that those who travel across the seas change their skies but not their minds, which remain as dull as when they left. Milton says that when he travels overseas he changes his skies—the skies of England for those of Italy—but never his mind. The trip north through France and home to England soon followed. Milton had fallen in love with Italy, with its language, its learning, its brilliant culture (perhaps especially its music), its affable scholars, and its astonishing sights and sounds. But his exposure in Italy to the oppressive spirit of the Counter-Reformation confirmed Milton in his hostility to Roman Catholicism and in his determination to oppose the Romanizing tendencies of the Anglican Church at home.

The next twenty years were tumultuous for Milton, as they were for England, which was first convulsed by a civil war that was atrociously destructive of human life and then governed by a regime that never achieved the one thing indispensable to a government if it is to last: legitimacy. The king was executed in 1649. The Long Parliament was reduced to a more compliant "Rump Parliament" (as it was derisively called) and then to a still smaller "Barebones Parliament" of religious fanatics, which would give way in turn to the "Protectorate" of Oliver Cromwell. Milton took up a means of livelihood as a schoolmaster; married seventeen-year-old Mary Powell (he was thirty-three at the time); became engaged in the bitter controversies over church government, which were, in effect, the opening salvos of the English civil war; was abandoned by his wife; wrote some remarkable works in prose (including *Reason of Church Government; Areopagitica*, the great work on intellectual freedom; and the forward-looking, but at the time notorious, pamphlets on divorce); and was reconciled with his wife. With her he had three daughters—Anne, Mary, and Deborah—and a son, John, who died when he was just over a year old. He also published *Poems of Mr. John Milton* (1646, dated 1645

because the year then changed in March), containing most of his
Latin and English poems up to that date. The collection also contains a Greek epigram and a translation into Greek of Psalm 114,
an early experiment (Milton did it as a teenager) in grafting the
style of the heroic epic onto the subject matter of the Hebrew scriptures. The subject of Psalm 114 was a favorite of Milton's: the exodus of the Hebrew nation from bondage in Egypt and its joyous
entry into the Promised Land. It would be Milton's metaphor for
the English Revolution.

Early in 1652, after some years of weakening eyesight, Milton
became totally blind. Only months later his wife, Mary, died after
the birth of their daughter Deborah. Thus it was that by the middle
of 1652, little more than a decade after returning to England young,
brilliant, ardently idealistic and hopeful, and with the best education
possible at that time (and equal to the best at any time), Milton found
himself widowed and blind with three daughters to raise, the oldest
of whom was six. For a devoted teacher and an accurate scholar, one
who had worked all his life with his eyes, Milton might well have
thought that his education and talents were now useless and his
ambition to serve God with his pen an unrealizable dream from his
past. Sonnet 19, "When I Consider How My Light Is Spent," is a
response to precisely these thoughts. Milton speaks first, with moving force, of the poetic talent that lies now useless within him, and
he asks, "Doth God exact day labor, light denied?" But to this the
voice of Patience answers from a place deeper within him:

> God doth not need
> Either man's work or His own gifts. Who best
> Bear His mild yoke, they serve Him best. His state
> Is kingly: thousands at His bidding speed
> And post o'er land and ocean without rest.
> They also serve who only stand and wait.

From 1649, after the execution of King Charles I, which he
defended in *The Tenure of Kings and Magistrates*, Milton had
worked for the new, revolutionary government as secretary for foreign
tongues to the Council of State. It was in this capacity that his
energies were absorbed, and his weak eyesight destroyed, defending
the new English Commonwealth against covert royalist attacks
from within and open attacks from abroad. He became famous for
his responses to the latter, fulminating across Europe in brilliant
Latin prose. Inevitably, his duties were relaxed after he went blind
(that they continued at all shows how indispensable he was), and he
was accorded an assistant in his work, the poet Andrew Marvell.

In 1656 Milton married Katherine Woodcock. Both she and the
child she bore to him died in 1658. She is remembered (if the

sonnet is addressed to her and not, as some scholars think, to Milton's first wife, Mary) in the moving sonnet 23, "Methought I Saw My Late-Espousèd Saint." If the sonnet is addressed to Katherine, it is particularly interesting to read when one recalls that Milton never saw her. He says that in sleep he thought he *saw* his wife come back to him from the grave. Her face, he thought, was veiled, and yet (as can happen in sleep) her entire person shone with more sweetness and love than could ever be expressed in a face:

> Her face was veiled, yet to my fancied sight
> Love, sweetness, goodness in her person shined
> So clear as in no face with more delight.
> But O! as to embrace me she inclined
> I waked, she fled, and day brought back my night.

With the death of his second wife the catastrophes of Milton's middle years were far from over. Later in 1658 the death of Oliver Cromwell, the brilliant general of the later phase of the civil war, the leader of the Council of State after the war, the perpetrator of brutal atrocities in Ireland, and, at his death, the reluctant, baffled dictator of the English Commonwealth, set in motion events that would lead, by 1660, to the Restoration: the triumphal return from the Continent of Charles II, the son of the executed Charles I. The mood of most of the English at Cromwell's death is reflected in the diary of John Evelyn, who says of the funeral (at which Milton, Marvell, and Dryden were official mourners) that it was "the joyfullest funeral that ever I saw for there was none that cried but dogs, which the soldiers hooted away." Whatever his shortcomings (old Puritans, including Milton, were shocked by the gay life at court), Charles II's return was immensely popular.

The Restoration was not so much the triumph of royal authority, however, which would henceforth be much more restricted, especially after the "Glorious Revolution" (*glorious* because it was bloodless) of 1688, as it was a triumph of representative, parliamentary rule. The Rump Parliament, itself only recently reinstated after its dismissal by Cromwell, was diluted when the members excluded in Pride's Purge (1648) were recalled, fatally weakening republican resistance to the return of the king. In his diary, Samuel Pepys describes the bonfires and roasting of pork rumps on the London street corners, celebrating the end of the Rump and also the end of the petty, interfering despotism of Cromwell's major generals. The revolution in which Milton had placed his hopes, comparing the English struggle for liberty to the Israelites' escape from Egypt and their journey through the wilderness to the Promised Land, had come to its inevitable, ignominious end. Yet the principles by which Milton was guided in defending the English Revolution, even in its last, indefensible stages, were important for the future of English liberalism and would also inspire the fathers of the American Revolution.

We do not know for certain when Milton began composing *Paradise Lost*, but sometime in 1658 may be supposed. In that year (as we saw) Milton's second wife (and their child) died and the political stability Cromwell had imposed on the realm, under the Protectorate, began to fail with the Protector himself. The moral questions of *Paradise Lost* cannot be reduced to narrowly political ones, but the political adventure of the interregnum—the period between the reigns of Charles I and Charles II—was the cause to which Milton devoted himself and for which he sacrificed his eyesight. It gave him the experience of the world—of practical affairs, of sharp conflict, of the conduct of people under intense responsibility and pressure—that is necessary for a poet to be great.

Why the revolution failed, why the English chose "a captain back for Egypt," in the stern phrase of *The Ready and Easy Way* (the courageous appeal Milton published—twice—in the months before the Restoration), is the question that inspired him and drove him on in the composition of *Paradise Lost*. The question is framed in the widest terms possible. The failure of the English people at their supreme moment of opportunity opened a radical reflection— *radical* in the sense of going to the root of the matter—on the meaning of history itself and the place of human liberty in it. History begins at the Fall, when Adam and Eve lose the perfect liberty they had in the garden of Eden. If God's plan for history is the increase of human liberty, partly by human means, partly by divine aid, what causes a nation to surrender its liberty? Is it cowardice or the desire for physical comfort, or both? To pose such questions is only to raise a deeper question: "What is evil?" That is the mysterious question of *Paradise Lost*. Milton's dogmatic answer—*disobedience of God*—never silences the question or dispels the aura of mystery it raises. That is so largely because the question is embodied in one of the grandest characters in English literature: Milton's rebel angel, his seductive antagonist, Satan.

In Milton's Satan we do not see the horrible figure of the medieval imagination, chewing and excreting the damned in Hell. We see the darkened splendor and the reserved, explosive power of an archangel: "He above the rest / In shape and gesture proudly eminent / Stood like a tower" (1.589–91). We may or may not agree with Baudelaire that this power, hardened by Satan's resolute vengefulness yet softened by his deep unhappiness, makes him "the most perfect type of virile beauty" (cited in Armand Himy, *John Milton*, pp. 480–81). But we cannot help being drawn to and fascinated by the commander who is so moved at the sight of his defeated companions in revolt: "Thrice he assayed [to speak] and thrice, in spite of scorn, / Tears such as angels weep burst forth" (1.619–20). Nor can we fail to be impressed when he exclaims, "Better to reign in Hell than serve in Heaven!" (1.263). Only gradually does Satan become what he is when we last see him, in the annual punishment to which he and the other devils are subjected, chewing the fruit that turns to dust and ashes in his mouth: "A monstrous serpent on his belly prone" (10.514).

Years before beginning *Paradise Lost*, indeed not long after he returned from Italy, Milton produced four drafts of a tragedy he called *Paradise Lost* and, alternatively, *Adam Unparadized*. At some later time Milton composed verses for the opening of this tragedy that survive in Book Four of *Paradise Lost* (lines 32–41) as Satan's address to the sun, which Satan delivers when he has just landed on Earth, on the top of Mount Niphates:

> O thou that with surpassing glory crowned
> Look'st from thy sole dominion like the god
> Of this new world, at whose sight all the stars
> Hide their diminished heads, to thee I call
> But with no friendly voice and add thy name,
> O Sun, to tell thee how I hate thy beams
> That bring to my remembrance from what state
> I fell, how glorious once above thy sphere
> Till pride and worse ambition threw me down,
> Warring in Heav'n against Heav'n's matchless King.

As much as anything Satan says in the epic, these verses convey the glamour, even the majesty of evil, without diminishing, so to speak, the evil of evil.

Somehow in this period Milton managed to complete, among other projects, a very interesting theological treatise, in Latin, on the foundations of Christian faith, with every argument and point tagged to a passage in the Bible. The authorship of *On Christian Doctrine* (*De Doctrina Christiana*) has recently been questioned, and persuasively defended, but in either case it provides a useful commentary on the ideas underlying *Paradise Lost*: on the death of the soul and the body together; on the materiality of all being, including the source of all being, God the Father; on the subordination of the Son to the Father; and, most important, on Christian liberty and reason.

Although a general amnesty was proclaimed at the Restoration, Milton's name was proposed in Parliament for the list of those excluded from amnesty and therefore liable to prosecution. His friends concealed him through the summer months, when a warrant was out for his arrest. Nine of the men who had signed Charles I's death warrant were executed (against Charles II's wishes, but on the insistence of Parliament) by the terrible punishment of disemboweling, drawing, and quartering. Another Commonwealth leader, Sir Henry Vane the Younger, to whom Milton had addressed a sonnet in 1652, would also be dispatched. In 1661 the corpses of Cromwell and two of Charles I's judges were exhumed, dragged to the place of execution on Tyburn hill, beheaded, and the heads exhibited on pikes. (These events are alluded to in *Samson Agonistes*, lines 680–96.) Through the influence of friends such as Marvell, who had gone into Parliament as the member for Hull, Milton's name was not among those formally excluded from the Act of Pardon at the end of August 1660. He could come out of hiding. But through a misunderstanding (if that is what it was), Milton was arrested anyway in November and imprisoned into December. His feelings in this period, which reveal his resolution as an artist and a prophet, are recorded in verses from the invocation to Book Seven (lines 24–28) of *Paradise Lost*:

> I sing with mortal voice unchanged
> To hoarse or mute though fall'n on evil days,
> On evil days though fall'n and evil tongues,
> In darkness and with dangers compassed round
> And solitude.

Were he more inclined to self-pity, Milton might have added "and poverty," since, with the collapse of the Excise Bank and other severe financial misfortunes, he was left after the Restoration in difficult circumstances, which were not eased by his being charged vindictively ruinous fees upon his release from prison.

Living now in relative obscurity, Milton gave his nights and his mornings to the composition of *Paradise Lost*, his afternoons to an increasing flow of visitors from the Continent, where his Latin defenses of the Commonwealth had made him famous. He also received a younger generation of English admirers and poets, such as John Dryden. In 1663 he married Elizabeth Minshull, who would outlive him, and by 1665, before retiring to the country during the Great Plague (1665–66), he completed *Paradise Lost*. Milton's young Quaker friend Thomas Ellwood, to whom he taught Latin in exchange for assistance with reading, recalls being asked, almost casually, to look over a certain manuscript, which the poet then called to have brought to him. It was the manuscript of *Paradise Lost*. Ellwood reports that when he next saw Milton they discussed the poem for some time before Ellwood asked, half in jest, what Milton could now say about "paradise found." Milton made no reply at that time, but he would answer with *Paradise Regained*. Unfortunately, Ellwood says nothing of the substance of their discussion of *Paradise Lost*.

Milton was back in London in 1666, in time to witness (for he could feel it and hear it) the apocalyptic destruction caused by the Great Fire, or Fire of London, in which his boyhood home on Bread Street, the only property left to him, was lost. The fire destroyed the whole city except for its eastern and northeastern edges, including eighty-nine of its ninety-seven parish churches. The great cathedral of Saint Paul's burned with the rest. Pepys's description of the event—of the noise and explosions, of the terrifying smoke and heat, of an entire city in panic, and of pigeons, as they flew, catching fire—is unforgettable.

The fire also destroyed the shops and equipment of many printers and booksellers, which were concentrated around Saint Paul's. When *Paradise Lost* was at last published, in 1667, after further delays obtaining a license (for Milton was still regarded with suspicion by the authorities), it was an immediate success, being mentioned in Parliament, accorded the highest praise by John Dryden, and, not incidentally, selling well. Even readers who were implacably hostile to Milton on political grounds acknowledged the poem's greatness.

In 1670 or 1671 (it was licensed in 1670) Milton published in a single volume the two other long poems of his mature years, *Paradise Regained*, the brilliant and still underappreciated sequel to *Paradise Lost* recounting Christ's mental fight with Satan in the desert, and *Samson Agonistes*, a tragedy intended for reading rather than for the stage. (The date of *Samson* has been contested in the past, but the evidence is strongly in favor of its being a post-Restoration work. It is generally accepted as the last poem Milton wrote.) The two poems complement each other and make a fascinating study in contrasts. Whereas *Paradise Regained* is subdued in tone and intensely cerebral, *Samson Agonistes* is an explosively passionate work, the poet's *cri de coeur* over the political disappointments and personal afflictions of his life. Yet *Samson* ends—and these are probably the last words of Milton's poetic career—with "calm of mind, all passion spent."

In 1673 Milton published an enlarged edition of the shorter poems of 1645–46, including, among other things, the superb political sonnets written in the intervening years, poems that would make Wordsworth wish Milton were "living at this hour." In the summer of 1674 the second and final edition (in the poet's lifetime) of *Paradise Lost* was published. Milton died the following November, perhaps on the ninth, a month before his sixty-sixth birthday. He was buried beside his father in the London church of Saint Giles, Cripplegate. For a revolutionary, an antimonarchist, and an enemy of the Anglican Church, the poets' corner in Westminster Abbey, where Edmund Spenser rests, was out of the question. But the funeral was attended, as a contemporary reported, by all classes of persons. There was an awareness that there had passed from the scene a great national poet who took, as he said, "these British islands as my world" (*YP* 1:812).

Before the publication of *Paradise Lost*, when he was almost sixty years old, Milton was hardly known as a poet, except to a small circle. He was known as a political controversialist, as a disestablishmentarian (someone who opposes an "established," state-run church), as an enemy of bishops and of "hireling priests" (ministers paid for their work), as a proponent of divorce, as a defender of regicide, and as the chief propagandist of the English Commonwealth under the dictatorship of Oliver Cromwell—in short, as a vigorous proponent of everything that, after 1660, was regarded by many in England as criminal and seditious. This view of Milton did not fade away after 1667, with the appearance of *Paradise Lost*. But it was entirely subordinated to the conviction, which would only grow more intense in the following century (during which about one hundred editions of *Paradise Lost* would be published), that Milton is one of the very greatest poets of the modern world. Yet he is a poet around whom argument and controversy on the most central issues—on religion, history, politics, and gender relations, in short, on freedom, authority, and power—have never ceased to rage.

The standard scholarly biography is Barbara K. Lewalski's *The Life of John Milton* (London, 2000). Valuable sources are Gordon Campbell, *A Milton Chronology* (London, 1997); John S. Diekhoff, ed., *Milton on Himself*, 2nd ed. (London, 1965); and Helen Darbishire, ed., *The Early Lives of Milton* (New York, 1965). Until Lewalski's *Life* appeared, the standard biography was William Riley Parker, *Milton: A Biography*, 2 vols. (Oxford, 1968; revised ed. Gordon Campbell, 1996). It is still worth consulting. All modern students of Milton are indebted to David Masson's monumental nineteenth-century work *The Life of John Milton, Narrated in Connexion with the Political, Ecclesiastical and Literary History of His Time*, 7 vols. (London, 1881–94). Excellent shorter biographies are A. N. Wilson, *The Life of John Milton* (Oxford, 1983), and Douglas Bush, *John Milton: A Sketch of His Life and Writings* (London, 1965). For readers of French there is an excellent biography by Armand Himy, *John Milton* (Paris, 2003), and a parallel-text translation, also by Himy, with a valuable critical introduction: *Le Paradis perdu* (Paris, 2001).

Valuable biographical works to appear since 2005 include Gordon Campbell and Thomas N. Corns, *John Milton: Life, Work, and Thought* (Oxford: 2008); Anna Beer, *Milton: Poet, Pamphleteer, and Patriot* (London: 2008); Edward Jones, ed., *Young Milton: The Emerging Author, 1620–1642* (Oxford: 2012); and William Poole, *Milton and the Making of "Paradise Lost"* (Cambridge, MA: 2017).

On the Text of *Paradise Lost*

In 1667, *Paradise Lost: A Poem Written in Ten Books by John Milton* appeared in quarto without either the "arguments" (the prose summaries at the head of each book) or the poet's note on the verse. Although the poem was divided into only ten books, it was substantially complete, only a handful of verses shorter than the later, twelve-book version. Of this first edition there were six issues (essentially reprintings, with minor alterations) between 1667 and 1669, after which the run of some thirteen hundred copies was sold out.

To the fourth issue of this first edition, in 1668, the arguments and the note on the verse were added to the front of the volume, in response to complaints (as the publisher informs us) that the narrative is hard to follow and that the poem "rhymes not." The new arguments could not be placed before their respective books until a new edition was published, which occurred in 1674, only months before the poet's death.

The title page of this second edition, in the smaller octavo format, reads *Paradise Lost: A Poem in Twelve Books. The Author John Milton . . . revised and augmented by the same author. Redistributed* would be a better term than *augmented*: Book Seven was divided to become Books Seven and Eight (accordingly, Book Eight became Nine and Nine became Ten), and the former Book Ten was divided to produce Books Eleven and Twelve. Brief transitional passages of three and a half and five lines, respectively, were added to the new Books Eight and Twelve, and three lines (485–87) were added to Book Eleven. Other changes were very minor.

The text on which this edition is based is 1674, with a few emendations and some adoptions, which are noted below, from the first edition and from the scribal manuscript of Book One, in the Pierpont Morgan Library, New York.

Textual Notes

1.230	The manuscript is punctuated to attach the clause *and such appeared in hue* to *fire* (229). Editions 1667 and 1674 imply that the clause is attached to what follows. The manuscript reading is more logical.
1.530	*fainting* 1674; *fainted* 1667 and manuscript
1.703	*founded* manuscript and 1667; *found out* 1674
1.754	*trumpets*'; *Trumpets* 1667, 1674; and *trumpets* manuscript
2.282	*where* 1667; *were* 1674
2.375	*originals* 1667; *original* 1674

2.483	*their* 1667; *her* 1674
2.527	*his* 1667; *this* 1674
2.1001	*your*, an early emendation; *our* 1667 and 1674
2.1039	*broken* 1667; *brok'd* 1674
3.592	*metal*; *medal* 1667, 1674
4.451	*on* 1667; *of* 1674
4.472	*shalt*; *shall* 1667 and 1674
4.928	*The* 1667; *Thy* 1674
6.352	*limn*; *Limb* 1667, 1674. (See note to this line and Shaw-cross, "A Note," p. 392.)
7.321	*swelling*, emendation of *smelling* 1667, 1674
7.366	*her* 1674; *his* 1667. Some editors adopt the 1667 reading, *his*, taking the "morning planet" to be Lucifer, not Venus. But the gender of the wearer of these *horns* appears to have been carefully corrected in 1674 to *her*.
7.370	Some editors transpose *his* and *the*, making it *the east and his lamp*. But the more difficult reading of 1667 and 1674 is preferable.
7.451	*soul* emendation of *Fowle* 1667 and *Foul* 1674. See line 388.
8.1–3	Added in 1674, when Book Seven became Books Seven and Eight.
8.4	1667 reads: "To whom thus Adam gratefully, repl'd."
9.213	*hear* 1667; *bear* 1674
9.394	*Likest* 1667; *Likeliest* 1674
9.1019	*we* 1667; *me* 1674
9.1092	*for* 1667; *from* 1674
9.1093	*from* 1667; *for* 1674
9.1183	*women* 1667, 1674. Sometimes emended to *woman*.
10.241	*avengers* 1667; *avenger* 1674
10.408	*prevail* 1667; *prevails* 1674
10.550	*fair fruit* 1667; *Fruit* 1674
10.989	*so Death*. In 1667, 1674 *So Death* begins line 990, rendering 989 too short and 990 too long.
11.427	*that sin* 1667; *that* 1674
11.485–87	Added in 1674.
11.651	*tacks* 1667; *makes* 1674
12.1–5	Added in 1674.
12.534	*Will* 1667; *Well* 1674

PARADISE LOST

3

The Verse

The measure is English heroic verse without rhyme, as that of Homer in Greek, and of Virgil in Latin, rhyme being no necessary adjunct or true ornament of poem or good verse, in longer works especially, but the invention of a barbarous age, to set off wretched matter and lame meter; graced indeed since by the use of some famous modern poets, carried away by custom, but much to their own vexation, hindrance and constraint to express many things otherwise, and for the most part worse than else they would have expressed them. Not without cause therefore some both Italian and Spanish poets of prime note have rejected rhyme both in longer and shorter works, as have also long since our best English tragedies, as a thing of it self, to all judicious ears, trivial and of no true musical delight, which consists only in apt numbers, fit quantity of syllables, and the sense variously drawn out from one verse into another, not in the jingling sound of like endings, a fault avoided by the learned ancients

The Verse.

    This somewhat aggressive note on the verse was added to a later issue (the fourth) of the first edition, in 1668, apparently in response to complaints that the poem, as the publisher said, "rhymes not."

1.   *English heroic verse* is a ten- to occasionally eleven-syllable sound row with alternating beats, or stresses, which in practice is much varied upon. The alternating beats are traditionally called *iambs* (unstressed/stressed, e.g., "Of Man's" [1.1]) and trochees (stressed/unstressed, e.g., "ever burning sulfur" [1.69]). An eleven-syllable row may occur—though not invariably, in Milton—when the final syllable is unaccented, e.g., 1.73: "As far removed from God and light of Heaven." More rarely, an eleven-syllable row may occur when an unaccented syllable falls before the caesura (the medial pause), e.g., 4.219: "High eminent bloom*ing* // ambrosial fruit," a subtlety picked up from Shakespeare. See George T. Wright, *Shakespeare's Metrical Art* (Berkeley University of California Press, 1988), pp. 227–28, and below, 2.261 n. Also important (see 13–14 n. below) is the natural but artistically enhanced alternation between pauses and run-ons—or, as these are called, *enjambments*—at the ends of lines, yielding such wonders as "Disparted Chaos overbuilt exclaimed / And with rebounding surge the bars assailed / That scorned his indignation" (10.416–18); and the description of Death crossing space toward earth, avidly sniffing out flesh: "So scented the grim feature and upturned / His nostril wide into the murky air, / Sagacious of his quarry from so far" (10.279–81).

4.   *a barbarous age*: the Middle Ages, after the fall of the Roman Empire and the disappearance of classical culture.

5–6. *famous modern poets*, such as Ariosto, Tasso, and Spenser, all of whom employed rhyme; *modern* means after the Middle Ages, in what we call the Renaissance.

11. *our best English tragedies* refers to Shakespeare principally, but also to Marlowe, Webster, and others.

13–14. *apt numbers* refers, probably, to the number of syllables in the line (usually ten; eleven for "feminine" lines, in which there is an extra, unaccented syllable). *fit quantity of syllables* refers, perhaps, to the length of time a syllable is sounded or to whether the vowel is long or short. (The term *quantity* alludes to Greek and Latin quantitative meter, which is entirely different from Milton's verse. He may have used the term here chiefly to intimidate.) *the sense variously drawn out from one verse into another*, the most important part of this statement, refers to the use of enjambment to run one line into another without a pause, allowing the rhythms of the syntax to assert themselves on a longer scale than that of the individual line. See 1 n., above.

15. The *learned ancients* avoided alliteration and rhyme, which they considered stylistic faults.

both in poetry and all good oratory. This neglect then of rhyme so little is to be taken for a defect, though it may seem so perhaps to vulgar readers, that it rather is to be esteemed an example set, the first in English, of ancient liberty recovered to heroic poem from the troublesome and modern bondage of rhyming.

Book One

The Argument

This first book proposes first, in brief, the whole subject: Man's disobedience and the loss thereupon of Paradise wherein he was placed; then touches the prime cause of his fall, the serpent, or rather Satan in the serpent, who revolting from God and drawing to his side many legions of angels was by the command of God driven out of Heaven with all his crew into the great deep. Which action passed over, the poem hastes into the midst of things, presenting Satan with his angels now fallen into Hell—described here, not in the center (for Heaven and Earth may be supposed as yet not made, certainly not yet accursed) but in a place of utter darkness fitliest called chaos. Here, Satan with his angels lying on the burning lake, thunder-struck and astonished, after a certain space recovers, as from confusion, calls up him who next in order and dignity lay by him. They confer of their miserable fall. Satan awakens all his legions, who lay till then in the same manner confounded. They rise: their numbers, array of battle, their chief leaders named, according to the idols known afterwards in Canaan and the countries adjoining. To these Satan directs his speech, comforts them with hope yet of regaining Heaven, but tells them lastly of a new world and new kind of creature to be created, according to an ancient prophecy or report in Heaven. (For that angels were long before this visible Creation was the opinion of many

Book One

　　The Argument. From the Latin *argumentum*, a summary of the underlying subject matter of a poetical work, often placed before a play. The action that is "passed over" is the War in Heaven, recounted in Book Six. The phrase "hastes into the midst of things" closely follows Horace's wording, in *Ars poetica* (lines 147–49). Horace says that Homer doesn't begin the tale of the Trojan War from the "double egg" (*nec gemino bellum troianum orditur ab ovo*) but always hastens to the main event and carries the reader into the midst of things (*semper ad eventum festinat et in medias res . . . auditorem rapit*). The egg is twinned because Helen of Troy and Clytemnestra were hatched from one of the two eggs laid by Leda, queen of Sparta, after Zeus, disguised as a swan, raped her. (The other egg contained the Dioscuri, Castor, and Pollux.) The cause of the Trojan War was Paris's carrying Helen away from her husband Menelaus. Helen's birth may therefore be thought of (Horace is being humorous) as the very beginning of the war. But to begin at the beginning, long deferring the war itself, would be tedious. It is better, Horace advises, to plunge into the action at the main event and have earlier episodes referred to retrospectively by characters in the course of the narrative. Milton will do so at length, in two entire books, Six and Seven, which contain Raphael's narrative of the War in Heaven and the Creation of the World (*PL* 5.561–8.3).

ancient fathers.) To find out the truth of this prophecy, and what to
determine thereon, he refers to a full council. What his associates
thence attempt: Pandemonium, the palace of Satan, rises, suddenly
built out of the deep. The infernal peers there sit in council.

Of Man's first disobedience and the fruit
Of that forbidden tree whose mortal taste
Brought death into the world and all our woe
With loss of Eden till one greater Man
Restore us and regain the blissful seat   5
Sing Heav'nly Muse, that on the secret top
Of Oreb or of Sinai didst inspire
That shepherd who first taught the chosen seed,
In the beginning, how the heav'ns and earth
Rose out of chaos. Or if Sion hill   10
Delight thee more and Siloa's brook that flowed
Fast by the oracle of God, I thence
Invoke thy aid to my advent'rous song
That with no middle flight intends to soar
Above th' Aonian mount while it pursues   15
Things unattempted yet in prose or rhyme.
And chiefly thou, O Spirit, that dost prefer
Before all temples th' upright heart and pure
Instruct me, for thou know'st, thou from the first
Wast present and with mighty wings outspread   20
Dove-like sat'st brooding on the vast abyss
And mad'st it pregnant. What in me is dark
Illumine, what is low raise and support,

---

4. *Man*: Jesus.
5. *seat*: home, throne.
6. *Muse*: recalling the epic muse of Homer and Virgil, but here the Holy Ghost, God's
    creative power.
7. *Oreb, Sinai*: Two names for the mountain on which Moses received from God the Ten
    Commandments and the Law. See 10 n., *Sion*, the mountain of Jerusalem, where
    King David composed the Psalms; and 15 n., Helicon, the mountain sacred to the
    classical muses, inspiring pre-Christian, Greek literature. For these and other proper
    names in the text, see Glossary of Names in *Paradise Lost*.
8. *shepherd*: Moses, who was first called by God (on Mount Oreb) while pasturing sheep.
    The account of Creation, in Genesis, was attributed to Moses.
10. *Sion*: After mentioning Sinai, the mountain associated with Moses' creation narrative
    in Genesis, the poet mentions Mount Zion, which is associated with the Psalms, attrib-
    uted to King David, some of which are concerned with Creation (e.g., Psalm 104).
12. *oracle*: on Mount Zion, in Jerusalem, where God inspired the kings David and Solo-
    mon. Recalls the oracle of Apollo at Delphi, also on a mountain, and the stream
    where Apollo prophesied through his priestess.
15. *Aonian mount*: See Glossary. Mount Helicon, sacred to the ancient Greek muses. The
    poet's Christian song will soar above the songs of his classical predecessors, Hesiod and
    Homer.
17. *Spirit*: the Holy Ghost, the *Muse* of line 6, the inner experience of faith.
18. *upright heart*: the temple of the Spirit. See Genesis 1:2.

That to the heighth of this great argument
I may assert Eternal Providence   25
And justify the ways of God to men.
    Say first, for Heav'n hides nothing from thy view,
Nor the deep tract of Hell, say first what cause
Moved our grand parents in that happy state,
Favored of Heav'n so highly, to fall off   30
From their Creator and transgress His will
For one restraint, lords of the world besides.
Who first seduced them to that foul revolt?
Th' infernal Serpent. He it was whose guile
Stirred up with envy and revenge deceived   35
The mother of mankind, what time his pride
Had cast him out from Heav'n with all his host
Of rebel angels, by whose aid aspiring
To set himself in glory 'bove his peers
He trusted to have equaled the Most High   40
If he opposed, and with ambitious aim
Against the throne and monarchy of God
Raised impious war in Heav'n and battle proud
With vain attempt. Him the Almighty Power
Hurled headlong flaming from th' ethereal sky   45
With hideous ruin and combustion down
To bottomless perdition, there to dwell
In adamantine chains and penal fire
Who durst defy th' Omnipotent to arms.
Nine times the space that measures day and night   50
To mortal men he with his horrid crew
Lay vanquished rolling in the fiery gulf
Confounded though immortal. But his doom
Reserved him to more wrath, for now the thought
Both of lost happiness and lasting pain   55
Torments him. Round he throws his baleful eyes
That witnessed huge affliction and dismay

24. *argument*: subject.
25. *Providence*: God's foresight and plan for history.
29. *grand parents*: Adam and Eve.
32. *one restraint*: the command not to eat the fruit of the Tree of Knowledge of Good and
Evil.
34. *Serpent*: In the Genesis account, the serpent tempts Eve to eat the fruit. In Christian
tradition this serpent was identified with Satan. See Revelation 12:9 and 20:1–3.
48. *adamantine*: made of the legendary hardest substance, *adamant*. The word is from
a Homeric epithet of the king of the underworld, Hades (*Iliad* 9.158): *adamastos*,
"untamble, incapable of being overpowered" (*a* "un" + *damnaō* "to overpower, subjugate,
master").
50. *Nine times*: recalls the Titans in Greek myth (Hesiod, *Theogony* 720–25), who fell
nine days to Earth and nine more into the pit of Tartarus. Milton's rebel angels are
not the devils of medieval myth but huge cosmic powers. See lines 197–200.

Mixed with obdúrate pride and steadfast hate.
At once as far as angels' ken he views
The dismal situation waste and wild: 60
A dungeon horrible on all sides round
As one great furnace flamed yet from those flames
No light but rather darkness visible
Served only to discover sights of woe,
Regions of sorrow, doleful shades, where peace   65
And rest can never dwell, hope never comes
That comes to all but torture without end
Still urges and a fiery deluge fed
With ever-burning sulfur unconsumed.
Such place Eternal Justice had prepared   70
For those rebellious, here their prison ordained
In utter darkness and their portion set
As far removed from God and light of Heaven
As from the center thrice to th' utmost pole.
O how unlike the place from whence they fell!   75
There the companions of his fall o'erwhelmed
With floods and whirlwinds of tempestuous fire
He soon discerns. And weltering by his side
One next himself in power and next in crime,
Long after known in Palestine and named   80
Beëlzebub. To whom th' Arch-Enemy,
And thence in Heav'n called *Satan*, with bold words
Breaking the horrid silence thus began:
   If thou beest he (but O how fall'n! how changed
From him who in the happy realms of light   85
Clothed with transcendent brightness didst outshine
Myriads, though bright!), if he whom mutual league,
United thoughts and counsels, equal hope
And hazard in the glorious enterprise
Joined with me once (now misery hath joined   90
In equal ruin), into what pit thou seest
From what heighth fall'n, so much the stronger proved
He with His thunder (and till then who knew
The force of those dire arms?), yet not for those

---

59. *ken*: sight. Possibly a verb ("can see"), probably a noun.
74. *center*: of the earth. *pole*: of the created universe, not of the earth. Milton's Hell is
   situated not in the interior of the earth but outside the created universe altogether,
   far off in chaos. The distance referred to here would be many times the distance from
   the center of the earth to the upper pole of the cosmos.
81–82. *Arch-Enemy . . . Satan*: Satan's name is from the Hebrew word for "adversary."
   Greek *archē* means a "beginning," a "first cause."
84–94. *If . . . if . . . into . . . yet . . .*: Milton makes Satan's syntax obscure to show passion
   dominating over reason. Satan will later use such syntax to confuse Eve.

Nor what the potent victor in His rage   95
Can else inflict do I repent or change,
Though changed in outward luster, that fixed mind
And high disdain from sense of injured merit
That with the Mightiest raised me to contend
And to the fierce contention brought along   100
Innumerable force of spirits armed
That durst dislike His reign and, me preferring,
His utmost power with adverse power opposed
In dubious battle on the plains of Heav'n
And shook His throne. What though the field be lost?   105
All is not lost: th' unconquerable will
And study of revenge, immortal hate
And courage never to submit or yield—
And what is else not to be overcome?
That glory never shall His wrath or might   110
Extort from me: to bow and sue for grace
With suppliant knee and deify His power
Who from the terror of this arm so late
Doubted His empire! That were low indeed,
That were an ignominy and shame beneath   115
This downfall, since by fate the strength of gods
And this empyreal substance cannot fail,
Since through experience of this great event,
In arms not worse, in foresight much advanced,
We may with more successful hope resolve   120
To wage by force or guile eternal war
Irreconcilable to our grand Foe
Who now triúmphs and in th' excess of joy
Sole reigning holds the tyranny of Heav'n.
      So spake th' Apostate Angel though in pain,   125
Vaunting aloud but racked with deep despair.
And him thus answered soon his bold compeer:
      O prince, O chief of many thronèd pow'rs
That led th' embattled seraphim to war
Under thy conduct and in dreadful deeds   130
Fearless endangered Heav'n's perpetual King
And put to proof His high supremacy

---

114. *Doubted*: feared the loss of. *Who* [God] is the subject of *Doubted*.
117. *empyreal substance*: the fiery, flexible material of which angels are made. (The Greek root *pyr* means "fire.") *fail*: perish.
125–26. These lines recall the moment in Virgil's *Aeneid* (1.208–9) when the Trojans, wrecked on the African shore, are cheered by their leader Aeneas, who conceals his dismay: *Talia voce refert, curisque ingentibus aeger / spem voltu simulat, premit altum corde dolorem.* In Dryden's deft translation, "These words he spoke, but spoke not from his heart; his outward smiles concealed his inward smart." As often with Milton, the moral difference from the source is as important as the verbal similarity.

(Whether upheld by strength, or chance, or fate)
Too well I see and rue the dire event
That with sad overthrow and foul defeat   135
Hath lost us Heav'n and all this mighty host
In horrible destruction laid thus low
As far as gods and Heav'nly essences
Can perish. For the mind and spirit remains
Invincible and vigor soon returns   140
Though all our glory extinct and happy state
Here swallowed up in endless misery.
But what if He our conqueror (whom I now
Of force believe almighty since no less
Than such could have o'erpow'red such force as ours)   145
Have left us this our spirit and strength entire
Strongly to suffer and support our pains
That we may so suffice His vengeful ire
Or do Him mightier service as His thralls
By right of war, whate'er His business be: 150
Here in the heart of Hell to work in fire
Or do His errands in the gloomy deep?
What can it then avail, though yet we feel
Strength undiminished or eternal being,
To undergo eternal punishment?   155
Whereto with speedy words th' Arch-Fiend replied:
    Fall'n cherub, to be weak is mis'rable,
Doing or suffering, but of this be sure:
To do aught good will never be our task
But ever to do ill our sole delight   160
As being the contrary to His high will
Whom we resist. If then His providence
Out of our evil seek to bring forth good
Our labor must be to pervert that end
And out of good still to find means of evil,   165
Which ofttimes may succeed so as perhaps
Shall grieve Him, if I fail not, and disturb
His inmost counsels from their destined aim.
But see! The angry victor hath recalled
His ministers of vengeance and pursuit   170
Back to the gates of Heav'n. The sulfurous hail
Shot after us in storm o'erblown hath laid
The fiery surge that from the precipice
Of Heav'n received us falling. And the thunder,

---

167. *fail*: mistake. Imitating a similar expression in Latin.
171–74. The storm of thunder that pursues the rebel angels through chaos shoots over
    them to form the lake into which they fall.

Winged with red lightning and impetuous rage,   175
Perhaps hath spent his shafts and ceases now
To bellow through the vast and boundless deep.
Let us not slip th' occasion, whether scorn
Or satiate fury yield it from our Foe.
Seest thou yon dreary plain forlorn and wild,   180
The seat of desolation, void of light
Save what the glimmering of these livid flames
Casts pale and dreadful? Thither let us tend
From off the tossing of these fiery waves,
There rest (if any rest can harbor there)   185
And reassembling our afflicted powers
Consult how we may henceforth most offend
Our Enemy, our own loss how repair,
How overcome this dire calamity,
What reinforcement we may gain from hope,   190
If not what resolution from despair.
   Thus Satan talking to his nearest mate
With head uplift above the wave and eyes
That sparkling blazed. His other parts besides,
Prone on the flood, extended long and large,   195
Lay floating many a rood in bulk as huge
As whom the fables name of monstrous size:
Titanian or Earth-born that warred on Jove,
Briareos or Typhon whom the den
By ancient Tarsus held or that sea-beast   200
Leviathan which God of all His works
Created hugest that swim the ocean stream.
Him haply slumb'ring on the Norway foam
The pilot of some small night-foundered skiff
Deeming some island, oft, as seamen tell,   205
With fixèd anchor in his scaly rind
Moors by his side, under the lee, while Night
Invests the sea and wishèd morn delays.
So stretched out huge in length the Arch-Fiend lay

196. *rood*: a measure of distance, six to eight yards.
198–202. Satan's monstrous size is compared to that of the Titans and giants of classical
   mythology who warred against Jove and the Olympians, and to the biblical sea-
   monster Leviathan, which is "king over all the children of pride" (Job 41:34). See
   Glossary, TARSUS and TYPHON.
203. The mention of Norway suggests Milton knew how plentiful whales were in northern latitudes.
204–8. *skiff*: a small seagoing rowboat carried on ships; used in whaling. *night-foundered*:
   separated from its ship and overcome by darkness. The sailors fasten anchor to what
   they suppose to be an island but is in fact a whale. The whale dives, dragging them
   down with it—a symbol of the devil.
208. *Invests*: covers, as with a robe.

Chained on the burning lake. Nor ever thence   210
Had risen or heaved his head but that the will
And high permission of all-ruling Heaven
Left him at large to his own dark designs
That with reiterated crimes he might
Heap on himself damnation while he sought   215
Evil to others and enraged might see
How all his malice served but to bring forth
Infinite goodness, grace, and mercy shown
On Man by him seduced, but on himself
Treble confusion, wrath and vengeance poured.   220
Forthwith upright he rears from off the pool
His mighty stature. On each hand the flames
Driv'n backward slope their pointing spires and, rolled
In billows, leave i' th' midst a horrid vale.
Then with expanded wings he steers his flight   225
Aloft incumbent on the dusky air
That felt unusual weight till on dry land
He lights—if it were land that ever burned
With solid as the lake with liquid fire,
And such appeared in hue. As when the force   230
Of subterranean wind transports a hill
Torn from Pelorus or the shattered side
Of thund'ring Etna whose combustible
And fueled entrails thence conceiving fire
Sublimed with mineral fury aid the winds   235
And leave a singèd bottom all involved
With stench and smoke: such resting found the sole
Of unblest feet. Him followed his next mate,
Both glorying to have 'scaped the Stygian flood
As gods and by their own recovered strength,   240
Not by the sufferance of Supernal Pow'r.
     Is this the region, this the soil, the clime,
Said then the lost archangel, this the seat
That we must change for Heav'n, this mournful gloom
For that celestial light? Be it so, since He   245
Who now is Sov'reign can dispose and bid

230–37. Milton's appropriation of a ranting passage in Virgil: "Aetna thunders with hor-
    rifying ruin while hurling forth black clouds and balls of flame that lick the stars,
    vomiting from its depths, with a roar, its entrails of boulders and liquefied stone"
    (*Aeneid* 3.571–77).
235. *Sublimed*: vaporized.
240. *gods*: The devils will set themselves up as gods in the world after the Fall. Milton
    follows the Christian tradition that the gods of the Greeks and Romans were devils
    in disguise. See 1.364–75.
241. *suff'rance*: permission.

What shall be right. Farthest from Him is best
Whom reason hath equaled, force hath made supreme
Above His equals. Farewell happy fields
Where joy forever dwells! Hail horrors, hail   250
Infernal world! And thou, profoundest Hell,
Receive thy new possessor, one who brings
A mind not to be changed by place or time!
The mind is its own place and in itself
Can make a Heav'n of Hell, a Hell of Heaven.   255
What matter where, if I be still the same
And what I should be: all but less than He
Whom thunder hath made greater? Here at least
We shall be free. Th' Almighty hath not built
Here for His envy, will not drive us hence.   260
Here we may reign secure, and in my choice
To reign is worth ambition, though in Hell:
Better to reign in Hell than serve in Heaven!
But wherefore let we then our faithful friends,
Th' associates and copartners of our loss,   265
Lie thus astonished on th' oblivious pool
And call them not to share with us their part
In this unhappy mansion or once more
With rallied arms to try what may be yet
Regained in Heaven or what more lost in Hell?   270
     So Satan spake and him Beëlzebub
Thus answered: Leader of those armies bright
Which but th' Omnipotent none could have foiled,
If once they hear that voice (their liveliest pledge
Of hope in fears and dangers, heard so oft   275
In worst extremes and on the perilous edge
Of battle when it raged, in all assaults
Their surest signal) they will soon resume
New courage and revive though now they lie
Grov'ling and prostrate on yon lake of fire   280
As we erewhile, astounded and amazed—
No wonder, fall'n such a pernicious heighth!
     He scarce had ceased when the superior fiend
Was moving toward the shore. His ponderous shield,
Ethereal temper, massy, large and round,   285

248–49. I.e., God, whom we have equaled with our reason, but whom mere force has
   raised above us.
254. A classic doctrine of the ancient Stoics.
262–63. "In heav'n they scorn'd to serve, so now in hell they reigne" (Phineas Fletcher,
   The Purple Island 7.10).
266. *oblivious pool* suggests one of the rivers of Hell: Lethe, "forgetfulness."
285. *Ethereal temper*: The shield is made of empyreal (fiery) substance of Heaven and
   tempered in the cool *aether* just beneath the region of fire.

Behind him cast. The broad circumference
Hung on his shoulders like the moon whose orb
Through optic glass the Tuscan artist views
At evening from the top of Fesolè
Or in Valdarno to descry new lands,   290
Rivers or mountains in her spotty globe.
His spear (to equal which the tallest pine
Hewn on Norwegian hills to be the mast
Of some great admiral were but a wand)
He walked with to support uneasy steps   295
Over the burning marl (not like those steps
On Heaven's azure) and the torrid clime
Smote on him sore besides, vaulted with fire.
Nathless he so endured till on the beach
Of that inflamèd sea he stood and called   300
His legions, angel forms who lay entranced
Thick as autumnal leaves that strew the brooks
In Vallombrosa where th' Etrurian shades
High overarched embow'r, or scattered sedge
Afloat when with fierce winds Orion armed   305
Hath vexed the Red Sea coast whose waves o'erthrew
Busiris and his Memphian chivalry
While with perfidious hatred they pursued
The sojourners of Goshen, who beheld
From the safe shore their floating carcasses   310
And broken chariot wheels. So thick bestrewn,
Abject and lost lay these, covering the flood,
Under amazement of their hideous change.
He called so loud that all the hollow deep
Of Hell resounded: Princes! Potentates!   315

---

286. *Behind*: Greek soldiers slung their shields behind them when in retreat.
288–90. *Tuscan artist*: Galileo, who was from the region of Tuscany in central Italy. In his
    last decade Galileo lived under house arrest in Arcetri, in the hills south of Florence,
    where the young Milton visited him in 1638–89. For *Fesolè* (Fiesole) and *Valdarno*
    (valley of the river Arno), see Glossary. Galileo is called *artist* in the sense of an
    artifex, one who invents mechanical devices. To observe the heavens, Galileo greatly
    improved the telescope, formerly a naval instrument.
294. *admiral*: the principal ship of a fleet, having the tallest mast (for signaling). Such a
    mast would be a mere wand in comparison with Satan's spear.
299. *Nathless*: nevertheless.
302–11. Two similes in succession, a natural followed by a biblical: (1) The devils cover
    the surface of the fiery lake as thickly as fallen leaves cover brooks in the shadowy
    vale (hence the name *Vallombrosa*) of Tuscany, the region of Italy anciently known as
    Etruria, the home of the pre-Roman Etruscans. (2) The devils are strewn on the fiery
    lake as reedy plants, uprooted by violent winds brought by the constellation Orion,
    strew the coast of the Red Sea. The Red Sea closed over the army of Pharoah
    (*Busiris*) and his Egyptian cavalry (*Memphian chivalry*) when they were pursuing the
    Israelites, who were formerly encamped at *Goshen* and who now behold the destruc-
    tion of their pursuers (Exodus 14:21–31).

Warriors! the flow'r of Heav'n once yours, now lost,
If such astonishment as this can seize
Eternal Spirits! Or have ye chos'n this place
After the toil of battle to repose
Your wearied virtue for the ease you find   320
To slumber here as in the vales of Heaven?
Or in this abject posture have ye sworn
T' adore the Conqueror, who now beholds
Cherub and seraph rolling in the flood
With scattered arms and ensigns till anon   325
His swift pursuers from Heaven gates discern
Th' advantage and descending tread us down,
Thus drooping, or with linkèd thunderbolts
Transfix us to the bottom of this gulf?
Awake! Arise, or be for ever fallen!   330
    They heard and were abashed and up they sprung
Upon the wing, as when men wont to watch
On duty, sleeping found by whom they dread,
Rouse and bestir themselves ere well awake.
Nor did they not perceive the evil plight   335
In which they were or the fierce pains not feel,
Yet to their general's voice they soon obeyed
Innumerable. As when the potent rod
Of Amram's son in Egypt's evil day
Waved round the coast upcalled a pitchy cloud   340
Of locusts warping on the eastern wind
That o'er the realm of impious Pharaoh hung
Like night and darkened all the land of Nile,
So numberless were those bad angels seen
Hovering on wing under the cope of Hell   345
'Twixt upper, nether, and surrounding fires
Till as a signal giv'n th' uplifted spear
Of their great sultan waving to direct
Their course in even balance down they light
On the firm brimstone and fill all the plain: 350
A multitude like which the populous north
Poured never from her frozen loins to pass
Rhene or the Danaw when her barb'rous sons

---

338. *potent rod*: Moses' staff, which has magical powers given by God. "And Moses
    stretched forth his rod over the land of Egypt . . . And the locusts went up over all
    the land of Egypt . . . they covered the face of the whole earth, so that the land was
    darkened" (Exodus 10:13–15).
339. *Amram's son*: Moses (Exodus 6:20).
351–55. The devils' landing on the solid ground of Hell is compared to the barbarian
    hordes that poured out of the north to destroy the Roman Empire, crossing the
    Rhine and Danube rivers and not only invading Italy but descending through Spain
    into North Africa.

Came like a deluge on the south and spread
Beneath Gibraltar to the Libyan sands.   355
Forthwith from every squadron and each band
The heads and leaders thither haste where stood
Their great commander: godlike shapes and forms
Excelling human, princely dignities
And pow'rs that erst in Heaven sat on thrones,   360
Though of their names in Heav'nly records now
Be no memorial, blotted out and razed
By their rebellion from the books of life.
Nor had they yet among the sons of Eve
Got them new names, till wand'ring o'er the earth   365
Through God's high suff'rance, for the trial of Man,
By falsities and lies the greatest part
Of mankind they corrupted to forsake
God their Creator and th' invisible
Glory of Him that made them, to transform   370
Oft to the image of a brute adorned
With gay religions full of pomp and gold,
And devils to adore for deities!
Then were they known to men by various names
And various idols through the heathen world.   375
    Say, Muse, their names then known, who first, who last,
Roused from the slumber on that fiery couch
At their great emperor's call, as next in worth,
Came singly where he stood on the bare strand
While the promiscuous crowd stood yet aloof.   380
The chief were those who from the pit of Hell
Roaming to seek their prey on Earth durst fix
Their seats long after next the seat of God,
Their altars by His altar, gods adored
Among the nations round, and durst abide   385
Jehovah thund'ring out of Zion throned

---

363. *books of life*: "Let them be blotted out of the book of the living, and not be written
with the righteous" (Psalm 69:28).

376. It is a convention of epic poetry to reinvoke the muse before any long, encyclopedic list.
Homer does so before the catalog of Achaean (Greek) leaders, who lay siege to Troy:
"Tell me now you Muses who have your homes on Olympus, for you are goddesses, and
are present to aid me, and you know all things" (*Iliad* 2.484–85). Virgil does so before
the catalog of ancient Italic leaders: "Spread open Helicon, O goddesses, and move your
song . . . for you, being goddesses, can remember and can tell" (*Aeneid* 7.641–45).

379. *singly*: one by one.

380. *promiscuous*: mixed, not distinguished from one another, as the leading devils will be.

383–91. Pagan deities worshipped near and even on the Temple Mount in Jerusalem,
brought thither by the foreign wives of kings such as Solomon: "Then did Solomon
build an high place for Chemosh, the abomination of Moab, in the hill that is before
Jerusalem, and for Molech, the abomination of the children of Ammon. And likewise did he for all his strange wives, which burnt incense and sacrificed unto their
gods" (I Kings 11:7–8).

385. *nations*: i.e., non-Hebrew peoples, gentiles.

Between the cherubim, yea, often placed
Within His sanctuary itself their shrines,
Abominations, and with cursèd things
His holy rites and solemn feasts profaned   390
And with their darkness durst affront His light.
First Moloch, horrid king, besmeared with blood
Of human sacrifice and parents' tears
Though for the noise of drums and timbrels loud
Their children's cries unheard that passed through fire   395
To his grim idol. Him the Ammonite
Worshipped in Rabba and her wat'ry plain,
In Argob and in Basan to the stream
Of utmost Arnon. Nor content with such
Audacious neighborhood the wisest heart   400
Of Solomon he led by fraud to build
His temple right against the temple of God
On that opprobrious hill and made his grove
The pleasant valley of Hinnom, Tophet thence
And black Gehenna called, the type of Hell.   405
    Next Chemos, th' óbscene dread of Moab's sons,
From Aroer to Nebo and the wild
Of southmost Abarim, in Hesebon
And Horonaim, Seon's realm, beyond
The flow'ry dale of Sibma clad with vines   410
And Elealè to th' Asphaltic Pool.
Peor his other name when he enticed
Israel in Sittim on their march from Nile
To do him wanton rites which cost them woe.

387. *cherubim*: gold statues in the Hebrew sanctuary (later in the temple) of angelic
    beings whose wings overshadow the mercy seat and the ark of the covenant. "Give
    ear, O Shepherd of Israel, . . . thou that dwellest between the cherubims, shine
    forth" (Psalm 80:1). See Exodus 37:7–8 and I Kings 8:6.
388. "[Manasseh] built altars in the house of the Lord . . . for all the host of heaven" (2
    Kings 21:4–5). "Host of heaven" here means false gods, not loyal angels.
403. *opprobrious hill*: the Mount of Olives, which faces the Temple Mount, Zion, to the
    west.
404. "And they have built the high places of Tophet, which is in the valley of the son of
    Hinnom, to burn their sons and their daughters in the fire" (Jeremiah 7:31).
406. *obscene*: ominous (Latin), but also repulsive, as might be said of a god whose priests
    were reputed to defecate ritually before his shrine. Chemos is associated with Peor,
    whose name means to open or to stretch out. Many of the horrific details of Milton's
    devils' future careers as the false gods of the Old Testament are from John Selden's
    De Diis Syriis (*On the Gods of Syria and Palestine,* 1617). Selden denies this detail
    about Chemos/Peor, however; Milton associates him with sexual license (line 415).
413. *march from Nile*: the Exodus from Egypt, during which the temptation to couple
    with foreign women and to worship foreign gods caused much trouble. "And Israel
    abode in Shittim, and the people began to commit whoredom with the daughters of
    Moab. And [the Moabites] called the people unto the sacrifices of their gods; and the
    people did eat, and bowed down to their gods" (Numbers 25:1–2).
414. *woe*: God sends a plague killing twenty-four thousand, until Phinehas spears
    through an Israelite man and Moabite woman as they copulate. This action, plus the
    general purge that follows, appeases the Lord (Numbers 25:4–12).

Yet thence his lustful orgies he enlarged   415
Ev'n to that hill of scandal by the grove
Of Moloch homicide (lust hard by hate)
Till good Josiah drove them thence to Hell.
   With these came they who from the bord'ring flood
Of old Euphrates to the brook that parts   420
Egypt from Syrian ground had general names
Of Baälim and Ashtaroth, those male,
These feminine, for spirits when they please
Can either sex assume or both, so soft
And uncompounded is their essence pure,   425
Not tied or manacled with joint or limb
Nor founded on the brittle strength of bones
Like cumbrous flesh but in what shape they choose,
Dilated or condensed, bright or obscure,
Can execute their airy purposes   430
And works of love or enmity fulfill.
For those the race of Israel oft forsook
Their Living Strength and unfrequented left
His righteous altar, bowing lowly down
To bestial gods, for which their heads as low   435
Bowed down in battle, sunk before the spear
Of despicable foes. With these in troop
Came Astoreth whom the Phoenicians called
Astartè, Queen of Heav'n, with crescent horns,
To whose bright image nightly by the moon   440
Sidonian virgins paid their vows and songs,
In Sion also not unsung where stood
Her temple on th' offensive mountain, built
By that uxorious king whose heart, though large,
Beguiled by fair idolatresses, fell   445
To idols foul. Thammuz came next behind
Whose annual wound in Lebanon allured
The Syrian damsels to lament his fate
In amorous ditties all a summer's day
While smooth Adonis from his native rock   450

---

418. "And the groves, and the carved images, and the molten images, [Josiah] brake in pieces, and made dust of them. . . . And he burnt the bones of the priests upon their altars, and cleansed Judah and Jerusalem" (2 Chronicles 34:4–5).

419–21. Throughout Palestine (Syria, as Milton called it), from the upper Euphrates in the north to the brook in the south that forms the boundary with Egypt.

444. *uxorious king*: i.e., Solomon (Latin *uxor*, "wife"). "And he had seven hundred wives, princesses, and three hundred concubines" (1 Kings 11:3). See lines 383–91 n.

450–52. The river Adonis was discolored annually, supposedly by the blood of the dying god Adonis, actually by ferrous mud stirred up by rains or, more poetically, by the petals of the anemone, or windflower, the Adonis (James G. Frazer, *Adonis, Attis, Osiris: Studies in Oriental Religion*, 3rd ed., vol. 1, p. 30). Since Milton says the river is *purple*, he is most likely thinking of the petals as the cause. The *love-tale* is the story, told (e.g., in Shakespeare's *Venus and Adonis*) of Venus's (Aphrodite's) love for

Ran purple to the sea, supposed with blood
Of Thammuz yearly wounded. The love-tale
Infected Sion's daughters with like heat
Whose wanton passions in the sacred porch
Ezekiel saw when by the vision led   455
His eye surveyed the dark idolatries
Of alienated Judah. Next came one
Who mourned in earnest when the captive ark
Maimed his brute image, head and hands lopped off
In his own temple on the grunsel edge   460
Where he fell flat and shamed his worshippers:
Dagon his name, sea monster, upward man
And downward fish, yet had his temple high
Reared in Azotus, dreaded through the coast
Of Palestine, in Gath and Ascalon   465
And Accaron and Gaza's frontier bounds.
   Him followed Rimmon whose delightful seat
Was fair Damascus on the fertile banks
Of Abbana and Pharphar, lucid streams.
He also 'gainst the house of God was bold.   470
A leper once he lost and gained a king,
Ahaz, his sottish conqueror, whom he drew
God's altar to disparage and displace
For one of Syrian mode whereon to burn
His odious offerings and adore the gods   475

---

the boy Adonis, who is killed by a boar. Venus changes Adonis into a flower, which
dies and revives annually.

452–57. In Ezekiel 8 the prophet is carried in spirit to Jerusalem and shown various sac-
rileges being committed there, among which were women sitting by the gate of the
temple precinct weeping for Thammuz (identified by Saint Jerome with Adonis) and
men inside the temple committing the *dark idolatries* of turning their backs to the
altar and facing east to worship the sun. In facing the physical light of the sun, they
are in mental and moral darkness. The kingdom of *Judah* is *alienated* because its
religious and political leaders, including Ezekiel, are in captivity in Babylon.

457–61. When the Philistines captured the ark of the covenant, they placed it in their
temple to Dagon: "And when they arose early on the morrow morning, behold,
Dagon was fallen upon his face to the ground before the ark of the Lord; and the
head of Dagon and both the palms of his hands were cut off upon the threshold; only
the stump of Dagon was left to him" (1 Samuel 5:4).

460. *grunsel*: threshold.

469. *Abbana and Pharphar*: See Glossary, DAMASCUS. That the streams are *lucid* 'Shining,
luminous' (OED; cf. 11.240) recalls Ariosto's description of them as "crystalline."
See *Orlando Furioso* 17.19 and 4.237–41 n.

471. *leper . . . king*: I.e., The Syrian god Rimmon loses as his worshipper the leper Naaman
but gains King Ahaz of Judah. Ahaz conquered Syria and its capital Damascus but
converted to Rimmon's worship, building an altar to him in the Jerusalem temple and
defacing the altar of God (2 Kings 16). Naaman was commander of the army of King
Rezin of Syria and a devout worshipper of Rimmon. But when at the prophet Elisha's
instructions he is cured of his leprosy by washing seven times in the river Jordan, Naaman changes his allegiance to the God of Israel. At first, Naaman was too proud to wash
in the Jordan, preferring the rivers of Damascus, Abbana, and Pharphar (2 Kings 5).

Whom he had vanquished. After these appeared
A crew who under names of old renown,
Osiris, Isis, Orus and their train,
With monstrous shapes and sorceries abused
Fanatic Egypt and her priests to seek   480
Their wand'ring gods disguised in brutish forms
Rather than human. Nor did Israel 'scape
Th' infection when their borrowed gold composed
The calf in Oreb and the rebel king
Doubled that sin in Bethel and in Dan,   485
Lik'ning his Maker to the grazèd ox,
Jehovah, who in one night when he passed
From Egypt marching equaled with one stroke
Both her first-born and all her bleating gods.
Belial came last, than whom a spirit more lewd   490
Fell not from Heaven or more gross to love
Vice for itself. To him no temple stood
Or altar smoked. Yet who more oft than he
In temples and at altars when the priest
Turns atheist, as did Eli's sons, who filled   495
With lust and violence the house of God?
In courts and palaces he also reigns
And in luxurious cities where the noise
Of riot ascends above their loftiest towers,
And injury and outrage. And when night   500
Darkens the streets then wander forth the sons

476–89. The gods of Egypt, especially debased in Milton's eyes because they have animal
heads. See Glossary, TYPHON. The Egyptian aberration was imitated by the Hebrews
when they worshipped the Golden Calf during the march out of Egypt (Exodus
32:1–6) and again when the *rebel king*, Jeroboam, *doubled* the sin by making two
calves. These were placed for worship in the northern- and southernmost points of
the northern kingdom: "Whereupon the king took counsel, and made two calves of
gold, and said unto them, It is too much for you to go up to Jerusalem: behold thy
gods, O Israel, which brought thee up out of the land of Egypt. And he set the one in
Bethel, and the other put he in Dan" (1 Kings 12:28–29).
488. *equaled*: killed. "For I will pass through the land of Egypt this night, and will smite
all the firstborn in the land of Egypt, both man and beast; and against all the gods of
Egypt I will execute judgment: I am the Lord" (Exodus 12:12).
492–98. Belial has no temple because he represents shamelessness and sexual violence,
which can occur anywhere, e.g., in the *courts, palaces*, and *luxurious cities*.
495–96. The sons of the high priest Eli were themselves priests: "Now the sons of Eli
were sons of Belial; they knew not the Lord" (1 Samuel 2:12).
500–5. The "sons of Belial" attempted to rape the angels who visited Lot in Sodom (Genesis
19:1–11). They later attempted to rape the Levite guest of a pious Jew in Gibeah. The
Levite sent his concubine out to them and they raped her to death (Judges 19). Milton
calls the concubine a "matron" because in the original Hebrew her status is uncertain. His grasp of the intention of this primitive and obscure tale—in particular,
that the rape and murder of the Levite, or of the daughter of the host, would have
been "worse" than the rape and murder of the woman—is accurate. But it is one
moment when the poet's legendarily strict morals are incoherent.

Of Belial flown with insolence and wine.
Witness the streets of Sodom and that night
In Gibeah when the hospitable door
Exposed a matron to avoid worse rape.   505
    These were the prime in order and in might.
The rest were long to tell though far renowned:
Th' Ionian gods of Javan's issue, held
Gods, yet confessed later than Heaven and Earth,
Their boasted parents: Titan, Heav'n's first-born,   510
With his enormous brood and birthright seized
By younger Saturn. He from mightier Jove
(His own and Rhea's son) like measure found:
So Jove usurping reigned. These first in Crete
And Ida known, thence on the snowy top   515
Of cold Olympus ruled the middle air,
Their highest heaven, or on the Delphian cliff
Or in Dodona and through all the bounds
Of Doric land, or who with Saturn old
Fled o'er Adria to th' Hesperian fields   520
And o'er the Celtic roamed the utmost isles.
All these and more came flocking but with looks
Downcast and damp, yet such wherein appeared
Obscure some glimpse of joy t' have found their chief
Not in despair, t' have found themselves not lost   525
In loss itself which on his count'nance cast
Like doubtful hue. But he his wonted pride
Soon recollecting with high words that bore
Semblance of worth, not substance, gently raised
Their fainting courage and dispelled their fears.   530
Then straight commands that at the warlike sound
Of trumpets loud and clarions be upreared
His mighty standard. That proud honor claimed
Azazel as his right, a cherub tall
Who forthwith from the glittering staff unfurled   535
Th' imperial ensign which full high advanced
Shone like a meteor streaming to the wind

---

502. *flown*: flushed.
508–21. The gods of Greek myth as described in Hesiod's *Theogony* (literally, "sexual
    generation of the gods"), maiming, mating with, and overthrowing one another. The
    Greeks were thought to descend from one of the three sons of Noah, Japhet.
    The Greek gods are to Milton obviously false gods because in Hesiod's account they
    are *later* than Heaven (*Ouranos*) and Earth (*Gaia*), from whom they are generated.
520–21. Over the Adriatic Sea, on Italy's east coast, to Italy herself, Hesperia. The *i* in
    Adria is long. Those gods who fled with Saturn from usurping Jove went north to the
    British Isles, i.e., the *Celtic* (fields) and the *utmost*, i.e., northernmost islands beyond,
    including the "stormy Hebrides" ("Lycidas," line 156) off Scotland's northwest coast.
536. *ensign*: military banner.

With gems and golden luster rich emblazed,
Seraphic arms and trophies, all the while
Sonorous metal blowing martial sounds   540
At which the universal host upsent
A shout that tore Hell's concave and beyond
Frighted the reign of Chaos and old Night.
    All in a moment through the gloom were seen
Ten thousand banners rise into the air   545
With orient colors waving. With them rose
A forest huge of spears; and thronging helms
Appeared and serried shields in thick array
Of depth immeasurable. Anon they move
In perfect phalanx to the Dorian mood   550
Of flutes and soft recorders, such as raised
To heighth of noblest temper heroes old
Arming to battle, and instead of rage
Deliberate valor breathed, firm and unmoved
With dread of death to flight or foul retreat,   555
Nor wanting pow'r to mitigate and swage
With solemn touches, troubled thoughts, and chase
Anguish and doubt and fear and sorrow and pain
From mortal or immortal minds. Thus they
Breathing united force with fixèd thought   560
Moved on in silence to soft pipes that charmed
Their painful steps o'er the burnt soil. And now
Advanced in view they stand a horrid front
Of dreadful length and dazzling arms in guise
Of warriors old with ordered spear and shield   565
Awaiting what command their mighty chief
Had to impose. He through the armèd files
Darts his experienced eye and soon traverse
The whole battalion views, their order due,
Their visages and stature as of gods,   570

---

546. *orient*: adjective describing the color of the sun rising in the east; lustrous, like a
    pearl.
548. *serried*: in close order.
550–55. *phalanx*: a tightly packed, heavily armed rank of foot soldiers in ancient Greek
    warfare. *Dorian mood*: a musical mode suited to military discipline, favored for this
    reason by Plato in the *Republic* (3.399a). The ancient Spartans, who were distin-
    guished for valor, went calmly into battle to the sound of flutes, impervious to fear or
    to rage (Plutarch, *Lycurgus* 22.3). In Homer, the clamorous Trojans are contrasted
    with the Achaeans (Greeks), who "move in silence, breathing strength" (*Iliad* 3.8).
554–55. *unmoved . . . retreat*: fear of death cannot move them to fly or to retreat.
563. *horrid front*: Latin *horridus*, "bristling, trembling and inspiring cold terror." Seen
    from the front, their ranks bristle with arms and cause a chill of horror.
567–68. *files . . . traverse*: Satan walks along the side of his army, darting his eye down the
    lanes between each rank to inspect it.
569. *battalion*: the main body of an army.

Their number last he sums. And now his heart
Distends with pride and, hard'ning in his strength,
Glories. For never since created Man
Met such embodied force as named with these
Could merit more than that small infantry   575
Warred on by cranes, though all the giant brood
Of Phlegra with th' heroic race were joined
That fought at Thebes and Ilium, on each side
Mixed with auxiliar gods, and what resounds
In fable or romance of Uther's son   580
Begirt with British and Armoric knights
And all who since, baptized or infidel,
Jousted in Aspramont or Montalban,
Damasco, or Morocc' or Trebisond,
Or whom Biserta sent from Afric shore   585
When Charlemagne with all his peerage fell
By Fontarrábia. Thus far these beyond
Compare of mortal prowess yet observed
Their dread commander. He above the rest
In shape and gesture proudly eminent   590
Stood like a tower. His form had yet not lost
All her original brightness nor appeared
Less than archangel ruined and th' excess
Of glory obscured, as when the sun, new risen,
Looks through the horizontal misty air   595
Shorn of his beams or from behind the moon
In dim eclipse disastrous twilight sheds
On half the nations and with fear of change
Perplexes monarchs. Darkened so, yet shone
Above them all th' archangel, but his face   600
Deep scars of thunder had entrenched and care
Sat on his faded cheek, but under brows
Of dauntless courage and considerate pride
Waiting revenge. Cruel his eye, but cast
Signs of remorse and passion to behold   605
The fellows of his crime, the followers rather
(Far other once beheld in bliss) condemned

573. *since created Man*: since Man was created.
573–87. I.e., To the largest army of men ever amassed add the following: the giants who
    fought the Olympians, all the heroes in two separate Greek wars (at Troy and at
    Thebes), the Olympian gods who became involved in those Greek wars, and all the
    knights of medieval romance. Such an army would still be as puny, compared with
    this army of rebel angels, as the army of pygmies (mentioned in *Iliad* 3.3–6), which
    fought against cranes.
594–99. In 1667 these lines were objected to—as much for their superstition as for per-
    plexed monarchs—by the royalist licenser of the poem. See Nicholas von Maltzahn,
    "The First Reception of *Paradise Lost*," *RES* 48.188 (1996): 479–99.
603. *considerate*: calculating.

For ever now to have their lot in pain:
Millions of spirits for his fault amerced
Of Heav'n and from eternal splendors flung   610
For his revolt. Yet faithful how they stood,
Their glory withered. As when heaven's fire
Hath scathed the forest oaks or mountain pines,
With singèd top their stately growth though bare
Stands on the blasted heath. He now prepared   615
To speak, whereat their doubled ranks they bend
From wing to wing and half enclose him round
With all his peers. Attention held them mute.
Thrice he assayed and thrice, in spite of scorn,
Tears such as angels weep burst forth. At last   620
Words interwove with sighs found out their way:
    O myriads of immortal spirits, O Pow'rs
Matchless but with th' Almighty (and that strife
Was not inglorious though th' event was dire
As this place testifies and this dire change,   625
Hateful to utter). But what pow'r of mind
Foreseeing or presaging from the depth
Of knowledge past or present could have feared
How such united force of gods, how such
As stood like these, could ever know repulse?   630
For who can yet believe, though after loss,
That all these puissant legions whose exíle
Hath emptied Heav'n shall fail to re-ascend,
Self-raised, and repossess their native seat?
For me be witness all the host of Heaven   635
If counsels different or danger shunned
By me have lost our hopes! But He who reigns
Monarch in Heaven till then as one secure
Sat on His throne upheld by old repute,
Consent or custom, and His regal state   640
Put forth at full but still His strength concealed,
Which tempted our attempt and wrought our fall.
Henceforth His might we know, and know our own,
So as not either to provoke or dread
New war provoked. Our better part remains   645
To work in close design by fraud or guile
What force effected not, that He no less
At length from us may find who overcomes
By force hath overcome but half His foe!

609. *amerced*: deprived.
632. *puissant*: powerful.
642. *tempted our attempt*: I.e., God's not revealing his strength is to blame for our fall, for that concealment tempted us to try to overthrow him.

Space may produce new worlds whereof so rife   650
There went a fame in Heav'n that He ere long
Intended to create and therein plant
A generation whom His choice regard
Should favor equal to the sons of Heaven.
Thither, if but to pry, shall be perhaps   655
Our first eruption, thither or elsewhere.
For this infernal pit shall never hold
Celestial spirits in bondage, nor th' abyss
Long under darkness cover! But these thoughts
Full counsel must mature. Peace is despaired,   660
For who can think submission? War then, war
Open or understood, must be resolved!
　　He spake, and to confirm his words out flew
Millions of flaming swords drawn from the thighs
Of mighty cherubim. The sudden blaze   665
Far round illumined Hell. Highly they raged
Against the High'st and fierce with graspèd arms
Clashed on their sounding shields the din of war,
Hurling defiance toward the vault of Heaven.
　　There stood a hill not far whose grisly top   670
Belched fire and rolling smoke. The rest entire
Shone with a glossy scurf, undoubted sign
That in his womb was hid metallic ore,
The work of sulfur. Thither winged with speed
A num'rous brígade hastened, as when bands   675
Of pioneers with spade and pickaxe armed
Forerun the royal camp to trench a field
Or cast a rampart. Mammon led them on,
Mammon the least erected spirit that fell
From Heav'n, for ev'n in Heav'n his looks and thoughts 680
Were always downward bent, admiring more
The riches of Heav'n's pavement, trodden gold,
Than aught divine or holy else enjoyed
In vision beatific. By him first
Men also, and by his suggestion taught,   685
Ransacked the center and with impious hands
Rifled the bowels of their mother Earth
For treasures better hid. Soon had his crew

---

651. *fame*: rumor.
653. *A generation*: i.e., human beings.
672. *scurf*: scaly crust.
674. *work of sulfur*: Metals were supposed to be formed by the combination of sulfur and
　　mercury.
676. *pioneers*: military engineers, sappers, responsible for fortifications, bridges, etc.

Opened into the hill a spacious wound
And digged out ribs of gold. Let none admire   690
That riches grow in Hell: that soil may best
Deserve the precious bane! And here let those
Who boast in mortal things and wond'ring tell
Of Babel and the works of Memphian kings
Learn how their greatest monuments of fame   695
And strength and art are easily outdone
By spirits reprobate, and in an hour
What in an age they with incessant toil
And hands innumerable scarce perform.
Nigh on the plain in many cells prepared   700
That underneath had veins of liquid fire
Sluiced from the lake, a second multitude
With wondrous art founded the massy ore,
Severing each kind, and scummed the bullion dross.
A third as soon had formed within the ground   705
A various mold and from the boiling cells
By strange conveyance filled each hollow nook,
As in an organ from one blast of wind
To many a row of pipes the soundboard breathes.
Anon out of the earth a fabric huge   710
Rose like an exhalation with the sound
Of dulcet symphonies and voices sweet,
Built like a temple where pilasters round
Were set and Doric pillars overlaid
With golden architrave, nor did there want   715
Cornice or frieze with bossy sculptures graven.
The roof was fretted gold. Not Babylon
Nor great Alcairo such magnificence
Equaled in all their glories to enshrine
Belus or Serapis their gods, or seat   720
Their kings, when Egypt with Assyria strove

690. *admire*: wonder at. Latin *admiror*. Compare 2.677.
694. References to the two great wicked construction works of the Bible, the Tower of
   Babel (Genesis 11:1–9) and Pharaoh's building project in Exodus.
698. *they*: the wicked builders.
700. *cells*: separated pools.
702. *Sluiced*: channeled.
703. *founded*: in the 1667 printing; *found out* in 1674. The change to *found out* was perhaps motivated by a desire to be more technically correct, since the ore is being
   separated from the rock. *Founded* is better. To *found* metal means to melt it and
   pour it into a mold, a meaning that is adequate to the process Milton describes.
705–17. Milton thinks of the rising of this palace of Hell as a kind of visual music. Hence
   the comparison with the organ (which Milton played), where one blast of air is sent
   over the *soundboard* into pipes of different length. From these pipes all kinds of
   musical structures develop, just as pillars, cornices, and friezes (architectural features) evolve as Satan's palace rises in the air.

In wealth and luxury. Th' ascending pile
Stood fixed her stately heighth, and straight the doors,
Op'ning their brazen folds, discover wide
Within her ample spaces o'er the smooth   725
And level pavement. From the archèd roof
Pendent by subtle magic many a row
Of starry lamps and blazing cressets fed
With naphtha and asphaltus yielded light
As from a sky. The hasty multitude   730
Admiring entered and the work some praise
And some the architect. His hand was known
In Heav'n by many a towered structure high
Where sceptred angels held their residence
And sat as princes, whom the Súpreme King   735
Exalted to such power and gave to rule
Each in his hierarchy the orders bright.
Nor was his name unheard or unadored
In ancient Greece and in Ausonian land.
Men called him Mulciber, and how he fell   740
From Heav'n they fabled, thrown by angry Jove
Sheer o'er the crystal battlements. From morn
To noon he fell, from noon to dewy eve,
A summer's day, and with the setting sun
Dropped from the zenith like a falling star   745
On Lemnós th' Aegéan isle. Thus they relate,
Erring. For he with his rebellious rout
Fell long before, nor aught availed him now
T' have built in Heav'n high tow'rs, nor did he 'scape
By all his engines but was headlong sent   750
With his industrious crew to build in Hell.
Meanwhile the wingèd heralds by command
Of sovereign pow'r with awful ceremony
And trumpets' sound throughout the host proclaim
A solemn council forthwith to be held   755

---

728. *cressets*: metal cups suspended from above, containing such flammable materials as
    naphtha and *asphaltus* (tar) in the next line.
732. *the architect*: Mammon, symbolizing worldly wealth and the overvaluing of wealth,
    is here aligned with the Greek and Roman gods of the forge, Hephaistos and Mul-
    ciber, or Vulcan.
740–46. The fall of Hephaistos, when Zeus threw him from heaven, is described by Heph-
    aistos himself in *Iliad* 1.591–93: "Seizing me by the foot, he threw me from the
    enchanted threshold of Olympos and I fell for an entire day, falling together with the
    sun, until I plunged down onto the isle of Lemnos."
746–48. Milton regards classical myths as deformations (often beautiful deformations)
    of biblical truth. Homer's account of Hephaistos being thrown from Olympos, which
    Hephaistos recounts amid divine laughter in the very place from which he was
    thrown, is a beautiful deformation of the stern truth that Mammon was driven into
    Hell by God's fiery thunder, never to return.

At Pandemonium the high capital
Of Satan and his peers. Their summons called
From every band and squarèd regiment
By place or choice the worthiest, they anon
With hundreds and with thousands trooping came   760
Attended. All accéss was thronged, the gates
And porches wide, but chief the spacious hall
(Though like a covered field where champions bold
Wont ride in armed and at the soldan's chair
Defied the best of paynim chivalry   765
To mortal combat or career with lance)
Thick swarmed, both on the ground and in the air,
Brushed with the hiss of rustling wings. As bees
In springtime when the sun with Taurus rides
Pour forth their populous youth about the hive   770
In clusters, they among fresh dews and flow'rs
Fly to and fro or on the smoothèd plank,
The suburb of their straw-built citadel,
New rubbed with balm, expatiate and confer
Their state affairs, so thick the airy crowd   775
Swarmed and were straitened, till the signal giv'n,
Behold, a wonder! They but now who seemed
In bigness to surpass Earth's giant sons
Now less than smallest dwarfs in narrow room
Throng numberless like that Pygméan race   780
Beyond the Indian mount or fairy elves
Whose midnight revels by a forest side
Or fountain some belated peasant sees,
Or dreams he sees, while overhead the moon
Sits arbitress and nearer to the earth   785
Wheels her pale course. They on their mirth and dance
Intent with jocund music charm his ear.
At once with joy and fear his heart rebounds!
Thus incorporeal spirits to smallest forms
Reduced their shapes immense and were at large,   790

756. *Pandemonium*: The word is Milton's coinage, formed from Greek *pan*, "all"; *daimon*, "demon, supernatural being"; and the suffix -*ion*, indicating a place of worship, a building.
761. *All accéss*: all entrances.
763. *covered field*: a field covered with a huge, decorated, sideless tent.
764–68. *soldan*: sultan. Christian knights boldly ride beneath the tent roof up to the sultan's throne, where they issue a challenge to fight the strongest pagan knights. Although the hall of Pandemonium is as large as such a covered field, still it is thick with swarming devils, whose wings brush the building and also one another.
765. *paynim*: pagan.
768–80. The comparison of the rebel angels to swarming bees leads to their actual diminution, making it possible for them all to enter Pandemonium.
786. *They*: the fairies.

Though without number still amidst the hall
Of that infernal court. But far within
And in their own dimensions like themselves
The great seraphic lords and cherubim
In close recess and secret conclave sat,   795
A thousand demi-gods on golden seats
Frequent and full. After short silence then
And summons read the great consult began.

Book Two

The Argument

The consultation begun, Satan debates whether another battle be
to be hazarded for the recovery of Heaven: some advise it, others
dissuade. A third proposal is preferred, mentioned before by Satan,
to search the truth of that prophecy or tradition in Heaven concerning another world and another kind of creature equal or not
much inferior to themselves, about this time to be created. Their
doubt who shall be sent on this difficult search. Satan, their chief,
undertakes alone the voyage, is honored and applauded. The council thus ended, the rest betake them several ways and to several
employments as their inclinations lead them to entertain the time
till Satan return. He passes on his journey to Hell gates, finds them
shut and who sat there to guard them, by whom at length they are
opened, and discover to him the great gulf between Hell and
Heaven. With what difficulty he passes through, directed by Chaos,
the power of that place, to the sight of this new world which he
sought.

High on a throne of royal state which far
Outshone the wealth of Ormus and of Ind
Or where the gorgeous East with richest hand
Show'rs on her kings barbaric pearl and gold
Satan exalted sat, by merit raised   5
To that bad eminence and from despair
Thus high uplifted beyond hope aspires
Beyond thus high, insatiate to pursue
Vain war with Heaven, and by success untaught
His proud imaginations thus displayed: 10
    Powers and Dominions, deities of Heaven,

---

793. *their own dimensions*: retaining their own size, unlike the less important rebel angels.
795. *conclave*: an assembly of Roman Catholic cardinals.
797. *Frequent*: crowded (Latin *frequens*, "full, crowded, thronging").

For since no deep within her gulf can hold
Immortal vigor, though oppressed and fall'n,
I give not Heav'n for lost. From this descent
Celestial Virtues rising will appear   15
More glorious and more dread than from no fall
And trust themselves to fear no second fate.
Me though just right and the fixed laws of Heaven
Did first create your leader, next free choice
With what besides in counsel or in fight   20
Hath been achieved of merit, yet this loss,
Thus far at least recovered, hath much more
Established in a safe unenvied throne
Yielded with full consent. The happier state
In Heav'n which follows dignity might draw   25
Envy from each inferior. But who here
Will envy whom the highest place exposes
Foremost to stand against the Thunderer's aim,
Your bulwark, and condemns to greatest share
Of endless pain? Where there is then no good   30
For which to strive no strife can grow up there
From faction. For none sure will claim in Hell
Precedence, none whose portion is so small
Of present pain that with ambitious mind
Will covet more! With this advantage then   35
To union and firm faith and firm accord
More than can be in Heav'n we now return
To claim our just inheritance of old,
Surer to prosper than prosperity
Could have assured us, and by what best way—   40
Whether of open war or covert guile—
We now debate. Who can advise may speak.
    He ceased, and next him Moloch, sceptered king
Stood up, the strongest and the fiercest spirit
That fought in Heaven, now fiercer by despair.   45

Book Two
    The Argument, final sentence. Satan is given directions by Chaos, who is the
    reigning power of the realm of chaos (*that place*). These directions lead Satan
    to the distant sight of the created universe (*this new world*), which Satan had been
    seeking. Once inside that universe Satan will seek out the earth, where Eve and
    Adam live.
15. *Celestial Virtues*: powers of heaven, referring to the rebel angels.
18–26. I.e., By the law of Heaven, by your own free choice, and by the merit of my own
    achievements, I am your leader. But our fall (though already we begin to undo it, as
    you see) has made me even more secure on my throne, which you readily consent to
    my having and do not envy, as you might envy me if I were on a happier throne (*hap-
    pier state*) in Heaven.
27. A "feminine" line (i.e., an eleven-syllable line in which the final syllable of the last
    word is unaccented).

His trust was with th' Eternal to be deemed
Equal in strength and rather than be less
Cared not to be at all. With that care lost
Went all his fear. Of God or Hell or worse
He recked not and these words thereafter spake: 50
 My sentence is for open war: of wiles
More unexpért I boast not: them let those
Contrive who need or when they need, not now.
For while they sit contriving shall the rest—
Millions that stand in arms and longing wait   55
The signal to ascend—sit lingering here
Heav'n's fugitives and for their dwelling place
Accept this dark opprobrious den of shame,
The prison of His tyranny who reigns
By our delay? No! Let us rather choose   60
Armed with hell flames and fury all at once
O'er Heav'n's high tow'rs to force resistless way,
Turning our tortures into horrid arms
Against the Torturer when to meet the noise
Of His almighty engine He shall hear   65
Infernal thunder and for lightning see
Black fire and horror shot with equal rage
Among His angels and His throne itself
Mixed with Tartarean sulphur and strange fire,
His own invented torments. But perhaps   70
The way seems difficult and steep to scale
With upright wing against a higher foe.
Let such bethink them (if the sleepy drench
Of that forgetful lake benumb not still)
That in our proper motion we ascend   75
Up to our native seat. Descent and fall
To us is adverse. Who but felt of late
When the fierce Foe hung on our broken rear
Insulting and pursued us through the deep
With what compulsion and laborious flight   80
We sunk thus low? Th' ascent is easy then.
Th' event is feared? Should we again provoke
Our Stronger some worse way His wrath may find
To our destruction—if there be in Hell

---

52. *unexpért*: unexperienced (in wiles).
65. *engine*: contrivance (the thunder with which the rebel angels were vanquished).
74. *forgetful lake*: the lake of fire on which the rebel angels lay unconscious, suggesting
 Lethe, the river of oblivion. Cf. 1.266, *oblivious pool*.
78. *rear*: rear guard of the army.
79. *Insulting*: springing upon and trampling.
82. *event*: consequence.

Fear to be worse destroyed! What can be worse   85
Than to dwell here, driven out from bliss, condemned
In this abhorrèd deep to utter woe
Where pain of unextinguishable fire
Must exercise us without hope of end,
The vassals of His anger, when the scourge   90
Inexorably and the torturing hour
Calls us to penance? More destroyed than thus
We should be quite abolished and expire.
What fear we then? What doubt we to incense
His utmost ire which to the heighth enraged   95
Will either quite consume us and reduce
To nothing this essential, happier far
Than, miserable, to have eternal being?
Or if our substance be indeed divine
And cannot cease to be we are at worst   100
On this side nothing and by proof we feel
Our power sufficient to disturb His Heaven
And with perpetual inroads to alarm,
Though inaccessible, His fatal throne,
Which if not victory is yet revenge.   105
    He ended frowning and his look denounced
Desperate revenge and battle dangerous
To less than gods. On th' other side up rose
Belial in act more graceful and humane:
A fairer person lost not Heav'n! He seemed   110
For dignity composed and high explóit,
But all was false and hollow though his tongue
Dropped manna and could make the worse appear
The better reason to perplex and dash
Maturest counsels. For his thoughts were low,   115
To vice industrious but to nobler deeds
Timorous and slothful. Yet he pleased the ear
And with persuasive accent thus began:
    I should be much for open war, O peers,

94. *doubt*: fear.
97. *essential*: fundamental substance. The immortal substance of angel's bodies.
100–101. I.e., We are already in the worst state possible, short of annihilation.
106. *denounced*: proclaimed.
113–14. *make the worse . . . reason*: In Cicero's *Brutus* (8.30) the Sophists are charged
       with teaching politicians how to make the inferior and (it is implied) the morally
       worse argument appear to be best. Aristotle (*Rhetoric* 1402a24) says this was what
       Protagoras professed to teach: "to make the weaker appear the stronger argument."
       His phrase is drawn verbatim from Plato's *Apology* (18b), in which Socrates defends
       himself against that charge. The expression was commonplace and casts Belial as a
       typical corrupt politician.

As not behind in hate, if what was urged   120
Main reason to persuade immediate war
Did not dissuade me most and seem to cast
Ominous conjecture on the whole success:
When he who most excels in fact of arms—
In what he counsels and in what excels   125
Mistrustful—grounds his courage on despair
And utter dissolution as the scope
Of all his aim after some dire revenge.
First, what revenge? The tow'rs of Heav'n are filled
With armèd watch that render all accéss   130
Impregnable. Oft on the bord'ring deep
Encamp their legions or with óbscure wing
Scout far and wide into the realm of Night,
Scorning surprise. Or could we break our way
By force and at our heels all Hell should rise   135
With blackest insurrection to confound
Heav'n's purest light, yet our great Enemy
All incorruptible would on His throne
Sit unpolluted and th' ethereal mould,
Incapable of stain, would soon expel   140
Her mischief and purge off the baser fire,
Victorious. Thus repulsed our final hope
Is flat despair: we must exasperate
Th' Almighty Victor to spend all His rage.
And that must end us, that must be our cure: 145
To be no more. Sad cure! For who would lose,
Though full of pain, this intellectual being,
Those thoughts that wander through eternity,
To perish rather, swallowed up and lost
In the wide womb of uncreated night   150
Devoid of sense and motion? And who knows,
Let this be good, whether our angry Foe
Can give it or will ever? How He can
Is doubtful. That He never will is sure.
Will He, so wise, let loose at once His ire,   155
Belike through impotence, or unaware,
To give His enemies their wish and end
Them in His anger whom His anger saves

120–23. I.e., if the reason given (by Moloch) for immediate counterattack were not the
best argument against it.
124. *fact of arms*: acts of valor (Latin *facio*, "to make, to do").
139. *ethereal mould*: heavenly structure, which would of itself expel the foreign substance
of infernal fire.
152. *Let this be good*: even if we allow annihilation to be desirable.

To punish endless? "Wherefore cease we then?"
Say they who counsel war, "We are decreed,   160
Reserved and destined to eternal woe
Whatever doing. What can we suffer more?
What can we suffer worse?" Is this then worst,
Thus sitting, thus consulting, thus in arms?
What, when we fled amain pursued and strook   165
With Heav'n's afflicting thunder and besought
The deep to shelter us? This Hell then seemed
A refuge from those wounds. Or when we lay
Chained on the burning lake? That sure was worse!
What if the breath that kindled those grim fires   170
Awaked should blow them into sev'nfold rage
And plunge us in the flames? Or from above
Should intermitted vengeance arm again
His red right hand to plague us? What if all
Her stores were opened and this firmament   175
Of Hell should spout her cataracts of fire,
Impendent horrors threat'ning hideous fall,
One day upon our heads while we, perhaps
Designing or exhorting glorious war,
Caught in a fiery tempest shall be hurled   180
Each on his rock transfixed, the sport and prey
Of racking whirlwinds, or for ever sunk
Under yon boiling ocean, wrapped in chains,
There to converse with everlasting groans,
Unréspited, unpitied, unreprieved,   185
Ages of hopeless end? This would be worse!
War, therefore, open or concealed alike
My voice dissuades. For what can force or guile
With Him? Or who deceive His mind, whose eye
Views all things at one view? He from Heav'n's heighth   190
All these our motions vain sees and derides,
Not more almighty to resist our might
Than wise to frustrate all our plots and wiles.
Shall we then live thus vile, the race of Heav'n
Thus trampled, thus expelled to suffer here   195

174. See Horace, *Odes* 1.2.2–3, where Jove strikes the sacred hills of Rome "with his red right hand."
175. *Her*: Hell's.
177. *Impendent*: overhanging.
188–89. The implied main verb is *accomplish*; i.e., what can force or guile accomplish against God?
191. "He that sitteth in the heavens shall laugh: the Lord shall have them in derision" (Psalm 2:4).
192–93. I.e., God is no less wise in anticipating our subterfuges than he is powerful to repel our attacks.

Chains and these torments? Better these than worse
By my advice since fate inevitable
Subdues us and omnipotent decree,
The victor's will. To suffer, as to do,
Our strength is equal nor the law unjust   200
That so ordains. This was at first resolved,
If we were wise, against so great a Foe
Contending and so doubtful what might fall.
I laugh when those who at the spear are bold
And vent'rous, if that fail them shrink and fear   205
What yet they know must follow: to endure
Exile or ignominy or bonds or pain,
The sentence of their conqueror. This is now
Our doom which if we can sustain and bear
Our súpreme Foe in time may much remit   210
His anger and perhaps thus far removed
Not mind us not offending, satisfied
With what is punished, whence these raging fires
Will slacken if His breath stir not their flames.
Our purer essence then will overcome   215
Their noxious vapor or inured not feel,
Or changed at length and to the place conformed
In temper and in nature will receive
Familiar the fierce heat. And void of pain
This horror will grow mild, this darkness light,   220
Besides what hope the never-ending flight
Of future days may bring, what chance, what change
Worth waiting since our present lot appears
For happy though but ill, for ill not worst,
If we procure not to ourselves more woe.   225
    Thus Belial with words clothed in reason's garb
Counseled ignoble ease and peaceful sloth,
Not peace, and after him thus Mammon spake:
    Either to disenthrone the King of Heav'n
We war, if war be best, or to regain   230
Our own right lost. Him to unthrone we then
May hope when everlasting Fate shall yield

197. A feminine line. See line 27 n.
203. *fall*: occur.
224–25. I.e., Although our condition now isn't a happy one, it is also not the worst. It will remain not the worst so long as we do not provoke God to further ire.
229–35. Mammon attributes both futile alternatives to the former two speakers: the first, war, is attributed to Moloch, the second, to wait for better times to overthrow God, to Belial. The latter is an inexact summary of Belial's position, since Belial does not propose overthrowing God at some time in the future. Yet this aim might still be attributed to Belial, as an inevitable consequence of his position. That is exactly what Mammon does in the sentence following. But his argument comes to much the same as Belial's: let us make the best of it in Hell.

To fickle Chance and Chaos judge the strife.
The former vain to hope argues as vain
The latter. For what place can be for us   235
Within Heav'n's bound unless Heav'n's Lord supreme
We overpower? Suppose He should relent
And publish grace to all on promise made
Of new subjection. With what eyes could we
Stand in His presence humble and receive   240
Strict laws imposed to celebrate His throne
With warbled hymns and to His Godhead sing
Forced hallelujahs while He lordly sits
Our envied sov'reign and His altar breathes
Ambrosial odors and ambrosial flowers,   245
Our servile offerings? This must be our task
In Heav'n, this our delight. How wearisome
Eternity so spent in worship paid
To whom we hate! Let us not then pursue—
By force impossible, by leave obtained   250
Unacceptable, though in Heav'n—our state
Of splendid vassalage but rather seek
Our own good from ourselves and from our own
Live to ourselves, though in this vast recess,
Free and to none accountable, preferring   255
Hard liberty before the easy yoke
Of servile pomp. Our greatness will appear
Then most conspicuous when great things of small—
Useful of hurtful, prosperous of adverse—
We can create and in what place soe'er   260
Thrive under evil and work ease out of pain
Through labor and endurance. This deep world
Of darkness do we dread? How oft amidst

---

252. *vassalage*: servility, as displayed by medieval vassals.
261. This verse may appear to be hypermetrical, having eleven syllables with a strong
accent on the last syllable, *pain*. The unaccented syllable that should normally come
at the end of an eleven-syllable line comes instead before the caesura, or medial
pause. But in *Paradise Lost* major pauses occur almost as frequently in the middle of
the line as they do at the end, thus allowing the medial placement of the extra, unaccented syllable. Furthermore, Milton arranges the verse with an acoustical arch of
three strong beats following the caesura: *and work ease*. The rhythm is familiar as an
element of one of several formulaic line endings in Homer: spondee, dactyl, spondee,
as in ἀρίστη φαίνετο βουλή (ar-IS-TE PHAIN-e-to BOU-LE), "seemed the best counsel" (*Iliad* 2.5, 7.325, 9.94; *Odyssey* 11.230): ⌣−−−−⌣⌣−−−. The two strong beats of
the spondee (IS-TE) combine with the strong first beat of the dactyl (PHAIN) to
make three strong beats, or long syllables, followed by the two light beats of the
dactyl (*e-to*) and then the terminal spondee (BOU-LE). This is nearly identical to
"AND WORK EASE out of PAIN," the only difference being the replacement of the
two-syllable spondee with the strong final beat, PAIN. The key is the sustain of the
three long syllables. Similar effects throughout the poem support Matthew Arnold's
claim (see p. 426) that reading Milton is as close as one can come in English to the
effect of reading Homer.

Thick clouds and dark doth Heav'n's all-ruling Sire
Choose to reside, His glory unobscured,   265
And with the majesty of darkness round
Covers His throne from whence deep thunders roar,
Must'ring their rage, and Heav'n resembles Hell?
As He our darkness, cannot we His light
Imitate when we please? This desert soil   270
Wants not her hidden luster: gems and gold!
Nor want we skill or art from whence to raise
Magnificence. And what can Heav'n show more?
Our torments also may in length of time
Become our elements, these piercing fires   275
As soft as now severe, our temper changed
Into their temper, which must needs remove
The sensible of pain. All things invite
To peaceful counsels and the settled state
Of order, how in safety best we may   280
Compose our present evils with regard
Of what we are and where, dismissing quite
All thoughts of war. Ye have what I advise.
    He scarce had finished when such murmur filled
Th' assembly as when hollow rocks retain   285
The sound of blust'ring winds which all night long
Had roused the sea, now with hoarse cadence lull
Seafaring men o'erwatched whose bark by chance
Or pinnace anchors in a craggy bay
After the tempest. Such applause was heard   290
As Mammon ended, and his sentence pleased,
Advising peace, for such another field
They dreaded worse than Hell, so much the fear
Of thunder and the sword of Michaël
Wrought still within them and, no less, desire   295
To found this nether empire which might rise
By policy and long procéss of time
In emulation opposite to Heaven.
Which when Beëlzebub perceived (than whom,
Satan except, none higher sat) with grave   300
Aspéct he rose and in his rising seemed
A pillar of state. Deep on his front engrav'n
Deliberation sat and public care
And princely counsel in his face yet shone,

284–88. Comparison of a murmuring crowd to a rising (or, here, a falling) storm at sea is
traditional in epic poetry. See *Iliad* 2.142–46; *Aeneid* 10.96–99.
287. The subject of *lull* is *winds*.
297. *policy*: political manipulation. *Procéss* an advance or forward march; Milton preserves the Latin military sense of the word. See p. 426.

Majestic though in ruin. Sage he stood   305
With Atlantéan shoulders fit to bear
The weight of mightiest monarchies. His look
Drew audience and attention still as night
Or summer's noontide air while thus he spake:
    Thrones and Imperial Pow'rs, offspring of Heav'n,   310
Ethereal Virtues, or these titles now
Must we renounce and changing style be called
Princes of Hell? For so the popular vote
Inclines here to continue and build up here
A growing empire. Doubtless! while we dream   315
And know not that the King of Heav'n hath doomed
This place our dungeon not our safe retreat
Beyond His potent arm to live exempt
From Heav'n's high jurisdiction in new league
Banded against His throne, but to remain   320
In strictest bondage, though thus far removed,
Under th' inevitable curb reserved,
His captive multitude. For He, be sure,
In heighth or depth still first and last will reign
Sole king and of His kingdom lose no part   325
By our revolt but over Hell extend
His empire and with iron scepter rule
Us here as with His golden those in Heaven.
What sit we then projecting peace and war?
War hath determined us and foiled with loss   330
Irreparable, terms of peace yet none
Vouchsafed or sought. For what peace will be giv'n
To us enslaved but custody severe
And stripes and arbitrary punishment
Inflicted? And what peace can we return   335
But to our pow'r hostility and hate,
Untamed reluctance and revenge, though slow,
Yet ever plotting how the Conqueror least
May reap His conquest and may least rejoice
In doing what we most in suffering feel?   340
Nor will occasion want nor shall we need
With dangerous expedition to invade

---

305. *Atlantéan*: like Atlas, who bears the weight of the sky on his shoulders.
312. *style*: written title; from Latin *stilus*, "pen."
314. *continue* and *and* are elided.
327. *scepter*: a rod, symbol of royal authority, but also a weapon. "Thou shalt break them
    with a rod of iron; thou shalt dash them in pieces like a potter's vessel" (Psalm 2:9).
334. *stripes*: from whipping.
336. *to our pow'r*: with all our might.
337. *reluctance*: struggling back, against. See 6.58 n.
338. *Conqueror* has two syllables.

Heav'n whose high walls fear no assault or siege
Or ambush from the deep. What if we find
Some easier enterprise? There is a place,   345
If ancient and prophetic fame in Heav'n
Err not, another world, the happy seat
Of some new race called Man about this time
To be created like to us though less
In pow'r and excellence but favored more   350
Of Him who rules above. So was His will
Pronounced among the gods and by an oath
That shook Heav'n's whole circumference confirmed.
Thither let us bend all our thoughts to learn
What creatures there inhabit, of what mould   355
Or substance, how endued and what their power
And where their weakness, how attempted best
By force or subtlety. Though Heav'n be shut
And Heav'n's high Arbitrator sit secure
In His own strength, this place may lie exposed,   360
The utmost border of His kingdom left
To their defense who hold it. Here perhaps
Some advantageous act may be achieved
By sudden onset, either with Hell fire
To waste His whole creation or possess   365
All as our own and drive, as we were driven,
The puny habitants, or if not drive
Seduce them to our party that their God
May prove their foe and with repenting hand
Abolish His own works. This would surpass   370
Common revenge and interrupt His joy
In our confusion and our joy upraise
In His disturbance when His darling sons
Hurled headlong to partake with us shall curse
Their frail originals and faded bliss—   375
Faded so soon! Advise if this be worth
Attempting or to sit in darkness here

345–53. It was debated whether humanity was created before or after the fall of the rebel angels. Milton has humanity created after the fall of the rebel angels. See Argument, Book One. The divine plan is for humans to rise eventually to heaven and there replace, to the exact number, the fallen angels. Milton invents a rumor in heaven by which Satan and Beëlzebub obtain this information (see 1.650–54). That rumor here becomes a formal pronouncement and oath by God.

353. The heavens shake when the king of the gods in classical verse—Zeus in Homer and Jove in Virgil—takes an oath. See *Iliad* 1.530 and *Aeneid* 9.106. Jehovah shakes heaven and earth too—not, however, when he takes an oath but when he exercises his wrath, a premonition of the apocalypse: "Therefore I will shake the heavens, and the earth shall remove out of her place, in the wrath of the Lord of Hosts, and in the day of his fierce anger" (Isaiah 13:13).

375. *frail originals*: Adam and Eve.

Hatching vain empires. Thus Beëlzebub
Pleaded his devilish counsel first devised
By Satan and in part proposed. For whence   380
But from the author of all ill could spring
So deep a malice to confound the race
Of mankind in one root and Earth with Hell
To mingle and involve, done all to spite
The great Creator? But their spite still serves   385
His glory to augment. The bold design
Pleased highly those infernal states and joy
Sparkled in all their eyes. With full assent
They vote, whereat his speech he thus renews:
    Well have ye judged, well ended long debate,   390
Synod of gods, and like to what ye are
Great things resolved which from the lowest deep
Will once more lift us up, in spite of fate,
Nearer our ancient seat, perhaps in view
Of those bright confines whence with neighboring arms   395
And opportune excursion we may chance
Re-enter Heav'n. Or else in some mild zone
Dwell not unvisited of Heav'n's fair light
Secure and at the bright'ning orient beam
Purge off this gloom. The soft delicious air   400
To heal the scar of these corrosive fires
Shall breathe her balm. But first whom shall we send
In search of this new world, whom shall we find
Sufficient? Who shall tempt with wand'ring feet
The dark unbottomed infinite abyss   405
And through the palpable obscure find out
His uncouth way or spread his airy flight
Upborne with indefatigable wings
Over the vast abrupt ere he arrive
The happy isle? What strength, what art can then   410
Suffice or what evasion bear him safe
Through the strict senteries and stations thick
Of angels watching round? Here he had need

391–92. I.e., Being great yourselves, you have resolved upon great actions.
397–402. As we see in *Paradise Regained*, after the Fall of Man the rebel angels will
   escape Hell and take up residence in the *soft delicious air*, the sky. That will be the
   base from which they will go to Earth to set themselves up as pagan gods and draw
   human worship away from the true God.
406. *obscure* (noun): darkness so thick it can be felt (*palpable*).
407. *uncouth*: unknown (from Old English *cunnan*, "to know").
409. *abrupt*: Latin *abruptus*, "broken off"; used of places that are steep (like a cliff), inaccessible (like the abyss), or all but impossible to cross (like the sea). *palpable obscure*
   (line 406) and *vast abrupt* are typically Miltonic, sublime locutions.
412. *senteries*: sentries.

All circumspection and we now no less
Choice in our suffrage, for on whom we send   415
The weight of all and our last hope relies.
   This said, he sat and expectation held
His look suspense, awaiting who appeared
To second or oppose or undertake
The perilous attempt. But all sat mute,   420
Pondering the danger with deep thoughts and each
In other's count'nance read his own dismay,
Astonished. None among the choice and prime
Of those Heav'n-warring champions could be found
So hardy as to proffer or accept   425
Alone the dreadful voyage till at last
Satan, whom now transcendent glory raised
Above his fellows with monarchal pride
Conscious of highest worth, unmoved thus spake:
   O progeny of Heaven, Empyreal Thrones,   430
With reason hath deep silence and demur
Seized us, though undismayed. Long is the way
And hard that out of Hell leads up to light.
Our prison strong, this huge convéx of fire
Outrageous to devour immures us round   435
Ninefold and gates of burning adamant
Barred over us prohibit all egress.
These passed (if any pass) the void profound
Of unessential Night receives him next
Wide gaping and with utter loss of being   440
Threatens him plunged in that abortive gulf.
If thence he 'scape into whatever world
Or unknown region what remains him less
Than unknown dangers and as hard escape?
But I should ill become this throne, O peers,   445
And this imperial sov'reignty adorned
With splendor, armed with pow'r, if aught proposed
And judged of public moment in the shape
Of difficulty or danger could deter
Me from attempting. Wherefore do I assume   450

432–33. Paraphrasing the famous lines of the sibyl in *Aeneid* 6.126–29: "Easy is the
   descent to Avernus, where night and day the door of the dark lord stands open, but
   to make one's way back up again and escape to the upper air, that is the task, that is
   the labor." See 3.19–21.
435. *Outrageous*: cruelly eager. *immures*: encloses with walls.
439. *unessential*: having no foundation in one substance.
441. *abortive*: Latin *abortivus*, "prematurely born." The meaning is that the gulf of chaos,
   which has not been created, is an actual thing or place only in an anticipatory and
   premature sense, for chaos is not really a thing or place at all.
449. *difficulty* and *or* are elided.

These royalties and not refuse to reign,
Refusing to accept as great a share
Of hazard as of honor, due alike
To him who reigns? And so much to him due
Of hazard more as he above the rest   455
High honored sits. Go therefore, mighty Pow'rs,
Terror of Heav'n though fall'n: intend at home
(While here shall be our home) what best may ease
The present misery and render Hell
More tolerable if there be cure or charm   460
To respite or deceive or slack the pain
Of this ill mansion. Intermit no watch
Against a wakeful foe while I abroad
Through all the coasts of dark destruction seek
Deliverance for us all! This enterprise   465
None shall partake with me. Thus saying rose
The monarch and prevented all reply:
Prudent, lest from his resolution raised
Others among the chief might offer now
(Certain to be refused) what erst they feared   470
And so refused might in opinion stand
His rivals, winning cheap the high repute
Which he through hazard huge must earn. But they
Dreaded not more th' adventure than his voice
Forbidding, and at once with him they rose.   475
Their rising all at once was as the sound
Of thunder heard remote. Towards him they bend
With awful reverence prone and as a god
Extol him equal to the High'st in Heav'n.
Nor failed they to express how much they praised   480
That for the gen'ral safety he despised
His own: for neither do the spirits damned
Lose all their virtue, lest bad men should boast
Their specious deeds on earth which glory excites,
Or close ambition varnished o'er with zeal.   485
    Thus they their doubtful consultations dark
Ended rejoicing in their matchless chief.
As when from mountain tops the dusky clouds
Ascending while the north wind sleeps o'erspread

452–56. *hazard* as well as *honor* is the ruler's due. The higher the ruler sits above those he
    rules, the more danger he should be willing to be exposed to.
457. *intend*: stretch your minds.
482–85. I.e., Fallen angels do not lose all their "virtue" (power). Otherwise, bad men who
    accomplish great deeds (though motivated thereto by concealed ambition and desire
    of glory) would be able to boast that their deeds alone make them good, not the inner
    intentions by which those deeds were accomplished.

Heav'n's cheerful face, the louring element   490
Scowls o'er the darkened landscape snow or show'r,
If chance the radiant sun with farewell sweet
Extend his evening beam, the fields revive,
The birds their notes renew and bleating herds
Attest their joy, that hill and valley rings.   495
O shame to men! Devil with devil damned
Firm concord holds. Men only disagree
Of creatures rational, though under hope
Of Heav'nly grace and, God proclaiming peace,
Yet live in hatred, enmity and strife   500
Among themselves and levy cruel wars,
Wasting the earth each other to destroy—
As if (which might induce us to accord)
Man had not hellish foes enow besides
That day and night for his destruction wait!   505
   The Stygian council thus dissolved and forth
In order came the grand infernal peers.
Midst came their mighty paramount and seemed
Alone th' Antagonist of Heav'n, nor less
Than Hell's dread Emperor with pomp supreme   510
And God-like imitated state. Him round
A globe of fiery seraphim enclosed
With bright emblazonry and horrent arms.
Then of their session ended they bid cry
With trumpets' regal sound the great result.   515
Towards the four winds four speedy cherubim
Put to their mouths the sounding alchemy
By herald's voice explained. The hollow abyss
Heard far and wide and all the host of Hell
With deaf'ning shout returned them loud acclaim.   520
Thence more at ease their minds and somewhat raised
By false presumptuous hope the rangèd pow'rs
Disband and wand'ring each his several way
Pursues as inclination or sad choice
Leads him perplexed where he may likeliest find   525
Truce to his restless thoughts and entertain

499–500. I.e., Although God proclaims peace, men live in hatred and at war.
513. *horrent*: bristling, standing upright (Latin *horresco*, "to stand on end, bristle, be rough"). Various forms of the word are often used of armies before battle or as an epithet of Mars, god of war.
517. *sounding alchemy*: trumpets fashioned of gold or of a metal resembling gold, obtained by alchemy.
523–24. *each . . . Pursues*: Note the change of focus from the rebel angels as a crowd, showing the psychology of crowds, to the solitude of each rebel angel's experience of Hell: *wand'ring, sad, perplexed, restless thoughts, irksome hours.*

The irksome hours till his great chief return.
Part on the plain or in the air sublime
Upon the wing or in swift race contend
As at th' Olympian games or Pythian fields.   530
Part curb their fiery steeds or shun the goal
With rapid wheels or fronted brigades form,
As when to warn proud cities war appears
Waged in the troubled sky and armies rush
To battle in the clouds. Before each van   535
Prick forth the airy knights and couch their spears
Till thickest legions close. With feats of arms
From either end of heav'n the welkin burns.
Others with vast Typhoean rage more fell
Rend up both rocks and hills and ride the air   540
In whirlwind: Hell scarce holds the wild uproar.
As when Alcides from Oechalia crowned
With conquest felt th' envenomed robe and tore
Through pain up by the roots Thessalian pines
And Lichas from the top of Oeta threw   545
Into th' Euboic Sea. Others more mild,
Retreated in a silent valley, sing
With notes angelical to many a harp
Their own heroic deeds and hapless fall
By doom of battle and complain that fate   550
Free virtue should enthrall to force or chance.
Their song was partial but the harmony
(What could it less when spirits immortal sing?)
Suspended Hell and took with ravishment
The thronging audience. In discourse more sweet   555
(For eloquence the soul, song charms the sense)
Others apart sat on a hill retired
In thoughts more elevate and reasoned high

---

530. *Olympian . . . Pythian*: The devils take up heroic games (a staple of epic poetry) such as those held in Greece at Olympia and at Delphi. *Olympian* has three syllables: 'ol-imp-yan,' and *Pythian* has two syllables: 'pyth-yan.'

536. *Prick*: ride (while "pricking" the sides of the horse with one's spurs). See Spenser, *Faerie Queene* 1.1.1: "A gentle knight was pricking on the plaine." The transition is from classical games to medieval jousts.

538. *heav'n*: the sky of hell, the *welkin*.

539. *Typhoean*: rage like that of the monster Typhon. See Glossary. Three syllables: 'ty-fee-an.'

542–46. *Alcides*: Hercules, who when returning from the conquest of Oechalia received from his wife a robe that she thought was infused with a love potion. It was infused with a poison, which caused Hercules the agony described, in the course of which he threw his friend Lichas into the sea.

550–51. The devils complain that their free will is enthralled to fate. Milton's reply would be that freedom is never safe and never easy: freedom can be lost (by rebelling against God), and freedom demands discipline to resist the work of fate.

552. *partial*: sung in several different parts.

Of providence, foreknowledge, will and fate,
Fixed fate, free will, foreknowledge absolute,   560
And found no end in wand'ring mazes lost.
Of good and evil much they argued then,
Of happiness and final misery,
Passion and apathy, and glory and shame:
Vain wisdom all and false philosophy!   565
Yet with a pleasing sorcery could charm
Pain for a while, or anguish, and excite
Fallacious hope or arm th' obdurèd breast
With stubborn patience as with triple steel.
　　Another part in squadrons and gross bands   570
On bold adventure to discover wide
That dismal world, if any clime perhaps
Might yield them easier habitation, bend
Four ways their flying march along the banks
Of four infernal rivers that disgorge   575
Into the burning lake their baleful streams:
Abhorrèd Styx, the flood of deadly hate,
Sad Acheron of sorrow black and deep,
Cocytus, named of lamentation loud
Heard on the rueful stream, fierce Phlegethon   580
Whose waves of torrent fire inflame with rage.
Far off from these a slow and silent stream,
Lethe the river of oblivion rolls
Her wat'ry labyrinth whereof who drinks
Forthwith his former state and being forgets,   585
Forgets both joy and grief, pleasure and pain.
Beyond this flood a frozen continent
Lies dark and wild, beat with perpetual storms
Of whirlwind and dire hail which on firm land
Thaws not but gathers heap and ruin seems   590
Of ancient pile. All else deep snow and ice,
A gulf profound as that Serbonian bog
Betwixt Damiata and Mount Casius old
Where armies whole have sunk. The parching air
Burns frore and cold performs th' effect of fire.   595

568. *obdurèd*: hardened.
570–76. *squadrons* and *bands* (not *part*) are the subject of *bend*: four squadrons bend, or
　　turn, in four directions, to explore the four rivers of Hell.
583. *Lethe* has two syllables.
591. *pile*: castle or fortress.
593. *Damiata* has three syllables, *Casius* two.
595. *frore*: sea frost that forms on a ship's lines and cables. The sensation *frore* gives to
　　the touch is of burning. See Spenser's Proteus, in *Faerie Queene* 3.8.30, whose
　　beard is "frory hoar." The word is still used in Newfoundland.

Thither by harpy-footed furies haled
At certain revolutions all the damned
Are brought and feel by turns the bitter change
Of fierce extremes, extremes by change more fierce:
From beds of raging fire to starve in ice   600
Their soft ethereal warmth and there to pine
Immovable, infixed and frozen round,
Periods of time, thence hurried back to fire.
They ferry over this Lethéan sound
Both to and fro, their sorrow to augment,   605
And wish and struggle as they pass to reach
The tempting stream with one small drop to lose
In sweet forgetfulness all pain and woe
All in one moment, and so near the brink.
But fate withstands and to oppose th' attempt   610
Medusa with gorgonian terror guards
The ford and of itself the water flies
All taste of living wight as once it fled
The lip of Tantalus. Thus roving on
In cónfused march forlorn th' advent'rous bands   615
With shudd'ring horror pale and eyes aghast
Viewed first their lamentable lot and found
No rest. Through many a dark and dreary vale
They passed and many a region dolorous,
O'er many a frozen, many a fiery alp,   620
Rocks, caves, lakes, fens, bogs, dens, and shades of death,
A universe of death which God by curse
Created evil, for evil only good,
Where all life dies, death lives, and nature breeds
Perverse all monstrous, all prodigious things,   625
Abominable, inutt'rable, and worse
Than fables yet have feigned or fear conceived:
Gorgons and hydras and chimeras dire.
    Meanwhile the Adversary of God and Man,
Satan, with thoughts inflamed of high'st design   630
Puts on swift wings and towards the gates of Hell

---

600. *starve*: to perish.
607. *tempting stream*: Lethe.
611. *gorgonian*. See Glossary, GORGON.
621. A line famous for the way its meter (especially in the first six syllables, up to the caesura) reproduces the feeling created by the landscape of Hell: of endlessness and sameness, even in variety.
626–28. I.e., The monsters of Hell are far worse than anything the human imagination has conceived, such as gorgons, hydras, and chimeras, bad as these are.
629. *Adversary*. See Glossary, SATAN.

Explores his solitary flight. Sometimes
He scours the right-hand coast, sometimes the left,
Now shaves with level wing the deep, then soars
Up to the fiery concave tow'ring high.   635
As when far off at sea a fleet descried
Hangs in the clouds by equinoctial winds
Close sailing from Bengala or the isles
Of Ternate and Tidore whence merchants bring
Their spicy drugs, they on the trading flood   640
Through the wide Ethiopian to the Cape
Ply stemming nightly toward the pole, so seemed
Far off the flying Fiend. At last appear
Hell bounds high reaching to the horrid roof
And thrice threefold the gates. Three folds were brass,   645
Three iron, three of adamantine rock
Impenetrable, impaled with circling fire
Yet unconsumed. Before the gates there sat
On either side a formidable shape:
The one seemed woman to the waist and fair   650
But ended foul in many a scaly fold
Voluminous and vast, a serpent armed
With mortal sting. About her middle round
A cry of hell-hounds never ceasing barked
With wide Cerberean mouths full loud and rung   655
A hideous peal. Yet when they list would creep
If aught disturbed their noise into her womb
And kennel there, yet there still barked and howled
Within unseen. Far less abhorred than these
Vexed Scylla bathing in the sea that parts   660

632. *Explores*: Milton intends the Latinate, military sense of *exploro*, "to spy, reconnoiter." Satan is spying out all the confines of Hell to find the way out.

634. *shaves with level wing the deep*: glides along close to the floor of Hell, which is like the ocean bottom.

635. *concave*: adjective ("curving in," like the surface under a dome) used here as a noun. From the inside, the roof of Hell is concave, like a dome. The whole of Hell seems to be spherical, the better to focus its intense flames on those within.

640–42. *trading flood*: the trade route on the Indian Ocean between northwestern India and northeastern Africa (Ethiopia). Once returning ships (laden with Indian spices) reach Ethiopia, they sail south to the Cape of Good Hope, the southern tip of Africa, i.e., *toward the [south] pole*. *stemming*: steering. Literally, directing the prow, the most forward point of a ship's bow, known as the *stem*, an upright timber to which the horizontal planks are joined at the bow.

647. *impaled*: surrounded by a fence of pillars, or upright poles (pales).

652. *Voluminous*: coiled.

655. *Cerberean*. See Glossary, CERBERUS.

656. *list*: wish.

659–66. The sea dogs of Sicily that chewed Scylla's private parts were far less horrible than these dogs, which tormented their mother's womb from the inside. Their mother (Sin) is uglier than the hags who fly to Lapland to murder children and drink their blood. See Glossary, SCYLLA.

Calabria from the hoarse Trinacrian shore.
Nor uglier follow the night-hag when, called
In secret, riding through the air she comes
Lured with the smell of infant blood to dance
With Lapland witches while the laboring moon   665
Eclipses at their charms. The other shape
(If shape it might be called that shape had none
Distinguishable in member, joint, or limb,
Or substance might be called that shadow seemed,
For each seemed either): black it stood as night,   670
Fierce as ten furies, terrible as Hell
And shook a dreadful dart. What seemed his head
The likeness of a kingly crown had on.
Satan was now at hand and from his seat
The monster moving onward came as fast   675
With horrid strides. Hell trembled as he strode!
Th' undaunted Fiend what this might be admired,
Admired, not feared. God and his Son except,
Created thing naught valued he, nor shunned,
And with disdainful look thus first began: 680
    Whence and what art thou, execrable shape,
That dar'st though grim and terrible advance
Thy miscreated front athwart my way
To yonder gates? Through them I mean to pass,
That be assured, without leave asked of thee.   685
Retire, or taste thy folly and learn by proof,
Hell-born, not to contend with spirits of Heav'n!
    To whom the goblin full of wrath replied:
Art thou that traitor angel, art thou he
Who first broke peace in Heav'n and faith, till then 690
Unbroken, and in proud rebellious arms
Drew after him the third part of Heav'n's sons
Conjured against the High'st for which both thou
And they outcast from God are here condemned
To waste eternal days in woe and pain?   695
And reckon'st thou thyself with spirits of Heav'n,
Hell-doomed, and breath'st defiance here and scorn
Where I reign king, and to enrage thee more,
Thy king and lord? Back to thy punishment,

---

665. *laboring moon*: the moon going into eclipse, struggling to survive.
669–70. I.e., If it can be called a substance, since it appeared instead to be a shadow, although its very shadowiness seemed substantial.
677. *admired*: wondered. See 1.690 n.
679. *he*: Satan.
693. *Conjured*: sworn together.

False fugitive, and to thy speed add wings   700
Lest with a whip of scorpions I pursue
Thy ling'ring or with one stroke of this dart
Strange horror seize thee and pangs unfelt before!
    So spake the grisly terror and in shape,
So speaking and so threat'ning, grew tenfold   705
More dreadful and deform. On th' other side
Incensed with indignation Satan stood
Unterrified and like a comet burned
That fires the length of Ophiucus huge
In th' arctic sky and from his horrid hair   710
Shakes pestilence and war. Each at the head
Levelled his deadly aim: their fatal hands
No second stroke intend. And such a frown
Each cast at th' other as when two black clouds
With heav'n's artillery fraught come rattling on   715
Over the Caspian, then stand front to front
Hov'ring a space till winds the signal blow
To join their dark encounter in mid air.
So frowned the mighty cómbatants that Hell
Grew darker at their frown. So matched they stood,   720
For never but once more was either like
To meet so great a foe. And now great deeds
Had been achieved whereof all Hell had rung,
Had not the snaky sorceress that sat
Fast by Hell gate and kept the fatal key   725
Ris'n and with hideous outcry rushed between:
    O Father, what intends thy hand, she cried,
Against thy only son? What fury, O Son,
Possesses thee to bend that mortal dart
Against thy father's head? And know'st for whom?   730
For Him who sits above and laughs the while
At thee ordained His drudge to execute
Whate'er His wrath (which He calls "justice") bids,
His wrath which one day will destroy ye both!
    She spake and at her words the hellish pest   735
Forbore. Then these to her Satan returned:

---

710. *horrid hair*: bristling like the hair of an enraged animal, such as a boar. The word
    comet is from Greek *komē*, "the hair," and *komētēs*, "long-haired." Comets were
    thought to be the portents or even the causes of disasters such as *pestilence* and *war*.
716. *Caspian*. See Glossary.
722. *so great a foe*: the Son. "For he [Christ] must reign, till he hath put all enemies under
    his feet. The last enemy that shall be destroyed is death" (1 Corinthians 15:25–26).
726. *hideous* has two syllables: 'hid-jus.'
735. *pest*: not Satan but his adversary.

    So strange thy outcry and thy words so strange
Thou interposes that my sudden hand
Prevented spares to tell thee yet by deeds
What it intends till first I know of thee   740
What thing thou art thus double-formed and why
In this infernal vale first met thou call'st
Me "father" and that phantasm call'st my son.
I know thee not nor ever saw till now
Sight more detestable than him and thee.   745
    T' whom thus the portress of Hell gate replied:
Hast thou forgot me then and do I seem
Now in thine eyes so foul, once deemed so fair
In Heav'n when at th' assembly and in sight
Of all the seraphim with thee combined   750
In bold conspiracy 'gainst Heaven's King?
All on a sudden miserable pain
Surprised thee; dim thine eyes and dizzy swum
In darkness while thy head flames thick and fast
Threw forth till on the left side op'ning wide,   755
Likest to thee in shape and count'nance bright
(Then shining Heav'nly fair) a goddess armed
Out of thy head I sprung. Amazement seized
All th' host of Heaven. Back they recoiled afraid
At first and called me "Sin" and for a sign   760
Portentous held me. But familiar grown
I pleased and with attractive graces won
The most averse (thee chiefly) who full oft
Thyself in me thy perfect image viewing
Becam'st enamoured and such joy thou took'st   765
With me in secret that my womb conceived
A growing burden. Meanwhile war arose
And fields were fought in Heav'n wherein remained
(For what could else) to our almighty Foe
Clear victory, to our part loss and rout   770
Through all the empyréan. Down they fell
Driv'n headlong from the pitch of Heaven, down
Into this deep and in the general fall
I also, at which time this pow'rful key
Into my hand was giv'n with charge to keep   775
These gates for ever shut which none can pass

737–40. I.e., Your words are so strange that they delay my (usually undelaying) hand from
    proclaiming, in the language of deeds, what it intends to do.
755–58. Like Athena, goddess of wisdom, who burst out of Zeus's head.
766–67. *conceived / A growing burden*: "Then when lust hath conceived, it bringeth forth
    sin: and sin, when it is finished, bringeth forth death" (James 1:15).

Without my op'ning. Pensive here I sat
Alone, but long I sat not till my womb—
Pregnant by thee and now excessive grown—
Prodigious motion felt and rueful throes.   780
At last this odious offspring whom thou seest,
Thine own begotten, breaking violent way
Tore through my entrails, that with fear and pain
Distorted all my nether shape thus grew
Transformed. But he my inbred enemy   785
Forth issued brandishing his fatal dart
Made to destroy. I fled and cried out "Death!"
Hell trembled at the hideous name and sighed
From all her caves and back resounded "Death!"
I fled but he pursued (though more, it seems,   790
Inflamed with lust than rage) and swifter far
Me overtook, his mother, all dismayed,
And in embraces forcible and foul
Engend'ring with me of that rape begot
These yelling monsters that with ceaseless cry   795
Surround me as thou saw'st, hourly conceived
And hourly born with sorrow infinite
To me. For when they list, into the womb
That bred them they return and howl and gnaw
My bowels, their repast, then bursting forth   800
Afresh with conscious terrors vex me round
That rest or intermission none I find.
Before mine eyes in opposition sits
Grim Death, my son and foe, who sets them on
And me his parent would full soon devour   805
For want of other prey but that he knows
His end with mine involved and knows that I
Should prove a bitter morsel and his bane
Whenever that shall be: so Fate pronounced.
But thou, O Father, I forewarn thee, shun   810
His deadly arrow. Neither vainly hope
To be invulnerable in those bright arms,
Though tempered Heav'nly, for that mortal dint,
Save He who reigns above, none can resist.
    She finished and the subtle Fiend his lore   815
Soon learned, now milder, and thus answered smooth:
    Dear Daughter, since thou claim'st me for thy sire
And my fair son here show'st me (the dear pledge
Of dalliance had with thee in Heav'n and joys

---

782. *Thine own begotten*: recalling the Son as the only begotten of the Father.

Then sweet, now sad to mention through dire change   820
Befall'n us unforeseen, unthought of), know
I come no enemy but to set free
From out this dark and dismal house of pain
Both him and thee and all the Heav'nly host
Of spirits that in our just pretenses armed   825
Fell with us from on high. From them I go
This uncouth errand sole and one for all
Myself expose with lonely steps to tread
Th' unfounded deep and through the void immense
To search with wand'ring quest a place foretold   830
Should be (and by concurring signs, ere now
Created, vast and round) a place of bliss
In the purlieus of Heaven and therein placed
A race of upstart creatures to supply
Perhaps our vacant room, though more removed,   835
Lest Heav'n surcharged with potent multitude
Might hap to move new broils. Be this or aught
Than this more secret now designed I haste
To know and this once known shall soon return
And bring ye to the place where thou and Death   840
Shall dwell at ease and up and down unseen
Wing silently the buxom air, embalmed
With odors. There ye shall be fed and filled
Immeasurably: all things shall be your prey!
    He ceased, for both seemed highly pleased, and Death   845
Grinned horrible a ghastly smile to hear
His famine should be filled and blest his maw
Destined to that good hour. No less rejoiced
His mother bad and thus bespake her sire:
    The key of this infernal pit by due   850
And by command of Heav'n's all-powerful King
I keep, by Him forbidden to unlock
These adamantine gates. Against all force
Death ready stands to interpose his dart,
Fearless to be o'ermatched by living might.   855
But what owe I to His commands above
Who hates me and hath hither thrust me down
Into this gloom of Tartarus profound

830–32. He seeks the created universe, which was foretold by prophecy in heaven, and
    which by reading other signs Satan knows has now been created.
833. *purlieus*: neighborhood. More precisely, a piece of land on the edge of a royal forest
    which might be turned over to private use under some restrictions; a fairly precise
    word for the legal status of the world Adam and Eve are given.
842. *buxom*: pliant. *embalmed*: made odorous, as with balm.

To sit in hateful office here confined,
Inhabitant of Heav'n and Heav'nly-born,   860
Here in perpetual agony and pain
With terrors and with clamors compassed round
Of mine own brood that on my bowels feed?
Thou art my father, thou my author, thou
My being gav'st me: whom should I obey   865
But thee, whom follow? Thou wilt bring me soon
To that new world of light and bliss among
The gods who live at ease, where I shall reign
At thy right hand voluptuous as beseems
Thy daughter and thy darling without end.   870
    Thus saying, from her side the fatal key,
Sad instrument of all our woe, she took
And towards the gate rolling her bestial train
Forthwith the huge portcullis high up drew
Which but herself not all the Stygian pow'rs   875
Could once have moved, then in the key-hole turns
Th' intrícate wards and every bolt and bar
Of massy iron or solid rock with ease
Unfastens. On a sudden open fly
With impetuous recoil and jarring sound   880
Th' infernal doors and on their hinges grate
Harsh thunder that the lowest bottom shook
Of Erebus. She opened, but to shut
Excelled her power. The gates wide open stood
That with extended wings a bannered host   885
Under spread ensigns marching might pass through
With horse and chariots ranked in loose array.
So wide they stood and like a furnace mouth
Cast forth redounding smoke and ruddy flame.
Before their eyes in sudden view appear   890
The secrets of the hoary deep, a dark
Illimitable ocean without bound,
Without dimension, where length, breadth, and heighth,
And time and place are lost, where eldest Night
And Chaos, áncestors of Nature, hold   895
Eternal anarchy amidst the noise
Of endless wars and by confusion stand.
For Hot, Cold, Moist, and Dry, four champions fierce
Strive here for mast'ry and to battle bring

---

869. *voluptuous*: an adverb modifying *reign*; Latin *voluptas*, "pleasure."
878. *iron* has one syllable.
879–83. The horrid sound made by the opening of Hell's gates imitates the grinding
    hinges of the gates of the temple of Mars, in *Aeneid* 6.573–74.

Their embryon atoms. They around the flag   900
Of each his faction in their several clans,
Light-armed or heavy, sharp, smooth, swift or slow,
Swarm populous, unnumbered as the sands
Of Barca or Cyrenè's torrid soil,
Levied to side with warring winds and poise   905
Their lighter wings. To whom these most adhere,
He rules a moment. Chaos umpire sits
And by decision more embroils the fray
By which he reigns. Next him high arbiter
Chance governs all. Into this wild abyss   910
(The womb of Nature and perhaps her grave)
Of neither sea, nor shore, nor air, nor fire,
But all these in their pregnant causes mixed
Confusedly, and which thus must ever fight
Unless th' Almighty Maker them ordain   915
His dark materials to create more worlds,
Into this wild abyss the wary Fiend
Stood on the brink of Hell and looked a while,
Pondering his voyage, for no narrow frith
He had to cross. Nor was his ear less pealed   920
With noises loud and ruinous (to compare
Great things with small) than when Bellona storms
With all her battering engines bent to raze
Some capital city—or less than if this frame
Of Heaven were falling and these elements   925
In mutiny had from her axle torn
The steadfast earth. At last his sail-broad vans
He spreads for flight and in the surging smoke
Uplifted spurns the ground, thence many a league
As in a cloudy chair ascending rides   930
Audacious but that seat soon failing meets
A vast vacuity. All unawares,
Flutt'ring his pennons vain, plumb down he drops
Ten thousand fathom deep and to this hour
Down had been falling had not by ill chance   935

900. *They*: the *embryon atoms.*
904. *Cyrenè*: All vowels are long: 'sigh-ree-nee.'
910–20. The main structure of the sentence is "Into this wild abyss the Fiend looked a
   while." The opening prepositional phrase, *into this wild abyss*, is repeated at line 917
   because of the heavy freight of descriptive ideas on the purpose and nature of Chaos
   borne in lines 911–16.
912. *Of*: composed of.
919. *frith*: firth, a long narrow arm of the sea, related to *fjord.*
920. *pealed*: battered with noise.
922. *Bellona*: Roman goddess of war.
924–25. *or less*: picking up from line 920, *Nor . . . less*: The sound of chaos was no less
   loud than if the earth imploded.
932. *unawares*: unexpectedly.

The strong rebuff of some tumultuous cloud
Instínct with fire and nitre hurried him
As many miles aloft. *That* fury stayed,
Quenched in a boggy Syrtis, neither sea
Nor good dry land, nigh foundered, on he fares   940
Treading the crude consistence half on foot,
Half flying: behooves him now both oar and sail!
As when a gryphon through the wilderness
With winged course o'er hill or moory dale
Pursues the Arimaspian who by stealth   945
Had from his wakeful custody purloined
The guarded gold, so eagerly the Fiend
O'er bog or steep, through strait, rough, dense, or rare,
With head, hands, wings, or feet pursues his way
And swims, or sinks, or wades, or creeps, or flies.   950
At length a universal hubbub wild
Of stunning sounds and voices all confused
Borne through the hollow dark assaults his ear
With loudest vehemence. Thither he plies
Undaunted to meet there whatever pow'r   955
Or spirit of the nethermost abyss
Might in that noise reside, of whom to ask
Which way the nearest coast of darkness lies,
Bord'ring on light, when straight, behold! the throne
Of Chaos and his dark pavilion spread   960
Wide on the wasteful deep. With him enthroned
Sat sable-vested Night, eldest of things,
The consort of his reign, and by them stood
Orcus and Ades and the dreaded name
Of Demogorgon, Rumor next and Chance   965
And Tumult and Confusion all embroiled
And Discord with a thousand various mouths.
    T' whom Satan turning boldly, thus: Ye pow'rs
And spirits of the nethermost abyss,
Chaos and ancient Night, I come no spy   970
With purpose to explore or to disturb
The secrets of your realm but by constraint,
Wand'ring this darksome desert (as my way
Lies through your spacious empire up to light)

943–47. The one-eyed Arimaspians steal gold from gryphons, fabled birds with an eagle's
wings and beak and a lion's body who stand guard over gold in northern India. See
Glossary, ARIMASPIAN.

948–50. The onomatopoeic meter of these lines has been justly praised. Lines 948 and
949 move into irregular rhythm, imitating the difficulty of the passage through
Chaos. Line 950 falls into mechanically regular iambic rhythm (something Milton
rarely does).

Alone and without guide, half lost, I seek   975
What readiest path leads where your gloomy bounds
Confine with Heav'n. Or if some other place
From your dominion won th' ethereal King
Possesses lately, thither to arrive
I travel this profound: direct my course!   980
Directed, no mean recompense it brings
To your behoof if I that region lost,
All usurpation thence expelled, reduce
To her original darkness and your sway
(Which is my present journey) and once more   985
Erect the standard there of ancient Night.
Yours be th' advantage all, mine the revenge!
    Thus Satan, and him thus the anarch old
With falt'ring speech and visage incomposed
Answered: I know thee, stranger, who thou art,   990
That mighty leading angel who of late
Made head against Heav'n's King, though overthrown.
I saw and heard, for such a num'rous host
Fled not in silence through the frighted deep
With ruin upon ruin, rout on rout,   995
Confusion worse confounded, and Heav'n gates
Poured out by millions her victorious bands
Pursuing. I upon my frontiers here
Keep residence. If all I can will serve
That little which is left so to defend,   1000
Encroached on still through your intestine broils,
Weak'ning the scepter of old Night: first Hell,
Your dungeon stretching far and wide beneath,
Now lately Heav'n and Earth, another world
Hung o'er my realm, linked in a golden chain   1005
To that side Heav'n from whence your legions fell.
If that way be your walk you have not far,
So much the nearer danger. Go and speed:
Havoc and spoil and ruin are my gain!
    He ceased and Satan stayed not to reply   1010
But glad now that his sea should find a shore
With fresh alacrity and force renewed
Springs upward like a pyramid of fire
Into the wide expanse and through the shock
Of fighting elements on all sides round   1015
Environed wins his way, harder beset
And more endangered than when Argo passed

1001. *your.* The 1667 and 1674 printings read *our.* Early editors emended to *your.*

Through Bosphorus betwixt the justling rocks
Or when Ulysses on the larboard shunned
Charybdis and by th' other whirlpool steered,   1020
So he with difficulty and labor hard
Moved on—with difficulty and labor he,
But he once passed, soon after when Man fell,
Strange alteration! Sin and Death amain
Following his track (such was the will of Heav'n)   1025
Paved after him a broad and beaten way,
Over the dark abyss whose boiling gulf
Tamely endured a bridge of wondrous length
From Hell continued reaching th' utmost orb
Of this frail world, by which the spirits perverse   1030
With easy intercourse pass to and fro
To tempt or punish mortals (except whom
God and good angels guard by special grace).
But now at last the sacred influence
Of light appears and from the walls of Heaven   1035
Shoots far into the bosom of dim night
A glimmering dawn. Here nature first begins
Her farthest verge and chaos to retire
As from her outmost works a broken foe
With tumult less and with less hostile din,   1040
That Satan with less toil and now with ease
Wafts on the calmer wave by dubious light
And like a weather-beaten vessel holds
Gladly the port, though shrouds and tackle torn,
Or in the emptier waste resembling air   1045
Weighs his spread wings, at leisure to behold
Far off th' empyreal Heav'n extended wide
In circuit, undetermined square or round,
With opal tow'rs and battlements adorned
Of living sapphire, once his native seat,   1050

1018. *justling*: jostling.
1021–26. *he*: Satan. Satan had difficulty but Sin and Death will make the way across
    Chaos easy for the devils after the fall of humanity.
1029–30. *utmost orb* / *Of this frail world*: the outside of the outermost sphere of the cre-
    ated universe.
1031. *intercourse*: passage back and forth. Latin *intercursus*, "a running between."
1034. *influence*: literally, a "flowing in." See 3.1–55.
1042. *Wafts*: floats gently, but moves.
1043. *holds*: heads for.
1048. *undetermined*: From Satan's viewpoint it is unclear whether heaven is square or
    round. The Bible (Revelation 21:16, based on Ezekiel 40) describes heaven as
    square. But Milton may be suggesting the form of heaven, which mystically unites
    the incompatible shapes of the square and the circle.

And fast by hanging in a golden chain
This pendent world in bigness as a star
Of smallest magnitude close by the moon.
Thither full fraught with mischievous revenge
Accurst, and in a cursèd hour, he hies.   1055

Book Three

The Argument

God sitting on His throne sees Satan flying towards this world, then
newly created, shows him to the Son who sat at His right hand, foretells the success of Satan in perverting Mankind, clears His own justice and wisdom from all imputation, having created Man free and
able enough to have withstood his tempter, yet declares His purpose
of grace towards him, in regard he fell not of his own malice as did
Satan, but by him seduced. The Son of God renders praises to his
Father for the manifestation of his gracious purpose towards Man but
God again declares that grace cannot be extended towards Man without the satisfaction of divine justice. Man hath offended the majesty
of God by aspiring to godhead and therefore, with all his progeny
devoted to death, must die unless someone can be found sufficient to
answer for his offence and undergo his punishment. The Son of God
freely offers Himself a ransom for Man. The Father accepts Him,
ordains His incarnation, pronounces His exaltation above all names
in Heaven and Earth, commands all the angels to adore Him. They
obey and, hymning to their harps in full choir, celebrate the Father
and the Son. Meanwhile Satan alights upon the bare convex of this
world's outermost orb where wand'ring he first finds a place since
called the Limbo of Vanity. What persons and things fly up thither.
Thence comes to the gate of Heaven, described ascending by stairs,
and the waters above the firmament that flow about it. His passage
thence to the orb of the sun: he finds there Uriel, the regent of that
orb, but first changes himself into the shape of a meaner angel, pretending a zealous desire to behold the new Creation and Man whom
God had placed here, inquires of him the place of his habitation and
is directed, alights first on Mount Niphates.

1051. *in*: by. The golden chain mentioned in the *Iliad* (8.18–27) became, for later inter-
    preters of the poem, a symbol of the unity and order of the universe on all its levels,
    leading up to God.
1052. *pendent*: hanging. *world*: universe.

Hail, holy Light, offspring of Heav'n, first-born,
Or of th' Eternal co-eternal beam
May I express thee unblamed? Since God is light
And never but in unapproachèd light
Dwelt from eternity, dwelt then in thee,   5
Bright effluence of bright essence increate.
Or hear'st thou rather pure ethereal stream
Whose fountain who shall tell? Before the sun,
Before the heavens thou wert and at the voice
Of God as with a mantle didst invest   10
The rising world of waters dark and deep,
Won from the void and formless infinite.
Thee I revisit now with bolder wing
Escaped the Stygian pool though long detained
In that obscure sojoúrn while in my flight   15
Through utter and through middle darkness borne
With other notes than to th' Orphéan lyre
I sung of Chaos and Eternal Night,
Taught by the Heav'nly Muse to venture down
The dark descent and up to reascend   20
Though hard and rare. Thee I revisit safe
And feel thy sovereign vital lamp but thou
Revisit'st not these eyes that roll in vain
To find thy piercing ray and find no dawn,

Book Three

1–55. This prayer to light is the most famous passage of *Paradise Lost* and the most personal. Its setting is the transition from the darkness of Hell and Chaos to the light of Heaven, first seen through Satan's eyes (2.1034–37). Now the light is greeted by the poet, who advances the startling claim that in making his poem he has flown to Hell and back, following Satan's track (lines 13–21). He then speaks of his blindness, which separates him from the beauty of nature but which no more stops him from making poetry than it did the poets and prophets of old. He asks the heavenly light to *shine inward* (line 52), and that request prepares for the main event of Book Three: the scene in heaven in which the Father reveals his plan for history and the Son offers himself as a sacrifice to rescue humanity.

1–8. Milton conjectures three things of light: (1) that light is the spontaneous growth, or "offspring," of heaven (line 1), (2) that light was never created because it has existed forever with God (lines 2–6), and (3) that light is mysterious in origin (lines 7–8). All three conflict with the Bible (Genesis 1:1–3), where light is created by God after the heaven and the earth. But see line 6 n. See also 7.243–51.

6. *effluence*: flowing forth. *essence*: unchanging, inner being of something. *increate*: never created. Radiant light is a flowing forth out of what is also bright but does not flow forth: the uncreated essence of light. The word *increate* suggests that while the essence of light is eternally with God, the *effluence* of that essence is created in Genesis 1:3: "Let there be light: and there was light." With this distinction between essential and radiant light Milton reconciles his mystical vision of the eternity of light with the literal text of the Bible.

7. *Or hear'st thou*: or are you called.

14. *Stygian*: of the infernal river Styx.

17. *Orphéan*: of Orpheus, alluding to an archaic Greek poem, "Hymn to Night," attributed to the legendary poet Orpheus, who, like the narrator of *Paradise Lost*, visited Hell.

19–21. See 2.432–33 and n.

So thick a drop serene hath quenched their orbs   25
Or dim suffusion veiled. Yet not the more
Cease I to wander where the muses haunt
Clear spring or shady grove or sunny hill,
Smit with the love of sacred song. But chief
Thee, Sion, and the flow'ry brooks beneath   30
That wash thy hallowed feet and warbling flow,
Nightly I visit nor sometimes forget
Those other two equaled with me in fate
(So were I equaled with them in renown)
Blind Thamyris and blind Maeonides,   35
And Tiresias and Phineus, prophets old.
Then feed on thoughts that voluntary move
Harmonious numbers as the wakeful bird
Sings darkling and in shadiest covert hid
Tunes her nocturnal note. Thus with the year   40
Seasons return but not to me returns
Day or the sweet approach of ev'n or morn
Or sight of vernal bloom or summer's rose
Or flocks or herds or human face divine
But cloud instead and ever-during dark   45
Surrounds me, from the cheerful ways of men
Cut off and, for the book of knowledge fair,
Presented with a universal blank
Of nature's works to me expunged and razed
And wisdom at one entrance quite shut out.   50
So much the rather thou, celestial Light,
Shine inward and the mind through all her powers
Irradiate. *There* plant eyes. All mist from thence
Purge and disperse, that I may see and tell
Of things invisible to mortal sight.   55
       Now had th' almighty Father from above,
From the pure empyréan where He sits
High throned above all heighth, bent down His eye
His own works and their works at once to view.

25–26. *drop serene . . . dim suffusion*: medical language of Milton's day that suggests he is
    uncertain whether he is permanently or temporarily blind, whether his sight is
    quenched or only *veiled*.
30. *Sion*: the mount of Jerusalem (Zion), associated with the Bible, especially the Psalms.
33–35. The reference is to Homer (*Maeonides*) and a legendary blind poet, Thamyris; i.e.,
    I am equal to them in blindness. So may I be equal to them in fame!
35. *Tiresias* and *Phineus* are blind prophets in Greek literature. In both figures, the power
    of prophecy and the affliction of blindness are linked.
37. *voluntary*: spontaneously.
38. *numbers*: metrical verse. *wakeful bird*: nightingale. Milton often composed at night.
47. *book of knowledge*: nature, traditionally regarded as a book in which the Creator's
    purpose can be read.
49. Note the vehement rhythm of this line. Compare 1.69.

About Him all the sanctities of Heav'n   60
Stood thick as stars and from His sight received
Beatitude past utterance. On His right
The radiant image of His glory sat,
His only Son. On Earth He first beheld
Our two first parents, yet the only two   65
Of mankind, in the happy garden placed,
Reaping immortal fruits of joy and love,
Uninterrupted joy, unrivaled love
In blissful solitude. He then surveyed
Hell and the gulf between and Satan there   70
Coasting the wall of Heav'n on this side night
In the dun air sublime and ready now
To stoop with wearied wings and willing feet
On the bare outside of this world that seemed
Firm land embosomed without firmament—   75
Uncertain which, in ocean or in air.
Him God beholding from His prospect high
(Wherein past, present, future He beholds)
Thus to His only Son foreseeing spake:
    Only begotten Son, seest thou what rage   80
Transports our Adversary whom no bounds
Prescribed, no bars of Hell nor all the chains
Heaped on him there nor yet the main abyss
Wide interrupt can hold, so bent he seems
On desperate revenge that shall redound   85
Upon his own rebellious head? And now
Through all restraint broke loose he wings his way
Not far off Heav'n in the precíncts of light
Directly towards the new created world
And Man there placed, with purpose to assay   90
If him by force he can destroy or worse
By some false guile pervert. And shall pervert,
For Man will hearken to his glozing lies
And easily transgress the sole command,
Sole pledge of his obedience. So will fall   95
He and his faithless progeny. Whose fault?

---

60. *sanctities*: blessed ones, angels.
64. *Son*: The Son of God, who will be incarnate as Jesus, is here the visible image of
    God's invisible glory. (See lines 139–40 and 6.680.)
73. *stoop*: descend. A term from hawking.
74. *world*: the entire created universe, not the earth. See lines 418–19.
75–76. *embosomed . . . air*: The outer, convex surface of the universe is directly exposed
    to chaos, without any protective *firmament*, or upper sky. The universe is thus *embos-
    omed* in the violence of chaos, which batters it like the ocean.
77. *Him*: Satan.
88. *precíncts*: the outskirts.

Whose but his own? Ingrate! He had of Me
All he could have. I made him just and right,
Sufficient to have stood though free to fall.
Such I created all th' ethereal pow'rs   100
And spirits, both them who stood and them who failed:
Freely they stood who stood and fell who fell.
Not free, what proof could they have giv'n sincere
Of true allegiance, constant faith or love
Where only what they needs must do appeared,   105
Not what they would? What praise could they receive?
What pleasure I from such obedience paid
When will and reason (reason also is choice)
Useless and vain, of freedom both despoiled,
Made passive both, had served necessity,   110
Not Me? They therefore, as to right belonged,
So were created, nor can justly accuse
Their Maker or their making or their fate,
As if predestination overruled
Their will disposed by absolute decree   115
Or high foreknowledge. They themselves decreed
Their own revolt, not I. If I foreknew
Foreknowledge had no influence on their fault
Which had no less proved certain unforeknown.
So without least impúlse or shadow of fate   120
Or aught by me immutably foreseen
They trespass, authors to themselves in all
Both what they judge and what they choose, for so
I formed them free and free they must remain
Till they enthrall themselves. I else must change   125
Their nature and revoke the high decree,
Unchangeable, eternal, which ordained
Their freedom: they themselves ordained their Fall.
The first sort by their own suggestion fell
Self-tempted, self-depraved. Man falls deceived   130
By th' other first: Man therefore shall find grace,
The other none. In mercy and justice both
Through Heav'n and Earth so shall my glory excel,

---

97. *Ingrate! . . . had*: Because God is in eternity he sees all events as present. This makes
    his use of tenses somewhat arbitrary. See Argument to Book Three: "Man hath
    offended." But he hasn't, yet.
100–101. *pow'rs / And spirits*: angels.
108. To make the most reasonable choice in any matter (e.g., whether to remain faithful
    to God) is still a free choice. See *Areopagitica*: "When God gave him reason, he gave
    him freedom to choose, for reason is but choosing" (below, p. 367).
112. *So*: free.
129. *first sort*: the rebel angels.
131. *other*: Satan, the head of the rebel angels.

But mercy first and last shall brightest shine.
   Thus while God spake ambrosial fragrance filled   135
All Heav'n and in the blessèd spirits elect
Sense of new joy ineffable diffused.
Beyond compare the Son of God was seen
Most glorious. In Him all His Father shone
Substantially expressed and in His face   140
Divine compassion visibly appeared:
Love without end and without measure grace,
Which uttering thus He to His Father spake:
   O Father, gracious was that word which closed
Thy sov'reign sentence, that Man should find grace,   145
For which both Heav'n and Earth shall high extol
Thy praises with th' inumerable sound
Of hymns and sacred songs wherewith Thy throne
Encompassed shall resound Thee ever blest.
For should Man finally be lost? Should Man,   150
Thy creature late so loved, Thy youngest son,
Fall circumvented thus by fraud, though joined
With his own folly? That be from Thee far,
That far be from Thee, Father, who art judge
Of all things made and judgest only right.   155
Or shall the Adversary thus obtain
His end and frustrate Thine? Shall he fulfill
His malice and Thy goodness bring to naught
Or proud return (though to his heavier doom,
Yet with revenge accomplished) and to Hell   160
Draw after him the whole race of mankind
By him corrupted? Or wilt Thou thyself
Abolish Thy creation and unmake
For him what for Thy glory Thou hast made?
So should Thy goodness and Thy greatness both   165
Be questioned and blasphémed without defense.
   To whom the great Creator thus replied:
O Son in whom my soul hath chief delight,
Son of my bosom, Son who art alone
My Word, my wisdom, and effectual might,   170
All hast thou spoken as my thoughts are, all
As my eternal purpose hath decreed.
Man shall not quite be lost but saved who will,

142. *grace*: salvation, forgiveness.
170. *Word*: "In the beginning was the Word, and the Word was with God, and the Word
was God. . . . All things were made by him" (John 1:1–3). See 7.163 and n. *effectual*:
producing effects. The Father's power acts through the Son.
173. *who will*: whoever chooses. God's grace softens the hard heart and makes one capable of choosing to be saved. See 11.2–5.

Yet not of will in him but grace in me
Freely vouchsafed. Once more I will renew   175
His lapsèd pow'rs though forfeit and enthralled
By sin to foul exorbitant desires.
Upheld by me, yet once more he shall stand
On even ground against his mortal foe,
By me upheld that he may know how frail   180
His fall'n condition is and to me owe
All his deliv'rance, and to none but me.
Some I have chosen of peculiar grace
Elect above the rest: so is my will.
The rest shall hear me call and oft be warned   185
Their sinful state and to appease betimes
Th' incensèd Deity while offered grace
Invites, for I will clear their senses dark
What may suffice and soften stony hearts
To pray, repent, and bring obedience due.   190
To prayer, repentance, and obedience due,
Though but endeavored with sincere intent,
Mine ear shall not be slow, mine eyes not shut.
And I will place within them as a guide
My umpire conscience whom if they will hear   195
Light after light well used they shall attain
And to the end persisting safe arrive.
This my long suff'rance and my day of grace
They who neglect and scorn shall never taste
But hard be hardened, blind be blinded more,   200
That they may stumble on and deeper fall:
And none but such from mercy I exclude!
But yet all is not done: Man disobeying
Disloyal breaks his fealty and sins
Against the high supremacy of Heaven,   205
Affecting godhead, and so, losing all,
To expiate his treason hath naught left
But to destruction sacred and devote

184. *Elect*: chosen.
185. *The rest*: those of mankind who will be saved, but are not of the *elect*, honored with *peculiar grace* (line 183).
189. "I will take the stony heart out of their flesh, and will give them an heart of flesh" (Ezekiel 11:19).
196. *Light after light well used*: I.e., they shall attain the light of true repentance by using the light of conscience.
202. *such*: *They* (line 199) who scorn God's offered grace.
206. *godhead*: the status of God. Man's crime is to intend to be like a god. *losing all*: having lost all goodness by this crime.
208. *sacred*: set apart and formally doomed. (One of the Latin senses of *sacer*.) *devote*: cursed formally and outlawed.

He with his whole posterity must die.
Die he or justice must, unless for him   210
Some other able and as willing pay
The rigid satisfaction, death for death.
Say, Heavn'ly Pow'rs, where shall we find such love?
Which of ye will be mortal to redeem
Man's mortal crime and, just, th' unjust to save?   215
Dwells in all Heaven charity so dear?
    He asked, but all the Heavn'ly choir stood mute
And silence was in Heaven. On Man's behalf
Patron or intercessor none appeared,
Much less that durst upon his own head draw   220
The deadly forfeiture and ransom set.
And now without redemption all mankind
Must have been lost, adjudged to death and Hell
By doom severe, had not the Son of God
In whom the fullness dwells of love divine   225
His dearest mediation thus renewed:
    Father, Thy word is past: Man shall find grace!
And shall grace not find means that finds her way
The speediest of Thy wingèd messengers
To visit all Thy creatures and to all   230
Comes unprevented, unimplored, unsought?
Happy for Man, so coming. He her aid
Can never seek once dead in sins and lost:
Atonement for himself or offering meet,
Indebted and undone, hath none to bring.   235
Behold Me then, Me for him, life for life
I offer. On Me let thine anger fall.
Account Me Man. I for his sake will leave
Thy bosom and this glory next to Thee
Freely put off and for him lastly die   240
Well pleased. On Me let Death wreck all his rage!
Under his gloomy pow'r I shall not long
Lie vanquished. Thou hast giv'n me to possess
Life in myself for ever. By Thee I live

209. *whole posterity*: all his children.
210. Man must die or justice will.
215. "For Christ also hath once suffered for sins, the just for the unjust" (1 Peter 3:18). The reference is to the Crucifixion.
216. *charity*: heavenly love (Latin *caritas*, trans. Greek *agapē*, disinterested, altruistic love, as opposed to *erōs*, erotic love). See line 225: *love divine*.
231. *unprevented*: not preceded (by prayer) (Latin *praevenio*, "to precede, anticipate"). Divine grace comes before Man knows he needs it, softening the heart, which has been hardened by sin.
232. *her*: grace's.
238–40. The Son will leave God's presence, become human, and die.

Though now to Death I yield and am his due: 245
All that of Me *can* die. Yet that debt paid
Thou wilt not leave me in the loathsome grave
His prey nor suffer my unspotted soul
For ever with corruption there to dwell
But I shall rise victorious and subdue   250
My vanquisher, spoiled of his vaunted spoil.
Death his death's wound shall then receive and stoop
Inglorious, of his mortal sting disarmed.
I through the ample air in triumph high
Shall lead Hell captive maugre Hell and show   255
The pow'rs of darkness bound. Thou at the sight
Pleased, out of Heaven shalt look down and smile
While by Thee raised I ruin all my foes,
Death last, and with his carcass glut the grave,
Then with the multitude of my redeemed   260
Shall enter Heav'n long absent and return,
Father, to see Thy face wherein no cloud
Of anger shall remain but peace assured
And reconcilement. Wrath shall be no more
Thenceforth but in Thy presence joy entire.   265
    His words here ended but his meek aspéct
Silent yet spake and breathed immortal love
To mortal men, above which only shone
Filial obedience. As a sacrifice,
Glad to be offered, He attends the will   270
Of his great Father. Admiration seized
All Heaven, what this might mean and whither tend,
Wondering. But soon th' Almighty thus replied:
    O Thou in Heav'n and Earth the only peace
Found out for mankind under wrath, O Thou   275
My sole complacence! Well Thou know'st how dear
To me are all my works nor Man the least,
Though last created, that for him I spare
Thee from My bosom and right hand to save,
By losing Thee a while, the whole race lost.   280
Thou therefore whom Thou only canst redeem
Their nature also to Thy nature join

247–49. "For thou wilt not leave my soul in hell; neither wilt thou suffer thine Holy One
    to see corruption" (Psalm 16:10).
252. "The last enemy that shall be destroyed is death" and "O death, where is thy sting? O
    grave, where is thy victory?" (1 Corinthians 15:26 and 55).
255. *maugre*: despite (French *malgré*). "Thou hast led captivity captive" (Psalm 68:18).
271. *Admiration*: wonder (Latinate sense: *admiror*, "to regard with wonder").
280. *lost*: which would otherwise be lost.
281–82. I.e., Join your nature to the nature of mankind, whom only you can redeem.

And be Thyself man among men on Earth,
Made flesh (when time shall be) of virgin seed
By wondrous birth. Be Thou in Adam's room   285
The head of all mankind though Adam's son.
As in him perish all men so in Thee
As from a second root shall be restored
As many as are restored, without Thee none.
His crime makes guilty all his sons. Thy merit   290
Imputed shall absolve them who renounce
Their own both righteous and unrighteous deeds
And live in Thee transplanted and from Thee
Receive new life. So Man, as is most just,
Shall satisfy for Man, be judged and die,   295
And dying rise and rising with Him raise
His brethren ransomed with His own dear life.
So heav'nly love shall outdo hellish hate,
Giving to death and dying to redeem
(So dearly to redeem) what hellish hate   300
So easily destroyed and still destroys
In those who, when they may, accept not grace.
Nor shalt Thou by descending to assume
Man's nature lessen or degrade thine own.
Because Thou hast, though throned in highest bliss   305
Equal to God and equally enjoying
God-like fruition, quitted all to save
A world from utter loss and hast been found
By merit more than birthright Son of God
(Found worthiest to be so by being good   310
Far more than great or high, because in Thee
Love hath abounded more than glory abounds)

284. The Son will be Jesus Christ, who is born of the virgin Mary.
285. *room*: place.
287–89. "For as in Adam all die, even so in Christ shall all be made alive" (1 Corinthians 15:22).
291. *Imputed*: attributed. Because the Son becomes a man himself, before he pays for the sins of mankind, his sacrifice is imputed to humanity.
292–93. From the Calvinist perspective, it is not enough to renounce one's unrighteous deeds. One must also renounce any credit, or merit, for one's righteous deeds, since these can be performed only with Christ's help. One must therefore *transplant* (line 293) oneself in Christ.
295. *be judged*: The reference is to Christ's trial before he is crucified.
296–97. Christ's rising from the grave after the Crucifixion is an assurance that humanity will rise from the dead at the end of time.
299. Christ gives himself to death to redeem mankind.
301. *and still destroys*: None of this has occurred yet. See line 97 n.
303–4 and 313–14. By becoming incarnate and mortal, as a man, the Son does not bring down his divinity to the level of the human but raises the human to the divine.
305–12. By voluntarily quitting the status of equality with God in order to save mankind, the Son earns his title, "Son of God," which was his before only by birthright.
307. *fruition*: enjoyment (Latin *fructus*, "enjoyment, delight, satisfaction").

Therefore thy humiliation shall exalt
With Thee thy manhood also to this throne.
Here shalt Thou sit incarnate, here shalt reign   315
Both God and Man, Son both of God and Man,
Anointed universal King. All pow'r
I give Thee: reign for ever and assume
Thy merits! Under Thee as Head Supreme
Thrones, princedoms, pow'rs, dominions I reduce: 320
All knees to Thee shall bow of them that bide
In Heaven or Earth or under Earth in Hell,
When Thou attended gloriously from Heav'n
Shalt in the sky appear and from Thee send
The summoning archangels to proclaim   325
Thy dread tribunal. Forthwith from all winds
The living and forthwith the cited dead
Of all past ages to the general doom
Shall hasten, such a peal shall rouse their sleep.
Then all Thy saints assembled, Thou shalt judge   330
Bad men and angels: they arraigned shall sink
Beneath Thy sentence. Hell, her numbers full,
Thenceforth shall be for ever shut. Meanwhile
The world shall burn and from her ashes spring
New Heav'n and Earth wherein the just shall dwell   335
And after all their tribulations long
See golden days fruitful of golden deeds
With Joy and Love triúmphing and fair Truth.
Then Thou thy regal scepter shalt lay by,
For regal scepter then no more shall need: 340
God shall be All in all. But all ye gods

314–17. After the resurrection, the Son will ascend to heaven in his human body and will sit beside the Father in that body.

321–22. "At the name of Jesus every knee should bow, of things in heaven, and things in earth, and things under the earth" (Philippians 2:10). The entire second chapter of Philippians underlies God's discourse here.

323–29. The Son's return to earth at the Last Judgment: "And they shall see the Son of man coming in the clouds of heaven with power and great glory" (Matthew 24:30). All people who have died rise from the dead and, joined by those who are still living, go up to judgment in their bodies. "For the Lord himself shall descend from heaven . . . and the dead in Christ shall rise first: Then we which are alive . . . shall be caught up together with them in the clouds, to meet the Lord in the air" (1 Thessalonians 4:16–17). "For the trumpet shall sound, and the dead shall be raised incorruptible" (1 Corinthians 15:52).

327. *cited*: summoned.

330. *saints assembled*: The faithful angels and the humans who have been saved will be gathered together to watch the Son damn the wicked.

334–35. "And I saw a new heaven and a new earth: for the first heaven and the first earth were passed away; and there was no more sea" (Revelation 21:1).

341. *All in all*: "And when all things shall be subdued unto him [the Son], then shall the Son also himself be subject unto him that put all things under him, that God may be all in all" (1 Corinthians 15:28). See 6.731–33 and n.

341. *gods*: angels.

Adore Him who to compass all this dies!
Adore the Son and honor Him as Me!
    No sooner had th' Almighty ceased but all
The multitude of angels with a shout   345
Loud as from numbers without number, sweet
As from blest voices uttering joy, Heaven rung
With jubilee and loud hosannas filled
Th' eternal regions. Lowly reverent
Towards either throne they bow and to the ground   350
With solemn adoration down they cast
Their crowns inwove with amarant and gold,
Immortal amarant, a flow'r which once
In Paradise fast by the Tree of Life
Began to bloom but soon for Man's offence   355
To Heav'n removed where first it grew, there grows
And flowers aloft, shading the Fount of Life
And where the river of bliss through midst of Heav'n
Rolls o'er Elysian flow'rs her amber stream.
With these that never fade the spirits elect   360
Bind their resplendent locks inwreathed with beams.
Now in loose garlands thick thrown off, the bright
Pavement, that like a sea of jasper shone,
Impurpled with celestial roses, smiled.
Then, crowned again, their golden harps they took   365
(Harps ever tuned that glittering by their side
Like quivers hung) and with preamble sweet
Of charming symphony they introduce
Their sacred song and waken raptures high.
No voice exempt, no voice but well could join   370
Melodious part, such concord is in Heav'n.
    Thee, Father, first they sung omnipotent,
Immutable, immortal, infinite,
Eternal King, Thee Author of all being,
Fountain of light, Thyself invisible   375
Admidst the glorious brightness where Thou sitt'st
Throned inaccessible but when Thou shad'st
The full blaze of thy beams and through a cloud
Drawn round about Thee like a radiant shrine,
Dark with excessive bright thy skirts appear   380

347. *rung*: rang. The syntax of lines 345–48 makes *Heav'n* the object, not the subject, of
    rung. I.e., With a shout, the angels made heaven ring with celebration.
353. *amarant*: the legendary, unfading flower, *amaranthus*, its name derived from the
    Greek *mainō*, "to wither, fade away." The Greek word is present in 1 Peter 5:4: "ye
    shall receive a crown of glory that fadeth not away."
359. *Elysian flow'rs*. See Glossary, ELYSIUM.
360. *these*: their amaranthus crowns (line 352).

Yet dazzle Heaven that brightest seraphim
Approach not but with both wings veil their eyes!
Thee next they sang of all Creation first,
Begotten Son, divine similitude,
In whose conspicuous countenance without cloud   385
Made visible th' almighty Father shines
Whom else no creature can behold. On Thee
Impressed th' effulgence of His glory abides;
Transfused on Thee his ample Spirit rests.
He Heav'n of heav'ns and all the pow'rs therein   390
By Thee created and by Thee threw down
Th' aspiring dominations. Thou that day
Thy Father's dreadful thunder didst not spare
Nor stop Thy flaming chariot wheels that shook
Heav'n's everlasting frame while o'er the necks   395
Thou drov'st of warring angels disarrayed.
Back from pursuit Thy pow'rs with loud acclaim
Thee only extolled, Son of thy Father's might,
To execute fierce vengeance on His foes.
Not so on Man! Him through their malice fall'n,   400
Father of mercy and grace, Thou didst not doom
So strictly but much more to pity incline.
No sooner did Thy dear and only Son
Perceive Thee purposed not to doom frail Man
So strictly, but much more to pity inclined,   405
He to appease Thy wrath and end the strife
Of Mercy and Justice in Thy face discerned,
Regardless of the bliss wherein He sat
Second to Thee, offered himself to die
For Man's offence. O unexampled love!   410
Love nowhere to be found less than divine!
Hail Son of God, Savior of men, thy name
Shall be the copious matter of my song

381–82. The seraphim, who contemplate God, must cover their faces with their wings: "Above it stood the seraphims: each one had six wings; with twain he covered his face, and with twain he covered his feet, and with twain he did fly. And one cried unto another, and said, Holy, holy, holy, is the Lord of hosts: the whole earth is full of his glory" (Isaiah 6:2–3).
384–92. *divine similitude . . . dominations*: "Who is the image of the invisible God, the firstborn of every creature: For by him were all things created, that are in heaven, and that are in earth, visible and invisible, whether they be thrones, or dominions, or principalities, or powers" (Colossians 1:15–16).
390–92. *He*: God the Father. *Thee . . . Thee*: the Son. God created the heavens and the angels through, or by means of, the Son.
392–96. In the same way, through the Son, God defeated the rebel angels, *th' aspiring dominations*. The action described here will be seen in Book Six.
401, 407. *mercy* and *and* are elided: 'merce-yand.'
402, 405. *pity* and *incline(d)* are elided: 'pit-yincline(d).'

Henceforth and never shall my harp thy praise
Forget nor from thy Father's praise disjoin!   415
   Thus they in Heav'n above the starry sphere
Their happy hours in joy and hymning spent.
Meanwhile upon the firm opacous globe
Of this round world whose first convéx divides
The luminous inferior orbs enclosed   420
From chaos and th' inroad of darkness old
Satan alighted walks. A globe far off
It seemed, now seems a boundless continent
Dark, waste, and wild, under the frown of Night
Starless exposed and ever threat'ning storms   425
Of chaos blust'ring round, inclement sky
Save on that side which from the wall of Heav'n
Though distant far some small reflection gains
Of glimm'ring air less vexed with tempest loud.
Here walked the Fiend at large in spacious field.   430
As when a vulture on Imaüs bred,
Whose snowy ridge the roving Tartar bounds,
Dislodging from a region scarce of prey
To gorge the flesh lambs or yeanling kids
On hills where flocks are fed, flies toward the springs   435
Of Ganges or Hydaspes, Indian streams,
But in his way lights on the barren plains
Of Sericana where Chineses drive
With sails and wind their cany wagons light,
So on this windy sea of land the Fiend   440
Walked up and down alone, bent on his prey.
Alone, for other creature in this place
Living or lifeless to be found was none,
None yet, but store hereafter from the earth
Up hither like aerïal vapors flew   445
Of all things transitory and vain when sin
With vanity had filled the works of men:
Both all things vain and all who in vain things
Build their fond hopes of glory or lasting fame
Or happiness in this or th' other life,   450

418. *opacous*: dark, opaque.
418–21. The outermost sphere of the universe encloses and protects the *inferior* (lower)
    orbs (the stars, the planets, the sun, the moon) from *chaos*.
422–23. See 2.1052–53, when Satan first catches sight of the universe, which seems no
    bigger than the smallest star.
431–41. Satan is compared to a vulture that flies in search of prey from northern Asia over
    the Himalayas to India, pausing in his flight on the high, arid plains of central China.
444–97. The Paradise of Fools, the chief anti-Catholic passage of the poem, is distantly
    inspired by the episode of Ariosto's *Orlando Furioso* (canto 34), in which the knight
    Astolfo visits the moon, where he finds all vain and forgotten things. See line 459.
    Milton's tone is much more serious.

All who have their reward on Earth, the fruits
Of painful superstition and blind zeal
(Naught seeking but the praise of men) here find
Fit retribution empty as their deeds.
All th' unaccomplished works of Nature's hand,   455
Abortive, monstrous, or unkindly mixed,
Dissolved on Earth, fleet hither and in vain
Till final dissolution wander here,
Not in the neighboring moon as some have dreamed.
Those argent fields more likely habitants   460
Translated saints or middle spirits hold
Betwixt th' angelical and human kind.
Hither of ill-joined sons and daughters born
First from the ancient world those giants came
With many a vain exploít though then renowned.   465
The builders next of Babel on the plain
Of Sennaär and still with vain design
New Babels, had they wherewithal, would build.
Others came single: he who to be deemed
A god leaped fondly into Etna flames,   470
Empedocles, and he who to enjoy
Plato's Elysium leaped into the sea,
Cleombrotus, and many more too long:
Embryos and idiots, eremites and friars,
White, black and grey with all their trumpery.   475
Here pilgrims roam that strayed so far to seek
In Golgotha Him dead who lives in Heav'n,
And they who to be sure of Paradise
Dying put on the weeds of Dominic

452. *painful*: laborious.
456. *unkindly*: unnaturally.
457. *fleet*: fly.
460. *argent*: silver.
461. *Translated saints*: those who have not died but have been carried off to heaven: Enoch
    (Genesis 5:24) and Elijah (2 Kings 2:11). *middle spirits*: beings between angels and
    humans. The plan for humans, before the Fall, is that they will gradually become like
    angels. The moon might be an intermediate place for such spirits to reside.
466–67. The Tower of Babel (Genesis 11:1–9), built in the plain of Shinar (*Sennaär*), in
    Babylonia, was a type of human folly and of the aspiration to compete with God.
469–73. Both suicides, Empedocles and Cleombrotus, are mentioned by the Christian
    fathers as examples of the vanity of pagan wishes.
472. *Plato's Elysium*: When he committed suicide the youthful Cleombrotus was reading
    Plato's "On the Soul," as the *Phaedo* was known in antiquity. In that dialogue, Ely-
    sium is located on islands in the region of the sky. See Glossary, CLEOMBROTUS and
    ELYSIUM.
473. *too long*: too long to tell.
474. *eremites*: hermits.
474–80. Examples of empty forms of hope in Roman Catholicism: the three orders of
    friars, the institution of pilgrimage to Jerusalem, and the practice of worldly men
    being buried in friar's robes or donning them shortly before dying. All are to Milton
    external and mechanical substitutes for inward sincerity.
477. *Golgotha*: "place of the skull"; the hill on which Christ was crucified.

Or in Franciscan think to pass disguised.   480
They pass the planets sev'n and pass the fixed
And that crystálline sphere whose balance weighs
The trepidation talked, and that first moved.
And now Saint Peter at Heav'n's wicket seems
To wait them with his keys and now at foot   485
Of Heav'n's ascent they lift their feet when, lo!
A violent crosswind from either coast
Blows them transverse ten thousand leagues awry
Into the devious air. Then might ye see
Cowls, hoods and habits with their wearers tossed   490
And fluttered into rags, then relics, beads,
Indulgences, dispenses, pardons, bulls,
The sport of winds. All these upwhirled aloft
Fly o'er the backside of the world far off
Into a limbo large and broad since called   495
The Paradise of Fools, to few unknown
Long after, now unpeopled and untrod.
　　All this dark globe the Fiend found as he passed
And long he wandered till at last a gleam
Of dawning light turned thitherward in haste   500
His traveled steps. Far distant he descries
Ascending by degrees magnificent
Up to the wall of Heav'n a structure high
At top whereof, but far more rich, appeared
The work as of a kingly palace gate   505
With frontispiece of diamond and gold
Embellished thick. With sparkling orient gems
The portal shone, inimitable on Earth
By model or by shading pencil drawn.
The stairs were such as whereon Jacob saw   510

481–83. The ten translucent spheres enclosing the earth: the seven planetary spheres; the sphere of the fixed stars, the ninth, or crystalline sphere; and the outermost, tenth sphere, *primum mobile* (first mover), which imparts motion to all the others. The nested, crystalline spheres of the medieval cosmos are imaginary, not real. They are what these foolish souls expect to see after they die, and so they shall. But it is all vanity, an illusion.

483. *trepidation*: Trembling in the cosmic spheres is said to be the cause of anomalies in astronomical observations. The word *talked* suggests that Milton thought it mere jargon.

484. *wicket*: gate. As Milton did not believe that Saint Peter guards heaven's gate, this image too is an example of vanity. The ascent through the spheres and the arrival at Saint Peter's gate are what the fools think they see.

490–92. Accoutrements of Roman Catholic devotion and papal arrogance.

494. *world*: universe.

506. *diamond* has three syllables.

508. *inimitable* and *on* are elided.

510–15. Jacob fled from his brother Esau, from whom he had stolen his birthright. One night on his journey, Jacob dreamed of a ladder extending from heaven to earth. He woke and said, "this is none other but the house of God, and this is the gate of heaven" (Genesis 28:17).

Angels ascending and descending, bands
Of guardians bright, when he from Esau fled
To Padan-Aram in the field of Luz,
Dreaming by night under the open sky,
And waking cried, "This is the gate of Heav'n!"   515
Each stair mysteriously was meant nor stood
There always but drawn up to Heav'n sometimes
Viewless, and underneath a bright sea flowed
Of jasper or of liquid pearl whereon
Who after came from Earth sailing arrived   520
Wafted by angels or flew o'er the lake
Rapt in a chariot drawn by fiery steeds.
    The stairs were then let down, whether to dare
The Fiend by easy ascent or aggravate
His sad exclusion from the doors of bliss.   525
Direct against, which opened from beneath,
Just o'er the blissful seat of Paradise,
A passage down to th' earth, a passage wide,
Wider by far than that of aftertimes
Over Mount Sion and, though that were large,   530
Over the Promised Land to God so dear
By which to visit oft those happy tribes
On high behests, His angels, to and fro
Passed frequent, and His eye with choice regard
From Paneas, the fount of Jordan's flood,   535
To Beërsaba where the Holy Land
Borders on Egypt and th' Arabian shore.
So wide the op'ning seemed, where bounds were set
To darkness, such as bound the ocean wave.
Satan from hence now on the lower stair   540
That scaled by steps of gold to Heaven gate
Looks down with wonder at the sudden view
Of all this world at once, as when a scout
Through dark and desert ways with peril gone
All night at last by break of cheerful dawn   545
Obtains the brow of some high climbing hill
Which to his eye discovers unaware
The goodly prospect of some foreign land
First seen, or some renowned metropolis
With glistering spires and pinnacles adorned   550

520–22. *Who*: humans who go to heaven. This account of how humans are transported to heaven is in contrast with the false idea of Peter's gate (line 484). Arrival by ship recalls the beginning of Dante's *Purgatorio*.
524. *easy* and *ascent* are elided: 'eas-yassent.'
535–37. The opening in the globe of the universe is wide enough to give God a clear view of the entire holy land, from the north, where the Jordan rises, to the south, which borders on Egypt and the Red Sea. The eastern shore is the shore of Arabia.

Which now the rising sun gilds with his beams.
Such wonder seized (though after Heaven seen)
The spirit malign but much more envy seized
At sight of all this world beheld so fair.
   Round he surveys (and well might where he stood   555
So high above the circling canopy
Of night's extended shade) from eastern point
Of Libra to the fleecy star that bears
Andromeda far off Atlantic seas
Beyond th' horizon. Then from pole to pole   560
He views in breadth and without longer pause
Down right into the world's first region throws
His flight precipitant and winds with ease
Through the pure marble air his óblique way
Amongst innumerable stars that shone—   565
Stars distant, but nigh hand seemed other worlds.
Or other worlds they seemed or happy isles
Like those Hesperian gardens famed of old,
Fortunate fields and groves and flow'ry vales,
Thrice happy isles, but who dwelt happy there   570
He stayed not to inquire. Above them all
The golden sun in splendor likest Heav'n
Allured his eye. Thither his course he bends
Through the calm firmament (but up or down
By center or eccentric, hard to tell,   575
Or longitude) where the great luminary
(Aloof the vulgar constellations thick
That from his lordly eye keep distance due)
Dispenses light from far. They as they move
Their starry dance in numbers that compute   580
Days, months and years, towards his all-cheering lamp
Turn swift their various motions or are turned
By his magnetic beam that gently warms
The universe and to each inward part
With gentle penetration, though unseen,   585

555–65. From his position at the opening into the universe, Satan is directly above these
    constellations and is looking down through them at the earth. Before plunging into
    the universe (the *world*, line 562) and descending through the *first region* (line 562)
    of liquid (*marble*, line 564) air, Satan views the interior of the entire universe, scan-
    ning *from pole to pole* (line 560).

567. *Or . . . or*: either . . . or. A Latin construction.

568–70. The western paradise, the garden of the Hesperides, can no longer be thought in
    Milton's day to be beyond the ocean, where the sun sets. Milton suggests that the
    myth may still be true, but in other worlds, in space. Milton thinks the stars could be
    distant worlds, like Earth, but not distant suns.

572–87. Despite his expanded cosmic vision, Milton still thinks there is only one sun,
    which turns the constellations and dispenses light and life (*virtue*, line 586) through-
    out the universe.

Shoots invisible virtue even to the deep:
So wondrously was set his station bright.
   There lands the Fiend: a spot like which perhaps
Astronomer in the sun's lucent orb
Through his glazed optic tube yet never saw.   590
The place he found beyond expression bright
Compared with aught on earth, metal or stone.
Not all parts like but all alike informed
With radiant light as glowing iron with fire.
If metal, part seemed gold, part silver clear.   595
If stone, carbuncle most or chrysolite,
Ruby or topaz, to the twelve that shone
In Aaron's breastplate and a stone besides
Imagined rather oft than elsewhere seen.
That stone, or like to that, which here below   600
Philosophers in vain so long have sought,
In vain though by their powerful art they bind
Volatile Hermes and call up unbound
In various shapes old Proteus from the sea,
Drained through a limbec to his native form.   605
What wonder then if fields and regions here
Breathe forth elixir pure and rivers run
Potable gold when with one virtuous touch
Th' arch-chemic sun so far from us remote
Produces with terrestrial humor mixed   610
Here in the dark so many precious things
Of color glorious and effect so rare?
Here matter new to gaze the Devil met
Undazzled. Far and wide his eye commands,
For sight no obstacle found here nor shade   615
But all sunshine (as when his beams at noon
Culminate from th' equator, as they now

---

598. The life-giving stones in the sun are like those in the high priest Aaron's breastplate in Exodus 28:17–20. *stone besides*: the "philosopher's stone" of the alchemists, which transforms ordinary metals into gold. Milton does not believe in the philosopher's stone, but he likens what is claimed for it to the real life-giving power of the sun. See lines 609–12.
601. *Philosophers*: alchemists.
603. *Hermes*: Mercury, which vaporizes readily, is used in alchemical research.
604. *Proteus*: The shape-shifter god is the symbol of the central idea of alchemy: that metals are convertible into one another.
605. *limbec*: alembic, glass instrument used in distilling and refining.
609–12. The sun's rays were thought to create precious stones in the earth, just as they bring living plants out of the earth. Milton would have been pleased to know that elements beyond helium on the periodic table were formed by synthesis in the interior of stars and that much heavier elements, such as precious metals, were formed in exploding supernovae.
615–19. As the sun's rays fall from directly overhead at the equator, leaving no shadow, so here the rays fly straight up and leave no shadow.

Shot upward still direct, whence no way round
Shadow from body opaque can fall) and th' air,
Nowhere so clear, sharpened his visual ray   620
To objects distant far, whereby he soon
Saw within ken a glorious angel stand,
The same whom John saw also in the sun.
His back was turned but not his brightness hid
Of beaming sunny rays, a golden tiar   625
Circled his head, nor less his locks behind
Illustrious on his shoulders (fledge with wings)
Lay waving round. On some great charge employed
He seemed or fixed in cogitation deep.
Glad was the spirit impure as now in hope   630
To find who might direct his wand'ring flight
To Paradise, the happy seat of Man,
His journey's end and our beginning woe.
But first he casts to change his proper shape
Which else might work him danger or delay: 635
And now a stripling cherub he appears,
Not of the prime yet such as in his face
Youth smiled celestial and to every limb
Suitable grace diffused, so well he feigned.
Under a coronet his flowing hair   640
In curls on either cheek played. Wings he wore
Of many a colored plume sprinkled with gold,
His habit fit for speed succinct, and held
Before his decent steps a silver wand.
He drew not nigh unheard: the angel bright   645
Ere he drew nigh his radiant visage turned
(Admonished by his ear) and straight was known
Th' Archangel Uriel, one of the sev'n
Who in God's presence nearest to His throne
Stand ready at command and are His eyes   650
That run through all the heav'ns or down to th' earth
Bear his swift errands over moist and dry,
O'er sea and land. Him Satan thus accosts:
    Uriel, for thou of those sev'n spirits that stand
In sight of God's high throne, gloriously bright,   655
The first art wont His great authentic will,
Interpreter, through highest Heav'n to bring
Where all His sons thy embassy attend

---

623. "And I saw an angel standing in the sun" (Revelation 19:17).
625. *tiar*: tiara, i.e., crown, or *coronet* (line 640).
643. *succinct*: drawn up and secured (Latin).

And here art likeliest by supreme decree
Like honor to obtain and as His eye   660
To visit oft this new Creation round:
Unspeakable desire to see and know
All these His wondrous works (but chiefly Man,
His chief delight and favor, him for whom
All these His works so wondrous He ordained)   665
Hath brought me from the choirs of cherubim
Alone thus wand'ring. Brightest Seraph, tell,
In which of all these shining orbs hath Man
His fixèd seat, or fixèd seat hath none
But all these shining orbs his choice to dwell,   670
That I may find him and with secret gaze
Or open admiration him behold
On whom the great Creator hath bestowed
Worlds and on whom hath all these graces poured,
That both in him and all things, as is meet,   675
The Universal Maker we may praise,
Who justly hath driv'n out His rebel foes
To deepest Hell and to repair that loss
Created this new happy race of men
To serve Him better: wise are all His ways!   680
    So spake the false dissembler unperceived,
For neither man nor angel can discern
Hypocrisy, the only evil that walks
Invisible except to God alone
By His permissive will through Heav'n and Earth.   685
And oft, though Wisdom wake, Suspicion sleeps
At Wisdom's gate and to Simplicity
Resigns her charge while Goodness thinks no ill
Where no ill seems, which now for once beguiled
Uriel, though regent of the sun and held   690
The sharpest sighted spirit of all in Heav'n,
Who to the fraudulent impostor foul
In his uprightness answer thus returned:
    Fair angel, thy desire which tends to know
The works of God thereby to glorify   695
The great Work-Master leads to no excess
That reaches blame but rather merits praise
The more it seems excess that led thee hither
From thy empyreal mansion thus alone
To witness with thine eyes what some perhaps   700

675. *him*: Man.
689. *which*: Hypocrisy, which beguiled Uriel.

Contented with report hear only in Heaven.
For wonderful indeed are all His works,
Pleasant to know and worthiest to be all
Had in remembrance, always with delight.
But what created mind can comprehend   705
Their number or the wisdom infinite
That brought them forth but hid their causes deep?
I saw when at His Word the formless mass,
This world's material mold, came to a heap.
Confusion heard His voice and Wild Uproar   710
Stood ruled, stood Vast Infinitude confined,
Till at His second bidding darkness fled,
Light shone, and order from disorder sprung.
Swift to their several quarters hasted then
The cumbrous elements, earth, flood, air, fire,   715
And this ethereal quíntessence of Heav'n
Flew upward, spirited with various forms
That rolled orbicular and turned to stars
Numberless, as thou seest, and how they move.
Each had his place appointed, each his course,   720
The rest in circuit walls this universe.
Look downward on that globe whose hither side
With light from hence though but reflected shines.
That place is Earth, the seat of Man, that light
His day, which else as th' other hemisphere   725
Night would invade. But there the neighboring Moon
(So call that opposite fair star) her aid
Timely interposes and her monthly round
Still ending, still renewing, through mid heav'n
With borrowed light her countenance triform,   730
Hence fills and empties to enlighten th' earth
And in her pale dominion checks the night.

710–13. Vestigial personifications in lines 710–11 fade into abstractions in 712–13.
716. *ethereal quíntessence:* Quintessence means a hidden "fifth element" beyond the four
observable ones already named in line 715. Associated with Heaven and with anything divine, such as the soul, as in *Hamlet* 2.2.298, the quintessence is associated
with the *ether*, the fiery and pure upper air. (From Greek αἴθήρ, *aithēr*, related to
aithō, "to burn," but also "to flash brightly," and ἀήρ, "air": *aithēr* is the upper atmosphere, *aēr* the lower.) The gods breathe the fiery ether as humans breath air. The
ether is associated with the *empyrean*, or heavenly region of fire (from πῦρ, "fire").
Milton refers to himself in *Reason of Church Government* (below, p.) as "a poet,
soaring in the high region of his fancies," who must now confine himself to "the cool
element of prose, a mortal thing . . . of no empyreal conceit." See 7.14–15 and n.
721. A reference to the sphere of the fixed stars, as opposed to those (actually planets and
the moon) that wander in the heavens.
723. *light from hence:* light from here, on the sun.
726. *there:* on the dark side of the earth.
730. *triform:* the three phases of the moon.
732. *checks:* prevents from becoming total.

That spot to which I point is Paradise,
Adam's abode, those lofty shades his bower.
Thy way thou canst not miss, me mine requires.   735
    Thus said he turned and Satan, bowing low
As to superior spirits is wont in Heaven
(Where honor due and reverence none neglects)
Took leave and toward the coast of Earth beneath,
Down from th' ecliptic, sped with hoped success,   740
Throws his steep flight in many an airy wheel,
Nor stayed till on Niphates' top he lights.

Book Four

The Argument

Satan, now in prospect of Eden, and nigh the place where he must
now attempt the bold enterprise which he undertook alone against
God and Man, falls into many doubts with himself and many
passions—fear, envy, and despair—but at length confirms himself
in evil, journeys on to Paradise (whose outward prospect and situation is described), overleaps the bounds, sits in the shape of a cormorant on the Tree of Life (as highest in the garden) to look about
him. The garden described; Satan's first sight of Adam and Eve; his
wonder at their excellent form and happy state, but with resolution
to work their Fall; overhears their discourse; thence gathers that
the Tree of Knowledge was forbidden them to eat of, under penalty
of death; and thereon intends to found his temptation, by seducing
them to transgress. Then leaves them a while, to know further of
their state by some other means. Meanwhile Uriel, descending on a
sunbeam, warns Gabriel, who had in charge the gate of Paradise,
that some evil spirit had escaped the deep and passed at noon by
his sphere in the shape of a good angel down to Paradise, discovered after by his furious gestures in the mount. Gabriel promises to
find him ere morning. Night coming on, Adam and Eve discourse of
going to their rest; their bower described; their evening worship.
Gabriel, drawing forth his bands of night-watch to walk the round

---

740. *ecliptic*: here, the orbit of the sun around the earth and therefore the point of departure for Satan's flight downward to earth. Satan flies down *from* the ecliptic. But this
point of departure is moving along the arc of the ecliptic, meaning that Satan's flight
will not be direct but must adjust to the altering positions of the sun and the earth.
Hence the splendid phrase describing Satan's devious flight, "in many an airy wheel"
(line 741). Milton is perhaps remembering Ariosto's sinister enchanter, Atlante, who
when flying the winged Hippogriff soars "with large circles" ("con large ruote")
before he lands. Cf. 9.62–66 and n. *sped*: impelled.
742. *Niphates*: a mountain in Assyria, near Eden, its name suggesting that its peak is
snow-covered, an appropriate backdrop for Satan's soliloquy there (4.32–113).

of Paradise, appoints two strong angels to Adam's bower, lest the
evil spirit should be there doing some harm to Adam or Eve sleeping. There they find him at the ear of Eve, tempting her in a dream,
and bring him, though unwilling, to Gabriel; by whom questioned,
he scornfully answers, prepares resistance, but hindered by a sign
from Heaven, flies out of Paradise.

O! for that warning voice which he who saw
Th' Apocalypse heard cry in Heav'n aloud
Then when the Dragon, put to second rout,
Came furious down to be revenged on men:
"Woe to the inhabitants on Earth!" That now,
While time was, our first parents had been warned
The coming of their secret foe and 'scaped,
Haply so 'scaped, his mortal snare. For now
Satan, now first inflamed with rage, came down
The tempter ere th' accuser of mankind   10
To wreck on innocent frail Man his loss
Of that first battle and his flight to Hell.
Yet not rejoicing in his speed, though bold,
Far off and fearless, nor with cause to boast
Begins his dire attempt which, nigh the birth,   15
Now rolling boils in his tumultuous breast
And like a devilish engine back recoils
Upon himself. Horror and doubt distract
His troubled thoughts and from the bottom stir
The Hell within him, for within him Hell   20
He brings and round about him, nor from Hell
One step no more than from himself can fly
By change of place. Now conscience wakes despair
That slumbered, wakes the bitter memory
Of what he was, what is, and what must be   25
Worse: of worse deeds worse sufferings must ensue.
Sometimes towards Eden which now in his view

Book Four
1. *he*: John, author of the book of Revelation, which recounts the visions he saw of the
    end of the world.
2. *Apocalypse*: "unveiling"; the Greek title of the book of Revelation.
3. *Dragon*: Satan. Revelation 12:3–9.
5. Revelation 12:12: "Woe to the inhabiters of the earth and of the sea! for the devil is come
    down unto you, having great wrath, because he knoweth that he hath but a short time."
8. *Haply*: perhaps; also, happily.
10. *accuser*: one of the meanings of the name *Satan*, in the sense of being God's prosecut-
    ing attorney, a role Satan performs in the first two chapters of the book of Job.
11. *his*: Satan's.
20–21. A famous borrowing from Marlowe's *Doctor Faustus*, scene 3, lines 75–76: "*Faus-
    tus*. How comes it then that thou art out of hell? / *Mephistophilis*. Why this is hell, nor
    am I out of it."

Lay pleasant his grieved look he fixes sad,
Sometimes towards Heav'n and the full-blazing sun
Which now sat high in his meridian tower.   30
Then much revolving thus in sighs began:
   O thou that with surpassing glory crowned
Look'st from thy sole dominion like the god
Of this new world, at whose sight all the stars
Hide their diminished heads, to thee I call   35
But with no friendly voice and add thy name,
O sun, to tell thee how I hate thy beams
That bring to my remembrance from what state
I fell, how glorious once above thy sphere
Till pride and worse ambition threw me down,   40
Warring in Heav'n against Heav'n's matchless King.
Ah wherefore! He deserved no such return
From me, whom He created what I was
In that bright eminence and with His good
Upbraided none. Nor was His service hard: 45
What could be less than to afford Him praise,
The easiest recompense, and pay Him thanks?
How due! Yet all His good proved ill in me
And wrought but malice. Lifted up so high
I 'sdeigned subjection and thought one step higher   50
Would set me high'st and in a moment quit
The debt immense of endless gratitude
So burdensome—still paying! still to owe!—
Forgetful what from Him I still received
And understood not that a grateful mind   55
By owing owes not but still pays, at once
Indebted and discharged. What burden then?
O had His pow'rful destiny ordained
Me some inferior angel! I had stood
Then happy: no unbounded hope had raised   60
Ambition. Yet why not? Some other pow'r
As great might have aspired and me, though mean,

---

31. *revolving*: turning over in himself many thoughts and many strong emotions.
32. *thou*: the sun, to whom the first part of this speech is addressed, as if the sun were a god himself and not something created by God.
32–41. According to Milton's nephew, Edward Phillips, Milton composed these lines when he was still thinking of making a tragedy, *Adam Unparadised*, rather than an epic. The lines recall addresses to the sun in two ancient tragedies: Aeschylus's *Prometheus Bound* (91) and Euripides' *Phoenissae* (1–3).
50. *'sdeigned*: disdained.
53–54. *still*: always, perpetually.
55–57. In the economy of heaven the debt one owes God for one's creation is discharged by gratitude, which, paradoxically, recognizes the continuing nature of the debt even as it pays it off.
62. *mean*: low-ranking.

Drawn to his part. But other pow'rs as great
Fell not but stand unshaken from within
Or from without to all temptations armed.   65
Hadst thou the same free will and pow'r to stand?
Thou hadst. Whom hast thou then or what t' accuse
But Heav'n's free love dealt equally to all?
Be then His love accursed, since love or hate
To me alike it deals eternal woe!   70
Nay cursed be thou since against His thy will
Chose freely what it now so justly rues.
Me miserable! Which way shall I fly
Infinite wrath and infinite despair?
Which way I fly is Hell, myself am Hell,   75
And in the lowest deep a lower deep
Still threat'ning to devour me opens wide,
To which the Hell I suffer seems a Heav'n.
O then at last relent! Is there no place
Left for repentance, none for pardon left?   80
None left but by submission and that word
Disdain forbids me and my dread of shame
Among the spirits beneath whom I seduced
With other promises and other vaunts
Than to submit, boasting I could subdue   85
Th' Omnipotent. Ay me! they little know
How dearly I abide that boast so vain,
Under what torments inwardly I groan
While they adore me on the throne of Hell
With diadem and scepter high advanced   90
The lower still I fall, only supreme
In misery. Such joy ambition finds.
But say I could repent and could obtain
By act of grace my former state. How soon
Would heighth recall high thoughts? How soon unsay   95
What feigned submission swore? Ease would recant
Vows made in pain as violent and void
(For never can true reconcilement grow
Where wounds of deadly hate have pierced so deep)

63. *as great*: as eminent as Satan was. For Milton, Lucifer before his fall was among
     the highest angels but was not the highest. See 5.659–60.
66. *thou*: you. Satan is speaking to himself.
73–74. I.e., In what direction can I fly from wrath and despair?
88–92. An example of Milton's compressed syntax, where two distinct sentences coincide
     in one: 'I groan while they adore me with my diadem and scepter raised' and 'the
     higher my diadem and scepter are raised the lower I fall.'
90. *diadem*: crown. *scepter*: a rod borne in the hand as an emblem of royal authority.
96–97. Once restored to blessedness, I would recant my vow of faith as invalid, since it
     was made under duress.

Which would but lead me to a worse relapse   100
And heavier fall. So should I purchase dear
Short intermission bought with double smart.
This knows my punisher. Therefore as far
From granting He as I from begging peace.
All hope excluded thus, behold instead   105
Of us outcast, exiled, His new delight:
Mankind created and for him this world.
So farewell hope and with hope farewell fear!
Farewell remorse! All good to me is lost.
Evil, be thou my good. By thee at least   110
Divided empire with Heav'n's King I hold
By thee, and more than half perhaps will reign,
As man ere long and this new world shall know.
      Thus while he spake each passion dimmed his face
Thrice changed with pale ire, envy and despair,   115
Which marred his borrowed visage and betrayed
Him counterfeit if any eye beheld,
For Heav'nly minds from such distempers foul
Are ever clear. Whereof he soon aware
Each perturbation smoothed with outward calm,   120
Artíficer of fraud, and was the first
That practiced falsehood: under saintly show
Deep malice to conceal couched with revenge.
Yet not enough had practiced to deceive
Uriel once warned, whose eye pursued him down   125
The way he went and on th' Assyrian mount
Saw him disfigured more than could befall
Spirit of happy sort. His gestures fierce
He marked and mad demeanor, then alone,
As he supposed, all unobserved, unseen.   130
So on he fares and to the border comes
Of Eden where delicious Paradise,
Now nearer, crowns with her enclosure green
As with a rural mound the champaign head
Of a steep wilderness whose hairy sides   135

---

102. *double smart:* redoubled agony.
110. Isaiah 5:20: "Woe unto them that call evil good, and good evil!"
116. *borrowed visage:* Satan is still disguised as the *stripling cherub* of 3.636.
126. *Assyrian mount:* Niphates (3.742).
129. *He:* Uriel.
130. *he:* Satan.
131. *he:* Satan.
132. *Eden* and *Paradise:* See Glossary.
132–35. I.e., The garden, *Paradise,* enclosed with trees, lies on the broad plain (*champaign*) that surmounts a steep hill overgrown with thickets.

With thicket overgrown, grotesque and wild,
Access denied. And overhead up grew
Insuperable heighth of loftiest shade,
Cedar and pine and fir and branching palm,
A sylvan scene, and as the ranks ascend   140
Shade above shade, a woody theater
Of stateliest view. Yet higher than their tops
The verdurous wall of Paradise up sprung
Which to our gen'ral sire gave prospect large
Into his nether empire neighboring round.   145
And higher than that wall a circling row
Of goodliest trees loaden with fairest fruit
Blossoms, and fruits at once of golden hue
Appeared with gay enameled colors mixed,
On which the sun more glad impressed his beams   150
Than in fair evening cloud or humid bow
When God hath show'red the earth, so lovely seemed
That landscip. And of pure now purer air
Meets his approach and to the heart inspires
Vernal delight and joy, able to drive   155
All sadness but despair. Now gentle gales
Fanning their odoriferous wings dispense
Native perfumes and whisper whence they stole
Those balmy spoils. As when to them who sail
Beyond the Cape of Hope and now are passed   160
Mozámbique, off at sea, northeast winds blow
Sabéan odors from the spicy shore
Of Araby the blest—with such delay
Well pleased they slack their course and many a league
Cheered with the grateful smell old Ocean smiles—   165
So entertained those odorous sweets the Fiend

136. *grotesque*: full of caves (grottos) as well as like the decorative, tangled growth
    depicted on Roman wall paintings.
137. The wilderness on the side of the paradisal mountain denied access to Paradise at
    the top.
137–42. *overhead*: As *ranks* of trees *ascend* the mountainside, each rank overshadows the
    last (*shade above shade*) so that the trees appear to form a kind of theater. Milton
    follows closely a description of trees in the *Aeneid* 1.164–65, capturing the phrase
    silvis scaena in *sylvan scene* (line 140).
143. *verdurous*: green. The wall is overgrown with plants.
144. *our gen'ral sire*: the father of us all, Adam.
146. *circling row*: fruit trees within the encircling wall of Paradise, rising above that wall
    so that their tops are visible from without.
149. *enameled*: gleaming and variegated, bejeweled.
153. *landscip*: land view. The Dutch word for "landscape," a new, fashionable term in
    Milton's day.
154. *his*: Satan's. This entire description of Eden as we first see it, up to line 356, is seen,
    with impressive irony, through Satan's eyes. See lines 194–207.
162. *Sabéan odors*: from Arabian myrrh. See Glossary.

Who came their bane, though with them better pleased
Than Asmodeus with the fishy fume
That drove him, though enamored, from the spouse
Of Tobit's son and with a vengeance sent   170
From Media post to Egypt, there fast bound.
    Now to th' ascent of that steep savage hill
Satan had journeyed on, pensive and slow,
But further way found none, so thick entwined
As one continued brake the undergrowth   175
Of shrubs and tangling bushes had perplexed
All path of man or beast that passed that way.
One gate there only was and that looked east
On th' other side. Which when th' arch-felon saw
Due entrance he disdained and in contempt   180
At one slight bound high overleaped all bound
Of hill or highest wall and sheer within
Lights on his feet. As when a prowling wolf
Whom hunger drives to seek new haunt for prey,
Watching where shepherds pen their flocks at eve   185
In hurdled cotes amid the field secure,
Leaps o'er the fence with ease into the fold,
Or as a thief bent to unhoard the cash
Of some rich burgher, whose substantial doors
Cross-barred and bolted fast fear no assault,   190
In at the window climbs or o'er the tiles:
So clomb this first grand thief into God's fold:
So since into His Church lewd hirelings climb!
Thence up he flew and on the Tree of Life,
The middle tree and highest there that grew,   195
Sat like a cormorant. Yet not true life
Thereby regained but sat devising death

---

170 and 171. *sent* and *bound*: The object of these verbs is *Asmodeus*. The smell drives him from Persia to Egypt, where he is bound.
172. *savage*: adorned with trees, from Latin *silvaticus*. Milton is likely thinking of Italian *selvaggio*, as applied to agreeably wild landscapes.
179. *other side*: Satan approaches Paradise from the west, in the direction opposite to that of the sun.
186. *hurdled*: made of interlaced branches. *cotes*: movable pens in which sheep are kept at night.
187. *fold*: an enclosure for sheep.
189. *burgher*: town dweller.
193. *lewd*: poorly educated, vulgar, and base. *hirelings*: priests, such as those in the Church of England, who accept pay or other emolument for their pastoral work. As Milton notes in "Lycidas," wolves climb into the fold to snatch their prey. The image is biblical, John 10:1–11.
195. *middle*: in the center of the garden.
196. *cormorant*: large, ugly, voracious seabird.

To them who lived. Nor on the virtue thought
Of that life-giving plant but only used
For prospect what well used had been the pledge   200
Of immortality. So little knows
Any but God alone to value right
The good before him but perverts best things
To worst abuse or to their meanest use.
Beneath him with new wonder now he views   205
To all delight of human sense exposed
In narrow room Nature's whole wealth, yea more,
A Heav'n on Earth, for blissful Paradise
Of God the garden was by Him in th' east
Of Eden planted. Eden stretched her line   210
From Auran eastward to the royal towers
Of great Seleucia built by Grecian kings
Or where the sons of Eden long before
Dwelt in Telassar. In this pleasant soil
His far more pleasant garden God ordained.   215
Out of the fertile ground He caused to grow
All trees of noblest kind for sight, smell, taste
And all amid them stood the Tree of Life
High eminent blooming ambrosial fruit
Of vegetable gold. And next to Life   220
Our death, the Tree of Knowledge, grew fast by:
Knowledge of good bought dear by knowing ill.
Southward through Eden went a river large
Nor changed his course but through the shaggy hill
Passed underneath engulfed, for God had thrown   225
That mountain as His garden mold high raised
Upon the rapid current which through veins
Of porous earth with kindly thirst up drawn
Rose a fresh fountain and with many a rill
Watered the garden; thence united fell   230
Down the steep glade and met the nether flood
Which from his darksome passage now appears,
And now divided into four main streams
Runs diverse wand'ring many a famous realm

198–201. Satan uses the tree only to get a good view (*prospect*) of the garden, not for its
power to confer immortality. But immortality is Satan's biggest problem.
221. *Our death*: the cause of our death.
222. This formulation Milton worked out many years before in *Areopagitica*: "this is that
doom which Adam fell into of knowing good and evil, that is to say of knowing good
by evil" (below, p. 362).
223–35. I.e., The streams of Paradise are fed by a river that flows under the mount. They
flow together again south of the garden and become a waterfall, the source of the
major rivers of the world.

And country. Whereof here needs no account   235
But rather to tell how, if art could tell,
How from that sapphire fount the crispèd brooks
Rolling on orient pearl and sands of gold
With mazy error under pendent shades
Ran nectar, visiting each plant, and fed   240
Flow'rs worthy of Paradise which not nice art
In beds and curious knots, but Nature boon
Poured forth profuse on hill and dale and plain,
Both where the morning sun first warmly smote
The open field and where th' unpiercèd shade   245
Embrowned the noontide bowers. Thus was this place
A happy rural seat of various view,
Groves whose rich trees wept odorous gums and balm,
Others whose fruit, burnished with golden rind,
Hung amiable: Hesperian fables true,   250
If true, here only, and of delicious taste.
Betwixt them lawns or level downs and flocks
Grazing the tender herb were interposed
Or palmy hillock or the flow'ry lap
Of some irriguous valley spread her store—   255
Flow'rs of all hue and without thorn the rose.
Another side umbrageous grots and caves
Of cool recéss o'er which the mantling vine
Lays forth her purple grape and gently creeps
Luxuriant. Meanwhile murmuring waters fall   260
Down the slope hills, dispersed, or in a lake
That to the fringèd bank with myrtle crowned
Her crystal mirror holds unite their streams.
The birds their choir apply. Airs, vernal airs,
Breathing the smell of field and grove attune   265

237. *crispèd*: Latin *crispus*, "curled, waving, trembling," often of hair.
237–41. Like the two crystalline streams of Damascus, watering every garden in the city. See Ariosto, *Orlando Furioso* 17.19 and Glossary, DAMASCUS.
238. *orient*: irridescent, lustrous, like the dawn in the eastern sky.
239. *error*: wandering, meandering (Latin).
241. *nice art*: fussy calculation, by which flowers would be planted in carefully arranged beds and entangling designs (*curious knots*, line 242).
250–51. I.e., If the classical fables of the magical fruit of the Hesperides are true, they are true only because they refer to this place, Paradise.
252. *them*: the groves.
255. *irriguous*: well-watered.
260–63. *waters* is the subject of two successive principal clauses, the main verbs of which are *fall* and *unite*; i.e., Waters falling downhill either disperse in various directions or they flow together (*unite their streams*) in a lake, a calm lake that holds its mirror up to the bank, which is fringed with myrtle.
264. *apply*: add to the scene or fold into the scene, with the suggestion that the birds' choral singing is not in unison but folded together in several parts, like counterpoint.

The trembling leaves while universal Pan
Knit with the Graces and the Hours in dance
Led on th' eternal spring. Not that fair field
Of Enna where Prosérpine gath'ring flow'rs,
Herself a fairer flow'r, by gloomy Dis   270
Was gathered, which cost Ceres all that pain
To seek her through the world, nor that sweet grove
Of Daphne by Orontes and th' inspired
Castalian spring might with this paradise
Of Eden strive, nor that Nyseian isle   275
Girt with the river Triton where old Cham
(Whom Gentiles Ammon call and Libyan Jove)
Hid Amalthéa and her florid son,
Young Bacchus, from his stepdame Rhea's eye,
Nor where Abássin kings their issue guard,   280
Mount Amara, though this by some supposed
True Paradise, under the Ethiop line
By Nilus' head, enclosed with shining rock
A whole day's journey high, but wide remote
From this Assyrian garden where the Fiend   285
Saw undelighted all delight, all kind
Of living creatures new to sight and strange.
   Two of far nobler shape erect and tall,
Godlike erect with native honor clad
In naked majesty, seemed lords of all.   290
And worthy seemed for in their looks divine
The image of their glorious Maker shone:
Truth, wisdom, sanctitude severe and pure,
Severe, but in true filial freedom placed,
Whence true authority in men. Though both   295
Not equal as their sex not equal seemed:
For contemplation he and valor formed,
For softness she and sweet attractive grace:
He for God only, she for God in him.

266. *Pan*: the goat god, symbolizing universal nature (his name in Greek means "all").
268–87. A series of four mythical paradises negatively compared with the Paradise Milton describes. The main verb with its auxiliary, *might . . . strive* (lines 274–75), is set in the middle, with two comparisons before it (*Not . . . nor*, lines 268 and 272) and two after (*nor . . . Nor*, lines 275 and 280). The symmetrical structure of the sentence is then given over to the forward movement of the action by the clause beginning *but wide remote* (line 284) and by the sudden reappearance of Satan. At this moment, Adam and Eve are introduced (line 288).
278. *florid*: red-complexioned, flushed with wine; associated with blooming flowers.
292. *image*: "So God created man in his own image, in the image of God created he him; male and female created he them" (Genesis 1:27).
296. See 8.383–87.
299. See 1 Cor. 11:3: "the head of every man is Christ; and the head of the woman is the man; and the head of Christ is God." For hair, see verses 14–15.

His fair large front and eye sublime declared   300
Absolute rule, and hyacinthine locks
Round from his parted forelock manly hung
Clust'ring but not beneath his shoulders broad.
She as a veil down to the slender waist
Her unadornèd golden tresses wore   305
Dishevelled but in wanton ringlets waved
As the vine curls her tendrils, which implied
Subjection, but required with gentle sway
And by her yielded, by him best received,
Yielded with coy submission, modest pride,   310
And sweet reluctant amorous delay.
Nor those mysterious parts were then concealed:
Then was not guilty shame, dishonest shame
Of nature's works, honor dishonorable,
Sin-bred. How have ye troubled all mankind   315
With shows instead—mere shows of seeming pure!—
And banished from Man's life his happiest life:
Simplicity and spotless innocence.
So passed they naked on nor shunned the sight
Of God or angel, for they thought no ill.   320
So hand in hand they passed, the loveliest pair
That ever since in love's embraces met:
Adam the goodliest man of men since born
His sons, the fairest of her daughters Eve.
Under a tuft of shade that on a green   325
Stood whispering soft by a fresh fountain side
They sat them down and after no more toil
Of their sweet gard'ning labor than sufficed
To recommend cool Zephyr and made ease
More easy, wholesome thirst and appetite   330
More grateful, to their supper fruits they fell:
Nectarine fruits which the compliant boughs
Yielded them sidelong as they sat recline

301. *hyacinthine locks*: rich, dark hair. A Homeric expression: Odysseus's hair, improved by Athena. See *Odyssey* 6.230–31.
308. *Subjection*: Eve's long, beautiful hair is a sign of her submission to Adam's authority. Adam and Eve are not equals but exist, like everything else in Milton's idea of divine Creation, in hierarchy. "Doth not even nature itself teach you, that, if a man have long hair, it is a shame unto him? But if a woman have long hair, it is a glory to her: for her hair is given her for a covering" (1 Corinthians 11:14–15). *sway*: rule.
314. *honor dishonorable*: decently covering one's genitals is indecent because doing so acknowledges the shame that came with the Fall.
315. *ye*: i.e., *shame* and *honor*.
323–24. *goodliest . . . fairest*: Adam and Eve are the best physical specimens of humanity that ever were.

On the soft downy bank, damasked with flowers.
The savory pulp they chew and in the rind   335
Still as they thirsted scoop the brimming stream.
Nor gentle purpose nor endearing smiles
Wanted, nor youthful dalliance as beseems
Fair couple linked in happy nuptial league,
Alone as they. About them frisking played   340
All beasts of th' earth, since wild, and of all chase
In wood or wilderness, forest or den.
Sporting the lion ramped and in his paw
Dandled the kid. Bears, tigers, ounces, pards
Gamboled before them. Th' unwieldy elephant   345
To make them mirth used all his might and wreathed
His lithe proboscis. Close the serpent sly
Insinuating wove with Gordian twine
His braided train and of his fatal guile
Gave proof unheeded. Others on the grass   350
Couched and now filled with pasture gazing sat
Or bedward ruminating, for the sun,
Declined, was hasting now with prone career
To th' ocean isles and in th' ascending scale
Of Heav'n the stars that usher evening rose.   355
When Satan, still in gaze as first he stood,
Scarce thus at length failed speech recovered sad:
    O Hell! What do mine eyes with grief behold?
Into our room of bliss thus high advanced
Creatures of other mold, earth-born perhaps,   360
Not spirits, yet to Heav'nly spirits bright
Little inferior, whom my thoughts pursue
With wonder and could love, so lively shines
In them divine resemblance and such grace
The hand that formed them on their shape hath poured.   365
Ah, gentle pair, ye little think how nigh
Your change approaches when all these delights
Will vanish and deliver ye to woe,
More woe the more your taste is now of joy!

---

338. *Wanted*: lacked. *dalliance*: flirtation.
341. *all chase*: every habitat, as in a wildlife preserve (*chase*).
344. *ounces*: snow leopards (*OED2*). *pards*: leopards.
347. *lithe proboscis*: flexible snout, i.e., trunk.
348. *Insinuating*: winding, with a suggestion of our sense of the word. The serpent must
     be seen here as innocent because it is uninhabited by Satan. But the serpent's natu-
     rally subtle character makes it the perfect vessel for Satan's fraud.
351. *pasture*: food.
353. *prone career*: headfirst, downward course.
359. *room*: place.

Happy, but for so happy ill secured   370
Long to continue and this high seat, your Heaven,
Ill fenced for Heav'n to keep out such a foe
As now is entered! Yet no purposed foe
To you whom I could pity, thus forlorn,
Though I unpitied. League with you I seek   375
And mutual amity so strait, so close,
That I with you must dwell or you with me
Henceforth. My dwelling haply may not please,
Like this fair Paradise, your sense, yet such
Accept your Maker's work. He gave it me   380
Which I as freely give. Hell shall unfold
To entertain you two her widest gates
And send forth all her kings. There will be room
Not like these narrow limits to receive
Your numerous offspring. If no better place,   385
Thank Him who puts me, loath to this revenge,
On you who wrong me not for Him who wronged.
And should I at your harmless innocence
Melt, as I do, yet public reason just,
Honor and empire with revenge enlarged   390
By conquering this new world compels me now
To do what else, though damned, I should abhor.
    So spake the Fiend and with necessity,
The tyrant's plea, excused his dev'lish deeds.
Then from his lofty stand on that high tree   395
Down he alights among the sportful herd
Of those four-footed kinds, himself now one,
Now other, as their shape served best his end
Nearer to view his prey and unespied
To mark what of their state he more might learn   400
By word or action marked. About them round
A lion now he stalks with fiery glare,
Then as a tiger who by chance hath spied
In some purlieu two gentle fawns at play,
Straight couches close, then rising changes oft   405
His couchant watch as one who chose his ground

370. *Happy*: I.e., You are happy.
374. *thus forlorn*: I.e., I could pity you, Adam and Eve, since you are abandoned here without protection from me.
380. *your Maker's work*: Hell.
385–87. I.e., If you do not like Hell, blame (*Thank*) God, who forces me unwillingly to take revenge on you, who never wronged me, instead of on God, who did wrong me.
389. *Melt*: weep.
404. *purlieu*: land on the skirts of the forest.
406. *couchant*: lying close to the ground, ready to pounce. When Satan is inside them, the animals become more like the predators they will be after the Fall.

Whence rushing he might surest seize them both
Gripped in each paw, when Adam first of men
To first of women Eve, thus moving speech
Turned him, all ear to hear new utterance flow: 410
    Sole partner and sole part of all these joys,
Dearer thyself than all, needs must the Power
That made us and for us this ample world
Be infinitely good. And of His good
As liberal and free as infinite   415
That raised us from the dust and placed us here
In all this happiness who at His hand
Have nothing merited nor can perform
Aught whereof He hath need, He who requires
From us no other service than to keep   420
This one, this easy charge, of all the trees
In Paradise that bear delicious fruit
So various, not to taste that only Tree
Of Knowledge planted by the Tree of Life.
So near grows death to life, whate'er death is,   425
Some dreadful thing no doubt, for well thou know'st
God hath pronounced it death to taste that tree,
The only sign of our obedience left
Among so many signs of pow'r and rule
Conferred upon us, and dominion given   430
Over all other creatures that possess
Earth, air, and sea. Then let us not think hard
One easy prohibition who enjoy
Free leave so large to all things else and choice
Unlimited of manifold delights.   435
But let us ever praise Him and extol
His bounty, following our delightful task
To prune these growing plants and tend these flowers
Which, were it toilsome, yet with thee were sweet.
    To whom thus Eve replied: O thou for whom   440
And from whom I was formed flesh of thy flesh
And without whom am to no end, my guide
And head, what thou hast said is just and right.
For we to Him indeed all praises owe
And daily thanks, I chiefly who enjoy   445
So far the happier lot, enjoying thee
Preëminent by so much odds while thou

409–10. Adam turns as he starts to speak and Eve is "all ear" to hear what he says.
442. *am to no end*: without whom my being has no purpose.
443. *head*: "The head of every man is Christ; and the head of the woman is the man; and
    the head of Christ is God" (1 Corinthians 11:3).

Like consort to thyself canst nowhere find.
That day I oft remember when from sleep
I first awaked and found myself reposed   450
Under a shade on flow'rs, much wond'ring where
And what I was, whence thither brought and how.
Not distant far from thence a murmuring sound
Of waters issued from a cave and spread
Into a liquid plain, then stood unmoved   455
Pure as th' expanse of heav'n. I thither went
With unexperienced thought and laid me down
On the green bank to look into the clear
Smooth lake that to me seemed another sky.
As I bent down to look, just opposite   460
A shape within the wat'ry gleam appeared
Bending to look on me. I started back,
It started back, but pleased I soon returned,
Pleased *it* returned as soon with answering looks
Of sympathy and love. There I had fixed   465
Mine eyes till now and pined with vain desire
Had not a Voice thus warned me: "What thou seest,
What there thou seest, fair creature, is thyself:
With thee it came and goes. But follow me
And I will bring thee where no shadow stays   470
Thy coming and thy soft embraces. He
Whose image thou art, him thou shalt enjoy
Inseparably thine. To him shalt bear
Multitudes like thyself and thence be called
Mother of human race." What could I do   475
But follow straight, invisibly thus led?
Till I espied thee (fair indeed, and tall!)
Under a platan. Yet methought less fair,
Less winning soft, less amiably mild
Than that smooth wat'ry image: back I turned.   480
Thou following cried'st aloud: "Return, fair Eve!
Whom fli'st thou? Whom thou fli'st, of him thou art,
His flesh, his bone. To give thee being I lent
Out of my side to thee, nearest my heart,
Substantial life to have thee by my side   485
Henceforth an individual solace dear.
Part of my soul I seek thee and thee claim

465–66. The episode closely follows that of Narcissus, in Ovid, *Metamorphoses* 3.407–36, the crucial difference being that Eve is rescued and does not *pine with vain desire* for herself.

478. *platan:* a stately Near Eastern fruit tree, *Platanus orientalis*, related to the plane trees Milton would have seen in Europe.

My other half." With that thy gentle hand
Seized mine, I yielded, and from that time see
How beauty is excelled by manly grace   490
And wisdom which alone is truly fair.
   So spake our general mother and with eyes
Of conjugal attraction unreproved
And meek surrender half embracing leaned
On our first father. Half her swelling breast   495
Naked met his under the flowing gold
Of her loose tresses hid. He in delight
Both of her beauty and submissive charms
Smiled with superior love as Jupiter
On Juno smiles when he impregns the clouds   500
That shed May flow'rs, and pressed her matron lip
With kisses pure. Aside the Devil turned
For envy, yet with jealous leer malign
Eyed them askance and to himself thus plained:
   Sight hateful! sight tormenting! Thus these two   505
Imparadised in one another's arms,
The happier Eden, shall enjoy their fill
Of bliss on bliss while I to Hell am thrust
Where neither joy nor love but fierce desire
(Among our other torments not the least)   510
Still unfulfilled with pain of longing pines.
Yet let me not forget what I have gained
From their own mouths. All is not theirs it seems.
One fatal Tree there stands of Knowledge called
Forbidden them to taste. Knowledge forbidden?   515
Suspicious, reasonless. Why should their Lord
Envy them that? Can it be sin to know?
Can it be death? And do they only stand
By ignorance? Is that their happy state,
The proof of their obedience and their faith?   520
O fair foundation laid whereon to build
Their ruin! Hence I will excite their minds
With more desire to know and to reject
Envious commands invented with design
To keep them low whom knowledge might exalt   525
Equal with gods. Aspiring to be such,
They taste and die: what likelier can ensue?

492. *our general mother*: the mother of us all.
499. *superior*: from above.
499–501. *Jupiter . . . flow'rs*: an example of the rationalizing interpretation of classical
    myth: Jupiter impregnates the clouds with the seeds of the flowers that grow after rain.
509. *fierce desire*: sexual desire, one of the torments of the devils.

But first with narrow search I must walk round
This garden and no corner leave unspied.
A chance but chance may lead where I may meet   530
Some wand'ring spirit of Heav'n by fountain side
Or in thick shade retired from him to draw
What further would be learnt. Live while ye may
Yet happy pair! Enjoy, till I return,
Short pleasures, for long woes are to succeed!   535
So saying his proud step he scornful turned
But with sly circumspection and began
Through wood, through waste, o'er hill, o'er dale his roam.
   Meanwhile in utmost longitude, where heav'n
With earth and ocean meets, the setting sun   540
Slowly descended and with right aspéct
Against the eastern gate of Paradise
Leveled his evening rays. It was a rock
Of alabaster piled up to the clouds,
Conspicuous far, winding with one ascent   545
Accessible from earth, one entrance high.
The rest was craggy cliff that overhung
Still as it rose, impossible to climb.
Betwixt these rocky pillars Gabriel sat,
Chief of th' angelic guards, awaiting night.   550
About him exercised heroic games
The unarmed youth of Heav'n but nigh at hand
Celestial armory, shields, helms and spears
Hung high with diamond flaming and with gold.
Thither came Uriel gliding through the even   555
On a sunbeam, swift as a shooting star
In autumn thwarts the night when vapors fired
Impress the air and shows the mariner
From what point of his compass to beware
Impetuous winds. He thus began in haste: 560
   Gabriel, to thee thy course by lot hath giv'n
Charge and strict watch that to this happy place
No evil thing approach or enter in.
This day at heighth of noon came to my sphere
A spirit zealous as he seemed to know   565
More of th' Almighty's works, and chiefly Man,

---

530. *A chance but chance*: by chance, with luck.
539–43. As the sun set in the west, its rays passed level through Paradise to strike (and
    cause to glow) the white, eastern gate of Paradise.
544. *alabaster*: smooth, white stone.
549. *rocky pillars*: the alabaster gateposts.
557. *thwarts*: cuts across.
558. *Impress*: compress.

God's latest image. I described his way
Bent on all speed and marked his airy gait
But in the mount that lies from Eden north
Where he first lighted soon discerned his looks   570
Alien from Heav'n with passions foul obscured.
Mine eye pursued him still but under shade
Lost sight of him. One of the banished crew
I fear hath ventured from the deep to raise
New troubles: him thy care must be to find!   575
   To whom the wingèd warrior thus returned:
Uriel, no wonder if thy perfect sight
Amid the sun's bright circle where thou sitt'st
See far and wide. In at this gate none pass
The vigilance here placed but such as come   580
Well known from Heav'n and since meridian hour
No creature thence. If spirit of other sort
So minded have o'erleaped these earthy bounds
On purpose, hard thou know'st it to exclude
Spiritual substance with corporeal bar.   585
But if within the circuit of these walks,
In whatsoever shape he lurk of whom
Thou tell'st, by morrow dawning I shall know.
   So promised he, and Uriel to his charge
Returned on that bright beam whose point now raised   590
Bore him slope downward to the sun now fall'n
Beneath the Azores. Whither the prime orb,
Incredible how swift, had thither rolled
Diurnal or this less voluble earth
By shorter flight to th' east had left him there   595
Arraying with reflected purple and gold
The clouds that on his western throne attend.
Now came still evening on and twilight grey
Had in her sober livery all things clad.
Silence accompanied, for beast and bird,   600
They to their grassy couch, these to their nests
Were slunk—all but the wakeful nightingale.
She all night long her amorous descant sung:
Silence was pleased. Now glowed the firmament
With living sapphires. Hesperus that led   605

---

567. *latest*: The angels are also made in God's image. *described*: descried, carefully noted.
590–95. Uriel must tilt his sunbeam so that it will carry him to the west, where the sun
    now sets. Either the sun rolled around the earth to the west or the earth itself
    rotated to the east, leaving the stationary sun behind, in the west. In Milton's eyes
    one point in favor of the latter, Copernican system is that it does not require the
    celestial orbs to move with *incredible* (line 593) swiftness.
603. *descant*: melody.

The starry host rode brightest till the Moon,
Rising in clouded majesty, at length
Apparent queen, unveiled her peerless light
And o'er the dark her silver mantle threw.
   When Adam thus to Eve: Fair consort, th' hour   610
Of night and all things now retired to rest
Mind us of like repose since God hath set
Labor and rest as day and night to men
Successive. And the timely dew of sleep
Now falling with soft slumberous weight inclines   615
Our eyelids. Other creatures all day long
Rove idle unemployed and less need rest.
Man hath his daily work of body or mind
Appointed which declares his dignity
And the regard of Heav'n on all his ways   620
While other animals unactive range
And of their doings God takes no account.
Tomorrow ere fresh morning streak the east
With first approach of light we must be ris'n
And at our pleasant labor to reform   625
Yon flow'ry arbors, yonder alleys green,
Our walk at noon with branches overgrown
That mock our scant manuring and require
More hands than ours to lop their wanton growth.
Those blossoms also and those dropping gums   630
That lie bestrewn unsightly and unsmooth
Ask riddance if we mean to tread with ease.
Meanwhile as nature wills night bids us rest.
   To whom thus Eve with perfect beauty adorned:
My author and disposer, what thou bidst   635
Unargued I obey: so God ordains.
God is thy law, thou mine. To know no more
Is woman's happiest knowledge and her praise.
With thee conversing I forget all time,
All seasons and their change all please alike.   640
Sweet is the breath of morn, her rising sweet
With charm of earliest birds. Pleasant the sun
When first on this delightful land he spreads
His orient beams on herb, tree, fruit and flower
Glist'ring with dew. Fragrant the fertile earth   645

628. *manuring*: manual labor. Old French *manoeuvrer*, "to work with the hands"; Latin *manus*, "hand." The etymological reference is picked up in the verse following: *More hands than ours.*

635. *author and disposer*: origin and commander, arranger.

639–56. The last seven lines of this elaborate poem (lines 650–56), beginning *But neither*, gather up in summary the things and events Eve has described as *sweet*.

After soft showers and sweet the coming on
Of grateful evening mild, then silent night
With this her solemn bird and this fair moon
And these, the gems of heav'n, her starry train!
But neither breath of morn when she ascends   650
With charm of earliest birds, nor rising sun
On this delightful land, nor herb, fruit, flower
Glist'ring with dew, nor fragrance after showers,
Nor grateful evening mild, nor silent night
With this her solemn bird, nor walk by moon   655
Or glitt'ring starlight without thee is sweet.
But wherefore all night long shine these? For whom
This glorious sight when sleep hath shut all eyes?
     To whom our gen'ral ancestor replied:
Daughter of God and Man, accomplished Eve,   660
Those have their course to finish round the Earth
By morrow evening and from land to land
In order, though to nations yet unborn,
Minist'ring light prepared they set and rise
Lest total darkness should by night regain   665
Her old possession and extinguish life
In nature and all things which these soft fires
Not only enlighten but with kindly heat
Of various influence foment and warm,
Temper or nourish, or in part shed down   670
Their stellar virtue on all kinds that grow
On Earth, made hereby apter to receive
Perfection from the Sun's more potent ray.
These then though unbeheld in deep of night
Shine not in vain. Nor think, though men were none,   675
That Heav'n would want spectators, God want praise!
Millions of spiritual creatures walk the earth
Unseen both when we wake and when we sleep.
All these with ceaseless praise His works behold
Both day and night. How often from the steep   680
Of echoing hill or thicket have we heard
Celestial voices to the midnight air,

651. *charm*: song.
657. *these*: the stars.
657–58. Although the suddenness of this question is jarring, it follows logically from the
     statement Eve has made in her poem: that things are not of value in themselves but
     only as they are perceived and shared.
660. *accomplished*: perfected. See 10.867 n.
661–73. The stars shine on countries where humans will live in the future. The stars also
     shed their invisible streams, their influences (Latin *in + fluo*, "to flow in"), to nourish
     plants and prepare them to receive the light of the sun.
675. *though men were none*: even if there were no humans.

Sole or responsive each to other's note,
Singing their great Creator. Oft in bands,
While they keep watch or nightly rounding walk,   685
With Heav'nly touch of instrumental sounds
In full harmonic number joined their songs
Divide the night and lift our thoughts to Heav'n.
    Thus talking hand in hand alone they passed
On to their blissful bow'r. It was a place   690
Chos'n by the sov'reign planter when He framed
All things to Man's delightful use. The roof
Of thickest covert was inwoven shade,
Laurel and myrtle, and what higher grew
Of firm and fragrant leaf. On either side   695
Acanthus and each odorous bushy shrub
Fenced up the verdant wall. Each beauteous flower,
Iris all hues, roses and jessamine
Reared high their flourished heads between and wrought
Mosaic. Underfoot the violet,   700
Crocus and hyacinth with rich inlay
Broidered the ground more colored than with stone
Of costliest emblem. Other creature here
Beast, bird, insect or worm durst enter none,
Such was their awe of Man. In shady bow'r   705
More sacred and sequestered, though but feigned,
Pan or Silvanus never slept nor nymph
Nor Faunus haunted. Here in close recess
With flowers, garlands and sweet-smelling herbs
Espousèd Eve decked first her nuptial bed   710
And Heav'nly choirs the hymenéan sung,
What day the genial angel to our sire
Brought her in naked beauty more adorned,
More lovely than Pandora whom the gods
Endowed with all their gifts—and O! too like   715

700. *Mosaic.* Cf. line 149. Milton would have seen gleaming mosaics in Rome.
703. *emblem*: inlay.
706. *though but feigned*: Another reference to classical myth as untrue except as it dimly
    recalls the truth of Paradise.
711. *hymenéan*: marriage song, after the Greek and Roman god of marriage, Hymen.
712. *genial angel*: procreative messenger. In Adam's later account of Eve's creation, it is
    the Creator who leads Eve to Adam. See 8.484–85. But in the Hebrew scriptures
    God sometimes appears as an angel, or as three angels.
714. *Pandora*: meaning "gifts from all [the gods]." To avenge the theft of fire from the
    gods, Zeus sends Pandora to Earth. She is a beautiful virgin endowed with gifts
    from all the gods, e.g., beauty, given by Aphrodite, and skill at lying, given by
    Hermes. She is also provided with a jar containing all the evils that assail human-
    ity. She opens it and the evils escape. The story is told in Hesiod, *Works and Days*
    70–104.
715. *too like*: As events will show, Eve proves to be *too like* Pandora.

In sad event when to th' unwiser son
Of Japhet, brought by Hermes, she ensnared
Mankind with her fair looks to be avenged
On him who had stole Jove's authentic fire.
   Thus at their shady lodge arrived both stood,   720
Both turned, and under open sky adored
The God who made both sky, air, earth and heav'n
Which they beheld, the moon's resplendent globe
And starry pole: Thou also mad'st the night,
Maker Omnipotent, and Thou the day   725
Which we in our appointed work employed
Have finished happy in our mutual help
And mutual love, the crown of all our bliss
Ordained by Thee, and this delicious place
For us too large where Thy abundance wants   730
Partakers and uncropped falls to the ground.
But Thou hast promised from us two a race
To fill the earth who shall with us extol
Thy goodness infinite both when we wake
And when we seek, as now, Thy gift of sleep.   735
   This said unanimous and other rites
Observing none but adoration pure
Which God likes best into their inmost bower
Handed they went and, eased the putting off
These troublesome disguises which we wear,   740
Straight side by side were laid. Nor turned I ween
Adam from his fair spouse nor Eve the rites
Mysterious of connubial love refused,
Whatever hypocrites austerely talk
Of purity and place and innocence,   745
Defaming as impure what God declares
Pure and commands to some, leaves free to all.
Our Maker bids increase. Who bids abstain

716–17. *unwiser son*: Epimetheus ("after-thought"), as opposed to his wiser brother, Prometheus ("fore-thought"). *Japhet*, one of the three sons of Noah, thought to be the
father of the Greeks and other non-Semitic and non-African peoples, has a name
similar to that of the father of Prometheus and Epimetheus: Iapetos. Zeus calls Prometheus "son of Iapetos" (Hesiod, *Works and Days* 54).
719. *him*: Prometheus, who in pity for mankind stole fire from Heaven.
724–35. Adam and Eve's evening prayer, in which they praise the Creator and recall that
their own progeny will fill the earth and praise the Creator too.
736. *unanimous*: with one voice, but also with one spirit, Latin *anima*.
739. *eased*: a participle; i.e., and being eased of the burden of removing their clothes,
since they wore none, they lay down side by side.
741. *ween*: expect, suppose.
743. *connubial*: conjugal, married.
748. "And God blessed them, and God said unto them, Be fruitful and multiply, and
replenish the earth" (Genesis 1:28).

But our destroyer, foe to God and Man?
Hail wedded love, mysterious law, true source   750
Of human offspring, sole propriety
In Paradise, of all things common else!
By thee adult'rous lust was driv'n from men
Among the bestial herds to range. By thee
Founded in reason, loyal, just and pure,   755
Relations dear and all the charities
Of father, son and brother first were known.
Far be it that I should write thee sin or blame
Or think thee unbefitting holiest place,
Perpetual fountain of domestic sweets   760
Whose bed is undefiled and chaste pronounced,
Present or past, as saints and patriarchs used.
Here Love his golden shaft employs, here lights
His constant lamp and waves his purple wings,
Reigns here and revels, not in the bought smile   765
Of harlots, loveless, joyless, unendeared,
Casual fruition, nor in court amours,
Mixed dance or wanton masque or midnight ball
Or serenade which the starved lover sings
To his proud fair, best quitted with disdain.   770
These lulled by nightingales embracing slept
And on their naked limbs the flow'ry roof
Show'red roses which the morn repaired. Sleep on
Blest pair and O yet happiest if ye seek
No happier state and know to know no more!   775
    Now had night measured with her shadowy cone
Half way up hill this vast sublunar vault
And from their ivory port the cherubim
Forth issuing at th' accustomed hour stood armed
To their night watches in warlike parade   780

751–52. *propriety . . . common*: Wedded love is the only private possession, all other things being held in common. The distinction doesn't mean much yet, but it will when more people are born.
761. "Marriage is honourable in all, and the bed undefiled: but whoremongers and adulterers God will judge" (Hebrews 13:4).
763. *shaft*: arrow (of Cupid).
767. *court amours*: affairs at the royal court.
768. *Mixed dance*: dance in which partners are frequently changed, giving opportunity for assignations. *wanton masque*: theatrical performance at court in which courtiers (often in masks) participated.
771. *These*: Adam and Eve.
775. *know no more*: The knowledge referred to here is knowledge of the sexual anxieties, pleasures, and stimulants described in the previous lines.
776–77. The vault of the sky under the moon has been half darkened (in the east) by night. The shadow of night, which is cast by the earth, is cone-shaped.
778. *ivory port*: the eastern gate of Paradise, which, whether made of ivory or *alabaster* (line 544), is white.

When Gabriel to his next in pow'r thus spake:
    Uzziel, half these draw off and coast the south
With strictest watch, these other wheel the north!
Our circuit meets full west. As flame they part,
Half wheeling to the shield half to the spear.   785
From these two strong and subtle spirits he called
That near him stood and gave them thus in charge:
    Ithuriel and Zephon, with winged speed
Search through this garden! Leave unsearched no nook
But chiefly where those two fair creatures lodge,   790
Now laid perhaps asleep secure of harm.
This evening from the sun's decline arrived
Who tells of some infernal spirit seen
Hitherward bent (who could have thought?) escaped
The bars of Hell, on errand bad, no doubt.   795
Such where ye find, seize fast and hither bring!
    So saying, on he led his radiant files,
Dazzling the moon, these to the bow'r direct
In search of whom they sought. Him there they found
Squat like a toad close at the ear of Eve   800
Assaying by his develish art to reach
The organs of her fancy and with them forge
Illusions as he list, phantasms and dreams,
Or if inspiring venom he might taint
Th' animal spirits that from pure blood arise   805
Like gentle breaths from rivers pure, thence raise
At least distempered, discontented thoughts,
Vain hopes, vain aims, inordinate desires
Blown up with high conceits engend'ring pride.
Him thus intent Ithuriel with his spear   810
Touched lightly, for no falsehood can endure
Touch of celestial temper but returns
Of force to its own likeness. Up he starts
Discovered and surprised. As when a spark
Lights on a heap of nitrous powder laid   815
Fit for the tun (some magazine to store
Against a rumored war) the smutty grain

---

782. Uzziel is commanded to draw off half the troop of angels and lead it round the gar-
    den to the south, meeting the other half of the troop, led by Gabriel, in the west,
    opposite their point of departure.
786. *he*: Gabriel.
791. *secure*: unaware.
793. *Who*: Uriel.
798. *These*: Ithuriel and Zephon.
799. *whom* and *Him*: the infernal spirit (Satan).
802. *organs*: instruments, in this case in the brain or *fancy*, the power of imagination.
816. *tun*: cask. *magazine*: a secure place for storing weapons and ammunition.

With sudden blaze diffused inflames the air,
So started up in his own shape the Fiend.
Back stepped those two fair angels half amazed   820
So sudden to behold the grisly king
Yet thus unmoved with fear accost him soon:
    Which of those rebel spirits adjudged to Hell
Com'st thou, escaped thy prison and transformed?
Why sat'st thou like an enemy in wait   825
Here watching at the head of these that sleep?
    Know ye not then, said Satan, filled with scorn,
Know ye not me? Ye knew me once no mate
For you, there sitting where ye durst not soar.
Not to know me argues yourselves unknown: 830
The lowest of your throng! Or if ye know
Why ask ye and superfluous begin
Your message, like to end as much in vain?
    To whom thus Zephon answering scorn with scorn:
Think not, revolted spirit, thy shape the same   835
Or undiminished brightness to be known
As when thou stood'st in Heav'n upright and pure!
That glory then when thou no more wast good
Departed from thee and thou resemblest now
Thy sin and place of doom obscure and foul.   840
But come! For thou, be sure, shalt give account
To him who sent us, whose charge is to keep
This place inviolable and these from harm.
    So spake the cherub and his grave rebuke
Severe in youthful beauty added grace   845
Invincible. Abashed the devil stood
And felt how awful goodness is and saw
Virtue in her shape how lovely, saw and pined
His loss, but chiefly to find here observed
His luster visibly impaired. Yet seemed   850
Undaunted: If I must contend, said he,
Best with the best, the sender not the sent,
Or all at once, more glory will be won
Or less be lost. Thy fear, said Zephon bold,
Will save us trial what the least can do   855
Single against thee wicked and thence weak.
    The Fiend replied not, overcome with rage,
But like a proud steed reined went haughty on

---

829. *durst*: dared.
855. *the least*: the weakest (i.e., as you account me).
856. *Single*: alone, in single combat.

Champing his iron curb. To strive or fly
He held it vain. Awe from above had quelled   860
His heart not else dismayed. Now drew they nigh
The western point where those half-rounding guards
Just met and closing stood in squadron joined
Awaiting next command. To whom their chief,
Gabriel, from the front thus called aloud: 865
     O friends, I hear the tread of nimble feet
Hasting this way and now by glimpse discern
Ithuriel and Zephon through the shade
And with them comes a third of regal port
But faded splendor wan who by his gait   870
And fierce demeanor seems the Prince of Hell,
Not likely to part hence without contést.
Stand firm, for in his look defiance lours!
     He scarce had ended when those two approached
And brief related whom they brought, where found,   875
How busied, in what form and posture couched.
     To whom with stern regard thus Gabriel spake:
Why hast thou, Satan, broke the bounds prescribed
To thy transgressions and disturbed the charge
Of others who approve not to transgress   880
By thy example but have pow'r and right
To question thy bold entrance on this place,
Employed, it seems, to violate sleep and those
Whose dwelling God hath planted here in bliss?
     To whom thus Satan with contemptuous brow: 885
Gabriel, thou had'st in Heav'n th' esteem of wise
And such I held thee, but this question asked
Puts me in doubt. Lives there who loves his pain?
Who would not, finding way, break loose from Hell
Though thither doomed? Thou wouldst thyself, no doubt,   890
And boldly venture to whatever place
Farthest from pain where thou might'st hope to change
Torment with ease and soonest recompense
Dole with delight, which in this place I sought.
To thee no reason, who knowst only good   895
But evil hast not tried. And wilt object
His will who bound us? Let Him surer bar
His iron gates if He intends our stay

---

862. *The western point*: Gabriel has divided the force of angels into two wings, one led by
him, one by Uzziel (see line 782 n.). Starting in the east of Paradise, they encircle
the garden on either side and meet again in the extreme west, where Ithuriel and
Zephon conduct Satan.
883. *it*: Satan's escape from Hell and intrusion in Paradise.

In that dark durance: thus much what was asked.
The rest is true, they found me where they say.   900
But that implies not violence or harm.
    Thus he in scorn. The warlike angel, moved
Disdainfuly, half smiling thus replied:
O loss of one in Heav'n to judge of wise
Since Satan fell, whom folly overthrew!   905
And now returns him from his prison 'scaped
Gravely in doubt whether to hold them wise
Or not who ask what boldness brought him hither
Unlicensed from his bounds in Hell prescribed?
So wise he judges it to fly from pain   910
However, and to 'scape his punishment.
So judge thou still, presumptuous, till the wrath
Which thou incurr'st by flying meet that flight
Sevenfold and scourge that wisdom back to Hell
Which taught thee yet no better that no pain   915
Can equal anger infinite provoked!
But wherefore thou alone? Wherefore with thee
Came not all Hell broke loose? Is pain to them
Less pain, less to be fled, or thou than they
Less hardy to endure? Courageous chief: 920
The first in flight from pain! Hadst thou alleged
To thy deserted host this cause of flight
Thou surely hadst not come sole fugitive.
    To which the Fiend thus answered frowning stern:
Not that I less endure or shrink from pain,   925
Insulting angel, well thou know'st I stood
Thy fiercest when in battle to thy aid
The blasting volleyed thunder made all speed
And seconded thy else not dreaded spear.
But still thy words at random, as before,   930
Argue thy inexperience what behooves
From hard assays and ill successes past
A faithful leader, not to hazard all
Through ways of danger by himself untried.
I therefore, I alone first undertook   935
To wing the desolate abyss and spy
This new-created world whereof in Hell

899. *durance*: imprisonment. *thus much*: so much for what you asked.
902. *moved*: being moved (to anger).
904–5. Gabriel's reply is ironical: What a pity we have lost from Heaven one who is as
    good a judge of wisdom as you are. The irony continues in the repetition of *wise* and
    wisdom (lines 907, 910, and 914).
911. *However*: by any means possible.
928. I.e., The Son's thunderbolts drove us all to flight.

Fame is not silent, here in hope to find
Better abode and my afflicted powers
To settle here on earth or in mid air,   940
Though for possession put to try once more
What thou and thy gay legions dare against,
Whose easier business were to serve their Lord
High up in Heav'n with songs to hymn His throne
And practiced distances to cringe, not fight.   945
    To whom the warrior angel soon replied:
To say and straight unsay—pretending first
Wise to fly pain, professing next the spy—
Argues no leader but a liar traced,
Satan. And couldst thou "faithful" add? O name,   950
O sacred name of *faithfulness* profaned!
Faithful to whom? to thy rebellious crew,
Army of fiends? Fit body to fit head!
Was this your discipline and faith engaged,
Your military obedience, to dissolve   955
Allegiance to th' acknowledged Power Supreme?
And thou, sly hypocrite, who now wouldst seem
Patron of liberty, who more than thou
Once fawned, and cringed, and servilely adored
Heav'n's awful Monarch? Wherefore but in hope   960
To dispossess Him and thyself to reign?
But mark what I aread thee now: avaunt!
Fly thither whence thou fledst! If from this hour
Within these hallowed limits thou appear,
Back to th' infernal pit I drag thee chained   965
And seal thee so as henceforth not to scorn
The facile gates of Hell too slightly barred!
    So threatened he but Satan to no threats
Gave heed but waxing more in rage replied:
    Then when I *am* thy captive talk of chains,   970
Proud limitary cherub! But ere then
Far heavier load thyself expect to feel
From my prevailing arm though Heaven's King
Ride on thy wings and thou with thy compeers,
Used to the yoke, draw'st his triumphant wheels   975
In progress through the road of Heav'n star-paved!
    While thus he spake th' angelic squadron bright

---

941. *possession*: of the earth and middle air.
945. *practiced distances*: courtly bows.
950. *faithful*: See line 933.
962. *aread*: advise (ironical), decree. *avaunt!*: away!
971. *limitary*: guarding the frontier.

Turned fiery red, sharp'ning in moonèd horns
Their phalanx and began to hem him round
With ported spears as thick as when a field   980
Of Ceres ripe for harvest waving bends
Her bearded grove of ears which way the wind
Sways them. The careful ploughman doubting stands
Lest on the threshing floor his hopeful sheaves
Prove chaff. On th' other side Satan alarmed,   985
Collecting all his might, dilated stood
Like Teneriffe or Atlas unremoved.
His stature reached the sky and on his crest
Sat Horror plumed. Nor wanted in his grasp
What seemed both spear and shield. Now dreadful deeds   990
Might have ensued. Nor only Paradise
In this commotion but the starry cope
Of heav'n perhaps or all the elements
At least had gone to wrack, disturbed and torn
With violence of this conflict, had not soon   995
Th' Eternal to prevent such horrid fray
Hung forth in heav'n His golden scales, yet seen
Betwixt Astraea and the Scorpion sign,
Wherein all things created first He weighed
(The pendulous round earth with balanced air   1000
In counterpoise), now ponders all events,
Battles and realms. In these He put two weights,
The sequel each of parting and of fight.
The latter quick up flew and kicked the beam
Which Gabriel spying thus bespake the Fiend: 1005
    Satan, I know thy strength and thou know'st mine:
Neither our own, but giv'n. What folly then
To boast what arms can do since thine no more

979. *phalanx*: a tight formation of heavily armed infantry (Greek). See 1.549–55 n.
980. *ported*: held up and forward at an angle, in the ready position.
983–85. *careful*: full of care. The ploughman worries that in the strong wind the kernels will be blown out of the husks so that when the sheaves are brought in to be threshed there will be nothing but chaff.
986. *dilated*: expanded. See 1.429.
987. *Teneriffe* and *Atlas* are mountains.
989. From Latin *horror*; the cognate adjective is *horridus*, frequently used to describe "bristling," dreadful arms. See line 996 and 1.563 n.
997–1014. *golden scales*: See *Iliad* 22.209–13, where Zeus weighs the fates of Hector and Achilles in his golden scales (cf. 8.69–77), and *Aeneid* 12.725–27, where Jove weighs the fates of Turnus and Aeneas. In the classical epics, the sinking scale means death, and the rising scale victory. In Milton, the rising scale indicates weakness (line 1012) and certain defeat. In the Hebrew tradition, the scales are implied in the Creation, when God weighs "the mountains in scales, and the hills in a balance" (Isaiah 40:12). Milton says that God first used the scales in the work of Creation and now uses them to weigh events in human history (line 1002). *ponders*: weighs (Latin *pondus*, "weight").
1007. Neither your strength nor mine is owned by us but is given from God.

Than Heav'n permits—nor mine, though doubled now
To trample thee as mire. For proof look up   1010
And read thy lot in yon celestial sign
Where thou art weighed and shown how light, how weak,
If thou resist. The Fiend looked up and knew
His mounted scale aloft. Nor more, but fled
Murmuring, and with him fled the shades of night.   1015

Book Five

The Argument

Morning approached, Eve relates to Adam her troublesome dream.
He likes it not, yet comforts her. They come forth to their day
labors: their morning hymn at the door of their bower. God, to render man inexcusable, sends Raphael to admonish him of his obedience, of his free state, of his enemy near at hand, who he is, and
why his enemy, and whatever else may avail Adam to know. Raphael
comes down to Paradise, his appearance described, his coming discerned by Adam afar off, sitting at the door of his bower. He goes
out to meet him, brings him to his lodge, entertains him with the
choicest fruits of Paradise got together by Eve. Their discourse at
table. Raphael performs his message, minds Adam of his state and
of his enemy, relates at Adam's request who that enemy is and how
he came to be so, beginning from his first revolt in Heaven and the
occasion thereof. How he drew his legions after him to the parts of
the North and there incited them to rebel with him, persuading all
but only Abdiel, a seraph, who in argument dissuades and opposes
him, then forsakes him.

Now Morn her rosy steps in th' eastern clime
Advancing sowed the earth with orient pearl
When Adam waked, so customed, for his sleep
Was airy light from pure digestion bred
And temperate vapors bland which th' only sound   5
Of leaves and fuming rills, Aurora's fan,

1013–14. Satan knew that it was his side of the scales that had risen aloft, thus showing
     him to be weaker than Gabriel.
1014. *Nor more*: He said no more.
   Book Five
1–2. A Homeric description of dawn. But see Psalm 97:11: "light is sown for the righteous."
5. *vapors bland*: mild exhalations. A discreet answer to the perennial question of Edenic
     excretion. Adam's sleep is light because his digestion is so efficient that nothing is left
     over as waste except mild vapors emitted through the pores, which the goddess of the
     dawn, Aurora, disperses with her fan. Aurora's fan is the mere sound of leaves, rushing
     streams, and birdsong.

Lightly dispersed and the shrill matin song
Of birds on every bough. So much the more
His wonder was to find unwakened Eve
With tresses discomposed and glowing cheek   10
As through unquiet rest. He on his side
Leaning half-raised with looks of cordial love
Hung over her enamored and beheld
Beauty which whether waking or asleep
Shot forth peculiar graces. Then with voice   15
Mild as when Zephyrus on Flora breathes
Her hand soft touching whispered thus: Awake,
My fairest, my espoused, my latest found,
Heav'n's last best gift, my ever new delight,
Awake! The morning shines and the fresh field   20
Calls us. We lose the prime to mark how spring
Our tended plants, how blows the citron grove,
What drops the myrrh and what the balmy reed,
How Nature paints her colors, how the bee
Sits on the bloom extracting liquid sweet.   25
    Such whispering waked her, but with startled eye
On Adam, whom embracing, thus she spake:
    O sole in whom my thoughts find all repose,
My glory, my perfection, glad I see
Thy face and morn returned, for I this night   30
(Such night till this I never passed) have dreamed,
If dreamed, not as I oft am wont, of thee,
Works of day past or morrow's next design
But of offense and trouble which my mind
Knew never till this irksome night. Methought   35
Close at mine ear one called me forth to walk
With gentle voice. I thought it thine. It said,
"Why sleep'st thou, Eve? Now is the pleasant time,
The cool, the silent, save where silence yields
To the night-warbling bird that now awake   40
Tunes sweetest his love-labored song. Now reigns
Full orbed the moon and with more pleasing light

15. *peculiar*: unique to her.
16. I.e., as when the west wind blows on the flowers.
17–25. *Awake*: Adam's words are a spontaneous aubade, a love song calling the beloved to awake, as in Herrick's "Corinna's Going A-Maying." But Adam calls Eve to a day of delightful work in Eden, not leisurely maying in the woods and fields, disapproved of by Puritans. See Nathaniel Hawthorne, "The May Pole of Merry Mount." Milton's thought is that in Eden humans are spontaneous poets, doing naturally what later poets would have to strive to achieve with arduous craft. For a serenade, or evening wooing song, see lines 38–47. Milton mentions the serenade form with disapproval at 4.769. For a spontaneous poem by Eve that celebrates togetherness from dawn to evening, see 4.639–56. For the highest kind of poetry, psalms of praise to the Creator, see lines 153–208 and n.

Shadowy sets off the face of things—in vain
If none regard! Heav'n wakes with all his eyes
Whom to behold but thee, Nature's desire,   45
In whose sight all things joy with ravishment,
Attracted by thy beauty still to gaze."
I rose as at thy call but found thee not.
To find thee I directed then my walk
And on methought alone I passed through ways   50
That brought me on a sudden to the Tree
Of interdicted Knowledge. Fair it seemed,
Much fairer to my fancy than by day.
And as I wond'ring looked, beside it stood
One shaped and winged like one of those from Heav'n   55
By us oft seen. His dewy locks distilled
Ambrosia. On that tree he also gazed
And "O fair plant," said he, "with fruit surcharged,
Deigns none to ease thy load and taste thy sweet,
Nor god, nor man? Is knowledge so despised?   60
Or envy or what reserve forbids to taste?
Forbid who will, none shall from me withhold
Longer thy offered good: why else set here?"
This said, he paused not but with vent'rous arm
He plucked, he tasted. Me damp horror chilled   65
At such bold words vouched with a deed so bold.
But he thus overjoyed, "O fruit divine,
Sweet of thyself but much more sweet thus cropped,
Forbidden here it seems as only fit
For gods yet able to make gods of men.   70
And why not gods of men since good the more
Communicated more abundant grows,
The Author not impaired but honored more?
Here, happy creature, fair angelic Eve,
Partake thou also! Happy though thou art,   75
Happier thou may'st be, worthier canst not be.
Taste this and be henceforth among the gods
Thyself a goddess, not to earth confined
But sometimes in the air as we! Sometimes
Ascend to Heav'n, by merit thine, and see   80

44–47. I.e., The voice says, Whom does Heaven stay awake to see, if not you, on whom all things gaze with joy at your beauty?

61. *Or . . . or:* a Latinate construction. I.e., Is it envy or some other reason of God's that forbids you to taste?

71–72. I.e., Since goodness increases the more it is shared, why should not this good, the fruit, make gods of men? The unstated assumption of the last clause is that to make gods of men—in our terms, to increase human power indefinitely—is in itself a good thing.

What life the gods live there—and such live thou!"
So saying he drew nigh and to me held,
E'en to my mouth, of that same fruit held part
Which he had plucked. The pleasant savory smell
So quickened appetite that I, methought,   85
Could not but taste. Forthwith up to the clouds
With him I flew and underneath beheld
The earth outstretched immense, a prospect wide
And various, wond'ring at my flight and change
To this high exaltation. Suddenly   90
My guide was gone and I, methought, sunk down
And fell asleep. But O how glad I waked
To find this but a dream! Thus Eve her night
Related and thus Adam answered sad:
    Best image of myself and dearer half,   95
The trouble of thy thoughts this night in sleep
Affects me equally. Nor can I like
This uncouth dream, of evil sprung I fear.
Yet evil whence? In thee can harbor none,
Created pure. But know that in the soul   100
Are many lesser faculties that serve
Reason as chief. Among these Fancy next
Her office holds. Of all external things
Which the five watchful senses represent
She forms imaginations, airy shapes   105
Which Reason joining or disjoining frames
All what we affirm or what deny and call
Our knowledge or opinion, then retires
Into her private cell when nature rests.
Oft in her absence mimic Fancy wakes   110
To imitate her but misjoining shapes
Wild work produces oft, and most in dreams,

---

81. I.e., See what kind of life the gods live in heaven, which is where *you* should be, and
     live that life yourself. Note the subtle appeal to envy.
82–83. *held . . . held*: Either the verb *held* is being repeated for dramatic emphasis or the
     second *held* means "deemed," "supposed." The effect captures the quality of dreams:
     Eve says she *supposed* the fruit held to her mouth was a piece of the fruit the speaker
     had plucked. She wasn't sure. See lines 85–86.
85–86. Eve does not taste the fruit in her dream. There is a break in her consciousness
     between the moment when she feels she can do nothing other than taste and the
     moment when she finds herself soaring to the clouds. This break is important.
94. *sad*: seriously.
102. *next*: beneath.
105. *She*: fancy. *imaginations*: mental images.
106. *frames*: makes, fashions.
108–12. *retires*: The subject of this verb is *Reason* (line 106), not *She* (line 105). Reason
     retires when we go to sleep, i.e., *when* [human] nature rests. Fancy, like the sorcerer's
     apprentice, then imitates Reason but misjoins the mental images.

Ill matching words and deeds long past or late.
Some such resemblances methinks I find
Of our last evening's talk in this thy dream   115
But with addition strange. Yet be not sad:
Evil into the mind of god or man
May come and go, so unapproved, and leave
No spot or blame behind. Which gives me hope
That what in sleep thou didst abhor to dream   120
Waking thou never wilt consent to do.
Be not disheartened then nor cloud those looks
That wont to be more cheerful and serene
Than when fair morning first smiles on the world!
And let us to our fresh employments rise   125
Among the groves, the fountains and the flow'rs
That open now their choicest bosomed smells
Reserved from night and kept for thee in store.
    So cheered he his fair spouse and she was cheered
But silently a gentle tear let fall   130
From either eye and wiped them with her hair.
Two other precious drops that ready stood
Each in their crystal sluice he ere they fell
Kissed as the gracious signs of sweet remorse
And pious awe that feared to have offended.   135
    So all was cleared and to the field they haste.
But first from under shady arborous roof
Soon as they forth were come to open sight
Of day-spring and the sun (who scarce up risen
With wheels yet hovering o'er the ocean brim   140
Shot parallel to th' earth his dewy ray,
Discov'ring in wide landscape all the east
Of Paradise and Eden's happy plains)
Lowly they bowed adoring and began
Their orisons, each morning duly paid   145
In various style. For neither various style
Nor holy rapture wanted they to praise

---

113. *late*: recent.
115–16. *last evening's talk*, in which Adam spoke of *spiritual creatures* (4.677), angels, who walk the earth at night, keeping watch and making music in praise of the Creator. Yet the spiritual creatures show no interest in the tree with the forbidden fruit; that is the *addition strange* that Adam discerns in Eve's dream and that cannot be explained psychologically. The explanation is that Satan overheard Adam speaking to Eve of the prohibition. See 4.419–35.
117. *god*: angel.
128. *Reserved from night*: The flowers close at night to hold in their smells and open in the day to release them for Eve. Elsewhere (9.193–97), the smell of the opening flowers is directed to God in *silent praise*, filling his nostrils with *grateful [welcome] smell*.
147. *wanted*: lacked.

Their Maker in fit strains pronounced or sung
Unmeditated. Such prompt eloquence
Flowed from their lips in prose or num'rous verse   150
More tuneable than needed lute or harp
To add more sweetness. And they thus began:
   These are thy glorious works, Parent of Good,
Almighty, thine this universal frame
Thus wondrous fair. Thyself how wondrous then,   155
Unspeakable, who sitt'st above these heavens
To us invisible or dimly seen
In these Thy lowest works! Yet these declare
Thy goodness beyond thought and power divine.
Speak ye who best can tell, ye sons of light,   160
Angels, for ye behold Him and with songs
And choral symphonies day without night
Circle His throne rejoicing, ye in Heaven!
On earth join all ye creatures to extol
Him first, Him last, Him midst and without end!   165
Fairest of stars, last in the train of night
(If better thou belong not to the dawn,
Sure pledge of day) that crown'st the smiling Morn
With thy bright circlet, praise Him in thy sphere
While day arises, that sweet hour of prime!   170
Thou, Sun, of this great World both eye and soul,
Acknowledge Him thy greater, sound His praise
In thy eternal course both when thou climb'st
And when high noon hast gained and when thou fall'st!
Moon that now meet'st the orient sun, now fli'st   175
With the fixed stars fixed in their orb that flies
And ye five other wand'ring fires that move

149. *Unmeditated*: spontaneous, improvised. Adam and Eve are natural poets: they do spontaneously what later poets, however talented, must study long and labor hard to do.
153–208. For Milton, the deepest impulse for poetry is not imitation but praise, especially praise of the Creator of the world. Adam and Eve's morning hymn is based on the language of praise in Psalms 104 and 148 and the first verse of 19: "The heavens declare the glory of God; and the firmament sheweth his handywork." Milton regards the Psalms as humanity's highest achievement in poetry and as the actual (though "ill imitated") source of classical poetry. See *Paradise Regained* 4.336–38 and 347.
166. *Fairest of stars*: Hesperus (*Iliad* 22.318), or the planet Venus, seen in the evening, as the first "star" to appear, and at dawn, as the last "star" to disappear. Adam and Eve say that this star may be better called the first light of the day rather than the last light of the night.
170. *prime*: first light.
175. *orient*: in the east. As the sun rises in the east, the moon, which faces (*meets*) the sun in the west, retreats over the western horizon, followed by the stars, which do not change position with respect to each other but are *fixed* on their crystal *orb*. Milton no longer believes this ancient and medieval cosmology, but it seems reasonable to him that Adam and Eve would.
177. *wand'ring fires*: planets, or "wanderers," from Greek *planaō*, "to wander."

In mystic dance, not without song, resound
His praise who out of darkness called up light!
Air and ye elements, the eldest birth   180
Of Nature's womb that in quaternion run
Perpetual circle multiform and mix
And nourish all things, let your ceaseless change
Vary to our Great Maker still new praise!
Ye mists and exhalations that now rise   185
From hill or steaming lake, dusky or grey,
Till the sun paint your fleecy skirts with gold
In honor to the world's Great Author, rise!
Whether to deck with clouds th' uncolored sky
Or wet the thirsty Earth with falling showers: 190
Rising or falling, still advance His praise!
His praise ye winds that from four quarters blow
Breathe soft or loud! And wave your tops, ye pines,
With every plant: in sign of worship wave!
Fountains, and ye that warble as ye flow   195
Melodious murmurs, warbling tune His praise!
Join voices all ye living souls, ye birds
That singing up to Heaven gate ascend
Bear on your wings and in your notes His praise!
Ye that in waters glide and ye that walk   200
The earth and stately tread or lowly creep
Witness if I be silent, morn or ev'n,
To hill or valley, fountain or fresh shade
Made vocal by my song and taught His praise!
Hail Universal Lord! Be bounteous still   205
To give us only good! And if the night
Have gathered aught of evil or concealed,
Disperse it as now light dispels the dark!
   So prayed they innocent and to their thoughts
Firm peace recovered soon and wonted calm.   210
On to their morning's rural work they haste
Among sweet dews and flow'rs where any row
Of fruit-trees over-woody reached too far
Their pampered boughs and needed hands to check
Fruitless embraces. Or they led the vine   215

181–82. *quaternion*: fourfold intercombination. The four elements of medieval and
   Renaissance science—air, water, earth, and fire—are combined in all things in
   nature and are continually mixing and adjusting their balance.
196. *warbling*: singing.
197. *living souls*: animate creatures (Genesis 2:7).
215–19. The ancient practice of winding grape vines around and up the trunks of elms
   was a commonplace in Roman literature. See Virgil, *Georgics* 1.2; 2.221, 360–61,
   367; Horace, *Odes* 4.5.30, *Epodes* 2.9–10.

To wed her elm: she spoused about him twines
Her marriageable arms and with her brings
Her dow'r, th' adopted clusters, to adorn
His barren leaves. Them thus employed beheld
With pity Heav'n's high King and to Him called   220
Raphael the sociable spirit that deigned
To travel with Tobias and secured
His marriage with the sev'n-times-wedded maid.
   Raphael, said He, thou hear'st what stir on Earth
Satan from Hell 'scaped through the darksome gulf   225
Hath raised in Paradise and how disturbed
This night the human pair, how he designs
In them at once to ruin all mankind.
Go therefore: half this day as friend with friend
Converse with Adam in what bow'r or shade   230
Thou find'st him from the heat of noon retired
To respite his day-labor with repast
Or with repose and such discourse bring on
As may advise him of his happy state,
Happiness in his pow'r left free to will,   235
Left to his own free will, his will though free
Yet mutable. Whence warn him to beware
He swerve not too secure. Tell him withal
His danger and from whom, what enemy
Late fall'n himself from Heav'n is plotting now   240
The fall of others from like state of bliss:
By violence, no, for that shall be withstood,
But by deceit and lies. This let him know
Lest willfully transgressing he pretend
Surprisal unadmonished, unforewarned.   245
   So spake th' Eternal Father and fulfilled
All justice. Nor delayed the wingèd saint
After his charge received but from among
Thousand celestial ardors where he stood
Veiled with his gorgeous wings up springing light   250
Flew through the midst of Heav'n. Th' angelic choirs
On each hand parting to his speed gave way
Through all th' empyreal road till at the gate
Of Heav'n arrived. The gate self-opened wide

---

216. *she*: the grapevine.
222–23. See Glossary, ASMODEUS. A romantic story from the biblical Apocrypha, in
    which the young Tobias is aided by the angel Raphael against a demon who has
    killed Sarah's seven successive husbands (Tobit 7:11). See 4.167–71.
235–37. Happiness depends on freedom of the will. But free will is not free from the
    danger of changing into something less than free.
249. *ardors*: flames, angels aflame with divine love.

On golden hinges turning as by work   255
Divine the Sov'reign Architect had framed.
From hence (no cloud or to obstruct his sight
Star interposed, however small) he sees,
Not unconform to other shining globes,
Earth and the gard'n of God with cedars crowned   260
Above all hills. As when by night the glass
Of Galileo, less assured, observes
Imagined lands and regions in the moon,
Or pilot from amidst the Cycladës,
Delos or Samos first appearing, kens   265
A cloudy spot. Down thither prone in flight
He speeds and through the vast ethereal sky
Sails between worlds and worlds with steady wing
Now on the polar winds then with quick fan
Winnows the buxom air till, within soar   270
Of tow'ring eagles, to all fowls he seems
A phoenix: gazed by all as that sole bird
When to enshrine his relics in the Sun's
Bright temple to Egyptian Thebes he flies.
At once on th' eastern cliff of Paradise   275
He lights and to his proper shape returns
A seraph winged. Six wings he wore to shade
His lineaments divine: the pair that clad
Each shoulder broad came mantling o'er his breast
With regal ornament. The middle pair   280
Girt like a starry zone his waist and round

---

256. *Sov'reign Architect*: the Son, who puts the Father's will into effect.

262. *less assured*: less clear sight. Across a "distance inexpressible / By numbers that have name" (8.113–14), Raphael's angelic vision gives perfect knowledge of whatever it is focused on. The comparisons that follow—to Galileo's telescope and to the keen-eyed Aegean sailor—are examples of imperfect vision.

269–70. *polar winds . . . buxom air*: These are the contrasting conditions through which Raphael flies. He needs both great strength and delicacy of touch, strength for steering on the high winds blowing down from chaos (see 3.425–26) and delicacy of touch for rapidly fanning the more rarefied, "flexible" (the old sense of *buxom*) air above the earth. *Winnows*: verb; a fanning action used to separate chaff from grain. The principles of flight were poorly understood in Milton's day. This passage, which works by analogy to propulsion through water, shows remarkable powers of hypothesis.

270. *within soar*: descended to the height to which the highest soaring eagles attain.

272–74. *phoenix*: mythical bird of Arabia, of which there is only one of the species alive at any time (hence *sole*, line 272). It lives five hundred years and then constructs an aromatic nest in which it expires or, in some accounts, burns up. From the body or the ashes a new phoenix rises to continue the cycle. Herodotus (2.73) reports that the new phoenix was said to make a ball of precious myrrh in which it carried the old phoenix's body through the air to the temple of the sun, in Egypt. According to Ovid (*Metamorphoses* 15.406), the temple is located in the city of Hyperion, i.e., Heliopolis, in Lower Egypt. (The Greek name means "city of the sun.") Milton locates the temple of the sun in *Egyptian Thebes* (line 274), in Upper Egypt. See Glossary, THEBES, EGYPTIAN.

277–85. See 3.381–82 n.

281. *zone*: belt.

Skirted his loins and thighs with downy gold
And colors dipped in Heaven. The third his feet
Shadowed from either heel with feathered mail,
Sky-tinctured grain. Like Maia's son he stood   285
And shook his plumes that Heav'nly fragrance filled
The circuit wide. Straight knew him all the bands
Of angels under watch and to his state
And to his message high in honor rise,
For on some message high they guessed him bound.   290
Their glitt'ring tents he passed and now is come
Into the blissful field through groves of myrrh
And flow'ring odors, cassia, nard and balm,
A wilderness of sweets, for Nature here
Wantoned as in her prime and played at will   295
Her virgin fancies pouring forth more sweet,
Wild above rule or art, enormous bliss.
Him through the spicy forest onward come
Adam discerned as in the door he sat
Of his cool bow'r while now the mounted sun   300
Shot down direct his fervid rays to warm
Earth's inmost womb, more warmth than Adam needs.
And Eve within, due at her hour, prepared
For dinner savory fruits of taste to please
True appetite and not disrelish thirst   305
Of nectarous draughts between from milky stream,
Berry or grape. To whom thus Adam called:
    Haste hither Eve and worth thy sight behold
Eastward among those trees what glorious shape
Comes this way moving! Seems another morn   310
Ris'n on mid-noon. Some great behest from Heav'n
To us perhaps he brings and will vouchsafe
This day to be our guest. But go with speed
And what thy stores contain bring forth and pour
Abundance fit to honor and receive   315
Our Heav'nly stranger. Well we may afford
Our givers their own gifts and large bestow
From large bestowed where nature multiplies
Her fertile growth and by disburd'ning grows

287–88. *bands / Of angels*: These are the troops of angels, under Gabriel's command, guarding Paradise at its eastern gate (4.541–59).
295. *Wantoned*: played. *prime*: beginning, dawn.
298. *Him . . . come*: I.e., Raphael, having come onward through the forest. *spicy*: aromatic.
299. Abraham is visited by the divine presence when "he sat in the tent door in the heat of the day" (Genesis 18:1).
306. *draughts between*: drinks taken between courses of fruit. *nectarous* has two syllables: 'nec-trous.'

More fruitful, which instructs us not to spare.   320
   To whom thus Eve: Adam, earth's hallowed mold,
Of God inspired, small store will serve where store
All seasons ripe for use hangs on the stalk,
Save what by frugal storing firmness gains
To nourish and superfluous moist consumes.   325
But I will haste and from each bough and brake,
Each plant and juiciest gourd, will pluck such choice
To entertain our angel guest as he
Beholding shall confess that here on Earth
God hath dispensed His bounties as in Heav'n.   330
   So saying with dispatchful looks in haste
She turns, on hospitáble thoughts intent
What choice to choose for delicacy best,
What order so contrived as not to mix
Tastes not well joined, inelegant, but bring   335
Taste after taste upheld with kindliest change.
Bestirs her then and from each tender stalk
Whatever Earth all-bearing mother yields
In India east or west, or middle shore
In Pontus or the Punic coast, or where   340
Alcinous reigned, fruit of all kinds in coat
(Rough or smooth rined or bearded husk or shell)
She gathers tribute large and on the board
Heaps with unsparing hand. For drink the grape
She crushes, inoffensive must, and meaths   345
From many a berry, and from sweet kernels pressed
She tempers dulcet creams nor these to hold
Wants her fit vessels pure, then strews the ground
With rose and odors from the shrub unfumed.
Meanwhile our primitive great sire to meet   350
His godlike guest walks forth without more train
Accompanied than with his own complete
Perfections. In himself was all his state
More solemn than the tedious pomp that waits
On princes when their rich retínue long   355
Of horses led and grooms besmeared with gold
Dazzles the crowd and sets them all agape.

321–22. *hallowed mold, / Of God inspired:* i.e., you who are formed of the sacred earth and animated by God's breath.

339. *middle shore:* the shores of the Mediterranean, situated on the globe between the East and West Indies, India, and North America.

345. *inoffensive must:* unfermented wine and so not intoxicating. *meaths:* sweet drinks.

349. *unfumed:* not burned, as an incense, since Adam and Eve have no fire. In Eden the twigs of shrubs give odors as rich as burning incense.

350. *primitive:* original, first (Latin *primus,* "first").

Nearer his presence Adam, though not awed,
Yet with submiss approach and reverence meek
As to a superior nature bowing low   360
Thus said: Native of Heaven, for other place
None can than Heav'n such glorious shape contain,
Since by descending from the thrones above
Those happy places thou hast deigned a while
To want and honor these, vouchsafe with us   365
Two only, who yet by sov'reign gift possess
This spacious ground, in yonder shady bow'r
To rest and what the garden choicest bears
To sit and taste till this meridian heat
Be over and the sun more cool decline.   370
   Whom thus th' angelic virtue answered mild:
Adam, I therefore came, nor art thou such
Created or such place hast here to dwell
As may not oft invite, though spirits of Heav'n,
To visit thee. Lead on then where thy bow'r   375
O'ershades, for these mid-hours till evening rise
I have at will. So to the sylvan lodge
They came that like Pomona's arbor smiled
With flow'rets decked and fragrant smells. But Eve
(Undecked save with herself, more lovely fair   380
Than wood-nymph or the fairest goddess feigned
Of three that in Mount Ida naked strove)
Stood to entertain her guest from Heav'n. No veil
She needed, virtue-proof, no thought infirm
Altered her cheek. On whom the angel "Hail!"   385
Bestowed, the holy salutation used
Long after to blest Mary, second Eve:
   Hail Mother of Mankind whose fruitful womb
Shall fill the world more numerous with thy sons
Than with these various fruits the trees of God   390
Have heaped this table! Raised of grassy turf
Their table was and mossy seats had round

---

365. *To want*: to be absent from. *these*: places on earth.
369. *meridian*: midday.
372. *therefore*: for that purpose (to socialize with you).
372–75. A good example of Milton's compressed syntax; i.e., Although they are spirits of
    heaven, you, Adam, are created so nobly that it is suitable for you to invite spirits of
    heaven to visit.
378. *Pomona*: Roman goddess of fruit trees.
380. *Undecked*: unclothed.
381. *feigned*: pretended by the classical poets. Aphrodite, Athena, and Hera strove for the
    prize of beauty on Mount Ida, where the Trojan prince Paris awarded the prize to
    Aphrodite in return for the love of Helen, an event that caused the Trojan War.
384. *virtue-proof*: being guarded by her virtue.

And on her ample square from side to side
All autumn piled, though spring and autumn here
Danced hand in hand. A while discourse they hold   395
(No fear lest dinner cool) when thus began
Our author: Heav'nly stranger, please to taste
These bounties which our Nourisher (from whom
All perfect good unmeasured out descends
To us for food and for delight) hath caused   400
The earth to yield, unsavory food perhaps
To spiritual natures. Only this I know:
That one celestial Father gives to all.
    To whom the angel: Therefore what He gives
(Whose praise be ever sung) to Man in part   405
Spiritual may of purest spirits be found
No ingrateful food. And food alike those pure
Intelligential substances require
As doth your rational and both contain
Within them every lower faculty   410
Of sense whereby they hear, see, smell, touch, taste,
Tasting concoct, digest, assimilate,
And corporeal to incorporeal turn.
For know whatever was created needs
To be sustained and fed. Of elements   415
The grosser feeds the purer: Earth the Sea,
Earth and the Sea feed Air, the Air those Fires
Ethereal and as lowest first the Moon,
Whence in her visage round those spots unpurged,
Vapors not yet into her substance turned.   420
Nor doth the Moon no nourishment exhale
From her moist continent to higher orbs.
The Sun that light imparts to all receives

393. *her*: the table's.
397. *Our author*: our first father.
404–7. The food God gives to humans, who are partly spiritual beings, is welcome to the
    purest spirits as well.
408. *Intelligential substances*: angels' bodies, which, being material (though the highest
    degree of matter), need food.
409. *both*: *Intelligential* and *rational* substances: angelic and human bodies.
413. *incorporeal*: material, or substantial, but in a higher degree of existence than body,
    which has fixed boundaries and specialized parts. Through digestion the corporeal
    matter of fruits is refined into the incorporeal substance of angelic bodies and, in
    humans, into the reasoning power.
416. *grosser*: denser.
417–20. *Fires / Ethereal*: the liquid fire of the upper air, the empyrean, as well as the planets
    and stars. The lowest of these fires, the moon, is between the cool air of the upper atmo-
    sphere and the empyrean. Because the moon is on the border between the two realms,
    we can see in her face (*visage*) the as yet undigested vapors of the air being assimilated
    to her. The dark spots in the moon are the moon's food: atmospheric vapors.
423–26. The sun is sustained by vapors from all things, to which it gives nourishing light.

From all his alimental recompense
In humid exhalations and at ev'n   425
Sups with the Ocean. Though in Heav'n the trees
Of life ambrosial fruitage bear and vines
Yield nectar, though from off the boughs each morn
We brush mellifluous dews and find the ground
Covered with pearly grain, yet God hath here   430
Varied His bounty so with new delights
As may compare with Heaven—and to taste
Think not I shall be nice! So down they sat
And to their viands fell, nor seemingly
The angel nor in mist (the common gloss   435
Of theologians) but with keen dispatch
Of real hunger and concoctive heat
To transubstantiate. What redounds transpires
Through spirits with ease. Nor wonder if by fire
Of sooty coal th' empiric alchemist   440
Can turn, or holds it possible to turn,
Metals of drossiest ore to perfect gold
As from the mine. Meanwhile at table Eve
Ministered naked and their flowing cups
With pleasant liquors crowned. O innocence   445
Deserving Paradise! If ever, then,
Then had the sons of God excuse t' have been
Enamoured at that sight. But in those hearts
Love unlibidinous reigned nor jealousy.
Was understood, the injured lover's Hell.   450
      Thus when with meats and drinks they had sufficed,

430. *here*: on earth.
433. *nice*: disinclined and fussy.
434. *viands*: food.
435. *in mist*: symbolically.
437. *concoctive*: cooking. The angel cooks his meal inside him.
438. *transubstantiate*: turn one substance into another, in this case a higher. A loaded term in Milton's day, denoting for Roman Catholics the changing of the bread and wine of the mass into Christ's body and blood. For Milton, true transubstantiation exists in the natural world, in the processes of digestion and in the entire movement of creatures upward on the scale of being toward their Creator. *redounds*: is in excess. *transpires*: is breathed or radiated out. See line 5 n.
440. *empiric alchemist*: one who attempts by trial and error to convert supposedly lower metals, such as lead, into supposedly higher metals, ultimately gold. Many alchemists were charlatans, as in Jonson's play *The Alchemist*, and Milton at the very least doubts what they claim.
445. *crowned*: cups filled with noble drink.
447. *sons of God*: rogue angels who became enamored of human women—"the sons of God saw the daughters of men that they were fair" (Genesis 6:2)—and mated with them, bringing forth a race of mighty men, which was destroyed in the Flood. Milton's point here is that if ever the sons of God (e.g., Raphael) had excuse for being attracted to human women it was here, where Eve *ministered naked*. See Glossary, RAMIEL.
448. *those*: Adam's and Eve's.
449. *unlibidinous*: not lustful.

Not burdened nature, sudden mind arose
In Adam not to let th' occasion pass
Giv'n him by this great conference to know
Of things above his world and of their being   455
Who dwell in Heav'n whose excellence he saw
Transcend his own so far, whose radiant forms'
Divine effulgence, whose high pow'r so far
Exceeded human, and his wary speech
Thus to th' empyreal minister he framed: 460
     Inhabitant with God, now know I well
Thy favor in this honor done to Man
Under whose lowly roof thou hast vouchsafed
To enter and these earthly fruits to taste,
Food not of angels yet accepted so   465
As that more willingly thou couldst not seem
At Heav'n's high feasts t' have fed, yet what compare?
     To whom the wingèd hierarch replied:
O Adam! one Almighty is, from whom
All things proceed and up to Him return   470
If not depraved from good, created all
Such to perfection, one first matter all
Endued with various forms, various degrees
Of substance and in things that live of life,
But more refined, more spirituous and pure   475
As nearer to Him placed or nearer tending,
Each in their several active spheres assigned
Till body up to spirit work in bounds
Proportioned to each kind. So from the root
Springs lighter the green stalk, from thence the leaves   480
More airy, last the bright consummate flower
Spirits odorous breathes: flow'rs and their fruit,
Man's nourishment, by gradual scale sublimed
To vital spirits aspire, to animal,
To intellectual, give both life and sense,   485
Fancy and understanding, whence the soul
Reason receives, and reason is her being,
Discursive or intuitive: discourse

---

455. *their*: the angels'.
465. *accepted so*: I.e., You accepted and enjoyed our lower, human food as willingly as you
     would the food served at heaven's feasts.
479–90. This famous, broken simile of the flower begins as a model of the cosmos, the
     hierarchy of *All things* (line 470). With *flow'rs and their fruit* (line 482), however,
     the model is pulled back into the realm of the things it once modeled, representing a
     part of the whole it has formerly described, like the romantic symbol. Coleridge
     quotes this passage (lines 469–88) at the head of the thirteenth chapter of *Bio-
     graphia Literaria*, "On the Imagination, or Esemplastic Power."

Is oftest yours, the latter most is ours,
Differing but in degree, of kind the same.   490
Wonder not then what God for you saw good
If I refuse not but convert as you
To proper substance. Time may come when men
With angels may participate and find
No inconvenient diet nor too light fare.   495
And from these corporal nutriments perhaps
Your bodies may at last turn all to spirit,
Improved by tract of time, and winged ascend
Ethereal as we, or may at choice
Here or in Heav'nly paradises dwell—   500
If ye be found obedient and retain
Unalterably firm His love entire
Whose progeny you are. Meanwhile enjoy
Your fill what happiness this happy state
Can comprehend, incapable of more.   505
    To whom the patriarch of mankind replied:
O favorable Spirit, propitious guest,
Well hast thou taught the way that might direct
Our knowledge and the scale of nature set
From center to circumference whereon   510
In contemplation of created things
By steps we may ascend to God. But say,
What meant that caution joined, "if ye be found
Obedient"? Can we want obedience then
To Him or possibly His love desert   515
Who formed us from the dust and placed us here
Full to the utmost measure of what bliss
Human desires can seek or apprehend?
    To whom the angel: Son of Heav'n and Earth,
Attend! That thou art happy owe to God.   520
That thou continuest such owe to thyself,

---

493. *To proper substance*: to one's own body.
494. *participate*: a learned pun: "to share meals with" or "to be of like substance with."
495. *inconvenient*: inappropriate.
497. *spirit*: highest, most refined degree of substance.
498–99. *winged*: being winged. *ascend / Ethereal as we*: ascend so high as to become ethereal, as we are.
503. *Whose progeny you are*: Strictly speaking, Adam and Eve are not God's offspring (only the Son is) but His creatures: they are beings God has made. Raphael's phrase is meant figuratively, as it is in its source, Saint Paul's sermon to the Athenians, on "Mars' hill," the Areopagus; Acts 17:28: "For in him we live, and move, and have our being; as certain also of your own poets have said, For we are also his offspring."
505. *incapable*: unable, given your present bodily structure, to be happier than you now are. This thought is in Dante's *Paradiso* (4.31–36), where the souls at different levels all experience bliss equally, that is, to the maximum of their capacity.
509. *scale*: Latin *scala*, "ladder."

That is, to thy obedience: therein stand!
This was that caution giv'n thee. Be advised!
God made thee perfect, not immutable,
And good He made thee. But to persevere   525
He left it in thy pow'r, ordained thy will
By nature free, not overruled by fate
Inextricable or strict necessity.
Our voluntary service He requires,
Not our necessitated: such with Him   530
Finds no acceptance, nor *can* find. For how
Can hearts, not free, be tried whether they serve
Willing or no, who will but what they must
By destiny and can no other choose?
Myself and all th' angelic host that stand   535
In sight of God enthroned our happy state
Hold as you yours while our obedience holds,
On other surety none. Freely we serve
Because we freely love as in our will
To love or not: in this we stand or fall.   540
And some *are* fall'n, to disobedience fallen
And so from Heav'n to deepest Hell. O fall
From what high state of bliss into what woe!
    To whom our great progenitor: Thy words
Attentive and with more delighted ear,   545
Divine instructor, I have heard than when
Cherubic songs by night from neighboring hills
Aerial music send. Nor knew I not
To be both will and deed created free.
Yet that we never shall forget to love   550
Our Maker and obey Him whose command
Single is yet so just, my constant thoughts
Assured me and still assure, though what thou tell'st
Hath passed in Heav'n some doubt within me move
But more desire to hear, if thou consent,   555
The full relation which must needs be strange,
Worthy of sacred silence to be heard!
And we have yet large day, for scarce the Sun
Hath finished half his journey and scarce begins

538–40. Raphael says that the angels, like humanity, serve God freely because they love God. Angels are free to choose to love God. They are not compelled to do so either by God or by their own nature.
557. An expression from Horace, *Odes* 2.13.29, describing songs worthy of being heard in sacred silence, *sacro digna silentio.*
559. *journey* and *and* are elided: 'journ-yand.'

His other half in the great zone of Heav'n.   560
   Thus Adam made request and Raphael
After short pause assenting thus began:
   High matter thou enjoin'st me O Prime of Men,
Sad task and hard, for how shall I relate
To human sense th' invisible explóits   565
Of warring spirits, how without remorse
The ruin of so many glorious once
And perfect while they stood, how last unfold
The secrets of another world perhaps
Not lawful to reveal? Yet for thy good   570
This is dispensed, and what surmounts the reach
Of human sense I shall delineate so
By lik'ning spiritual to corporal forms
As may express them best. Though what if Earth
Be but the shadow of Heav'n and things therein   575
Each to other like more than on Earth is thought?
   As yet this world was not and chaos wild
Reigned where these heav'ns now roll, where Earth now rests
Upon her center poised, when on a day
(For time, though in eternity, applied   580
To motion measures all things durable
By present, past and future) on such day
As Heav'n's Great Year brings forth th' empyreal host
Of angels, by imperial summons called,
Innum'rable before th' Almighty's throne,   585
Forthwith from all the ends of Heav'n appeared
Under their hierarchs in orders bright,
Ten thousand thousand ensigns high advanced,
Standards and gonfalons 'twixt van and rear
Stream in the air and for distinction serve   590
Of hierarchies, of orders and degrees
Or in their glittering tissues bear imblazed
Holy memorials, acts of zeal and love
Recorded eminent. Thus when in orbs

---

560. *great zone:* belt of the zodiac, through whose signs the sun travels through the day.
564. *Sad task:* Raphael's preface recalls Aeneas's words to Dido before recounting, at her request, the fall of Troy. *Aeneid* 2.3: "Unspeakable, O queen, is the grief you command me to revive."
570–74. The war in heaven will be recounted in terms that are at once figurative and literal: figurative because the events described entirely exceed anything on the level of the human senses, literal because the events as described cannot be translated into other terms (such as concepts) or apprehended by the human mind in any other way.
581. *durable:* having extension in time.
583. *Great Year:* a period of 36,000 earth years, when the stars return to their original positions. Plato, *Timaeus* 37c–39e and *Republic* 8.546b–c.
589. *gonfalons:* banners suspended from crossbars. *van:* the front line of troops. See 6.558 n.
592. *tissues:* woven fabrics.

Of circuit inexpressible they stood,   595
Orb within orb, the Father Infinite,
By whom in bliss embosomed sat the Son,
Amidst as from a flaming mount whose top
Brightness had made invisible, thus spake:
    "Hear all ye angels, progeny of light,   600
Thrones, Dominations, Princedoms, Virtues, Powers,
Hear My decree, which unrevoked shall stand!
This day I have begot whom I declare
My only Son and on this holy hill
Him have anointed whom ye now behold   605
At My right hand. Your head I Him appoint
And by Myself have sworn to Him shall bow
All knees in Heav'n and shall confess Him Lord.
Under His great vicegerent reign abide
United as one individual soul   610
For ever happy. Him who disobeys
Me disobeys, breaks union, and that day,
Cast out from God and blessèd vision, falls
Into utter darkness, deep engulfed, his place
Ordained without redemption, without end."   615
    So spake th' Omnipotent and with His words
All seemed well pleased: all seemed but were not all.
That day as other solemn days they spent
In song and dance about the sacred hill,
Mystical dance which yonder starry sphere   620
Of planets and of fixed in all her wheels
Resembles nearest, mazes intricate,
Eccentric, intervolved, yet regular

598–99. *flaming mount . . . invisible*: recalls Mount Sinai, where Moses received the
    Hebrew Law (Exodus 19:19–20).
603. "The Lord hath said unto me, Thou art my Son; this day I have begotten thee" (Psalm
    2:7). This event, the proclamation of the Son as Messiah and king over the angels, is
    the earliest in the action of the poem. The Son is not literally begotten by the Father at
    this time but is revealed to the angels as such. In fact, the Son created the angels, act-
    ing as the Father's instrument, or Word, when doing so (lines 835–37).
605. *anointed*: Anointing is ritual pouring of oil over the head to inaugurate a high priest
    or king. See line 664 and n., line 777, and 12.359. In Hebrew prophecy, a special
    Messiah, a descendant of David, will enter Jerusalem by the east gate and establish
    an age of peace. See, e.g, Isaiah 2:4–17 and 26:19; Ezekiel 36:29–30; Amos 9:13;
    Zechariah 8:23. For Christians, the Messiah is likewise a son of David but also the
    "only Son" (line 604) of God. He creates the universe (7.192–231); he becomes
    incarnate as Jesus Christ (12.358–60) to die on the cross; and at the end of history
    he will judge humanity (12.540–51). These three roles—Creator, Savior, and
    Judge—are described in Milton's poem "On the Morning of Christ's Nativity."
607–8. "I have sworn by myself . . . that unto me every knee shall bow" (Isaiah 45:23).
    "God also hath highly exalted him, and given him a name which is above every
    name: That at the name of Jesus every knee should bow" (Philippians 2:9–10).
621. *fixed*: stars fixed on their crystal sphere. They do not change position with respect to
    each other.

Then most when most irregular they seem
And in their motions harmony divine   625
So smooths her charming tones that God's own ear
Listens delighted. Evening now approached
(For we have also our evening and our morn,
We ours for change delectable, not need),
Forthwith from dance to sweet repast they turn   630
Desirous. All in circles as they stood
Tables are set and on a sudden piled
With angels' food and rubied nectar flows
In pearl, in diamond and massy gold,
Fruit of delicious vines, the growth of Heav'n.   635
On flow'rs reposed and with fresh flow'rets crowned
They eat, they drink, and in communion sweet
Quaff immortality and joy (secure
Of surfeit where full measure only bounds
Excess) before th' all-bounteous King, who show'red   640
With copious hand, rejoicing in their joy.
    Now when ambrosial night with clouds exhaled
From that high Mount of God (whence light and shade
Spring both) the face of brightest Heav'n had changed
To grateful twilight (for night comes not there   645
In darker veil) and roseate dews disposed
All but th' unsleeping eyes of God to rest,
Wide over all the plain and wider far
Than all the globous Earth in plain outspread
(Such are the courts of God) th' angelic throng,   650
Dispersed in bands and files, their camp extend
By living streams among the trees of life,

---

627. *Listens delighted*: This phrase (τέρπετ' ἀκούων) concludes the beautiful scene in the *Iliad* (1.472–74) in which an entire day is devoted by the Achaean youths to appeasing the god Apollo with sacred dance and holy song (paean); "and the god's heart was delighted as he listened."

633. *nectar*: in Homer the drink of the gods.

636–40. Lines 636 and 638–39 were added in 1674. *in communion sweet* (line 637) replaced *with refection sweet* and *Excess* (line 640) replaced *Are filled*. The parenthetical clause, "secure / Of surfeit where full measure only bounds / Excess," appears to mean the angels are in no danger of overeating or drinking to excess, because the vessels mentioned in line 634, when full, hold just enough to satisfy. The substitution of *communion*, a sharing, for *refection*, which etymologically means a restoring or remaking of the individual, adds a spiritual overtone to this scene, one that includes an abundance that falls short of excess, as in Psalm 36:8: "They shall be abundantly satisfied with the fatness of thy house; and thou shalt make them drink of the river of thy pleasures." For Milton the materialist monist, spiritual and substantial nourishment are in Heaven one and the same.

642–44. I.e., when night changed the face of heaven.

642–57. This sentence opens with a complex subordinate clause (governed by *when*) extending from line 642 to line 647. The subject is *throng* (line 650), the main verb *reared* (line 653), and the direct object *Pavilions*: 'the angelic throng reared their pavilions.' (The force of *extend*, line 651, is participial: 'their camp being extended.')

Pavilions numberless and sudden reared,
Celestial tabernacles where they slept
Fanned with cool winds, save those who in their course   655
Melodious hymns about the sov'reign throne
Alternate all night long. But not so waked
Satan (so call him now: his former name
Is heard no more in Heav'n). He of the first
If not the first archangel great in power,   660
In favor, and preëminence, yet fraught
With envy 'gainst the Son of God that day
Honored by His great Father and proclaimed
Messiah, King Anointed, could not bear
Through pride that sight and thought himself impaired.   665
Deep malice thence conceiving and disdain,
Soon as midnight brought on the dusky hour
Friendliest to sleep and silence, he resolved
With all his legions to dislodge and leave
Unworshipped, unobeyed, the throne supreme,   670
Contemptuous, and his next subordinate
Awak'ning, thus to him in secret spake:
    "Sleep'st thou, companion dear? What sleep can close
Thy eyelids? And remember'st what decree
Of yesterday so late hath passed the lips   675
Of Heav'n's Almighty? Thou to me thy thoughts
Wast wont, I mine to thee was wont t' impart:
Both waking we were one. How then can now
Thy sleep dissent? New laws thou seest imposed,
New laws from Him who reigns new minds may raise   680
In us who serve, new counsels, to debate
What doubtful may ensue. More in this place
To utter is not safe. Assemble thou
Of all those myriads which we lead the chief.
Tell them that by command ere yet dim night   685
Her shadowy cloud withdraws I am to haste,
And all who under me their banners wave,

---

658. *his former name*: *Lucifer*, "light-bearer": "How art thou fallen from heaven, O Lucifer,
    son of the morning!" (Isaiah 14:12). But Raphael may mean another, more mysteri-
    ous name as well. See lines 760–62.
659–60. Milton's Satan is not necessarily as in Christian tradition the head of the angels
    before his fall. But he is one of the archangels.
664. *King Anointed* is the meaning of *Messiah* and a formula from Hebrew prophecy,
    melech ha-mashiach (מלך המשיח).
671. *Contemptuous*: either an adjective modifying *he* (line 668) or an adverb modifying
    leave (line 669): he, being contemptuous, left; or, he left, contemptuously. *next subor-
    dinate*: Beëlzebub.
680–81. I.e., New laws will raise new ways of thinking (*minds*) in us who serve. (We may,
    for example, think of serving no more.)

Homeward with flying march where we possess
The quarters of the north, there to prepare
Fit entertainment to receive our King   690
The great Messiah and His new commands,
Who speedily through all the hierarchies
Intends to pass triumphant and give laws."
    So spake the false archangel and infused
Bad influence into th' unwary breast   695
Of his associate. He together calls,
Or several one by one, the regent powers,
Under him regent, tells as he was taught
That the Most High Commanding now ere night,
Now ere dim night had disencumbered Heav'n,   700
The great hierarchal standard was to move,
Tells the suggested cause and casts between
Ambiguous words and jealousies to sound
Or taint integrity. But all obeyed
The wonted signal and superior voice   705
Of their great potentate. For great indeed
His name and high was his degree in Heav'n!
His count'nance as the morning star that guides
The starry flock allured them and with lies
Drew after him the third part of Heav'n's host.   710
Meanwhile th' Eternal Eye whose sight discerns
Abstrusest thoughts from forth His holy mount
And from within the golden lamps that burn
Nightly before Him saw without their light
Rebellion rising, saw in whom, how spread   715
Among the sons of morn, what multitudes
Were banded to oppose His high decree
And smiling to His only Son thus said:
    "Son, Thou in whom My glory I behold

---

689. *north*: "For thou hast said in thine heart . . . I will exalt my throne above the stars of God: I will sit also upon the mount of the congregation, in the sides of the north" (Isaiah 14:13).
690. *Fit entertainment*: suitable greeting, whether peaceful or warlike. An example of Satan's ambiguous way of speaking.
692. *hierarchies*: orders of angels.
693. *give laws*: a classical expression, evoking the image of a Roman general conquering new territories and imposing laws (and taxes).
696–98. *He . . . him . . . he*: Beëlzebub, who is *regent* (one who rules in another's name) under Satan.
699. *the Most High Commanding*: tendentious title of Satan.
707. *His name*: Satan's name, Lucifer. See 658 n.
708. *morning star*: Hesperus, the planet Venus, which in the morning appears to lead the stars from the sky. See "On the Morning of Christ's Nativity," stanza 6.
710. *third part*: "and [the dragon's] tail drew the third part of the stars of heaven, and did cast them to the earth" (Revelation 12:4). See 2.692.
714. *their*: the lamps'.

In full resplendence, heir of all My might,   720
Nearly it now concerns us to be sure
Of our omnipotence and with what arms
We mean to hold what anciently we claim
Of deity or empire, such a foe
Is rising who intends t' erect his throne   725
Equal to ours throughout the spacious north!
Nor so content hath in his thought to try
In battle what our pow'r is or our right.
Let us advise and to this hazard draw
With speed what force is left and all employ   730
In our defense, lest unawares we lose
This our high place, our sanctuary, our hill."
    To whom the Son with calm aspect and clear,
Lightning divine, ineffable, serene,
Made answer: "Mighty Father, thou thy foes   735
Justly hast in derision and, secure,
Laugh'st at their vain designs and tumults vain,
Matter to Me of glory whom their hate
Illústrates when they see all regal power
Giv'n Me to quell their pride and in event   740
Know whether I be dextrous to subdue
Thy rebels or be found the worst in Heav'n."
    So spake the Son. But Satan with his pow'rs
Far was advanced on wingèd speed, an host
Innumerable as the stars of night   745
Or stars of morning, dew-drops which the sun
Impearls on every leaf and every flower.
Regions they passed, the mighty regencies
Of seraphim and potentates and thrones
In their triple degrees, regions to which   750
All thy dominion, Adam, is no more
Than what this garden is to all the Earth

727–28. Nor so content . . . right: 'and not being content with having his own empire in the
    north (which he has not yet achieved), intends to fight us here.' That God says this
    smiling (line 718) shows that he holds Satan's plans in derision. See also the Son's
    reply at lines 735–37. That there is any real danger God does not for a moment sup-
    pose. Yet for dramatic purposes Milton must give the impression that some danger
    exists, that Satan's powers are real.
729–32. There is an unavoidable contradiction between what God is as a character in a story
    and what God must be theologically. Is God truly worried about the safety of our hill?
    If he is worried, then he is not omnipotent. If he is not worried, then his irony (unlike,
    e.g., Gabriel's at 4.904–11) is unpleasant. The Son takes the latter view, that God is not
    worried, and the Son is, of course, theologically correct (lines 735–37). But we cannot
    so easily dispel this apparition of a God who laughs at the weakness of his foes.
740. in event: when the issue is put to the test.
741. be dextrous: have the power (Latin dextera or dextra, "the right hand," metaphor-
    ically applied to military force).

And all the sea from one entire globose
Stretched into longitude! Which having passed
At length into the limits of the north   755
They came and Satan to his royal seat
(High on a hill far blazing as a mount
Raised on a mount with pyramids and tow'rs
From diamond quarries hewn and rocks of gold)
The palace of great Lucifer (so call   760
That structure in the dialect of men
Interpreted) which not long after he
(Affecting all equality with God
In imitation of that mount whereon
Messiah was declared in sight of Heav'n)   765
The Mountain of the Congregation called;
For thither he assembled all his train
(Pretending so commanded to consult
About the great reception of their King
Thither to come) and with calumnious art   770
Of counterfeited truth thus held their ears:
    "Thrones, Dominations, Princedoms, Virtues, Powers,
If these magnific titles yet remain
Not merely titular since by decree
Another now hath to himself engrossed   775
All power and us eclipsed under the name
Of King Anointed for whom all this haste
Of midnight march and hurried meeting here,
This only to consult how we may best
With what may be devised of honors new   780
Receive Him coming to receive from us
Knee-tribute yet unpaid—prostration vile!
Too much to one but double how endured,
To one and to His image now proclaimed!
But what if better counsels might erect   785
Our minds and teach us to cast off this yoke?
Will ye submit your necks and choose to bend
The supple knee? Ye will not if I trust
To know ye right or if ye know yourselves
Natives and sons of Heav'n possessed before   790
By none, and if not equal all, yet free,

753–54. *one entire globose . . . into longitude*: the sea from an entire globe (like this
    earth) stretched out flat.
754–71. I.e., Satan came to his royal seat, the palace of Lucifer. Not long after, Satan
    called it the Mountain of the Congregation.
777. *King Anointed*: Messiah. See lines 605 n. and 664 n.
777–78. *for whom . . . meeting here*: This is a lie: Satan has commanded the haste, the
    march, and the meeting. See lines 754–71 n.
783–84. *one*: God the Father. *double*: the Father and the Son. *His image*: the Son.

Equally free, for orders and degrees
Jar not with liberty but well consist.
Who can in reason then or right assume
Monarchy over such as live by right   795
His equals if, in power and splendor less,
In freedom equal? Or can introduce
Law and edíct on us who without law
Err not, much less for this to be our lord
And look for adoration to th' abuse   800
Of those imperial titles which assert
Our being ordained to govern, not to serve?"
     Thus far his bold discourse without control
Had audience when among the seraphim
Abdiel (than whom none with more zeal adored   805
The Deity and divine commands obeyed)
Stood up and in a flame of zeal severe
The current of his fury thus opposed:
     "O argument blasphémous, false and proud!
Words which no ear ever to hear in Heav'n   810
Expected, least of all from thee, ingrate,
In place thyself so high above thy peers!
Canst thou with impious obloquy condemn
The just decree of God pronounced and sworn
That to His only Son by right endued   815
With regal scepter every soul in Heav'n
Shall bend the knee and in that honor due
Confess Him rightful King? Unjust thou say'st,
Flatly unjust, to bind with laws the free
And equal over equals to let reign,   820
One over all with unsucceeded pow'r.
Shalt thou give law to God, shalt thou dispute

792–97. Satan attempts to conceal a contradiction in what he says. Because he intends to
     preserve his ascendancy over the rebel angels, Satan says that hierarchy is not
     inconsistent with freedom. Yet he also says that it is unjust for the Son to assume
     monarchy over those who are his equals. Abdiel catches this contradiction at line 812.
796–98. I.e., Who can in reason impose laws and commands on us when we do nothing
     wrong, nothing such laws would forbid? Cf. Adam's remark to Michael at 12.283:
     "So many laws argue so many sins."
797. Or can: The implied subject is who.
800. And look: The implied subject is who and the implied auxiliary verb is can: "who can look?"
802. to govern, not to serve: But this is not an either/or choice: the disjunction is false.
808. his: Satan's.
813. obloquy: abusive language.
821. unsucceeded: not supplanted by another, a successor, and not nearly approached by
     any other.
822–25. Romans 9:20: "Shall the thing formed say to him that formed it, Why hast thou
     made me thus?" The main moral idea of Paradise Lost and the foundation of the
     poem's religious ethic: all beings are created beings and are therefore subject to their
     Creator. See lines 894–95 and n.

With Him the points of liberty who made
Thee what thou art and formed the pow'rs of Heav'n
Such as He pleased and circumscribed their being?   825
Yet by experience taught we know how good
And of our good and of our dignity
How provident He is, how far from thought
To make us less, bent rather to exalt
Our happy state under one head more near   830
United. But to grant it thee unjust
That equal over equals monarch reign:
Thyself though great and glorious dost thou count,
Or all angelic nature joined in one,
Equal to him, begotten Son, by whom   835
As by His Word the mighty Father made
All things, ev'n thee, and all the spirits of Heav'n
By Him created in their bright degrees,
Crowned them with glory and to their glory named
Thrones, Dominations, Princedoms, Virtues, Powers,   840
Essential Powers, nor by His reign obscured
But more illustrious made since He, the Head,
One of our number thus reduced becomes,
His laws our laws: all honor to Him done
Returns our own. Cease then this impious rage   845
And tempt not these but hasten to appease
Th' incensèd Father and th' incensèd Son
While pardon may be found in time besought!"
    So spake the fervent angel but his zeal
None seconded as out of season judged   850
Or singular and rash, whereat rejoiced
Th' Apostate and more haughty thus replied:
"That we were formed then say'st thou? And the work
Of secondary hands by task transferred
From Father to His Son? Strange point and new!   855
Doctrine which we would know whence learnt: who saw
When this Creation was? Remember'st thou
Thy making while the Maker gave thee being?
We know no time when we were not as now,

---

825. *circumscribed*: established the limits to.
841. *Essential*: constituting the very being of those powers.
853–63. With some justice Satan points out that there is no evidence for, because no angelic witness of, what Abdiel affirms: the Son's creation of the angels. But such evidence is by definition impossible to obtain: Abdiel cannot witness his own creation because he isn't there to be a witness until he is made, when it's too late. Satan's objection to Abdiel's statement recoils on his own: if direct witness is the only valid evidence, Satan can have no evidence for his claim about his own generation, *self-begot . . . By . . . quick'ning power.*

Know none before us, self-begot, self-raised   860
By our own quick'ning power when fatal course
Had circled his full orb, the birth mature
Of this our native Heav'n, ethereal sons.
Our puissance is our own. Our own right hand
Shall teach us highest deeds by proof to try   865
Who is our equal. Then thou shalt behold
Whether by supplication we intend
Address and to begirt th' almighty throne
Beseeching or besieging! This report,
These tidings carry to th' Anointed King—   870
And fly, ere evil intercept thy flight!"
  He said, and as the sound of waters deep
Hoarse murmur echoed to his words applause
Through the infinite host. Nor less for that
The flaming seraph fearless though alone,   875
Encompassed round with foes, thus answered bold:
  "O alienate from God! O spirit accurst,
Forsaken of all good! I see thy fall
Determined and thy hapless crew involved
In this perfidious fraud, contagion spread   880
Both of thy crime and punishment! Henceforth
No more be troubled how to quit the yoke
Of God's Messiah: those indulgent laws
Will not be now vouchsafed! Other decrees
Against thee are gone forth without recall.   885
That golden scepter which thou didst reject
Is now an iron rod to bruise and break
Thy disobedience. Well thou didst advise,
Yet not for thy advice or threats I fly
These wicked tents devoted, lest the wrath   890
Impendent raging into sudden flame
Distinguish not. For soon expect to feel

---

869. *Beseeching or besieging*: a rhetorical effect typical of Satan's ambiguous language: the two words sound almost identical but are opposite in meaning. Cf. *entertainment* (line 690 and n.).

880. *contagion*: Satan's fraud is like a disease that will be rapidly spread by the crimes to follow (rebellion against God, destruction of Man) and even by the punishment of those crimes.

884–88. Abdiel here speaks as a prophet. He has no direct information on what he says (*Other decrees / Against thee are gone forth*) but is inspired to knowledge.

887. *iron rod*: Psalm 2:9: "Thou shalt break them with a rod of iron; thou shalt dash them in pieces."

890. *wicked tents*: Moses' words to the Hebrews in the wilderness when rebellion rose among them: "Depart, I pray you, from the tents of these wicked men, and touch nothing of theirs, lest ye be consumed in all their sins" (Numbers 16:26). See Psalm 84:10: "I had rather be a doorkeeper in the house of my God, than to dwell in the tents of wickedness."

His thunder on thy head, devouring fire!
Then who created thee lamenting learn
When who can uncreate thee thou shalt know!"   895
   So spake the seraph Abdiel faithful found
Among the faithless, faithful only he
Among innumerable false. Unmoved,
Unshaken, unseduced, unterrified
His loyalty he kept, his love, his zeal.   900
Nor number nor example with him wrought
To swerve from truth or change his constant mind
Though single. From amidst them forth he passed
Long way through hostile scorn which he sustained
Superior, nor of violence feared aught   905
And with retorted scorn his back he turned
On those proud tow'rs to swift destruction doomed.

Book Six

The Argument

Raphael continues to relate how Michael and Gabriel were sent forth to battle against Satan and his angels. The first fight described. Satan and his powers retire under night, he calls a council, invents devilish engines which in the second day's fight put Michael and his angels to some disorder. But they at length pulling up mountains overwhelmed both the force and machines of Satan. Yet the tumult not so ending, God on the third day sends Messiah his Son for whom He had reserved the glory of that victory. He in the power of his Father coming to the place and causing all His legions to stand still on either side, with His chariot and thunder driving into the midst of his enemies, pursues them unable to resist towards the wall of Heaven. Which opening, they leap down with horror and

---

894–95. This magnificent rebuke gives dramatic force to Milton's creationist ethic. See lines 822–25 n.

901. *Nor . . . nor*: neither . . . nor. Neither the quantity of those rebelling nor their example affected Abdiel's judgment.

903. *Though single*: although he was alone.

906. *retorted*: Latin *retorqueo*, "to turn back, to throw back." This word can refer either to Abdiel's verbal response, which has been thrown back at Satan, or to Abdiel's physical gesture of turning his back in scorn, or to both.

907. *proud tow'rs*: one of the boldest metaphors in the epic. As Abdiel departs, the rebel angels are seen as gigantic, sinister towers, recalling the Tower of Babel (Genesis 11:1–9). See also 2 Peter 2:1: "false prophets [and] false teachers . . . who . . . bring upon themselves swift destruction." To Milton, false teaching is even worse than open war, to which it leads. Although the rebel angels will conduct an actual war against God, the root cause of their destruction is not that they rebel but that they succumb to Satan's false arguments.

confusion into the place of punishment prepared for them in the
deep. Messiah returns with triumph to his Father.

All night the dreadless angel unpursued
Through Heav'n's wide champaign held his way till Morn,
Waked by the circling Hours, with rosy hand
Unbarred the gates of light. There is a cave
Within the Mount of God fast by His throne   5
Where light and darkness in perpetual round
Lodge and dislodge by turns which makes through Heaven
Grateful vicissitude like day and night:
Light issues forth and at the other door
Obsequious darkness enters till her hour   10
To veil the Heav'n, though darkness there might well
Seem twilight here. And now went forth the Morn
Such as in highest Heav'n, arrayed in gold
Empyreal. From before her vanished Night,
Shot through with orient beams, when all the plain,   15
Covered with thick embattled squadrons bright,
Chariots and flaming arms and fiery steeds
Reflecting blaze on blaze, first met his view.
War he perceived, war in procinct, and found
Already known what he for news had thought   20
To have reported. Gladly then he mixed
Among those friendly pow'rs who him received
With joy and acclamations loud, that one
That of so many myriads fall'n—yet one!—
Returned not lost. Onto the sacred hill   25
They led him high applauded and present
Before the Seat Supreme, from whence a Voice
From midst a golden cloud thus mild was heard:
    "Servant of God, well done, well hast thou fought
The better fight, who single hast maintained   30
Against revolted multitudes the cause
Of truth, in word mightier than they in arms,
And for the testimony of truth hast borne
Universal reproach, far worse to bear
Than violence. For this was all thy care: 35
To stand approved in sight of God though worlds
Judged thee perverse. The easier conquest now
Remains thee, aided by this host of friends:

Book Six
8. *Grateful vicissitude*: welcome change.
18. *his*: Abdiel's.
19. *in procinct*: Latin *in procinctu*, girded up in readiness for battle.

Back on thy foes more glorious to return
Than scorned thou didst depart and to subdue   40
By force who reason for their law refuse,
Right reason for their law and for their King
Messiah who by right of merit reigns.
Go, Michael, of celestial armies prince
And thou in military prowess next,   45
Gabriel, lead forth to battle these my sons
Invincible, lead forth my armèd saints
By thousands and by millions ranged for fight
Equal in number to that godless crew
Rebellious! Them with fire and hostile arms   50
Fearless assault and to the brow of Heaven
Pursuing drive them out from God and bliss
Into their place of punishment, the gulf
Of Tartarus which ready opens wide
His fiery chaos to receive their fall!"   55
    So spake the Sov'reign Voice and clouds began
To darken all the hill and smoke to roll
In dusky wreaths, reluctant flames, the sign
Of wrath awaked. Nor with less dread the loud
Ethereal trumpet from on high gan blow,   60
At which command the powers militant
That stood for Heav'n, in mighty quadrate joined
Of union irresistible, moved on
In silence their bright legions to the sound
Of instrumental harmony that breathed   65
Heroic ardor to advent'rous deeds
Under their godlike leaders in the cause
Of God and His Messiah. On they move
Indíssolubly firm, nor obvious hill,
Nor strait'ning vale, nor wood nor stream divides   70
Their perfect ranks. For high above the ground
Their march was and the passive air upbore
Their nimble tread as when the total kind
Of birds in orderly array on wing

---

41. *their*: the rebel angels'.
54. *Tartarus*: in Greek myth, a deeper Hell for gods. See Glossary.
58. *reluctant*: Latin *reluceo*, "to blaze, shine, glow," as in Livy 22.17.2, "relucens flamma," but also the Latin deponent verb *reluctor*, "to struggle against"—i.e., the brightness of the flames struggles against the darkness of the smoke. Cf. 2.337.
60. *gan*: began.
62. *quadrate*: square, a Roman formation.
64–66. The angels advance silently to martial music, like Homer's Achaeans in contrast to the Trojans and their confederates, who advance making a loud noise, like flocks of cranes (*Iliad* 3.1–9).
69. *obvious*: blocking the way.

Came summoned over Eden to receive   75
Their names of thee. So over many a tract
Of Heav'n they marched and many a province wide
Tenfold the length of this terrene. At last
Far in th' horizon to the north appeared
From skirt to skirt a fiery region stretched   80
In battailous aspéct and, nearer view,
Bristled with upright beams innumerable
Of rigid spears and helmets thronged and shields
Various with boastful argument portrayed,
The banded powers of Satan hasting on   85
With furious expedition. For they weened
That selfsame day by fight or by surprise
To win the Mount of God and on His throne
To set the envier of His state, the proud
Aspirer, but their thoughts proved fond and vain   90
In the mid way, though strange to us it seemed
At first that angel should with angel war
And in fierce hosting meet who wont to meet
So oft in festivals of joy and love
Unanimous as sons of one great Sire,   95
Hymning th' Eternal Father. But the shout
Of battle now began and rushing sound
Of onset ended soon each milder thought.
High in the midst exalted as a god
Th' Apostate in his sun-bright chariot sat,   100
Idol of majesty divine, enclosed
With flaming cherubim and golden shields,
Then lighted from his gorgeous throne, for now
Twixt host and host but narrow space was left,
A dreadful interval, and front to front   105
Presented stood in terrible array
Of hideous length. Before the cloudy van
On the rough edge of battle ere it joined
Satan, with vast and haughty strides advanced,
Came tow'ring armed in adamant and gold.   110
Abdiel that sight endured not where he stood

76. *thee*: Adam, to whom Raphael is speaking.
78. *this terrene*: this earth. I.e., The provinces of Heaven which the angels cross are ten times wider than this earth.
80. *From skirt to skirt*: from one edge to the other.
91. *mid way*: The rebel angels' intentions proved to be empty before their attempt to fulfill those intentions was half complete.
93. *hosting*: as in *hostile*, playing on the ambiguity in many languages, e.g., Old English (*gæst*) and Latin (*hospes*), by which the same word is used for *enemy*, *guest*, and *host*. See also the archaic word for an army, *host*, line 104. *wont*: were accustomed.
100. *Apostate*: Satan, "he who stands apart."

Among the mightiest bent on highest deeds
And thus his own undaunted heart explores:
   "O Heaven! That such resemblance of the High'st
Should yet remain where faith and realty   115
Remain not! Wherefore should not strength and might
There fail where virtue fails or weakest prove
Where boldest, though to sight unconquerable?
His puissance, trusting in th' Almighty's aid,
I mean to try whose reason I have tried   120
Unsound and false. Nor is it aught but just
That he who in debate of truth hath won
Should win in arms, in both disputes alike
Victor, though brutish that contést and foul
When reason hath to deal with force, yet so   125
Most reason is that reason overcome."
   So pondering and from his armèd peers
Forth stepping opposite half way he met
His daring foe, at this prevention more
Incensed, and thus securely him defied: 130
   "Proud, art thou met? Thy hope was to have reached
The heighth of thy aspiring unopposed,
The Throne of God unguarded and His side
Abandoned at the terror of thy power
Or potent tongue. Fool! Not to think how vain   135
Against th' Omnipotent to rise in arms
Who out of smallest things could without end
Have raised incessant armies to defeat
Thy folly or with solitary hand,
Reaching beyond all limit, at one blow   140
Unaided could have finished thee and whelmed
Thy legions under darkness! But thou seest
All are not of thy train: there be who faith
Prefer and piety to God though then
To thee not visible when I alone   145
Seemed in thy world erroneous to dissent
From all. My sect thou seest: now learn too late
How few sometimes may know when thousands err!"

---

113. *explores*: pours forth.
115. *realty*: Anglo-Norman *reauté*, "royal dignity," and *realté*, "real existence" (*OED*), the
    latter opposed to false *resemblance* (line 114). *fealty* is an early emendation.
119. *His*: Satan's.
120–26. Abdiel is saying that since conflict in arms is inferior to conflict by reason, he
    who wins by force of reason should also win by force of arms.
129. *prevention*: coming foremost, beforehand. Abdiel is incensed at Satan's boldness in
    stepping forward between the armies before the fight begins.
147. *sect*: adherents to a party or a cause, especially, in Milton's day, in religion.

Whom the grand Foe with scornful eye askance
Thus answered: "Ill for thee, but in wished hour   150
Of my revenge first sought, for thou return'st
From flight, seditious angel, to receive
Thy merited reward, the first assay
Of this right hand provoked since first that tongue
Inspired with contradiction durst oppose   155
A third part of the gods in synod met
Their deities to assert who while they feel
Vigor divine within them can allow
Omnipotence to none! But well thou com'st
Before thy fellows ámbitious to win   160
From me some plume that thy success may show
Destruction to the rest. This pause between
(Unanswered lest thou boast) to let thee know:
At first I thought that liberty and Heav'n
To heav'nly souls had been all one but now   165
I see that most through sloth had rather serve,
Minist'ring spirits trained up in feast and song.
Such hast thou armed—the minstrelsy of Heaven!—
Servility with freedom to contend,
As both their deeds compared this day shall prove."   170
    To whom in brief thus Abdiel stern replied:
"Apostate, still thou err'st nor end wilt find
Of erring, from the path of truth remote!
Unjustly thou deprav'st it with the name
Of servitude to serve whom God ordains   175
Or Nature: God and Nature bid the same
When he who rules is worthiest and excels
Them whom he governs. This is servitude:
To serve th' unwise or him who hath rebelled
Against his worthier as thine now serve thee,   180
Thyself not free but to thyself enthralled,

150–56. I.e., That you should be the first enemy I meet is unlucky for you, Abdiel, but happy for me, for I will punish you for daring to contradict me and my confederates during our meeting last night.

160. *ámbitious* is an adverb modifying *com'st* (line 159), not an adjective modifying *fellows*. Abdiel comes ambitious for success.

164–70. I.e., I once thought that for angels freedom and being in Heaven were one and the same. Now I see that for some angels Heaven is making music (and eating feasts) to flatter God. These are the sort you have now placed in arms—musicians, not soldiers! You have armed them for the war between the cause of servility, which you champion, and the cause of freedom, which we champion: we shall see today which cause makes better fighters.

177. *he*: God, although the principle expressed is a general one: it is only natural that the best should govern.

181. *Thyself not free but to thyself enthralled*: Another example of Abdiel speaking from a point of view close to the poet's own. Compare 5.894–95 and n. This sentence is the fruit of two decades of thinking and writing about liberty.

Yet lewdly dar'st our minist'ring upbraid.
Reign thou in Hell thy kingdom, let me serve
In Heav'n God ever blest and His divine
Behests obey, worthiest to be obeyed.   185
Yet chains in Hell, not realms, expect! Meanwhile
From me returned, as erst thou saidst, from flight,
This greeting on thy impious crest receive!"
    So saying, a noble stoke he lifted high
Which hung not but so swift with tempest fell   190
On the proud crest of Satan that no sight
Nor motion of swift thought (less could his shield)
Such ruin intercept. Ten paces huge
He back recoiled, the tenth on bended knee
His massy spear upstayed, as if on Earth   195
Winds under ground or waters forcing way
Sidelong had pushed a mountain from his seat
Half sunk with all his pines. Amazement seized
The rebel thrones but greater rage to see
Thus foiled their mightiest. Ours joy filled and shout,   200
Presage of victory and fierce desire
Of battle, whereat Michaël bid sound
Th' archangel trumpet. Through the vast of Heaven
It sounded and the faithful armies rung
Hosanna to the Highest. Nor stood at gaze   205
The adverse legions nor less hideous joined
The horrid shock. Now storming fury rose
And clamor such as heard in Heav'n till now
Was never: arms on armor clashing brayed
Horrible discord and the madding wheels   210
Of brazen chariots raged. Dire was the noise
Of conflict. Overhead the dismal hiss
Of fiery darts in flaming volleys flew
And flying vaulted either host with fire.
So under fiery cope together rushed   215
Both battles main with ruinous assault
And inextinguishable rage. All Heaven
Resounded and had earth been then, all earth
Had to her center shook. What wonder? When
Millions of fierce encount'ring angels fought   220
On either side the least of whom could wield
These elements and arm him with the force
Of all their regions. How much more of power

221–23. Even the least of the angels could wield the elements of the cosmos, such as stars, for weapons.

Army against army numberless to raise
Dreadful combustion warring and disturb,   225
Though not destroy, their happy native seat,
Had not th' Eternal King Omnipotent
From His stronghóld of Heaven high overruled
And limited their might, though numbered such
As each divided legion might have seemed   230
A num'rous host, in strength each armèd hand
A legion. Led in fight, yet leader seemed
Each warrior, single as in chief, expért
When to advance or stand or turn the sway
Of battle, open when and when to close   235
The ridges of grim war: no thought of flight,
None of retreat, no unbecoming deed
That argued fear. Each on himself relied
As only in his arm the moment lay
Of victory. Deeds of eternal fame   240
Were done, but infinite, for wide was spread
That war and various. Sometimes on firm ground
A standing fight, then soaring on main wing
Tormented all the air: all air seemed then
Conflicting fire. Long time in even scale   245
The battle hung till Satan, who that day
Prodigious power had shown and met in arms
No equal, ranging through the dire attack
Of fighting seraphim confused at length,
Saw where the sword of Michael smote and felled   250
Squadrons at once with huge two-handed sway:
Brandished aloft the horrid edge came down
Wide wasting. Such destruction to withstand
He hasted and opposed the rocky orb
Of tenfold adamant, his ample shield,   255
A vast circumference. At his approach
The great archangel from his warlike toil
Surceased and glad as hoping here to end
Intestine war in Heav'n, th' arch-foe subdued
Or captive dragged in chains, with hostile frown   260
And visage all inflamed first thus began:
   "Author of evil unknown till thy revolt,

239. *moment*: turning point.
244. *Tormented*: Latin *torqueo*, "to twist." Roman war engines, ballistas, propelled large
    stones and flaming balls of pitch, etc., by means of energy stored by torsion, or
    twisted ropes.
254. *He*: Satan. *rocky orb*: Satan's shield, made of adamant; see 1.48 n.
258–60. *glad as hoping . . . dragged in chains*: Michael is glad at Satan's approach because
    Michael hopes that by *subduing* Satan or making him *captive* the war in Heaven can
    be ended. The syntax is clearer if one understands "being" before *subdued* (line 259).

Unnamed in Heav'n, now plenteous, as thou seest:
These acts of hateful strife, hateful to all
Though heaviest by just measure on thyself   265
And thy adherents. How hast thou disturbed
Heav'n's blessèd peace and into nature brought
Misery uncreated till the crime
Of thy rebellion! How hast thou instilled
Thy malice into thousands once upright   270
And faithful, now proved false! But think not here
To trouble holy rest: Heaven casts thee out
From all her confines. Heav'n the seat of bliss
Brooks not the works of violence and war.
Hence then, and evil go with thee along,   275
Thy offspring, to the place of evil, Hell,
Thou and thy wicked crew! There mingle broils
Ere this avenging sword begin thy doom
Or some more sudden vengeance winged from God
Precipitate thee with augmented pain!"   280
   So spake the Prince of Angels. To whom thus
The Adversary: "Nor think thou with wind
Of airy threats to awe whom yet with deeds
Thou canst not! Hast thou turned the least of these
To flight or, if to fall, but that they rise   285
Unvanquished, easier to transact with me
That thou shouldst hope, imperious, and with threats
To chase me hence? Err not that so shall end
The strife which thou call'st evil but we style
The strife of glory, which we mean to win   290
Or turn this Heav'n itself into the Hell
Thou fablest, here however to dwell free,
If not to reign. Meanwhile thy utmost force—
And join Him named Almighty to thy aid—
I fly not but have sought thee far and nigh."   295
   They ended parley and both addressed for fight
Unspeakable. For who though with the tongue
Of angels can relate or to what things
Liken on Earth conspicuous that may lift
Human imagination to such heighth   300
Of godlike pow'r! For likest gods they seemed,
Stood they or moved, in stature, motion, arms,
Fit to decide the empire of great Heaven.

263. The subject of *Unnamed* and *plenteous* is *evil*.
286. *easier to transact with me*: Do you think it easier to fight me?
289. *style*: call; literally "write" (Latin *stilus*, "pen").
296. *parley*: discussion or negotiation before battle (like most military terms, French).
   Elided with *and. addressed*: prepared.

Now waved their fiery swords and in the air
Made horrid circles. Two broad suns their shields   305
Blazed opposite while Expectation stood
In horror. From each hand with speed retired
Where erst was thickest fight th' angelic throng
And left large field, unsafe within the wind
Of such commotion, such as (to set forth   310
Great things by small) if, nature's concord broke,
Among the constellations war were sprung,
Two planets rushing from aspéct malign
Of fiercest opposition in mid sky
Should combat and their jarring spheres confound.   315
Together both with next to almighty arm
Uplifted imminent one stroke they aimed
That might determine and not need repeat
As not of power at once, nor odds appeared
In might or swift prevention. But the sword   320
Of Michael from the armory of God
Was giv'n him tempered so that neither keen
Nor solid might resist that edge. It met
The sword of Satan with steep force to smite
Descending and in half cut sheer, nor stayed   325
But with swift wheel reverse deep ent'ring shared
All his right side. Then Satan first knew pain
And writhed him to and fro convolved, so sore
The griding sword with discontinuous wound
Passed through him. But th' ethereal substance closed,   330
Not long divisible, and from the gash
A stream of nectarous humor issuing flowed
Sanguine, such as celestial spirits may bleed,
And all his armor stained, erewhile so bright.
Forthwith on all sides to his aid was run   335
By angels many and strong who interposed
Defense while others bore him on their shields
Back to his chariot where it stood retired
From off the files of war. There they him laid

310–15. *such as . . . if . . . confound*: The syntax of the two clauses—*war were sprung* and
planets should combat—will be clearer if one imagines an *or* between them.
319. *As not of power at once*: as not having any power if not victorious in one stroke.
323. *It*: the sword's edge.
325–27. With a downstroke Michael cuts Satan's sword in half. Then with an upstroke he
cuts open Satan's right side.
329. *discontinuous*: breaking the unity of the body.
332. *nectarous humor*: the blood of angels, from Homeric *ichor*, the blood of the gods, and
nectar, the drink of the gods. *humor*: vital fluid. *Nectarous* and *issuing* have each two
syllables.
333. *Sanguine*: bloodred.

Gnashing for anguish and despite and shame   340
To find himself not matchless and his pride
Humbled by such rebuke so far beneath
His confidence to equal God in power.
Yet soon he healed, for spirits that live throughout
Vital in every part—not as frail man   345
In entrails, heart or head, liver or reins—
Cannot but by annihilating die
Nor in their liquid texture mortal wound
Receive no more than can the fluid air:
All heart they live, all head, all eye, all ear,   350
All intellect, all sense, and as they please
They limn themselves and color, shape or size
Assume as likes them best, condense or rare.
    Meanwhile in other parts like deeds deserved
Memorial: where the might of Gabriel fought   355
And with fierce ensigns pierced the deep array
Of Moloch furious king who him defied
And at his chariot wheels to drag him bound
Threatened, nor from the Holy One of Heaven
Refrained his tongue blasphémous, but anon   360
Down cloven to the waist with shattered arms
And uncouth pain fled bellowing. On each wing
Uriel and Raphael his vaunting foe—
Though huge and in a rock of diamond armed—
Vanquished Adramelech and Asmadai,   365
Two potent thrones that to be less than gods
Disdained but meaner thoughts learned in their flight,

344–53. Spiritual beings are material, and *Vital*, but they are not organic in the sense of
having parts specialized for various functions, such as seeing. All functions are per-
formable everywhere in them. They can, moreover, alter their entire appearance into
any form they choose: *They limn themselves.* They are like *liquid* in being able to
take any shape. But spiritual beings are like *air* in being able to be compressed into
small space or spread out thinly over a large area: *condense* or *rare.*

346. *reins*: kidneys.

352. *limn*: an emendation of *limb* (1667, 1674; Shawcross, ed., *Paradise Lost*, p. 392). The
angels can refashion their total appearance, as when a pliable substance is modeled.
Milton uses the word in this sense in *Reason of Church Government* (YP 1:777–78)
when he speaks of the prelates, who would "frame of their own heads as it were with
wax a kinde of Mimic Bishop limm'd out to the life." The primary sense of *limn* is
from painting, but its broader, metaphorical sense, "to bring to life and to refashion
by conscious art," was current, as when Thomas Nashe speaks of the essence of writing being the ability "with life and spirit to limn deadness itself" (*Four Letters Con-
futed,* in *Works,* ed. Ronald B. McKerrow and F. P. Wilson [Oxford, 1958] 1.282.33).

356. *ensigns*: military banners. Gabriel's powers, marked by their several banners, cut
through Moloch's troop formations.

358. *chariot wheels*: In the *Iliad*, Achilles drags the dead Hector behind his chariot.

360. *anon*: soon.

363–65. Uriel and Raphael each vanquished his vaunting foe: Uriel beat Adramelech and
Raphael beat Asmadai.

Mangled with ghastly wounds through plate and mail.
Nor stood unmindful Abdiel to annoy
The atheist crew but with redoubled blow   370
Ariel and Arioch and the violence
Of Ramiel, scorched and blasted, overthrew.
I might relate of thousands and their names
Eternize here on Earth but those elect
Angels, contented with their fame in Heaven,   375
Seek not the praise of men. The other sort,
In might though wondrous and in acts of war,
Nor of renown less eager, yet by doom
Cancelled from Heav'n and sacred memory,
Nameless in dark oblivion let them dwell.   380
For strength, from truth divided and from just,
Illaudable, naught merits but dispraise
And ignominy, yet to glory aspires
Vainglorious and through infamy seeks fame:
Therefore eternal silence be their doom.   385
    And now their mightiest quelled, the battle swerved
With many an inroad gored. Deformèd rout
Entered and foul disorder. All the ground
With shivered armor strewn and on a heap
Chariot and charioteer lay overturned   390
And fiery foaming steeds. What stood, recoiled
O'er-wearied, through the faint Satanic host
Defensive scarce or with pale fear surprised,
Then first with fear surprised and sense of pain
Fled ignominious, to such evil brought   395
By sin of disobedience, till that hour
Not liable to fear or flight or pain.
Far otherwise th' inviolable saints
In cubic phalanx firm advanced entire,

---

369. *annoy*: injure (*OED* 4a).
376. *other sort*: the rebel angels, now devils in Hell.
382. *Illaudable*: unworthy of praise, a predicate of *strength*. I.e., Strength divided from truth and justice merits no praise.
386. *their*: the devils'.
386–99. This passage contrasts the disarray of the rebel angels' formations, and their shameful flight, with the aggressive order of the faithful angels' army.
387. *inroad*: area into which the faithful angels have penetrated the rebel angels' formations, as a bull gores with its horns. *rout*: defeat, causing deformity and disorder in the rebel angels' formations.
391–97. *What stood*: Those rebel angels left standing fled, exhausted, through the troops behind them. And even these troops, who had not yet been in the battle, were scarcely able to mount any defense, being surprised with fear. For their sin of disobedience to God, giving them guilty consciences, makes them susceptible to fear.
399. *cubic*: Because angels are airborne when they fight, their military formations can improve by one dimension on the Roman square, or *quadrate* (see line 62 and n.). *phalanx*: an ancient Greek formation of heavily armed, closely ranked infantry. Cf. 1.549–55 and n.

Invulnerable, impenetrably armed, 400
Such high advantages their innocence
Gave them above their foes not to have sinned,
Not to have disobeyed. In fight they stood
Unwearied, unobnoxious to be pained
By wound though from their place by violence moved. 405
   Now Night her course began and over Heaven
Inducing darkness grateful truce imposed
And silence on the odious din of war.
Under her cloudy covert both retired,
Victor and vanquished. On the foughten field 410
Michaël and his angels prevalent
Encamping placed in guard their watches round,
Cherubic waving fires. On th' other part
Satan with his rebellious disappeared
Far in the dark, dislodged and void of rest, 415
His potentates to council called by night
And in the midst thus undismayed began:
   "O now in danger tried, now known in arms
Not to be overpow'red, companions dear,
Found worthy not of liberty alone, 420
Too mean pretense, but what we more affect,
Honor, dominion, glory and renown
Who have sustained one day in doubtful fight
(And if one day, why not eternal days?)
What Heaven's Lord had pow'rfullest to send 425
Against us from about His throne and judged
Sufficient to subdue us to His will,
But proves not so! Then fallible it seems
Of future we may deem Him though till now
Omniscient thought. True is, less firmly armed, 430
Some disadvantage we endured and pain
Till now not known, but known as soon contemned
Since now we find this our empyreal form
Incapable of mortal injury,
Imperishable, and though pierced with wound 435

---

404. *unobnoxious:* unable. The faithful angels experience the force (*violence*) of blows but not the pain such blows cause the rebel angels.
409. *her:* Night's.
414–16. The principal verb following *Satan* is *called*, not *disappeared*. I.e., Satan, having disappeared into the dark with his rebellious troops, called his potentates. It is possible, however, that Milton intends the reader first to take *disappeared* as the main verb ("Satan disappeared") and then to take *called* as the main verb ("Satan called"), thus condensing two actions into one sentence.
428–29. *fallible . . . Of future:* Because God couldn't predict our having survived today, He is shown to be capable of error.
432. *contemned:* despised.
433. *empyreal:* of the sky, the empyrean.

Soon closing and by native vigor healed.
Of evil then so small as easy think
The remedy! Perhaps more valid arms,
Weapons more violent when next we meet,
May serve to better us and worse our foes   440
Or equal what between us made the odds—
In nature none. If other hidden cause
Left them superior, while we can preserve
Unhurt our minds and understanding sound,
Due search and consultation will disclose."   445
    He sat and in th' assembly next upstood
Nisroch of principalities the prime.
As one he stood escaped from cruel fight
Sore toiled, his riven arms to havoc hewn
And cloudy in aspéct, thus answering spake: 450
"Deliv'rer from new lords, leader to free
Enjoyment of our right as gods, yet hard
For gods and too unequal work we find
Against unequal arms to fight in pain
Against unpained, impassive, from which evil   455
Ruin must needs ensue. For what avails
Valor or strength, though matchless, quelled with pain
Which all subdues and makes remiss the hands
Of mightiest? Sense of pleasure we may well
Spare out of life perhaps and not repine   460
But live content, which is the calmest life.
But pain is perfect misery, the worst
Of evils, and, excessive, overturns
All patience. He who therefore can invent
With what more forcible we may offend   465
Our yet unwounded enemies or arm
Ourselves with like defense to me deserves
No less than for deliverance what we owe."
    Whereto with look composed Satan replied:
"Not uninvented that which thou aright   470
Believ'st so main to our success I bring.
Which of us who beholds the bright surface
Of this ethereous mold whereon we stand,

439. *when next we meet*: when our armies fight next.
441–42. *what between us made the odds—In nature none*: Whatever it was that gave them
    the advantage today, since they don't have any natural advantage over us.
451. *new lords*: referring to the Son, whose proclamation as the angels' "Lord" occasioned
    the rebellion. Nisroch makes it seem as if many lords, rather than one, have been
    placed over the angels.
458. *remiss*: slack, slow, incapable of action.
459–60. The first indication that the rebel angels can no longer experience pleasure.

This continent of spacious Heav'n adorned
With plant, fruit, flow'r ambrosial, gems and gold—   475
Whose eye so superficially surveys
These things as not to mind from whence they grow
Deep under ground, materials dark and crude
Of spiritous and fiery spume, till touched
With Heaven's ray and tempered they shoot forth   480
So beauteous, op'ning to the ambient light?
These in their dark nativity the deep
Shall yield us pregnant with infernal flame
Which into hollow engines long and round
Thick-rammed, at th' other bore with touch of fire   485
Dilated and infuriate shall send forth
From far with thund'ring noise among our foes
Such implements of mischief as shall dash
To pieces and o'erwhelm whatever stands
Adverse, that they shall fear we have disarmed   490
The Thund'rer of His only dreaded bolt.
Nor long shall be our labor yet: ere dawn
Effect shall end our wish. Meanwhile, revive!
Abandon fear! To strength and counsel joined
Think nothing hard, much less to be despaired!"   495
    He ended, and his words their drooping cheer
Enlightened and their languished hope revived.
Th' invention all admired and each how he
To be th' inventor missed, so easy it seemed
Once found which yet unfound most would have thought   500
Impossible. Yet haply of thy race
In future days if malice should abound
Someone intent on mischief or inspired
With dev'lish machination might devise
Like instrument to plague the sons of men   505
For sin, on war and mutual slaughter bent.

482–91. *These*: the *materials dark* (line 478), *pregnant with infernal flame* (line 483). Under normal conditions, when activated by the sun's rays, the materials bloom as flowers, *gems*, and *gold* (line 475). They are now to be made into gunpowder, *rammed* (line 485) into one end of a hollow cylinder (*hollow engines*, line 484), and ignited from the other end, the *other bore* (line 485), so they will expand (*dilate*) with growing fury (line 486). This sense of *infuriate* from *infuriare*, "to grow in fury," is in John Florio's Italian dictionary of 1611 (*OED*). The cannon, invented in the Renaissance, was widely regarded as a diabolic invention and as marking the end of chivalric martial values. See Ariosto's *Orlando Furioso* 9.91, where the paragon of chivalric martial valor, Orlando, delivers an oration against the cannon and sinks one in the ocean.
493. *Effect*: result.
496. *their*: the rebel angels'.
501–6. *thy race*: humanity, the children of Eve and Adam. Weapons such as artillery—and far worse, as we now know—will be invented by humans, should they fall into sin. Raphael is again performing his commission, given at 5.237–45.

Forthwith from council to the work they flew:
None arguing stood! Innumerable hands
Were ready. In a moment up they turned
Wide the celestial soil and saw beneath   510
Th' originals of nature in their crude
Conception: sulfurous and nitrous foam
They found, they mingled, and with subtle art
Concocted and adusted they reduced
To blackest grain and into store conveyed.   515
Part hidden veins digged up (nor hath this Earth
Entrails unlike) of mineral and stone
Whereof to found their engines and their balls
Of missive ruin, part incentive reed
Provide pernicious with one touch to fire.   520
So all ere day-spring under conscious night
Secret they finished and in order set
With silent circumspection unespied.
    Now when fair morn orient in Heav'n appeared
Up rose the victor angels and to arms   525
The matin trumpet sung. In arms they stood
Of golden panoply, refulgent host
Soon banded. Others from the dawning hills
Looked round and scouts each coast light-armèd scour,
Each quarter, to descry the distant foe   530
Where lodged or whither fled or if for fight
In motion or in halt. Him soon they met
Under spread ensigns moving nigh in slow
But firm battalion. Back with speediest sail
Zophiel of Cherubim the swiftest wing   535
Came flying and in mid air aloud thus cried:
    "Arm, warriors, arm for fight! The foe at hand
Whom fled we thought will save us long pursuit
This day. Fear not his flight! So thick a cloud
He comes and settled in his face I see   540
Sad resolution and secure. Let each
His adamantine coat gird well and each

516–19. *Part . . . part*: "Some [do this] . . . some [do that]," a Virgilianism.
518. *engines*: "ingenious constructions," here cannons.
519. *missive*: missile. *incentive*: flammable. A tar-soaked reed is used to ignite the charge
    in the cannon.
521. *day-spring*: dawn. *conscious night*: night witnessing their work, an expression from
    Ovid, *Metamorphoses* 13.15: "of which night alone is witness" (*quorum nox conscia
    sola est*).
525. *victor angels*: the army of the faithful angels.
532. *Him*: the enemy army, the rebel angels.
541. *Sad*: sober, grim.

Fit well his helm, grip fast his orbèd shield
Borne ev'n or high! For this day will pour down,
If I conjecture aught, no drizzling show'r   545
But rattling storm of arrows barbed with fire!"
So warned he them aware themselves and soon
In order, quit of all impediment,
Instant without disturb they took alarm
And onward move embattled when, behold!   550
Not distant far with heavy pace the foe
Approaching gross and huge in hollow cube
Training his dev'lish engin'ry impaled
On every side with shadowing squadrons deep
To hide the fraud. At interview both stood   555
A while but suddenly at head appeared
Satan and thus was heard commanding loud:
    "Vanguard to right and left the front unfold
That all may see who hate us how we seek
Peace and composure and with open breast   560
Stand ready to receive them if they like
Our overture and turn not back perverse!
But that I doubt. However, witness Heaven,
Heav'n witness thou anon while we discharge
Freely our part! Ye who appointed stand   565
Do as ye have in charge and briefly touch
What we propound—and loud, that all may hear!"
    So scoffing in ambiguous words he scarce
Had ended when to right and left the front
Divided and to either flank retired,   570

---

544. *ev'n or high*: held directly in front (even) or over the head, to protect against missiles.
In the Roman formation, the *testudo* (tortoise), shields were held overhead by tightly
packed formations, making a roof against missiles.
548. *impediment*: military baggage and supplies, a term much used in Caesar's accounts
of his wars.
552. *hollow cube*: a formation imitating the *cubic phalanx* (line 399) of the faithful
angels, but hollow within, where the cannons are concealed.
553. *impaled*: surrounded, as by a fence, with troops.
555. *interview*: within sight of each other.
558. *Vanguard*: advance guard, or front rank, of an army.
559–67. *how we seek / Peace . . . overture . . . turn not back . . . discharge . . . touch . . .
propound . . . loud*: With laborious irony, Satan speaks the language of negotiation
and peace while his meaning is violent. The rebel angels seek peace, but peace by
victory, via cannon. Their opening bombardment is an *overture*, though not to negotiation but to battle. If the faithful angels like this overture, they will not *turn back*
(i.e., be driven back by cannonballs). The rebel angels will *discharge* not their part in
a negotiation but their cannons. The rebel angels' artillery officers are told to *briefly
touch* not on the conditions for peace but rather to touch, with their flaming reeds,
the fuses at the bases of the cannons. What the rebel angels *propound* (Latin, "to
put forward") is not the terms of peace but a hail of cannonballs, and these proposi-
tions will be *loud*. See Landor (below, p. 422).

Which to our eyes discovered new and strange,
A triple-mounted row of pillars laid
On wheels (for like to pillars most they seemed
Or hollowed bodies made of oak or fir
With branches lopped in wood or mountain felled),   575
Brass, iron, stony mold, had not their mouths
With hideous orifice gaped on us wide,
Portending hollow truce. At each behind
A seraph stood and in his hand a reed
Stood waving tipped with fire while we suspense   580
Collected stood within our thoughts amused
Not long, for sudden all at once their reeds
Put forth and to a narrow vent applied
With nicest touch. Immediate in a flame,
But soon obscured with smoke, all Heav'n appeared   585
From those deep-throated engines belched, whose roar
Embowelled with outrageous noise the air
And all her entrails tore disgorging foul
Their dev'lish glut: chained thunderbolts and hail
Of iron globes which on the victor host   590
Leveled with such impetuous fury smote
That whom they hit none on their feet might stand
Though standing else as rocks. But down they fell
By thousands, angel on archangel rolled
The sooner for their arms. Unarmed they might   595
Have easily as spirits evaded swift
By quick contraction or remove but now
Foul dissipation followed and forced rout—
Nor served it to relax their serried files!
What should they do? If on they rushed repulse   600
Repeated and indecent overthrow
Doubled would render them yet more despised
And to their foes a laughter, for in view
Stood ranked of seraphim another row

571. *our*: Raphael was among the armies of the faithful angels and a participant in the events he describes. The plural possessive pronoun reminds us of this fact, since Raphael, being like the other angels "contented with [his] fame in Heaven" (line 375), will recount none of his own deeds in the war.
578. *hollow truce*: Raphael here catches the infection of Satan's verbal play. The cannons are literally hollow, like the truce Satan speaks of.
581. *amused*: puzzled.
589. *glut*: contents of the cannons. *chained*: an allusion to chain shot: missiles joined by chains so as to cut a swath through the enemy's formations.
591. *Leveled*: aimed (*OED*, "level," 7a).
598. *dissipation*: scattering.
599. *relax their serried files*: allow the ranks of the faithful angels to spread out, thus presenting a less concentrated target to the rebel angel's artillery.
604. *seraphim*: rebel seraphim, not the faithful ones.

In posture to displode their second tire   605
Of thunder. Back defeated to return
They worse abhorred. Satan beheld their plight
And to his mates thus in derision called:
    "O friends! why come not on these victors proud?
Erewhile they fierce were coming and when we   610
To entertain them fair with open front
And breast (what could we more?) propounded terms
Of composition, straight they changed their minds,
Flew off, and into strange vagaries fell
As they would dance! Yet for a dance they seemed   615
Somewhat extravagant and wild, perhaps
For joy of offered peace. But I suppose
If our proposals once again were heard
We should compel them to a quick result!"
    To whom thus Belial in like gamesome mood: 620
"Leader, the terms we sent were terms of weight,
Of hard conténts and full of force urged home
Such as we might perceive amused them all
And stumbled many. Who receives them right
Had need from head to foot well understand.   625
Not understood, this gift they have besides:
They show us when our foes walk not upright."
    So they among themselves in pleasant vein
Stood scoffing, heightened in their thoughts beyond
All doubt of victory. Eternal Might   630
To match with their inventions they presumed
So easy and of His thunder made a scorn
And all His host derided while they stood
Awhile in trouble. But they stood not long.
Rage prompted them at length and found them arms   635
Against such hellish mischief fit t' oppose.
Forthwith—behold the excellence, the power
Which God hath in His mighty angels placed!—
Their arms away they threw and to the hills

---

605. *displode*: explode, fire. *tire*: volley.
614. *vagaries*: wanderings. Digressions from the point under discussion, i.e., the *pro-pounded terms / of composition* (lines 612–13), or agreement.
621–27. Belial continues Satan's jest, comparing the artillery assault to a verbal state-ment of terms of truce. The terms were hard to understand and forcefully presented. The terms therefore confused (*amused*) their recipients and caused many to miscon-strue them (*stumbled many*). Whoever correctly understands the terms of truce (i.e., *receives* a direct hit) must understand them from beginning to end (*from head to foot*). Then he will *well understand* (i.e., be overthrown and no longer stand). The truce terms have, however, another benefit for us. When the terms are not under-stood, they show us when our foes are not dealing honestly with us (*walk not upright*) in negotiation—for they have fallen down.

(For Earth hath this variety from Heaven,   640
Of pleasure situate in hill and dale)
Light as the lightning glimpse they ran, they flew:
From their foundations loos'ning to and fro
They plucked the seated hills with all their load,
Rocks, waters, woods, and by the shaggy tops   645
Uplifting bore them in their hands. Amaze,
Be sure, and terror seized the rebel host
When coming tówards them so dread they saw
The bottom of the mountains upward turned
Till on those cursèd engines' triple row   650
They saw them whelmed and all their confidence
Under the weight of mountains buried deep,
Themselves invaded next and on their heads
Main promontories flung which in the air
Came shadowing and oppressed whole legions armed.   655
Their armor helped their harm, crushed in and bruised
Into their substance pent which wrought them pain
Implacable and many a dolorous groan
Long struggling underneath ere they could wind
Out of such prison though spirits of purest light,   660
Purest at first, now gross by sinning grown.
The rest in imitation to like arms
Betook them and the neighboring hills uptore:
So hills amid the air encountered hills
Hurled to and fro with jaculation dire   665
That under ground they fought in dismal shade,
Infernal noise. War seemed a civil game
To this uproar. Horrid confusion heaped
Upon confusion rose and now all Heav'n
Had gone to wrack with ruin overspread   670
Had not th' Almighty Father where He sits
Shrined in His sanctuary of Heav'n secure

---

640. The pleasant variety of hills and valleys on earth is derived from Heaven, where it
    existed first. The statement reminds us Raphael is speaking to Adam.
651. *them*: the cannons.
656. *helped their harm*: The reason is given at line 661.
660. *prison* (i.e., their armor) has two syllables, *spirits* has one ('spearts'). This is an eleven-
    syllable line with the second, unstressed syllable of *prison* before the caesura.
661. *gross*: densely material. The rebel angels have already become more *condense*, as
    opposed to *rare* (line 353). They therefore not only suffer more when crushed in their
    armor but have a harder time squeezing out.
665. *jaculation*: throwing (Latin *iacio*). In classical authors, hills are used as missiles in
    the wars between the Olympians and the giants and between the Olympians and the
    Titans.
666. *under ground*: the fighting continues beneath the hills that have been thrown, in
    darkness and amid terrible noise. Milton may intend this detail to be understood as
    the source of the later notion that Hell is deep within the earth.

Consulting on the sum of things forseen
This tumult and permitted all advised,
That His great purpose He might so fulfill   675
To honor his Anointed Son avenged
Upon His enemies and to declare
All power on Him transferred, whence to his Son,
Th' assessor of his throne, He thus began:
    "Effulgence of my glory, Son beloved,   680
Son in whose face invisible is beheld
Visibly what by deity I am
And in whose hand what by decree I do,
Second Omnipotence, two days are passed,
Two days as we compute the days of Heav'n,   685
Since Michael and his powers went forth to tame
These disobedient. Sore hath been their fight
As likeliest was when two such foes met armed,
For to themselves I left them and thou know'st
Equal in their creation they were formed   690
Save what sin hath impaired which yet hath wrought
Insensibly, for I suspend their doom
Whence in perpetual fight they needs must last
Endless and no solution will be found.
War, wearied, hath performed what war can do   695
And to disordered rage let loose the reins
With mountains as with weapons armed which makes
Wild work in Heav'n and dangerous to the main.
Two days are therefore passed, the third is thine.
For Thee I have ordained it and thus far   700
Have suffered that the glory may be thine
Of ending this great war since none but Thou
Can end it. Into Thee such virtue and grace
Immense I have transfused that all may know
In Heav'n and Hell thy pow'r above compare   705
And this perverse commotion governed thus
To manifest Thee worthiest to be Heir
Of all things, to be Heir and to be King
By sacred unction, thy deservèd right.
Go then Thou mightiest in thy Father's might!   710

---

679. *assessor*: "he who sits beside."
691–92. *impaired*: changed for the worse. *Insensibly*: without being noticed. But see line
    661 and n.
698. *main*: the whole (structure of Heaven). God observes that a continued rumpus will
    destroy not only things in Heaven but the very walls and foundations of Heaven.
701. *suffered*: put up with [the war].
709. *sacred unction*: anointing with oil, the biblical act of creating a king. The Hebrew
    word *messiah* and the Greek word *christos* both mean "anointed one."

Ascend My chariot, guide the rapid wheels
That shake Heav'n's basis! Bring forth all my war,
My bow and thunder, my almighty arms
Gird on and sword upon thy puissant thigh!
Pursue these sons of darkness, drive them out   715
From all Heav'n's bounds into the utter deep!
There let them learn as likes them to despise
God and Messiah, his Anointed King."
    He said, and on his Son with rays direct
Shone full: he all his Father full expressed,   720
Ineffably into his face received,
And thus the Filial Godhead answering spake:
    "O Father, O Supreme of Heav'nly thrones,
First, highest, holiest, best, Thou always seek'st
To glorify thy Son, I always Thee,   725
As is most just. This I my glory account,
My exaltation and my whole delight,
That Thou in Me well pleased declar'st thy will
Fulfilled which to fulfil is all my bliss.
Scepter and pow'r, thy giving, I assume   730
And gladlier shall resign when in the end
Thou shalt be all in all and I in Thee
For ever, and in Me all whom Thou lov'st.
But whom Thou hat'st I hate and can put on
Thy terrors as I put thy mildness on,   735
Image of Thee in all things, and shall soon,
Armed with thy might, rid Heav'n of these rebelled
To their prepared ill mansion driven down,
To chains of darkness and th' undying worm,
That from thy just obedience could revolt   740
Whom to obey is happiness entire.

720–22. I.e., The Father cannot be perceived in himself. But when the Father shines on
    the Son, the Son's face becomes the full expression of the Father's nature.
728. well pleased: the gospel phrase with which the Father acknowledges Jesus as His son
    (Matthew 3:17 and 17:5; Mark 1:11).
730–33. Milton here sets forth his eschatology, his vision of the end of time, and his non-
    Trinitarian theory of the relation of the Son to the Father. At the end of time, all crea-
    tures will return to God the Father, as their substantial origin (see 7.168–73 n.).
    Conscious created beings, angels and humans, will return to the Father by first entering
    the Son, who will then enter the Father. Ontologically, the Son is not the equal of the
    Father. But morally, i.e., by merit, he is. The Father promotes the Son to equality with
    him by delegating to him authority over all creatures—all things, living and not living,
    which the Son has created. Hence, at the Last Judgment, the Son will judge all humans.
    The Father has also delegated to the Son his, the Father's, authority over the angels.
    This was the cause of Satan's rebellion and the war in Heaven. After the Last Judgment,
    the Son will willingly relinquish his authority and be "subject unto him [i.e., the Father]
    that put all things under him [i.e., the Son]" (1 Corinthians 15:28). See 3.339–41.
739. Mark 9:48: Hell, "where their worm dieth not."

Then shall thy saints unmixed and from th' impure
Far separate, circling thy Holy Mount,
Unfeignèd hallelujahs to Thee sing,
Hymns of high praise, and I among them chief."   745
    So said, He o'er his scepter bowing rose
From the right hand of glory where He sat
And the third sacred morn began to shine,
Dawning through Heav'n. Forth rushed with whirlwind sound
The Chariot of Paternal Deity   750
Flashing thick flames, wheel within wheel undrawn,
Itself instínct with spirit but convoyed
By four cherubic shapes. Four faces each
Had wondrous. As with stars their bodies all
And wings were set with eyes, with eyes the wheels   755
Of beryl and careering fires between;
Over their heads a crystal firmament
Whereon a sapphire throne inlaid with pure
Amber and colors of the show'ry arch.
    He in celestial panoply all armed   760
Of radiant Urim, work divinely wrought,
Ascended. At his right hand Victory
Sat eagle-winged, beside Him hung his bow
And quiver with three-bolted thunder stored
And from about Him fierce effusion rolled   765
Of smoke and bickering flame and sparkles dire.
Attended with ten thousand thousand saints
He onward came. Far off his coming shone
And twenty thousand (I their number heard)
Chariots of God half on each hand were seen.   770
He on the wings of cherub rode sublime
On the crystálline sky in sapphire throned,
Illustrious far and wide but by his own
First seen. Them unexpected joy surprised

---

742. *saints*: literally, "sanctified ones," all the conscious beings in heaven who are not God, or the Son, or the Holy Ghost: the faithful angels and all humans who have been saved.
749–59. The description of the chariot is based on the visions in Ezekiel 1 and 10. "And when I looked, behold the four wheels by the cherubims, one wheel by one cherub, and another wheel by another cherub: and the appearance of the wheels was as the colour of a beryl stone. And as for their appearances, they four had one likeness, as if a wheel had been in the midst of a wheel" (Ezekiel 10:9–10).
751. *undrawn*: not pulled by horses but powered from within by *spirit* (line 752).
752. *instínct*: standing within. *convoyed*: accompanied.
762–66. After the biblical imagery of the chariot, Milton adds to his depiction of the Son the imagery of the classical Jove, attended by the eagle and armed with thunderbolts.
769. *I*: Raphael, a reminder that what we see is being related by the angel to Adam.
773. *his own*: the faithful angels.

When the great ensign of Messiah blazed   775
Aloft by angels borne, his sign in Heav'n,
Under whose conduct Michael soon reduced
His army circumfused on either wing
Under their Head embodied all in one.
Before Him pow'r divine his way prepared.   780
At his command th' uprooted hills retired
Each to his place: they heard his voice and went
Obsequious. Heav'n his wonted face renewed
And with fresh flow'rets hill and valley smiled.
This saw his hapless foes but stood obdured   785
And to rebellious fight rallied their powers
Insensate, hope conceiving from despair:
In Heav'nly spirits could such perverseness dwell?
But to convince the proud what signs avail
Or wonders move th' obdúrate to relent?   790
They, hardened more by what might most reclaim,
Grieving to see his glory, at the sight
Took envy and aspiring to his heighth
Stood re-embattled fierce by force or fraud
Weening to prosper and at length prevail   795
Against God and Messiah or to fall
In universal ruin last. And now
To final battle drew, disdaining flight
Or faint retreat, when the great Son of God
To all his host on either hand thus spake: 800
    "Stand still in bright array, ye saints, here stand
Ye angels armed, this day from battle rest!
Faithful hath been your warfare and of God
Accepted, fearless in his righteous cause,
And as ye have received so have ye done   805
Invincibly. But of this cursèd crew
The punishment to other hand belongs.
Vengeance is his or whose He sole appoints.
Number to this day's work is not ordained
Nor multitude: stand only and behold   810

---

777. *reduced*: led back.
778–79. *circumfused*: joined together in a great circle so that the army is now like one
    body, with the Son, like a head, at its center and above the mass.
785. *obdured*: hardened.
788. A famous epic phrase, derived from Virgil, *Aeneid*: 1.11: "in heavenly beings [gods]
    can so much anger dwell?" See 9.729–30 and n.
791. *what might most reclaim*: the Son, submission to whom is their only chance of being
    restored from sin to faithfulness.
794. *re-embattled*: returned to their ranks.
795. *Weening*: imagining, hoping.
808. *Vengeance*: "Vengeance is mine" (Romans 12:19; Deuteronomy 32:35; Psalm 94:1).

God's indignation on these godless poured
By Me! Not you but Me they have despised,
Yet envied. Against Me is all their rage
Because the Father, t' whom in Heav'n supreme
Kingdom and pow'r and glory appertains,   815
Hath honored Me according to his will.
Therefore to Me their doom He hath assigned
That they may have their wish to try with Me
In battle which the stronger proves, they all
Or I alone against them, since by strength   820
They measure all, of other excellence
Not emulous, nor care who them excels—
Nor other strife with them do I vouchsafe."
     So spake the Son and into terror changed
His count'nance too severe to be beheld   825
And full of wrath bent on his enemies.
At once the four spread out their starry wings
With dreadful shade contiguous and the orbs
Of his fierce chariot rolled as with the sound
Of torrent floods or of a num'rous host.   830
He on his impious foes right onward drove
Gloomy as night. Under his burning wheels
The steadfast empyréan shook throughout
All but the throne itself of God. Full soon
Among them He arrived, in his right hand   835
Grasping ten thousand thunders which He sent
Before Him such as in their souls infixed
Plagues. They, astonished, all resistance lost,
All courage: down their idle weapons dropped.
O'er shields and helms and helmèd heads He rode   840
Of thrones and mighty seraphim prostrate
That wished the mountains now might be again
Thrown on them as a shelter from his ire.
Nor less on either side tempestuous fell
His arrows from the fourfold-visaged four   845
Distinct with eyes and from the living wheels
Distinct alike with multitude of eyes.

818–23. I.e., Since the rebel angels value only physical power and care nothing for other
  (and higher) forms of excellence, such as wisdom, they shall have what they desire: a
  physical contest of power with me. Nor would I allow them to strive with me in any
  other way (such as in debate).
827. *four*: cherubim.
832. *Gloomy as night* captures νυκτὶ ἐοικώς, "like night" (*Iliad* 1.47), describing Apollo's
  angry descent from Olympus.
833. *steadfast empyréan*: the solid foundation of heaven, as opposed to the fiery region of
  the upper air.

One spirit in them ruled and every eye
Glared lightning and shot forth pernicious fire
Among th' accurst that withered all their strength   850
And of their wonted vigor left them drained,
Exhausted, spiritless, afflicted, fallen.
Yet half his strength he put not forth but checked
His thunder in mid volley for He meant
Not to destroy but root them out of Heaven.   855
The overthrown He raised and as a herd
Of goats or timorous flock together thronged
Drove them before him thunderstruck, pursued
With terrors and with furies to the bounds
And crystal wall of Heaven which op'ning wide   860
Rolled inward and a spacious gap disclosed
Into the wasteful deep. The monstrous sight
Strook them with horror backward but far worse
Urged them behind: headlong themselves they threw
Down from the verge of Heaven. Eternal wrath   865
Burnt after them to the bottomless pit.
     Hell heard th' unsufferable noise. Hell saw
Heav'n ruining from Heaven and would have fled
Affrighted but strict Fate had cast too deep
Her dark foundations and too fast had bound.   870
Nine days they fell. Confounded, Chaos roared
And felt tenfold confusion in their fall
Through his wild anarchy, so huge a rout
Encumbered him with ruin. Hell at last
Yawning received them whole and on them closed,   875
Hell their fit habitation fraught with fire
Unquenchable, the house of woe and pain.
Disburdened, Heav'n rejoiced and soon repaired
Her mural breach returning whence it rolled.
Sole Victor, from th' expulsion of his foes   880
Messiah his triumphal chariot turned.
To meet Him all his saints who silent stood
Eye witnesses of his almighty acts
With jubilee advancèd as they went
Shaded with branching palm. Each order bright   885
Sung triumph and Him sung Victorious King,
Son, Heir and Lord, to him dominion given,

852. *afflicted*: cast down.
873–74. *his* and *him*: Chaos.
879. *mural breach*: hole in the wall. Part of the wall rolled out; now that part rolls back.
884. *jubilee*: a song calling for rejoicing.
885. *palm*: The procession is meant to recall Christ's entry into Jerusalem.

Worthiest to reign. He, celebrated, rode
Triumphant through mid Heav'n into the courts
And temple of his mighty Father throned   890
On high who into glory Him received
Where now He sits at the right hand of bliss.
   Thus measuring things in Heav'n by things on Earth,
At thy request, and that thou may'st beware
By what is past to thee I have revealed   895
What might have else to human race been hid:
The discord which befell and war in Heav'n
Among th' angelic pow'rs and the deep fall
Of those too high aspiring who rebelled
With Satan, he who envies now thy state,   900
Who now is plotting how he may seduce
Thee also from obedience, that with him
Bereaved of happiness thou may'st partake
His punishment, eternal misery,
Which would be all his solace and revenge   905
As a despite done against the Most High,
Thee once to gain companion of his woe.
But listen not to his temptations! Warn
Thy weaker! Let it profit thee t' have heard
By terrible example the reward   910
Of disobedience! Firm they might have stood,
Yet fell. Remember, and fear to transgress!

Book Seven

The Argument

Raphael, at the request of Adam, relates how and wherefore this
world was first created: that God, after the expelling of Satan and
his angels out of Heaven, declared his pleasure to create another
world and other creatures to dwell therein; sends his Son with glory
and attendance of angels to perform the work of Creation in six
days; the angels celebrate with hymns the performance thereof,
and His reascension into Heaven.

---

892. *He:* the Son.
900–912. *envies now . . . now is plotting . . . fear to transgress:* Note the shift in these lines
    to the present tense, for urgency. Raphael returns to his commission, which is to warn
    Adam of imminent danger from his enemy; to explain the enemy's motive for seeking
    to destroy them (and in them the human race); to suggest that Eve, as the "weaker ves-
    sel" (1 Peter 3:7), is the likelier first target of the assault; to remind Adam that the
    story of the war in Heaven is to give a *terrible example* (line 910); and also to remind
    Adam that the rebel angels were free and *might have stood, / Yet fell* (lines 911–12).
911. *they:* the rebel angels.

Descend from Heav'n, Urania, by that name
If rightly thou art called, whose voice divine
Following above th' Olympian hill I soar,
Above the flight of Pegaséan wing.
The meaning not the name I call for thou   5
Nor of the Muses nine nor on the top
Of old Olympus dwell'st but Heav'nly born.
Before the hills appeared or fountain flowed
Thou with eternal Wisdom didst converse,
Wisdom thy sister, and with her didst play   10
In presence of th' Almighty Father, pleased
With thy celestial song. Up led by thee
Into the Heav'n of Heav'ns I have presumed
An earthly guest and drawn empyreal air,
Thy temp'ring. With like safety guided down   15
Return me to my native element
Lest from this flying steed unreined (as once
Bellerophon, though from a lower clime)
Dismounted on th' Aleian field I fall
Erroneous there to wander and forlorn.   20
Half yet remains unsung but narrower bound
Within the visible diurnal sphere:
Standing on earth, not rapt above the pole

Book Seven

1. Changing the name of the muse from Calliope to Urania, the opening half verse
    translates Horace's invocation in *Odes* 3.4.1–2: *Descende caelo . . . Calliope*. The
    theme of Horace's ode, the power of wisdom and learning in subduing violence, is
    also Milton's theme.

1–7. *Urania*: the Christian muse and muse of astronomy; Mount *Olympus*, the home of
    the gods; *Pegaséan wing*, alluding to the winged horse Pegasus, commonly associated
    with poetry; and the classical *Muses*, see Glossary. Because *Urania* is of the sky (*oura-
    nos*), she is higher than the classical muses, which are associated with things beneath
    the sky: *hills*, such as Olympus and Parnassus, and *fountain[s]* (line 8), such as Hip-
    pocrene, the "horse spring," on Mount Helicon. Hippocrene was opened by a strike
    from Pegasus's hoof.

8–10. *Urania* is not only higher than the classical Muses but older, too. She existed before
    the world was created, playing with her sister, eternal Wisdom. In the Bible, Wisdom
    says, "Before the mountains were settled, before the hills was I brought forth. . . .
    When he prepared the heavens, I was there: when he set a compass upon the face of
    the depth . . . I was daily his delight, rejoicing always before him" (Proverbs 8:25–30).
    For the compasses, see lines 225–27.

14–15. The poet has breathed the fiery element of the empyrean (*aether*, from a Greek root
    meaning to burn), which has been cooled, or tempered for him by the muse. The Latin
    empyrius, "of the highest heavens," is frequently used by Augustine and later Christian
    writers, a loan word from Greek, ἐμπύριος, "fiery," or "in fire," πύρ (*OED*). See line 73.

15–20. Resuming the Pegasus reference of line 4, the poet's flight beyond the confines of
    the world is now seen as a dangerous undertaking unless guided by the heavenly
    muse. When Bellerophon presumed to ride Pegasus up Mount Olympus and join the
    gods, Zeus sent a gadfly to sting the flying horse, which threw its rider. Bellerophon
    fell to earth on the *Aleian* (line 19) plain, where he went eating his heart out and
    shunning human pathways (*Iliad* 6.200–3).

22. *visible diurnal sphere*: the sphere of the heavens that is visible from earth.

23. *rapt*: caught up. *pole*: the pole of the universe, not of the earth.

More safe I sing with mortal voice unchanged
To hoarse or mute though fall'n on evil days,   25
On evil days though fall'n and evil tongues,
In darkness and with dangers compassed round
And solitude. Yet not alone while thou
Visit'st my slumbers nightly or when morn
Purples the east. Still govern thou my song,   30
Urania, and fit audience find, though few!
But drive far off the barbarous dissonance
Of Bacchus and his revelers, the race
Of that wild rout that tore the Thracian bard
In Rhodopè where woods and rocks had ears   35
To rapture till the savage clamor drowned
Both harp and voice, nor could the Muse defend
Her son. So fail not thou who thee implores,
For thou art Heav'nly, she an empty dream.
    Say, Goddess, what ensued when Raphaël   40
The affable archangel had forewarned
Adam by dire example to beware
Apostasy by what befell in Heaven
To those apostates lest the like befall
In Paradise to Adam or his race,   45
Charged not to touch the interdicted tree
If they transgress and slight that sole command
So easily obeyed amid the choice
Of all tastes else to please their appetite,
Though wand'ring. He with his consorted Eve   50
The story heard attentive and was filled
With admiration and deep muse to hear
Of things so high and strange, things to their thought
So unimaginable as hate in Heav'n
And war so near the peace of God in bliss   55
With such confusion. But the evil soon
Driv'n back redounded as a flood on those
From whom it sprung, impossible to mix

25–28. *evil days . . . evil tongues . . . darkness . . . solitude*: After the Restoration (the return of Charles II, which Milton publicly opposed) the blind poet spent a period of time in hiding and, later, several weeks in prison. After his release, his blindness rendered him vulnerable to assassination.
29. *nightly . . . morn*: New verses often came to Milton at night or in the early morning.
30. *govern*: guide, steer, as a ship (Greek *kubernaō*).
32–38. As in "Lycidas," Milton fears sharing the fate of Orpheus. Orpheus was torn to pieces by the bacchantes, Thracian worshippers of Bacchus (Dionysus).
39. *thou*: the heavenly muse. *she*: the muse of epic poetry, Calliope, the mother of Orpheus.
43. *Apostasy*: literally, "standing apart," but implying also betrayal.
50. *wand'ring*: seeking variety.

With blessedness, whence Adam soon repealed
The doubts that in his heart arose and now   60
Led on, yet sinless, with desire to know
What nearer might concern him: how this world
Of Heav'n and Earth conspicuous first began,
When and whereof created, for what cause,
What within Eden or without was done   65
Before his memory, as one whose drouth
Yet scarce allayed still eyes the current stream
Whose liquid murmur heard new thirst excites
Proceeded thus to ask his Heav'nly guest:
    Great things and full of wonder in our ears   70
Far differing from this world thou hast revealed,
Divine Interpreter, by favor sent
Down from the empyréan to forewarn
Us timely of what might else have been our loss,
Unknown, which human knowledge could not reach,   75
For which to th' Infinitely Good we owe
Immortal thanks and His admonishment
Receive with solemn purpose to observe
Immutably His sov'reign will, the end
Of what we are. But since thou hast vouchsafed   80
Gently for our instruction to impart
Things above earthly thought (which yet concerned
Our knowing, as to Highest Wisdom seemed)
Deign to descend now lower and relate
What may no less perhaps avail us known: 85
How first began this heav'n which we behold
Distant so high with moving fires adorned
Innumerable and this which yields or fills
All space, the ambient air wide interfused
Embracing round this florid earth? What cause   90
Moved the Creator in His holy rest

62–63. *world . . . conspicuous*: the visible world of the sky and the earth. *conspicuous*: seen together. See line 22 n.
66. *drouth*: thirst.
67. *current*: running.
69. *Proceeded*: The subject is *Adam*, line 59.
72. *Interpreter*: mediator, message bearer. Adam remembers that what Raphael tells him is accommodated to his human understanding. See 5.570–74 and n.
79. *end*: Greek *telos*, "ultimate purpose."
83. *as to Highest Wisdom seemed*: I.e., It seemed to God that it is not only instructive but necessary for us to know what we could not apprehend by our unaided intellectual powers (e.g., Satan's revolt).
88–89. The air *yields* to physical objects, which take up space within it, and the air *fills* the space between those objects.
89. *interfused*: Latin *interfusus*, "poured between."
90. *florid*: blooming.

Through all eternity so late to build
In chaos and, the work begun, how soon
Absolved? If unforbid thou may'st unfold
What we, not to explore the secrets ask   95
Of His eternal empire but the more
To magnify His works the more we know.
And the great light of day yet wants to run
Much of his race, though steep, suspense in heav'n
Held by thy voice: thy potent voice he hears   100
And longer will delay to hear thee tell
His generation and the rising birth
Of Nature from the unapparent deep.
Or if the star of evening and the Moon
Haste to thy audience Night with her will bring   105
Silence; and Sleep, list'ning to thee, will watch,
Or we can bid his absence till thy song
End and dismiss thee ere the morning shine.
   Thus Adam his illustrious guest besought
And thus the godlike angel answered mild: 110
This also thy request with caution asked
Obtain, though to recount almighty works
What words or tongue of seraph can suffice
Or heart of man suffice to comprehend?
Yet what thou canst attain which best may serve   115
To glorify the Maker and infer
Thee also happier shall not be withheld
Thy hearing, such commission from above
I have received to answer thy desire
Of knowledge within bounds. Beyond abstain   120
To ask nor let thine own inventions hope
Things not revealed which the invisible King
Only omniscient hath suppressed in night,
To none communicable in Earth or Heaven:
Enough is left besides to search and know.   125
But knowledge is as food and needs no less

94. Absolved: completed.
98–101. The sun has begun his *steep* descent from his noonday height but delays his
    course (*suspense in heav'n*) to hear Raphael speak.
103. *unapparent*: invisible. *deep*: chaos, abyss.
104. *star of evening*: Hesperus.
106. *watch*: remain awake.
107. *his*: Sleep's.
115. *attain*: understand.
116–17. *infer / Thee also happier*: lead you to conclude that you are happier than you now
    know.
121. *inventions*: speculations. *hope*, with the implied verb, "to grasp." I.e., neither ask to
    know nor hope to grasp by your own intellectual powers what God has hid.

Her temperance over appetite to know
In measure what the mind may well contain,
Oppresses else with surfeit and soon turns
Wisdom to folly as nourishment to wind.   130
　　Know then that after Lucifer from Heaven
(So call him, brighter once amidst the host
Of angels than that star the stars among)
Fell with his flaming legions through the deep
Into his place and the great Son returned   135
Victorious with His saints, th' Omnipotent
Eternal Father from His throne beheld
Their multitude and to his Son thus spake:
　　"At least our envious foe hath failed who thought
All like himself rebellious, by whose aid   140
This inaccessible high strength, the seat
Of Deity supreme, us dispossessed,
He trusted to have seized and into fraud
Drew many whom their place knows here no more.
Yet far the greater part have kept, I see,   145
Their station. Heav'n yet populous retains
Number sufficient to possess her realms,
Though wide, and this high temple to frequént
With ministéries due and solemn rites.
But lest his heart exalt him in the harm   150
Already done to have dispeopled Heaven
(My damage fondly deemed) I can repair
That detriment (if such it be to lose
Self-lost) and in a moment will create

129–30. As eating too much results in flatulence, so knowing too much results in folly. The subject of *Oppresses* is *knowledge* (line 126).

131. *Lucifer*: "light bearer"; the name of Satan before his fall. "How art thou fallen from heaven, O Lucifer, son of the morning!" (Isaiah 14:12). See 5.708 and 5.658 n.

132–33. I.e., You may call him *Lucifer*. He shone even more brightly in comparison to the other angels than does the evening star among the other stars.

136. *saints*: "sacred ones," the angels in Heaven. (Human saints are so called because they are deemed to be among the angels in Heaven.)

139. *At least*: An ironical understatement: at the very least, Satan failed in his plan to rule Heaven. But Satan's failure was much greater than that, as he was expelled from Heaven into Hell.

142. *us dispossessed*: once we had been dispossessed (of heaven). God is saying (with continuing irony), 'as if dispossessing us were a foregone conclusion.'

148. *this high temple*. The place of the presence of God, where the angels worship Him.

150–61. A third of the angels joined Satan and fell. The remaining angels are sufficient in number to occupy Heaven. But lest Satan boast the contrary, God will create humans, who will eventually rise up to Heaven and replace the precise number of angels who fell. The earth will become more like Heaven, until the two places are united. See lines 188–90 and 5.493–500.

152. *fondly*: foolishly.

153–54. I.e., if the loss of those who have lost themselves can be counted a loss to me too, which it can't.

Another world, out of one man a race   155
Of men innumerable there to dwell,
Not here, till by degrees of merit raised
They open to themselves at length the way
Up hither, under long obedience tried,
And Earth be changed to Heav'n and Heav'n to Earth,   160
One Kingdom, joy and union without end.
Meanwhile inhabit lax, ye pow'rs of Heaven,
And Thou my Word, begotten Son, by Thee
This I perform: speak Thou and be it done!
My overshadowing Spirit and might with Thee   165
I send along: ride forth and bid the deep
Within appointed bounds be Heav'n and Earth!
Boundless the deep because I am who fill
Infinitude, nor vacuous the space
(Though I uncircumscribed Myself retire   170
And put not forth My goodness which is free
To act or not): necessity and chance
Approach not Me, and what I will is fate."
   So spake th' Almighty and to what He spake
His Word, the Filial Godhead, gave effect.   175
Immediate are the acts of God, more swift
Than time or motion but to human ears
Cannot without process of speech be told
(So told as earthly notion can receive).
Great triumph and rejoicing was in Heaven   180
When such was heard declared th' Almighty's will.

---

162. *inhabit lax*: spread out. (To fill the space formerly occupied by the angels who rebelled.)
163. The Creation now begins. It is performed by God's Son, who is also the *Word*, the power of command by which God brings his creatures into being (John 1:1–3). See 3.170 and n.
165. *Spirit*: God's creative power, which the poet invokes to his aid at the beginning of *Paradise Lost* (1.17 and n.). Milton means the power named in Genesis 1:2: "And the Spirit of God moved upon the face of the waters," which in orthodox Christian doctrine is the Holy Ghost, the third person of the trinity.
168–73. In the very beginning God is totality and fills, to infinity, all space. Space is therefore not empty (*vacuous*) but filled with the substance of God, his essential being. God withdraws from totality to the place of his presence in Heaven, *this high temple* (line 148), leaving a residue, which was formerly (but is no longer) God's substance. The residue is instead the substance of chaos, which is ruled by *necessity* (compulsion, force) and *chance*. God now confronts this chaos of substance and may (or may not) *put forth [his] goodness* by creating new beings and even giving them freedom. This *goodness* is manifested in the Son, who will now create the universe, all creatures in it, and human beings.
173. *fate*: Fate, which includes the laws of the universe and the more inscrutable laws governing human actions, is not prior to God's will but is the expression of God's will. Richard Hooker (*The Laws of Ecclesiastical Polity* 1.2.6) describes fate as "that order which God before all ages hath set down with himself, for himself to do all things by."
175. *His Word, the Filial Godhead*: the Son.
176–79. The Creation, which is now to be described, happened in an instant but will be told in a narrative so that it may be grasped by Adam's human mind.

Glory they sung to the Most High, good will
To future men and in their dwellings peace,
Glory to Him whose just avenging ire
Had driven out th' ungodly from His sight   185
And th' habitations of the just, to Him
Glory and praise whose wisdom had ordained
Good out of evil to create: instead
Of spirits malign a better race to bring
Into their vacant room and thence diffuse   190
His good to worlds and ages infinite.
So sang the hierarchies. Meanwhile the Son
On his great expedition now appeared
Girt with omnipotence, with radiance crowned
Of majesty divine, sapience and love   195
Immense, and all his Father in him shone.
About his chariot numberless were poured
Cherub and seraph, potentates and thrones,
And virtues, wingèd spirits, and chariots winged
From th' armory of God where stand of old   200
Myriads between two brazen mountains lodged
Against a solemn day, harnessed at hand,
Celestial equipage, and now came forth
Spontaneous (for within them Spirit lived)
Attendant on their Lord. Heav'n opened wide   205
Her ever-during gates, harmonious sound
On golden hinges moving, to let forth
The King of Glory in his powerful Word
And Spirit coming to create new worlds.
On Heav'nly ground they stood and from the shore   210
They viewed the vast immeasurable abyss
Outrageous as a sea, dark, wasteful, wild,
Up from the bottom turned by furious winds
And surging waves as mountains to assault
Heav'n's heighth and with the center mix the pole.   215
   "Silence, ye troubled waves and thou, deep, peace!"
Said then th' Omnific Word, "Your discord end!"
   Nor stayed but on the wings of cherubim
Uplifted in paternal glory rode

188–90. See lines 150–61 n.
203. *equipage*: chariots with horses. "Behold, there came four chariots out from between
    two mountains; and the mountains were mountains of brass" (Zechariah 6:1).
208. *King of Glory*: the Father. *Word*: the Son.
209. *Spirit*: creative power of God. See line 165 and n.
216. "And he arose, and rebuked the wind, and said unto the sea, Peace, be still. And the
    wind ceased, and there was a great calm" (Mark 4:39).
217. *Omnific*: all-making.

Far into chaos and the world unborn.   220
For chaos heard his voice. Him all his train
Followed in bright procession to behold
Creation and the wonders of his might.
Then stayed the fervid wheels and in his hand
He took the golden compasses prepared   225
In God's eternal store to circumscribe
This universe and all created things.
One foot He centered and the other turned
Round through the vast profundity obscure
And said, "Thus far extend, thus far thy bounds,   230
This be thy just circumference, O world!"
Thus God the heav'n created, thus the earth,
Matter unformed and void. Darkness profound
Covered th' abyss but on the wat'ry calm
His brooding wings the Spirit of God outspread   235
And vital virtue infused and vital warmth
Throughout the fluid mass but downward purged
The black tartareous cold infernal dregs
Adverse to life, then founded, then conglobed
Like things to like, the rest to several place   240
Disparted and between spun out the air,
And Earth self-balanced on her center hung.
     "Let there be light," said God, and forthwith light
Ethereal, first of things, quintessence pure,
Sprung from the deep and from her native east   245
To journey through the airy gloom began,
Sphered in a radiant cloud, for yet the sun
Was not: she in a cloudy tabernacle
Sojourned the while. God saw the light was good
And light from darkness by the hemisphere   250

221. *Him*: the Son, probably.
224. *fervid*: burning.
224–27. "He set a compass upon the face of the depth" (Proverbs 8:27). Famously, William
   Blake captures this scene in his frontispiece to *Europe*, "The Ancient of Days" (Daniel
   7:9). But Blake's old man with the compasses is Urizen, one of the four Zoas representing the aspects of God, the symbol of abstract reason setting a limit to creative energy:
   "He formed golden compasses / And began to explore the Abyss" (*The Book of Urizen*,
   chap. 7, 8; plate 20.8). Strikingly, Milton has the youthful Son perform this task.
224–550. The account of creation that follows is a vast imaginative amplification of the
   first two chapters of Genesis. See selections from the Bible, pp. 313–36.
225. See lines 7–12 n.
233. *Matter*: out of matter.
236. *virtue* and *infused* are elided: 'virch-infused.'
242. "He . . . hangeth the earth upon nothing" (Job 26:7): The earth is balanced around a
   vertical axis, as a standing person is balanced. But the earth is balanced laterally as
   well, so that it can be suspended in space without support from below. Milton still
   thinks of space as having an "up" and a "down."
248. *she*: the sun.

Divided: light the "day" and darkness "night"
He named. Thus was the first day, ev'n and morn.
Nor passed uncelebrated nor unsung
By the celestial choirs when orient light
Exhaling first from darkness they beheld,   255
Birthday of Heav'n and Earth. With joy and shout
The hollow universal orb they filled
And touched their golden harps and hymning praised
God and His works: "Creator" him they sung
Both when first evening was and when first morn.   260
    Again God said: "Let there be firmament
Amid the waters and let it divide
The waters from the waters." And God made
The firmament, expanse of liquid, pure,
Transparent, elemental air diffused   265
In circuit to the uttermost convéx
Of this great round, partition firm and sure,
The waters underneath from those above
Dividing. For as earth, so he the world
Built on circumfluous waters calm in wide   270
Crystálline ocean and the loud misrule
Of chaos far removed lest fierce extremes
Contiguous might distemper the whole frame.
And heav'n he named the "firmament." So ev'n
And morning chorus sung the second day.   275
    The Earth was formed but in the womb as yet
Of waters—embryon immature, involved—
Appeared not. Over all the face of Earth
Main ocean flowed not idle but with warm
Prolific humor, soft'ning all her globe,   280
Fermented the Great Mother to conceive,
Satiate with genial moisture, when God said,
"Be gathered now, ye waters under heav'n,
Into one place and let dry land appear!"
Immediately the mountains huge appear   285
Emergent and their broad bare backs upheave
Into the clouds, their tops ascend the sky.
So high as heaved the tumid hills, so low

263. *The waters from the waters*: the waters on the earth from the waters supposed to be
    above the sky, making the sky appear blue.
267. *great round*: the sphere of the universe, which is supposed to be filled with liquid air.
270–73. Just as the continents on the earth rest on the surrounding seas, so the universe
    (*world*) rests on liquid aether, which functions as a buffer between creation and chaos.
276–77. The earth, like a human embryo, was formed but still immature, and still sunk
    (*involved*) within the waters.
280. *Prolific humor*: life-giving liquid.

Down sunk a hollow bottom broad and deep,
Capacious bed of waters. Thither they   290
Hasted with glad precipitance, uprolled
As drops on dust conglobing from the dry.
Part rise in crystal wall or ridge direct
For haste, such flight the great command impressed
On the swift floods. As armies at the call   295
Of trumpet (for of armies thou hast heard)
Troop to their standard, so the wat'ry throng,
Wave rolling after wave, where way they found:
If steep, with torrent rapture, if through plain,
Soft ebbing. Nor withstood them rock or hill   300
But they or under ground or circuit wide
With serpent error wand'ring found their way
And on the washy ooze deep channels wore
Easy ere God had bid the ground be dry,
All but within those banks where rivers now   305
Stream, and perpetual draw their humid train.
The dry land, earth, and the great receptácle
Of congregated waters he called "seas"
And saw that it was good and said, "Let th' earth
Put forth the verdant grass, herb yielding seed   310
And fruit tree yielding fruit after her kind
Whose seed is in herself upon the earth!"
He scarce had said when the bare earth till then
Desert and bare, unsightly, unadorned,
Brought forth the tender grass whose verdure clad   315
Her universal face with pleasant green,
Then herbs of every leaf that sudden flow'red
Op'ning their various colors and made gay
Her bosom smelling sweet. And these scarce blown
Forth flourished thick the clust'ring vine, forth crept   320
The swelling gourd, up stood the corny reed
Embattled in her field and th' humble shrub
And bush with frizzled hair implicit. Last
Rose as in dance the stately trees and spread

---

290. *they*: the waters.
291. *precipitance*: rushing headlong.
292. The waters roll up into huge balls resembling water drops. These balls roll down into
the ocean beds and fill the oceans. "[The waters] go down by the valleys unto the
place which thou hast founded for them" (Psalm 104:8).
296. *thou hast heard*: one of the moments when the poet reminds us we are hearing a narrative spoken by Raphael to Adam. Adam first heard of armies when Raphael told
him of the war in heaven.
321. *swelling*: an early emendation of *smelling* (1667, 1674) by Richard Bentley. Some
scholars defend the aromatic gourd.

Their branches hung with copious fruit or gemmed   325
Their blossoms. With high woods the hills were crowned,
With tufts the valleys and each fountain side,
With borders long the rivers, that Earth now
Seemed like to Heav'n, a seat where gods might dwell
Or wander with delight and love to haunt   330
Her sacred shades, though God had not yet rained
Upon the earth and man to till the ground
None was, but from the earth a dewy mist
Went up and watered all the ground and each
Plant of the field which ere 't was in the earth   335
God made and every herb before it grew
On the green stem. God saw that it was good.
So ev'n and morn recorded the third day.
    Again th' Almighty spake: "Let there be lights
High in th' expanse of heaven to divide   340
The day from night and let them be for signs,
For seasons, and for days and circling years,
And let them be for lights as I ordain
Their office in the firmament of heaven
To give light on the earth!" And it was so.   345
And God made two great lights, great for their use
To Man, the greater to have rule by day,
The less by night altern, and made the stars
And set them in the firmament of heav'n
T' illuminate the earth and rule the day   350
In their vicissitude and rule the night
And light from darkness to divide. God saw,
Surveying his great work, that it was good.
For of celestial bodies first the sun
A mighty sphere he framed, unlightsome first   355
Though of ethereal mold, then formed the moon
Globose and every magnitude of stars
And sowed with stars the heav'n thick as a field.
Of light by far the greater part he took
Transplanted from her cloudy shrine and placed   360
In the sun's orb, made porous to receive

---

325. *gemmed*: budded.
331–34. See Genesis 2:5.
348. *altern*: The sun and moon rule day and night alternately.
355. *unlightsome*: not yet giving off light.
358. "All sowd with glistring stars more thicke than grasse" (Spenser, "An Hymne of Heavenly Beautie," line 53).
361–62. *porous . . . firm*: The sun is porous so that it can soak up light, which Milton conceives of as a liquid. Through these pores light will radiate out in controlled amounts. The sun is also firm so that all the light will not escape it at once.

And drink the liquid light, firm to retain
Her gathered beams, great palace now of light.
Hither as to their fountain other stars
Repairing in their golden urns draw light   365
And hence the morning planet gilds her horns.
By tincture or reflection they augment
Their small peculiar though from human sight
So far remote with diminution seen.
First in his east the glorious lamp was seen,   370
Regent of day and all th' horizon round
Invested with bright rays, jocund to run
His longitude through heav'n's high road. The grey
Dawn and the Pleiades before him danced
Shedding sweet influence. Less bright the moon   375
(But opposite in leveled west was set)
His mirror with full face borrowing her light
From him, for other light she needed none
In that aspéct and still that distance keeps
Till night. Then in the east her turn she shines   380
Revolved on heav'n's great axle and her reign
With thousand lesser lights dividual holds,
With thousand thousand stars that then appeared
Spangling the hemisphere. Then first adorned
With their bright luminaries that set and rose,   385
Glad Evening and glad Morn crowned the fourth day.
    And God said, "Let the waters generate
Reptile with spawn abundant, living soul,
And let fowl fly above the earth with wings
Displayed on th' open firmament of heav'n!"   390
And God created the great whales and each

364–66. The stars come to the palace of the sun to obtain light, just as the moon receives
    light from the sun. Galileo discovered that Venus, the *morning planet*, has moonlike
    phases, hence golden *horns*.
367–69. Each star has a little light of its own (its small portion, or *peculiar*). But each star
    increases this amount by borrowing light from the sun. This light is borrowed either
    by reflection, as with the moon, or by direct infusion (*tincture*).
370. *lamp*: the sun.
374–75. *Pleiades . . . sweet influence*: "Canst thou bind the sweet influence of Pleiades, or
    loose the bands of Orion?" (Job 38:31). See Glossary, PLEIADES.
376. *leveled west*: due west.
377. *His mirror* modifies *moon* (line 375): The moon is the sun's mirror because she reflects
    his light.
379. *In that aspéct*: from that angle.
381. *axle*: a reference to the great but invisible whorl to which all the celestial bodies are
    fixed and by which their movements are governed (Plato, *Republic* 10.616d–e).
382. *dividual*: shared, modifying *reign* (line 381).
384–86. When they crown the fourth day, evening and morning are adorned with stars
    and celestial bodies that rise and set.
388. *living soul*: principle of life in beings, whether reptiles and fish or humans, that move
    and make decisions.

Soul living, each that crept, which plenteously
The waters generated by their kinds,
And every bird of wing after his kind,
And saw that it was good and blessed them saying,   395
"Be fruitful, multiply, and in the seas
And lakes and running streams the waters fill!
And let the fowl be multiplied on th' earth!"
Forthwith the sounds and seas, each creek and bay,
With fry innumerable swarm and shoals   400
Of fish that with their fins and shining scales
Glide under the green wave in schools that oft
Bank the mid sea. Part single or with mate
Graze the seaweed their pasture and through groves
Of coral stray or sporting with quick glance   405
Show to the sun their waved coats dropped with gold
Or in their pearly shells at ease attend
Moist nutriment or under rocks their food
In jointed armor watch. On smooth, the seal
And bended dolphins play, part huge of bulk   410
Wallowing unwieldy, enormous in their gait,
Tempest the ocean. There Leviathan,
Hugest of living creatures, on the deep
Stretched like a promontory sleeps or swims
And seems a moving land and at his gills   415
Draws in and at his trunk spouts out a sea.
Meanwhile the tepid caves and fens and shores
Their brood as num'rous hatch from th' egg that soon
Bursting with kindly rupture forth disclosed
Their callow young, but feathered soon and fledge   420
They summed their pens and soaring th' air sublime
With clang despised the ground under a cloud
In prospect. There the eagle and the stork
On cliffs and cedar tops their eyries build.
Part loosely wing the region, part, more wise,   425

400. *fry*: hatchling fish.
406. *dropped*: flecked.
409. *jointed armor*: shellfish. *On smooth*: on the calm surface.
412. *Leviathan*: the whale.
417. *tepid*: moist.
419. *kindly*: natural.
420. *callow*: immature. *fledge*: able to fly.
421. *summed their pens*: Their pinions reached full growth.
422. *clang*: noise (Greek *klangē*, loud sharp sound, associated with the screeching of birds).
422–23. *despised*: looked down upon. *under a cloud*: The birds are above a cloud, looking down at the earth below it. Despite the cloud, the earth remains in view (*in prospect*).

In common ranged, in figure wedge their way
Intelligent of seasons and set forth
Their airy caravan, high over seas
Flying and over lands with mutual wing
Easing their flight. So steers the prudent crane   430
Her annual voyage, borne on winds. The air
Floats as they pass, fanned with unnumbered plumes.
From branch to branch the smaller birds with song
Solaced the woods and spread their painted wings
Till ev'n, nor then the solemn nightingale   435
Ceased warbling but all night tuned her soft lays.
Others on silver lakes and rivers bathed
Their downy breast: the swan with archèd neck
Between her white wings mantling proudly rows
Her state with oary feet. Yet oft they quit   440
The dank, and rising on still pennons tow'r
The mid aerïal sky. Others on ground
Walked firm: the crested cock whose clarion sounds
The silent hours and th' other whose gay train
Adorns him colored with the florid hue   445
Of rainbows and starry eyes. The waters thus
With fish replenished and the air with fowl,
Evening and Morn solémnized the fifth day.
    The sixth and of Creation last arose
With evening harps and matin when God said,   450
"Let th' Earth bring forth soul living in her kind,
Cattle and creeping things and beast of th' earth
Each in their kind. The Earth obeyed and straight,
Op'ning her fertile womb, teemed at a birth
Innumerous living creatures, perfect forms,   455
Limbed and full-grown. Out of the ground uprose
As from his lair the wild beast where he wons
In forest wild, in thicket, brake or den.
Among the trees in pairs they rose, they walked,
The cattle in the fields and meadows green,   460
Those rare and solitary, these in flocks
Pasturing at once and in broad herds upsprung.
The grassy clods now calved, now half appeared

---

426. They travel in flocks and in wedge formations.
429. *mutual wing*: flying together and beating the air in time with one another.
441. *dank*: water. *pennons*: wings, pinions.
450. *matin*: morning song of angels.
451. *soul*: 1667 *Fowle*; 1674 *Foul*. See line 388 and n.
457. *wons*: dwells.

The tawny lion pawing to get free
His hinder parts, then springs as broke from bonds   465
And rampant shakes his brinded mane. The ounce,
The libbard and the tiger, as the mole
Rising, the crumbled earth above them threw
In hillocks. The swift stag from under ground
Bore up his branching head. Scarce from his mold   470
Behemoth, biggest born of earth, upheaved
His vastness. Fleeced the flocks and bleating rose,
As plants. Ambiguous between sea and land
The river horse and scaly crocodile.
At once came forth whatever creeps the ground,   475
Insect or worm. Those waved their limber fans
For wings and smallest lineaments exact
In all the liveries decked of summer's pride
With spots of gold and purple, azure and green.
These as a line their long dimension drew   480
Streaking the ground with sinuous trace. Not all
Minims of nature: some of serpent kind
Wondrous in length and corpulence involved
Their snaky folds and added wings. First crept
The parsimonious emmet, provident   485
Of future, in small room large heart enclosed,
Pattern of just equality perhaps
Hereafter, joined in her popular tribes
Of commonalty. Swarming next appeared
The female bee that feeds her husband drone   490
Deliciously and builds her waxen cells
With honey stored. The rest are numberless
And thou their natures know'st and gav'st them names,
Needless to thee repeated. Nor unknown
The serpent, subtlest beast of all the field,   495

---

466. *rampant*: a heraldic term meaning "erect," "on hind legs." *brinded*: brown, or tawny, with stripes, as if from burning. See 4.344 n.
467. *libbard*: leopard.
471. *Behemoth*: an imaginary biblical land beast. "Behold now behemoth, which I made with thee; . . . his strength is in his loins, and his force is in the navel of his belly. He moveth his tail like a cedar: the sinews of his stones are wrapped together . . . his bones are like bars of iron. He is the chief of the ways of God" (Job 40:15–19).
473. *Ambiguous*: It is unclear whether these beasts are sea or land creatures, since they inhabit both.
474. *river horse*: a literal translation of the Greek word *hippopotamus*.
476. *Those*: the insects.
480. *These*: the worms.
481–82. Not all the worms were minute creatures (*minims*). Some were big snakes.
485. *emmet*: ant.
495. The last of the animals mentioned by Raphael is the serpent. The serpent is *subtle* (intelligent) but not harmful (*noxious*), despite its brassy eyes and its frightening (*terrific*) hairy mane. See *Aeneid* 2.206–7.

Of huge extent sometimes with brazen eyes
And hairy mane terrific though to thee
Not noxious but obedient at thy call.
   Now Heav'n in all her glory shone and rolled
Her motions as the great First Mover's hand   500
First wheeled their course. Earth in her rich attire
Consúmmate lovely smiled. Air, water, earth,
By fowl, fish, beast, was flown, was swum, was walked
Frequent. And of the sixth day yet remained
There wanted yet the master work, the end   505
Of all yet done: a creature who not prone
And brute as other creatures but endued
With sanctity of reason might erect
His stature and, upright with front serene,
Govern the rest, self-knowing, and from thence   510
Magnanimous to correspond with Heaven,
But grateful to acknowledge whence his good
Descends; thither with heart and voice and eyes
Directed in devotion to adore
And worship God supreme who made him chief   515
Of all His works. Therefore th' Omnipotent
Eternal Father (for where is not He
Present?) thus to his Son audibly spake:
   "Let us now make Man in our image, Man
In our similitude, and let them rule   520
Over the fish and fowl of sea and air,
Beast of the field and over all the earth
And every creeping thing that creeps the ground."
This said, He formed thee, Adam, thee O Man,
Dust of the ground, and in thy nostrils breathed   525
The breath of life. In His own image He
Created thee, in the image of God
Express, and thou becam'st a living soul.
Male He created thee but thy consort
Female for race, then blessed mankind and said,   530

504–5. *yet remained . . . wanted yet*: In the time remaining on the sixth day, the creation
    of the *master work*, humans, remained to be done.
508. The subject of *erect* is *creature* (line 506), i.e., Man.
509. *front*: forehead.
511. *Magnanimous*: of great and noble mind. *correspond*: to be in regular communication
    with, and eventually to be like.
512. *grateful* modifies *creature*.
516–19. Although in Book Seven generally it is the Son who performs the Creation while
    the Father remains in Heaven (see lines 163–67), Milton here makes the Father pres-
    ent, on the scene of Creation, at the crucial moment when Man is created. Doing so
    allows Milton to be more faithful to the literal text of Genesis, in which God alone
    creates the world and humanity. See 8.403 n.
528. *Express*: represented.

"Be fruitful, multiply, and fill the earth,
Subdue it and throughout dominion hold
Over fish of the sea and fowl of the air
And every living thing that moves on the earth!"
Wherever thus created, for no place   535
Is yet distinct by name, thence as thou know'st
He brought thee into this delicious grove,
This garden planted with the trees of God
Delectable both to behold and taste,
And freely all their pleasant fruit for food   540
Gave thee. All sorts are here that all th' earth yields,
Variety without end, but of the tree
Which tasted works knowledge of good and evil
Thou may'st not. In the day thou eat'st, thou diest:
Death is the penalty imposed. Beware!   545
And govern well thy appetite lest Sin
Surprise thee and her black attendant Death.
    Here finished He and all that he had made
Viewed and, behold! all was entirely good.
So ev'n and morn accomplished the sixth day,   550
Yet not till the Creator from his work
Desisting, though unwearied, up returned,
Up to the Heav'n of Heav'ns his high abode
Thence to behold this new created world,
Th' addition of his empire, how it showed   555
In prospect from his throne, how good, how fair,
Answering his great idea. Up He rode
Followed with acclamation and the sound
Symphonious of ten thousand harps that tuned
Angelic harmonies. The earth, the air   560
Resounded (thou remember'st, for thou heard'st),
The heav'ns and all the constellations rung,
The planets in their station list'ning stood
While the bright pomp ascended jubilant.

535–37. Adam is not made in the garden, Paradise, but somewhere else on the earth.
After Adam is made, he is transported to the garden. See 8.300–6. Milton follows
the second creation account in Genesis, where only after God has created Man does
God plant the garden and place Man in it: "And the Lord God planted a garden eastward in Eden; and there he put the man whom he had formed" (2:8).
556. *In prospect*: in view. Cf. line 423.
557. *idea*: a thing that is seen before the mind's eye, the Platonic form. This is the only
occurrence of the word in Milton's English poetry. (He did write a Latin poem called
"On the Platonic Idea as Aristotle Understood It.") Milton uses the term here in a very
un-Platonic sense: the created world, far from being a poor copy of the realm of ideas,
is a perfect material realization of the mental plan the Son formed beforehand. And
the created world is more excellent than the plan. For historical background, see
Erwin Panofsky, *Idea: A Concept in Art Theory*, trans. Joseph J. S. Peake (1968).

"Open, ye everlasting gates!" they sung,   565
"Open, ye Heaven, your living doors! Let in
The great Creator from his work returned
Magnificent, his six days' work, a world!
Open, and henceforth oft! For God will deign
To visit oft the dwellings of just men   570
Delighted and with frequent intercourse
Thither will send his wingèd messengers
On errands of supernal grace." So sung
The glorious train ascending. He through Heav'n
That opened wide her blazing portals led   575
To God's eternal house direct the way,
A broad and ample road whose dust is gold
And pavement stars, as stars to thee appear
Seen in the galaxy, that Milky Way
Which nightly as a circling zone thou seest   580
Powdered with stars. And now on earth the seventh
Evening arose in Eden for the sun
Was set and twilight from the east came on
Forerunning night when at the holy mount
Of Heav'n's high-seated top, th' imperial throne   585
Of Godhead fixed for ever firm and sure,
The Filial Pow'r arrived and sat Him down
With his great Father (for He also went
Invisible, yet stayed—such privilege
Hath omnipresence—and the work ordained,   590
Author and end of all things) and from work
Now resting, blessed and hallowed the seventh day,
As resting on that day from all his work.
But not in silence holy kept: the harp
Had work and rested not, the solemn pipe,   595
And dulcimer, all organs of sweet stop,
All sounds on fret by string or golden wire
Tempered soft tunings intermixed with voice

---

565. *they*: the angels. The angels sing; the constellations resonate to the song, like instruments; and the planets stop to listen.

565–67. "Lift up your heads, O ye gates; and be ye lift up, ye everlasting doors; and the King of glory shall come in" (Psalm 24:7).

571. *intercourse*: going (running) back and forth (Latin *intercursus*). The word suggests mutual visiting between heaven and earth but also the eventual sharing of natures, a blending of the human and divine.

578–81. The Milky Way we see in the night sky is like the road of stars on which the Son returns to Heaven.

580. *zone*: belt.

588. See lines 516–19 n.

594–95. *the harp / Had work and rested not*: The Sabbath in Heaven is a day of rest, but the angels make music, for making music is not work, although their instruments do work. (With humorous intent.)

Choral or unison. Of incense clouds
Fuming from golden censers hid the Mount.   600
Creation and the six days' acts they sung:
   "Great are thy works, Jehovah, infinite
Thy pow'r! What thought can measure Thee or tongue
Relate Thee, greater now in thy return
Than from the giant angels? Thee that day   605
Thy thunders magnified; but to create
Is greater than created to destroy.
Who can impair Thee, Mighty King, or bound
Thy empire? Easily the proud attempt
Of spirits apostate and their counsels vain   610
Thou hast repelled while impiously they thought
Thee to diminish and from Thee withdraw
The number of thy worshippers. Who seeks
To lessen Thee against his purpose serves
To manifest the more thy might, his evil   615
Thou usest and from thence creat'st more good.
Witness this new-made world, another Heaven
From Heaven gate not far, founded in view
On the clear hyaline, the glassy sea
Of amplitude almost immense, with stars   620
Numerous and every star perhaps a world
Of destined habitation. But Thou know'st
Their seasons. Among these the seat of men,
Earth, with her nether ocean circumfused,
Their pleasant dwelling place. Thrice happy men   625
And sons of men whom God hath thus advanced,
Created in His image there to dwell
And worship Him and in reward to rule
Over his works on earth, in sea, or air,
And multiply a race of worshippers   630
Holy and just! Thrice happy if they know
Their happiness and persevere upright!"
   So sung they and the empyréan rung

600. *censers*: holders for burning incense.
605. *giant angels*: rebel angels, with an allusion to the giants of classical myth who warred against the Olympians. See 1.573–87 and n.
606. *magnified*: praised. On the day the Son defeated the rebel angels, his own thunderbolts spoke his, the Son's, praise. But on this day our song praises him.
608. *impair*: diminish.
613. *Who*: whoever.
619. *hyaline*: the cosmic sea of liquid air, the waters above the firmament. Cf. *crystalline ocean*, line 271 and n., and line 624 and n. Greek *hyalinos*, "made of glass"; Latin *hyalus*, "glass." Glass in antiquity was green; hence the use of this word for the sea when calm.
624. *nether ocean*: lower terrestrial ocean, as distinct from the "upper" ocean of the waters above the firmament.

With hallelujahs. Thus was Sabbath kept.
And thy request think now fulfilled that asked   635
How first this world and face of things began
And what before thy memory was done
From the beginning, that posterity
Informed by thee might know. If else thou seek'st
Aught not surpassing human measure, say.   640

Book Eight

The Argument

Adam inquires concerning celestial motions, is doubtfully answered
and exhorted to search rather things more worthy of knowledge.
Adam assents and, still desirous to detain Raphael, relates to him
what he remembered since his own creation, his placing in Paradise, his talk with God concerning solitude and fit society, his first
meeting and nuptials with Eve, his discourse with the angel thereupon who, after admonitions repeated, departs.

The angel ended and in Adam's ear
So charming left his voice that he a while
Thought him still speaking, still stood fixed to hear,
Then as new waked thus gratefully replied:
What thanks sufficient or what recompense   5
Equal have I to render thee, divine
Historian, who thus largely hast allayed
The thirst I had of knowledge and vouchsafed
This friendly condescension to relate
Things else by me unsearchable, now heard   10
With wonder, but delight, and, as is due,
With glory attribúted to the High
Creator. Something yet of doubt remains

Book Eight
2. *charming*: spellbinding. *he*: Adam.
3. *him*: Raphael.
13–38. The question Adam now puts to Raphael implies a *doubt* (line 13) of the effi-
    ciency of divine creation. Why should the heavenly bodies be compelled to circle
    the earth, at vast distances and unimaginable speeds, merely to bring light to this
    one tiny spot? Would it not be more *frugal* (line 26) and less *superfluous* (line 27) for
    the earth to move instead? Eve has already raised this doubt (4.657–58), asking why
    the stars shine at night when there is no one to see them, since she and Adam are
    asleep. But perhaps God has created the universe on such a vast scale to teach
    mankind humility: "That Man may know he dwells not in his own, / An edifice too
    large for him to fill" (lines 103–4). This, of course, would mean the universe was
    created for mankind after all, but as a lesson in human limits rather than as a thing
    for human use.

Which only thy solution can resolve:
When I behold this goodly frame, this world   15
Of heav'n and earth consisting and compute
Their magnitudes, this earth a spot, a grain,
An atom with the firmament compared
And all her numbered stars that seem to roll
Spaces incomprehensible (for such   20
Their distance argues and their swift return
Diurnal) merely to officiate light
Round this opacous earth, this punctual spot
One day and night, in all their vast survéy
Useless besides, reasoning I oft admire   25
How Nature wise and frugal could commit
Such disproportions with superfluous hand:
So many nobler bodies to create
Greater so manifold to this one use
(For aught appears) and on their orbs impose   30
Such restless revolution day by day
Repeated while the sedentary earth
(That better might with far less compass move,
Served by more noble than herself) attains
Her end without least motion and receives   35
As tribute (such a sumless journey brought
Of incorporeal speed) her warmth and light—
Speed to describe whose swiftness number fails!
    So spake our sire and by his count'nance seemed
Ent'ring on studious thoughts abstruse, which Eve   40
Perceiving where she sat retired in sight
With lowliness majestic from her seat
And grace that won who saw to wish her stay,
Rose and went forth among her fruits and flow'rs
To visit how they prospered, bud and bloom,   45
Her nursery. They at her coming sprung
And touched by her fair tendance gladlier grew.
Yet went she not as not with such discourse
Delighted or not capable her ear
Of what was high. Such pleasure she reserved,   50
Adam relating, she sole auditress:

15. *goodly frame*: cf. Spenser, *Faerie Queene* 2.12.1: "Now gins this goodly frame of Temperance / Fairly to rise." *frame*: constructed thing. *world*: universe.
19. *her*: the firmament's.
23. *opacous*: opaque, not a source of direct light.
24. *vast survéy*: nonearthly regions over which the stars look.
28. *nobler*: than the earth.
29. *Greater so manifold*: capable of so much more. *this one use*: to serve the earth.
36. *sumless*: incalculable.
37. *incorporeal speed*: speed greater than would seem possible to bodies with mass.
44–47. Compare 9.427–31 and 11.273–79.

Her husband the relater she preferred
Before the angel and of him to ask
Chose rather. He, she knew, would intermix
Grateful digressions and solve high dispute 55
With conjugal caresses (from his lip
Not words alone pleased her). O when meet now
Such pairs in love and mutual honor joined?
With goddess-like demeanor forth she went,
Not unattended for on her as queen 60
A pomp of winning graces waited still
And from about her shot darts of desire
Into all eyes to wish her still in sight.
And Raphael now to Adam's doubt proposed
Benevolent and facile thus replied: 65
    To ask or search I blame thee not for heav'n
Is as the book of God before thee set
Wherein to read his wondrous works and learn
His seasons, hours or days or months or years.
This to attain, whether heav'n move or earth, 70
Imports not if thou reckon right. The rest
From man or angel the Great Architect
Did wisely to conceal and not divulge
His secrets to be scanned by them who ought
Rather admire. Or if they list to try 75
Conjecture He his fabric of the heav'ns
Hath left to their disputes perhaps to move
His laughter at their quaint opinions wide
Hereafter when they come to model heav'n
And calculate the stars, how they will wield 80
The mighty frame, how build, unbuild, contrive
To save appearances, how gird the sphere
With centric and eccentric scribbled o'er

---

61. *pomp*: formal procession. In classical mythology the *graces*, daughters of Zeus, are goddesses of beauty and attendants of Aphrodite (Venus). *waited*: attended.
62. The subject of *shot* is *graces* (line 61).
65. *facile*: friendly, easygoing.
70. *attain*: know.
79. *Hereafter*: in the future, i.e., in Milton's day, when many scientific conjectures about the universe and the stars will be ventured.
80. *wield*: an ironical choice of verb; i.e., in speculating about the universe, men will suppose they can master it for their use and wield it like a tool.
81. *build, unbuild* continues the irony of *wield* (line 80).
82. *save appearances*: a technical term from ancient Greek science (*sōzein ta phainomena*); to reconcile new observations with an existing theoretical model. Raphael now describes the increasingly desperate attempts of astronomers in later times to reconcile new observations with the earth-centered, Ptolemaic system.
82. *gird the sphere*: add to the cosmic sphere.
83. *centric*: a sphere centered on the earth. *eccentric*: a sphere enclosing the earth but not centered on the earth.

Cycle and epicycle, orb in orb.
Already by thy reasoning this I guess,   85
Who art to lead thy offspring, and supposest
That bodies bright and greater should not serve
The less not bright nor heav'n such journeys run,
Earth sitting still when she alone receives
The benefit. Consider first that great   90
Or bright infers not excellence: the earth
Though in comparison of heav'n so small,
Nor glistering, may of solid good contain
More plenty than the sun that barren shines
Whose virtue on itself works no effect   95
But in the fruitful earth: there first received
His beams, unactive else, their vigor find.
Yet not to earth are those bright luminaries
Officious but to thee earth's habitant.
And for the heav'n's wide circuit: let it speak   100
The Maker's high magnificence who built
So spacious and His line stretched out so far
That Man may know he dwells not in his own,
An edifice too large for him to fill,
Lodged in a small partition and the rest   105
Ordained for uses to his Lord best known.
The swiftness of those circles áttribute,
Though numberless, to His omnipotence,
That to corporeal substances could add
Speed almost spiritual. Me thou think'st not slow   110
Who since the morning hour set out from Heav'n
Where God resides and ere mid-day arrived
In Eden, distance inexpressible
By numbers that have name. But this I urge,
Admitting motion in the heavens, to show   115
Invalid that which thee to doubt it moved,
Not that I so affirm, though so it seem
To thee who hast thy dwelling here on earth.
God to remove His ways from human sense

84. Cycle: orbit of a planet. *epicycle*: orbit of a planet (such as Mars) that has its center not
     on the earth but on the circumference of another orbit that *is* centered on the earth. An
     epicycle is like the circle partly described by the swinging of a chair on a Ferris wheel.
96. *There*: on earth.
97. *His*: the sun's.
105. *small partition*: the earth.
109–10. *corporeal . . . spiritual*. See line 37 n.
114–18. I.e., For the sake of argument, let us suppose that the heavenly bodies actually do
     move, rather than seeming to move because the earth does. Even if your assumption
     of such motion is true, your conclusion, that nature is wasteful, does not follow.
116. *it*: Read "has." I.e., to show that what has moved you to doubt is an invalid proposition.

Placed heav'n from earth so far that earthly sight   120
If it presume might err in things too high
And no advantage gain. What if the sun
Be center to the world and other stars
By his attractive virtue and their own
Incited dance about him various rounds?   125
Their wand'ring course now high, now low, then hid,
Progressive, retrograde or standing still
In six thou seest. And what if seventh to these
The planet earth, so steadfast though she seem,
Insensibly three different motions move,   130
Which else to several spheres thou must ascribe,
Moved cóntrary with thwart obliquities
Or save the sun his labor and that swift
Nocturnal and diurnal rhomb supposed,
Invisible else above all stars, the wheel   135
Of day and night, which needs not thy belief
If Earth industrious of herself fetch day
Traveling east and with her part averse
From the sun's beam meet night, her other part
Still luminous by his ray. What if that light   140
Sent from her through the wide transpicuous air
To the terrestrial moon be as a star
Enlight'ning her by day as she by night
This earth reciprocal if land be there,
Fields and inhabitants? Her spots thou seest   145

122–58. After showing that the geocentric system is consistent with God's creative wisdom, Raphael expounds the heliocentric system to show that it too is consistent with God's creative wisdom.

126. *Their* now means planets, not stars, as the phrase "wand'ring course" indicates. See 5.177 n.

128–29. *six*: Moon, Mercury, Venus, Mars, Jupiter, Saturn. I.e., What if earth is the seventh planet, instead of the sun, around which all the planets revolve?

130. *three different motions*: daily rotation around the earth's axis, annual orbiting of the sun, and seasonal rotation of the ends of the earth's axis. The earth spins, travels, and wobbles. That this third motion does not begin until after the Fall (10.668–71), making it meaningless for Raphael to mention it here, should not be taken as a mistake on Milton's part but rather as a fold in the poem's frames of reference. Raphael is indeed speaking to Adam before the Fall, but Milton is also in these passages speaking to his contemporaries, who were as concerned about the consequences for Christian faith of the struggle between the Ptolemaic and Copernican systems as, two centuries later, people would be about the struggle between biblical Genesis and Darwinian evolution.

131–40. *several spheres*: different spherical structures beyond the earth, providing an alternative (but overelaborate) explanation for the three motions of the earth. Such motion would *save the sun his labor* by not requiring the sun to move at all. *rhomb*: Greek *rhombos*, anything that spins, like a top. The *wheel of day and night* (lines 135–36) need not be believed in if the earth is understood simply to rotate to the east: by rotating, the earth moves toward day, rather than day moving toward the earth. Night would then fall on the side of the earth (*her part averse*) that is shielded from the sun.

144. *reciprocal*: i.e., As the moon gives light to the inhabitants of the earth, so the earth may give light to the inhabitants of the moon.

As clouds and clouds may rain and rain produce
Fruits in her softened soil for some to eat
Allotted there. And other suns perhaps
With their attendant moons thou wilt descry
Communicating male and female light   150
(Which two great sexes animate the world)
Stored in each orb perhaps with some that live.
For such vast room in nature unpossessed
By living soul, desért and desolate,
Only to shine yet scarce to cóntribute   155
Each orb a glimpse of light conveyed so far
Down to this habitable, which returns
Light back to them, is obvious to dispute.
But whether thus these things or whether not,
Whether the sun predominant in heav'n   160
Rise on the earth or earth rise on the sun,
He from the east his flaming road begin
Or she from west her silent course advance
With inoffensive pace that spinning sleeps
On her soft axle while she paces ev'n   165
And bears thee soft with the smooth air along,
Solicit not thy thoughts with matters hid.
Leave them to God above. Him serve and fear!
Of other creatures as Him pleases best,
Wherever placed, let Him dispose. Joy thou.   170
In what He gives to thee: this Paradise
And thy fair Eve. Heav'n is for thee too high
To know what passes there. Be lowly wise:
Think only what concerns thee and thy being.
Dream not of other worlds, what creatures there   175
Live in what state, condition or degree,
Contented that thus far hath been revealed
Not of earth only but of highest Heav'n.
    To whom thus Adam cleared of doubt replied:
How fully hast thou satisfied me, pure   180
Intelligence of Heav'n, angel serene,

148–49. An allusion to the moons of Jupiter, discovered by Galileo.
150. *male and female light*: direct and reflected light, like the light of the sun and the moon.
153–58. Raphael here allows some validity to Adam's doubt: 'It would indeed be strange if
    the vast universe has no life in it and its innumerable stars exist only to afford a
    glimpse of their light here, on earth. But in that case it is more reasonable to suppose
    that there are inhabitants of other planets than to suppose that nature is wasteful.'
167–78. *Solicit not thy thoughts*: The Latinate meaning of *solicit* is to shake up, agitate.
    Milton is not imposing general limits on knowledge in all times and circumstances.
    Nothing could be more unlike him. Raphael is keeping to his commission, which is
    to focus Adam's attention—in the present, emergency circumstances—on the immi-
    nent danger. But see lines 188–97 and n.

And freed from intricacies, taught to live
The easiest way nor with perplexing thoughts
To interrupt the sweet of life from which
God hath bid dwell far off all anxious cares   185
And not molest us, unless we ourselves
Seek them with wand'ring thoughts and notions vain.
But apt the mind or fancy is to rove
Unchecked and of her roving is no end
Till warned or by experience taught she learn   190
That not to know at large of things remote
From use, obscure and subtle, but to know
That which before us lies in daily life
Is the prime wisdom. What is more is fume
Or emptiness or fond impertinence   195
And renders us in things that most concern
Unpracticed, unprepared and still to seek.
Therefore from this high pitch let us descend
A lower flight and speak of things at hand
Useful, whence haply mention may arise   200
Of something not unseasonable to ask
By sufferance and thy wonted favor deigned.
Thee I have heard relating what was done
Ere my remembrance. Now hear me relate
My story which perhaps thou hast not heard,   205
And day is yet not spent. Till then thou seest
How subtly to detain thee I devise,
Inviting thee to hear while I relate—
Fond, were it not in hope of thy reply!
For while I sit with thee I seem in Heaven   210
And sweeter thy discourse is to my ear
Than fruits of palm tree pleasantest to thirst
And hunger both from labor at the hour
Of sweet repast: they satiate and soon fill,
Though pleasant, but thy words with grace divine   215
Imbued bring to their sweetness no satiety.
    To whom thus Raphael answered Heav'nly meek:
Nor are thy lips ungraceful, Sire of Men,
Nor tongue ineloquent. For God on thee
Abundantly His gifts hath also poured   220

188–97. *apt the mind . . . to rove . . . still to seek*: Against castles in the air, Milton holds
    that knowledge is for use.
195. *fond*: foolish. *impertinence*: irrelevance.
209. *Fond*: to no purpose.
214. *they*: the *fruits* (line 212). *Satiate* has two syllables: 'say-shut.'

Inward and outward both, His image fair.
Speaking or mute, all comeliness and grace
Attends thee and each word, each motion forms.
Nor less think we in Heav'n of thee on Earth
Than of our fellow servant and inquire   225
Gladly into the ways of God with Man:
For God we see hath honored thee and set
On Man His equal love. Say therefore on!
For I that day was absent, as befell,
Bound on a voyage uncouth and obscure   230
Far on excursion toward the gates of Hell.
Squared in full legion such command we had
To see that none thence issued forth a spy
Or enemy while God was in His work
Lest He incensed at such eruption bold   235
Destruction with Creation might have mixed.
Not that they durst without His leave attempt,
But us He sends upon His high behests
For state, as Sov'reign King, and to inure
Our prompt obedience. Fast we found, fast shut   240
The dismal gates and barricadoed strong.
But long ere our approaching heard within
Noise other than the sound of dance or song,
Torment and loud lament and furious rage.
Glad we returned up to the coasts of light   245
Ere Sabbath evening, so we had in charge.
But thy relation now! For I attend
Pleased with thy words no less than thou with mine.
    So spake the godlike pow'r. And thus our sire:
For Man to tell how human life began   250
Is hard: for who himself beginning knew?
Desire with thee still longer to converse
Induced me. As new waked from soundest sleep
Soft on the flow'ry herb I found me laid
In balmy sweat which with his beams the sun   255
Soon dried and on the reeking moisture fed.
Straight toward heav'n my wond'ring eyes I turned
And gazed a while the ample sky till raised
By quick instinctive motion up I sprung

---

221. Adam is the image of God not only outwardly, in his appearance, but inwardly too,
    in his reason and eloquence.
232. *Squared in full legion*: Raphael was part of a full legion (an army division) formed in
    a square—or cube.
254. *herb*: grass.
255. *balmy*: sweet-smelling.
256. *reeking*: evaporating. The word does not have the negative sense it now has.

As thitherward endeavoring and upright   260
Stood on my feet. About me round I saw
Hill, dale, and shady woods and sunny plains
And liquid lapse of murmuring streams; by these,
Creatures that lived and moved and walked or flew,
Birds on the branches warbling. All things smiled.   265
With fragrance and with joy my heart o'erflowed!
Myself I then perused and limb by limb
Surveyed and sometimes went and sometimes ran
With supple joints and lively vigor led.
But who I was, or where, or from what cause   270
Knew not. To speak I tried and forthwith spake:
My tongue obeyed and readily could name
Whate'er I saw. "Thou Sun," said I, "fair light,
And thou enlightened Earth so fresh and gay,
Ye hills and dales, ye rivers, woods and plains,   275
And ye that live and move, fair creatures, tell,
Tell if ye saw how came I thus, how here.
Not of myself: by some great Maker, then,
In goodness and in pow'r preëminent.
Tell me how may I know Him, how adore,   280
From whom I have that thus I move and live
And feel that I am happier than I know!"
While thus I called and strayed I knew not whither
From where I first drew air and first beheld
This happy light, when answer none returned,   285
On a green shady bank profuse of flowers
Pensive I sat me down. There gentle sleep
First found me and with soft oppression seized
My drowsèd sense untroubled, though I thought
I then was passing to my former state   290
Insensible and forthwith to dissolve.
When suddenly stood at my head a dream
Whose inward apparition gently moved
My fancy to believe I yet had being
And lived. One came, methought, of shape divine   295
And said, "Thy mansion wants thee, Adam. Rise,
First man of men innum'rable ordained,
First father! Called by thee I come thy guide

260. *thitherward*: toward heaven.
267. *perused*: considered, looked at.
268. *went*: walked.
278–82. *some great Maker . . . than I know*: God-given instinct tells Adam that his bare existence, like his happiness, is due to someone who made him.
297. Two things are *ordained* (commanded): that Adam shall be the first man, and that men, Adam's sons, shall be innumerable.

To the garden of bliss, thy seat prepared."
So saying, by the hand He took me raised   300
And over fields and waters as in air
Smooth sliding without step, last led me up
A woody mountain whose high top was plain,
A circuit wide enclosed, with goodliest trees
Planted, with walks and bow'rs, that what I saw   305
Of earth before scarce pleasant seemed! Each tree
Loaden with fairest fruit that hung to th' eye
Tempting stirred in me sudden appetite
To pluck and eat, whereat I waked and found
Before mine eyes all real as the dream   310
Had lively shadowed. Here had new begun
My wand'ring had not He who was my guide
Up hither from among the trees appeared,
Presence Divine. Rejoicing, but with awe
In adoration, at His feet I fell   315
Submiss. He reared me and, "Whom thou sought'st I am,"
Said mildly, "Author of all this thou seest
Above or round about thee or beneath.
This Paradise I give thee, count it thine
To till and keep and of the fruit to eat.   320
Of every tree that in the garden grows
Eat freely with glad heart: fear here no dearth!
But of the tree whose operation brings
Knowledge of good and ill (which I have set
The pledge of thy obedience and thy faith   325
Amid the garden by the Tree of Life)
Remember what I warn thee: shun to taste
And shun the bitter consequence! For know,
The day thou eat'st thereof, my sole command
Transgressed, inevitably thou shalt die,   330
From that day mortal and this happy state
Shalt lose, expelled from hence into a world
Of woe and sorrow." Sternly He pronounced
The rigid interdiction which resounds
Yet dreadful in mine ear, though in my choice   335
Not to incur. But soon His clear aspéct
Returned and gracious purpose thus renewed:
"Not only these fair bounds but all the Earth
To thee and to thy race I give. As lords
Possess it and all things that therein live,   340

329–32. Adam will not die on the very day he eats the fruit. But on that day he will
 become mortal and his death inevitable.

Or live in sea or air, beast, fish and fowl,
In sign whereof each bird and beast behold
After their kinds. I bring them to receive
From thee their names and pay thee fealty
With low subjection. Understand the same   345
Of fish within their wat'ry residence,
Not hither summoned since they cannot change
Their element to draw the thinner air."
As thus He spake each bird and beast behold!
Approaching two and two, these cow'ring low   350
With blandishment, each bird stooped on his wing.
I named them as they passed and understood
Their nature: with such knowledge God endued
My sudden apprehension. But in these
I found not what methought I wanted still   355
And to the Heav'nly Vision thus presumed:
   "O by what name (for Thou above all these,
Above mankind or aught than mankind higher,
Surpassest far my naming) how may I
Adore Thee, Author of this universe   360
And all this good to Man for whose well being
So amply and with hands so liberal
Thou hast provided all things? But with me
I see not who partakes. In solitude
What happiness? Who can enjoy alone   365
Or all enjoying what contentment find?"
Thus I presumptuous, and the Vision bright
As with a smile more brightened thus replied:
   "What call'st thou solitude? Is not the earth
With various living creatures and the air   370
Replenished? And all these at thy command
To come and play before thee? Know'st thou not
Their language and their ways? They also know
And reason not contemptibly. With these
Find pastime and bear rule: thy realm is large!"   375
So spake the Universal Lord and seemed
So ordering. I with leave of speech implored

341. *Or live in*: whether they live in.
345–48. It is typical of Milton's love of complete explanations that he should have God explain to Adam why the fish are not being summoned into Adam's presence to be given their names.
350. *these*: the beasts.
351. *stooped*: descended, or dove. A term from hawking.
355. *wanted*: lacked.
358. *aught than Mankind higher*: i.e., angels.
371. *Replenished*: filled.

And humble deprecation thus replied:
   "Let not my words offend Thee, Heav'nly Power,
My Maker, be propitious while I speak.   380
Hast Thou not made me here Thy substitute
And these inferior far beneath me set?
Among unequals what society
Can sort, what harmony or true delight,
Which must be mutual in proportion due   385
Given and received? But in disparity—
The one intense, the other still remiss—
Cannot well suit with either but soon prove
Tedious alike. Of fellowship I speak
Such as I seek, fit to participate   390
All rational delight wherein the brute
Cannot be human consort. They rejoice
Each with their kind, lion with lioness,
So fitly them in pairs thou hast combined;
Much less can bird with beast or fish with fowl   395
So well converse, nor with the ox the ape:
Worse then can Man with beast, and least of all!"
   Whereto th' Almighty answered not displeased:
"A nice and subtle happiness I see
Thou to thyself proposest in the choice   400
Of thy associates, Adam, and wilt taste
No pleasure, though in pleasure, solitary.
What think'st thou then of Me and this My state?
Seem I to thee sufficiently possessed
Of happiness, or not, who am alone   405

380. *propitious*: favorable.
382. *these*: the animals.
383–87 *unequals*. A passage anticipating Milton's idealized but unequal notion of marriage. See 4.295–96. The difference referred to here is between animals and humans, which is so great it is impossible for them to engage in mutual concord. Eve and Adam, however, will be equals in Milton's musical but nonmathematical sense of the word. The differences between them complement one another, as harmonious differences of musical pitch (*proportion due*, line 385) are complementary, not identical.
386. A feminine line. See 2.27 n. Neither *Given* nor *disparity* is shortened.
387. *intense*: in tune, like the taut string of an instrument. *remiss*: out of tune, like a string that has gone slack.
395–97. Conversation between Man and beast is even more absurd than social interaction between beasts of different kind, such as birds and fish.
401–2. I.e., You will taste no pleasure alone (*solitary*), although you are in the place of pleasure itself. The name *Eden* was interpreted by allegorical commentators to mean *pleasure* (Greek *hēdonē*).
403. The Son, not the Father, is present to Adam, but the Son speaks as the Father. Milton is keeping to the account of Creation in Genesis, in which the Father creates. That the Father creates through the person of the Son is the later, Christian interpretation of the Creation in Genesis, based on the opening of John's gospel (1.1–3). See 7.516–19 n.

From all eternity? For none I know
Second to Me or like, equal much less.
How have I then with whom to hold converse
Save with the creatures which I made, and those
To me inferior, infinite descents   410
Beneath what other creatures are to thee?"
   He ceased, I lowly answered: "To attain
The heighth and depth of Thy eternal ways
All human thoughts come short, Supreme of Things.
Thou in Thyself art perfect and in Thee   415
Is no deficience found. Not so is Man
But in degree, the cause of his desire
By conversation with his like to help
Or solace his defects. No need that Thou
Shouldst propagate, already infinite   420
And through all numbers absolute, though One.
But Man by number is to manifest
His single imperfection and beget
Like of his like, his image multiplied
In unity defective which requires   425
Collateral love and dearest amity.
Thou in Thy secrecy, although alone,
Best with Thyself accompanied, seek'st not
Social communication. Yet, so pleased,
Canst raise thy creature to what heighth Thou wilt   430
Of union or communion deified.
I by conversing cannot these erect
From prone, nor in their ways complacence find."
Thus I emboldened spake and freedom used
Permissive and acceptance found which gained   435
This answer from the gracious Voice Divine:
   "Thus far to try thee, Adam, I was pleased
And find thee knowing not of beasts alone

416–19. *in degree*: Adam argues that Man, unlike God, is in the hierarchy of created
beings and is, therefore, open to improvement. Married persons can help each other
improve while accepting, with mutual love, the *defects* they have in respect of higher
beings, such as angels.

420–21. *already infinite . . . though One*: God's oneness is perfection because it encom-
passes all, as in the Pythagorean notion that the number "1" contains all other numbers
in itself. Being complete, there is no need for God to multiply, or *propagate* himself. See
George Chapman's continuation of Christopher Marlowe's *Hero and Leander*: "For one
no number is; but thence doth flow / The powerful race of number" (5.339–40).

422–26. *Man by number is to manifest / His single imperfection*: Because they do (or
rather will) *multiply* (line 424) themselves, human beings are imperfect alone, and
perfect themselves through love (line 426). In his portion of *Hero and Leander* Marlowe has the seductive Leander say to Hero, "One is no number: maids are nothing
then / Without the sweet society of men" (1.255–56).

432. *these*: animals.

Which thou hast rightly named but of thyself,
Expressing well the spirit within thee free,   440
My image, not imparted to the brute
Whose fellowship therefore, unmeet for thee,
Good reason was thou freely shouldst dislike:
And be so minded still! I, ere thou spak'st,
Knew it not good for Man to be alone   445
And no such company as then thou saw'st
Intended thee—for trial only brought
To see how thou could'st judge of fit and meet.
What next I bring shall please thee, be assured,
Thy likeness, thy fit help, thy other self,   450
Thy wish exactly to thy heart's desire."
    He ended or I heard no more for now
My earthly by His Heav'nly overpowered
Which it had long stood under, strained to th' heighth
In that celestial colloquy sublime   455
As with an object that excels the sense,
Dazzled and spent, sunk down, and sought repair
Of sleep which instantly fell on me, called
By nature as in aid, and closed mine eyes.
Mine eyes He closed but open left the cell   460
Of fancy my internal sight by which
Abstráct as in a trance methought I saw
(Though sleeping where I lay) and saw the Shape
Still glorious before whom awake I stood,
Who stooping opened my left side and took   465
From thence a rib with cordial spirits warm
And life-blood streaming fresh. Wide was the wound
But suddenly with flesh filled up and healed.
The rib He formed and fashioned with His hands,
Under His forming hands a creature grew   470
Manlike but different sex, so lovely fair
That what seemed fair in all the world seemed now
Mean—or in her summed up, in her contained
And in her looks, which from that time infused
Sweetness into my heart, unfelt before,   475
And into all things from her air inspired

440–41. Adam's inner freedom, which permits him to reason and to question, is God's image in him, an image not imparted to the animals, which are therefore unsuitable company for Adam.
455. *colloquy*: conversation.
466. *cordial*: of the heart, life-giving.
471–77. The syntax imitates the dream state. All that is fair is summed up in Eve's person and also in her *looks* (474), her glances, and her carriage, or *air* (476), which go out from her as a *sweetness* that is poured into Adam's *heart* (475).

The spirit of love and amorous delight.
She disappeared and left me dark. I waked
To find her or for ever to deplore
Her loss and other pleasures all abjure   480
When out of hope behold her not far off
Such as I saw her in my dream, adorned
With what all Earth or Heaven could bestow
To make her amiable. On she came
Led by her Heav'nly Maker, though unseen,   485
And guided by His voice, nor uninformed
Of nuptial sanctity and marriage rites.
Grace was in all her steps, Heav'n in her eye,
In every gesture dignity and love.
I overjoyed could not forbear aloud: 490
    "This turn hath made amends, thou hast fulfilled
Thy words, Creator bounteous and benign,
Giver of all things fair but fairest this
Of all Thy gifts, nor enviest. I now see
Bone of my bone, flesh of my flesh, my self   495
Before me: *Woman* is her name, of Man
Extracted. For this cause he shall forgo
Father and mother and to his wife adhere
And they shall be one flesh, one heart, one soul."
    She heard me thus and though divinely brought   500
Yet innocence and virgin modesty,
Her virtue and the conscience of her worth
That would be wooed and not unsought be won,
Not obvious, not obtrusive, but retired
The more desirable, or to say all,   505
Nature herself though pure of sinful thought
Wrought in her so that seeing me she turned.
I followed her: she what was honor knew
And with obsequious majesty approved
My pleaded reason. To the nuptial bow'r   510
I led her blushing like the morn. All heav'n
And happy constellations on that hour
Shed their selectest influence. The earth

486–87. *nor uninformed . . . marriage rites*: See 4.470–75.

496–97. *Woman* means "of Man": "she shall be called woman, because she was taken out of Man" (Genesis 2:23). See 10.867–68 n.

500–7. Compare Adam's speculation on Eve's motive for turning away from him with Eve's account of this moment (4.477–80).

509. *obsequious*: accommodating. The Latin sense of the word (*obsequor*, "to accommodate oneself to another's will") is not negative, as it is in English. Since *sequor* means "to follow," we picture Eve following, or going along with Adam, but majestically.

510. *pleaded* has here the sense of arguing a case, as in court. For what Adam says, see 4.481–88.

Gave sign of gratulation, and each hill.
Joyous the birds, fresh gales and gentle airs   515
Whispered it to the woods and from their wings
Flung rose, flung odors from the spicy shrub
Disporting till the amorous bird of night
Sung spousal and bid haste the evening star
On his hill top to light the bridal lamp.   520
   Thus I have told thee all my state and brought
My story to the sum of earthly bliss
Which I enjoy and must confess to find
In all things else delight indeed but such
As, used or not, works in the mind no change   525
Nor vehement desire. These delicacies
I mean of taste, sight, smell, herbs, fruits and flowers,
Walks, and the melody of birds. But here
Far otherwise: transported I behold,
Transported touch. Here passion first I felt,   530
Commotion strange! In all enjoyments else
Superior and unmoved, here only weak
Against the charm of beauty's powerful glance.
Or nature failed in me and left some part
Not proof enough such object to sustain   535
Or from my side subducting took perhaps
More than enough, at least on her bestowed
Too much of ornament, in outward show
Elaborate, of inward less exact.
For well I understand in the prime end   540
Of nature her th' inferior in the mind
And inward faculties which most excel,
In outward also her resembling less
His image who made both and less expressing
The character of that dominion giv'n   545

516. *it*: news of the marriage.
518. *bird of night*: the nightingale.
519. *evening star*: Venus, the goddess of love.
520. *his*: the nightingale's.
528. *here*: in this pleasure, love.
529. *transported*: carried out of himself.
530–33. Adam is superior to all other pleasures (which he names in lines 527–28) and not
carried away by them, but not to the pleasure of beauty's glance. See lines 471–77 n.
See Spenser, "An Hymn in Honour of Beautie": the beauty of nature does not "move
such affection [passion] in the inward mind / That it can rob both sense and reason
blind" (lines 76–77).
534–36. *Or . . . Or . . .* : Following Latin usage. Either Nature left me internally weak in
some part or took more than was necessary out of my side, which made Eve's beauty
overwhelming.
536. *subducting*: drawing out, from under.
539. *exact*: "well-ordered, complete." Cf. Adam's use of *exact* at 9.1017.
544. *His*: God's.
545. *character*: visual appearance, as of a mask. I.e., Adam's face, less beautiful than Eve's,
is more excellent because it has on it the look of command and royal authority.

O'er other creatures. Yet when I approach
Her loveliness so absolute she seems
And in herself complete so well to know
Her own that what she wills to do or say
Seems wisest, virtuousest, discreetest, best.   550
All higher knowledge in her presence falls
Degraded. Wisdom in discourse with her
Loses discount'nanced and like folly shows.
Authority and Reason on her wait
As one intended first, not after made   555
Occasionally. And to consúmmate all,
Greatness of mind and nobleness their seat
Build in her loveliest and create an awe
About her as a guard angelic placed.
To whom the angel with contracted brow: 560
    Accuse not Nature: she hath done her part,
Do thou but thine and be not diffident
Of Wisdom! She deserts thee not if thou
Dismiss not her when most thou need'st her nigh
By áttributing overmuch to things   565
Less excellent as thou thyself perceiv'st.
For what admir'st thou, what transports thee so,
An outside? Fair no doubt and worthy well
Thy cherishing, thy honoring, and thy love,
Not thy subjection. Weigh with her thyself,   570
Then value. Oft times nothing profits more
Than self-esteem grounded on just and right
Well managed. Of that skill the more thou know'st
The more she will acknowledge thee her head
And to realities yield all her shows   575
Made so adorn for thy delight the more,
So awful that with honor thou may'st love
Thy mate, who sees when thou art seen least wise.
But if the sense of touch whereby mankind
Is propagated seem such dear delight   580
Beyond all other, think the same vouchsafed

---

550. *virtuousest*: most virtuous; pronounced in three syllables, the first and last accented: 'vírchus-ést.' Milton makes Adam inelegantly hiss to indicate a slight moral deviation, which the following lines (lines 551–59) show.
552. *Degraded*: The word is placed at the beginning of the line, after an enjambment, for a more shocking effect.
554–56. Divine *Authority* and natural *Reason* are prior conditions of Eve's being. Adam is troubled because he knows that the opposite can't be true, yet his senses tell him otherwise.
557. *seat*: Latin *sedes*, "dwelling place, throne."
562. *diffident*: lacking in confidence; Latin *fides*, "trust." Cf. the important use of this word at 9.293.
563. *She*: wisdom.
577. *awful*: awe-inspiring.

To cattle and each beast, which would not be
To them made common and divulged if aught
Therein enjoyed were worthy to subdue
The soul of Man or passion in him move.   585
What higher in her society thou find'st
Attractive, human, rational, love still.
In loving thou dost well, in passion not,
Wherein true love consists not. Love refines
The thoughts and heart enlarges, hath his seat   590
In reason and is judicious, is the scale
By which to Heav'nly love thou may'st ascend,
Not sunk in carnal pleasure, for which cause
Among the beasts no mate for thee was found.
   To whom thus half abashed Adam replied: 595
Neither her outside formed so fair nor aught
In procreation common to all kinds
(Though higher of the genial bed by far
And with mysterious reverence I deem)
So much delights me as those graceful acts,   600
Those thousand decencies that daily flow
From all her words and actions mixed with love
And sweet compliance, which declare unfeigned
Union of mind or in us both one soul.
Harmony to behold in wedded pair   605
More grateful than harmonious sound to th' ear,
Yet these subject not. I to thee disclose
What inward thence I feel: not therefore foiled
Who meet with various objects from the sense
Variously representing, yet still free   610
Approve the best and follow what I approve.
To love thou blam'st me not for love thou say'st
Leads up to Heaven, is both the way and guide.
Bear with me then if lawful what I ask:
Love not the Heav'nly spirits? And how their love   615
Express they? By looks only or do they mix
Irradiance? Virtual or immediate touch?

---

583. *made common*: made available to all equally. *divulged* (Latin *divulgo*) has the same
meaning, "to spread among all."

585. Raphael says sex is not supposed to cause passion. See line 588. Milton portrays sex
before the Fall, but not excitement, which Raphael condemns as beastly (line 594).
See 4.741–70 and compare 9.1034–45. At lines 598–99 we learn that Adam does not
agree with Raphael's condemnation of sexual excitement as beastly.

598. *genial bed*: marriage bed, Latin *lectus genialis* (OED), pertaining to generation.

608–11. We remain free to choose among our mental representations, according to reason.

611. *follow* has one syllable, elided with *what*: 'foll-what.'

617. *Virtual or immediate*: I.e., Do angels when they love touch each other only virtually,
for example, by looks—or do they touch each other directly, without intermediary—
for example, by mixing their *Irradiance[s]*, their bodies of light?

To whom the angel with a smile that glowed
Celestial rosy red, love's proper hue,
Answered: Let it suffice thee that thou know'st   620
Us happy and without love no happiness.
Whatever pure thou in the body enjoy'st
(And pure thou wert created) we enjoy
In eminence and obstacle find none
Of membrane, joint or limb, exclusive bars.   625
Easier than air with air, if spirits embrace,
Total they mix, union of pure with pure
Desiring, nor restrained conveyance need
As flesh to mix with flesh or soul with soul.
But I can now no more: the parting sun   630
Beyond the earth's green cape and verdant isles
Hesperian sets, my signal to depart.
Be strong, live happy and love, but first of all
Him whom to love is to obey, and keep
His great command! Take heed lest passion sway   635
Thy judgment to do aught which else free will
Would not admit! Thine and of all thy sons
The weal or woe in thee is placed: beware!
I in thy persevering shall rejoice
And all the blest. Stand fast! To stand or fall   640
Free in thine own arbítrement it lies.
Perfect within, no outward aid require
And all temptation to transgress repel!
    So saying he arose, whom Adam thus
Followed with benediction: Since to part,   645
Go Heav'nly guest, ethereal messenger,
Sent from whose sov'reign goodness I adore.
Gentle to me and affable hath been
Thy condescension and shall be honored ever
With grateful memory. Thou to mankind   650
Be good and friendly still, and oft return!
    So parted they, the angel up to Heaven
From the thick shade and Adam to his bower.

---

628. *restrained conveyance*: sexual organs for conducting a part of one body into a part of
another. This is a restraint in comparison with angels, who mix totally (line 627).
633. *happy* and *and* are elided.
634. *Him*: love Him; i.e., Love each other, but first love God.
640. *all the blest*: all the other angels.
641. *arbitrement*: choice.
642. I.e., Since you are perfect in yourselves, you need no help from without.
645. *benediction*: farewell blessing.
649. A feminine line, the final syllable of *ever* being unstressed. See 2.27 n. *Condescension* and *and* are elided.
653. *thick shade*: a foreboding image of the evening coming on.

Book Nine

The Argument

Satan, having compassed the earth with meditated guile returns as a mist by night into Paradise; enters into the serpent sleeping. Adam and Eve in the morning go forth to their labors, which Eve proposes to divide in several places, each laboring apart. Adam consents not, alleging the danger lest that enemy of whom they were forewarned should attempt her, found alone. Eve, loath to be thought not circumspect or firm enough, urges her going apart, the rather desirous to make trial of her strength; Adam at last yields. The serpent finds her alone; his subtle approach, first gazing then speaking with much flattery, extolling Eve above all other creatures. Eve, wondering to hear the serpent speak, asks how he attained to human speech and such understanding, not till now. The serpent answers that by tasting of a certain tree in the garden he attained both to speech and reason, till then void of both. Eve requires him to bring her to that tree and finds it to be the Tree of Knowledge forbidden. The serpent, now grown bolder, with many wiles and arguments induces her at length to eat. She, pleased with the taste, deliberates a while whether to impart thereof to Adam or not; at last brings him of the fruit; relates what persuaded her to eat thereof. Adam, at first amazed but perceiving her lost, resolves through vehemence of love to perish with her and, extenuating the trespass, eats also of the fruit. The effects thereof in them both. They seek to cover their nakedness, then fall to variance and accusation of one another.

No more of talk where God or angel guest
With Man as with his friend familiar used
To sit indulgent and with him partake
Rural repast, permitting him the while
Venial discourse unblamed. I now must change   5
Those notes to tragic: foul distrust and breach
Disloyal on the part of Man, revolt
And disobedience. On the part of Heaven,
Now alienated, distance and distaste,
Anger and just rebuke and judgment given   10
That brought into this world a world of woe,
Sin and her shadow Death, and Misery,

Book Nine
4. *him*: Man.
5. *Venial discourse*: talk that is graciously permitted to range freely (Latin *venia*, "grace, favor, indulgence").

Death's harbinger. Sad task! Yet argument
Not less but more heroic than the wrath
Of stern Achilles on his foe pursued   15
Thrice fugitive about Troy wall or rage
Of Turnus for Lavinia disespoused,
Or Neptune's ire or Juno's that so long
Perplexed the Greek and Cytheréa's son,
If answerable style I can obtain   20
Of my celestial patroness who deigns
Her nightly visitation unimplored
And díctates to me slumb'ring or inspires
Easy my unpremeditated verse,
Since first this subject for heroic song   25
Pleased me, long choosing and beginning late,
Not sedulous by nature to indite
Wars, hitherto the only argument
Heroic deemed, chief mast'ry to dissect
With long and tedious havoc fabled knights   30
In battles feigned, the better fortitude
Of patience and heroic martyrdom
Unsung. Or to describe races and games
Or tilting furniture, emblazoned shields,
Impreses quaint, caparisons and steeds,   35
Bases and tinsel trappings, gorgeous knights
At joust and tournament, then marshaled feast
Served up in hall with sewers and seneschals:
The skill of artifice or office mean,

13. *harbinger*: one sent before to prepare the way for an army, a monarch, or other digni-
    tary. See George Herbert's poem "The Forerunners."
14–19. The epic poems referred to by these names are the *Iliad*, in which Hector is pur-
    sued about the walls of Troy and killed; the *Aeneid*, in the second half of which Tur-
    nus leads an Italian alliance against Aeneas and the Trojans; the *Odyssey*, in which
    Poseidon (in Latin, *Neptune*) is angry at Odysseus (*the Greek*); and the *Aeneid* again,
    in the first half of which Juno opposes Aeneas's efforts to reach Italy. (Aeneas is the
    son of Venus, or *Cytherea*.)
21. *celestial patroness*: Urania, Milton's muse. See 7.1–7 and 28–30.
26. Milton did not begin *Paradise Lost* until he was in his late forties.
27. *sedulous*: diligent, busy. The word is used here mockingly.
34. *tilting furniture*: equipment for jousting. *emblazoned*: decorated with heraldic imagery.
34–39. Milton moves from ancient epic to medieval and Renaissance romances: very
    long, elaborate tales of knights, ladies, tournaments, and feasts.
35. *Impreses*: Italian *imprese* (heraldic devices). *quaint*: strange, riddling; the word is used
    here mockingly, dismissing such devices as trivial. *caparisons*: decorative coverings
    for a horse's harness.
36. *Bases*: decorated coverings for the body of a horse, complementing the *caparisons* above.
37. *marshaled feast*: a very large, highly organized feast, with marshals to seat guests in
    their assigned places.
38. *sewers*: stewards overseeing waiters at a feast (Anglo-French *asseour*, "seater"). *sene-
    schals*: head servants (like a head butler) in a medieval household.
39. I.e., To describe such things requires only technical skill or personal experience as a
    waiter, a low occupation (*office mean*).

Not that which justly gives heroic name   40
To person or to poem. Me of these
Nor skilled nor studious, higher argument
Remains sufficient of itself to raise
That name unless an age too late or cold
Climate or years damp my intended wing   45
Depressed, and much they may if all be mine,
Not hers who brings it nightly to my ear.
   The sun was sunk and after him the star
Of Hesperus whose office is to bring
Twilight upon the earth, short arbiter   50
'Twixt day and night. And now from end to end
Night's hemisphere had veiled th' horizon round
When Satan who late fled before the threats
Of Gabriel out of Eden, now improved
In meditated fraud and malice bent   55
On Man's destruction, maugre what might hap
Of heavier on himself, fearless returned.
By night he fled and at midníght returned
From compassing the Earth, cautious of day
Since Uriel regent of the sun descried   60
His entrance and forewarned the cherubim
That kept their watch. Thence full of anguish driven
The space of seven continued nights he rode

41–44. I.e., A higher subject remains for me to take up, since I am unskilled in these
   lower, trivial things; and that subject is sufficient in itself, even if I were not particularly skilled, to deserve the name *heroic* (line 40).
44. *That name: heroic* (line 40).
44–46. Three things may weigh Milton down and keep him from completing his heroic
   poem: (1) he lives too late in history for such a poem to succeed; (2) he lives too far
   north, in a cold climate, rather than near the warm Mediterranean sea, where all
   great epics have hitherto been written; and (3) he is himself too old.
46. *Depressed*: pushed down (to earth).
50. *arbiter*: one who decides, in this case when day shall end and night officially begin.
56. *maugre*: despite. French *malgré*.
63–66. *rode / With darkness*: So as not to be seen by Uriel, who stands on the sun, or by
   any other angels (lines 60–61), Satan flies for one week in the earth's cone-shaped
   shadow. First, for three days, he flies over the equator, the *equinoctial line* (line 64),
   keeping dusk ahead and dawn behind. Next, for four days, he flies around the north
   and south poles, *traversing*, i.e., "following" *each colure* (line 66), the lines of longitude that cross at right angles at the poles. (For *traversing* as "going along" see *OED*,
   traverse, verb, 2a, citing this passage.)
      During the first, or equatorial, stage of his flight, Satan seems to himself to be in
   motion, propelling himself around the equator. But in truth he flies in place as the
   earth turns, treading air so he can remain always opposite the sun. (The orbital
   motion of the earth around the sun is not a factor.)
      Beginning the second stage, Satan flies from the equator up to the pole (doubtless
   to his favorite pole, the North) to make four complete circuits along the two colures,
   completing each half circuit (pole to pole) in exactly twelve hours, just before the
   semicircular line of longitude he has been flying along swings around into the light.
   He can then complete the other half circuit of the colure as it swings around through
   the dark. Even with perfect timing, he will flash briefly into sight at the poles.

With darkness, thrice the equinoctial line
He circled, four times crossed the car of Night   65
From pole to pole traversing each colure,
On th' eighth returned and on the coast averse
From entrance or cherubic watch by stealth
Found unsuspected way. There was a place,
Now not (though sin, not time, first wrought the change)   70
Where Tigris at the foot of Paradise
Into a gulf shot underground till part
Rose up a fountain by the Tree of Life.
In with the river sunk and with it rose
Satan involved in rising mist, then sought   75
Where to lie hid. Sea he had searched and land
From Eden over Pontus and the pool
Maeotis up beyond the river Ob,
Downward as far Antarctic and in length
West from Orontes to the ocean barred   80
At Darien, thence to the land where flows
Ganges and Indus. Thus the orb he roamed
With narrow search and with inspection deep
Considered every creature: which of all
Most opportune might serve his wiles and found   85
The serpent subtlest beast of all the field.

Four times on this second phase of his flight Satan must cross the path of the
chariot, or *car* (line 65), of *Night* (a vestigial personification), always just after it has
passed. Night is to be imagined on the western, horizontal line between light and
dark, facing the light and seeming to pull the darkness along, although of course,
from an external point of view, the chariot does not move. For Satan, the flight along
a colure describes a great circle, like a Ferris wheel. But from an external point of
view, Satan turns continuously left, veering to the sinister side.

67. *coast averse*: the western side of the garden, farthest from the eastern gate where
Gabriel and his troop of cherubs are on watch.

85–86. *and found / The serpent*: cf. line 182, *soon he found*. It may be considering "too
curiously to consider so" (*Hamlet* 5.1.190), but Satan appears to find two serpents.
The first he finds before he had entered the garden, during his search of all the creatures on the earth ("Sea he *had* searched and land," line 76), looking for the creature
that *might serve his wiles*: "and found / The serpent subtlest beast of all the field" (lines
85–86). After deciding to use it, he begins his long, passionate speech, *O Earth!* (lines
99–178). This speech is begun when Satan stands over the serpent, somewhere on the
earth outside the garden before entering it "in rising mist" (75). When, however, Satan
completes his speech—"So saying through each thicket dank or dry" (line 179)—he is
already inside the garden, and now moves through the thickets in search of the serpent, which he finds: "Him fast sleeping soon he found" (line 182). He now enters the
serpent, not disturbing its sleep, and waits for dawn to begin his attack. The first serpent is an example of what he needs; the second serpent is the actual vessel, although
the poet appears to elide them. This elision occurs because Satan's speech, "O Earth!"
begins in one location, on the wide earth, and ends in another, in the Garden of Eden.
The unaccountable change of location is the result of Milton's opening his description
of Satan's voyage over the earth in the past tense after Satan has already entered the
garden: "Sea *he had searched* and land." We do not need to suppose Milton simply
forgot where Satan was while speaking. With justifiable poetic license (since commentators appear not to have noticed), Milton elides the speech across the two loca-
tions so that his narrative can resume with greater urgency.

Him after long debate irresolute
Of thoughts revolved his final sentence chose
Fit vessel, fittest imp of fraud in whom
To enter and his dark suggestions hide   90
From sharpest sight for in the wily snake
Whatever sleights none would suspicious mark,
As from his wit and native subtlety
Proceeding which in other beasts observed
Doubt might beget of diabolic pow'r   95
Active within beyond the sense of brute.
Thus he resolved but first from inward grief
His bursting passion into plaints thus poured:
     O Earth! how like to Heav'n if not preferred
More justly, seat worthier of gods as built   100
With second thoughts reforming what was old!
For what god after better worse would build?
Terrestrial heav'n danced round by other heav'ns
That shine yet bear their bright officious lamps,
Light above light for thee alone, as seems   105
In thee concent'ring all their precious beams
Of sacred influence! As God in Heav'n
Is center yet extends to all, so thou
Cent'ring receiv'st from all those orbs. In thee,
Not in themselves, all their known virtue appears   110
Productive in herb, plant, and nobler birth
Of creatures animate with gradual life
Of growth, sense, reason: all summed up in Man!
With what delight could I have walked thee round
(If I could joy in aught) sweet interchange   115
Of hill and valley, rivers, woods and plains,
Now land, now sea and shores with forest crowned,
Rocks, dens and caves! But I in none of these
Find place or refuge and the more I see
Pleasures about me so much more I feel   120
Torment within me as from the hateful siege
Of cóntraries: all good to me becomes
Bane, and in Heav'n much worse would be my state.

87. *Him*: the serpent.
88. *final sentence*: concluding decision.
89. *imp*: not a devil but the archaic sense of the word as "offspring, shoot, or graft" (Old English *impian*, "to graft"). Spenser, *Faerie Queene* 4.9.4: "That headlesse tyrants tronke he reard from ground, / And hauing ympt the head to it agayne. / Vpon his vsuall beast it firmely bound." The serpent is the fittest shoot for Satan to graft his fraud with. Once the serpent has been grafted to fraud it is "vitiated in nature" (10.169).
105. *thee*: Earth.
118. *Rocks, dens and caves!*: A telling conclusion to Satan's list of nature's beauties.

But neither here seek I, no, nor in Heav'n
To dwell (unless by mast'ring Heav'n's Supreme),   125
Nor hope to be myself less miserable
By what I seek but others to make such
As I, though thereby worse to me redound.
For only in destroying I find ease
To my relentless thoughts. And him destroyed   130
Or won to what may work his utter loss
For whom all this was made, all this will soon
Follow as to him linked in weal or woe:
In woe then, that destruction wide may range!
To me shall be the glory sole among   135
Th' infernal pow'rs in one day to have marred
What He, "Almighty" styled, six nights and days
Continued making. And who knows how long
Before had been contriving? Though perhaps
Not longer than since I in one night freed   140
From servitude inglorious well nigh half
Th' angelic name and thinner left the throng
Of His adorers. He to be avenged
And to repair His numbers thus impaired,
Whether such virtue, spent of old, now failed   145
More angels to create (if they at least
Are His created), or to spite us more,
Determined to advance into our room
A creature formed of earth and him endow,
Exalted from so base original,   150
With Heav'nly spoils—*our* spoils! What He decreed
He effected: Man He made and for him built
Magnificent this world and Earth his seat,
Him "lord" pronounced and (O indignity!)
Subjected to his service angel wings   155
And flaming ministers to watch and tend
Their earthy charge. Of these the vigilance
I dread and to elude thus wrapped in mist

130. *him*: Man, "for whom all this was made" (line 132).
132. *all this . . . all this*: all nature, all things on *Earth*, as just described (lines 99–118).
133. *weal*: happiness.
137. *styled*: titled.
141. *half*: in fact, one-third.
142. *angelic name*: those named "angels."
145. *virtue*: creative power.
146–47. See 5.857–61, where Satan questions whether God made the angels. *They* refers to the angels whom Satan has just now, inadvertently, spoken of as created. In the parenthesis, he catches himself and puts the matter back into question.
153–54. *his . . . Him*: Man.
156. *flaming ministers*: "Who maketh his angels spirits; his ministers a flaming fire" (Psalm 104:4). The exact phrase (in the singular) is in *Othello* 5.2.8.

Of midnight vapor glide obscure and pry
In every bush and brake where hap may find   160
The serpent sleeping in whose mazy folds
To hide me and the dark intent I bring.
O foul descent! That I who erst contended
With gods to sit the high'st am now constrained
Into a beast and mixed with bestial slime,   165
This essence to incarnate and imbrute
That to the heighth of deity aspired!
But what will not ambition and revenge
Descend to? Who aspires must down as low
As high he soared, obnoxious first or last   170
To basest things. Revenge at first though sweet
Bitter ere long back on itself recoils.
Let it! I reck not, so it light well aimed
(Since higher I fall short) on him who next
Provokes my envy: this new favorite   175
Of Heav'n, this man of clay, son of despite
Whom us the more to spite his Maker raised
From dust. Spite then with spite is best repaid!
    So saying through each thicket dank or dry
Like a black mist low creeping he held on   180
His midnight search where soonest he might find
The serpent. Him fast sleeping soon he found
In labyrinth of many a round self-rolled,
His head the midst well stored with subtle wiles.
Not yet in horrid shade or dismal den   185
Nor nocent yet but on the grassy herb
Fearless unfeared he slept. In at his mouth
The Devil entered and his brutal sense
In heart or head possessing soon inspired
With act intelligential, but his sleep   190
Disturbed not, waiting close th' approach of morn.
    Now when as sacred light began to dawn
In Eden on the humid flow'rs that breathed
Their morning incense, when all things that breathe
From th' Earth's great altar send up silent praise   195
To the Creator and His nostrils fill
With grateful smell, forth came the human pair

---

163. *erst*: erstwhile, formerly.
170. *obnoxious*: exposed, subject to.
174. *Since higher I fall short*: i.e., since his revenge on God is unsuccessful.
186. *nocent*: harmful (Latin *noceo*, "to injure, harm").
187–90. *his*: All three occurrences of *his* refer to the serpent.

And joined their vocal worship to the choir
Of creatures wanting voice; that done, partake
The season prime for sweetest scents and airs;   200
Then cómmune how that day they best may ply
Their growing work. For much their work outgrew
The hands' dispatch of two, gardening so wide,
And Eve first to her husband thus began:
    Adam, well may we labor still to dress   205
This garden, still to tend plant, herb and flow'r,
Our pleasant task enjoined, but till more hands
Aid us, the work under our labor grows
Luxurious by restraint: what we by day
Lop overgrown or prune or prop or bind   210
One night or two with wanton growth derides,
Tending to wild. Thou therefore now advise
Or hear what to my mind first thoughts present:
Let us divide our labors, thou where choice
Leads thee or where most needs, whether to wind   215
The woodbine round this arbor or direct
The clasping ivy where to climb, while I
In yonder spring of roses intermixed
With myrtle find what to redress till noon.
For while so near each other thus all day   220
Our task we choose what wonder if, so near,
Looks intervene and smiles or object new
Casual discóurse draw on which intermits
Our day's work brought to little, though begun
Early, and th' hour of supper come unearned.   225
    To whom mild answer Adam thus returned:
Sole Eve, associate soul, to me beyond
Compare above all living creatures dear,
Well hast thou motioned, well thy thoughts employed
How we might best fulfil the work which here   230
God hath assigned us, nor of me shalt pass
Unpraised, for nothing lovelier can be found
In woman than to study household good
And good works in her husband to promote.
Yet not so strictly hath our Lord imposed   235
Labor as to debar us when we need
Refreshment, whether food or talk between,

198–99. *choir / Of creatures:* the flowers. *wanting:* lacking. The smell of the flowers is "silent praise" (line 195).
232–34. "She looketh well to the ways of her household, and eateth not the bread of idleness" (Proverbs 31:27).

Food of the mind or this sweet intercourse
Of looks and smiles, for smiles from reason flow,
To brute denied, and are of love the food,   240
Love not the lowest end of human life.
For not to irksome toil but to delight
He made us and delight to reason joined.
These paths and bow'rs, doubt not but our joint hands
Will keep from wilderness with ease as wide   245
As we need walk till younger hands ere long
Assist us. But if much convérse perhaps
Thee satiate, to short absence I could yield,
For solitude sometimes is best society
And short retirement urges sweet return.   250
But other doubt possesses me lest harm
Befall thee severed from me for thou know'st
What hath been warned us, what malicious foe,
Envying our happiness and of his own
Despairing, seeks to work us woe and shame   255
By sly assault and somewhere nigh at hand
Watches no doubt with greedy hope to find
His wish and best advantage, us asunder,
Hopeless to circumvent us joined where each
To other speedy aid might lend at need,   260
Whether his first design be to withdraw
Our fealty from God or to disturb
Conjugal love, than which perhaps no bliss
Enjoyed by us excites his envy more.
Or this or worse, leave not the faithful side   265
That gave thee being, still shades thee and protects!
The wife where danger or dishonor lurks
Safest and seemliest by her husband stays
Who guards her or with her the worst endures.
　　To whom the virgin majesty of Eve   270
As one who loves and some unkindness meets
With sweet austere composure thus replied:
　　Offspring of Heav'n and Earth and all Earth's lord,
That such an enemy we have who seeks
Our ruin both by thee informed I learn   275
And from the parting angel overheard
As in a shady nook I stood behind

238. *intercourse*: exchange; literally "running between" (Latin).
246. *younger hands*: those of their children.
262–64. Adam guesses correctly. Satan envies Adam and Eve's physical love and men-
　　tions that relentless "fierce desire" is one of the torments of Hell (4.509–11).

Just then returned at shut of evening flow'rs.
But that thou shouldst my firmness therefore doubt
To God or thee because we have a foe   280
May tempt it I expected not to hear.
His violence thou fear'st not, being such
As we, not capable of death or pain,
Can either not receive or can repel.
His fraud is then thy fear, which plain infers   285
Thy equal fear that my firm faith and love
Can by his fraud be shaken or seduced!—
Thoughts which, how found they harbor in thy breast,
Adam, misthought of her to thee so dear.
    To whom with healing words Adam replied: 290
Daughter of God and Man, immortal Eve,
For such thou art, from sin and blame entire:
Not diffident of thee do I dissuade
Thy absence from my sight but to avoid
Th' attempt itself intended by our foe.   295
For he who tempts, though in vain, at least asperses
The tempted with dishonor foul, supposed
Not incorruptible of faith, not proof
Against temptation. Thou thyself with scorn
And anger would'st resent the offered wrong   300
Though ineffectual found. Misdeem not then
If such affront I labor to avert
From thee alone which on us both at once
The enemy, though bold, will hardly dare
Or, daring, first on me th' assault shall light.   305
Nor thou his malice and false guile condemn:
Subtle he needs must be who could seduce
Angels. Nor think superfluous others' aid:
I from the influence of thy looks receive
Accéss in every virtue, in thy sight   310
More wise, more watchful, stronger if need were
Of outward strength while shame, thou looking on
(Shame to be overcome or overreached)

282–83. The implied subject of *being* is *we*. I.e., We, being as we are incapable of death or
    pain.
284. The object of *receive* and *repel* is *violence* (line 282).
288–89. I.e., However those thoughts came into your breast, Adam, they are *misthought*
    of me, who am to you so dear.
292. *entire*: untouched.
293. *diffident*: distrusting.
306. *condemn*: despise, underestimate.
310. *Accéss*: increased power.
312–14. Shame would arouse Adam's greatest reserves of strength while Eve is looking on.

Would utmost vigor raise and, raised, unite.
Why shouldst not thou like sense within thee feel   315
When I am present and thy trial choose
With me, best witness of thy virtue tried?
So spake domestic Adam in his care
And matrimonial love. But Eve who thought
Less áttributed to her faith sincere   320
Thus her reply with accent sweet renewed:
     If this be our condition thus to dwell
In narrow circuit straitened by a foe
Subtle or violent, we not endued
Single with like defence wherever met,   325
How are we happy, still in fear of harm?
But harm precedes not sin: only our foe
Tempting affronts us with his foul esteem
Of our integrity. His foul esteem
Sticks no dishonor on our front but turns   330
Foul on himself! Then wherefore shunned or feared
By us who rather double honor gain
From his surmise proved false, find peace within,
Favor from Heav'n, our witness, from th' event?
And what is faith, love, virtue unassayed,   335
Alone, without exterior help sustained?
Let us not then suspect our happy state
Left so imperfect by the Maker wise
As not secure to single or combined.
Frail is our happiness if this be so   340
And Eden were no Eden thus exposed!
     To whom thus Adam fervently replied:
O Woman! best are all things as the will
Of God ordained them. His creating hand
Nothing imperfect or deficient left   345
Of all that He created, much less Man
Or aught that might his happy state secure,
Secure from outward force. Within himself
The danger lies, yet lies within his power:

---

326. *still*: always.
335–36. I.e., Of what value are faith, love, and virtue if they remain alone and are not put
     to the test by what is outside them? Whatever tempts virtue helps virtue to be more
     clearly what it is. This statement, the argument of Milton's *Areopagitica*, describes
     the dialectical conditions in which virtue operates after the Fall, but not before.
     (See below, pp. 362.) Even so, we are struck by the nobility and good sense of her
     statement.
348. *Secure*: They are safe from any direct violence (*outward force*). But because they are
     free, they are not safe from inward treason (lines 351–52).

Against his will he can receive no harm.   350
But God left free the will, for what obeys
Reason is free, and reason he made right
But bid her well beware and still erect
Lest by some fair appearing good surprised
She díctate false and misinform the will   355
To do what God expressly hath forbid.
Not then mistrust but tender love enjoins
That I should mind thee oft—and mind thou me!
Firm we subsist, yet possible to swerve
Since reason not impossibly may meet   360
Some specious object by the foe suborned
And fall into deception unaware,
Not keeping strictest watch as she was warned.
Seek not temptation, then, which to avoid
Were better and most likely if from me   365
Thou sever not: trial will come unsought.
Wouldst thou approve thy constancy? Approve
First thy obedience! Th' other who can know
Not seeing thee attempted, who attest?
But if thou think trial unsought may find   370
Us both securer than thus warned thou seem'st,
Go, for thy stay, not free, absents thee more.
Go in thy native innocence, rely
On what thou hast of virtue, summon all,
For God towards thee hath done his part: do thine!   375
　　So spake the patriarch of mankind. But Eve
Persisted; yet submiss, though last, replied:
　　With thy permission then and thus forewarned
Chiefly by what thy own last reasoning words

363. *she*: reason.
368. *Th' other*: constancy.
370–72. *But if thou think . . . Go . . . absents thee more*: Commentators are at some vari-
　　ance on the exact sense of the first part of this statement, in particular *trial unsought*
　　(line 370) and *securer* (line 371). The first means an assault that is unlooked for
　　because the defenders, working separately, are not on their guard. The second does
　　not mean "overconfident," but "safer." (See lines 347–48 n. and 11.746.) Adam is
　　saying, 'If you suppose that by not being on our guard, by not being on the lookout
　　together for trouble (i.e., *trial*), we are safer than you seem to be (since, despite hav-
　　ing been warned, you are not taking this matter seriously enough), go. Staying
　　against your will divides us even more than physical separation can do.'
377. I.e., Although she continued verbally to express submission to Adam, Eve spoke last.
　　Milton implies that Eve's verbal submission to Adam is not borne out by her insis-
　　tence on going. Milton offers the subtle thought that it is possible, even in the state
　　of innocence, to make a mistake. (It is also possible to lose your temper, as Adam
　　does at line 342, when he replies *fervently*.) The difference is that in the state of
　　innocence no mistake has necessary or irreversible consequences. After the Fall,
　　mistakes are irreversible and cannot be set right.

Touched only, that our trial when least sought   380
May find us both perhaps far less prepared,
The willinger I go, nor much expect
A foe so proud will first the weaker seek:
So bent, the more shall shame him his repulse.
Thus saying, from her husband's hand her hand   385
Soft she withdrew and like a wood-nymph light,
Oread or Dryad, or of Delia's train,
Betook her to the groves, but Delia's self
In gait surpassed and goddess-like deport,
Though not, as she, with bow and quiver armed   390
But with such gard'ning tools as art yet rude,
Guiltless of fire, had formed, or angels brought.
To Pales or Pomona thus adorned
Likest she seemed (Pomona when she fled
Vertumnus) or to Ceres in her prime   395
Yet virgin of Prosérpina from Jove.
Her long with ardent look his eye pursued
Delighted but desiring more her stay.
Oft he to her his charge of quick return
Repeated, she to him as oft engaged   400
To be returned by noon amid the bow'r
And all things in best order to invite
Noontide repast or afternoon's repose.
O much deceived, much failing, hapless Eve,
Of thy presumed return! Event perverse!   405
Thou never from that hour in Paradise
Found'st either sweet repast or sound repose,
Such ambush hid among sweet flow'rs and shades,
Waited with hellish rancor imminent
To intercept thy way or send thee back   410
Despoiled of innocence, of faith, of bliss.
    For now and since first break of dawn the Fiend,
Mere serpent in appearance, forth was come
And on his quest where likeliest he might find
The only two of mankind (but in them   415
The whole included race) his purposed prey.

---

390. *she*: Delia.
391–92. A good example of Milton's wish to leave no practical detail unexplained. Since there was no fire in Eden, there was no forge to make iron tools. Therefore either Adam and Eve made *rude* stone tools themselves or the angels brought them rather better ones from heaven.
392. *Guiltless*: Iron tools were made in the forge, but so were weapons. Fire is therefore seen as a symptom of the Fall, of human guilt.
393–96. Goddesses associated with fertility.
396. *Yet virgin*: before Proserpina (Persephone) was born, and therefore before winter. See 892–93 n.

In bow'r and field he sought where any tuft
Of grove or garden plot more pleasant lay
Their tendance or plantation for delight.
By fountain or by shady rivulet   420
He sought them both but wished his hap might find
Eve separate. He wished, but not with hope
Of what so seldom chanced when to his wish
Beyond his hope Eve separate he spies
Veiled in a cloud of fragrance where she stood,   425
Half spied, so thick the roses bushing round
About her glowed, oft stooping to support
Each flow'r of slender stalk whose head, though gay
Carnation, purple, azure or specked with gold
Hung drooping unsustained. Them she upstays   430
Gently with myrtle band, mindless the while
Herself though fairest unsupported flow'r
From her best prop so far and storm so nigh.
Nearer he drew and many a walk traversed
Of stateliest covert, cedar, pine or palm,   435
Then voluble and bold, now hid, now seen,
Among thick-woven arborets and flow'rs
Embordered on each bank, the hand of Eve,
Spot more delicious than those gardens feigned
Or of revived Adonis or renowned   440
Alcinous host of old Laertes' son
Or that, not mystic, where the sapient king
Held dalliance with his fair Egyptian spouse.
Much he the place admired, the person more.
As one who long in populous city pent   445
Where houses thick and sewers annoy the air
Forth issuing on a summer's morn to breathe
Among the pleasant villages and farms
Adjoined, from each thing met conceives delight—
The smell of grain or tedded grass, or kine   450

417. *bow'r*: overhanging wood (not Adam and Eve's nuptial bower).
417–18. *tuft / Of grove*: cluster of trees.
421. *wished his hap*: wished he would have the luck.
431. *myrtle band*: rods from the myrtle bush, which, like the roses these myrtles support, are sacred to Venus, the goddess of love.
438. *the hand of Eve*: done by Eve's hand.
439. *gardens feigned*: cf. 4.250–51 and n.
442. *not mystic*: not imagined ("feigned," line 439), like the gardens just mentioned, but real, because biblical.
442–43. *sapient king*: Solomon, legendary for his wisdom and also for his many wives, one of whom was an Egyptian princess.
444. *he*: Satan. *the person*: Eve.
450. *tedded grass*: hay spread out to dry before storage.

Or dairy, each rural sight, each rural sound—
If chance with nymph-like step fair virgin pass
What pleasing seemed, for her now pleases more,
She most, and in her look sums all delight.
Such pleasure took the serpent to behold   455
This flow'ry plat the sweet recess of Eve,
Thus early, thus alone. Her Heav'nly form
Angelic but more soft and feminine,
Her graceful innocence, her every air
Of gesture or least action overawed   460
His malice and with rapine sweet bereaved
His fierceness of the fierce intent it brought.
That space the evil one abstracted stood
From his own evil and for the time remained
Stupidly good, of enmity disarmed,   465
Of guile, of hate, of envy, of revenge.
But the hot Hell that always in him burns,
Though in mid-Heav'n, soon ended his delight
And tortures him now more the more he sees
Of pleasure not for him ordained. Then soon   470
Fierce hate he recollects and all his thoughts
Of mischief gratulating thus excites:
    Thoughts, whither have ye led me, with what sweet
Compulsion thus transported to forget
What hither brought us? Hate, not love! Nor hope   475
Of Paradise for Hell, hope here to taste
Of pleasure, but all pleasure to destroy
Save what is in destroying! Other joy
To me is lost. Then let me not let pass
Occasion which now smiles: behold alone   480
The woman opportune to all attempts,
Her husband (for I view far round) not nigh,
Whose higher intellectual more I shun
And strength of courage haughty and of limb
Heroic built though of terrestrial mould,   485
Foe not informidable, exempt from wound,
I not, so much hath Hell debased and pain
Enfeebled me to what I was in Heaven.
She fair, divinely fair, fit love for gods,

451. *dairy* and *each* are elided.
461. *rapine*: a seizing, a rapture.
465. *Stupidly good*: good because he is in a stupor. *Stupid* here does not mean "unintelli-
        gent"; it means "stunned."
472. *gratulating*: taking pleasure in. The object of *excites* (Latin *excito*, "to wake, rouse,
        call forth") is *thoughts* (line 471).
480. *Occasion*: opportunity.

Not terrible, though terror be in love   490
And beauty not approached by stronger hate,
Hate stronger under show of love well-feigned,
The way which to her ruin now I tend.
 So spake the enemy of mankind, enclosed
In serpent, inmate bad, and tóward Eve   495
Addressed his way not with indented wave
Prone on the ground, as since, but on his rear,
Circular base of rising folds that towered
Fold above fold, a surging maze. His head
Crested aloft and carbuncle his eyes   500
With burnished neck of verdant gold erect
Amidst his circling spires that on the grass
Floated redundant. Pleasing was his shape
And lovely, never since of serpent kind
Lovelier, not those that in Illyria changed   505
Hermione and Cadmus or the god
In Epidaurus, nor to which transformed
Ammonian Jove or Capitoline was seen,
He with Olympias this with her who bore
Scipio the heighth of Rome. With tract oblique,   510
At first as one who sought accéss but feared
To interrupt, sidelong he works his way.
As when a ship by skilful steersman wrought
Nigh river's mouth or foreland where the wind
Veers oft, as oft so steers and shifts her sail,   515
So varied he and of his tortuous train
Curled many a wanton wreath in sight of Eve
To lure her eye. She, busied, heard the sound
Of rustling leaves but minded not as used
To such disport before her through the field   520

490–92. Love (and beauty) can inspire a kind of terror in the lover, unless the lover secretly hates whom he pretends to love: the logic of misogyny.

496. *indented*: cf. *As You Like It* 4.3.111, for the snake that "with indented glides did slip away."

498–99. *surging maze*: This picture of the rising, moving, complicatedly twisting loops of the serpent's body is among the finest poetic images in the poem.

500. *carbuncle*: red, like burning coals (Latin *carbo*, "a coal").

501. *verdant*: green. A greenish tint to the serpent's lustrous, gold neck.

502. The head is in the center of a circle of folds, which rise like spires. The architectural image suggests a moving castle.

503. *redundant*: pouring over one another.

505–10. A passage of virtuosic classical allusion. In the serpents were concealed a king and his queen, the god of healing, and the king of the gods, who as a serpent begot (on separate occasions) Alexander the Great and Scipio, Rome's greatest military hero. See Glossary, ILLYRIA, CADMUS, and EPIDAURUS.

510–14. Possibly an acrostic hiding the word *SATAN*, as Satan is hidden in the serpent. See Paul J. Klemp, *Milton Quarterly* 11 (1977): 91–92.

519. *minded not*: paid no attention.

From every beast more duteous at her call
Than at Circean call the herd disguised.
He bolder now uncalled before her stood
But as in gaze admiring. Oft he bowed
His turret crest and sleek enamelled neck,   525
Fawning, and licked the ground whereon she trod.
His gentle dumb expression turned at length
The eye of Eve to mark his play. He, glad
Of her attention gained, with serpent tongue
Organic or impúlse of vocal air   530
His fraudulent temptation thus began:
    Wonder not, Sovereign Mistress, if perhaps
Thou canst, who art sole wonder, much less arm
Thy looks, the heav'n of mildness, with disdain,
Displeased that I approach thee thus and gaze   535
Insatiate, I thus single, nor have feared
Thy awful brow, more awful thus retired!
Fairest resemblance of thy Maker fair,
Thee all things living gaze on (all things thine
By gift) and thy celestial beauty adore   540
With ravishment beheld, there best beheld
Where universally admired. But here
In this enclosure wild these beasts among
(Beholders rude and shallow to discern
Half what in thee is fair), one man except,   545
Who sees thee? (and what is one?), who shouldst be seen
A goddess among gods adored and served
By angels numberless thy daily train!
    So glozed the Tempter and his proem tuned.
Into the heart of Eve his words made way   550
Though at the voice much marveling. At length
Not unamazed she thus in answer spake:
    What may this mean? Language of man pronounced
By tongue of brute and human sense expressed?
The first at least of these I thought denied   555
To beasts whom God on their creation-day
Created mute to all articulate sound,

529–30. Satan emits sound through the serpent either by using the serpent's tongue or by emitting pulses of air, which make sound by vibrating in the elongated tube of the serpent's body.
538. We are to recall that Adam, not Eve, is made in God's image. Eve is made in the image of Adam's desire.
545. *one man except*: i.e., Adam.
546. *what is one?*: See 8.422–26 n.
549. *glozed*: spoke deceitfully. *proem*: prelude, introduction.
555. *first*: language.

The latter I demur for in their looks
Much reason and in their actions oft appears.
Thee, Serpent, subtlest beast of all the field   560
I knew, but not with human voice endued.
Redouble then this miracle and say
How cam'st thou speakable of mute and how
To me so friendly grown above the rest
Of brutal kind that daily are in sight?   565
Say, for such wonder claims attention due.
    To whom the guileful Tempter thus replied:
Empress of this fair world, resplendent Eve,
Easy to me it is to tell thee all
What thou command'st and right thou shouldst be obeyed. 570
I was at first as other beasts that graze
The trodden herb: of abject thoughts and low,
As was my food, nor aught but food discerned,
Or sex, and apprehended nothing high.
Till on a day roving the field I chanced   575
A goodly tree far distant to behold
Loaden with fruit of fairest colors mixed,
Ruddy and gold. I nearer drew to gaze
When from the boughs a savory odor blown,
Grateful to appetite, more pleased my sense   580
Than smell of sweetest fennel or the teats
Of ewe or goat dropping with milk at ev'n
Unsucked of lamb or kid that tend their play.
To satisfy the sharp desire I had
Of tasting those fair apples I resolved   585
Not to defer. Hunger and thirst at once,
Powerful persuaders, quickened by the scent
Of that alluring fruit, urged me so keen.
About the mossy trunk I wound me soon
For high from ground the branches would require   590
Thy utmost reach or Adam's. Round the tree
All other beasts that saw with like desire
Longing and envying stood but could not reach.
Amid the tree now got, where plenty hung
Tempting so nigh, to pluck and eat my fill   595
I spared not, for such pleasure till that hour
At feed or fountain never had I found.

---

558. *latter: human sense* (line 554), meaning.
581–82. Snakes were popularly supposed to suck milk from sheep and goats.
585. The forbidden fruit is here for the first time referred to as *apples*. Satan will do so
      again at 10.487.
593. Satan introduces Eve to the pleasure of hoarding what others desire.

Sated at length ere long I might perceive
Strange alteration in me to degree
Of reason in my inward pow'rs, and speech   600
Wanted not long though to this shape retained.
Thenceforth to speculations high or deep
I turned my thoughts and with capacious mind
Considered all things visible in heav'n
Or earth or middle, all things fair and good.   605
But all that fair and good in thy divine
Semblance and in thy beauty's heav'nly ray
United I beheld, no fair to thine
Equivalent or second, which compelled
Me thus though importune perhaps to come   610
And gaze and worship thee, of right declared
Sovereign of creatures, universal dame!
    So talked the spirited sly snake and Eve
Yet more amazed unwary thus replied:
    Serpent, thy overpraising leaves in doubt   615
The virtue of that fruit in thee first proved.
But say, where grows that tree, from hence how far?
For many are the trees of God that grow
In Paradise and various yet unknown
To us: in such abundance lies our choice   620
As leaves a greater store of fruit untouched,
Still hanging incorruptible till men
Grow up to their provision and more hands
Help to disburden Nature of her bearth.
    To whom the wily adder blithe and glad: 625
Empress, the way is ready and not long:
Beyond a row of myrtles on a flat
Fast by a fountain, one small thicket past
Of blowing myrrh and balm. If thou accept
My conduct I can bring thee thither soon.   630
    Lead then, said Eve. He leading swiftly rolled
In tangles and made intricate seem straight,
To mischief swift. Hope elevates and joy
Brightens his crest. As when a wand'ring fire,
Compáct of unctuous vapor which the night   635

601. Although he gained the power of speech, that power remained confined to the form
    (*shape*) of a serpent.
605. *middle*: the air between earth and heaven.
612. *universal dame*: lady, and ruler of the universe.
624. *bearth*: "birth" but also "burden," which Earth *bears*, as the nineteenth-century edi-
    tor David Masson noted.
634–42. *wand'ring fire*: fairy light: phosphorescent swamp gas that misleads travelers at
    night, thought to be the malicious work of fairies. Typically, Milton gives a scientific
    account of the phenomenon before mentioning the folkloric account, which he then
    darkens by making an *evil spirit* (line 638) responsible.

Condenses and the cold environs round,
Kindled through agitation to a flame
Which oft, they say, some evil spirit attends,
Hovering and blazing with delusive light,
Misleads th' amazed night-wanderer from his way   640
To bogs and mires and oft through pond or pool,
There swallowed up and lost from succor far,
So glistered the dire snake and into fraud
Led Eve our credulous mother to the Tree
Of Prohibition, root of all our woe.   645
Which when she saw thus to her guide she spake:
    Serpent, we might have spared our coming hither,
Fruitless to me though fruit be here t' excess,
The credit of whose virtue rest with thee,
Wondrous indeed if cause of such effects.   650
But of this tree we may not taste nor touch:
God so commanded and left that command
Sole daughter of His voice. The rest we live
Law to ourselves: our reason is our law.
    To whom the Tempter guilefully replied: 655
Indeed? Hath God then said that of the fruit
Of all these garden trees ye shall not eat
Yet lords declared of all in earth or air?
To whom thus Eve yet sinless: Of the fruit
Of each tree in the garden we may eat   660
But of the fruit of this fair tree amidst
The garden God hath said, "Ye shall not eat
Thereof nor shall ye touch it, lest ye die."
    She scarce had said, though brief, when now more bold 665
The Tempter but with show of zeal and love
To man and indignation at his wrong
New part puts on and as to passion moved
Fluctuates disturbed, yet comely, and in act
Raised as of some great matter to begin.
As when of old some orator renowned   670
In Athens or free Rome where eloquence
Flourished (since mute) to some great cause addressed
Stood in himself collected while each part,
Motion, each act won audience ere the tongue,
Sometimes in heighth began as no delay   675

653–54. *The rest*: I.e., As to the rest of the natural world, we do as we please, governed by
our own reason, which is our only law. "For when the Gentiles, which have not the law,
do by nature the things contained in the law, these, having not the law, are a law unto
themselves: Which show the work of the law written in their hearts" (Romans
2:14–15).
668. *in act*: by his actions seemed.
671. *free Rome*: Rome of the Republic, before the emperors.

Of preface brooking through his zeal of right,
So standing, moving, or to heighth upgrown
The Tempter all impassioned thus began:
    O sacred, wise, and wisdom-giving plant,
Mother of science, now I feel thy pow'r   680
Within me clear not only to discern
Things in their causes but to trace the ways
Of highest agents deemed however wise!
Queen of this universe, do not believe
Those rigid threats of death! Ye shall not die.   685
How should ye? By the fruit? It gives you life
To knowledge. By the Threatener? Look on me!
Me who have touched and tasted yet both live
And life more perfect have attained than fate
Meant me by vent'ring higher than my lot.   690
Shall that be shut to Man which to the beast
Is open? Or will God incense His ire
For such a petty trespass and not praise
Rather your dauntless virtue whom the pain
Of death denounced (whatever thing death be)   695
Deterred not from achieving what might lead
To happier life, knowledge of good and evil?
Of good, how just? Of evil (if what is evil
Be real) why not known since easier shunned?
God therefore cannot hurt ye and be just: 700
Not just, not God! Not feared then, nor obeyed.
Your fear itself of death removes the fear!
Why then was this forbid? Why but to awe,
Why but to keep ye low and ignorant,
His worshippers? He knows that in the day   705
Ye eat thereof your eyes, that seem so clear
Yet are but dim, shall perfectly be then
Opened and cleared and ye shall be as gods
Knowing both good and evil as they know.
That ye should be as gods since I as Man,   710
Internal Man, is but proportion meet:

---

683. *highest agents*: God, whom Satan refers to in the plural, the first of Satan's efforts to
    instill polytheism and idolatry in the human mind. See line 709 and n. and lines
    716–19. We see Satan's success at line 804.
702. What appears to be a chain of necessary consequences is drawn into a circle: i.e.,
    God would not allow anything fearful to exist. Because you fear death, death must
    not exist: your fear therefore proves that there is nothing to fear.
709. *they*: God and the angels. The plural is biblical: "And the Lord God said, Behold, the
    man is become as one of us, to know good and evil" (Genesis 3:22). But Satan's aim
    is to suggest multiplicity in God, in order to make it easier for the rebel angels to
    present themselves on Earth as gods. See lines 716–19.

I of brute human, ye of human gods.
So ye shall die perhaps by putting off
Human to put on gods: death to be wished,
Though threatened, which no worse than this can bring!   715
And what are gods that Man may not become
As they, participating godlike food?
The gods are first and that advantage use
On our belief that all from them proceeds.
I question it, for this fair earth I see   720
Warmed by the sun producing every kind,
Them nothing. If they all things, *who* enclosed
Knowledge of good and evil in this tree
That whoso eats thereof forthwith attains
Wisdom without their leave? And wherein lies   725
Th' offence that Man should thus attain to know?
What can your knowledge hurt Him or this tree
Impart against His will *if* all be His?
Or is it envy? And can envy dwell
In Heav'nly breasts? These, these and many more   730
Causes import your need of this fair fruit.
Goddess humane, reach then and freely taste!
     He ended and his words replete with guile
Into her heart too easy entrance won.
Fixed on the fruit she gazed which to behold   735
Might tempt alone and in her ears the sound
Yet rung of his persuasive words impregned
With reason (to her seeming) and with truth.
Meanwhile the hour of noon drew on and waked
An eager appetite raised by the smell   740
So savory of that fruit which with desire
Inclinable now grown to touch or taste
Solicited her longing eye. Yet first

712. *of*: from. The understood verbs are *was made* and *shall be made*: 'As I was made
    human from an animal, so you shall be made gods from humans.'
713–14. "For this corruptible matter must put on incorruption, and this mortal must put
    on immortality" (1 Corinthians 15:53).
716–19. The earlier suggestion that God is plural becomes explicit in these lines.
718–19. This is essentially the same argument Satan uses at 5.856–60, where he suggests
    that the idea that God created the angels is a fiction devised by God to get an advan-
    tage over the angels.
722–30. The insinuation in these lines is that the gods enclosed knowledge of good and
    evil in the tree, and forbade eating its fruit, to conceal the lie that all things proceed
    from the gods. If Eve were to eat the fruit, she would see the lie of Creation exposed.
729–30. *can envy . . . breasts?*: A conspicuous allusion to the question of Virgil's *Aeneid*
    (I.11). The poet tells of Juno's hostility to Aeneas and asks, "Can so much anger
    dwell in heavenly breasts?" See 6.788 and n.
731. *need*: a telling word. Like advertising, temptation works by persuading the tempted
    that she or he has a need not recognized before. See line 755: *our want*.
737. *impregned*: filled with, impregnated with.

Pausing a while thus to herself she mused:
    Great are thy virtues doubtless, best of fruits,   745
Though kept from Man, and worthy to be admired,
Whose taste too long forborne at first assay
Gave elocution to the mute and taught
The tongue not made for speech to speak thy praise.
Thy praise He also who forbids thy use   750
Conceals not from us, naming thee the Tree
Of Knowledge, knowledge both of good and evil,
Forbids us then to taste, but His forbidding
Commends thee more while it infers the good
By thee communicated and our want.   755
For good unknown sure is not had or had
And yet unknown is as not had at all!
In plain then what forbids He but to know,
Forbids us good, forbids us to be wise?
Such prohibitions bind not! But if death   760
Bind us with after-bands what profits then
Our inward freedom? In the day we eat
Of this fair fruit our doom is we shall die.
How dies the serpent? He hath eat'n and lives
And knows, and speaks, and reasons and discerns,   765
Irrational till then. For us alone
Was death invented? Or to us denied
This intellectual food for beasts reserved?
For beasts it seems: yet that one beast which first
Hath tasted envies not but brings with joy   770
The good befall'n him, author unsuspect,
Friendly to man, far from deceit or guile.
What fear I then, rather what know to fear
Under this ignorance of good and evil,
Of God or death, of law or penalty?   775
Here grows the cure of all: this fruit divine,
Fair to the eye, inviting to the taste,
Of virtue to make wise. What hinders then
To reach and feed at once both body and mind?
    So saying, her rash hand in evil hour   780
Forth reaching to the fruit, she plucked, she eat:
Earth felt the wound and Nature from her seat
Sighing through all her works gave signs of woe

---

771. *author*: authority (the serpent).
773–75. I.e., Since I do not know the difference between good and evil, it can't be evil of
    me to eat the fruit. And I can't possibly fear death when I don't know what it is.
778. *Of virtue*: having the power.

That all was lost. Back to the thicket slunk
The guilty serpent and well might for Eve   785
Intent now wholly on her taste naught else
Regarded, such delight till then as seemed
In fruit she never tasted whether true
Or fancied so, through expectation high
Of knowledge, nor was godhead from her thought.   790
Greedily she engorged without restraint
And knew not eating death. Satiate at length
And heightened as with wine, jocund and boon,
Thus to herself she pleasingly began:
    O sovereign, virtuous, precious of all trees   795
In Paradise, of operation blest
To sapience, hitherto obscured, infamed,
And thy fair fruit let hang as to no end
Created! But henceforth my early care,
Not without song each morning and due praise,   800
Shall tend thee and the fertile burden ease
Of thy full branches offered free to all
Till dieted by thee I grow mature
In knowledge as the gods who all things know,
Though others envy what they cannot give,   805
For had the gift been theirs it had not here
Thus grown. Experience next, to thee I owe,
Best guide. Not foll'wing thee, I had remained
In ignorance. Thou open'st wisdom's way
And giv'st accéss though secret she retire.   810
And I perhaps am secret: Heav'n is high,
High and remote to see from thence distinct
Each thing on Earth and other care perhaps
May have diverted from continual watch
Our great Forbidder, safe with all His spies   815
About Him. But to Adam in what sort
Shall I appear? Shall I to him make known
As yet my change and give him to partake
Full happiness with me? Or rather not,

793. *jocund and boon*: cheerful, gay, convivial.
797. *sapience*: knowledge, wisdom (Latin *sapientia*); but also, as is relevant here, the sense of taste, Latin *sapor*, "flavor."
805. *others*: the gods.
807. *next*: Eve thanks the tree first and experience (as opposed to reason, or precept) next. She knows the fruit is good because she has experienced its goodness in herself. Milton takes a dim view of empiricism. See 988.
816–17. *But to Adam . . . appear*: The influence of the English stage, especially of Shakespeare, becomes clearer as this speech proceeds.

But keep the odds of knowledge in my pow'r   820
Without copartner so to add what wants
In female sex, the more to draw his love
And render me more equal and, perhaps,
A thing not undesirable, sometime
Superior: for inferior who is free?   825
This may be well. But what if God have seen
And death ensue? Then I shall be no more
And Adam wedded to another Eve
Shall live with her enjoying, I extinct:
A death to think! Confirmed then I resolve   830
Adam shall share with me in bliss or woe.
So dear I love him that with him all deaths
I could endure, without him live no life.

   So saying from the tree her step she turned,
But first low reverence done as to the pow'r   835
That dwelt within whose presence had infused
Into the plant sciential sap derived
From nectar, drink of gods. Adam the while
Waiting desirous her return had wove
Of choicest flow'rs a garland to adorn   840
Her tresses and her rural labors crown
As reapers oft are wont their harvest queen.
Great joy he promised to his thoughts and new
Solace in her return so long delayed.
Yet oft his heart, divine of something ill,   845
Misgave him: he the falt'ring measure felt
And forth to meet her went the way she took
That morn when first they parted. By the Tree
Of Knowledge he must pass. There he her met
Scarce from the tree returning, in her hand   850
A bough of fairest fruit that downy smiled
New gathered and ambrosial smell diffused.
To him she hasted. In her face excuse
Came prologue and apology too prompt

---

822. *the more to draw his love.* This shows the beginnings of insecurity in marriage.

826–27. Eve's hope of being sometimes superior to Adam depends on God's not seeing her take the fruit. For if God does, she will die.

830. *A death to think!*: I.e., It is as horrible as death merely to *think* of Adam with another wife. (Perhaps not.)

835. The first act of idolatry: Eve worships the tree, supposing there to be a godlike *power* within it.

835–38. *as to the pow'r . . . gods*: These lines show Eve supposing divine and magical properties dwell in the tree. Milton intends to show where and how false ideas in religion (e.g. notions of the real presence of Christ in the Eucharist) get started.

845. *divine*: divining.

846. *Misgave him*: caused him misgivings. *falt'ring measure*: irregular heartbeat.

852. *ambrosial smell*: smell of the food of the gods, ambrosia.

Which with bland words at will she thus addressed: 855
　　Hast thou not wondered, Adam, at my stay?
Thee I have missed and thought it long, deprived
Thy presence, agony of love till now
Not felt, nor shall be twice, for never more
Mean I to try what rash untried I sought: 860
The pain of absence from thy sight. But strange
Hath been the cause and wonderful to hear!
This tree is not as we are told a tree
Of danger tasted nor to evil unknown
Op'ning the way but of divine effect   865
To open eyes and make them gods who taste,
And hath been tasted such! The serpent wise,
Or not restrained as we or not obeying,
Hath eaten of the fruit and is become
Not dead, as we are threatened, but thenceforth   870
Endued with human voice and human sense
Reasoning to admiration and with me
Persuasively hath so prevailed that I
Have also tasted and have also found
Th' effects to correspond: opener mine eyes,   875
Dim erst, dilated spirits, ampler heart
And growing up to godhead which for thee
Chiefly I sought, without thee can despise.
For bliss, as thou hast part, to me is bliss,
Tedious unshared with thee and odious soon.   880
Thou therefore also taste that equal lot
May join us, equal joy as equal love,
Lest thou not tasting, different degree
Disjoin us and I then too late renounce
Deity for thee when fate will not permit.   885
　　Thus Eve with count'nance blithe her story told
But in her cheek distemper flushing glowed.
On th' other side Adam, soon as he heard
The fatal trespass done by Eve, amazed,
Astonied stood and blank while horror chill   890

---

876. *erst:* formerly. *dilated:* expanded, increased. *ampler heart:* more courageous, generous.
877. *godhead:* divine status.
887. *distemper:* imbalance of elements in the body.
890. *Astonied:* "turned to stone" and "thunderstruck" (Latin *tono,* "to thunder") are popular etymologies of this word.
890–91. See *Aeneid* I.92: "Immediately Aeneas's limbs were dissolved with cold" (*Extemplo Aeneae solvuntur frigore membra*).
892–93. Cf. Ovid, *Metamorphoses* 5.398–401, where Proserpina, in her childish simplicity, laments the loss of her gathered flowers, which spill from her ripped tunic when she is seized and carried off by Dis: "*conlecti flores tunicis cedidere remissis*" (5.399). Adam doesn't notice his fallen flowers.

Ran through his veins and all his joints relaxed.
From his slack hand the garland wreathed for Eve
Down dropped and all the faded roses shed.
Speechless he stood and pale till thus at length
First to himself he inward silence broke: 895
    O fairest of Creation, last and best
Of all God's works, creature in whom excelled
Whatever can to sight or thought be formed,
Holy, divine, good, amiable or sweet!
How art thou lost, how on a sudden lost,   900
Defaced, deflow'red, and now to death devote?
Rather how hast thou yielded to transgress
The strict forbiddance, how to violate
The sacred fruit forbidden? Some cursèd fraud
Of enemy hath beguiled thee, yet unknown,   905
And me with thee hath ruined, for with thee
Certain my resolution is to die!
How can I live without thee, how forgo
Thy sweet convérse and love so dearly joined
To live again in these wild woods forlorn?   910
Should God create another Eve and I
Another rib afford, yet loss of thee
Would never from my heart. No! No! I feel
The link of nature draw me, flesh of flesh,
Bone of my bone thou art and from thy state   915
Mine never shall be parted, bliss or woe.
    So having said as one from sad dismay
Recomforted and after thoughts disturbed
Submitting to what seemed remédiless
Thus in calm mood his words to Eve he turned: 920

895. *to himself*: A new phenomenon in marriage enters here: one thing is thought and another is said.

896–97. Eve is the *last* of all God's works, but not in Milton's view the *best*. Adam is about to change that. We are meant to recall Raphael's warning. See 8.560–78.

901. Note the unusual (for Milton) emphatic alliteration, suggesting the four-beat Anglo-Saxon line.

905. *yet unknown* can refer to the *fraud*, or trick, which is not yet known; to the *enemy*, whose identity is not yet known for certain; or to *thee*, Eve: that you have been deceived is as yet unknown to you.

910. *these wild woods*: Adam's mistake is to think the Fall has already occurred, that there is no point in resistance or in seeking higher aid. He thinks of himself as already fallen, and of the garden as already a wilderness. Yet there is dignity and pathos in his words. Cf. 1084–90.

914–15. "And Adam said, This is now bone of my bones, and flesh of my flesh: she shall be called Woman, because she was taken out of Man. Therefore shall a man leave his father and mother, and shall cleave unto his wife: and they shall be one flesh" (Genesis 2:23–24). The biblical passage gives still more emphasis to the tragic inevitability of Adam's decision. But see 955–59.

916. *bliss or woe*. Cf. 831.

   Bold deed thou hast presumed, advent'rous Eve,
And peril great provoked who thus hath dared,
Had it been only coveting, to eye
That sacred fruit, sacred to abstinence,
Much more to taste it under ban to touch.   925
But past who can recall or done undo?
Not God omnipotent nor fate. Yet so
Perhaps thou shalt not die. Perhaps the fact
Is not so heinous now: foretasted fruit,
Profaned first by the serpent, by him first   930
Made common and unhallowed ere our taste,
Nor yet on him found deadly—he yet lives,
Lives as thou saidst and gains to live as man
Higher degree of life, inducement strong
To us as likely tasting to attain   935
Proportional ascent which cannot be
But to be gods or angels, demigods.
Nor can I think that God, creator wise,
Though threat'ning, will in earnest so destroy
Us His prime creatures, dignified so high,   940
Set over all His works which in our Fall
For us created needs with us must fail,
Dependent made: so God shall uncreate,
Be frustrate, do, undo, and labor lose.
Not well conceived of God who though His power   945
Creation could repeat yet would be loath
Us to abolish lest the Adversary
Triumph and say, "Fickle their state whom God
Most favors! Who can please Him long? Me first
He ruined, now mankind! Whom will He next?"   950
Matter of scorn not to be giv'n the foe.
However, I with thee have fixed my lot
Certain to undergo like doom. If death
Consort with thee death is to me as life,
So forcible within my heart I feel   955
The bond of nature draw me to my own,
My own in thee, for what thou art is mine.
Our state cannot be severed. We are one,
One flesh: to lose thee were to lose myself.
   So Adam, and thus Eve to him replied: 960
O glorious trial of exceeding love,

926–27. While it is true that God himself cannot undo what has been done, God can, and
    will, overcome what has been done.
928. *fact*: deed (substantive of Latin *facio*, "to make, do"). See 2.124 and n. and line 980.
959. *One flesh*: See lines 914–15 n.

Illustrious evidence, example high,
Engaging me to emulate! But short
Of thy perfection how shall I attain,
Adam, from whose dear side I boast me sprung   965
And gladly of our union hear thee speak,
One heart, one soul in both whereof good proof
This day affords, declaring thee resolved
Rather than death or aught than death more dread
Shall separate us, linked in love so dear,   970
To undergo with me one guilt, one crime
(If any be) of tasting this fair fruit
Whose virtue (for of good still good proceeds)
Direct or by occasion hath presented
This happy trial of thy love which else   975
So eminently never had been known.
Were it I thought death menaced would ensue
This my attempt, I would sustain alone
The worst and not persuade thee, rather die
Deserted than oblige thee with a fact   980
Pernicious to thy peace, chiefly assured
Remarkably so late of thy so true,
So faithful love unequaled. But I feel
Far otherwise th' event: not death but life
Augmented, opened eyes, new hopes, new joys,   985
Taste so divine that what of sweet before
Hath touched my sense flat seems to this and harsh.
On my experience, Adam, freely taste
And fear of death deliver to the winds!
    So saying she embraced him and for joy   990
Tenderly wept, much won that he his love
Had so ennobled as of choice t' incur
Divine displeasure for her sake, or death.
In recompense (for such compliance bad
Such recompense best merits) from the bough   995
She gave him of that fair enticing fruit
With liberal hand. He scrupled not to eat,
Against his better knowledge, not deceived

973–76. I.e., Because good comes out of good, the power of the goodness (*virtue*, line
   973) in this fruit either has directly caused this trial of your love or has indirectly
   been the occasion for that trial. In either case, the height of your love would never
   have been known if the fruit had not been eaten.
977–83. I.e., If I really believed eating the fruit would cause us to die, I would die alone
   rather than make you die with me, and I would be comforted for the loss of my life by
   the assurance of your unequaled love and faith. Lines 826–33 may put this assertion
   in question, but there is little doubt she means it now.
980. *oblige thee with a fact*: compel you with a *fait accompli*.

But fondly overcome with female charm.
Earth trembled from her entrails as again   1000
In pangs and Nature gave a second groan.
Sky loured and mutt'ring thunder some sad drops
Wept at completing of the mortal sin
Original while Adam took no thought,
Eating his fill. Nor Eve to iterate   1005
Her former trespass feared, the more to soothe
Him with her loved society that now
As with new wine intoxicated both
They swim in mirth and fancy that they feel
Divinity within them breeding wings   1010
Wherewith to scorn the earth. But that false fruit
Far other operation first displayed,
Carnal desire inflaming. He on Eve
Began to cast lascivious eyes, she him
As wantonly repaid: in lust they burn   1015
Till Adam thus gan Eve to dalliance move:
    Eve, now I see thou art exact of taste
And elegant of sapience no small part
Since to each meaning savor we apply
And palate call judicious. I the praise   1020
Yield thee, so well this day thou hast purveyed.
Much pleasure we have lost while we abstained
From this delightful fruit, nor known till now
True relish tasting. If such pleasure be
In things to us forbidden it might be wished   1025
For this one tree had been forbidden ten!
But come, so well refreshed now let us play
As meet is after such delicious fare,
For never did thy beauty since the day
I saw thee first and wedded thee adorned   1030
With all perfections so inflame my sense
With ardor to enjoy thee, fairer now
Than ever, bounty of this virtuous tree!
    So said he and forbore not glance or toy
Of amorous intent, well understood   1035
Of Eve whose eye darted contagious fire.
Her hand he seized and to a shady bank

1018. *sapience*: a play on the double meaning of the Latin *sapientia*, "good taste, knowledge."
1027. *play*: have sex; meant to recall the Hebrews when, after they worshipped the golden calf, they "sat down to eat and to drink, and rose up to play" (Exodus 32:6).
1027–33. The language of Adam's proposal echoes Paris's words to Helen in the *Iliad* 3.441–42: "For never before has eros so entangled and veiled my mind, not even when I first seized you and carried you away from Sparta."

Thick overhead with verdant roof embow'red
He led her nothing loath. Flowers were the couch,
Pansies and violets and asphodel   1040
And hyacinth, Earth's freshest softest lap.
There they their fill of love and love's disport
Took largely, of their mutual guilt the seal,
The solace of their sin, till dewy sleep
Oppressed them, wearied with their am'rous play.   1045
Soon as the force of that fallacious fruit
That with exhilarating vapor bland
About their spirits had played and inmost pow'rs
Made err was now exhaled and grosser sleep
Bred of unkindly fumes with conscious dreams   1050
Encumbered now had left them, up they rose
As from unrest and each the other viewing
Soon found their eyes how opened and their minds
How darkened. Innocence that as a veil
Had shadowed them from knowing ill was gone,   1055
Just Confidence and Native Righteousness
And Honor from about them, naked left
To guilty Shame: he covered but his robe
Uncovered more. So rose the Danite strong,
Herculean Samson, from the harlot-lap   1060
Of Philistéan Dálilah and waked
Shorn of his strength—they, destitute and bare
Of all their virtue. Silent and in face
Confounded long they sat as strucken mute
Till Adam though not less than Eve abashed   1065
At length gave utterance to these words constrained:
    O Eve, in evil hour thou didst give ear
To that false worm of whomsoever taught
To counterfeit man's voice, true in our Fall,
False in our promised rising, since our eyes   1070
Opened we find indeed and find we know
Both good and evil: good lost, and evil got!
Bad fruit of knowledge if this be to know
Which leaves us naked thus, of honor void,
Of innocence, of faith, of purity,   1075
Our wonted ornaments now soiled and stained

1039–41. This scene, with its flowers, is similar to the *Iliad* 14.346–51, when the earth
    pushes up flowers beneath Zeus and Hera as they make love.
1054–59. *Innocence, Confidence, Righteousness,* and *Honor* no longer shield their naked
    shame. Yet Shame also covers them, but only with exposure of their sin. "Let mine
    adversaries be clothed with shame" (Psalm 109:29).
1061. Delilah, Samson's lover, has a servant shave off the seven locks of Samson's hair, in
    which his strength resided (Judges 16:19).

And in our faces evident the signs
Of foul concupiscence, whence evil store,
Ev'n shame the last of evils—of the first
Be sure then! How shall I behold the face   1080
Henceforth of God or angel, erst with joy
And rapture so oft beheld? Those Heav'nly shapes
Will dazzle now this earthly with their blaze
Insufferably bright. O might I here
In solitude live savage in some glade   1085
Obscured where highest woods impenetrable
To star or sunlight spread their umbrage broad
And brown as evening! Cover me ye pines,
Ye cedars, with innumerable boughs
Hide me where I may never see them more!   1090
But let us now as in bad plight devise
What best may for the present serve to hide
The parts of each from other that seem most
To shame obnoxious and unseemliest seen:
Some tree whose broad smooth leaves together sewed   1095
And girded on our loins may cover round
Those middle parts that this newcomer, Shame,
There sit not and reproach us as unclean.
    So counseled he and both together went
Into the thickest wood, there soon they chose   1100
The fig-tree: not that kind for fruit renowned
But such as at this day to Indians known
In Malabar or Deccan spreads her arms
Branching so broad and long that in the ground
The bended twigs take root and daughters grow   1105
About the mother tree, a pillared shade
High overarched and echoing walks between.
There oft the Indian herdsman shunning heat
Shelters in cool and tends his pasturing herds
At loopholes cut through thickest shade. Those leaves   1110
They gathered broad as Amazonian targe

1078. *concupiscence*: lust.
1079–80. Shame is the last of evils because it comes only after one has committed
crimes. But it is among the first of evils because it is involved in crimes as the
effect is involved in its cause.
1086–87. *Faerie Queene* 1.7.6: "Not perceable with power of any starre."
1088–90. "They shall say to the mountains, Cover us; and to the hills, Fall on us" (Hosea
10:8). Echoed in Luke 23:30 and in Revelation 6:16.
1102–3 and 1116. Milton knowledgeably refers to residents of *Malabar* and *Deccan* (see
Glossary) as *Indians* and to Native peoples of the Americas as *American*. See Glossary, COLUMBUS.
1111. The leaves are as broad as the shields of Amazons, female warriors of Greek
legend.

And with what skill they had together sewed
To gird their waist, vain covering if to hide
Their guilt and dreaded shame. O how unlike
To that first naked glory! Such of late   1115
Columbus found th' American so girt
With feathered cincture, naked else and wild
Among the trees on isles and woody shores.
Thus fenced and, as they thought, their shame in part
Covered, but not at rest or ease of mind   1120
They sat them down to weep. Nor only tears
Rained at their eyes but high winds worse within
Began to rise, high passions—anger, hate,
Mistrust, suspicion, discord—and shook sore
Their inward state of mind, calm region once   1125
And full of peace, now tossed and turbulent:
For Understanding ruled not and the Will
Heard not her lore, both in subjection now
To sensual Appetite who from beneath
Usurping over sov'reign Reason claimed   1130
Superior sway. From thus distempered breast
Adam estranged in look and altered style
Speech intermitted thus to Eve renewed:
     Would thou hadst hearkened to my words and stayed
With me as I besought thee when that strange   1135
Desire of wandering this unhappy morn
(I know not whence) possessed thee! We had then
Remained still happy, not as now despoiled
Of all our good, shamed, naked, miserable!
Let none henceforth seek needless cause t' approve   1140
The faith they owe. When earnestly they seek
Such proof, conclude they then begin to fail.
     To whom soon moved with touch of blame thus Eve:
What words have passed thy lips, Adam severe?
Imput'st thou that to my default (or will   1145
Of wandering as thou call'st it) which who knows
But might as ill have happened thou being by
Or to thyself perhaps? Hadst thou been there,

1117. *cincture*: belt around the waist.
1121. "By the rivers of Babylon, there we sat down, yea, we wept, when we remembered Zion" (Psalm 137:1).
1127–31. In the proper hierarchy of the faculties, reason is at the top, governing the will, which in turn governs the appetites. When the hierarchy is upset, when a lower faculty gains control over a higher, the passions are roused and the balance of the whole constitution—the body, its faculties, and its passions—is *distempered* (line 1131). See line 887 and n.
1144. *What words . . .* : a Homeric formula.

Or here th' attempt, thou couldst not have discerned
Fraud in the serpent, speaking as he spake,   1150
No ground of enmity between us known,
Why he should mean me ill or seek to harm?
Was I t' have never parted from thy side?
As good have grown there still a lifeless rib!
Being as I am, why didst not thou, the head,   1155
Command me absolutely not to go,
Going into such danger as thou saidst?
Too facile then thou didst not much gainsay,
Nay, didst permit, approve, and fair dismiss!
Hadst thou been firm and fixed in thy dissent   1160
Neither had I transgressed nor thou with me.
    To whom then first incensed Adam replied:
Is this the love, is this the recompense
Of mine to thee, ingrateful Eve, expressed
Immutable when *thou* wert lost, not I,   1165
Who might have lived and joyed immortal bliss
Yet willingly chose rather death with thee?
And am I now upbraided as the cause
Of thy transgressing, not enough severe
It seems in thy restraint? What could I more?   1170
I warned thee, I admonished thee, foretold
The danger and the lurking enemy
That lay in wait. Beyond this had been force
And force upon free will hath here no place.
But confidence then bore thee on secure   1175
Either to meet no danger or to find
Matter of glorious trial. And perhaps
I also erred in overmuch admiring
What seem'd in thee so perfect that I thought
No evil durst attempt thee. But I rue   1180
That error now which is become my crime
And thou th' accuser. Thus it shall befall
Him who to worth in women overtrusting
Lets her will rule! Restraint she will not brook
And left t' herself if evil thence ensue   1185
She first his weak indulgence will accuse.
    Thus they in mutual accusation spent
The fruitless hours, but neither self-condemning,
And of their vain contést appeared no end.

1158. *facile*: easygoing.

Book Ten

The Argument

Man's transgression known, the guardian angels forsake Paradise and return up to Heaven to approve their vigilance, and are approved, God declaring that the entrance of Satan could not be by them prevented. He sends his Son to judge the transgressors, who descends and gives sentence accordingly; then, in pity, clothes them both and reascends. Sin and Death, sitting till then at the gates of Hell, by wondrous sympathy feeling the success of Satan in this new world, and the sin by man there committed, resolve to sit no longer confined in Hell but to follow Satan their sire up to the place of Man. To make the way easier from Hell to and fro, they pave a broad highway or bridge over chaos according to the track that Satan first made. Then, preparing for Earth, they meet him, proud of his success, returning to Hell; their mutual gratulation. Satan arrives at Pandemonium, in full assembly relates with boasting his success against Man; instead of applause is entertained with a general hiss by all his audience, transformed with himself also suddenly into serpents, according to his doom, given in Paradise. Then, deluded with a show of the Forbidden Tree springing up before them, they greedily reaching to take of the fruit, chew dust and bitter ashes. The proceedings of Sin and Death. God foretells the final victory of his Son over them and the renewing of all things; but for the present commands his angels to make several alterations in the heavens and elements. Adam more and more perceiving his fallen condition, heavily bewails, rejects the condolement of Eve; she persists and at length appeases him; then to evade the curse likely to fall on their offspring, proposes to Adam violent ways which he approves not, but conceiving better hope, puts her in mind of the late promise made them that her seed should be revenged on the serpent, and exhorts her with him to seek peace of the offended Deity by repentance and supplication.

Meanwhile the heinous and despiteful act
Of Satan done in Paradise and how
He in the serpent had perverted Eve,
Her husband she, to taste the fatal fruit
Was known in Heaven. For what can 'scape the eye   5
Of God all-seeing or deceive His heart
Omniscient who, in all things wise and just,
Hindered not Satan to attempt the mind
Of Man with strength entire and free will armed
Complete to have discovered and repulsed   10
Whatever wiles of foe or seeming friend.

For still they knew and ought t' have still remembered
The high injunction not to taste that fruit,
Whoever tempted, which they not obeying
Incurred (what could they less?) the penalty   15
And, manifold in sin, deserved to fall.
Up into Heav'n from Paradise in haste
Th' angelic guards ascended mute and sad
For Man; for of his state by this they knew,
Much wond'ring how the subtle Fiend had stolen   20
Entrance unseen. Soon as th' unwelcome news
From Earth arrived at Heaven gate, displeased
All were who heard: dim sadness did not spare
That time celestial visages, yet mixed
With pity violated not their bliss.   25
About the new-arrived in multitudes
Th' ethereal people ran to hear and know
How all befell. They towards the throne supreme
Accountable made haste to make appear
With righteous plea their utmost vigilance,   30
And easily approved when the Most High
Eternal Father from His secret cloud
Amidst in thunder uttered thus His voice:
    Assembled angels and ye pow'rs returned
From unsuccessful charge, be not dismayed   35
Nor troubled at these tidings from the Earth
Which your sincerest care could not prevent,
Foretold so lately what would come to pass
When first this tempter crossed the gulf from Hell.
I told ye then he should prevail and speed   40
On his bad errand, Man should be seduced
And flattered out of all, believing lies
Against his Maker, no decree of mine
Concurring to necessitate his Fall
Or touch with lightest moment of impulse   45
His free will, to her own inclining left
In even scale. But fall'n he is. And now
What rests but that the mortal sentence pass
On his transgression: death denounced that day
Which he presumes already vain and void   50
Because not yet inflicted as he feared
By some immediate stroke but soon shall find

Book Ten
27. *ethereal people*: angels.
31. *approved*: vindicated.

Forbearance no acquittance ere day end.
Justice shall not return as bounty, scorned.
But whom send I to judge them? Whom but thee   55
Vicegerent Son, to thee I have transferred
All judgment whether in Heav'n, or Earth, or Hell.
Easy it might be seen that I intend
Mercy colléague with justice, sending thee
Man's friend, his Mediator, his designed   60
Both ransom and Redeemer voluntary
And destined man himself to judge Man fallen.
     So spake the Father and unfolding bright
Toward the right hand his glory on the Son
Blazed forth unclouded deity. He full   65
Resplendent all his Father manifest
Expressed, and thus divinely answered mild:
     Father Eternal, Thine is to decree,
Mine both in Heav'n and Earth to do Thy will
Supreme, that Thou in Me thy Son beloved   70
May'st ever rest well pleased. I go to judge
On Earth these Thy transgressors but Thou know'st,
Whoever judged, the worst on Me must light
When time shall be, for so I undertook
Before Thee and, not repenting, this obtain   75
Of right: that I may mitigate their doom
On Me derived. Yet I shall temper so
Justice with mercy as may illústrate most
Them fully satisfied and Thee appease.
Attendance none shall need, nor train, where none   80
Are to behold the judgment but the judged,
Those two. The third, best absent, is condemned,
Convict by flight and rebel to all law.
Conviction to the serpent none belongs.
     Thus saying from his radiant seat he rose   85
Of high collateral glory. Him thrones and powers,
Princedoms and dominations ministrant
Accompanied to Heaven gate from whence
Eden and all the coast in prospect lay.
Down he descended straight. The speed of gods   90

54. I.e., I sent my bounty to earth and it was scorned, and so returned to heaven. Now I will send my justice: let's see them try send *that* back!
56. *Vicegerent*: officer appointed as assistant to a supreme commander.
62. I.e., The Son is destined to be a man, Jesus.
77. *derived*: diverted.
82. *third*: Satan.
84. I.e., The serpent, being merely Satan's instrument, is not convicted of any crime. But see lines 164–69 and n.

Time counts not though with swiftest minutes winged.
Now was the sun in western cadence low
From noon and gentle airs due at their hour
To fan the earth now waked and usher in
The evening cool when he, from wrath more cool,   95
Came the mild Judge and Intercessor both
To sentence Man. The voice of God they heard
Now walking in the garden by soft winds
Brought to their ears while day declined. They heard
And from his presence hid themselves among   100
The thickest trees, both man and wife, till God
Approaching thus to Adam called aloud:
    Where art thou, Adam, wont with joy to meet
My coming seen far off? I miss thee here,
Not pleased thus entertained with solitude   105
Where obvious duty erewhile appeared unsought.
Or come I less conspicuous or what change
Absents thee or what chance detains? Come forth!
He came and with him Eve more loath, though first
T' offend, discount'nanced both and discomposed.   110
Love was not in their looks either to God
Or to each other but apparent guilt
And shame and perturbation and despair,
Anger and obstinacy and hate and guile.
Whence Adam falt'ring long thus answered brief: 115
    I heard Thee in the garden and of Thy voice
Afraid, being naked, hid myself. To whom
The gracious Judge without revile replied:
    My voice thou oft hast heard and hast not feared
But still rejoiced. How is it now become   120
So dreadful to thee? That thou art naked, who
Hath told thee? Hast thou eaten of the tree
Whereof I gave thee charge thou shouldst not eat?
    To whom thus Adam sore beset replied:
O Heav'n! in evil straight this day I stand   125
Before my Judge, either to undergo
Myself the total crime or to accuse
My other self, the partner of my life,
Whose failing while her faith to me remains
I should conceal and not expose to blame   130
By my complaint! But strict necessity
Subdues me and calamitous constraint

  92. *cadence*: descent.
  106. *obvious*: coming in the way, to meet.

Lest on my head both sin and punishment
However insupportable be all
Devolved; though should I hold my peace yet Thou   135
Wouldst easily detect what I conceal.
This woman whom Thou mad'st to be my help
And gav'st me as Thy perfect gift so good,
So fit, so acceptáble, so divine
That from her hand I could suspect no ill,   140
And what she did, whatever in itself,
Her doing seemed to justify the deed,
She gave me of the tree and I did eat.
    To whom the sov'reign Presence thus replied:
Was she thy God that her thou didst obey   145
Before His voice? Or was she made thy guide
Superior, or but equal, that to her
Thou didst resign thy manhood and the place
Wherein God set thee 'bove her, made of thee
And for thee, whose perfection far excelled   150
Hers in all real dignity? Adorned
She was indeed and lovely to attract
Thy love, not thy subjection, and her gifts
Were such as under government well seemed,
Unseemly to bear rule, which was thy part   155
And person hadst thou known thyself aright.
    So having said, he thus to Eve in few:
Say, woman, what is this which thou hast done?
    To whom sad Eve with shame nigh overwhelmed
Confessing soon, yet not before her Judge   160
Bold or loquacious, thus abashed replied:
    The serpent me beguiled and I did eat.
    Which when the Lord God heard without delay
To judgment he proceeded on th' accused

---

150. *whose*: Adam's.

153–56. Eve's gifts, though good in themselves, were such that it would be unseemly for
    them to be seen in a ruler. The hierarchical, sexist anthropology of the poem, sum-
    marized at 4.299—"He for God only, she for God in him"—is here reaffirmed, based
    on 1 Corinthians 11:3: "the head of every man is Christ; and the head of the woman
    is the man." By joining Eve in her crime, Milton holds, Adam forgot his superiority
    to her. His transgression is therefore more abject than hers. Eve falls first, deceived,
    but Adam, not being deceived but clear-eyed, resigns his "manhood" (148) and falls
    farther. His moving sympathy and love for Eve is not factored in to this moral
    calculation.

164–69. Although God said the serpent is not liable to conviction (line 84), the Son is
    unable to transfer from the serpent to Satan the guilt for having tempted Eve. The
    serpent is therefore *vitiated* (line 169) for having been Satan's *instrument* (line 166).
    This is Milton's somewhat contorted but stubbornly honest effort to come to terms
    with a major discrepancy between the Christian story and the account in Genesis
    (3:14–15), where Satan is unheard of. The tension between the simple tale of Genesis
    and the later, Jewish and Christian interpretation of it continues in lines 182–91.

Serpent, though brute, unable to transfer   165
The guilt on him who made him instrument
Of mischief and polluted from the end
Of his creation: justly then accurst
As vitiated in nature. More to know
Concerned not Man (since he no further knew)   170
Nor altered his offence. Yet God at last
To Satan, first in sin, His doom applied,
Though in mysterious terms judged as then best
And on the serpent thus His curse let fall:
    Because thou hast done this thou art accurst   175
Above all cattle, each beast of the field.
Upon thy belly groveling thou shalt go
And dust shalt eat all the days of thy life.
Between thee and the woman I will put
Enmity and between thine and her seed: 180
Her seed shall bruise thy head, thou bruise his heel.
    So spake this oracle, then verified
When Jesus son of Mary, second Eve,
Saw Satan fall like lightning down from Heav'n,
Prince of the Air; then rising from His grave   185
Spoiled principalities and pow'rs, triúmphed
In open show, and with ascension bright
Captivity led captive through the air,
The realm itself of Satan long usurped,
Whom he shall tread at last under our feet,   190
Ev'n he who now foretold his fatal bruise,
And to the woman thus his sentence turned:
    Thy sorrow I will greatly multiply
By thy conception: children thou shalt bring
In sorrow forth and to thy husband's will   195
Thine shall submit: he over thee shall rule.
    On Adam last thus judgment he pronounced:
Because thou hast harkened to the voice of thy wife
And eaten of the tree concerning which
I charged thee saying, "Thou shalt not eat thereof,"   200
Cursed is the ground for thy sake, thou in sorrow

---

166. The first *him* is Satan, the second the serpent.
170. *no further knew*: did not know that the serpent was inhabited by Satan.
184. "And he said unto them, I beheld Satan as lightning fall from heaven" (Luke 10:18).
A prophecy of the apocalypse, when Satan will lose his power in the air and be
driven into Hell forever. See lines 188–89.
188. "Thou hast ascended on high, thou hast led captivity captive" (Psalm 68:18).
190. Since the Son retains his human nature, when he treads Satan under his feet it is
our feet as well that do so. "And the God of peace shall bruise Satan under your feet
shortly" (Romans 16:20).

Shalt eat thereof all the days of thy life.
Thorns also and thistles it shall bring thee forth
Unbid and thou shalt eat th' herb of the field.
In the sweat of thy face shalt thou eat bread   205
Till thou return unto the ground for thou
Out of the ground wast taken. Know thy birth,
For dust thou art and shalt to dust return.
    So judged he Man, both Judge and Savior sent
And th' instant stroke of death, denounced that day,   210
Removed far off. Then, pitying how they stood
Before him naked to the air that now
Must suffer change disdained not to begin
Thenceforth the form of Servant to assume
As when he washed his servants' feet, so now   215
As father of his family he clad
Their nakedness with skins of beasts, or slain
Or as the snake with youthful coat repaid,
And thought not much to clothe his enemies.
Nor he their outward only with the skins   220
Of beasts but inward nakedness much more
Opprobrious with his robe of righteousness
Arraying covered from his Father's sight.
    To Him with swift ascent he up returned,
Into His blissful bosom reassumed   225
In glory as of old. To Him, appeased,
All, though all-knowing, what had passed with Man
Recounted, mixing intercession sweet.
Meanwhile, ere thus was sinned and judged on Earth,
Within the gates of Hell sat Sin and Death,   230
In counterview, within the gates that now
Stood open wide, belching outrageous flame
Far into chaos since the Fiend passed through,
Sin op'ning, who thus now to Death began:
    O son, why sit we here each other viewing   235

204. *herb of the field*: grass, wheat made into bread.
210. *denounced*: pronounced.
217–18. *or slain / Or as the snake*: The Son either kills some beasts to make garments for
    Adam and Eve or picks up skins that have been shed, like a snake's skin. "Unto Adam
    also and to his wife did the Lord God make coats of skins, and clothed them" (Gen-
    esis 3:21).
222. "He hath covered me with the robe of righteousness" (Isaiah 61:10).
224–28. After the Son has ascended to the Father and resumed his place of glory in the
    Father's bosom, he tells the Father, whose justice is now appeased, what occurred
    during the judgment of Man.
226–28. The direct object of *Recounted* (line 228) is *All* (line 227) and the indirect object
    is *Him* (line 226): i.e., The Son recounted all to the all-knowing Father.

Idly while Satan our great author thrives
In other worlds and happier seat provides
For us his offspring dear? It cannot be
But that success attends him. If mishap,
Ere this he had returned with fury driv'n   240
By his avengers since no place like this
Can fit his punishment or their revenge.
Methinks I feel new strength within me rise,
Wings growing and dominion giv'n me large
Beyond this deep, whatever draws me on,   245
Or sympathy or some connatural force
Pow'rful at greatest distance to unite
With secret amity things of like kind
By secretest conveyance. Thou my shade
Inseparable must with me along,   250
For Death from Sin no pow'r can separate.
But lest the difficulty of passing back
Stay his return perhaps over this gulf
Impassable, impervious, let us try
Advent'rous work yet to thy pow'r and mine   255
Not unagreeable: to found a path
Over this main from Hell to that new world
Where Satan now prevails, a monument
Of merit high to all th' infernal host,
Easing their passage hence for intercourse   260
Or transmigration as their lot shall lead.
Nor can I miss the way so strongly drawn
By this new felt attraction and instínct.
    Whom thus the meagre shadow answered soon:
Go whither fate and inclination strong   265
Leads thee! I shall not lag behind nor err
The way, thou leading, such a scent I draw
Of carnage, prey innumerable, and taste
The savor of death from all things there that live.
Nor shall I to the work thou enterprisest   270
Be wanting but afford thee equal aid.
    So saying with delight he snuffed the smell
Of mortal change on Earth. As when a flock
Of rav'nous fowl though many a league remote
Against the day of battle to a field   275
Where armies lie encamped come flying, lured
With scent of living carcasses designed
For death the following day in bloody fight,
So scented the grim feature and upturned

His nostril wide into the murky air,   280
Sagacious of his quarry from so far.
Then both from out Hell gates into the waste
Wide anarchy of chaos damp and dark
Flew diverse and with pow'r (their pow'r was great)
Hovering upon the waters. What they met   285
Solid or slimy as in raging sea
Tossed up and down together crowded drove
From each side shoaling towards the mouth of Hell,
As when two polar winds blowing adverse
Upon the Cronian Sea together drive   290
Mountains of ice that stop th' imagined way
Beyond Petsora eastward to the rich
Cathayan coast. The aggregated soil
Death with his mace petrific, cold and dry,
As with a trident smote and fixed as firm   295
As Delos floating once. The rest his look
Bound with gorgonian rigor not to move
And with asphaltic slime. Broad as the gate,
Deep to the roots of Hell, the gathered beach
They fastened and the mole immense wrought on   300
Over the foaming deep, high arched a bridge
Of length prodigious joining to the wall
Immovable of this now fenceless world
Forfeit to Death. From hence a passage broad,
Smooth, easy, inoffensive down to Hell.   305
So if great things to small may be compared
Xerxes the liberty of Greece to yoke
From Susa his Memnonian palace high
Came to the sea and over Hellespont
Bridging his way Europe with Asia joined   310
And scourged with many a stroke th' indignant waves.

281. *Sagacious*: knowing, sensing.
290. *Cronian Sea*: Arctic Ocean, named after Cronus, who fled there. The ice blocks the
     passage eastward to Russia, via the river *Petsora* (see Glossary), and eventually to
     China (Cathay).
294. *petrific*: turning to stone.
296. *Delos*: a floating island, which Zeus fastened to the bottom of the sea. See Glossary.
297. *gorgonian*: like a gorgon, whose face turned whoever saw it to stone.
299. *roots*: echoing Aeschylus's "pressed down with crushing weight by the roots of Etna."
     (*Prometheus Bound* 365).
300. *mole*: a massive, solid structure built in the water, a seawall.
300–303. I.e., They *wrought* the *mole* onward *and* (understood) they joined a high-arching
     bridge to the outer wall of the universe. We are to imagine a gigantic seawall extend-
     ing outward into Chaos from the gate of Hell and providing the footing for one end of
     the bridge, the other end being fixed to the universe with *pins of adamant* (line 318).
305. *inoffensive*: having no obstacles.
306–11. The Persian king Xerxes, angry at the destruction of his bridge of ships over the
     Hellespont, commanded that the waves be flogged. A traditional example of hubris.

Now had they brought the work by wondrous art
Pontifical, a ridge of pendent rock
Over the vexed abyss following the track
Of Satan to the selfsame place where he   315
First lighted from his wing and landed safe
From out of chaos to the outside bare
Of this round world. With pins of adamant
And chains they made all fast: too fast they made,
And durable! And now in little space   320
The confines met of empyréan Heav'n
And of this world, and on the left hand Hell
With long reach interposed: three several ways
In sight to each of these three places led.
And now their way to Earth they had descried,   325
To Paradise first tending when, behold!
Satan in likeness of an angel bright
Betwixt the Centaur and the Scorpion steering
His zenith while the sun in Aries rose.

   Disguised he came but those his children dear   330
Their parent soon discerned though in disguise.
He, after Eve seduced, unminded slunk
Into the wood fast by and changing shape
T' observe the sequel saw his guileful act
By Eve, though all unweeting, seconded   335
Upon her husband, saw their shame that sought
Vain covertures. But when he saw descend
The Son of God to judge them, terrified
He fled, not hoping to escape but shun
The present, fearing, guilty, what His wrath   340
Might suddenly inflict. That past, returned
By night and list'ning where the hapless pair
Sat in their sad discourse and various plaint,
Thence gathered his own doom, which understood
Not instant but of future time. With joy   345
And tidings fraught to Hell he now returned
And at the brink of chaos near the foot
Of this new wondrous pontifice unhoped

---

313. *Pontifical:* having to do with a bridge, Latin *pons*. A Roman high priest was called a
     pontifex, or "bridge maker," and the title was assumed by the bishop of Rome, as
     pontiff.
328–29. Between the two constellations Satan steers his course from a mark taken above
     him on the stellar sphere. This places him in the constellation Anguis, the serpent. See
     Alastair Fowler, ed., *Paradise Lost*, 2nd ed. (1998). See 2.709 and Glossary, OPHIUCHUS.
332. *unminded:* not paid attention to any longer by Adam and Eve.
344. Satan understands his doom to be reserved for a future time. This is what torments
     him in *Paradise Regained*.

Met who to meet him came, his offspring dear.
Great joy was at their meeting and at sight   350
Of that stupendious bridge his joy increased.
Long he admiring stood till Sin his fair
Enchanting daughter thus the silence broke:
　　O parent, these are thy magnific deeds,
Thy trophies which thou view'st as not thine own: 355
Thou art their author and prime architect,
For I no sooner in my heart divined
(My heart which by a secret harmony
Still moves with thine joined in connection sweet)
That thou on Earth hadst prospered (which thy looks   360
Now also evidence) but straight I felt,
Though distant from thee worlds between, yet felt
That I must after thee with this thy son,
Such fatal consequence unites us three.
Hell could no longer hold us in her bounds,   365
Nor this unvoyageable gulf obscure
Detain from following thy illustrious track.
Thou hast achieved our liberty, confined
Within Hell gates till now, thou us empow'red
To fortify thus far and overlay   370
With this portentous bridge the dark abyss.
Thine now is all this world, thy virtue hath won
That thy hands builded not, thy wisdom gained
With odds what war hath lost and fully avenged
Our foil in Heav'n. Here thou shalt monarch reign,   375
There didst not. There let Him still victor sway
As battle hath adjudged, from this new world
Retiring by His own doom alienated,
And henceforth monarchy with thee divide
Of all things parted by th' empyreal bounds,   380
His quadrature from thy orbicular world,
Or try thee now more dangrous to his throne.
　　Whom thus the Prince of Darkness answered glad:
Fair daughter and thou son and grandchild both,
High proof ye now have giv'n to be the race   385
Of Satan (for I glory in the name
"Antagonist of Heav'n's Almighty King"),

375. *Our foil*: He who foiled us.
378. I.e., The Son has withdrawn from this world, which has been further separated from
　　him by his judgment on it.
379–82. I.e., Either accept a divided hegemony, God ruling in heaven and you here in the
　　universe, or attempt something that will threaten God's throne.
381. *quadrature*: cube-shaped heaven. *orbicular world*: the created universe.
387. See 1.81–82 and n.

Amply have merited of me, of all
Th' infernal empire, that so near Heav'n's door
Triumphal with triumphal act have met   390
Mine with this glorious work and made one realm
Hell and this world, one realm, one continent
Of easy thoroughfare. Therefore while I
Descend through darkness on your road with ease
To my associate pow'rs, them to acquaint   395
With these successes and with them rejoice,
You two this way among these numerous orbs
All yours right down to Paradise descend.
There dwell and reign in bliss! Thence on the earth
Dominion exercise and in the air,   400
Chiefly on Man, sole lord of all declared:
Him first make sure your thrall and lastly kill.
My substitutes I send ye and create
Plenipotent on Earth, of matchless might
Issuing from me. On your joint vigor now   405
My hold of this new kingdom all depends
Through Sin to Death exposed by my explóit.
If your joint pow'r prevail th' affairs of Hell
No detriment need fear. Go, and be strong!
   So saying he dismissed them. They with speed   410
Their course through thickest constellations held
Spreading their bane. The blasted stars looked wan
And planets, planet-strook, real eclipse
Then suffered. Th' other way Satan went down
The causey to Hell gate. On either side   415
Disparted Chaos overbuilt exclaimed
And with rebounding surge the bars assailed
That scorned his indignation. Through the gate
Wide open and unguarded Satan passed
And all about found desolate, for those   420
Appointed to sit there had left their charge,
Flown to the upper world. The rest were all
Far to th' inlánd retired about the walls
Of Pandemonium, city and proud seat

---

391. *this glorious work*: the bridge.
397. *these numerous orbs*: the heavenly bodies inside the globe of the universe which are
    visible through the aperture mentioned at 3.525–28 and 3.542.
404. *Plenipotent*: "invested with or possessing full power or authority" (*OED*).
413. *planet-strook*: struck by the invisible influence, or "flowing-in," of a planet. Diseases
    and other catastrophes were thought to be caused by planetary influences. See lines
    660–62 and 662 n. Now the planets themselves are stricken.
415. *causey*: causeway, bridge.
416–18. Chaos assails the bars of the bridge. The bars scorn Chaos's indignation.

Of Lucifer (so by allusion called   425
Of that bright star to Satan paragoned).
There kept their watch the legions while the grand
In council sat, solicitous what chance
Might intercept their emperor sent: so he
Departing gave command and they observed.   430
As when the Tartar from his Russian foe
By Astracan over the snowy plains
Retires, or Bactrian Sophy from the horns
Of Turkish crescent leaves all waste beyond
The realm of Aladule in his retreat   435
To Tauris or Casbeen, so these the late
Heav'n-banished host left desert utmost Hell
Many a dark league reduced in careful watch
Round their metropolis, and now expecting
Each hour their great adventurer from the search   440
Of foreign worlds. He through the midst unmarked
In show plebeian angel militant
Of lowest order passed and from the door
Of that Plutonian hall invisible
Ascended his high throne which under state   445
Of richest texture spread at th' upper end
Was placed in regal luster. Down a while
He sat and round about him saw unseen.
At last as from a cloud his fulgent head
And shape star-bright appeared, or brighter, clad   450
With what permissive glory since his fall
Was left him, or false glitter. All amazed
At that so sudden blaze the Stygian throng
Bent their aspéct and whom they wished beheld:
Their mighty chief returned. Loud was th' acclaim.   455
Forth rushed in haste the great consulting peers
Raised from their dark divan and with like joy
Congratulant approached him who with hand
Silence and with these words attention won:
    Thrones, Dominations, Princedoms, Virtues, Powers!   460

431–36. Examples of barbaric warfare in Asia—a passage of florid orientalism.
432. *Astracan*: Astrakhan. City near the mouth of the Volga, on the Caspian Sea.
433–34. *Bactrian . . . crescent*: Persian king, from the crescent moon emblem on the
    Turkish flag.
435–36. *Aladule . . . Casbeen*: places in central Asia.
438. The devils are "drawn back" (the Latinate sense of *reduced*) around Pandemonium.
444. *Plutonian*: of Hell.
454. *Bent their aspéct*: turned their gaze.
457. *divan* denotes both a council of state held by Turkish leaders and the long, low, cush-
    ioned seat on which such a council is held.

For in possession such, not only of right,
I call ye and declare ye now, returned
Successful beyond hope to lead ye forth
Triumphant out of this infernal pit
Abominable, accurst, the house of woe   465
And dungeon of our Tyrant. Now possess
As lords a spacious world to our native Heaven
Little inferior, by my adventure hard
With peril great achieved. Long were to tell
What I have done, what suffered, with what pain   470
Voyaged th' unreal, vast, unbounded deep
Of horrible confusion over which
By Sin and Death a broad way now is paved
To expedite your glorious march. But I
Toiled out my uncouth passage, forced to ride   475
Th' intractable abyss, plunged in the womb
Of unoriginal Night and Chaos wild
That jealous of their secrets fiercely opposed
My journey strange with clamorous uproar
Protesting fate supreme. Thence how I found   480
The new created world which fame in Heav'n
Long had foretold, a fabric wonderful
Of absolute perfection, therein Man
Placed in a Paradise, by our exíle
Made happy. Him by fraud I have seduced   485
From his Creator and the more t' increase
Your wonder, with an apple! He thereat
Offended, worth your laughter, hath giv'n up
Both his beloved Man and all his world
To Sin and Death a prey and so to us   490
Without our hazard, labor, or alarm
To range in and to dwell and over Man
To rule as over all he should have ruled.
True is, me also he hath judged or rather
Me not—but the brute serpent in whose shape   495
Man I deceived. That which to me belongs
Is enmity which he will put between
Me and mankind: I am to bruise his heel;

461–62. I.e., I call you by these titles not just because you have a right to them but
    because you now possess the realms they signify.
475. *uncouth*: unknown.
478. *fiercely* and *opposed* are elided: 'fierce-lopposed.'
482. *fabric*: construction.
487. *apple*: See 9.585 n. *He*: God.
493. *he*: Man.
498–99. In both lines *his* refers to Man.

His Seed (when is not set) shall bruise my head.
A world who would not purchase with a bruise   500
Or much more grievous pain? Ye have th' account
Of my performance: what remains, ye gods,
But up and enter now into full bliss!
    So having said, a while he stood expecting
Their universal shout and high applause   505
To fill his ear when cóntrary he hears
On all sides from innumerable tongues
A dismal universal hiss, the sound
Of public scorn. He wondered but not long
Had leisure, wond'ring at himself now more: 510
His visage drawn he felt to sharp and spare,
His arms clung to his ribs, his legs entwining
Each other till supplanted down he fell
A monstrous serpent on his belly prone
Reluctant but in vain: a greater pow'r   515
Now ruled him, punished in the shape he sinned
According to his doom. He would have spoke
But hiss for hiss returned with forkèd tongue
To forkèd tongue, for now were all transformed
Alike to serpents, all as accessóries   520
To his bold riot. Dreadful was the din
Of hissing through the hall thick swarming now
With complicated monsters, head and tail,
Scorpion and asp and amphisbaena dire,
Cerastes horned, hydrus and ellops drear   525
And dipsas. (Not so thick swarmed once the soil
Bedropped with blood of Gorgon or the isle
Ophiusa.) But still greatest he the midst

500–1. Satan speaks here of a literal *bruise*, knowing, as he shows in *Paradise Regained*, that the bruise is a prophetic figure of something much more serious.
511–15. Satan's transformation closely follows that of Cadmus in Ovid's *Metamorphoses* (4.576–89).
514. *on his belly prone* translates Ovid's *in pectusque cadit pronus* (4.579).
517–18. The shock experienced when trying to speak and hissing instead is also in Ovid's transformation of Cadmus (4.587–89).
521. *riot*: rebellion.
521–28. The catalog of serpents, many of them fabulous, is inspired by a much longer catalog in Lucan's *Pharsalia* (9.696–733). In Lucan, the snakes spring from the drops of blood that fall in the Libyan desert when Perseus flies over, bearing Medusa's severed head. Another important source for this passage is Phineas Fletcher's *Purple Island*, book 7, stanza 11, in which it is Adam and Eve who are turned into serpents by their tempter, a "dragon fell": "Thus while the snake they heare they turn to snakes: / To make them gods he boasts, but beasts, and devils makes."
527–28. Snakes sprang from the drops of blood that fell on the Libyan desert as Perseus flew by bearing Medusa's severed head.
528. *Ophiusa*: "serpent isle" (Greek *ophis*, "snake").

Now dragon grown larger than whom the sun
Engendered in the Pythian vale on slime,   530
Huge Python, and his pow'r no less he seemed
Above the rest still to retain. They all
Him followed issuing forth to th' open field
Where all yet left of that revolted rout,
Heav'n-fall'n, in station stood or just array   535
Sublime with expectation when to see
In triumph issuing forth their glorious chief.
They saw, but other sight instead: a crowd
Of ugly serpents. Horror on them fell
And horrid sympathy for what they saw   540
They felt themselves now changing: down their arms,
Down fell both spear and shield, down they as fast
And the dire hiss renewed and the dire form
Catched by contagion, like in punishment
As in their crime. Thus was th' applause they meant   545
Turned to exploding hiss, triumph to shame
Cast on themselves from their own mouths. There stood
A grove hard by sprung up with this their change
(His will who reigns above to aggravate
Their penance) laden with fair fruit like that   550
Which grew in Paradise, the bait of Eve
Used by the Tempter. On that prospect strange
Their earnest eyes they fixed, imagining
For one forbidden tree a multitude
Now ris'n to work them further woe or shame.   555
Yet parched with scalding thirst and hunger fierce,
Though to delude them sent, could not abstain,
But on they rolled in heaps and up the trees
Climbing sat thicker than the snaky locks
That curled Megaera. Greedily they plucked   560
The fruitage fair to sight like that which grew
Near that bituminous lake where Sodom flamed.
This, more delusive, not the touch but taste
Deceived. They, fondly thinking to allay

529–31. The great serpent, Python, engendered from the drying action of the sun on the slime left after Deucalion's flood, was killed by the arrows of the god Apollo. See Ovid, *Metamorphoses* 1.434–47.
536. *Sublime*: raised up, exalted. They are both physically raised up and emotionally exalted, a prelude to their ignominious collapse.
545–46. *applause . . . exploding hiss*: In Latin the theater word *explodo* ("to hiss away") is the opposite of *plaudo* ("to applaud"): *explodo: ex + plaudo*.
560. *That curled Megaera*: that curled about the head of the fury Megaera.
562. Near the shore of the Dead Sea, where Sodom stood before it was destroyed by fire from heaven (Genesis 19:24), a fruit was said to grow that when touched turned to ashes.

Their appetite with gust, instead of fruit   565
Chewed bitter ashes which th' offended taste
With spattering noise rejected. Oft they assayed,
Hunger and thirst constraining, drugged as oft
With hatefullest disrelish writhed their jaws
With soot and cinders filled: so oft they fell   570
Into the same illusion, not as Man,
Whom they triúmphed, once lapsed. Thus were they plagued
And worn with famine long and ceaseless hiss
Till their lost shape permitted they resumed,
Yearly enjoined, some say, to undergo   575
This annual humbling certain numbered days
To dash their pride and joy for Man seduced.
However some tradition they dispersed
Among the heathen of their purchase got
And fabled how the serpent whom they called   580
Ophion with Eurynome the wide-
Encroaching, Eve perhaps, had first the rule
Of high Olympus, thence by Saturn driv'n
And Ops ere yet Dictaean Jove was born.
   Meanwhile in Paradise the hellish pair   585
Too soon arrived, Sin there in pow'r before,
Once actual, now in body, and to dwell
Habitual habitant. Behind her Death
Close following pace for pace, not mounted yet
On his pale horse, to whom Sin thus began: 590
   Second of Satan sprung, all-conquering Death,
What think'st thou of our empire now, though earned
With travail difficult? Not better far
Than still at Hell's dark threshold t' have sat watch,

565. *gust*: taste.
568. *drugged*: parched, or violently nauseated.
572. *triúmphed*: exulted over.
575. *some say*. Milton invented this episode entirely, plucking details from a heteroge-
     neous array of biblical and para-biblical sources. See notes in Alastair Fowler, ed.
     Paradise Lost.
577. *for Man seduced*: for having seduced Man.
578. *some tradition*: some have said. Parallel with *some say* (line 575). *dispersed*: spread the
     story.
578–84. *their purchase got*: their return for seducing Adam and Eve, i.e., their punish-
     ment. I.e., Some have said the devils spread among the pagans a lying fable about
     what was, in truth, their punishment for seducing Adam and Eve. Their story was
     that before Saturn and Ops (Rhea) ruled Olympus, and before Jove was born, a pri-
     mordial serpent, Ophion, ruled Olympus with his consort, Eurynome, whose name
     means "wide-ruling," but who is perhaps Eve. The devils exploit their humiliating
     punishment to suggest that they are the oldest, most legitimate, gods.
587. *actual*: in action. Sin's power was in Paradise before, in the act committed by Adam
     and Eve. Now Sin is there in her own body.
590. "And I looked, and behold a pale horse: and his name that sat on him was Death, and
     Hell followed with him" (Revelation 6:8).

Unnamed, undreaded, and thyself half-starved? 595
    Whom thus the Sin-born monster answered soon:
To me who with eternal famine pine
Alike is Hell or Paradise or Heav'n,
There best where most with ravin I may meet,
Which here though plenteous all too little seems 600
To stuff this maw, this vast unhidebound corpse.
    To whom th' incestuous mother thus replied:
Now therefore on these herbs and fruits and flow'rs
Feed first, on each beast next and fish and fowl,
No homely morsels, and whatever thing 605
The scythe of Time mows down devour unspared
Till I in Man residing through the race,
His thoughts, his looks, words, actions all infect
And season him thy last and sweetest prey.
    This said they both betook them several ways, 610
Both to destroy or unimmortal make
All kinds and for destruction to mature
Sooner or later, which th' Almighty seeing
From His transcendent seat the saints among
To those bright orders uttered thus His voice: 615
    See with what heat these dogs of Hell advance
To waste and havoc yonder world which I
So fair and good created and had still
Kept in that state had not the folly of Man
Let in these wasteful furies who impute 620
Folly to me! So doth the Prince of Hell
And his adherents that with so much ease
I suffer them to enter and possess
A place so Heav'nly, and conniving seem
To gratify my scornful enemies 625
That laugh, as if transported with some fit
Of passion I to them had quitted all,
At random yielded up to their misrule,
And know not that I called and drew them thither,
My Hell-hounds, to lick up the draff and filth 630
Which man's polluting sin with taint hath shed
On what was pure, till crammed and gorged, nigh burst

---

601. *unhidebound*: loose-skinned.
607. *race*: species.
609. *season*: to prepare game meat by hanging for a period of time, during which it dries and partly decays. Cf. Shakespeare, *Measure for Measure* (2.2.172): "corrupt with virtuous season."
615. *orders*: ranks of angels.
623. *them*: Sin and Death. Also lines 627 and 629.
630. *draff*: lees or refuse from brewing.

With sucked and glutted offal, at one sling
Of thy victorious arm, well-pleasing Son,
Both Sin and Death and yawning grave at last   635
Through chaos hurled obstruct the mouth of Hell
For ever and seal up his ravenous jaws.
Then Heav'n and Earth renewed shall be made pure
To sanctity that shall receive no stain.
Till then the curse pronounced on both precedes.   640
   He ended and the Heav'nly audience loud
Sung hallelujah as the sound of seas
Through multitude that sung: Just are Thy ways,
Righteous are Thy decrees on all Thy works!
Who can extenuate Thee? Next, to the Son,   645
Destined restorer of mankind by whom
New Heav'n and Earth shall to the ages rise
Or down from Heav'n descend. Such was their song
While the Creator calling forth by name
His mighty angels gave them several charge   650
As sorted best with present things. The sun
Had first his precept so to move, so shine
As might affect the Earth with cold and heat
Scarce tolerable and from the north to call
Decrepit winter, from the south to bring   655
Solstitial summer's heat. To the blank moon
Her office they prescribed, to th' other five
Their planetary motions and aspécts
In sextile, square and trine and opposite
Of noxious efficacy and when to join   660
In synod unbenign, and taught the fixed
Their influence malignant when to show'r,
Which of them rising with the sun or falling

---

633. *offal*: inedible parts of a butchered animal.
637. *his*: Hell's. At the end of time, when the Son blocks the mouth of Hell with the bodies of Sin and Death (and the grave), the jaws of Hell will no longer be open to receive damned people. (The damned will be already in Hell.)
638. "We, according to his promise, look for new heavens and a new earth, wherein dwelleth righteousness" (2 Peter 3:13). "And I saw a new heaven and a new earth: for the first heaven and the first earth were passed away; and there was no more sea" (Revelation 21:1).
640. *both*: the earth and the heavens, the latter understood as skies, within the universe, not heaven, the home of God. *precedes*: remains in effect.
645. *extenuate*: diminish.
647–48. See line 638 n.
656. *Solstitial*: of the solstice, when the sun has traveled to the farthest point north.
659. Astrological jargon concerning the angular positions of the planets as seen from the earth.
662. *influence malignant*: adjustments in the heavenly bodies, both wandering planets and stars fixed on the stellar sphere, causing bad influences on earth, such as diseases. Hence the word *influenza*, from stellar *influence*. See 4.661–73 n.

Should prove tempestuous. To the winds they set
Their corners, when with bluster to confound   665
Sea, air and shore, the thunder when to roll
With terror through the dark aerïal hall.
　　Some say He bid his angels turn askance
The poles of earth twice ten degrees and more
From the sun's axle: they with labor pushed   670
Oblique the centric globe. Some say the sun
Was bid turn reins from th' equinoctial road
Like distant breadth to Taurus with the sev'n
Atlantic Sisters and the Spartan Twins
Up to the tropic Crab, thence down amain   675
By Leo and the Virgin and the Scales
As deep as Capricorn to bring in change
Of seasons to each clime. Else had the spring
Perpetual smiled on earth with vernant flowers
Equal in days and nights except to those   680
Beyond the polar circles. To them day
Had unbenighted shone while the low sun
To recompense his distance in their sight
Had rounded still th' horizon and not known
Or east or west, which had forbid the snow   685
From cold Estótiland and south as far
Beneath Magellan. At that tasted fruit
The sun as from Thyéstean banquet turned
His course intended, else how had the world
Inhabited, though sinless, more than now   690
Avoided pinching cold and scorching heat?
These changes in the heav'ns, though slow, produced
Like change on sea and land, sidereal blast,
Vapor and mist and exhalation hot,
Corrupt and pestilent. Now from the north   695
Of Norumbega and the Samoed shore,
Bursting their brazen dungeon armed with ice
And snow and hail and stormy gust and flaw,
Boreas and Cacias and Argestes loud

668–78. Milton presents both the post-Copernican and the outdated (but more poetic)
　　Ptolemaic accounts of the seasons, the former supposing the earth's axis to wobble,
　　the latter supposing the sun to deviate in its course through the signs of the zodiac
　　(*th' equinoctial road*) between the signs Cancer and Capricorn.
679. *vernant*: vernal.
686–87. *Estótiland*: northern Canada. *Magellan*: the strait of Magellan, which rounds the
　　tip of the South American mainland.
693. *sidereal blast*: maleficent influence of stars (Latin *sideralis*, "of or belonging to
　　stars"). See line 662 n.
696. *Norumbega . . . Samoed shore*: northern Canada and northern Russia, Siberia.
699–706. A catalog of violent and maleficent winds.

And Thrascias rend the woods and seas upturn.   700
With adverse blast upturns them from the south
Notus and Afer black with thund'rous clouds
From Serraliona. Thwart of these as fierce
Forth rush the Lévant and the Pónent winds,
Eurus and Zephyr with their lateral noise,   705
Sirocco and Libecchio. Thus began
Outrage from lifeless things. But Discord, first
Daughter of Sin, among th' irrational
Death introduced through fierce antipathy:
Beast now with beast gan war and fowl with fowl   710
And fish with fish. To graze the herb all leaving
Devoured each other, nor stood much in awe
Of Man but fled him or with count'nance grim
Glared on him passing. These were from without
The growing miseries which Adam saw   715
Already in part though hid in gloomiest shade,
To sorrow abandoned, but worse felt within
And in a troubled sea of passion tossed
Thus to disburden sought with sad complaint:
    O miserable of happy! Is this the end   720
Of this new glorious world and me so late
The glory of that glory, who now, become
Accurst of blessèd, hide me from the face
Of God whom to behold was then my heighth
Of happiness? Yet well if here would end   725
The misery: I deserved it and would bear
My own deservings. But this will not serve:
All that I eat or drink or shall beget
Is propagated curse. O voice once heard
Delightfully, "increase and multiply,"   730
Now death to hear! For what can I increase
Or multiply but curses on my head?
Who of all ages to succeed but, feeling
The evil on him brought by me, will curse
My head: "ill fare our ancestor impure,   735
For this we may thank Adam." But his thanks
Shall be the execration. So besides
Mine own that bide upon me, all from me
Shall with a fierce reflux on me redound,

703. *Thwart of:* across.
704. *Lévant:* from the east. *Pónent:* from the west.
707–9. Death introduces discord first among irrational beings, animals.
729. *propagated:* Latinate sense of multiplied and extended by generation.
738. *Mine own:* evils, curses.

On me as on their natural center light,   740
Heavy though in their place. O fleeting joys
Of Paradise dear bought with lasting woes!
Did I request Thee, Maker, from my clay
To mold me Man? Did I solicit Thee
From darkness to promote me or here place   745
In this delicious garden? As my will
Concurred not to my being it were but right
And equal to reduce me to my dust,
Desirous to resign and render back
All I received, unable to perform   750
Thy terms too hard by which I was to hold
The good I sought not. To the loss of that,
Sufficient penalty, why hast thou added
The sense of endless woes? Inexplicable
Thy justice seems! Yet to say truth too late   755
I thus contést. Then should have been refused
Those terms whatever when they were proposed.
Thou didst accept them: wilt thou enjoy the good,
Then cavil the conditions? And though God
Made thee without thy leave, what if thy son   760
Prove disobedient and, reproved, retort
"Wherefore didst thou beget me? I sought it not."
Wouldst thou admit for his contempt of thee
That proud excuse? Yet him not thy election
But natural necessity begot.   765
God made thee of choice His own and of His own
To serve Him. Thy reward was of His grace:
Thy punishment then justly is at His will.
Be it so, for I submit, His doom is fair:
That dust I am and shall to dust return.   770
O welcome hour whenever! Why delays
His hand to execute what His decree
Fixed on this day? Why do I overlive?

---

741. *Heavy though in their place*: In pre-Newtonian physics, objects are not moved by external forces but are drawn to their natural places, where they are at rest. Fire rises, seeking its home above the air, and earth sinks, seeking its home beneath the water. The principle has been invoked by Moloch: "in our proper motion we ascend / Up to our native seat. Descent and fall / To us is adverse" (2.75–77). The evils and curses find their natural place in Adam, their origin and center, but they are still heavy, crushing him with their weight.

766. *thee* and *of* are elided.

766–68. I.e., Because God made you, you owe him absolute service (as an implement is made only for the use of its maker). But God gave you a reward for your service: your freedom. Your punishment, therefore, is entirely up to him.

768. *justly* and *is* are elided.

773. *this day*: "For in the day that thou eatest thereof thou shalt surely die" (Genesis 2:17). See 7.544; 8.329–30.

Why am I mocked with death and lengthened out
To deathless pain? How gladly would I meet   775
Mortality my sentence and be earth
Insensible, how glad would lay me down
As in my mother's lap! There I should rest
And sleep secure. His dreadful voice no more
Would thunder in my ears. No fear of worse   780
To me and to my offspring would torment me
With cruel expectation. Yet one doubt
Pursues me still: lest all I cannot die,
Lest that pure breath of life, the spirit of Man
Which God inspired cannot together perish   785
With this corporeal clod. Then in the grave
Or in some other dismal place, who knows
But I shall die a living death? O thought
Horrid if true! Yet why? It was but breath
Of life that sinned: what dies but what had life   790
And sin? The body properly hath neither.
All of me then shall die. Let this appease
The doubt since human reach no further knows.
For though the Lord of All be infinite,
Is His wrath also? Be it, Man is not so   795
But mortal doomed. How can He exercise
Wrath without end on Man whom death must end?
Can He make deathless death? That were to make
Strange contradiction, which to God himself
Impossible is held, as argument   800
Of weakness not of power. Will He draw out
For anger's sake finite to infinite
In punished Man to satisfy His rigor,
Satisfied never? That were to extend

782–93. Milton held that when we die we are entirely dead and remain so until the resurrection and last judgment. (For the resurrection of the body, see I Corinthians 15.) There is no place, such as purgatory, where a disembodied soul might live out the time in between, a thought that fills Adam with horror (lines 783–89). (Milton's denial that any part of us lives after we die, until the resurrection, is the so-called mortalist heresy. See Milton's *On Christian Doctrine*, book 1, chapter 13; YP 6:399–414.) Adam reasons that because it is the soul, not the body, that sins ("It was but breath / Of life that sinned," lines 789–90), the soul must bear the punishment, which is death: "All of me then shall die" (line 792). Adam has no idea that death is anything but final until Michael alludes to the resurrection: "Well may then thy Lord appeased / Redeem thee quite from Death's rapacious claim" (11.257–58).
785. *inspired*: breathed in to me.
796–98. Having reached the conclusion that all of him will die, Adam wonders how God's wrath, which like everything in God is infinite, could possibly extend beyond his, Adam's, death. See lines 804–8 n.
804–8. *That were to extend . . . own sphere. Dust*, or matter, and *nature's law* are themselves causes on which other causes depend (*all causes else*) depend and by which other causes are bounded, each in its own limited *sphere*. (For example, plants can grow and reproduce

His sentence beyond dust and nature's law   805
By which all causes else, according still
To the reception of their matter, act,
Not to th' extent of their own sphere. But say
That death be not one stroke as I supposed
Bereaving sense but endless misery   810
From this day onward which I feel begun
Both in me and without me, and so last
To perpetuity. Ay me! that fear
Comes thund'ring back with dreadful revolution
On my defenseless head! Both Death and I   815
Am found eternal and incorporate both,
Nor I on my part single: in me all
Posterity stands cursed. Fair patrimony
That I must leave ye, sons! O were I able
To waste it all myself and leave ye none!   820
So disinherited, how would ye bless
Me now your curse! Ah, why should all mankind
For one man's fault thus guiltless be condemned
If guiltless? But from me what can proceed
But all corrupt, both mind and will depraved,   825
Not to do only but to will the same
With me? How can they then acquitted stand
In sight of God? Him after all disputes
Forced I absolve: all my evasions vain
And reasonings, though through mazes, lead me still   830
But to my own conviction. First and last
On me, me only, as the source and spring
Of all corruption, all the blame lights due.
So might the wrath. Fond wish! Couldst thou support
That burden heavier than the earth to bear,   835
Than all the world much heavier, though divided
With that bad woman? Thus what thou desir'st
And what thou fear'st alike destroys all hope

because growth and reproduction are in the sphere of plants' action; but mountains
can't, because growth and reproduction aren't in their sphere.) Even God's wrath,
which causes bodily death, cannot act beyond the sphere of the living organism, which
is made of dust and operates by nature's law. God is infinite but death cannot be (see
lines 794–98).

808–13. Adam intuits eternal punishment in Hell.

816. *Am*: The singular verb expresses the unity of Adam and Death, since Adam is to die
eternally. The grammatical distortion illustrates the point, as in Rimbaud's *Je est un
autre* ("I is another").

820. *waste*: continues the irony of *patrimony*, inheritance. Adam wishes he could spend
all the guilt himself, instead of passing it on to his children.

826. Adam's descendants will not only do evil but will wish to do evil.

837–38. Adam both desires the wrath to fall on him alone and fears it absolutely. The
contradiction within himself leaves him abject.

Of refuge and concludes thee miserable
Beyond all past example and futúre,   840
To Satan only like both crime and doom.
O conscience, into what abyss of fears
And horrors hast thou driv'n me, out of which
I find no way, from deep to deeper plunged!
    Thus Adam to himself lamented loud   845
Through the still night, not now as ere Man fell,
Wholesome and cool and mild, but with black air
Accompanied, with damps and dreadful gloom
Which to his evil conscience represented
All things with double terror. On the ground   850
Outstretched he lay, on the cold ground, and oft
Cursed his creation, Death as oft accused
Of tardy execution since denounced
The day of his offence: Why comes not Death,
Said he, with one thrice-accéptáble stroke   855
To end me? Shall Truth fail to keep her word,
Justice divine not hasten to be just?
But Death comes not at call, Justice divine
Mends not her slowest pace for prayers or cries.
O woods, O fountains, hillocks, dales and bow'rs,   860
With other echo late I taught your shades
To answer and resound far other song!
    Whom thus afflicted when sad Eve beheld,
Desolate where she sat, approaching nigh,
Soft words to his fierce passion she assayed.   865
But her with stern regard he thus repelled:
    Out of my sight, thou serpent! That name best

841–44. *To Satan only like*: The inner contradiction makes Adam like Satan. In the lines
    following (842–44), Adam's cry is strikingly like Satan's at 4.73–78.
854–56. Sophocles, *Philoctetes* 797–98: "O Death! Death! How is it that I call you every
    day and yet you cannot come?"
860–62. *O woods . . . resound far other song*: a pastoral commonplace, as in Virgil: *For-
    mosam resonare doces Amaryllida silvas*, "you teach the woods to re-echo [the name]
    fair Amaryllis" (*Eclogues* 1.5); *non canimus surdis, respondent omnia silvae*, "we do
    not sing to deaf ears; the woods respond to all [by echoing]" (*Eclogues* 10.8).
867–68. *serpent! That name best / Befits thee*: a sonic resemblance in Aramaic, picked up
    by the Greek fathers of the church, Clement of Alexandria and Eusebius, whom
    Milton studied. See J. Leonard, *Naming in Paradise*, pp. 229–30; D. C. Allen, "Mil-
    ton and the Name of Eve," *Modern Language Notes* 74.8 (1959): 681–83. In ancient
    Hebrew *Chavah*, "Eve," bears no resemblance to *nachash*, "serpent." In Genesis
    3:20, after her condemnation to "sorrow" in childbearing, Adam names her "Eve
    (*Chavah*); because she was the mother of all living (*Chai*)." In the Septuagint Eve is
    Zōē, "life," because she is *mēter pantōn tōn zōntōn*, "mother of all animals." Milton's
    Adam, however, calls Eve by name when he first sees her (4.481). The "woman" of
    Genesis 2:23 is a label reserved for when Adam is incensed, at 9.343. Because God
    is the creator of all living, Milton judges that in context *all living* means all human
    beings. God titles Eve "Mother of human race" (4.475); and Raphael addresses her as
    "Mother of Mankind" (5.388). Adam uses this title only after their reconciliation,

Befits thee with him leagued, thyself as false
And hateful! Nothing wants but that thy shape
Like his and color serpentine may show   870
Thy inward fraud to warn all creatures from thee
Henceforth, lest that too Heav'nly form pretended
To hellish falsehood snare them! But for thee
I had persisted happy, had not thy pride
And wand'ring vanity when least was safe   875
Rejected my forewarning and disdained
Not to be trusted, longing to be seen,
Though by the Devil himself, him overweening
To overreach, but with the serpent meeting
Fooled and beguiled: by him thou, I by thee,   880
To trust thee from my side, imagined wise,
Constant, mature, proof against all assaults,
And understood not all was but a show
Rather than solid virtue, all but a rib
Crooked by nature, bent, as now appears   885
More to the part sinister from me drawn,
Well if thrown out as supernumerary
To my just number found. O why did God,
Creator wise, that peopled highest Heav'n
With spirits masculine, create at last   890
This novelty on earth, this fair defect
Of nature, and not fill the world at once
With men as angels, without feminine,
Or find some other way to generate
Mankind? This mischief had not then befall'n   895
And more that shall befall: innumerable
Disturbances on earth through female snares
And strait conjunction with this sex. For either
He never shall find out fit mate but such
As some misfortune brings him, or mistake,   900

---

when he calls Eve "*Mother of all Mankind*" (11.159) and explains the true meaning of
"Mother of all things living" (11.160): "all things" will "live for Man" (11.161). See
also 4.660 and 8.496–97.

872–73. *pretended / To*: Latin *prae*, "before," + *tendo*, "to extend." In English usage, *pretended* hangs off *Heav'nly form*, i.e., Eve's heavenly form is pretended. In Latin
usage, Eve's *Heav'nly form* is extended to cover *hellish falsehood* (line 873). Old editors cite Virgil's "to set a protective hedge before a crop," *segeti praetendere saepem*
(*Georgics* 1.270; cf. *Aeneid* 6.60). As often in *Paradise Lost*, a slight blurring of Latin
and English usage provides resonance.

884–88. In postbiblical tradition Adam was supposed to have had an extra rib on the left
(*sinister*) side, from which Eve was made.

888–98. Adam's angry speech, at first directed at Eve's act, here modulates into misogyny,
which the poet expects us to recognize as an effect of Adam's Fall. In the following
lines (898–908), Milton rehearses arguments he had made over two decades previous
in favor of divorce.

898. *strait conjunction*: forced union.

Or whom he wishes most shall seldom gain
Through her perverseness but shall see her gained
By a far worse or, if she love, withheld
By parents, or his happiest choice too late
Shall meet already linked and wedlock-bound   905
To a fell adversary, his hate or shame,
Which infinite calamity shall cause
To human life and household peace confound.
   He added not and from her turned, but Eve,
Not so repulsed, with tears that ceased not flowing   910
And tresses all disordered at his feet
Fell humble and embracing them besought
His peace and thus proceeded in her plaint:
   Forsake me not thus, Adam, witness Heaven,
What love sincere and reverence in my heart   915
I bear thee, and unweeting have offended,
Unhappily deceived. Thy suppliant,
I beg and clasp thy knees. Bereave me not
Whereon I live: thy gentle looks, thy aid,
Thy counsel, in this uttermost distress   920
My only strength and stay! Forlorn of thee,
Whither shall I betake me, where subsist?
While yet we live scarce one short hour perhaps
Between us two let there be peace, both joining,
As joined in injuries, one enmity   925
Against a foe by doom express assigned us,
That cruel serpent. On me exercise not
Thy hatred for this misery befall'n
On me, already lost, me than thyself
More miserable! Both have sinned, but thou   930
Against God only, I against God and thee,
And to the place of judgment will return,
There with my cries importune Heav'n that all
The sentence from thy head removed may light
On me, sole cause to thee of all this woe,   935
Me, me only just object of his ire!
   She ended weeping and her lowly plight,
Immovable till peace obtained from fault
Acknowledged and deplored, in Adam wrought

910–12. "A woman in the city . . . stood at his feet behind him weeping, and began to
wash his feet with tears, and did wipe them with the hairs of her head, and kissed
his feet, and anointed them with the ointment" (Luke 7:37–38).
214–31. The noble simplicity of Eve's words, her directness and honesty—and her practi-
cality concerning their common enemy (926)—contrasts with Adam's tirade.
927. *cruel serpent*: See 1032–35 and n.

Commiseration. Soon his heart relented   940
Towards her, His life so late and sole delight
Now at his feet submissive in distress,
Creature so fair his reconcilement seeking,
His counsel whom she had displeased, his aid.
As one disarmed his anger all he lost   945
And thus with peaceful words upraised her soon:
   Unwary, and too desirous as before,
So now, of what thou know'st not, who desir'st
The punishment all on thyself; Alas!
Bear thine own first, ill able to sustain   950
His full wrath whose thou feel'st as yet least part
And my displeasure bear'st so ill. If prayers
Could alter high decrees I to that place
Would speed before thee and be louder heard
That on my head all might be visited,   955
Thy frailty and infirmer sex forgiven,
To me committed and by me exposed.
But rise, let us no more contend, nor blame
Each other, blamed enough elsewhere, but strive
In offices of love how we may lighten   960
Each other's burden in our share of woe
Since this day's death denounced, if aught I see,
Will prove no sudden but a slow-paced evil,
A long day's dying to augment our pain
And to our seed (O hapless seed!) derived.   965
   To whom thus Eve recovering heart replied:
Adam, by sad experiment I know
How little weight my words with thee can find,
Found so erroneous, thence by just event
Found so unfortunate. Nevertheless,   970
Restored by thee, vile as I am, to place
Of new acceptance, hopeful to regain
Thy love the sole contentment of my heart,
Living or dying, from thee I will not hide
What thoughts in my unquiet breast are risen,   975
Tending to some relief of our extremes,
Or end, though sharp and sad, yet tolerable,
As in our evils and of easier choice.
If care of our descent perplex us most

943–44. I.e., Eve seeks Adam's *reconcilement, counsel,* and *aid.*
951. *whose:* which.
961. "Bear ye one another's burdens, and so fulfil the law of Christ" (Galatians 6:2).
978. *in our evils:* among our evils. She is referring to death and contemplating suicide, an
   easier choice than living to bear cursed offspring.

Which must be born to certain woe, devoured   980
By Death at last (and mis'rable it is
To be to others cause of misery),
Our own begotten, and of our loins to bring
Into this cursèd world a woeful race
That after wretched life must be at last   985
Food for so foul a monster, in thy power
It lies yet ere conception to prevent
The race unblest, to being yet unbegot.
Childless thou art, childless remain! So Death
Shall be deceived his glut and with us two   990
Be forced to satisfy his rav'nous maw.
But if thou judge it hard and difficult,
Conversing, looking, loving to abstain
From love's due rites, nuptial embraces sweet,
And with desire to languish without hope   995
Before the present object languishing
With like desire, which would be misery
And torment less than none of what we dread,
Then, both ourselves and seed at once to free
From what we fear for both, let us make short,   1000
Let us seek Death, or, he not found, supply
With our own hands his office on ourselves.
Why stand we longer shiv'ring under fears
That show no end but death and have the pow'r
Of many ways to die, the shortest choosing,   1005
Destruction with destruction to destroy?
    She ended here or vehement despair
Broke off the rest, so much of death her thoughts
Had entertained as dyed her cheeks with pale.
But Adam with such counsel nothing swayed   1010
To better hopes his more attentive mind
Laboring had raised and thus to Eve replied:
    Eve, thy contempt of life and pleasure seems
To argue in thee something more sublime
And excellent than what thy mind contemns.   1015
But self-destruction therefore sought refutes
That excellence thought in thee, and implies
Not thy contempt but anguish and regret

988.   *to being yet unbegot*: not yet conceived, not yet destined to exist.
1004. *and have*: when we have.
1013–15. A seemingly paradoxical but in fact sound argument: Eve's courage in rejecting
         pleasure and life itself shows that there is something in life, in human nature,
         worth preserving: nobility.
1015. *contemns*: condemns. The older form is kept for harmony with *contempt* (line
         1013).

For loss of life and pleasure overloved.
Or if thou covet death as utmost end   1020
Of misery, so thinking to evade
The penalty pronounced, doubt not but God
Hath wiselier armed His vengeful ire than so
To be forestalled. Much more I fear lest death
So snatched will not exempt us from the pain   1025
We are by doom to pay. Rather such acts
Of contumacy will provoke the Highest
To make Death in us live. Then let us seek
Some safer resolution which methinks
I have in view, calling to mind with heed   1030
Part of our sentence, that thy Seed shall bruise
The serpent's head, piteous amends unless
Be meant whom I conjecture, our grand foe
Satan, who in the serpent hath contrived
Against us this deceit. To crush *his* head   1035
Would be revenge indeed, which will be lost
By death brought on our selves or childless days
Resolved as thou proposest. So our foe
Shall 'scape his punishment ordained and we
Instead shall double ours upon our heads.   1040
No more be mentioned then of violence
Against ourselves and willful barrenness
That cuts us off from hope and savors only
Rancor and pride, impatience and despite,
Reluctance against God and His just yoke   1045
Laid on our necks. Remember with what mild
And gracious temper He both heard and judged
Without wrath or reviling. We expected
Immediate dissolution which we thought
Was meant by death that day when, lo! to thee   1050
Pains only in childbearing were foretold
And bringing forth soon recompensed with joy,
Fruit of thy womb. On me the curse aslope
Glanced on the ground: with labor I must earn
My bread. What harm? Idleness had been worse.   1055
My labor will sustain me and lest cold

1027. *contumacy*: "perverse and obstinate resistance of or disobedience to authority; rebellious stubbornness" (*OED*).
1031. *thy seed*: Jesus.
1032–35. This is the first indication that Adam suspects Satan was hidden in the serpent.
1052. "A woman when she is in travail hath sorrow . . . but as soon as she is delivered of the child, she remembereth no more the anguish, for joy that a man is born into the world" (John 16:21). "man" in the King James Version means 'human being, female or male, as in the original Greek, *anthrōpos*.

Or heat should injure us His timely care
Hath unbesought provided and His hands
Clothed us unworthy, pitying while He judged.
How much more if we pray Him will His ear 1060
Be open and His heart to pity incline
And teach us further by what means to shun
Th' inclement seasons, rain, ice, hail and snow,
Which now the sky with various face begins
To show us in this mountain while the winds 1065
Blow moist and keen, shattering the graceful locks
Of these fair spreading trees, which bids us seek
Some better shroud, some better warmth to cherish
Our limbs benumbed ere this diurnal star
Leave cold the night, how we his gathered beams 1070
Reflected may with matter sere foment,
Or by collision of two bodies grind
The air attrite to fire, as late the clouds
Justling or pushed with winds rude in their shock
Tine the slant lightning whose thwart flame, driv'n down, 1075
Kindles the gummy bark of fir or pine
And sends a comfortable heat from far
Which might supply the sun. Such fire to use
And what may else be remedy or cure
To evils which our own misdeeds have wrought 1080
He will instruct us praying and of grace
Beseeching Him so as we need not fear
To pass commodiously this life, sustained
By Him with many comforts till we end
In dust, our final rest and native home. 1085
What better can we do than to the place
Repairing where He judged us prostrate fall
Before Him reverent and there confess
Humbly our faults and pardon beg, with tears
Watering the ground and with our sighs the air 1090
Frequenting, sent from hearts contrite in sign

1069. *diurnal star*: the sun.
1070–73. Adam conceives the two means by which fire can be kindled: focusing of the sun's beams through a lens and friction to produce sparks.
1071. *sere*: dry, withered. *foment*: heat to ignition point.
1073. *attrite*: rubbed, for heating by friction.
1075. *Tine*: the prong of a fork, here used as a verb—"to make pronged." *thwart*: moving across [the sky]. Whereas fire on earth naturally flies up, in the sky fire naturally moves sideways, as lightning. But lightning can be *driv'n down* to strike a tree. See line 741 n.
1078. *supply the sun*: take the place of sun (at night) by giving heat.
1083. *commodiously*: suitably, in due measure, decently. The word is carefully chosen as a step below "happily."
1091. *Frequenting*: crowding, assiduously attending.

Of sorrow unfeigned and humiliation meek?
Undoubtedly He will relent and turn
From His displeasure, in whose look serene
When angry most He seemed and most severe   1095
What else but favor, grace and mercy shown?
     So spake our father penitent, nor Eve
Felt less remorse. They forthwith to the place
Repairing where He judged them prostrate fell
Before Him reverent and both confessed   1100
Humbly their faults and pardon begged, with tears
Watering the ground and with their sighs the air
Frequenting, sent from hearts contrite in sign
Of sorrow unfeigned and humiliation meek.

Book Eleven

The Argument

The Son of God presents to his Father the prayers of our first parents, now repenting, and intercedes for them. God accepts them,
but declares that they must no longer abide in Paradise, sends
Michael with a band of cherubim to dispossess them, but first to
reveal to Adam future things. Michael's coming down. Adam shows
to Eve certain ominous signs; he discerns Michael's approach, goes
out to meet him. The angel denounces their departure. Eve's lamentation. Adam pleads, but submits. The angel leads him up to a
high hill, sets before him in vision what shall happen till the Flood.

Thus they in lowliest plight repentant stood
Praying for from the mercy-seat above
Prevenient grace descending had removed
The stony from their hearts and made new flesh
Regenerate grow instead that sighs now breathed   5

1098–104. The repetition of lines 1086–92 is Homeric. It also emphasizes the ritual
    nature of prayer in the future and contrasts with the easy eloquence of the prayers
    that Adam and Eve sing before the Fall: the evening prayer at 4.724–35 and the
    morning prayer at 5.153–208.

Book Eleven
1. *stood*: Adam and Eve were last seen *prostrate* (10.1099).
2. *mercy-seat*: throne of God. See Exodus 25:17.
3. *Prevenient grace*: the grace that is sent beforehand from God to soften the heart and
    make the sinner capable of repentance. *Prevenient*: that which comes before.
4. "A new heart also will I give you, and a new spirit will I put within you: and I will take away
    the stony heart out of your flesh, and I will give you an heart of flesh" (Ezekiel 36:26).
5. *Regenerate*: an adjective modifying *flesh*.

Unutterable which the spirit of prayer
Inspired and winged for Heav'n with speedier flight
Than loudest oratory. Yet their port
Not of mean suitors nor important less
Seemed their petition than when th' ancient pair   10
In fables old, less ancient yet than these,
Deucalion and chaste Pyrrha, to restore
The race of mankind drowned before the shrine
Of Themis stood devout. To Heav'n their prayers
Flew up nor missed the way by envious winds   15
Blown vagabond or frustrate. In they passed
Dimensionless through Heav'nly doors, then clad
With incense where the golden altar fumed
By their great Intercessor came in sight
Before the Father's throne. Them the glad Son   20
Presenting thus to intercede began:
    See, Father, what first fruits on Earth are sprung
From Thy implanted grace in Man, these sighs
And prayers which in this golden censer mixed
With incense I Thy priest before Thee bring,   25
Fruits of more pleasing savor from Thy seed
Sown with contrition in his heart than those
Which his own hand manuring all the trees
Of Paradise could have produced ere fall'n
From innocence. Now therefore bend Thine ear   30
To supplication, hear his sighs though mute,
Unskillful with what words to pray. Let me
Interpret for him, me his advocate

6–8. *spirit of prayer*: a vestigial personification. (See Preface, p. xv.) This spirit of prayer, a
    special function of the Holy Ghost, inspires the sighs of Eve and Adam. The spirit of
    prayer then gives those sighs wings to fly to Heaven, where they enter with the dignity
    of eloquent ambassadors (lines 8–9). "We know not what we should pray for as we
    ought: but the Spirit itself maketh intercession for us with groanings which cannot be
    uttered" (Romans 8:26).
8. *their*: the prayers of Adam and Eve, personified as ambassadors. *port*: bearing.
12. *Deucalion and Pyrrha* repopulated the world after the Flood by casting stones over
    their shoulders. The stones became men and women.
14. *Themis*: goddess of justice.
14–21. *To Heav'n their prayers / Flew up . . . began*: A rare passage of truly baroque exuber-
    ance. For another, see 3.345–69. The *envious winds* (line 15) recall the Limbo of Van-
    ity's *violent crosswind* (3.487). The clouds of incense on the golden altar in which the
    prayers are attired by the Son recall the incense offered on the golden altar "before the
    throne" in Revelation, accompanied by "the prayers of the saints" (Revelation 8:3–4).
17. *Dimensionless*: The prayers have no bodies and so occupy no space.
19. *Intercessor*: The Son clothes the prayers in incense, as he clothed Adam and Eve in
    skins. In both instances the Son confers dignity on the abject.
28. *manuring*: working by hand, fertilizing (French *manoeuvrer*). In his prose works Mil-
    ton uses this word to signify careful diligence.
33–34. *advocate / And propitiation*: "We have an advocate with the Father, Jesus Christ
    the righteous: and he is the propitiation for our sins: and not for ours only, but also for
    the sins of the whole world" (1 John 2:1–2).

And propitiation, all his works on me
Good or not good ingraft: my merit those   35
Shall perfect and for these my death shall pay.
Accept me and in me from these receive
The smell of peace toward mankind! Let him live
Before Thee reconciled at least his days
Numbered, though sad, till death his doom (which I   40
To mitigate thus plead, not to reverse)
To better life shall yield him where with me
All my redeemed may dwell in joy and bliss,
Made one with me as I with Thee am one.
   To whom the Father without cloud, serene: 45
All thy request for Man, accepted Son,
Obtain: all thy request was my decree.
But longer in that Paradise to dwell
The law I gave to nature him forbids:
Those pure immortal elements that know   50
No gross, no unharmonious mixture foul
Eject him tainted now and purge him off
As a distemper gross to air as gross
And mortal food as may dispose him best
For dissolution wrought by sin, that first   55
Distempered all things and of incorrupt
Corrupted. I at first with two fair gifts
Created him, endowed with happiness
And immortality. That fondly lost,
This other served but to eternize woe   60
Till I provided death. So death becomes
His final remedy and after life,
Tried in sharp tribulation and refined
By faith and faithful works, to second life,
Waked in the renovation of the just,   65
Resigns him up with Heav'n and Earth renewed.
But let us call to synod all the blest
Through Heav'n's wide bounds. From them I will not hide
My judgments, how with mankind I proceed

---

34. *propitiation* has four syllables.
34–36. *all his works*: By becoming incarnate (as he will do) the Son joins to himself all human
   deeds, good and evil. Because we are sinful, our good deeds will have to be perfected
   by the *merit* (line 35) of the Son. Our bad deeds will be paid for by his crucifixion.
37. *these*: the prayers.
51. *gross*: thickened, unrefined, impure.
53. *to air as gross*: as gross as he is.
59. *That*: happiness.
60. *This*: immortality.
66. The subject of *Resigns* is *death* (line 61).
68. *them*: the loyal angels.

As how with peccant angels late they saw   70
And in their state, though firm, stood more confirmed.
   He ended and the Son gave signal high
To the bright minister that watched. He blew
His trumpet, heard in Oreb since perhaps
When God descended and perhaps once more   75
To sound at gen'ral doom. Th' angelic blast
Filled all the regions. From their blissful bow'rs
Of amarantine shade, fountain or spring,
By the waters of life where'er they sat
In fellowships of joy, the sons of light   80
Hasted resorting to the summons high
And took their seats, till from His throne supreme
Th' Almighty thus pronounced His sov'reign will:
   O sons! like one of us Man is become
To know both good and evil since his taste   85
Of that defended fruit. But let him boast
His knowledge of good lost and evil got,
Happier had it sufficed him to have known
Good by itself and evil not at all!
He sorrows now, repents and prays contrite,   90
My motions in him. Longer than they move
His heart I know, how variable and vain
Self-left. Lest therefore his now bolder hand
Reach also of the Tree of Life and eat
And live for ever, dream at least to live   95
For ever, to remove him I decree
And send him from the garden forth to till
The ground whence he was taken, fitter soil.
   Michael, this my behest have thou in charge:
Take to thee from among the cherubim   100

70. *peccant*: sinning.
71. *their*: the loyal angels'.
74. *Oreb*: Sinai. "There were thunders and lightnings, and a thick cloud upon the mount . . . And when the voice of the trumpet sounded long, and waxed louder and louder, Moses spake, and God answered him by a voice. And the Lord came down upon mount Sinai" (Exodus 19:16, 19–21). *since*: formerly.
76. *gen'ral doom*: Last Judgment (Old English *dôm*, "judgment, law").
78. *amarantine*: See 3.353 n.
86. *defended*: forbidden.
91. *My motions*: prevenient grace. See line 3 and n.
91–93. *Longer than they move . . . Self-left*: I.e., I know how much longer repentance will move Man: not much longer. Left to himself, without my grace to help him, Man's heart is variable and vain.
93–98. "And the Lord God said, Behold, the man is become as one of us, to know good and evil: and now, lest he put forth his hand, and take also of the tree of life, and eat, and live for ever: Therefore the Lord God sent him forth from the garden of Eden, to till the ground from whence he was taken. So he drove out the man; and he placed at the east of the garden of Eden Cherubims, and a flaming sword which turned every way, to keep the way of the tree of life" (Genesis 3:22–24).

Thy choice of flaming warriors lest the Fiend
Or in behalf of Man or to invade
Vacant possession some new trouble raise.
Haste thee and from the Paradise of God
Without remorse drive out the sinful pair,   105
From hallowed ground th' unholy, and denounce
To them and to their progeny from thence
Perpetual banishment. Yet lest they faint
At the sad sentence rigorously urged
(For I behold them softened and with tears   110
Bewailing their excess) all terror hide.
If patiently thy bidding they obey,
Dismiss them not disconsolate. Reveal
To Adam what shall come in future days
As I shall thee enlighten. Intermix   115
My covenant in the woman's seed renewed.
So send them forth—though sorrowing, yet in peace—
And on the east side of the garden place,
Where entrance up from Eden easiest climbs,
Cherubic watch and of a sword the flame   120
Wide waving all approach far off to fright
And guard all passage to the Tree of Life
Lest Paradise a receptacle prove
To spirits foul and all my trees their prey
With whose stol'n fruit Man once more to delude.   125
    He ceased and th' archangelic pow'r prepared
For swift descent, with him the cohort bright
Of watchful cherubim. Four faces each
Had like a double Janus, all their shape
Spangled with eyes more numerous than those   130
Of Argus and more wakeful than to drowse,
Charmed with Arcadian pipe, the pastoral reed

---

115. Lewalski notes that God reveals the future to Michael at the same time he, Michael, reveals it to Adam. This lends to the angel's narration a dramatic force that is increased when, in Book Twelve, Michael can see but Adam cannot. See, e.g., 12.128, where Michael first catches sight of Abraham but doesn't yet know his name. It comes to him—the first name to do so—at 12.152. See line 434 and n.

116. *covenant*: a formal relationship between Man and God (also *testament*). The vision of history in Books Eleven and Twelve is that of a progression of covenants. The forbidden fruit, although it was not called that, was the first covenant. Others are the rainbow, the promised land, the law given to Moses, and the new covenant in Jesus Christ, which replaces that of the law. This last is the covenant *in the woman's seed*.

119. *from Eden*: Eden is a large country in which the garden on the mountaintop, Paradise, is only one place.

129. *Janus*, the Roman god of doorways, has two faces.

131–33. *Argus*: a giant with one hundred eyes who was charmed to sleep and killed by Hermes. The cherubim, as guardians, have more eyes than Argus does and cannot be put to sleep. Ovid, *Metamorphoses* 1.713–23. *opiate rod*: the caduceus, infused with somiferous drugs.

Of Hermes or his opiate rod. Meanwhile
To resalute the world with sacred light
Leucothea waked and with fresh dews embalmed   135
The earth when Adam and first matron Eve
Had ended now their orisons and found
Strength added from above, new hope to spring
Out of despair, joy but with fear yet linked,
Which thus to Eve his welcome words renewed: 140
　　Eve, easily may faith admit that all
The good which we enjoy from Heav'n descends
But that from us aught should ascend to Heav'n
So prevalent as to concern the mind
Of God high-blest or to incline His will   145
Hard to belief may seem. Yet this will prayer
Or one short sigh of human breath upborn
Ev'n to the seat of God. For since I sought
By prayer th' offended Deity to appease,
Kneeled and before Him humbled all my heart,   150
Methought I saw Him placable and mild
Bending His ear. Persuasion in me grew
That I was heard with favor. Peace returned
Home to my breast and to my memory
His promise that thy Seed shall bruise our foe,   155
Which then not minded in dismay yet now
Assures me that the bitterness of death
Is past and we shall live. Whence hail to thee,
Eve, rightly called *Mother of all Mankind,*
Mother of all things living, since by thee   160
Man is to live and all things live for Man.
　　To whom thus Eve with sad demeanor meek:
Ill worthy, I, such title should belong
To me transgressor who for thee ordained
A help became thy snare. To me reproach   165
Rather belongs, distrust and all dispraise.
But infinite in pardon was my Judge,
That I who first brought death on all am graced
The source of life. Next favorable thou

135. *Leucothea*: Her name means "White Goddess", but Greek *leukos* also means "bright,
　　clear, joyful". Identified with Matuta, Roman goddess of first light. See 173–75. Not
　　the sea goddess of the *Odyssey*.
146. *this will prayer*: The understood verb is *do*—prayer will incline God's will to do what
　　we ask.
151. *placable*: inclined to peace.
155. *promise*: See 10.179–81.
159–61. *Mother*: See 10.867 n.
163–65. I.e., I am unworthy of such an exalted title, having been made to help you and
　　having snared you instead.

Who highly thus t' entitle me vouchsaf'st,   170
Far other name deserving. But the field
To labor calls us now with sweat imposed
Though after sleepless night. For see! the Morn,
All unconcerned with our unrest begins
Her rosy progress smiling. Let us forth,   175
I never from thy side henceforth to stray,
Where'er our day's work lies, though now enjoined
Laborious till day droop. While here we dwell
What can be toilsome in these pleasant walks?
Here let us live, though in fall'n state, content.   180
    So spake, so wished much-humbled Eve, but Fate
Subscribed not: Nature first gave signs impressed
On bird, beast, air, air suddenly eclipsed
After short blush of morn. Nigh in her sight
The bird of Jove, stooped from his airy tow'r,   185
Two birds of gayest plume before him drove.
Down from a hill the beast that reigns in woods,
First hunter then, pursued a gentle brace,
Goodliest of all the forest, hart and hind:
Direct to th' eastern gate was bent their flight.   190
Adam observed and with his eye the chase
Pursuing not unmoved to Eve thus spake:
    O Eve, some further change awaits us nigh
Which Heav'n by these mute signs in nature shows
Forerunners of his purpose or to warn   195
Us, haply too secure of our discharge
From penalty because from death released
Some days. How long and what till then our life
Who knows, or more than this: that we are dust
And thither must return and be no more.   200
Why else this double object in our sight
Of flight pursued in th' air and o'er the ground
One way the self-same hour? Why in the east
Darkness ere day's mid course and morning light
More orient in yon western cloud that draws   205
O'er the blue firmament a radiant white

177. *though now enjoined*: Work is now required.
185. *bird of Jove*: the eagle. *stooped*: plunged. *airy tow'r*: highest point to which he soars
    before plunging.
188. *brace*: pair.
198. *what till then our life*: I.e., what our life will be like until we die. Observing the ani-
    mals beginning to prey on one another, Adam suggests that Eve's imagining a life of
    pastoral contentment in the garden is *too secure* (line 196): this life will be worse
    than they can imagine.
203–7. While cloud darkens the dawn in the east, a white light appears in the west: the
    descending troop of cherubim, under Michael's command.

And slow descends with something Heav'nly fraught?
   He erred not, for by this the Heav'nly bands
Down from a sky of jasper lighted now
In Paradise and on a hill made halt,   210
A glorious apparition, had not doubt
And carnal fear that day dimmed Adam's eye.
Not that more glorious when the angels met
Jacob in Mahanaïm where he saw
The field pavilioned with his guardians bright,   215
Nor that which on the flaming mount appeared
In Dothan covered with a camp of fire
Against the Syrian king who to surprise
One man assassin-like had levied war,
War unproclaimed. The princely hierarch   220
In their bright stand there left his pow'rs to seize
Possession of the garden. He alone
To find where Adam sheltered took his way
Not unperceived of Adam who to Eve,
While the great visitant approached, thus spake: 225
   Eve, now expect great tidings which perhaps
Of us will soon determine or impose
New laws to be observed, for I descry
From yonder blazing cloud that veils the hill
One of the Heav'nly host and by his gait   230
None of the meanest, some great potentate
Or of the thrones above, such majesty
Invests him coming. Yet not terrible
That I should fear nor sociably mild
As Raphael that I should much confide,   235
But solemn and sublime, whom not t' offend,
With reverence I must meet and thou retire.
He ended and th' archangel soon drew nigh,
Not in his shape celestial but as man
Clad to meet man: over his lucid arms   240
A military vest of purple flowed
Livelier than Meliboean or the grain
Of Sarra worn by kings and heroes old

213–15. Jacob meets God's army of angels, which will protect him: "And when Jacob saw
   them, he said, This is God's host: and he called the name of that place Mahanaim
   [two camps]" (Genesis 32:2). *pavilioned*: encamped with military tents erected.
216–20. When the Syrian king sent an army to Dothan to capture the prophet Elisha,
   God sent an army for Elisha's protection: "and, behold, the mountain was full of
   horses and chariots of fire round about Elisha" (2 Kings 6:17).
220. *princely hierarch*: Michael.
233. *Invests him*: surrounds him.
242–43. The places named are famous for their fine purple dye, which was exceedingly
   rare. See Glossary.

In time of truce. Iris had dipped the woof.
His starry helm unbuckled showed him prime   245
In manhood where youth ended. By his side
As in a glist'ring zodiac hung the sword,
Satan's dire dread, and in his hand the spear.
Adam bowed low. He kingly from his state
Inclined not but his coming thus declared: 250
   Adam, Heaven's high behest no preface needs:
Sufficient that thy prayers are heard and death
Then due by sentence when thou didst transgress
Defeated of his seizure many days
Giv'n thee of grace wherein thou may'st repent   255
And one bad act with many deeds well done
May'st cover. Well may then thy Lord appeased
Redeem thee quite from Death's rapacious claim.
But longer in this Paradise to dwell
Permits not. To remove thee I am come   260
And send thee from the garden forth to till
The ground whence thou wast taken, fitter soil.
   He added not, for Adam at the news
Heart-strook with chilling gripe of sorrow stood
That all his senses bound. Eve who unseen   265
Yet all had heard with audible lament
Discovered soon the place of her retire:
   O! unexpected stroke worse than of death!
Must I thus leave thee, Paradise? Thus leave
Thee, native soil, these happy walks and shades,   270
Fit haunt of gods, where I had hope to spend
Quiet though sad the respite of that day
That must be mortal to us both? O flowers,
That never will in other climate grow,
My early visitation and my last   275
At ev'n which I bred up with tender hand
From the first op'ning bud and gave ye names,
Who now shall rear ye to the sun or rank
Your tribes and water from th' ambrosial fount?
Thee lastly, nuptial bow'r, by me adorned   280
With what to sight or smell was sweet, from thee
How shall I part and whither wander down

---

244. *Iris*: goddess of the rainbow and, in the *Iliad*, a messenger of Zeus who repeats Zeus's
    messages verbatim. See lines 261–62 n. *woof*: woven fabric.
254. *his*: Death's. *seizure*: a legal term for taking possession of property.
257–58. An important moment: the first indication to Adam that death may not be final.
261–62. Cf. lines 97–98. The repetition of the exact words of the divine command is a
    Homeric effect. See line 244 n.

Into a lower world, to this obscure
And wild? How shall we breath in other air
Less pure, accustomed to immortal fruits?   285
    Whom thus the angel interrupted mild:
Lament not, Eve, but patiently resign
What justly thou hast lost nor set thy heart
Thus over-fond on that which is not thine.
Thy going is not lonely: with thee goes   290
Thy husband. Him to follow thou art bound.
Where he abides think there thy native soil.
    Adam, by this from the cold sudden damp
Recovering and his scattered spirits returned,
To Michael thus his humble words addressed: 295
    Celestial, whether among the thrones or named
Of them the highest, for such of shape may seem
Prince above princes, gently hast thou told
Thy message which might else in telling wound
And in performing end us. What besides   300
Of sorrow and dejection and despair
Our frailty can sustain thy tidings bring:
Departure from this happy place, our sweet
Recess and only consolation left
Familiar to our eyes. All places else   305
Inhospitable appear and desolate,
Nor knowing us nor known. And if by prayer
Incessant I could hope to change the will
Of Him who all things can I would not cease
To weary Him with my assiduous cries.   310
But prayer against His absolute decree
No more avails than breath against the wind
Blown stifling back on him that breathes it forth.
Therefore to His great bidding I submit.
This most afflicts me: that departing hence   315
As from His face I shall be hid, deprived
His blessèd countenance. Here I could frequent
With worship place by place where He vouchsafed
Presence divine and to my sons relate,
"On this mount He appeared, under this tree   320
Stood visible, among these pines His voice
I heard, here with Him at this fountain talked."
So many grateful altars I would rear
Of grassy turf and pile up every stone

283. *to this*: compared to this.
296. *thrones*: the order of angels beneath the cherubim.
297. *the high'st*: seraphim, the order of angels above the cherubim.

Of luster from the brook in memory   325
Or monument to ages and thereon
Offer sweet-smelling gums and fruits and flowers.
In yonder nether world where shall I seek
His bright appearances or footstep trace?
For though I fled him angry, yet recalled   330
To life prolonged and promised race I now
Gladly behold though but His utmost skirts
Of glory, and far off His steps adore.
   To whom thus Michael with regard benign:
Adam, thou know'st Heav'n His and all the Earth,   335
Not this rock only: His omnipresence fills
Land, sea, and air and every kind that lives,
Fomented by His virtual pow'r and warmed.
All th' Earth He gave thee to possess and rule,
No despicable gift. Surmise not then   340
His presence to these narrow bounds confined
Of Paradise or Eden. This had been
Perhaps thy capital seat from whence had spread
All generations and had hither come
From all the ends of th' earth to celebrate   345
And reverence thee their great progenitor.
But this preëminence thou hast lost, brought down
To dwell on even ground now with thy sons.
Yet doubt not but in valley and in plain
God is as here and will be found alike   350
Present and of His presence many a sign
Still following thee, still compassing thee round
With goodness and paternal love, His face
Express, and of His steps the track divine.
Which that thou may'st believe and be confirmed   355
Ere thou from hence depart, know I am sent
To show thee what shall come in future days
To thee and to thy offspring. Good with bad
Expect to hear, supernal grace contending
With sinfulness of men thereby to learn   360
True patience and to temper joy with fear
And pious sorrow, equally inured

---

333. *far off His steps adore*: a phrase from the conclusion of the Statius's epic poem the *Thebaid*, in which the poet instructs his poem not to rival the *Aeneid* but to follow its example from afar and always to adore its steps: *sed longe sequere et vestigia semper adora* (12.817).
340. *No despicable gift*: a nice understatement, considering that much of history will be a violent, unsuccessful struggle for world domination.
342–46. An intriguing glimpse into what might have been had Adam and Eve not fallen.
353–54. *His face / Express*: natural signs that will express, though indirectly, the face of God.

By moderation either state to bear,
Prosperous or adverse. So shalt thou lead
Safest thy life and best prepared endure   365
Thy mortal passage when it comes. Ascend
This hill. Let Eve (for I have drenched her eyes)
Here sleep below while thou to foresight wak'st,
As once thou slept'st while she to life was formed.
   To whom thus Adam gratefully replied: 370
Ascend! I follow thee, safe guide, the path
Thou lead'st me, and to the hand of Heav'n submit,
However chast'ning, to the evil turn
My obvious breast arming to overcome
By suffering and earn rest from labor won   375
If so I may attain. So both ascend
In the visions of God. It was a hill
Of Paradise the highest from whose top
The hemisphere of Earth in clearest ken
Stretched out to th' amplest reach of prospect lay.   380
Not higher that hill nor wider looking round
Whereon for different cause the Tempter set
Our Second Adam in the wilderness
To show him all Earth's kingdoms and their glory.
His eye might there command wherever stood   385
City of old or modern fame, the seat
Of mightiest empire from the destined walls
Of Cambalu, seat of Cathaian Khan,
And Samarkand by Oxus, Temir's throne,
To Paquin of Sinaean kings and thence   390
To Agra and Lahore of Great Mogul
Down to the golden Chersonese, or where
The Persian in Ecbátan sat or since
In Hispahan, or where the Russian Czar
In Moscow or the Sultan in Bizance,   395
Turkestan-born. Nor could his eye not ken

---

374. *obvious*: exposed, in the path of the approaching evil. In the sentence spanning the lines 371 to 376, *My obvious breast* can be the object of *submit* (line 372) or the subject of a participle *arming* (line 374). He submits his exposed breast to the coming evil, or he arms his exposed breast by suffering. Cf. 12.569–570: "suffering for Truth's sake / Is fortitude."

377. *In the visions of God*: "In the visions of God brought he me into the land of Israel, and set me upon a very high mountain" (Ezekiel 40:2).

377–80. The hill is so high that fully half the earth can be seen from its top, the other half falling beneath the horizon.

383. *Second Adam*: Jesus Christ, so called because he undoes the effects of Adam's sin.

388–96. Virtuosic catalog of kingdoms in Asia, from China in the far east to the region bordering Europe, around the Hellespont and Bosphorus.

Th' empire of Negus to his utmost port,
Ercoco, and the less maritime kings,
Mombaza and Quiloa and Melind,
And Sofala, thought Ophir, to the realm   400
Of Congo and Angola farthest south.
Or thence from Niger flood to Atlas mount
The kingdoms of Almansor, Fez and Sus,
Morocco and Algiers and Tremisen;
On Europe thence and where Rome was to sway   405
The world. In spirit perhaps he also saw
Rich Mexico, the seat of Montezume,
And Cusco in Peru, the richer seat
Of Atabálipa and yet unspoiled
Guiana whose great city Geryon's sons   410
Call El Dorado. But to nobler sights
Michael from Adam's eyes the film removed
Which that false fruit that promised clearer sight
Had bred, then purged with euphrasy and rue
The visual nerve (for he had much to see)   415
And from the Well of Life three drops instilled.
So deep the power of these ingredients pierced
Even to the inmost seat of mental sight
That Adam now enforced to close his eyes
Sunk down and all his spirits became entranced.   420
But him the gentle angel by the hand
Soon raised and his attention thus recalled:
    Adam, now ope thine eyes and first behold
Th' effects which thy original crime hath wrought
In some to spring from thee who never touched   425
Th' excepted tree nor with the snake conspired
Nor sinned thy sin, yet from that sin derive
Corruption to bring forth more violent deeds.
    His eyes he opened and beheld a field
Part arable and tilth whereon were sheaves   430
New-reaped, the other part sheep-walks and folds.

397–404. Moving from Asia to the southwest, the catalog continues with kingdoms in Africa, from the Red Sea facing the Arabian Peninsula to the Atlas mountains across from Gibraltar, the nearest point to Europe.
398. *kings*: kingdoms.
405–11. After the mention of Rome, Adam is then shown the great kingdoms of North and South America that were destroyed by the Spaniards (*Geryon's sons*). But because these would have been over the horizon from the point where Adam stands, they were seen, if seen, *in spirit* (line 406).
414. *euphrasy and rue*: herbs medicinal to the sight.
424. *original crime*: Compare 12.83.
430. *tilth*: cultivated land.

I' th' midst an altar as the landmark stood
Rustic of grassy sward. Thither anon
A sweaty reaper from his tillage brought
First fruits, the green ear and the yellow sheaf   435
Unculled as came to hand. A shepherd next
More meek came with the firstlings of his flock
Choicest and best, then sacrificing laid
The innards and their fat with incense strewed
On the cleft wood and all due rites performed.   440
His off'ring soon propitious fire from Heav'n
Consumed with nimble glance and grateful steam,
The other's not for his was not sincere,
Whereat he inly raged and as they talked
Smote him into the midriff with a stone   445
That beat out life: he fell and deadly pale
Groaned out his soul with gushing blood effused.
Much at that sight was Adam in his heart
Dismayed and thus in haste to th' angel cried:
    O teacher! some great mischief hath befall'n   450
To that meek man who well had sacrificed.
Is piety thus and pure devotion paid?
    To whom Michael thus, he also moved, replied:
These two are brethren, Adam, and to come
Out of thy loins. Th' unjust the just hath slain   455
For envy that his brother's off'ring found
From Heav'n acceptance. But the bloody fact
Will be avenged and th' other's faith, approved,
Lose no reward though here thou see him die,
Rolling in dust and gore. To which our sire: 460
    Alas, both for the deed and for the cause!
But have I now seen death? Is this the way
I must return to native dust? O sight
Of terror foul and ugly to behold,
Horrid to think, how horrible to feel!   465
    To whom thus Michaël: Death thou hast seen

---

433. *sward*: turf.
434. *sweaty reaper*: Cain. This cinematic vision of the future begins to include names
    only after the Flood. See line 115 n. *tillage*: harvest from cultivated land. Cain, the
    first murderer, is represented in the Bible as an agriculturalist. As a pastoral people,
    the early Hebrews were at odds with the large, powerful, agricultural civilizations to
    the east and southwest, Babylon and Egypt.
436. *Unculled*: The grain has not been winnowed and separated from the chaff. This is
    Milton's rationalization for God's finding Cain's sacrifice unacceptable (Genesis 4:3–
    7). In the Bible, no reason is given. See line 434 n. *shepherd*: Abel, Cain's brother.
442. *glance*: flame. *steam*: smoke.
445. *him*: Abel.
459. *Lose no reward*: Another indication that death is not final.

In his first shape on Man. But many shapes
Of Death and many are the ways that lead
To his grim cave, all dismal, yet to sense
More terrible at the entrance than within.   470
Some as thou saw'st by violent stroke shall die,
By fire, flood, famine; by intemp'rance more
In meats and drinks which on the earth shall bring
Diseases dire, of which a monstrous crew
Before thee shall appear that thou may'st know   475
What misery th' inabstinence of Eve
Shall bring on men. Immediately a place
Before his eyes appeared, sad, noisome, dark.
A lazar-house it seemed wherein were laid
Numbers of all diseased, all maladies   480
Of ghastly spasm or racking torture, qualms
Of heart-sick agony, all feverous kinds,
Convulsions, epilepsies, fierce catarrhs,
Intestine stone and ulcer, colic pangs,
Demoniac frenzy, moping melancholy   485
And moon-struck madness, pining atrophy,
Marasmus and wide-wasting pestilence,
Dropsies and asthmas and joint-racking rheums.
Dire was the tossing, deep the groans. Despair
Tended the sick busiest from couch to couch   490
And over them triumphant Death his dart
Shook, but delayed to strike though oft invoked
With vows as their chief good and final hope.
Sight so deform what heart of rock could long
Dry-eyed behold? Adam could not, but wept,   495
Though not of woman born. Compassion quelled
His best of man and gave him up to tears
A space till firmer thoughts restrained excess,
And scarce recovering words his plaint renewed:
    O miserable mankind! To what fall   500
Degraded, to what wretched state reserved!

479. *lazar-house*: place of confinement for victims of leprosy.
480–88. A virtuosic catalog of diseases. Lines 485–87 were added in 1674. The *pestilence* (line 487), or Great Plague of London (1665–66), killed 100,000 people, about a quarter of the population of the city. Previous major visitations in Milton's lifetime were in 1625 (25,000 deaths) and 1636 (10,000 deaths). The dreadful scene opening Milton's Latin elegy for Bishop Lancelot Andrewes (1626), with Libertina, goddess of corpses, spreading havoc, and Death marching through marble palaces scything down princes, recalls the events of the previous year, when grass grew in the streets. See John Carey, *Complete Shorter Poems "Elegiatertia,"* lines 3–8 and n. The phrase "slaughtering pestilence" from "On the Death of a Fair Infant" (line 68) recalls the same visitation.
496. *not of woman born*: Because Adam is the only man without a mother, he is supposed to be less inclined to weep than other men.

Better end here unborn. Why is life giv'n
To be thus wrested from us? Rather why
Obtruded on us thus? who if we knew
What we receive would either not accept   505
Life offered or soon beg to lay it down,
Glad to be so dismissed in peace. Can thus
The image of God in Man created once
So goodly and erect, though faulty since,
To such unsightly sufferings be debased   510
Under inhuman pains? Why should not Man
Retaining still divine similitude
In part from such deformities be free
And for his Maker's image sake exempt?
   Their Maker's image, answered Michael, then   515
Forsook them when themselves they vilified
To serve ungoverned appetite and took
His image whom they served, a brutish vice,
Inductive mainly to the sin of Eve.
Therefore so abject is their punishment,   520
Disfiguring not God's likeness but their own
Or *if* His likeness, by themselves defaced
While they pervert pure nature's healthful rules
To loathsome sickness—worthily, since they
God's image did not reverence in themselves.   525
   I yield it just, said Adam, and submit.
But is there yet no other way besides
These painful passages how we may come
To death and mix with our connatural dust?
   There is, said Michael, if thou well observe   530
The rule of not too much by temp'rance taught
In what thou eat'st and drink'st, seeking from thence
Due nourishment, not gluttonous delight,
Till many years over thy head return.
So may'st thou live till like ripe fruit thou drop   535
Into thy mother's lap or be with ease
Gathered, not harshly plucked, for death mature.
This is old age, but then thou must outlive
Thy youth, thy strength, thy beauty which will change
To withered, weak and grey. Thy senses, then   540
Obtuse, all taste of pleasure must forgo
To what thou hast. And for the air of youth,
Hopeful and cheerful, in thy blood will reign
A melancholy damp of cold and dry

---

518. *vice*: gluttony.
519. *Inductive . . . to*: brought in from.
542. *To what thou hast*: i.e., in comparison with what you know of pleasure now.

To weigh thy spirits down and last consume   545
The balm of life. To whom our ancestor:
   Henceforth I fly not death nor would prolong
Life much, bent rather how I may be quit
Fairest and easiest of this cumbrous charge
Which I must keep till my appointed day   550
Of rend'ring up, and patiently attend
My dissolution. Michaël replied:
   Nor love thy life nor hate but what thou liv'st
Live well, how long or short permit to Heaven.
And now prepare thee for another sight.   555
   He looked and saw a spacious plain whereon
Were tents of various hue. By some were herds
Of cattle grazing, others whence the sound
Of instruments that made melodious chime
Was heard of harp and organ and who moved   560
Their stops and chords was seen: his volant touch
Instínct through all proportions low and high
Fled and pursued transverse the resonant fugue.
In other part stood one who at the forge
Laboring two massy clods of iron and brass   565
Had melted, whether found where casual fire
Had wasted woods on mountain or in vale
Down to the veins of earth, thence gliding hot
To some cave's mouth or whether washed by stream
From underground. The liquid ore he drained   570
Into fit molds prepared from which he formed
First his own tools, then what might else be wrought
Fusile or grav'n in metal. After these
But on the hither side, a different sort
From the high neighb'ring hills which was their seat   575
Down to the plain descended. By their guise
Just men they seemed and all their study bent
To worship God aright and know his works
Not hid, nor those things last which might preserve
Freedom and peace to men. They on the plain   580
Long had not walked when from the tents behold
A bevy of fair women richly gay

---

549. *cumbrous charge*: the body. I.e., 'This bothersome responsibility.'
556–73. The beginnings of the arts and sciences, of music, and of the work of the forge,
    useful for peace and war.
573. *Fusile*: melted and poured in a mold.
574. *a different sort*: the sons of Cain.
577. *study*: effort, concentration.
579–80. *nor those things last . . . men*: Nor did they neglect the study of political wisdom.
582. *bevy*: a group, usually of women.
582–92. Loosely based on Genesis 6:1–2, where angels ("sons of God"), seeing how
    attractive women are, beget giants on them (lines 623–25). Milton takes the "sons of

In gems and wanton dress. To the harp they sung
Soft amorous ditties and in dance came on.
The men, though grave, eyed them and let their eyes   585
Rove without rein till in the amorous net
Fast caught they like and each his liking chose.
And now of love they treat till th' evening star,
Love's harbinger, appeared, then all in heat
They light the nuptial torch and bid invoke   590
Hymen, then first to marriage rites invoked:
With feast and music all the tents resound.
Such happy interview and fair event
Of love and youth not lost, songs, garlands, flow'rs,
And charming symphonies attached the heart   595
Of Adam soon inclined t' admit delight,
The bent of nature, which he thus expressed:
   True opener of mine eyes, prime angel blest,
Much better seems this vision and more hope
Of peaceful days portends than those two past: 600
Those were of hate and death or pain much worse,
Here Nature seems fulfilled in all her ends.
   To whom thus Michael: Judge not what is best
By pleasure though to nature seeming meet,
Created as thou art to nobler end   605
Holy and pure, conformity divine.
Those tents thou saw'st so pleasant were the tents
Of wickedness wherein shall dwell his race
Who slew his brother. Studious they appear
Of arts that polish life, inventors rare,   610
Unmindful of their Maker though his Spirit
Taught them. But they his gifts acknowledged none.
Yet they a beauteous offspring shall beget,
For that fair female troop thou saw'st that seemed
Of goddesses so blithe, so smooth, so gay,   615
Yet empty of all good wherein consists
Woman's domestic honor and chief praise,
Bred only and completed to the taste
Of lustful áppetence: to sing, to dance,
To dress and troll the tongue and roll the eye.   620
To these that sober race of men whose lives
Religious titled them the sons of God

God" as men, descendants of Cain (line 609). The offspring of these amours are the
first tyrants, figuratively represented as giants (line 642). For Milton, the inward
tyranny of vice leads inevitably to outward, political tyranny. See lines 714–18 and
12.83–101. See Glossary, RAMIEL.
606. *conformity divine:* I.e., You are like God in nobility and purity, not in pleasure.
612. *acknowledged none:* This is arguably inconsistent with lines 577–78.
619. *áppetence:* desire.

Shall yield up all their virtue, all their fame
Ignobly to the trains and to the smiles
Of these fair atheists, and now swim in joy   625
(Erelong to swim at large) and laugh, for which
The world erelong a world of tears must weep.
  To whom thus Adam of short joy bereft:
O pity and shame that they who to live well
Entered so fair should turn aside to tread   630
Paths indirect or in the mid-way faint!
But still I see the tenor of man's woe
Holds on the same from woman to begin.
  From man's effeminate slackness it begins,
Said th' angel, who should better hold his place   635
By wisdom and superior gifts received.
But now prepare thee for another scene.
  He looked and saw wide territory spread
Before him, towns and rural works between,
Cities of men with lofty gates and towers,   640
Concourse in arms, fierce faces threat'ning war,
Giants of mighty bone and bold emprise.
Part wield their arms, part curb the foaming steed
Single or in array of battle ranged
Both horse and foot, nor idly must'ring stood.   645
One way a band select from forage drives
A herd of beeves, fair oxen and fair kine
From a fat meadow ground, or fleecy flock,
Ewes and their bleating lambs, over the plain,
Their booty. Scarce with life the shepherds fly   650
But call in aid which tacks a bloody fray:
With cruel tournament the squadrons join.
Where cattle pastured late now scattered lies
With carcasses and arms th' ensanguined field
Deserted. Others to a city strong   655
Lay siege encamped, by batt'ry, scale and mine
Assaulting. Others from the wall defend
With dart and javelin, stones and sulph'rous fire.

---

626. *Erelong to swim at large:* a grim foreboding of the Flood, in which they will all drown.
645. *mus'tring:* assembling (of troops). Latin *monstro*, "to show."
651. *tacks:* 1667; *makes* 1674. The change from the technical *tacks* ("joins in battle") to
    the more banal *makes* may or may not have been Milton's decision, prompted by
    complaint against the more obscure word. But the common word *makes,* in contrast
    to the technical word *tacks,* suggests a disorganized brawl rather than an engage-
    ment between trained soldiers, which is what the following line suggests. In *Of Ref-*
    ormation Milton uses *tack* as a noun: "holding tack against two of the king's
    generals" (*YP* 1:530).
654. *ensanguined:* soaked with blood.
656. *batt'ry, scale and mine:* battering ram, scaling ladders, and tunnels under the walls.

On each hand slaughter and gigantic deeds.
In other part the sceptred heralds call   660
To council in the city gates. Anon
Grey-headed men and grave with warriors mixed
Assemble and harangues are heard, but soon
In factious opposition, till at last
Of middle age one rising, eminent   665
In wise deport, spake much of right and wrong,
Of justice, of religion, truth and peace,
And judgment from above. Him old and young
Exploded and had seized with violent hands
Had not a cloud descending snatched him thence   670
Unseen amid the throng. So violence
Proceeded and oppression and sword-law
Through all the plain, and refuge none was found.
Adam was all in tears and to his guide
Lamenting turned full sad: O what are these,   675
Death's ministers not men who thus deal death
Inhumanly to men and multiply
Ten thousandfold the sin of him who slew
His brother? For of whom such massacre
Make they but of their brethren, men of men?   680
But who was that just man whom had not Heaven
Rescued had in his righteousness been lost?
    To whom thus Michael: These are the product
Of those ill-mated marriages thou saw'st,
Where good with bad were matched, who of themselves   685
Abhor to join and by imprudence mixed
Produce prodigious births of body or mind.
Such were these giants, men of high renown,
For in those days might only shall be admired
And "valor" and "heroic virtue" called.   690
To overcome in battle and subdue
Nations and bring home spoils with infinite
Manslaughter shall be held the highest pitch
Of human glory and for glory done
Of triumph to be styled great conquerors,   695
Patrons of mankind, gods, and sons of gods:

665. Enoch whom, like Elijah, God raised to Heaven without his having first to suffer
death (Genesis 5:21–24). Without precedent in Genesis, Milton makes Enoch a figure of political courage not unlike Abdiel and not unlike himself. For Enoch's
prophesying against the ungodly, see Jude 14–16.
669. *Exploded*: hissed out (Latin *explodo*, a theater term, opposite of *plaudo*, "to applaud").
See 10.545–46 n.
685–86. *of themselves / Abhor to join*: abhor to marry their own kind but mix with women
of foreign race.

Destroyers rightlier called and plagues of men!
Thus fame shall be achieved, renown on earth,
And what most merits fame in silence hid.
But he the sev'nth from thee, whom thou beheld'st,   700
The only righteous in a world perverse
And therefore hated, therefore so beset
With foes for daring single to be just
And utter odious truth that God would come
To judge them with his saints, him the Most High,   705
Rapt in a balmy cloud with wingèd steeds,
Did, as thou saw'st, receive to walk with God
High in salvation and the climes of bliss
Exempt from death, to show thee what reward
Awaits the good, the rest what punishment,   710
Which now direct thine eyes and soon behold.
    He looked and saw the face of things quite changed:
The brazen throat of war had ceased to roar.
All now was turned to jollity and game,
To luxury and riot, feast and dance,   715
Marrying or prostituting as befell,
Rape or adultery where passing fair
Allured them: thence from cups to civil broils.
At length a reverend sire among them came
And of their doings great dislike declared   720
And testified against their ways. He oft
Frequented their assemblies whereso met,
Triumphs or festivals, and to them preached
Conversion and repentance as to souls
In prison under judgments imminent.   725
But all in vain, which when he saw he ceased
Contending and removed his tents far off.
Then from the mountain hewing timber tall
Began to build a vessel of huge bulk
Measured by cubit, length, and breadth, and heighth,   730
Smeared round with pitch and in the side a door
Contrived, and of provisions laid in large
For man and beast, when, lo, a wonder strange!
Of every beast and bird and insect small
Came sevens and pairs and entered in as taught   735
Their order, last the sire and his three sons
With their four wives, and God made fast the door.

700–710. Enoch. See line 665 and n.
719. *reverend sire*: Noah (Genesis 6:9–9:29).
735. "Of every clean beast thou shalt take to thee by sevens, the male and his female: and
    of beasts that are not clean by two, the male and his female" (Genesis 7:2).

Meanwhile the south wind rose and with black wings
Wide hovering all the clouds together drove
From under heaven. The hills to their supply   740
Vapor and exhalation, dusk and moist
Sent up amain. And now the thickened sky
Like a dark ceiling stood. Down rushed the rain
Impetuous and continued till the earth
No more was seen. The floating vessel swum   745
Uplifted and secure with beakèd prow
Rode tilting o'er the waves. All dwellings else
Flood overwhelmed and them with all their pomp
Deep under water rolled. Sea covered sea,
Sea without shore, and in their palaces   750
Where luxury late reigned sea-monsters whelped
And stabled. Of mankind, so numerous late,
All left in one small bottom swum embarked.
How didst thou grieve then, Adam, to behold
The end of all thy offspring, end so sad,   755
Depopulation! Thee another flood
Of tears and sorrow, a flood thee also drowned
And sunk thee as thy sons, till gently reared
By th' angel on thy feet thou stood'st at last,
Though comfortless as when a father mourns   760
His children all in view destroyed at once,
And scarce to th' angel utter'dst thus thy plaint:
    O visions ill foreseen! Better had I
Lived ignorant of future, so had borne
My part of evil only, each day's lot   765
Enough to bear! Those now that were dispensed,
The burden of many ages, on me light
At once, by my foreknowledge gaining birth
Abortive to torment me, ere their being,
With thought that they must be! Let no man seek   770
Henceforth to be foretold what shall befall
Him or his children: evil he may be sure,
Which neither his foreknowing can prevent
And he the future evil shall no less
In apprehension than in substance feel   775

738–39. *south wind*: Ovid describes Notus, the south wind, flying on soaking wings, his
    beard heavy with rain and his terrifying face covered with pitchy cloud (*Metamor-*
    phoses 1.264–67).
740. *their supply*: the clouds' load of stored rain.
746. The syntax is clearer, but less resonant, if a comma is placed after *Uplifted*.
753. *bottom*: ship's hull.
766. *dispensed*: killed.
773. *neither*: not a *neither . . . nor* construction, but a simple negative.

Grievous to bear. But that care now is past:
Man is not whom to warn. Those few escaped
Famine and anguish will at last consume
Wand'ring that wat'ry desert! I had hope
When violence was ceased and war on earth, 780
All would have then gone well: peace would have crowned
With length of happy days the race of Man.
But I was far deceived, for now I see
Peace to corrupt no less than war to waste.
How comes it thus? Unfold, celestial guide, 785
And whether here the race of Man will end.
　　To whom thus Michael: Those whom last thou saw'st
In triumph and luxurious wealth are they
First seen in acts of prowess eminent
And great exploits but of true virtue void, 790
Who having spilt much blood and done much waste
Subduing nations and achieved thereby
Fame in the world, high titles and rich prey,
Shall change their course to pleasure, ease and sloth,
Surfeit and lust till wantonness and pride 795
Raise out of friendship hostile deeds in peace.
The conquered also and enslaved by war
Shall with their freedom lost all virtue lose
And fear of God from whom their piety feigned
In sharp contést of battle found no aid 800
Against invaders. Therefore cooled in zeal
Thenceforth shall practice how to live secure,
Worldly or dissolute on what their lords
Shall leave them to enjoy, for th' earth shall bear
More than enough that temp'rance may be tried. 805
So all shall turn degenerate, all depraved,
Justice and temp'rance, truth and faith forgot,
One man except, the only son of light
In a dark age against example good,
Against allurement, custom and a world 810
Offended, fearless of reproach and scorn
Or violence. He of their wicked ways
Shall them admonish and before them set

777. Man . . . warn: No man now lives who can be warned of this calamity, the Flood.
797–807. The conquered . . . faith forgot: The concentrated thought in these lines summarizes Milton's political philosophy, arrived at after long meditation on the history of Israel in the Bible's historical books (Joshua to Nehemiah) and the struggle for liberty during the failed English Revolution. No exact parallels with either are intended: Milton is giving a richer picture of what builds up great societies and what destroys them.
808–12. One man: Noah. Michael gives Noah's story in more clearly moral terms, making him another isolated champion, like Enoch, of moral courage. See line 655 n.

The paths of righteousness, how much more safe
And full of peace, denouncing wrath to come   815
On their impenitence, and shall return,
Of them derided but of God observed,
The one just man alive. By His command
Shall build a wondrous ark as thou beheld'st
To save himself and household from amidst   820
A world devote to universal wrack.
No sooner he with them of man and beast
Select for life shall in the ark be lodged
And sheltered round but all the cataracts
Of heav'n set open on the earth shall pour   825
Rain day and night, all fountains of the deep
Broke up shall heave the ocean to usurp
Beyond all bounds till inundation rise
Above the highest hills. Then shall this mount
Of Paradise by might of waves be moved   830
Out of his place, pushed by the hornèd Flood
With all his verdure spoiled and trees adrift
Down the great river to the opening gulf
And there take root an island salt and bare,
The haunt of seals and orcs and sea-mews' clang,   835
To teach thee that God áttributes to place
No sanctity if none be thither brought
By men who there frequent or therein dwell.
And now what further shall ensue, behold.
   He looked and saw the ark hull on the Flood   840
Which now abated for the clouds were fled
Driv'n by a keen north wind that blowing dry
Wrinkled the face of Deluge, as decayed,
And the clear sun on his wide wat'ry glass
Gazed hot and of the fresh wave largely drew   845
As after thirst, which made their flowing shrink
From standing lake to tripping ebb that stole
With soft foot towards the deep who now had stopped

---

821. *devote*: condemned.
831–35. *hornèd Flood*: rushing waters that divide in two courses around the mount of
   Paradise, tearing it from its foundations. The mount is driven down the swollen
   Euphrates River into the Arabian Gulf, where it is reduced to a bare rock. *orcs*: sea
   monsters, whales. *sea-mews*: seagulls. *clang*: noise made by a multitude, often used
   of birds (Greek *klangē*). See 7.422 n.
840. *hull*: a verb, used of a ship drifting on its bottom, or hull, without propulsion from sails.
843. A drying north wind wrinkles the surface of the Flood, as if the Flood were aging
   and close to its death, which it is. Milton admired the Metaphysical poet Cowley,
   and this image, though it is untypical of Milton, is a typical Metaphysical conceit.
844. *glass*: The Flood is the sun's mirror.
846. *their*: the waters of the Flood.
847. *tripping*: With quick steps and pleasant rhythm, the waters slip back toward the ocean.

His sluices as the heav'n his windows shut.
The ark no more now floats but seems on ground   850
Fast on the top of some high mountain fixed.
And now the tops of hills as rocks appear.
With clamor thence the rapid currents drive
Towards the retreating sea their furious tide.
Forthwith from out the ark a raven flies   855
And after him the surer messenger:
A dove sent forth once and again to spy
Green tree or ground whereon his foot may light.
The second time returning, in his bill
An olive leaf he brings, pacific sign.   860
Anon dry ground appears and from his ark
The ancient sire descends with all his train.
Then with uplifted hands and eyes devout,
Grateful to Heav'n, over his head beholds
A dewy cloud and in the cloud a bow   865
Conspicuous with three listed colors gay
Betok'ning peace from God and cov'nant new.
Whereat the heart of Adam erst so sad
Greatly rejoiced and thus his joy broke forth:
    O thou who future things canst represent   870
As present, Heav'nly instructor, I revive
At this last sight, assured that Man shall live
With all the creatures and their seed preserve.
Far less I now lament for one whole world
Of wicked sons destroyed than I rejoice   875
For one man found so perfect and so just
That God vouchsafes to raise another world
From him and all His anger to forget.
But say, what mean those colored streaks in heav'n
Distended as the brow of God appeased,   880
Or serve they as a flow'ry verge to bind
The fluid skirts of that same wat'ry cloud
Lest it again dissolve and show'r the Earth?
    To whom th' Archangel: Dexterously thou aim'st.
So willingly doth God remit His ire,   885
Though late repenting Him of man depraved,

---

851. *some high mountain*: Ararat (Genesis 8:4). We recall that Michael sees future events
    but does not know names. See lines 115 n. and 434 n.
860. *pacific sign*: the sign of peace.
862. *train*: followers.
874–78. Adam's language, applied to Noah, anticipates the Son's establishing of "a new
    heaven and a new earth" (Revelation 21:1). Likewise, the covenant of the rainbow
    anticipates the better covenant of the new testament in Christ. See lines 890–98.
879–83. Adam wonders if the rainbow is a sign that God's wrath is appeased or if it serves
    as a cord to tie the clouds closed.

Grieved at His heart when looking down He saw
The whole Earth filled with violence and all flesh
Corrupting each their way. Yet those removed,
Such grace shall one just man find in His sight   890
That He relents, not to blot out mankind,
And makes a covenant never to destroy
The Earth again by flood nor let the sea
Surpass his bounds nor rain to drown the world
With Man therein or beast; but when He brings   895
Over the Earth a cloud will therein set
His triple-colored bow whereon to look
And call to mind His covenant: day and night,
Seed time and harvest, heat and hoary frost
Shall hold their course till fire purge all things new,   900
Both Heav'n and Earth, wherein the just shall dwell.

Book Twelve

The Argument

The angel Michael continues from the Flood to relate what shall succeed. Then, in the mention of Abraham, comes by degrees to explain who that Seed of the woman shall be which was promised Adam and Eve in the Fall: His Incarnation, Death, Resurrection, and Ascension, the state of the Church till His Second Coming. Adam, greatly satisfied and recomforted by these relations and promises, descends the hill with Michael, wakens Eve who all this while had slept, but with gentle dreams composed to quietness of mind and submission. Michael in either hand leads them out of Paradise, the fiery sword waving behind them and the cherubim taking their stations to guard the place.

As one who in his journey bates at noon,
Though bent on speed, so here th' archangel paused
Betwixt the world destroyed and world restored

---

900. *till fire . . . new*: "Looking for and hasting unto the coming of the day of God, wherein the heavens being on fire shall be dissolved, and the elements shall melt with fervent heat . . . we, according to his promise, look for new heavens and a new earth, wherein dwelleth righteousness" (2 Peter 3:12–13).

Book Twelve
1–5. These lines were added in the second edition, 1674, when the final book of the first edition (1667) was divided in two. The division falls at a natural point for the narrative of history and for its audience, Adam. First, the Flood has wiped the slate clean and history begins anew, with Noah and his sons. Second, Adam, experiencing the effects of his mortality, is no longer capable of seeing visions. Michael continues to see them and relates them to Adam in words: "faith cometh by hearing" (Romans 10:17). See 11.115 n.
1. *bates*: halts.

If Adam aught perhaps might interpose,
Then with transition sweet new speech resumes: 5
   Thus thou hast seen one world begin and end
And Man as from a second stock proceed.
Much thou hast yet to see, but I perceive
Thy mortal sight to fail: objects divine
Must needs impair and weary human sense.   10
Henceforth what is to come I will relate:
Thou therefore give due audience and attend!
   This second source of men while yet but few
And while the dread of judgment past remains
Fresh in their minds, fearing the Deity   15
With some regard to what is just and right,
Shall lead their lives and multiply apace,
Laboring the soil and reaping plenteous crop,
Corn, wine, and oil, and from the herd or flock
Oft sacrificing bullock, lamb or kid   20
With large wine off'rings poured and sacred feast,
Shall spend their days in joy unblamed and dwell
Long time in peace by families and tribes
Under paternal rule. Till one shall rise
Of proud ambitious heart who not content   25
With fair equality, fraternal state,
Will arrogate dominion undeserved
Over his brethren and quite dispossess
Concord and law of Nature from the Earth,
Hunting (and men not beasts shall be his game)   30
With war and hostile snare such as refuse
Subjection to his empire tyrannous.
"A mighty hunter" thence shall he be styled
"Before the Lord" as in despite of Heaven
Or from Heaven claiming second sovereignty,   35
And from rebellion shall derive his name

11. *relate*: narrate, instead of show in visions.
19. *Corn*: grain. Compare Keats's Ruth, who, "sick for home, . . . stood in tears amid the alien corn" ("Ode to a Nightingale," lines 66–67).
24. *one*: Nimrod. By legend the first warrior-tyrant after the Flood and the first builder of great cities in Babylonia (Shinar): "And Cush begat Nimrod: he began to be a mighty one in the earth. He was a mighty hunter before the Lord . . . And the beginning of his kingdom was Babel, and Erech, and Accad, and Caineh, in the land of Shinar" (Genesis 10:8–10).
34–35. *in despite . . . second sovereignty*: Either Nimrod defies God entirely, *in despite of Heaven*, or he claims the second place after God, ruling by the blasphemous doctrine of the divine right of kings, as did the Stuart kings, James I (who was king when Milton was born) and Charles I, whose trial and execution by the revolutionary government Milton defended.
36. *shall derive his name*: not a false linkage, as commentators claim. Milton correctly follows rabbinic commentators who say the name נמרוד, Nimrod (Genesis 10:8), is from the Hebrew verb "to rebel," the two words sharing the same root, *marad* (מרד). How can a king be a rebel? By going against a higher principle, such as law, or against

Though of rebellion others he accuse.
He with a crew whom like ambition joins
With him or under him to tyrannize,
Marching from Eden towards the west shall find   40
The plain wherein a black bituminous gurge
Boils out from underground, the mouth of Hell.
Of brick and of that stuff they cast to build
A city and tow'r whose top may reach to Heav'n
And get themselves a name, lest far dispersed   45
In foreign lands their memory be lost,
Regardless whether good or evil fame.
But God, who oft descends to visit men
Unseen and through their habitations walks
To mark their doings, them beholding soon,   50
Comes down to see their city ere the tow'r
Obstruct Heav'n's tow'rs and in derision sets
Upon their tongues a various spirit to raze
Quite out their native language and instead
To sow a jangling noise of words unknown.   55
Forthwith a hideous gabble rises loud
Among the builders: each to other calls
Not understood, till hoarse and all in rage,
As mocked, they storm. Great laughter was in Heav'n
And looking down to see the hubbub strange   60
And hear the din, thus was the building left
Ridiculous and the work "Confusion" named.
   Whereto thus Adam fatherly displeased:
O execrable son so to aspire
Above his brethren, to himself assuming   65
Authority usurped from God not giv'n:
He gave us only over beast, fish, fowl
Dominion absolute. That right we hold
By His donation. But man over men
He made not lord, such title to himself   70
Reserving, human left from human free.
But this usurper his encroachment proud

God. See *rebel king* (1.484). In *Tenure of Kings and Magistrates* Milton calls Charles I
"a rebel to law and an enemy to the state" (*YP* 3:230).

38–62. The story of the Tower of Babel: "And they said, Go to, let us build a city and a
tower, whose top may reach unto heaven; and let us make us a name, lest we be scattered abroad upon the face of the whole earth" (Genesis 11:4). Although Nimrod is not
named in the story, Milton identifies those who "found a plain in the land of Shinar"
with Nimrod's founding his kingdom "in the land of Shinar" (Genesis 11:2, 10:10).

62. *"Confusion" named*: "Therefore is the name of it called Babel; because the Lord did
there confound the language of all the earth: and from thence did the Lord scatter
them abroad upon the face of all the earth" (Genesis 11:9). *Babel* (Hebrew *bavel*) is
from the same root as *balal*, "confound" or "confuse," "to mix all together."

Stays not on Man: to God his tow'r intends
Siege and defiance. Wretched man! what food
Will he convey up thither to sustain   75
Himself and his rash army where thin air
Above the clouds will pine his entrails gross
And famish him of breath if not of bread?
    To whom thus Michael: Justly thou abhorr'st
That son who on the quiet state of men   80
Such trouble brought, affecting to subdue
Rational liberty. Yet know withal,
Since thy original lapse true liberty
Is lost which always with right reason dwells
Twinned and from her hath no dividual being.   85
Reason in man obscured or not obeyed
Immediately inordinate desires
And upstart passions catch the government
From reason and to servitude reduce
Man till then free. Therefore since he permits   90
Within himself unworthy pow'rs to reign
Over free reason God in judgment just
Subjects him from without to violent lords
Who oft as undeservedly enthrall
His outward freedom. Tyranny must be,   95
Though to the tyrant thereby no excuse.
Yet sometimes nations will decline so low
From virtue, which is reason, that no wrong
But justice and some fatal curse annexed
Deprives them of their outward liberty,   100
Their inward lost: witness th' irreverent son
Of him who built the ark who for the shame
Done to his father heard this heavy curse,
"Servant of servants," on his vicious race.

83–101. These lines state the principal lesson of *Paradise Lost* (but see lines 561–73): that
    outward political liberty and inward moral self-command are reciprocal, and that
    both are under reason. When inward moral self-command is lost, outward political
    liberty is too. See 9.1127–31 and the opening of *Tenure of Kings and Magistrates*: "If
    men within themselves would be governed by reason, and not generally give up their
    understanding to a double tyranny, of custom from without and blind affections [pas-
    sions] within, they would discern better what it is to favor and uphold the tyrant of a
    nation . . . For indeed none can love freedom heartily but good men" (YP 3:190).
84. *right reason*: the philosophic conscience, implanted in us by God.
101–4. Noah's son Ham saw his drunken father naked and asleep. Ham's brothers, Japhet
    and Shem, placed a covering on their shoulders, walked backward into the tent so
    that they would not see Noah naked, and laid the covering on him. "And Noah awoke
    from his wine, and knew what his younger son [Ham] had done unto him. And he
    said, Cursed be Canaan [Ham's son]; a servant of servants shall he be unto his breth-
    ren. And he said, Blessed be the Lord God of Shem; and Canaan shall be his servant"
    (Genesis 9:24–26). The Canaanites are the inhabitants of the Promised Land, which
    is conquered by the Hebrews in the book of Judges. See lines 260–62 n.

Thus will this latter as the former world   105
Still tend from bad to worse till God at last
Wearied with their iniquities withdraw
His presence from among them and avert
His holy eyes, resolving from thenceforth
To leave them to their own polluted ways   110
And one peculiar nation to select
From all the rest of whom to be invoked,
A nation from one faithful man to spring,
Him on this side Euphrates yet residing,
Bred up in idol worship. Oh! that men   115
(Canst thou believe?) should be so stupid grown
While yet the patriarch lived who 'scaped the flood
As to forsake the living God and fall
To worship their own work in wood and stone
For gods! Yet him God the Most High vouchsafes   120
To call by vision from his father's house,
His kindred and false gods, into a land
Which he will show him and from him will raise
A mighty nation and upon him show'r
His benediction so that in his seed   125
All nations shall be blest. He straight obeys,
Not knowing to what land, yet firm believes.
I see him (but thou canst not) with what faith
He leaves his gods, his friends, and native soil,
Ur of Chaldea, passing now the ford   130
To Haran, after him a cumbrous train
Of herds and flocks and numerous servitude,
Not wand'ring poor but trusting all his wealth
With God who called him in a land unknown.
Canaan he now attains: I see his tents   135
Pitched about Shechem and the neighb'ring plain
Of Moreh. There by promise he receives
Gift to his progeny of all that land:

105. *latter . . . former world*: the world after and before the Flood.
111. *nation*: the Hebrews. *Nation* here means not a political but a biological entity: the
    seed of Abraham.
113. *one faithful man*: Abraham, who lives in Ur on the lower Euphrates, below Babylon,
    near the Arabian Gulf. He is called *Abram* until God renames him *Abraham*, "father
    of many nations" (Genesis 17:5). See line 152.
120–37. Milton skillfully compresses the biblical tale. In the Bible, Abram's father, Terah,
    travels from Ur up the Euphrates valley to Haran, north of Canaan, taking his son,
    Abram, and his grandson, Lot. Called thence by God into "a land that I will show thee"
    (Genesis 12:1), Abram travels south into Canaan, making camp at Shechem, where
    God promises the land to him and his descendants: "Unto thy seed will I give this
    land" (Genesis 12:7). The promise is later renewed as a formal covenant: "In the same
    day the Lord made a covenant with Abram, saying, Unto thy seed have I given this
    land, from the river of Egypt unto the great river, the river Euphrates" (Genesis 15:18).

From Hamath northward to the desert south
(Things by their names I call, though yet unnamed)   140
From Hermon east to the great western sea.
Mount Hermon, yonder sea, each place behold
In prospect as I point them: on the shore
Mount Carmel, here the double-founted stream
Jordan, true limit eastward, but his sons   145
Shall dwell to Senir, that long ridge of hills.
This ponder: that all nations of the earth
Shall in his seed be blessèd. (By that Seed
Is meant thy great Deliverer who shall bruise
The Serpent's head, whereof to thee anon   150
Plainlier shall be revealed.) This patriarch blest,
Whom faithful Abraham due time shall call,
A son and of his son a grandchild leaves
Like him in faith, in wisdom and renown.
The grandchild with twelve sons increased departs   155
From Canaan to a land hereafter called
Egypt, divided by the river Nile.
See where it flows disgorging at sev'n mouths
Into the sea! To sojourn in that land
He comes invited by a younger son   160
In time of dearth, a son whose worthy deeds
Raise him to be the second in that realm
Of Pharaoh. There he dies and leaves his race
Growing into a nation and, now grown,
Suspected to a sequent king who seeks   165
To stop their overgrowth, as inmate guests

139–46. The holy land, Palestine, is delineated, extending from Syria (Hamath) in the
north to the Sinai desert bordering Egypt in the south, and from Mount Hermon,
which Milton (following his sources) supposed was in the east, to the Mediterranean
Sea in the west. (Hermon, the highest peak in Palestine, is in the north.) Mount
Carmel, on the Mediterranean, is the promontory near modern Haifa. The eastern
boundary, the Jordan River, flows south into the Dead Sea. The Hebrews will inhabit
the hill country (*that long ridge of hills*) to the west of the Jordan, in the heart of
ancient Judea.
147–51. After Abraham has shown his willingness to sacrifice his son Isaac (an episode
Milton omits), God blesses Abraham again and says that not only Abraham's children
but all the nations of the earth will be blessed: "I will multiply thy seed as the stars
of the heaven, and as the sand which is upon the sea shore . . . and in thy seed shall
all the nations of the earth be blessed" (Genesis 22:17–18). Christians interpreted
the second use of *thy seed* in this passage as Jesus Christ, who will extend God's
blessing from Israel to all nations. "Now to Abraham and his seed were the promises
made. He saith not, And to seeds, as of many; but as of one, And to thy seed, which
is Christ" (Galatians 3:16).
152. *faithful Abraham*: so he will be called in *due time*, that is, far in the future, by Saint
Paul (Galatians 3:9). See 11.115 n. and 11.434 n.
153. *son*: Isaac. *grandchild*: Jacob.
160. *younger son*: Joseph.
163. *he*: Joseph.
165. *sequent king*: later pharaoh.

Too num'rous, whence of guests he makes them slaves
Inhospitably and kills their infant males,
Till by two brethren (those two brethren call
Moses and Aaron) sent from God to claim   170
His people from enthrallment they return
With glory and spoil back to their promised land.
But first the lawless tyrant who denies
To know their God or message to regard
Must be compelled by signs and judgments dire: 175
To blood unshed the rivers must be turned;
Frogs, lice and flies must all his palace fill
With loathed intrusion and fill all the land;
His cattle must of rot and murrain die;
Botches and blains must all his flesh emboss   180
And all his people; thunder mixed with hail,
Hail mixed with fire must rend th' Egyptian sky
And wheel on th' earth devouring where it rolls;
What it devours not, herb or fruit or grain,
A darksome cloud of locusts swarming down   185
Must eat and on the ground leave nothing green;
Darkness must overshadow all his bounds,
Palpable darkness, and blot out three days;
Last with one midnight stroke all the first-born
Of Egypt must lie dead. Thus with ten wounds   190
The river-dragon tamed at length submits
To let his sojourners depart and oft
Humbles his stubborn heart, but still as ice
More hardened after thaw till in his rage,
Pursuing whom he late dismissed, the sea   195
Swallows him with his host but *them* lets pass
As on dry land between two crystal walls,
Awed by the rod of Moses so to stand
Divided till his rescued gain their shore.
Such wondrous pow'r God to His saint will lend,   200
Though present in His angel, who shall go

172. *spoil*: "and they borrowed of the Egyptians jewels of silver, and jewels of gold, and raiment. . . . And they spoiled the Egyptians" (Exodus 12:35–36).
173. *tyrant*: Pharaoh.
175–90. The ten plagues of Egypt, recounted in Exodus 7–12, by which Pharaoh was at last compelled to let the Israelites leave Egypt for the Promised Land.
191. *river-dragon*: Pharaoh. "I am against thee, Pharaoh king of Egypt, the great dragon that lieth in the midst of his rivers, which hath said, My river is mine own, and I have made it for myself" (Ezekiel 29:3).
194–214. In Exodus 14, the Israelites, pursued by Pharaoh and his army, cross the Red Sea, which at Moses' signal, the extending of *his potent rod* (line 211), divides for them. Once the Israelites have crossed, Moses causes the sea to close again over Pharaoh's pursuing army. Cf. 1.306–11.

Before them in a cloud and pillar of fire,
By day a cloud, by night a pillar of fire
To guide them in their journey and remove
Behind them while th' obdúrate king pursues.   205
All night he will pursue but his approach
Darkness defends between till morning watch.
Then through the fiery pillar and the cloud
God looking forth will trouble all his host
And craze their chariot wheels when by command   210
Moses once more his potent rod extends
Over the sea. The sea his rod obeys:
On their embattled ranks the waves return
And overwhelm their war. The race elect
Safe towards Canaan from the shore advance   215
Through the wild desert, not the readiest way,
Lest ent'ring on the Canaanite alarmed
War terrify them inexpért and fear
Return them back to Egypt, choosing rather
Inglorious life with servitude, for life   220
To noble and ignoble is more sweet
Untrained in arms where rashness leads not on.
This also shall they gain by their delay
In the wide wilderness: there they shall found
Their government and their great senate choose   225
Through the twelve tribes to rule by laws ordained.
God from the Mount of Sinai, whose grey top
Shall tremble, He descending will himself
In thunder, lightning and loud trumpet's sound
Ordain them laws, part such as appertain   230
To civil justice, part religious rites
Of sacrifice, informing them by types
And shadows of that destined Seed to bruise
The Serpent, by what means He shall achieve
Mankind's deliverance. But the voice of God   235
To mortal ear is dreadful: they beseech

215–16. The Israelites begin their forty years' journey in the wilderness.
216–26. By taking the more indirect and extremely harsh route to Canaan, through the
   Sinai and the country to the east of the Dead Sea, the Israelites become tough and
   warlike. But they also become a nation governed by laws delivered to Moses on
   Mount Sinai, where God descends (Exodus 19–23). Milton places more emphasis on
   their political organization than on their religious rites.
231–35. The religious rites given to the Israelites in the law are seen by Christians as
   mysterious types (historical symbols) of the new covenant to come in Jesus Christ,
   the *destined Seed* (line 233), who will deliver humanity from the power of Satan.
235–44. Moses' ascending Mount Sinai alone, because God is too dreadful for the people
   to encounter directly, is a type of Christ's being a mediator between God and
   humanity. Moses bears Christ's *high office* (line 240) symbolically (*in figure* [line
   241]).

That Moses might report to them His will
And terror cease. He grants what they besought,
Instructed that to God is no accéss
Without Mediator, whose high office now   240
Moses in figure bears to introduce
One greater, of whose day he shall foretell,
And all the prophets in their age the times
Of great Messiah shall sing. Thus laws and rites
Established, such delight hath God in men   245
Obedient to His will that He vouchsafes
Among them to set up His tabernacle,
The Holy One with mortal men to dwell.
By His prescript a sanctuary is framed
Of cedar overlaid with gold, therein   250
An ark and in the ark his testimony,
The records of His cov'nant. Over these
A mercy-seat of gold between the wings
Of two bright cherubim. Before Him burn
Sev'n lamps as in a zodiac representing   255
The heav'nly fires. Over the tent a cloud
Shall rest by day, a fiery gleam by night,
Save when they journey, and at length they come
Conducted by His angel to the land
Promised to Abraham and his seed. The rest   260
Were long to tell: how many battles fought,
How many kings destroyed and kingdoms won,
Or how the sun shall in mid heav'n stand still
A day entire and night's due course adjourn,
Man's voice commanding, "Sun in Gibeon stand   265
And thou, Moon, in the vale of Aialon
Till Israel overcome." So call the third
From Abraham son of Isaac and from him
His whole descent, who thus shall Canaan win.

242. *he*: Moses.
243. *in their age*: The age of the prophets, who will foretell the Messiah more openly than
      do the *types and shadows* (lines 232–33) of the ritual law, is much later. The suggestion
      is that as history goes forward, God's purpose for history becomes increasingly clear.
247. *tabernacle*: the enclosure for the ark of the covenant, the box in which the tablets of the
      law were carried. The ark is kept in the sanctuary and is considered to be the presence
      of God, who has come down from heaven to live among his people (Exodus 24–27).
260. *Abraham* is pronounced with two syllables here and hereafter.
260–62. The Israelites cross the Jordan into the Promised Land, led by Joshua (see lines
      307–14 and n.), and conquer the people there, the Canaanites, who have been
      cursed by Noah.
265–67. "Then spake Joshua to the Lord in the day when the Lord delivered up the Amo-
      rites before the children of Israel, and he said in the sight of Israel, Sun, stand thou
      still upon Gibeon; and thou, Moon, in the valley of Ajalon" (Joshua 10:12).
267–69. *So call the third*: Jacob is the son of Isaac and is later called *Israel*. His twelve
      sons are the children of Israel.

Here Adam interposed: O sent from Heav'n,   270
Enlight'ner of my darkness, gracious things
Thou hast revealed, those chiefly which concern
Just Abraham and his seed. Now first I find
Mine eyes true op'ning and my heart much eased,
Erewhile perplexed with thoughts what would become   275
Of me and all mankind, but now I see
His Day in whom all nations shall be blest,
Favor unmerited by me who sought
Forbidden knowledge by forbidden means.
This yet I apprehend not, why to those   280
Among whom God will deign to dwell on Earth
So many and so various laws are giv'n?
So many laws argue so many sins
Among them: how can God with such reside?
    To whom thus Michael: Doubt not but that sin   285
Will reign among them as of thee begot
And therefore was Law giv'n them to evince
Their natural pravity by stirring up
Sin against Law to fight that when they see
Law can discover sin but not remove   290
Save by those shadowy expiations weak,
The blood of bulls and goats, they may conclude
Some blood more precious must be paid for Man,
Just for unjust, that in such righteousness,
To them by faith imputed, they may find   295
Justification towards God and peace
Of conscience, which the Law by ceremonies
Cannot appease nor Man the moral part
Perform and, not performing, cannot live.
So Law appears imperfect and but giv'n   300
With purpose to resign them in full time

277. *His Day*: the Day of the Lord, the Last Judgment.
287–88. The Law was given to the Hebrews, says Saint Paul, not with the expectation that it could be obeyed but with the aim of convincing the Hebrews of their sinfulness. "By the deeds of the law there shall no flesh be justified in his sight: for by the law is the knowledge of sin" (Romans 3:20). See lines 300–2 and n.
293. *blood more precious*: Christ's blood shed on the cross. The repetitive nature of animal sacrifice shows that the expiation of sin is never complete. But Christ's sacrifice need occur only once: "For if the blood of bulls and of goats, and the ashes of an heifer sprinkling the unclean, sanctifieth to the purifying of the flesh: How much more shall the blood of Christ, who through the eternal Spirit offered himself without spot to God, purge your conscience from dead works to serve the living God?" (Hebrews 9:13–14).
294–98. Christ's righteousness is attributed (*imputed*) to Man, who will be saved through faith in Christ rather than by obedience to the law. Justification by faith is the great theme of Paul's Epistle to the Romans and of the Protestant Reformation.
300–302. *Law appears imperfect*: Because the Law cannot be obeyed, it is an incomplete covenant, given only to be replaced by a *better covenant* (line 302), that of Christ's sacrifice. See lines 287–88 n.

Up to a better covenant, disciplined
From shadowy types to truth, from flesh to spirit,
From imposition of strict laws to free
Acceptance of large grace, from servile fear   305
To filial, works of law to works of faith.
And therefore shall not Moses, though of God
Highly beloved, being but the minister
Of Law, his people into Canaan lead,
But Joshua, whom the Gentiles "Jesus" call,   310
His name and office bearing who shall quell
The Adversary Serpent and bring back
Through the world's wilderness long wandered Man
Safe to Eternal Paradise of rest.
Meanwhile they in their earthly Canaan placed   315
Long time shall dwell and prosper, but when sins
National interrupt their public peace,
Provoking God to raise them enemies,
From whom as oft He saves them penitent,
By judges first, then under kings, of whom   320
The second both for piety renowned
And puissant deeds a promise shall receive
Irrevocable: that his regal throne
For ever shall endure. The like shall sing
All prophecy: that of the royal stock   325

303–6. *From . . . to:* Each of these five transitions contrasts the old covenant, under Moses, with the new covenant, under Christ.

305–6. *servile . . . filial:* the transition from slaves to sons.

307–14. Moses is not allowed to lead the people into the Promised Land because he is a symbol of the Law, which can only condemn. Instead, Joshua leads the Hebrews into the Promised Land. Joshua's name, *Yeshua,* is *Iesous* in Greek and *Jesus* in Latin. Joshua's leading the Hebrews into Canaan is therefore a type, a historical symbol, of Jesus' leading humanity into heaven.

311. *His name:* Jesus' name. *who:* Jesus.

313. *wilderness:* the wilderness of human history from the Fall to the apocalypse. History is symbolized by the wilderness through which the Israelites wander for forty years.

315. *earthly Canaan:* See lines 307–10 and 307–14 n.

316–17. *sins / National:* sins committed by the entire nation, worshipping the idols and false gods of the surrounding peoples. "If they break my statutes, and keep not my commandments; Then I will visit their transgression with the rod, and their iniquity with stripes. Nevertheless my lovingkindness will I not utterly take from him, nor suffer my faithfulness to fail" (Psalm 89:31–34).

320. *judges:* In the biblical book of that name, judges are military leaders (one of whom is Samson) who in time of crisis unite the tribes and lead them as a nation. *kings:* The people ask the prophet Samuel to give them a king, and the first king chosen is Saul. Milton follows the history of the kingdom of Israel (later, of the two kingdoms, Israel and Judea) until the conquest of Jerusalem by the king of Babylon, Nebuchadnezzar, and the carrying away of the Hebrews into captivity in Babylon.

321. *second:* David, who comes to the throne after Saul. Jesus will be a king in David's line.

325–30. *All prophecy:* E.g., "For unto us a child is born. . . . Of the increase of his government and peace there shall be no end, upon the throne of David" (Isaiah 9:6–7). "I saw in the night visions, and, behold, one like the Son of man came with the clouds of heaven. . . . And there was given him dominion, and glory, and a kingdom, that all

Of David (so I name this king) shall rise
A son, the woman's Seed to thee foretold,
Foretold to Abraham, as in whom shall trust
All nations, and to kings foretold—of kings
The last, for of his reign shall be no end.   330
But first a long succession must ensue
And his next son, for wealth and wisdom famed,
The clouded ark of God till then in tents,
Wand'ring, shall in a glorious temple enshrine.
Such follow him as shall be registered   335
Part good, part bad, of bad the longer scroll
Whose foul idolatries and other faults
Heaped to the popular sum will so incense
God as to leave them and expose their land,
Their city, His temple and His holy ark   340
With all His sacred things a scorn and prey
To that proud city whose high walls thou saw'st
Left in confusion, Babylon thence called.
There in captivity He lets them dwell
The space of seventy years, then brings them back,   345
Rememb'ring mercy and His cov'nant sworn
To David, 'stablished as the days of Heav'n.
Returned from Babylon by leave of kings
Their lords (whom God disposed) the house of God

---

people, nations, and languages should serve him: his dominion is an everlasting dominion, which shall not pass away" (Daniel 7:13–14).

327–28. *Seed . . . Abraham*: See lines 147–51 n.

329–30. *of kings / The last*: For Milton, who defended the execution of King Charles I, Jesus is the last legitimate king. All subsequent kings are usurpers of Jesus' right.

332. *next son*: Solomon, who built the temple to house the ark of the covenant.

335–36. *Such follow him*: the kings that come after Solomon.

340–43. The conquest of Jerusalem by the king of Babylon, Nebuchadnezzar, who carries the Hebrews into captivity.

348. *kings*: Cyrus, king of Persia, who conquers Babylon and allows the Hebrews to return to Jerusalem. Cyrus is succeeded by Darius and Artaxerxes. ". . . The Lord stirred up the spirit of Cyrus king of Persia, that he made a proclamation. . . . All the kingdoms of the earth hath the Lord God of heaven given me; and he hath charged me to build him an house in Jerusalem, which is in Judah. Who is there among you of all his people? The Lord his God be with him, and let him go up" (2 Chronicles 36:22–23).

349–60. Milton now covers the mostly intertestamental period beginning with the building of the Second Temple, *the house of god* (line 349), in the canonical books of Ezra and Nehemiah, these being the last historical books of the Old Testament. After returning from captivity in Babylon to freedom in Jerusalem, the Israelites are poor but virtuous and devout. Their growing wealth leads to *strife* (line 355), even among the priests, who "should most / Endeavor peace" (lines 354–55). The familiar pattern of moral decline leading to political abjection and religious pollution reflects only distantly on the poet's own experience of the English Revolution. (He makes no allusion, for example, to the Maccabean revolt, 167–160 B.C.E.) The period between the testaments ends with the birth of Jesus, which opens the New Testament (Matthew 1:18–2:23). Jesus is a king in David's royal line (Matthew 1:17 and 2:2) but is *Barred of His right* (line 360) by the Roman puppet king, Herod, the descendant of an Idumean (Edomite) *stranger* (line 358). Milton's sources are the apocryphal books

They first re-edify and for a while   350
In mean estate live moderate, till grown
In wealth and multitude, factious they grow.
But first among the priests dissension springs,
Men who attend the altar and should most
Endeavor peace. Their strife pollution brings   355
Upon the temple itself. At last they seize
The scepter and regard not David's sons,
Then lose it to a stranger, that the true
Anointed King, Messiah, might be born
Barred of His right. Yet at His birth a star   360
Unseen before in Heav'n proclaims Him come
And guides the eastern sages who inquire
His place to offer incense, myrrh and gold.
His place of birth a solemn angel tells
To simple shepherds keeping watch by night.   365
They gladly thither haste and by a choir
Of squadroned angels hear His carol sung.
A virgin is His mother but His sire
The Pow'r of the Most High. He shall ascend
The throne hereditary and bound His reign   370
With earth's wide bounds, His glory with the heav'ns.
    He ceased, discerning Adam with such joy
Surcharged as had like grief been dewed in tears
Without the vent of words, which these he breathed:
    O prophet of glad tidings, finisher   375
Of utmost hope! Now clear I understand
What oft my steadiest thoughts have searched in vain,
Why our great expectation should be called
The Seed of woman: Virgin Mother, hail!
High in the love of Heav'n, yet from my loins   380
Thou shalt proceed and from thy womb the Son
Of God Most High: so God with Man unites!
Needs must the serpent now his capital bruise
Expect with mortal pain. Say where and when

---

    1 and 2 Maccabees and the writings of the great Jewish historian Josephus. See
especially 2 Maccabees 4–6:11 and Josephus, *Antiquities of the Jews* 12–20.
359. *Messiah*: anointed one, king; although in David's royal line, Jesus is born in humble
    circumstances under the Roman domination of Palestine. See 5.605 n. and 5.664 n.
360–67. The story of Jesus' birth, summarized here, is told in Matthew 2 and Luke 2.
379–80. "And the angel came in unto her, and said, Hail, thou that art highly favoured,
    the Lord is with thee: blessed art thou among women. . . . And, behold, thou shalt
    conceive in thy womb, and bring forth a son, and shalt call his name JESUS. He
    shall be great, and shall be called the Son of the Highest: and the Lord God shall
    give unto him the throne of his father David: . . . and of his kingdom there shall be
    no end" (Luke 1:28, 31–33).
383. *capital*: of the head (Latin *caput*, "head").

Their fight! What stroke shall bruise the Victor's heel?   385
    To whom thus Michael: Dream not of their fight
As of a duel or the local wounds
Of head or heel. Not therefore joins the Son
Manhood to Godhead with more strength to foil
Thy enemy nor so is overcome   390
Satan, whose fall from Heav'n—a deadlier bruise—
Disabled not to give thee thy death's wound,
Which he who comes thy Savior shall recure
Not by destroying Satan but his works
In thee and in thy seed. Nor can this be   395
But by fulfilling that which thou didst want:
Obedience to the Law of God imposed
On penalty of death, and suffering death,
The penalty to thy transgression due,
And due to theirs which out of thine will grow: 400
So only can high justice rest apaid.
The Law of God exact He shall fulfill
Both by obedience and by love, though love
Alone fulfill the Law. Thy punishment
He shall endure by coming in the flesh   405
To a reproachful life and cursèd, death,
Proclaiming life to all who shall believe
In his Redemption and that his obedience
Imputed becomes theirs by faith, his merits
To save them, not their own, though legal works.   410
For this He shall live hated, be blasphemed,
Seized on by force, judged and to death condemned,
A shameful and accurst, nailed to the cross
By his own nation, slain for bringing life.
But to the cross He nails thy enemies: 415
The Law that is against thee and the sins
Of all mankind with him there crucified,
Never to hurt them more who rightly trust

394–401. The Son will defeat Satan's works in human beings by being perfectly obedient
to God (as no other human can) and by taking on himself the punishment for disobedience, death.

396. *want*: lack, fail.

397–401. Justice can be fulfilled because the Son will do two things: he will obey the law
of God (which Adam failed to do) and he will suffer death to pay for the crime of
Adam and the crimes of humanity.

407–10. We cannot obey God on our own, but if we believe in Christ his obedience will
be attributed (*imputed*) to us. Christians are saved by Christ's obedience and love,
not by *legal works* (obedience either to the Law or to ordinances of the church). Milton saw Roman Catholic and Anglican formalities as outward, legal works of the
same kind as the Jewish law. See line 512 n.

415–17. "Blotting out the handwriting of the ordinances that was against us; which was
contrary to us, and took it out of the way, nailing it to his cross" (Colossians 2:14).

In this his satisfaction. So He dies
But soon revives: Death over him no pow'r   420
Shall long usurp. Ere the third dawning light
Return the stars of morn shall see him rise
Out of his grave, fresh as the dawning light,
Thy ransom paid which Man from death redeems,
His death for Man: as many as offered life   425
Neglect not and the benefit embrace
By faith not void of works. This godlike act
Annuls thy doom, the death thou shouldst have died
In sin for ever lost from life. This act
Shall bruise the head of Satan, crush his strength,   430
Defeating Sin and Death, his two main arms,
And fix far deeper in his head their stings
Than temporal death shall bruise the Victor's heel
Or theirs whom He redeems, a death like sleep,
A gentle wafting to immortal life.   435
Nor after Resurrection shall He stay
Longer on Earth than certain times t' appear
To his disciples, men who in his life
Still followed him. To them shall leave in charge
To teach all nations what of him they learned   440
And his salvation, them who shall believe
Baptizing in the profluent stream, the sign
Of washing them from guilt of sin to life
Pure, and in mind prepared, if so befall,
For death like that which the Redeemer died.   445
All nations they shall teach, for from that day
Not only to the sons of Abraham's loins
Salvation shall be preached but to the sons
Of Abraham's faith wherever through the world:
So in his Seed all nations shall be blest.   450
Then to the Heav'n of Heav'ns He shall ascend

421. *third dawning light*: "In the end of the sabbath, as it began to dawn toward the first day of the week" (Matthew 28:1), i.e., Sunday at dawn. It is by the ancient inclusive way of counting that Jesus rose on the third day (Matthew 20:19; 1 Corinthians 15:4); by the modern way of counting he rose on the second. Compare Plato's statement that art—imitation of the real, which is imitation of the true—is at a third remove from reality (*Republic* 10.602c), when by our way of counting Plato means two. By any way of counting Jesus rose not at the *third* but the second *dawning light*.

432–33. I.e., The stings of Sin and Death shall strike Satan's head, a more serious and permanent wound than will be the temporary death of Jesus or of those whom Jesus has redeemed from death.

439–45. The ministry of the apostles, who establish the church and spread it throughout the nations, baptizing all believers and giving them the courage to face martyrdom.

447–49. The Christian Church will be open not only to the descendants of Abraham through his son Isaac but to all people who have Abraham's faith. But that faith is now faith in Jesus' sacrifice of himself for the salvation of humanity.

450. *his*: Abraham's. *Seed*: Jesus.

With victory triúmphing through the air
Over his foes and thine; there shall surprise
The Serpent, Prince of Air, and drag in chains
Through all his realm and there confounded leave,   455
Then enter into glory and resume
His seat at God's right hand, exalted high
Above all names in Heav'n, and thence shall come
When this world's dissolution shall be ripe
With glory and pow'r to judge both quick and dead: 460
To judge th' unfaithful dead but to reward
His faithful and receive them into bliss
Whether in Heav'n or Earth, for then the Earth
Shall all be Paradise, far happier place
Than this of Eden, and far happier days.   465
   So spake th' archangel Michaël, then paused
As at the world's great period, and our sire
Replete with joy and wonder thus replied:
   O goodness infinite, goodness immense!
That all this good of evil shall produce   470
And evil turn to good more wonderful
Than that which by Creation first brought forth
Light out of darkness! Full of doubt I stand,
Whether I should repent me now of sin
By me done and occasioned or rejoice   475
Much more that much more good thereof shall spring,
To God more glory, more good will to men
From God, and over wrath grace shall abound!
But say, if our Deliverer up to Heav'n
Must reascend, what will betide the few   480
His faithful left among th' unfaithful herd,
The enemies of truth? Who then shall guide
His people, who defend? Will they not deal
Worse with his followers than with Him they dealt?
   Be sure they will, said th' angel, but from Heav'n   485
He to his own a Comforter will send,

453–55. I.e., After his resurrection and ascension Christ will banish Satan and the devils from their kingdom in the air and drag them to Hell.

458–60. The Last Judgment.

473–78. A version of the medieval idea of a "fortunate fall." Milton doesn't take the idea seriously but uses it to express how Adam feels at this moment.

478. "Moreover the law entered, that the offence might abound. But where sin abounded, grace did much more abound" (Romans 5:20).

486–92. *Comforter*: the Paraclete, Holy Spirit, which comes from the Father and is sent by the Son (John 14:16–17, 26; 15:26; 16:7). Milton understands the Paraclete to be the source of our conscience, the law of God written in the heart, and of the fortitude to hold to what is right. "I will put my laws into their mind, and write them in their hearts" (Hebrews 8:10).

The promise of his Father, who shall dwell
His Spirit within them and the Law of Faith,
Working through love, upon their hearts shall write
To guide them in all truth and also arm   490
With spiritual armor able to resist
Satan's assaults and quench his fiery darts,
What Man can do against them, not afraid,
Though to the death, against such cruelties
With inward consolations recompensed   495
And oft supported so as shall amaze
Their proudest persecutors. For the Spirit
Poured first on his apostles whom he sends
T' evangelize the nations, then on all
Baptized, shall them with wondrous gifts endue   500
To speak all tongues and do all miracles
As did their Lord before them. Thus they win
Great numbers of each nation to receive
With joy the tidings brought from Heav'n. At length,
Their ministry performed and race well run,   505
Their doctrine and their story written left,
They die, but in their room as they forewarn
Wolves shall succeed for teachers, grievous wolves
Who all the sacred mysteries of Heav'n
To their own vile advantages shall turn   510
Of lucre and ambition and the truth
With superstitions and traditions taint,
Left only in those written records pure
Though not but by the Spirit understood.
Then shall they seek t' avail themselves of names,   515
Places and titles and with these to join
Secular power though feigning still to act

---

492. *Satan's assaults* and *fiery darts* are the cruelties and persecutions visited upon Christians in this world.

497–502. "And when the day of Pentecost was fully come . . . there appeared unto them cloven tongues like as of fire, and it sat upon each of them. And they were all filled with the Holy Ghost, and began to speak with other tongues, as the Spirit gave them utterance" (Acts 2:1, 3–4). The apostles are given the power to speak all languages in order to bring the good news to all nations.

499. *evangelize:* convert to Christ by bringing the "good news" (Greek *eu*, "good,"+*angelia*, "message").

508. *Wolves:* corrupt churchmen, who will devour the flock rather than feeding it. St. Paul, who organized the church in its early years, settling its doctrine and bringing the gospel to the gentiles, said, "For I know this, that after my departing shall grievous wolves enter in among you, not sparing the flock" (Acts 20:29).

512. In addition to enriching themselves, the wolves will introduce into the church practices that are merely external and formal, polluting the only legitimate traditions, those left in the Bible. See lines 407–10 n.

517–21. *Secular power . . . carnal pow'r:* the argument of Milton's late tract *A Treatise of Civil Power in Ecclesiastical Causes* (1659), which he probably wrote when newly embarked on the composition of *Paradise Lost*.

By spiritual, to themselves appropriating
The Spirit of God promised alike and giv'n
To all believers and from that pretense   520
Spiritual laws by carnal pow'r shall force
On every conscience, laws which none shall find
Left them enrolled or what the Spirit within
Shall on the heart engrave. What will they then
But force the Spirit of Grace itself and bind   525
His consort Liberty? What but unbuild
His living temples built by faith to stand,
Their own faith not another's? For on Earth
Who against faith and conscience can be heard
Infallible? Yet many will presume,   530
Whence heavy persecution shall arise
On all who in the worship persevere
Of Spirit and Truth. The rest, far greater part,
Will deem in outward rites and specious forms
Religion satisfied. Truth shall retire   535
Bestuck with sland'rous darts and works of faith
Rarely to be found. So shall the world go on,
To good malignant, to bad men benign,
Under her own weight groaning till the day
Appear of respiration to the just   540
And vengeance to the wicked at return
Of Him so lately promised to thy aid,
The woman's Seed, obscurely then foretold,
Now amplier known thy Savior and thy Lord,
Last in the clouds from Heav'n to be revealed   545
In glory of the Father to dissolve
Satan with his perverted world, then raise
From the conflagrant mass, purged and refined,

521–24. The wolves will use physical force—war, the Inquisition—to impose spiritual laws on others. These new laws will be neither in the scriptures nor in the human conscience.

527. Each Christian is a *living temple*, surpassing the temple at Jerusalem (which was destroyed by the Romans in 70 c.e.). "For the temple of God is holy, which temple ye are" (1 Corinthians 3:17).

539–51. The apocalypse, recounted in the book of Revelation, brings Milton's account of history to its end (line 552). For the *day* (line 539) of the Lord, see 2 Peter 3:10–13: "But the day of the Lord will come as a thief in the night; in which the heavens shall pass away with a great noise, and the elements shall melt with fervent heat, the earth also and the works that are therein shall be burned up. . . . Nevertheless we . . . look for new heavens and a new earth, wherein dwelleth righteousness." At the Last Judgment the Son, who is the *woman's Seed* (line 543), is enthroned *in the clouds* (line 545) and judges the *just* and the *wicked* (lines 540–41; Revelation 20:11–15). The wicked are thrown with Satan into the sea of fire (Revelation 20:10). That is the bruising of the serpent's head *obscurely then foretold* (line 543; cf. 10:181). The world is destroyed or, in Milton's materialist, chemical terms, *dissolve[d]* (line 546), *purged*, and *refined* (line 548) before a new world is raised (line 547; Revelation 21:1), in which the just will live in *eternal bliss* (line 551).

New Heavens, new Earth, ages of endless date
Founded in righteousness and peace and love   550
To bring forth fruits, joy and eternal bliss.
   He ended, and thus Adam last replied:
How soon hath thy prediction, seer blest,
Measured this transient world, the race of time
Till time stand fixed. Beyond all is abyss,   555
Eternity, whose end no eye can reach.
Greatly instructed I shall hence depart,
Greatly in peace of thought and have my fill
Of knowledge, what this vessel can contain,
Beyond which was my folly to aspire.   560
Henceforth I learn that to obey is best,
And love with fear the only God, to walk
As in His presence, ever to observe
His providence and on Him sole depend,
Merciful over all His works, with good   565
Still overcoming evil and by small
Accomplishing great things, by things deemed weak
Subverting worldly strong, and worldly wise
By simply meek, that suffering for Truth's sake
Is fortitude to highest victory   570
And to the faithful death the gate of life:
Taught this by His example whom I now
Acknowledge my Redeemer ever blest.
   To whom thus also th' angel last replied:
This having learned thou hast attained the sum   575
Of wisdom. Hope no higher, though all the stars
Thou knew'st by name and all th' ethereal powers,
All secrets of the deep, all nature's works
Or works of God in Heav'n, air, earth or sea,
And all the riches of this world enjoy'dst   580
And all the rule, one empire. Only add
Deeds to thy knowledge answerable, add faith,
Add virtue, patience, temperance, add love,
By name to come called charity, the soul

---

551. This line is unpunctuated in 1667 and 1674. Since the eighteenth century, most editors place a comma after *fruits*. Paul says we are to "bring forth fruit unto God" (Romans 7:4). Cf. John 4:36, "fruit unto life eternal." For "fruit of the Spirit," see Galatians 5:22–23.

559. *this vessel*: the body and mind, the container of the soul.

567–68. "God hath chosen the weak things of the world to confound the things which are mighty" (1 Corinthians 1:27).

581–84. "Add to your faith virtue; and to virtue knowledge; and to knowledge temperance; and to temperance patience; and to patience godliness; and to godliness brotherly kindness; and to brotherly kindness charity" (2 Peter 1.5–7).

584–85. *charity*, Latin *caritas*, in the biblical Greek, *agapē*, often rendered in English as *love*, i.e., caring for and kindness toward others. "Though I speak with the tongues of men and of angels, and have not charity, I am become as sounding brass, or a

Of all the rest. Then wilt thou not be loath   585
To leave this Paradise but shalt possess
A paradise within thee, happier far.
Let us descend now therefore from this top
Of speculation for the hour precise
Exacts our parting hence. And see! the guards   590
By me encamped on yonder hill expect
Their motion, at whose front a flaming sword
In signal of remove waves fiercely round:
We may no longer stay. Go, waken Eve.
Her also I with gentle dreams have calmed   595
Portending good and all her spirits composed
To meek submission. Thou at season fit
Let her with thee partake what thou hast heard,
Chiefly what may concern her faith to know:
The great deliv'rance by her Seed to come   600
(For by the woman's Seed) on all mankind,
That ye may live, which will be many days,
Both in one faith unanimous, though sad
With cause for evils past, yet much more cheered
With meditation on the happy end.   605
    He ended, and they both descend the hill.
Descended, Adam to the bow'r where Eve
Lay sleeping ran before but found her waked,
And thus with words not sad she him received:
    Whence thou return'st and whither went'st I know,   610
For God is also in sleep and dreams advise
Which he hath sent propitious, some great good
Presaging, since with sorrow and heart's distress
Wearied I fell asleep. But now lead on.
In me is no delay. With thee to go   615

---

tinkling cymbal"; "And now abideth faith, hope, charity, these three; but the greatest
of these is charity" (1 Corinthians 13:1 and 13).
588–89. *top / Of speculation*: high place for viewing. The word *speculation* here implies
prophetic vision but not theoretical reflection (Latin *specula*, "watchtower").
592–93. "And he placed at the east of the garden of Eden Cherubims, and a flaming
sword which turned every way" (Genesis 3:24). God says the flaming sword and
troop of cherubim are to protect the garden from Satan and "spirits foul" (11.100–3
and 118–25), not, as in the Bible, to frighten Eve and Adam and warn off their
descendants.
601. *(For by the woman's seed)*: This grammatically detached parenthesis, interrupting
the phrase, "to come [O]n all mankind," is in both 1667 and 1674. It appears to have
survived revision, perhaps because the half line it occupied was never filled in. At
any rate, it shows Milton's effort to counter Christian misogyny by emphasizing that
the catastrophe of *Paradise Lost* is repaired by the *woman's* seed.
611. "I the Lord . . . will speak unto him in a dream" (Numbers 12:6). A closer echo is the
Iliad 1.63, where Achilles says, "for a dream also is from Zeus."
615. *In me is no delay* translates (changing only the tense) Virgil's *in me mora non erit ulla*
(*Eclogues* 3.52).
615–18. Eve's words recall Ruth's to Naomi: "Intreat me not to leave thee, or to return
from following after thee: for whither thou goest, I will go; and where thou lodgest,

Is to stay here; without thee here to stay
Is to go hence unwilling. Thou to me
Art all things under Heaven, all places thou,
Who for my willful crime art banished hence.
This further consolation yet secure   620
I carry hence: though all by me is lost,
Such favor I unworthy am vouchsafed,
By me the promised Seed shall all restore.
   So spake our mother Eve and Adam heard
Well pleased but answered not. For now too nigh   625
Th' archangel stood and from the other hill
To their fixed station all in bright array
The cherubim descended, on the ground
Gliding metéorous as eve'ning mist
Ris'n from a river o'er the marish glides   630
And gathers ground fast at the laborer's heel
Homeward returning. High in front advanced,
The brandished sword of God before them blazed
Fierce as a comet which with torrid heat
And vapor as the Libyan air adust   635
Began to parch that temperate clime. Whereat
In either hand the hast'ning angel caught
Our ling'ring parents and to the eastern gate
Led them direct and down the cliff as fast
To the subjected plain, then disappeared.   640
They, looking back, all th' eastern side beheld
Of Paradise, so late their happy seat,
Waved over by that flaming brand. The gate
With dreadful faces thronged and fiery arms.
Some natural tears they dropped but wiped them soon.   645
The world was all before them, where to choose
Their place of rest, and Providence their guide.
They hand in hand with wand'ring steps and slow
Through Eden took their solitary way.

   I will lodge: thy people shall be my people, and thy God my God" (Ruth 1:16). In the
   Iliad, Andromache says to her husband, Hector, "You are to me father and mother
   and brother, you who are my young husband" (6.429–30).
629. *meteorous*: in midair (the Greek etymological sense of the word).
632–34. See lines 592–93 n.
635. *adust*: dry from having been burned by the sun.
640. *subjected*: lying below.
649. *Through Eden*: Eden is not the garden paradise but the large country in which that
   paradise is contained. Outside the garden, on the plain beneath it, Adam and Eve
   move through the country of Eden. See Glossary, EDEN and PARADISE.

SOURCES AND
BACKGROUNDS

Selections from the Bible[†]

Genesis

1

In the beginning God created the heaven and the earth.

2 And the earth was without form, and void; and darkness was upon the face of the deep. And the Spirit of God moved upon the face of the waters.

3 And God said, Let there be light: and there was light.

4 And God saw the light, that it was good: and God divided the light from the darkness.

5 And God called the light Day, and the darkness he called Night. And the evening and the morning were the first day.

6 And God said, Let there be a firmament in the midst of the waters, and let it divide the waters from the waters.

7 And God made the firmament, and divided the waters which were under the firmament from the waters which were above the firmament: and it was so.

8 And God called the firmament Heaven. And the evening and the morning were the second day.

9 And God said, Let the waters under the heaven be gathered together unto one place, and let the dry land appear: and it was so.

10 And God called the dry land Earth; and the gathering together of the waters called he Seas: and God saw that it was good.

11 And God said, Let the earth bring forth grass, the herb yielding seed, and the fruit tree yielding fruit after his kind, whose seed is in itself, upon the earth: and it was so.

12 And the earth brought forth grass, and herb yielding seed after his kind, and the tree yielding fruit, whose seed was in itself, after his kind: and God saw that it was good.

13 And the evening and the morning were the third day.

† Excerpted from *The Bible: Authorized King James Version*, ed. Robert Carroll and Stephen Prickett, Oxford World's Classics (Oxford: Oxford University Press, 1997; rpt., 2008), pp. 1–4, 11–12, 36, 82–83, 165–66, 219–21, 309–10, 316–19, 697–98, 704–5, 722, 770, 773, 800–1, 903–5. Extracts from the Authorized Version of the Bible (The King James Bible), the rights in which are vested in the Crown, are reproduced by permission of Crown's Patentee, Cambridge University Press.

14 And God said, Let there be lights in the firmament of the heaven to divide the day from the night; and let them be for signs, and for seasons, and for days, and years:

15 And let them be for lights in the firmament of the heaven to give light upon the earth: and it was so.

16 And God made two great lights; the greater light to rule the day, and the lesser light to rule the night: he made the stars also.

17 And God set them in the firmament of the heaven to give light upon the earth,

18 And to rule over the day and over the night, and to divide the light from the darkness: and God saw that it was good.

19 And the evening and the morning were the fourth day.

20 And God said, Let the waters bring forth abundantly the moving creature that hath life, and fowl that may fly above the earth in the open firmament of heaven.

21 And God created great whales, and every living creature that moveth, which the waters brought forth abundantly, after their kind, and every winged fowl after his kind: and God saw that it was good.

22 And God blessed them, saying, Be fruitful, and multiply, and fill the waters in the seas, and let fowl multiply in the earth.

23 And the evening and the morning were the fifth day.

24 And God said, Let the earth bring forth the living creature after his kind, cattle, and creeping thing, and beast of the earth after his kind; and it was so.

25 And God made the beast of the earth after his kind, and cattle after their kind, and every thing that creepeth upon the earth after his kind: and God saw that it was good.

26 And God said, Let us make man in our image, after our likeness: and let them have dominion over the fish of the sea, and over the fowl of the air, and over the cattle, and over all the earth, and over every creeping thing that creepeth upon the earth.

27 So God created man in his own image, in the image of God created he him; male and female created he them.

28 And God blessed them, and God said unto them, Be fruitful, and multiply, and replenish the earth, and subdue it: and have dominion over the fish of the sea, and over the fowl of the air, and over every living thing that moveth upon the earth.

29 And God said, Behold, I have given you every herb bearing seed, which is upon the face of all the earth, and every tree, in the which is the fruit of a tree yielding seed; to you it shall be for meat.

30 And to every beast of the earth, and to every fowl of the air, and to every thing that creepeth upon the earth, wherein there is life, I have given every green herb for meat: and it was so.

31 And God saw every thing that he had made, and, behold, it was very good. And the evening and the morning were the sixth day.

2

Thus the heavens and the earth were finished, and all the host of them.

2 And on the seventh day God ended his work which he had made; and he rested on the seventh day from all his work which he had made.

3 And God blessed the seventh day, and sanctified it: because that in it he had rested from all his work which God created and made.

4 These are the generations of the heavens and of the earth when they were created, in the day that the LORD God made the earth and the heavens,

5 And every plant of the field before it was in the earth, and every herb of the field before it grew: for the LORD God had not caused it to rain upon the earth, and there was not a man to till the ground.

6 But there went up a mist from the earth, and watered the whole face of the ground.

7 And the LORD God formed man of the dust of the ground, and breathed into his nostrils the breath of life; and man became a living soul.

8 And the LORD God planted a garden eastward in Eden; and there he put the man whom he had formed.

9 And out of the ground made the LORD God to grow every tree that is pleasant to the sight, and good for food; the tree of life also in the midst of the garden, and the tree of knowledge of good and evil.

10 And a river went out of Eden to water the garden; and from thence it was parted, and became into four heads.

11 The name of the first is Pison: that is it which compasseth the whole land of Havilah, where there is gold;

12 And the gold of that land is good; there is bdellium and the onyx stone.

13 And the name of the second river is Gihon: the same is it that compasseth the whole land of Ethiopia.

14 And the name of the third river is Hiddekel: that is it which goeth toward the east of Assyria. And the fourth river is Euphrates.

15 And the LORD God took the man, and put him into the garden of Eden to dress[1] it and to keep it.

16 And the LORD God commanded the man, saying, Of every tree of the garden thou mayest freely eat.

17 But of the tree of the knowledge of good and evil, thou shalt not eat of it: for in the day that thou eatest thereof thou shalt surely die.

---

1. Manage, put in order.

18 And the Lord God said, It is not good that the man should be alone; I will make him an help meet for him.

19 And out of the ground the Lord God formed every beast of the field, and every fowl of the air; and brought them unto Adam to see what he would call them: and whatsoever Adam called every living creature, that was the name thereof.

20 And Adam gave names to all cattle, and to the fowl of the air, and to every beast of the field; but for Adam there was not found an help meet for him.

21 And the Lord God caused a deep sleep to fall upon Adam, and he slept: and he took one of his ribs, and closed up the flesh instead thereof;

22 And the rib, which the Lord God had taken from man, made he a woman, and brought her unto the man.

23 And Adam said, This is now bone of my bones, and flesh of my flesh: she shall be called Woman, because she was taken out of Man.

24 Therefore shall a man leave his father and his mother, and shall cleave unto his wife: and they shall be one flesh.

25 And they were both naked, the man and his wife, and were not ashamed.

3

Now the serpent was more subtil than any beast of the field which the Lord God had made. And he said unto the woman, Yea, hath God said, Ye shall not eat of every tree of the garden?

2 And the woman said unto the serpent, We may eat of the fruit of the trees of the garden:

3 But of the fruit of the tree which is in the midst of the garden, God hath said, Ye shall not eat of it, neither shall ye touch it, lest ye die.

4 And the serpent said unto the woman, Ye shall not surely die:

5 For God doth know that in the day ye eat thereof, then your eyes shall be opened, and ye shall be as gods, knowing good and evil.

6 And when the woman saw that the tree was good for food, and that it was pleasant to the eyes, and a tree to be desired to make one wise, she took of the fruit thereof, and did eat, and gave also unto her husband with her; and he did eat.

7 And the eyes of them both were opened, and they knew that they were naked; and they sewed fig leaves together, and made themselves aprons.

8 And they heard the voice of the Lord God walking in the garden in the cool of the day: and Adam and his wife hid themselves

from the presence of the LORD God amongst the trees of the garden.

9 And the LORD God called unto Adam, and said unto him, Where art thou?

10 And he said, I heard thy voice in the garden, and I was afraid, because I was naked; and I hid myself.

11 And he said, Who told thee that thou wast naked? Hast thou eaten of the tree, whereof I commanded thee that thou shouldest not eat?

12 And the man said, The woman whom thou gavest to be with me, she gave me of the tree, and I did eat.

13 And the LORD God said unto the woman, What is this that thou hast done? And the woman said, The serpent beguiled me, and I did eat.

14 And the LORD God said unto the serpent, Because thou hast done this, thou art cursed above all cattle, and above every beast of the field; upon thy belly shalt thou go, and dust shalt thou eat all the days of thy life:

15 And I will put enmity between thee and the woman, and between thy seed and her seed; it shall bruise thy head, and thou shalt bruise his heel.

16 Unto the woman he said, I will greatly multiply thy sorrow and thy conception; in sorrow thou shalt bring forth children; and thy desire shall be to thy husband, and he shall rule over thee.

17 And unto Adam he said, Because thou hast hearkened unto the voice of thy wife, and hast eaten of the tree, of which I commanded thee, saying, Thou shalt not eat of it: cursed is the ground for thy sake; in sorrow shalt thou eat of it all the days of thy life;

18 Thorns also and thistles shall it bring forth to thee; and thou shalt eat the herb of the field;

19 In the sweat of thy face shalt thou eat bread, till thou return unto the ground; for out of it wast thou taken: for dust thou art, and unto dust shalt thou return.

20 And Adam called his wife's name Eve; because she was the mother of all living.

21 Unto Adam also and to his wife did the LORD God make coats of skins, and clothed them.

22 And the LORD God said, Behold, the man is become as one of us, to know good and evil: and now, lest he put forth his hand, and take also of the tree of life, and eat, and live for ever:

23 Therefore the LORD God sent him forth from the garden of Eden, to till the ground from whence he was taken.

24 So he drove out the man; and he placed at the east of the garden of Eden Cherubims, and a flaming sword which turned every way, to keep the way of the tree of life.

From *11*

And the whole earth was of one language, and of one speech.

2 And it came to pass, as they journeyed from the east, that they found a plain in the land of Shinar; and they dwelt there.

3 And they said one to another, Go to, let us make brick, and burn them throughly. And they had brick for stone, and slime had they for morter.

4 And they said, Go to, let us build us a city and a tower, whose top may reach unto heaven; and let us make us a name, lest we be scattered abroad upon the face of the whole earth.

5 And the LORD came down to see the city and the tower, which the children of men builded.

6 And the LORD said, Behold, the people is one, and they have all one language; and this they begin to do: and now nothing will be restrained from them, which they have imagined to do.

7 Go to, let us go down, and there confound their language, that they may not understand one another's speech.

8 So the LORD scattered them abroad from thence upon the face of all the earth: and they left off to build the city.

9 Therefore is the name of it called Babel; because the LORD did there confound the language of all the earth: and from thence did the LORD scatter them abroad upon the face of all the earth.

*   *   *

From *12*

Now the LORD had said unto Abram, Get thee out of thy country, and from thy kindred, and from thy father's house, unto a land that I will shew thee:

2 And I will make of thee a great nation, and I will bless thee, and make thy name great; and thou shalt be a blessing:

3 And I will bless them that bless thee, and curse him that curseth thee: and in thee shall all families of the earth be blessed.

4 So Abram departed, as the LORD had spoken unto him; and Lot went with him: and Abram was seventy and five years old when he departed out of Haran.

5 And Abram took Sarai his wife, and Lot his brother's son, and all their substance that they had gathered, and the souls that they had gotten in Haran; and they went forth to go into the land of Canaan; and into the land of Canaan they came.

6 And Abram passed through the land unto the place of Sichem, unto the plain of Moreh. And the Canaanite was then in the land.

7 And the LORD appeared unto Abram, and said, Unto thy seed will I give this land: and there builded he an altar unto the LORD, who appeared unto him.

*   *   *

Exodus

14

And the LORD spake unto Moses, saying,

2 Speak unto the children of Israel, that they turn and encamp before Pi-hahiroth, between Migdol and the sea, over against Baal-zephon: before it shall ye encamp by the sea.

3 For Pharaoh will say of the children of Israel, They are entangled in the land, the wilderness hath shut them in.

4 And I will harden Pharaoh's heart, that he shall follow after them; and I will be honoured upon Pharaoh, and upon all his host; that the Egyptians may know that I am the LORD. And they did so.

5 And it was told the king of Egypt that the people fled: and the heart of Pharaoh and of his servants was turned against the people, and they said, Why have we done this, that we have let Israel go from serving us?

6 And he made ready his chariot, and took his people with him:

7 And he took six hundred chosen chariots, and all the chariots of Egypt, and captains over every one of them.

8 And the LORD hardened the heart of Pharaoh king of Egypt, and he pursued after the children of Israel: and the children of Israel went out with an high hand.

9 But the Egyptians pursued after them, all the horses and chariots of Pharaoh, and his horsemen, and his army, and overtook them encamping by the sea, beside Pi-hahiroth, before Baal-zephon.

10 And when Pharaoh drew nigh, the children of Israel lifted up their eyes, and, behold, the Egyptians marched after them; and they were sore afraid; and the children of Israel cried out unto the LORD.

11 And they said unto Moses, Because there were no graves in Egypt, hast thou taken us away to die in the wilderness? wherefore hast thou dealt thus with us, to carry us forth out of Egypt?

12 Is not this the word that we did tell thee in Egypt, saying, Let us alone, that we may serve the Egyptians? For it had been better for us to serve the Egyptians, than that we should die in the wilderness.

13 And Moses said unto the people, Fear ye not, stand still, and see the salvation of the LORD, which he will shew to you to day: for

the Egyptians whom ye have seen to day, ye shall see them again no more for ever.

14 The Lord shall fight for you, and ye shall hold your peace.

15 And the Lord said unto Moses, Wherefore criest thou unto me? speak unto the children of Israel, that they go forward:

16 But lift thou up thy rod, and stretch out thine hand over the sea, and divide it: and the children of Israel shall go on dry ground through the midst of the sea.

17 And I, behold, I will harden the hearts of the Egyptians, and they shall follow them: and I will get me honour upon Pharaoh, and upon all his host, upon his chariots, and upon his horsemen.

18 And the Egyptians shall know that I am the Lord, when I have gotten me honour upon Pharaoh, upon his chariots, and upon his horsemen.

19 And the angel of God, which went before the camp of Israel, removed and went behind them; and the pillar of the cloud went from before their face, and stood behind them:

20 And it came between the camp of the Egyptians and the camp of Israel; and it was a cloud and darkness to them, but it gave light by night to these: so that the one came not near the other all the night.

21 And Moses stretched out his hand over the sea; and the Lord caused the sea to go back by a strong east wind all that night, and made the sea dry land, and the waters were divided.

22 And the children of Israel went into the midst of the sea upon the dry ground: and the waters were a wall unto them on their right hand, and on their left.

23 And the Egyptians pursued, and went in after them to the midst of the sea, even all Pharaoh's horses, his chariots, and his horsemen.

24 And it came to pass, that in the morning watch the Lord looked unto the host of the Egyptians through the pillar of fire and of the cloud, and troubled the host of the Egyptians,

25 And took off their chariot wheels, that they drave them heavily; so that the Egyptians said, Let us flee from the face of Israel: for the Lord fighteth for them against the Egyptians.

26 And the Lord said unto Moses, Stretch out thine hand over the sea that the waters may come again upon the Egyptians, upon their chariots, and upon their horsemen.

27 And Moses stretched forth his hand over the sea, and the sea returned to his strength when the morning appeared; and the Egyptians fled against it; and the Lord overthrew the Egyptians in the midst of the sea.

28 And the waters returned, and covered the chariots, and the horsemen, and all the host of Pharaoh that came into the sea after them; there remained not so much as one of them.

29 But the children of Israel walked upon dry land in the midst of the sea; and the waters were a wall unto them on their right hand, and on their left.

30 Thus the Lord saved Israel that day out of the hand of the Egyptians, and Israel saw the Egyptians dead upon the sea shore.

31 And Israel saw that great work which the Lord did upon the Egyptians: and the people feared the Lord and believed the Lord, and his servant Moses.

Psalms

104

Bless the Lord, O my soul. O Lord my God, thou art very great; thou art clothed with honour and majesty.

2 Who coverest thyself with light as with a garment: who stretchest out the heavens like a curtain:

3 Who layeth the beams of his chambers in the waters: who maketh the clouds his chariot: who walketh upon the wings of the wind:

4 Who maketh his angels spirits; his ministers a flaming fire:

5 Who laid the foundations of the earth, that it should not be removed for ever.

6 Thou coveredst it with the deep as with a garment: the waters stood above the mountains.

7 At thy rebuke they fled; at the voice of thy thunder they hasted away.

8 They go up by the mountains; they go down by the valleys unto the place which thou hast founded for them.

9 Thou hast set a bound that they may not pass over; that they turn not again to cover the earth.

10 He sendeth the springs into the valleys, which run among the hills.

11 They give drink to every beast of the field: the wild asses quench their thirst.

12 By them shall the fowls of the heaven have their habitation, which sing among the branches.

13 He watereth the hills from his chambers: the earth is satisfied with the fruit of thy works.

14 He causeth the grass to grow for the cattle, and herb for the service of man: that he may bring forth food out of the earth;

15 And wine that maketh glad the heart of man, and oil to make his face to shine, and bread which strengtheneth man's heart.

16 The trees of the Lord are full of sap; the cedars of Lebanon, which he hath planted;

17 Where the birds make their nests: as for the stork, the fir trees are her house.

18 The high hills are a refuge for the wild goats; and the rocks for the conies.

19 He appointed the moon for seasons: the sun knoweth his going down.

20 Thou makest darkness, and it is night: wherein all the beasts of the forest do creep forth.

21 The young lions roar after their prey, and seek their meat from God.

22 The sun ariseth, they gather themselves together, and lay them down in their dens.

23 Man goeth forth unto his work and to his labour until the evening.

24 O Lord, how manifold are thy works! in wisdom hast thou made them all: the earth is full of thy riches.

25 So is this great and wide sea, wherein are things creeping innumerable, both small and great beasts.

26 There go the ships: there is that leviathan, whom thou hast made to play therein.

27 These wait all upon thee; that thou mayest give them their meat in due season.

28 That thou givest them they gather: thou openest thine hand, they are filled with good.

29 Thou hidest thy face, they are troubled: thou takest away their breath, they die, and return to their dust.

30 Thou sendest forth thy spirit, they are created: and thou renewest the face of the earth.

31 The glory of the Lord shall endure for ever: the Lord shall rejoice in his works.

32 He looketh on the earth, and it trembleth: he toucheth the hills, and they smoke.

33 I will sing unto the Lord as long as I live: I will sing praise to my God while I have my being.

34 My meditation of him shall be sweet: I will be glad in the Lord.
35 Let the sinners be consumed out of the earth, and let the wicked be no more. Bless thou the Lord, O my soul. Praise ye the Lord.

114

When Israel went out of Egypt, the house of Jacob from a people of strange language;
2 Judah was his sanctuary, and Israel his dominion.
3 The sea saw it, and fled: Jordan was driven back.
4 The mountains skipped like rams, and the little hills like lambs.

5 What ailed thee, O thou sea, that thou fleddest? thou Jordan, that thou wast driven back?

6 Ye mountains, that ye skipped like rams; and ye little hills, like lambs?

7 Tremble, thou earth, at the presence of the Lord, at the presence of the God of Jacob;

8 Which turned the rock into a standing water, the flint into a fountain of waters.

148

Praise ye the Lord. Praise ye the Lord from the heavens: praise him in the heights.

2 Praise ye him, all his angels: praise ye him, all his hosts.

3 Praise ye him, sun and moon: praise him, all ye stars of light.

4 Praise him, ye heavens of heavens, and ye waters that be above the heavens.

5 Let them praise the name of the Lord: for he commanded, and they were created.

6 He hath also stablished them for ever and ever: he hath made a decree which shall not pass.

7 Praise the Lord from the earth, ye dragons, and all deeps:

8 Fire, and hail; snow, and vapour; stormy wind fulfilling his word:

9 Mountains, and all hills; fruitful trees, and all cedars:

10 Beasts, and all cattle; creeping things, and flying fowl:

11 Kings of the earth, and all people; princes, and all judges of the earth:

12 Both young men, and maidens; old men, and children:

13 Let them praise the name of the Lord: for his name alone is excellent; his glory is above the earth and heaven.

14 He also exalteth the horn of his people, the praise of all his saints; even of the children of Israel, a people near unto him. Praise ye the Lord.

Isaiah

From 6

In the year that king Uzziah died I saw also the Lord sitting upon a throne, high and lifted up, and his train filled the temple.

2 Above it stood the seraphims: each one had six wings; with twain he covered his face, and with twain he covered his feet, and with twain he did fly.

3 And one cried unto another, and said, Holy, holy, holy, is the Lord of hosts: the whole earth is full of his glory.

4 And the posts of the door moved at the voice of him that cried, and the house was filled with smoke.

5 Then said I, Woe is me! for I am undone; because I am a man of unclean lips, and I dwell in the midst of a people of unclean lips: for mine eyes have seen the King, the Lord of hosts.

6 Then flew one of the seraphims unto me, having a live coal in his hand, which he had taken with the tongs from off the altar:

7 And he laid it upon my mouth, and said, Lo, this hath touched thy lips; and thine iniquity is taken away, and thy sin purged.

8 Also I heard the voice of the Lord, saying, Whom shall I send, and who will go for us? Then said I, Here am I: send me.

*   *   *

From 9

*   *   *

6 For unto us a child is born, unto us a son is given: and the government shall be upon his shoulder: and his name shall be called Wonderful, Counsellor, The mighty God, The everlasting Father, The Prince of Peace.

7 Of the increase of his government and peace there shall be no end, upon the throne of David, and upon his kingdom, to order it, and to establish it with judgment and with justice from henceforth even for ever. The zeal of the Lord of hosts will perform this.

*   *   *

From 40

Comfort ye, comfort ye my people, saith your God.

2 Speak ye comfortably to Jerusalem, and cry unto her, that her warfare is accomplished, that her iniquity is pardoned: for she hath received of the Lord's hand double for all her sins.

   3 The voice of him that crieth in the wilderness, Prepare ye the way of the Lord, make straight in the desert a highway for our God.

4 Every valley shall be exalted, and every mountain and hill shall be made low: and the crooked shall be made straight, and the rough places plain:

5 And the glory of the Lord shall be revealed, and all flesh shall see it together: for the mouth of the Lord hath spoken it.

6 The voice said, Cry. And he said, What shall I cry? All flesh is grass, and all the goodliness thereof is as the flower of the field:

7 The grass withereth, the flower fadeth: because the spirit of the Lord bloweth upon it: surely the people is grass.

8 The grass withereth, the flower fadeth: but the word of our God shall stand for ever.

*   *   *

Ezekiel

1

Now it came to pass in the thirtieth year, in the fourth month, in the fifth day of the month, as I was among the captives by the river of Chebar, that the heavens were opened, and I saw visions of God. 2 In the fifth day of the month, which was the fifth year of king Jehoiachin's captivity.

3 The word of the LORD came expressly unto Ezekiel the priest, the son of Buzi, in the land of the Chaldeans by the river Chebar; and the hand of the LORD was there upon him.

4 And I looked, and, behold, a whirlwind came out of the north, a great cloud, and a fire infolding itself, and a brightness was about it, and out of the midst thereof as the colour of amber, out of the midst of the fire.

5 Also out of the midst thereof came the likeness of four living creatures. And this was their appearance; they had the likeness of a man.

6 And every one had four faces, and every one had four wings.

7 And their feet were straight feet; and the sole of their feet was like the sole of a calf's foot: and they sparkled like the colour of burnished brass.

8 And they had the hands of a man under their wings on their four sides; and they four had their faces and their wings.

9 Their wings were joined one to another; they turned not when they went; they went every one straight forward.

10 As for the likeness of their faces, they four had the face of a man, and the face of a lion, on the right side: and they four had the face of an ox on the left side; they four also had the face of an eagle.

11 Thus were their faces: and their wings were stretched upward; two wings of every one were joined one to another, and two covered their bodies.

12 And they went every one straight forward: whither the spirit was to go, they went; and they turned not when they went.

13 As for the likeness of the living creatures, their appearance was like burning coals of fire, and like the appearance of lamps: it went up and down among the living creatures; and the fire was bright, and out of the fire went forth lightning.

14 And the living creatures ran and returned as the appearance of a flash of lightning.

15 Now as I beheld the living creatures, behold one wheel upon the earth by the living creatures, with his four faces.

16 The appearance of the wheels and their work was like unto the colour of a beryl: and they four had one likeness: and their appearance and their work was as it were a wheel in the middle of a wheel.

17 When they went, they went upon their four sides: and they turned not when they went.

18 As for their rings, they were so high that they were dreadful; and their rings were full of eyes round about them four.

19 And when the living creatures went, the wheels went by them: and when the living creatures were lifted up from the earth, the wheels were lifted up.

20 Whithersoever the spirit was to go, they went, thither was their spirit to go; and the wheels were lifted up over against them: for the spirit of the living creature was in the wheels.

21 When those went, these went; and when those stood, these stood; and when those were lifted up from the earth, the wheels were lifted up over against them: for the spirit of the living creature was in the wheels.

22 And the likeness of the firmament upon the heads of the living creature was as the colour of the terrible crystal, stretched forth over their heads above.

23 And under the firmament were their wings straight, the one toward the other: every one had two, which covered on this side, and every one had two, which covered on that side, their bodies.

24 And when they went, I heard the noise of their wings, like the noise of great waters, as the voice of the Almighty, the voice of speech, as the noise of an host: when they stood, they let down their wings.

25 And there was a voice from the firmament that was over their heads, when they stood, and had let down their wings.

26 And above the firmament that was over their heads was the likeness of a throne, as the appearance of a sapphire stone: and upon the likeness of the throne was the likeness as the appearance of a man above upon it.

27 And I saw as the colour of amber, as the appearance of fire round about within it, from the appearance of his loins even upward, and from the appearance of his loins even downward, I saw as it were the appearance of fire and it had brightness round about.

28 As the appearance of the bow that is in the cloud in the day of rain, so was the appearance of the brightness round about. This was the appearance of the likeness of the glory of the LORD. And when I saw it, I fell upon my face, and I heard a voice of one that spake.

Mark

From *13*

* * *

24 But in those days, after that tribulation, the sun shall be darkened, and the moon shall not give her light.

25 And the stars of heaven shall fall, and the powers that are in heaven shall be shaken.

26 And then shall they see the Son of man coming in the clouds with great power and glory.

27 And then shall he send his angels, and shall gather together his elect from the four winds, from the uttermost part of the earth to the uttermost part of heaven.

28 Now learn a parable of the fig tree; When her branch is yet tender, and putteth forth leaves, ye know that summer is near:

29 So ye in like manner, when ye shall see these things come to pass, know that it is nigh, even at the doors.

30 Verily I say unto you, that this generation shall not pass, till all these things be done.

31 Heaven and earth shall pass away: but my words shall not pass away.

* * *

Acts

From *13*

* * *

16 Then Paul stood up, and beckoning with his hand said, Men of Israel, and ye that fear God, give audience.

17 The God of this people of Israel chose our fathers, and exalted the people when they dwelt as strangers in the land of Egypt, and with an high arm brought he them out of it.

18 And about the time of forty years suffered he their manners in the wilderness.

19 And when he had destroyed seven nations in the land of Chanaan, he divided their land to them by lot.

20 And after that he gave unto them judges about the space of four hundred and fifty years, until Samuel the prophet.

21 And afterward they desired a king: and God gave unto them Saul the son of Cis, a man of the tribe of Benjamin, by the space of forty years.

22 And when he had removed him, he raised up onto them David to be their king; to whom also he gave testimony, and said, I have found David the son of Jesse, a man after mine own heart, which shall fulfil all my will.

23 Of this man's seed hath God according to his promise raised unto Israel a Saviour, Jesus:

24 When John had first preached before his coming the baptism of repentance to all the people of Israel.

25 And as John fulfilled his course, he said, Whom think ye that I am? I am not he. But, behold, there cometh one after me, whose shoes of his feet I am not worthy to loose.

26 Men and brethren, children of the stock of Abraham, and whosoever among you feareth God, to you is the word of this salvation sent.

27 For they that dwell at Jerusalem, and their rulers, because they knew him not, nor yet the voices of the prophets which are read every sabbath day, they have fulfilled them in condemning him.

28 And though they found no cause of death in him, yet desired they Pilate that he should be slain.

29 And when they had fulfilled all that was written of him, they took him down from the tree, and laid him in a sepulchre.

30 But God raised him from the dead:

31 And he was seen many days of them which came up with him from Galilee to Jerusalem, who are his witnesses unto the people.

32 And we declare unto you glad tidings, how that the promise which was made unto the fathers.

33 God hath fulfilled the same unto us their children, in that he hath raised up Jesus again; as it is also written in the second psalm, Thou art my Son, this day have I begotten thee.

34 And as concerning that he raised him up from the dead, now no more to return to corruption, he said on this wise, I will give you the sure mercies of David.

35 Wherefore he saith also in another psalm, Thou shalt not suffer thine Holy One to see corruption.

36 For David, after he had served his own generation by the will of God, fell on sleep, and was laid unto his fathers, and saw corruption:

37 But he, whom God raised again, saw no corruption.

*   *   *

I Corinthians

15

Moreover, brethren, I declare unto you the gospel which I preached unto you, which also ye have received, and wherein ye stand;

2 By which also ye are saved, if ye keep in memory what I preached unto you, unless ye have believed in vain.

3 For I delivered unto you first of all that which I also received, how that Christ died for our sins according to the scriptures;

4 And that he was buried, and that he rose again the third day according to the scriptures:

5 And that he was seen of Cephas, then of the twelve:

6 After that, he was seen of above five hundred brethren at once; of whom the greater part remain unto this present, but some are fallen asleep.

7 After that, he was seen of James; then of all the apostles.

8 And last of all he was seen of me also, as of one born out of due time.

9 For I am the least of the apostles, that am not meet to be called an apostle, because I persecuted the church of God.

10 But by the grace of God I am what I am: and his grace which was bestowed upon me was not in vain; but I laboured more abundantly than they all: yet not I, but the grace of God which was with me.

11 Therefore whether it were I or they, so we preach, and so ye believed.

12 Now if Christ be preached that he rose from the dead, how say some among you that there is no resurrection of the dead?

13 But if there be no resurrection of the dead, then is Christ not risen:

14 And if Christ be not risen, then is our preaching vain, and your faith is also vain.

15 Yea, and we are found false witnesses of God; because we have testified of God that he raised up Christ: whom he raised not up, if so be that the dead rise not.

16 For if the dead rise not, then is not Christ raised:

17 And if Christ be not raised, your faith is vain; ye are yet in your sins.

18 Then they also which are fallen asleep in Christ are perished.

19 If in this life only we have hope in Christ, we are of all men most miserable.

20 But now is Christ risen from the dead, and become the firstfruits of them that slept.

21 For since by man came death, by man came also the resurrection of the dead.

22 For as in Adam all die, even so in Christ shall all be made alive.

23 But every man in his own order: Christ the firstfruits; afterward they that are Christ's at his coming.

24 Then cometh the end, when he shall have delivered up the kingdom to God, even the Father; when he shall have put down all rule and all authority and power.

25 For he must reign, till he hath put all enemies under his feet.

26 The last enemy that shall be destroyed is death.

27 For he hath put all things under his feet. But when he saith all things are put under him, it is manifest that he is excepted, which did put all things under him.

28 And when all things shall be subdued unto him, then shall the Son also himself be subject unto him that put all things under him, that God may be all in all.

29 Else what shall they do which are baptized for the dead, if the dead rise not at all? why are they then baptized for the dead?

30 And why stand we in jeopardy every hour?

31 I protest by your rejoicing which I have in Christ Jesus our Lord, I die daily.

32 If after the manner of men I have fought with beasts at Ephesus, what advantageth it me, if the dead rise not? let us eat and drink; for to morrow we die.

33 Be not deceived: evil communications corrupt good manners.

34 Awake to righteousness, and sin not; for some have not the knowledge of God: I speak this to your shame.

35 But some man will say, How are the dead raised up? and with what body do they come?

36 Thou fool, that which thou sowest is not quickened, except it die:

37 And that which thou sowest, thou sowest not that body that shall be, but bare grain, it may chance of wheat, or of some other grain:

38 But God giveth it a body as it hath pleased him, and to every seed his own body.

39 All flesh is not the same flesh: but there is one kind of flesh of men, another flesh of beasts, another of fishes, and another of birds.

40 There are also celestial bodies, and bodies terrestrial: but the glory of the celestial is one, and the glory of the terrestrial is another.

41 There is one glory of the sun, and another glory of the moon, and another glory of the stars: for one star differeth from another star in glory.

42 So also is the resurrection of the dead. It is sown in corruption; it is raised in incorruption:

43 It is sown in dishonour; it is raised in glory: it is sown in weakness; it is raised in power:

44 It is sown a natural body; it is raised a spiritual body. There is a natural body, and there is a spiritual body.

45 And so it is written, The first man Adam was made a living soul; the last Adam was made a quickening spirit.

46 Howbeit that was not first which is spiritual, but that which is natural; and afterward that which is spiritual.

47 The first man is of the earth, earthy: the second man is the Lord from heaven.

48 As is the earthy, such are they also that are earthy: and as is the heavenly, such are they also that are heavenly.

49 And as we have borne the image of the earthy, we shall also bear the image of the heavenly.

50 Now this I say, brethren, that flesh and blood cannot inherit the kingdom of God; neither doth corruption inherit incorruption.

51 Behold, I shew you a mystery; We shall not all sleep, but we shall all be changed,

52 In a moment, in the twinkling of an eye, at the last trump: for the trumpet shall sound, and the dead shall be raised incorruptible, and we shall be changed.

53 For this corruptible must put on incorruption, and this mortal must put on immortality.

54 So when this corruptible shall have put on incorruption, and this mortal shall have put on immortality, then shall be brought to pass the saying that is written, Death is swallowed up in victory.

55 O death, where is thy sting? O grave, where is thy victory?

56 The sting of death is sin; and the strength of sin is the law.

57 But thanks be to God, which giveth us the victory through our Lord Jesus Christ.

58 Therefore, my beloved brethren, be ye stedfast, unmoveable, always abounding in the work of the Lord, forasmuch as ye know that your labour is not in vain in the Lord.

Revelation

12

And there appeared a great wonder in heaven; a woman clothed with the sun, and the moon under her feet, and upon her head a crown of twelve stars:

2 And she being with child cried, travailing in birth, and pained to be delivered.

3 And there appeared another wonder in heaven; and behold a great red dragon, having seven heads and ten horns, and seven crowns upon his heads.

4 And his tail drew the third part of the stars of heaven, and did cast them to the earth: and the dragon stood before the woman which was ready to be delivered, for to devour her child as soon as it was born.

5 And she brought forth a man child, who was to rule all nations with a rod of iron: and her child was caught up unto God, and to his throne.

6 And the woman fled into the wilderness, where she hath a place prepared of God, that they should feed her there a thousand two hundred and threescore days.

7 And there was war in heaven: Michael and his angels fought against the dragon; and the dragon fought and his angels.

8 And prevailed not; neither was their place found any more in heaven.

9 And the great dragon was cast out, that old serpent, called the Devil, and Satan, which deceiveth the whole world: he was cast out into the earth, and his angels were cast out with him.

10 And I heard a loud voice saying in heaven, Now is come salvation, and strength, and the kingdom of our God, and the power of his Christ: for the accuser of our brethren is cast down, which accused them before our God day and night.

11 And they overcame him by the blood of the Lamb, and by the word of their testimony; and they loved not their lives unto the death.

12 Therefore rejoice, ye heavens, and ye that dwell in them. Woe to the inhabiters of the earth and of the sea! for the devil is come down unto you, having great wrath, because he knoweth that he hath but a short time.

13 And when the dragon saw that he was cast unto the earth, he persecuted the woman which brought forth the man child.

14 And to the woman were given two wings of a great eagle, that she might fly into the wilderness, into her place, where she is nourished for a time, and times, and half a time, from the face of the serpent.

15 And the serpent cast out of his mouth water as a flood after the woman, that he might cause her to be carried away of the flood.

16 And the earth helped the woman, and the earth opened her mouth, and swallowed up the flood which the dragon cast out of his mouth.

17 And the dragon was wroth with the woman, and went to make war with the remnant of her seed, which keep the commandments of God, and have the testimony of Jesus Christ.

20

And I saw an angel come down from heaven, having the key of the bottomless pit and a great chain in his hand.

2 And he laid hold on the dragon, that old serpent, which is the Devil, and Satan, and bound him a thousand years.

3 And cast him into the bottomless pit, and shut him up, and set a seal upon him, that he should deceive the nations no more, till the thousand years should be fulfilled: and after that he must be loosed a little season.

4 And I saw thrones, and they sat upon them, and judgment was given unto them: and I saw the souls of them that were beheaded for the witness of Jesus, and for the word of God, and which had not worshipped the beast, neither his image, neither had received his mark upon their foreheads, or in their hands; and they lived and reigned with Christ a thousand years.

5 But the rest of the dead lived not again until the thousand years were finished. This is the first resurrection.

6 Blessed and holy is he that hath part in the first resurrection: on such the second death hath no power, but they shall be priests of God and of Christ, and shall reign with him a thousand years.

7 And when the thousand years are expired, Satan shall be loosed out of his prison.

8 And shall go out to deceive the nations which are in the four quarters of the earth, Gog and Magog, to gather them together to battle: the number of whom is as the sand of the sea.

9 And they went up on the breadth of the earth, and compassed the camp of the saints about, and the beloved city: and fire came down from God out of heaven, and devoured them.

10 And the devil that deceived them was cast into the lake of fire and brimstone, where the beast and the false prophet are, and shall be tormented day and night for ever and ever.

11 And I saw a great white throne, and him that sat on it, from whose face the earth and the heaven fled away; and there was found no place for them.

12 And I saw the dead, small and great, stand before God; and the books were opened: and another book was opened, which is the book of life: and the dead were judged out of those things which were written in the books, according to their works.

13 And the sea gave up the dead which were in it; and death and hell delivered up the dead which were in them: and they were judged every man according to their works.

14 And death and hell were cast into the lake of fire. This is the second death.

15 And whosoever was not found written in the book of life was cast into the lake of fire.

21

And I saw a new heaven and a new earth: for the first heaven and the first earth were passed away; and there was no more sea.

2 And I John saw the holy city, new Jerusalem, coming down from God out of heaven, prepared as a bride adorned for her husband.

3 And I heard a great voice out of heaven saying, Behold, the tabernacle of God is with men, and he will dwell with them, and they

shall be his people, and God himself shall be with them, and be their God.

4 And God shall wipe away all tears from their eyes; and there shall be no more death, neither sorrow, nor crying, neither shall there be any more pain: for the former things are passed away.

5 And he that sat upon the throne said, Behold, I make all things new. And he said unto me, Write: for these words are true and faithful.

6 And he said unto me, It is done. I am Alpha and Omega, the beginning and the end. I will give unto him that is athirst of the fountain of the water of life freely.

7 He that overcometh shall inherit all things; and I will be his God, and he shall be my son.

8 But the fearful, and unbelieving, and the abominable, and murderers, and whoremongers, and sorcerers, and idolaters, and all liars, shall have their part in the lake which burneth with fire and brimstone: which is the second death.

9 And there came unto me one of the seven angels which had the seven vials full of the seven last plagues, and talked with me, saying, Come hither, I will shew thee the bride, the Lamb's wife.

10 And he carried me away in the spirit to a great and high mountain, and shewed me that great city, the holy Jerusalem, descending out of heaven from God,

11 Having the glory of God: and her light was like unto a stone most precious, even like a jasper stone, clear as crystal;

12 And had a wall great and high, and had twelve gates, and at the gates twelve angels, and names written thereon, which are the names of the twelve tribes of the children of Israel:

13 On the east three gates; on the north three gates; on the south three gates; and on the west three gates.

14 And the wall of the city had twelve foundations, and in them the names of the twelve apostles of the Lamb.

15 And he that talked with me had a golden reed to measure the city, and the gates thereof, and the wall thereof.

16 And the city lieth foursquare, and the length is as large as the breadth: and he measured the city with the reed, twelve thousand furlongs. The length and the breadth and the height of it are equal.

17 And he measured the wall thereof, an hundred and forty and four cubits, according to the measure of a man, that is, of the angel.

18 And the building of the wall of it was of jasper: and the city was pure gold, like unto clear glass.

19 And the foundations of the wall of the city were garnished with all manner of precious stones. The first foundation was jasper; the second, sapphire; the third, a chalcedony; the fourth, an emerald;

20 The fifth, sardonyx; the sixth, sardius; the seventh, chrysolite; the eighth, beryl; the ninth, a topaz; the tenth, a chrysoprasus; the eleventh, a jacinth; the twelfth, an amethyst.

21 And the twelve gates were twelve pearls; every several gate was of one pearl: and the street of the city was pure gold, as it were transparent glass.

22 And I saw no temple therein: for the Lord God Almighty and the Lamb are the temple of it.

23 And the city had no need of the sun, neither of the moon, to shine in it: for the glory of God did lighten it, and the Lamb is the light thereof.

24 And the nations of them which are saved shall walk in the light of it: and the kings of the earth do bring their glory and honour into it.

25 And the gates of it shall not be shut at all by day: for there shall be no night there.

26 And they shall bring the glory and honour of the nations into it.

27 And there shall in no wise enter into it any thing that defileth, neither whatsoever worketh abomination, or maketh a lie: but they which are written in the Lamb's book of life.

22

And he shewed me a pure river of water of life, clear as crystal, proceeding out of the throne of God and of the Lamb.

2 In the midst of the street of it, and on either side of the river, was there the tree of life, which bare twelve manner of fruits, and yielded her fruit every month: and the leaves of the tree were for the healing of the nations.

3 And there shall be no more curse: but the throne of God and of the Lamb shall be in it; and his servants shall serve him:

4 And they shall see his face; and his name shall be in their foreheads.

5 And there shall be no night there; and they need no candle, neither light of the sun; for the Lord God giveth them light: and they shall reign for ever and ever.

6 And he said unto me, These sayings are faithful and true: and the Lord God of the holy prophets sent his angel to shew unto his servants the things which must shortly be done.

7 Behold, I come quickly: blessed is he that keepeth the sayings of the prophecy of this book.

8 And I John saw these things, and heard them. And when I had heard and seen, I fell down to worship before the feet of the angel which shewed me these things.

9 Then saith he unto me, See thou do it not: for I am thy fellow-servant, and of thy brethren the prophets, and of them which keep the sayings of this book: worship God.

10 And he saith unto me, Seal not the sayings of the prophecy of this book: for the time is at hand.

11 He that is unjust, let him be unjust still: and he which is filthy, let him be filthy still: and he that is righteous, let him be righteous still: and he that is holy, let him be holy still.

12 And, behold, I come quickly; and my reward is with me, to give every man according as his work shall be.

13 I am Alpha and Omega, the beginning and the end, the first and the last.

14 Blessed are they that do his commandments, that they may have right to the tree of life, and may enter in through the gates into the city.

15 For without are dogs, and sorcerers, and whoremongers, and murderers, and idolaters, and whosoever loveth and maketh a lie.

16 I Jesus have sent mine angel to testify unto you these things in the churches. I am the root and the offspring of David, and the bright and morning star.

17 And the Spirit and the bride say, Come. And let him that heareth say, Come. And let him that is athirst come. And whosoever will, let him take the water of life freely.

18 For I testify unto every man that heareth the words of the prophecy of this book, If any man shall add unto these things, God shall add unto him the plagues that are written in this book:

19 And if any man shall take away from the words of the book of this prophecy, God shall take away his part out of the book of life, and out of the holy city, and from the things which are written in this book.

20 He which testifieth these things saith, Surely I come quickly. Amen. Even so, come, Lord Jesus.

21 The grace of our Lord Jesus Christ be with you all. Amen.

Selections from Milton's Prose

From 1641 up to the threshold of the Restoration (1660), Milton wrote polemical pamphlets on various subjects, all animated by what the seventeenth-century biographer John Aubrey called "a pure zeal to the liberty of mankind, which he thought would be greater under a free state than under a monarchial government." The two selections offered here, from *The Reason of Church Government* (1642) and, in its entirety, *Areopagitica* (1644), address religious and intellectual liberty, respectively.

The Reason of Church Government is the longest and in every other sense the most substantial of Milton's "antiprelatical" tracts—that is, pamplets against the government of the church by bishops, because such government limits each Christian's freedom of conscience. It is especially interesting for students of *Paradise Lost*, however, for the long digression on poetry, and on the poet's personal ambitions, which opens the second book. The digression is presented here.

Milton discloses that he has been preparing his entire life (being now in his mid-thirties, recently returned from the European continent) to compose something in poetry "so written to aftertimes, as they should not willingly let it die" (p. 344). He speaks of the crisis in the church because of which his conscience has drawn him away from his private studies and poetic ambitions into controversy against the bishops. He was enjoying "a calm and pleasing solitariness" in which he beheld "the bright countenance of Truth in the quiet and still air of delightful studies." How unpleasant it was to leave that serene companionship for the brawling arena of public controversy, "a troubled sea of noises and hoarse disputes" (p. 347).

Even so, his destiny, when all such matters have been settled, is to write something for future ages that will "imbreed and cherish in a great people the seeds of virtue and public civility," celebrating "God's almightiness" and "the deeds and triumphs of just and pious nations doing valiantly through faith against the enemies of Christ" (p. 346). He will be inspired to sing on such themes not by the classical Muses on Mount Helicon—"Dame Memory and her siren daughters"—"but by devout prayer to that eternal Spirit, who can enrich with all utterance and knowledge, and sends out his Seraphim, with the hallowed fire of his altar, to touch and purify the lips of whom he pleases" (p. 347). Those are of course his lips, touched like the prophet Isaiah's. We may be tempted to smile at the idealistic self-confidence of the poet, evidently young for his age (he would grow up rapidly in the next

337

338   SELECTIONS FROM MILTON'S PROSE

two years), who, like his model, Spenser, intends to make Englishmen virtuous and inspire a crusade against the enemies of Christ—probably meaning Roman Catholics, not Muslims, although on his likely reckoning the one is no better than the other.

But the brilliance of expression, the idealism, the conviction, and the fire are real. As for the ideas—in particular the taking of poetry more seriously than any modern poet had taken it before, and the intention to surpass even the achievement of the Greeks, notably Homer—they will mature in the sublime poet of *Paradise Lost*. Setting Homer aside, it is amazing to think Milton made good on every one of his numerous boasts.

After the antiprelatical tracts on religious liberty (1641–42), Milton composed four tracts on domestic liberty, in particular divorce (1643–45). In these he argued, very much ahead of his time, that marriage is a free union of minds and spirits, not just of bodies. For this reason, the state and the law have no authority over the private affairs of married persons, including their wish to stay married or to divorce.

Milton's greatest prose work, reprinted here in full, is titled *Areopagitica*, after the hill of the Areopagus (*Areios pagos*, "hill of Ares") in Athens, where grave elders of the Athenian council of state met in the earliest days, and which later was the seat of Athens' highest court. Milton intended a compliment (which doubtless was lost on many of its recipients) to the body he addresses: the "High Court of Parliament" (p. 349). The occasion was the Long Parliament's issuing an ordinance (June 1643) requiring that all books, before they were printed, be approved by a government-appointed censor. The ordinance reflected the alarm of Parliament at the torrent of freethinking publication that followed the abolition in 1641 of the hated court of the Star Chamber, which among its other notorious activities under the Stuarts had regulated printing. In fact, Milton's tracts arguing for divorce were among the principal causes for this alarm. By ordering that licensing be renewed, the revolutionary government was already tending toward the repressive authoritarianism against which its members had fought.

Milton was therefore opposed to the order and composed *Areopagitica* in the vain hope of changing the Parliament's mind. He also opposed it, of course, because he was a professional writer. In publishing without a license, Milton defied the order in the very act of opposing it, and he boldly—and quite properly—put his name on the title page to show what he stood for. What is striking about *Areopagitica*—beyond its magnificent style—is the way it continually moves from specific arguments (e.g., that licensing is impractical, ineffective, destructive of learning, and typical of the worst regimes in the past, including the Holy Office of the Inquisition) to higher principles that have given this work such resonant fame in the modern world (invoked, for example, in defense of the freedom of the press). Limiting what people can think—and publishing is vital for thinking—reduces them to the condition of children, unfit for the adult responsibilities of managing the affairs of a great nation, of advancing our understanding of the world, and of continuing the highest human task, which is the struggle for truth. Truth is now a matter of struggle, of opposition and fighting. We have come a long way in just under three years from the retiring poet who believed that he could, on his own, contemplate "the bright countenance of Truth in the quiet and still air of delightful studies."

The managing of nations and the struggle for truth are impossible without the "liberty of unlicensed printing." That is because the road to truth is never a straight one: it proceeds dialectically, by continual encounter with error and by reflection upon error. Truth is set free out of conflict with all that opposes it. In a passage that is startling from an author who more than twenty years later would publish *Paradise Lost*, we read, "It was from out the rind of one apple tasted that the knowledge of good and evil, as two twins cleaving together, leaped forth into the world. And perhaps this is that doom which Adam fell into of knowing good and evil, that is to say, of knowing good by evil. . . . [W]hat wisdom can there be to choose, what continence to forbear without the knowledge of evil? He that can apprehend and consider vice with all her baits and seeming pleasures and yet abstain, and yet distinguish, and yet prefer that which is truly better, he is the true warfaring Christian. I cannot praise a fugitive and cloistered virtue, unexercised and unbreathed, that never sallies out and sees her adversary but slinks out of the race where that immortal garland is to be run for, not without dust and heat" (pp. 361–62).

As the latter part of this passage suggests, in *Areopagitica* Milton's mind is never far from the revolutionary situation in which he was writing, when London, besieged by royalist troops, was, or should have been, "the mansion house of liberty" (p. 383). In praising the courage of Londoners and of the "High Court" of Parliament, the poet, as we may here call him, rises to Blakean heights of revolutionary vision: "Methinks I see in my mind a noble and puissant nation rousing herself like a strong man after sleep and shaking her invincible locks: methinks I see her as an eagle mewing her mighty youth and kindling her undazzled eyes at the full midday beam, purging and unscaling her long-abused sight at the fountain itself of heavenly radiance, while the whole noise of timorous and flocking birds, with those also that love the twilight, flutter about, amazed at what she means" (p. 386).

From The Reason of Church Government
Urged against Prelaty[†]

Introduction to "The Second Book"

How happy were it for this frail and, as it may be truly called, mortal life of man, since all earthly things which have the name of good and convenient in our daily use are withal so cumbersome

---

[†] From *The Reason of Church-Goverenment Urg'd against Prelaty* (London, 1641). The title page is dated 1641 because the year then changed in March; by modern reckoning, the date is 1642. The text is based on a copy in the Houghton Library, Harvard. Spelling, punctuation, and paragraphing have been modernized for this edition.

and full of trouble, if knowledge, yet which is the best and light-somest possession of the mind, were, as the common saying is, no burden; and that what it wanted of being a load to any part of the body it did not with a heavy advantage overlay upon the spirit! For not to speak of that knowledge that rests in the contemplation of natural causes and dimensions, which must needs be a lower wis-dom, as the object is low, certain it is that he who hath obtained in more than the scantiest measure to know anything distinctly of God, and of his true worship; and what is infallibly good and happy in the state of man's life, what in itself evil and miserable, though vulgarly not so esteemed; he that hath obtained to know this, the only high valuable wisdom indeed, remembering also that God, even to a strictness, requires the improvement of these his entrusted gifts, cannot but sustain a sorer burden of mind, and more press-ing, than any supportable toil or weight which the body can labour under: how and in what manner he shall dispose and employ those sums of knowledge and illumination, which God hath sent him into this world to trade with.[1]

And that which aggravates the burden more is that, having received amongst his allotted parcels certain precious truths of such an orient lustre as no diamond can equal, which nevertheless he has in charge to put off at any cheap rate, yea for nothing to them that will; the great merchants of this world, fearing that this course would soon discover and disgrace the false glitter of their deceitful wares, wherewith they abuse the people, like poor Indians with beads and glasses, practise by all means how they may suppress the vending of such rarities, and at such a cheapness as would undo them, and turn their trash upon their hands.[2] Therefore, by gratifying the cor-rupt desires of men in fleshly doctrines, they stir them up to perse-cute with hatred and contempt all those that seek to bear themselves uprightly in this their spiritual factory: which they foreseeing, though they cannot but testify of truth, and the excellence of that heavenly traffic which they bring, against what opposition or dan-ger soever, yet needs must it sit heavily upon their spirits, that being, in God's prime intention and their own, selected heralds of peace and dispensers of treasure inestimable, without price, to them that have no pence, they find in the discharge of their com-mission that they are made the greatest variance and offence, a very sword and fire both in house and city over the whole earth.

---

1. An allusion to the parable of the talents, Matthew 25:14–30, which had personal mean-ing to Milton, who was fully aware of his unusual intellectual gifts and rare education. The "burden of mind" he refers to is "how and in what manner" he is to make use of them in his own life.
2. According to one account of 1626, the island of Manhattan was sold to the Dutch for $24 worth of beads and trinkets. *Their* refers back to "the great merchants of this world," who are the subject (*they*) of the following sentence.

This is that which the sad prophet Jeremiah laments: *Woe is me, my mother, that thou hast borne me, a man of strife and contention!*[3] And although divine inspiration must certainly have been sweet to those ancient prophets, yet the irksomeness of that truth which they brought was so unpleasant to them that everywhere they call it a burden. Yea, that mysterious book of Revelation, which the great Evangelist was bid to eat, as it had been some eye-brightening electuary of knowledge and foresight, though it were sweet in his mouth and in the learning, it was bitter in his belly, bitter in the denouncing.[4] Nor was this hid from the wise poet Sophocles, who in that place of his tragedy where Tiresias is called to resolve King Oedipus in a matter which he knew would be grievous, brings him in bemoaning his lot, that he knew more than other men.[5] For surely to every good and peaceable man, it must in nature needs be a hateful thing to be the displeaser and molester of thousands; much better would it like him doubtless to be the messenger of gladness and contentment, which is his chief intended business to all mankind, but that they resist and oppose their own true happiness.

But when God commands to take the trumpet and blow a dolorous or a jarring blast, it lies not in man's will what he shall say or what he shall conceal. If he shall think to be silent, as Jeremiah did, because of the reproach and derision he met with daily, *And all his familiar friends watched for his halting,*[6] to be revenged on him for speaking the truth, he would be forced to confess as he confessed: *His word was in my heart as a burning fire shut up in my bones; I was weary with forbearing, and could not stay.*[7] Which might teach these times not suddenly to condemn all things that are sharply spoken or vehemently written as proceeding out of stomach, virulence, and ill-nature; but to consider rather that, if the prelates have leave to say the worst that can be said, or do the worst that can be done, while they strive to keep to themselves, to their great pleasure and commodity, those things which they ought to render up, no man can be justly offended with him that shall endeavour to impart and bestow, without any gain to himself, those sharp but saving words which would be a terror and a torment in him to keep back.

For me, I have determined to lay up as the best treasure and solace of a good old age, if God vouchsafe it me, the honest liberty of free speech from my youth, where I shall think it available in so dear a concernment as the Church's good. For if I be, either by disposition or what other cause, too inquisitive, or suspicious of myself

---

3. Jeremiah 15:10.
4. Revelation 10:9–10. The "great Evangelist" is John, the book's purported author.
5. Sophocles, *Oedipus the King* 316–18.
6. See Jeremiah 20:10.
7. Jeremiah 20:9.

and mine own doings, who can help it? But this I foresee, that should the Church be brought under heavy oppression and God have given me ability the while to reason against that man that should be the author of so foul a deed; or should she, by blessing from above on the industry and courage of faithful men, change this her distracted estate into better days without the least furtherance or contribution of those few talents which God at that present had lent me, I foresee what stories I should hear within myself, all my life after, of discourage and reproach.

"Timorous and ungrateful, the Church of God is now again at the foot of her insulting enemies, and thou bewailest. What matters it for thee, or thy bewailing? When time was, thou couldst not find a syllable of all that thou hadst read, or studied, to utter in her behalf. Yet ease and leisure was given thee for thy retired thoughts out of the sweat of other men. Thou hadst the diligence, the parts, the language of a man, if a vain subject were to be adorned or beautified; but when the cause of God and his Church was to be pleaded, for which purpose that tongue was given thee which thou hast, God listened if he could hear thy voice among his zealous servants, but thou wert dumb as a beast: from henceforward be that which thine own brutish silence hath made thee."

Or else I should have heard on the other ear: "Slothful, and ever to be set light by, the Church hath now overcome her late distresses after the unwearied labours of many her true servants that stood up in her defence; thou also wouldst take upon thee to share amongst them of their joy: but wherefore thou? Where canst thou show any word or deed of thine which might have hastened her peace? Whatever thou dost now talk, or write, or look, is the alms of other men's active prudence and zeal. Dare not now to say or do anything better than thy former sloth and infancy; or if thou darest, thou dost impudently to make a thrifty purchase of boldness to thyself out of the painful merits of other men. What before was thy sin is now thy duty: to be abject and worthless."

These, and such like lessons as these, I know would have been my matins duly, and my evensong. But now by this little diligence, mark what a privilege I have gained with good men and saints: to claim my right of lamenting the tribulations of the Church, if she should suffer, when others, that have ventured nothing for her sake, have not the honour to be admitted mourners. But if she lift up her drooping head and prosper, among those that have something more than wished her welfare, I have my charter and freehold of rejoicing to me and my heirs.

Concerning therefore this wayward subject against prelaty, the touching whereof is so distasteful and disquietous to a number of men, as by what hath been said I may deserve of charitable readers to be credited that neither envy nor gall hath entered me upon this controversy, but the enforcement of conscience only, and a preventive fear lest the omitting of this duty should be against me, when I would store up to myself the good provision of peaceful hours. So, lest it be still imputed to me, as I have found it hath been, that some self-pleasing humour of vainglory hath incited me to contest with men of high estimation now while green years are upon my head; from this needless surmisal I shall hope to dissuade the intelligent and equal auditor if I can but say successfully that which in this exigent behooves me; although I would be heard only, if it might be, by the elegant and learned reader, to whom principally for a while I shall beg leave I may address myself.

To him it will be no new thing, though I tell him that if I hunted after praise, by the ostentation of wit and learning, I should not write thus out of mine own season when I have neither yet completed to my mind the full circle of my private studies, although I complain not of any insufficiency to the matter in hand; or were I ready to my wishes, it were a folly to commit anything elaborately composed to the careless and interrupted listening of these tumultuous times. Next, if I were wise only to my own ends, I would certainly take such a subject as of itself might catch applause, whereas this hath all the disadvantages on the contrary; and such a subject as the publishing whereof might be delayed at pleasure, and time enough to pencil it over with all the curious touches of art, even to the perfection of a faultless picture; whenas in this argument the not deferring is of great moment to the good speeding, that, if solidity have leisure to do her office, art cannot have much. Lastly, I should not choose this manner of writing, wherein knowing myself inferior to myself, led by the genial power of nature to another task, I have the use, as I may account it, but of my left hand.

And though I shall be foolish in saying more to this purpose, yet, since it will be such a folly as wisest men go about to commit, having only confessed and so committed, I may trust with more reason, because with more folly, to have courteous pardon. For although a poet, soaring in the high region of his fancies with his garland and singing robes about him might, without apology, speak more of himself than I mean to do; yet for me sitting here below in the cool element of prose, a mortal thing among many readers of no empyreal conceit, to venture and divulge unusual things of myself, I shall petition to the gentler sort, it may not be envy to me.

I must say, therefore, that after I had for my first years, by the ceaseless diligence and care of my father (whom God recompense!), been exercised to the tongues and some sciences, as my age would suffer, by sundry masters and teachers, both at home and at the schools, it was found that whether aught was imposed me by them that had the overlooking,[8] or betaken to of mine own choice in English, or other tongue, prosing or versing, but chiefly this latter, the style, by certain vital signs it had, was likely to live. But much latelier in the private academies of Italy, whither I was favoured to resort, perceiving that some trifles which I had in memory, composed at under twenty or thereabout (for the manner is, that everyone must give some proof of his wit and reading there), met with acceptance above what was looked for; and other things, which I had shifted in scarcity of books and conveniences to patch up amongst them, were received with written encomiums, which the Italian is not forward to bestow on men of this side the Alps,[9] I began thus far to assent both to them and divers of my friends here at home, and not less to an inward prompting which now grew daily upon me, that by labour and intense study (which I take to be my portion in this life), joined with the strong propensity of nature, I might perhaps leave something so written to aftertimes, as they should not willingly let it die.

These thoughts at once possessed me, and these other; that if I were certain to write as men buy leases, for three lives and downward, there ought no regard be sooner had than to God's glory, by the honour and instruction of my country. For which cause, and not only for that I knew it would be hard to arrive at the second rank among the Latins, I applied myself to that resolution, which Ariosto followed against the persuasions of Bembo,[1] to fix all the industry and art I could unite to the adorning of my native tongue; not to make verbal curiosities the end (that were a toilsome vanity), but to be an interpreter and relater of the best and sagest things among mine own citizens throughout this island in the mother dialect. That, what the greatest and choicest wits of Athens, Rome, or modern Italy, and those Hebrews of old did for their country, I, in my proportion, with this over and above, of being a Christian, might do for mine, not caring to be once named abroad, though perhaps I could attain to that, but content with these British islands as my world; whose fortune hath hitherto been that, if the Athenians, as some say, made their small deeds great and renowned by their eloquent writers, England hath had her noble achievements made small by the unskilful handling of monks and mechanics.

Time[2] serves not now, and perhaps I might seem too profuse, to give any certain account of what the mind at home, in the spacious

---

8. I.e., whenever any task was given me by my tutors.
9. During his Italian journey Milton was admired by the learned gentlemen belonging to the private academies of Florence not only for Latin but also for Italian poems of his own composition. A few years later—early in 1646—Milton would publish some of these "written encomiums" as a preface to his Latin *Poemata.*
1. Although the Italian cardinal and scholar Pietro Bembo wrote fine Latin lyrics, he, like his countryman Ariosto, promoted the vernacular as a literary language.
2. This is the only paragraph break in the original text of the introduction to The Second Book.

circuits of her musing, hath liberty to propose to herself, though of highest hope and hardest attempting; whether that epic form whereof the two poems of Homer, and those other two of Virgil and Tasso,[3] are a diffuse, and the book of Job a brief model: or whether the rules of Aristotle[4] herein are strictly to be kept, or nature to be followed, which in them that know art and use judgment is no transgression but an enriching of art; and lastly, what king or knight, before the conquest, might be chosen in whom to lay the pattern of a Christian hero. And as Tasso gave to a prince of Italy his choice whether he would command him to write of Godfrey's expedition against the Infidels, or Belisarius against the Goths, or Charlemain against the Lombards; if to the instinct of nature and the emboldening of art aught may be trusted, and that there be nothing adverse in our climate, or the fate of this age, it haply would be no rashness, from an equal diligence and inclination, to present the like offer in our own ancient stories.[5]

Or whether those dramatic constitutions, wherein Sophocles and Euripides reign, shall be found more doctrinal and exemplary to a nation, the scripture also affords us a divine pastoral drama in the Song of Solomon, consisting of two persons, and a double chorus, as Origen rightly judges.[6] And the Apocalypse of St. John is the majestic image of a high and stately tragedy, shutting up and intermingling her solemn scenes and acts with a sevenfold chorus of hallelujahs and harping symphonies: and this my opinion the grave authority of Paraeus,[7] commenting that book, is sufficient to confirm. Or if occasion shall lead, to imitate those magnific odes and hymns, wherein Pindarus and Callimachus[8] are in most things worthy, some others in their frame judicious, in their matter most an end faulty. But those frequent songs throughout the law and prophets beyond all these, not in their divine argument alone, but in the very critical art of composition, may be easily made appear over all the kinds of lyric poesy to be incomparable.

3. Torquato Tasso, whose Italian epic poem *Jerusalem Liberated* treats the capture of Jerusalem (1099) by Christian knights during the First Crusade. Virgil's epic is the *Aeneid*. Homer's two epics are the *Iliad* and the *Odyssey*.
4. As set forth in his *Poetics*.
5. On the effects of cold climate on genius, and on the decline of the world (and hence of poetry) since ancient times, see *Paradise Lost* 9.44–45 and n. By "our own ancient stories" Milton means subjects drawn from British legend and history. He was at this time meditating possible subjects for an epic poem he might himself compose on the ancient kings of his native land, as the Trinity Manuscript reveals; he considered King Alfred, whose need of disguise made him similar to Ulysses. In his recent Latin poems, Milton mentions King Arthur and the knights of the Round Table ("Mansus," lines 80–84), the coming of the Trojans to Britain, and the scheme of Merlin by which Arthur was born of Igraine ("Epitaphium Damonis," lines 155–68).
6. The third-century Alexandrian theologian Origen described the Song as a wedding poem in dialogue.
7. David Paraeus, sixteenth-century German Calvinist theologian who in his commentary on Romans 13 asserted the people's right to resist tyranny. King James had his books burned in 1622.
8. Ancient Greek lyric poets who composed choral odes.

These abilities, wheresoever they be found, are the inspired gift of God, rarely bestowed, but yet to some (though most abuse) in every nation; and are of power, beside the office of a pulpit, to imbreed and cherish in a great people the seeds of virtue and public civility, to allay the perturbations of the mind, and set the affections in right tune; to celebrate in glorious and lofty hymns the throne and equipage of God's almightiness, and what he works, and what he suffers to be wrought with high providence in his Church; to sing victorious agonies of martyrs and saints, the deeds and triumphs of just and pious nations doing valiantly through faith against the enemies of Christ; to deplore the general relapses of kingdoms and states from justice and God's true worship.

Lastly, whatsoever in religion is holy and sublime, in virtue amiable or grave, whatsoever hath passion or admiration in all the changes of that which is called fortune from without, or the wily subtleties and refluxes of man's thoughts from within; all these things with a solid and treatable smoothness to paint out and describe. Teaching over the whole book of sanctity and virtue, through all the instances of example, with such delight to those especially of soft and delicious temper, who will not so much as look upon Truth herself, unless they see her elegantly dressed, that whereas the paths of honesty and good life appear now rugged and difficult, though they be indeed easy and pleasant, they will then appear to all men both easy and pleasant, though they were rugged and difficult indeed. And what a benefit this would be to our youth and gentry may be soon guessed by what we know of the corruption and bane which they suck in daily from the writings and interludes of libidinous and ignorant poetasters; who, having scarce ever heard of that which is the main consistence of a true poem, the choice of such persons as they ought to introduce, and what is moral and decent to each one, do for the most part lap up vicious principles in sweet pills to be swallowed down, and make the taste of virtuous documents harsh and sour.

But because the spirit of man cannot demean itself lively in this body without some recreating intermission of labour and serious things, it were happy for the Commonwealth if our magistrates, as in those famous governments of old, would take into their care not only the deciding of our contentious law-cases and brawls but the managing of our public sports and festival pastimes; that they might be, not such as were authorized a while since, the provocations of drunkenness and lust, but such as may inure and harden our bodies by martial exercises to all warlike skill and performance, and may civilize, adorn, and make discreet our minds by the learned and affable meeting of frequent Academies, and the procurement of wise and artful recitations, sweetened with eloquent and graceful enticements to the love and practice of justice, temperance, and fortitude, instructing and bettering the nation at all opportunities, that the call of wisdom and virtue may be heard everywhere, as Solomon saith: *She crieth without, she uttereth her voice in the streets, in the top of high places, in the chief concourse, and in the openings of the gates.*[9] Whether this may not be, not only in pulpits, but after another persuasive method, at set and solemn paneguries,[1] in theatres, porches, or what other place or way may win most upon the people to receive at once both recreation and instruction, let them in authority consult.

The thing which I had to say, and those intentions which have lived within me ever since I could conceive myself anything worth to my country, I return to crave excuse that urgent reason hath plucked from me, by an abortive and foredated discovery. And the accomplishment of them lies not but in a power above man's to promise, but that none hath by more studious ways endeavoured, and with more unwearied spirit that none shall, that I dare almost aver of myself, as far as life and free leisure will extend; and that the land had once enfranchised herself from this impertinent yoke of prelaty, under whose inquisitorious and tyrannical duncery no free and splendid wit can flourish.

Neither do I think it shame to covenant with any knowing reader, that for some few years yet I may go on trust with him toward the payment of what I am now indebted, as being a work not to be raised from the heat of youth or the vapours of wine; like that which flows at waste from the pen of some vulgar amorist, or the trencher fury of a rhyming parasite; nor to be obtained by the invocation of Dame Memory and her siren daughters,[2] but by devout prayer to that eternal Spirit, who can enrich with all utterance and knowledge, and sends out his Seraphim, with the hallowed fire of his altar, to touch and purify the lips of whom he pleases:[3] to this must be added industrious and select reading, steady observation, insight into all seemly and generous arts and affairs; till which in some measure be compassed, at mine own peril and cost, I refuse not to sustain this expectation from as many as are not loath to hazard so much credulity upon the best pledges that I can give them.

Although it nothing content me to have disclosed thus much beforehand, but that I trust hereby to make it manifest with what small willingness I endure to interrupt the pursuit of no less hopes than these, and leave a calm and pleasing solitariness, fed with cheerful and confident thoughts, to embark in a troubled sea of noises and hoarse disputes, put from beholding the bright countenance of Truth in the quiet and still air of delightful studies, to come into the dim reflection of hollow antiquities sold by the seeming bulk, and there be fain to club quotations with men whose learning and belief lies in marginal

9. Proverbs 1:20–21; see also 8:2–3.
1. Religious festivals.
2. I.e., the Muses.
3. See Isaiah 6:5–7.

stuffings; who, when they have, like good sumpters, laid ye down their horse-loads of citations and fathers at your door with a rhapsody of who and who were bishops here or there, ye may take off their pack-saddles, their day's work is done, and episcopacy, as they think, stoutly vindicated. Let any gentle apprehension, that can distinguish learned pains from unlearned drudgery, imagine what pleasure or profound-ness can be in this, or what honour to deal against such adversaries.

But were it the meanest under-service, if God by his secretary Conscience enjoin it, it were sad for me if I should draw back; for me especially, now when all men offer their aid to help, ease, and lighten the difficult labours of the Church, to whose service, by the intentions of my parents and friends, I was destined of a child, and in mine own resolutions: till coming to some maturity of years, and perceiving what tyranny had invaded the Church, that he who would take orders must subscribe slave, and take an oath withal, which unless he took with a conscience that would retch, he must either straight perjure, or split his faith, I thought it better to prefer a blameless silence before the sacred office of speaking, bought and begun with servitude and forswearing. Howsoever thus Church-outed by the prelates, hence may appear the right I have to meddle in these matters, as before the necessity and constraint appeared.

Areopagitica[†] [1]

A Speech of Mr. John Milton for the Liberty of Unlicensed Printing, to the Parliament of England

τοὐλεύθερον δ' ἐκεῖνο: Τίς θέλει πόλει
χρηστόν τι βούλευμ' ἐς μέσον φέρειν ἔχων;
καὶ ταῦθ' ὁ χρῇζων λαμπρός ἐσθ', ὁ δ' οὐ θέλων
σιγᾷ. τί τούτων ἔστ' ἰσαίτερον πόλει;

Euripides. Hicetides.

[†] *Aeropagitica; A Speech of Mr. John Milton For the Liberty of Unlicens'd Printing, To the Parlament of England* (London, 1664). The text is based on the copy in the Thomason collection of English civil war pamphlets (Thomason E.18[9]) in the British Library. Spelling, punctuation, and paragraphing have been modernized for this edition.

1. The title, which is plural, means "matters concerning the Areopagitic court." The Areo-pagus is the "Hill of Ares" (*areios* + *pagos*) in Athens, near the Acropolis, where in ancient times the state's highest judicial court sat: the Council of the Areopagus. Mil-ton compliments the "High Court of Parliament" by likening that body to this most august of ancient courts, although he also likens Parliament to the Athenian assembly, or *ecclesia*. His literary precedent is the seventh oration of Isocrates, titled *Areopagiti-cus* (355 B.C.E.), which urged the Athenian assembly to restore the powers of the Areop-agitic court; in former times, it oversaw matters concerning religion and morals as well as trying cases of homicide. Like Milton's treatise, Isocrates' orations were literary productions never intended for live delivery. Isocrates calls for the restoration of the public spiritedness and the common decency (*eukosmia*) that prevailed under the old democracy and affirms the connection between them and the good of the state (7.28, 37). Much of Milton's social thinking, notably the distinction between bad and good kinds of equality, license, and liberty, can be found in Isocrates (7.21).

This is true liberty, when free-born men,
Having to advise the public, may speak free,
Which he who can, and will, deserves high praise;
Who neither can, nor will, may hold his peace:
What can be juster in a state than this?
                              Euripides, *Suppliant Women*.[2]

They who to states and governors of the commonwealth direct their
speech, High Court of Parliament, or, wanting such access in a private condition, write that which they foresee may advance the public
good; I suppose them, as at the beginning of no mean endeavour, not
a little altered and moved inwardly in their minds: some with doubt
of what will be the success, others with fear of what will be the censure, some with hope, others with confidence of what they have to
speak. And me perhaps each of these dispositions, as the subject was
whereon I entered may have at other times variously affected, and
likely might in these foremost expressions now also disclose which of
them swayed most, but that the very attempt of this address thus
made, and the thought of whom it hath recourse to, hath got the power
within me to a passion far more welcome than incidental to a preface.

Which though I stay not to confess ere any ask, I shall be blameless, if it be no other than the joy and gratulation which it brings
to all who wish and promote their country's liberty; whereof this
whole discourse proposed will be a certain testimony, if not a tro-
phy. For this is not the liberty which we can hope, that no grievance ever should arise in the Commonwealth—that let no man in
this world expect; but when complaints are freely heard, deeply
considered and speedily reformed, then is the utmost bound of civil
liberty attained that wise men look for. To which if I now manifest
by the very sound of this which I shall utter, that we are already in
good part arrived, and yet from such a steep disadvantage of tyranny and superstition grounded into our principles as was beyond

2. Lines 438–41. The first two lines expand on the formula with which the herald at the
ecclesia or Athenian democratic assembly (not the Areopagus) opened debate: "Who
wishes to speak?" (*tis agoreuein bouletai?*). Any citizen might do so. For his political
awareness, Euripides was Milton's favorite Greek tragedian. (Compare, e.g., *Orestes*
909–11, in which giving wise advice to the state, whether implemented or not, is said to
be good because it may prove useful in the future.) *The Suppliant Women* was performed in 423 B.C.E. during the Peloponnesian War between democratic Athens and
oligarchic Sparta, the implied parallel being to the present war between the English
Parliament and the royalist forces loyal to Charles I. In the play, Theseus, the legendary
founder of the Athenian state, says that "freedom" (*eleutheria*, Milton's "true liberty") is
this: when any citizen who wishes to give good counsel may do so, thus gaining political
distinction (Milton's "deserves high praise"), and anyone who chooses to remain silent is
not condemned for failing to speak out. In a free polity, what can be "more equal"
(*isaiteros*)—"juster," as Milton renders that word—than this? Despite his praise of the
Parliament for its being like the Athenian democracy, Milton defied its licensing order
of June 1643 by publishing *Areopagitica* without an *imprimatur* (an official stamp that
literally says in Latin "let it be printed") and by courageously putting his name to the
work. The Greek text is from *Euripides 3: Suppliant Women, Electra, Heracles*, ed. and
trans. David Kovacs, Loeb Classical Library (Cambridge, MA: Harvard UP 1998).

the manhood of a Roman recovery,[3] it will be attributed first, as is most due, to the strong assistance of God our deliverer, next to your faithful guidance and undaunted wisdom, Lords and Commons of England. Neither is it in God's esteem the diminution of his glory when honourable things are spoken of good men and worthy magistrates; which if I now first should begin to do, after so fair a progress of your laudable deeds, and such a long obligement upon the whole realm to your indefatigable virtues, I might be justly reckoned among the tardiest and the unwillingest of them that praise ye.

Nevertheless there being three principal things, without which all praising is but courtship and flattery: first, when that only is praised which is solidly worth praise; next, when greatest likelihoods are brought that such things are truly and really in those persons to whom they are ascribed; the other, when he who praises, by showing that such his actual persuasion is of whom he writes, can demonstrate that he flatters not. The former two of these I have heretofore endeavoured, rescuing the employment from him[4] who went about to impair your merits with a trivial and malignant encomium; the latter, as belonging chiefly to mine own acquittal that whom I so extolled I did not flatter, hath been reserved opportunely to this occasion.

For he who freely magnifies what hath been nobly done, and fears not to declare as freely what might be done better, gives ye the best covenant of his fidelity, and that his loyalest affection and his hope waits on your proceedings. His highest praising is not flattery, and his plainest advice is a kind of praising. For though I should affirm and hold by argument that it would fare better with truth, with learning and the Commonwealth, if one of your published Orders, which I should name, were called in; yet at the same time it could not but much redound to the lustre of your mild and equal government, whenas private persons are hereby animated to think ye better pleased with public advice than other statists have been delighted heretofore with public flattery. And men will then see what difference there is between the magnanimity of a triennial Parliament, and that jealous haughtiness of prelates and cabin counsellors[5] that usurped of late, whenas they shall observe ye in the midst of your victories and successes more gently brooking written exceptions against a voted Order than other courts, which had produced nothing worth memory but the weak ostentation of wealth, would have endured the least signified dislike at any sudden proclamation.

---

3. I.e., The Romans were unable to recover from the fall of their empire.
4. Bishop Joseph Hall, an old adversary of Milton's in the controversy over church government.
5. The counselors who advised Charles I during the years of the Personal Rule, 1629–40. The Triennial Act of February 1641 required the king to summon Parliament at least once every three years.

If I should thus far presume upon the meek demeanour of your civil and gentle greatness, Lords and Commons, as what your published Order hath directly said, that to gainsay, I might defend myself with ease, if any should accuse me of being new or insolent, did they but know how much better I find ye esteem it to imitate the old and elegant humanity of Greece than the barbaric pride of a Hunnish and Norwegian stateliness. And out of those ages, to whose polite wisdom and letters we owe that we are not yet Goths and Jutlanders, I could name him[6] who from his private house wrote that discourse to the Parliament of Athens that persuades them to change the form of democracy which was then established. Such honour was done in those days to men who professed the study of wisdom and eloquence, not only in their own country but in other lands, that cities and signiories heard them gladly, and with great respect, if they had aught in public to admonish the state. Thus did Dion Prusaeus, a stranger and a private orator, counsel the Rhodians against a former edict;[7] and I abound with other like examples, which to set here would be superfluous.

But if from the industry of a life wholly dedicated to studious labours, and those natural endowments haply not the worst for two and fifty degrees of northern latitude, so much must be derogated as to count me not equal to any of those who had this privilege, I would obtain to be thought not so inferior, as yourselves are superior to the most of them who received their counsel: and how far you excel them, be assured, Lords and Commons, there can no greater testimony appear, than when your prudent spirit acknowledges and obeys the voice of reason from what quarter soever it be heard speaking; and renders ye as willing to repeal any Act of your own setting forth, as any set forth by your predecessors.

If ye be thus resolved, as it were injury to think ye were not, I know not what should withhold me from presenting ye with a fit instance wherein to show both that love of truth which ye eminently profess, and that uprightness of your judgment which is not wont to be partial to yourselves, by judging over again that Order which ye have ordained to regulate printing:—that no book, pamphlet, or paper shall be henceforth printed, unless the same be first approved and licensed by such, or at least one of such, as shall be thereto appointed. For that part which preserves justly every man's copy[8] to himself, or provides for the poor, I touch not, only wish they be not made pretences to abuse and persecute honest and

<hr>

6. Isocrates.
7. The government of the island of Rhodes updated public statues by substituting new names for old, which Dion Prusaeus counseled against in his Rhodian Discourse. There was, however, no "former edict" allowing this practice.
8. Copyright.

painful men, who offend not in either of these particulars. But that
other clause of licensing books, which we thought had died with his
brother quadragesimal and matrimonial when the prelates expired,[9]
I shall now attend with such a homily as shall lay before ye, first,
the inventors of it to be those whom ye will be loath to own; next
what is to be thought in general of reading, whatever sort the books
be; and that this order avails nothing to the suppressing of scandalous, seditious, and libellous books which were mainly intended to
be suppressed. Last, that it will be primely to the discouragement
of all learning, and the stop of truth, not only by disexercising and
blunting our abilities in what we know already, but by hindering
and cropping the discovery that might be yet further made both in
religious and civil wisdom.

I deny not, but that it is of greatest concernment in the Church
and Commonwealth, to have a vigilant eye how books demean
themselves as well as men; and thereafter to confine, imprison, and
do sharpest justice on them as malefactors. For books are not absolutely dead things but do contain a potency of life in them to be as
active as that soul was whose progeny they are; nay, they do preserve as in a vial the purest efficacy and extraction of that living
intellect that bred them. I know they are as lively, and as vigorously
productive, as those fabulous dragon's teeth;[1] and being sown up
and down, may chance to spring up armed men. And yet, on the
other hand, unless wariness be used, as good almost kill a man as
kill a good book. Who kills a man kills a reasonable creature, God's
image; but he who destroys a good book, kills reason itself, kills the
image of God, as it were in the eye. Many a man lives a burden to
the earth; but a good book is the precious life-blood of a master
spirit, embalmed and treasured up on purpose to a life beyond life.
'Tis true, no age can restore a life, whereof perhaps there is no
great loss; and revolutions of ages do not oft recover the loss of a
rejected truth, for the want of which whole nations fare the worse.

We should be wary therefore what persecution we raise against
the living labours of public men, how we spill that seasoned life of
man, preserved and stored up in books; since we see a kind of homicide may be thus committed, sometimes a martyrdom, and if it
extend to the whole impression, a kind of massacre; whereof the execution ends not in the slaying of an elemental life, but strikes at that

9. Episcopal dispensations concerning the forty days of Lent and the publishing of marriage banns terminated when the power of the bishops was curtailed by their exclusion
   from the House of Lords in 1642. Episcopacy (i.e., a church governed by bishops and an
   archbishop) would be abolished in 1646.
1. The dragon's teeth sown by Cadmus, the founder of Thebes, sprang up as armed men.
   They fought and killed one another until five were left. These joined Cadmus in founding the city. See Ovid, *Metamorphoses* 3.101–30.

ethereal and fifth essence,[2] the breath of reason itself, slays an immortality rather than a life. But lest I should be condemned of introducing licence, while I oppose licensing, I refuse not the pains to be so much historical as will serve to show what hath been done by ancient and famous commonwealths against this disorder, till the very time that this project of licensing crept out of the Inquisition, was catched up by our prelates, and hath caught some of our presbyters.

In Athens, where books and wits were ever busier than in any other part of Greece, I find but only two sorts of writings which the magistrate cared to take notice of; those either blasphemous and atheistical, or libellous. Thus the books of Protagoras were by the judges of Areopagus commanded to be burnt, and himself banished the territory for a discourse begun with his confessing not to know *whether there were gods, or whether not.* And against defaming, it was decreed that none should be traduced by name, as was the manner of Vetus Comoedia,[3] whereby we may guess how they censured libelling. And this course was quick enough, as Cicero writes,[4] to quell both the desperate wits of other atheists, and the open way of defaming, as the event showed. Of other sects and opinions, though tending to voluptuousness, and the denying of divine Providence, they took no heed.

Therefore we do not read that either Epicurus, or that libertine school of Cyrene, or what the Cynic impudence uttered, was ever questioned by the laws. Neither is it recorded that the writings of those old comedians were suppressed, though the acting of them were forbid; and that Plato commended the reading of Aristophanes, the loosest of them all, to his royal scholar Dionysius, is commonly known,[5] and may be excused, if holy Chrysostom,[6] as is reported, nightly studied so much the same author and had the art to cleanse a scurrilous vehemence into the style of a rousing sermon.

That other leading city of Greece, Lacedaemon,[7] considering that Lycurgus their lawgiver was so addicted to elegant learning, as to

2. I.e., the quintessence, the ethereal substance of the heavenly bodies above the four material elements of the world: earth, air, fire, and water. See *PL* 3.714–17. But Milton's meaning here is closer to that of *Hamlet*'s "quintessence of dust" (2.2.298), the essence of a person, the breathing soul and life. As treasured wisdom, books are more than physical things having a merely "elemental life." For if all copies of a book are destroyed, so too is its essence.
3. "Old Comedy" (Latin): Greek plays of the fifth century B.C.E., the most famous by Aristophanes (ca. 450–ca. 385 B.C.E.). The Old Comedy ridiculed public figures by name, representing them on the stage, often obscenely.
4. See *On the Nature of the Gods* 1.23.
5. An anecdote from the anonymous *Life of Aristophanes* 6 (ca. 300 B.C.E.). Plato for a time advised and instructed Dionysius, the tyrant of Syracuse.
6. The Greek church father John Chrysostom (347–407 C.E.), whose honorific name means "golden mouthed." Famous for purity and eloquence, he nevertheless made a close study of the scurrilous and fanciful poetry of Aristophanes' plays.
7. I.e., Sparta.

have been the first that brought out of Ionia the scattered works of Homer,[8] and sent the poet Thales from Crete to prepare and mollify the Spartan surliness with his smooth songs and odes, the better to plant among them law and civility, it is to be wondered how muse-less and unbookish they were, minding nought but the feats of war. There needed no licensing of books among them, for they disliked all but their own laconic apophthegms, and took a slight occasion to chase Archilochus[9] out of their city, perhaps for composing in a higher strain than their own soldierly ballads and roundels could reach to. Or if it were for his broad verses, they were not therein so cautious but they were as dissolute in their promiscuous convers-ing; whence Euripides affirms in *Andromache*, that their women were all unchaste.[1] Thus much may give us light after what sort of books were prohibited among the Greeks.

The Romans also, for many ages trained up only to a military roughness resembling most the Lacedaemonian guise, knew of learning little but what their twelve Tables and the Pontific College[2] with their augurs and flamens taught them in religion and law; so unacquainted with other learning, that when Carneades and Crito-laus, with the Stoic Diogenes,[3] coming ambassadors to Rome, took thereby occasion to give the city a taste of their philosophy, they were suspected for seducers by no less a man than Cato the Censor,[4] who moved it in the Senate to dismiss them speedily, and to banish all such Attic babblers out of Italy. But Scipio and others of the noblest senators withstood him and his old Sabine austerity; hon-oured and admired the men; and the Censor himself at last, in his old age, fell to the study of that whereof before he was so scrupu-lous. And yet at the same time Naevius and Plautus, the first Latin comedians, had filled the city with all the borrowed scenes of Menander and Philemon.[5] Then began to be considered there also

---

8. In his biography of the semilegendary figure, Plutarch says that Lycurgus, during his travels in Ionia (the Greek islands off the coast of Asia), united the scattered fragments of the epics of Homer (*Life of Lycurgus* 4.3).

9. Archilochus of Paros (680–645 B.C.E.), archaic Greek poet and soldier.

1. *Andromache* 595–601. "Promiscuous" here means "mixed" without explicit sexual meaning (Latin *misceo*, "to mix"; see "books promiscuously read," p. 362). Spartan boys and girls exercised naked together although without sexual intercourse; the practice scandalized other Greeks.

2. The institution that regulated religious ceremonies, the calendar, and public works. "The Twelve Tables": tablets placed in the Roman forum on which were inscribed the earliest written Roman law, traditionally dated 451–450 B.C.E.

3. Greek philosophers. Carneades (214–129 B.C.E.), a skeptic, made two speeches, one proving and the other disproving the existence of justice.

4. Also known as Cato the Elder (234–149 B.C.E.), a Roman politician famous for his severe morals and simple life.

5. Greek dramatists, the best-known authors of New Comedy (written ca. 325–265 B.C.E.). They inspired the earliest authors of Roman comedy, Naevius (ca. 270–ca. 201 B.C.E.), whose plays are lost, and the father of European romantic comedy, Plautus (ca. 254–184 B.C.E.), twenty of whose plays survive. Milton later describes him as scurri-lous (p. 359), which he is in comparison with grave Cicero.

what was to be done to libellous books and authors; for Naevius was quickly cast into prison for his unbridled pen, and released by the tribunes upon his recantation; we read also that libels were burnt, and the makers punished, by Augustus. The like severity, no doubt, was used, if aught were impiously written against their esteemed gods. Except in these two points, how the world went in books the magistrate kept no reckoning.

And therefore Lucretius[6] without impeachment versifies his Epicurism to Memmius, and had the honour to be set forth the second time by Cicero, so great a father of the Commonwealth; although himself disputes against that opinion in his own writings. Nor was the satirical sharpness or naked plainness of Lucilius, or Catullus, or Flaccus,[7] by any order prohibited. And for matters of state, the story[8] of Titus Livius, though it extolled that part which Pompey held, was not therefore suppressed by Octavius Caesar[9] of the other faction. But that Naso[1] was by him banished in his old age, for the wanton poems of his youth, was but a mere covert of state over some secret cause: and besides, the books were neither banished nor called in. From hence we shall meet with little else but tyranny in the Roman empire, that we may not marvel, if not so often bad as good books were silenced. I shall therefore deem to have been large enough, in producing what among the ancients was punishable to write; save only which, all other arguments were free to treat on.

By this time the emperors were become Christians, whose discipline in this point I do not find to have been more severe than what was formerly in practice. The books of those whom they took to be grand heretics were examined, refuted, and condemned in the general Councils; and not till then were prohibited, or burnt, by authority of the emperor. As for the writings of heathen authors, unless they were plain invectives against Christianity, as those of Porphyrius and Proclus, they met with no interdict that can be cited, till about the year 400, in a Carthaginian Council, wherein bishops themselves were forbid to read the books of Gentiles, but heresies they might read; while others long before them, on the contrary, scrupled more the books of heretics than of Gentiles. And that the primitive Councils and bishops were wont only to declare what books were not commendable, passing no further, but leaving it to

---

6. Great Roman scientific poet, atheist, materialist, atomist (ca. 94–55 B.C.E.), follower of the doctrine of the Greek philosopher Epicurus (341–270 B.C.E.).
7. Horace.
8. History.
9. I.e., Augustus Caesar, formerly Octavian (63 B.C.E.–14 C.E.), who became the first emperor of Rome, ending the Roman Republic, which Pompey upheld.
1. The poet Ovid, in full Publius Ovidius Naso (43 B.C.E.–17 C.E.). The author of *Metamorphoses* was banished by Augustus, allegedly because of moral objections to his *Art of Love*, but perhaps truly for political reasons, as Milton speculates.

each one's conscience to read or to lay by, till after the year 800, is observed already by Padre Paolo, the great unmasker of the Trentine Council.[2]

After which time the Popes of Rome, engrossing what they pleased of political rule into their own hands, extended their dominion over men's eyes, as they had before over their judgments, burning and prohibiting to be read what they fancied not; yet sparing in their censures, and the books not many which they so dealt with: till Martin V., by his bull, not only prohibited, but was the first that excommunicated the reading of heretical books; for about that time Wickliffe and Huss,[3] growing terrible, were they who first drove the Papal Court to a stricter policy of prohibiting. Which course Leo X. and his successors followed, until the Council of Trent and the Spanish Inquisition engendering together brought forth, or perfected, those Catalogues and expurging Indexes that rake through the entrails of many an old good author with a violation worse than any could be offered to his tomb. Nor did they stay in matters heretical, but any subject that was not to their palate they either condemned in a Prohibition or had it straight into the new purgatory of an index.

To fill up the measure of encroachment, their[4] last invention was to ordain that no book, pamphlet, or paper should be printed (as if St. Peter had bequeathed them the keys of the press also out of Paradise) unless it were approved and licensed under the hands of two or three glutton friars. For example:

> Let the Chancellor Cini be pleased to see if in this present work be contained aught that may withstand the printing.
> VINCENT RABBATTA, *Vicar of Florence.*

> I have seen this present work, and find nothing athwart the Catholic faith and good manners: in witness whereof I have given, etc.
> NICOLÒ CINI, *Chancellor of Florence.*

> Attending the precedent relation, it is allowed that this present work of Davanzati may be printed.
> VINCENT RABBATTA, *etc.*

> It may be printed, July 15.
> FRIAR SIMON MOMPEI D'AMELIA, *Chancellor of the Holy Office in Florence.*

Sure they have a conceit, if he of the bottomless pit had not long since broke prison, that this quadruple exorcism would bar him down.

2. The Roman Catholic Council of Trent (1545–63) was convened to oppose Protestantism and reform the Roman Catholic Church. The Venetian humanist Paolo Sarpi (1552–1623) wrote *History of the Council of Trent*, which Milton relies on here and in what follows. Sarpi is highly critical of the council and of the church.
3. Two religious reformers, the English theologian John Wycliffe (ca. 1330–1384) and the Bohemian Jan Hus (ca. 1370–1415).
4. The popes'.

I fear their next design will be to get into their custody the licensing of that which they say Claudius intended, but went not through with.[5] Vouchsafe: to see another of their forms, the Roman stamp:

> Imprimatur,[6] If it seem good to the reverend Master of the Holy Palace.
> BELCASTRO, Vicegerent. Imprimatur, Friar Nicolo Rodolphi,
> Master of the Holy Palace.

Sometimes five Imprimaturs are seen together dialogue-wise in the piazza of one title-page, complimenting and ducking each to other with their shaven reverences, whether the author, who stands by in perplexity at the foot of his epistle, shall to the press or to the sponge. These are the pretty responsories, these are the dear antiphonies, that so bewitched of late our prelates and their chaplains with the goodly echo they made; and besotted us to the gay imitation of a lordly Imprimatur, one from Lambeth House, another from the west end of Paul's,[7] so apishly Romanizing, that the word of command still was set down in Latin as if the learned grammatical pen that wrote it would cast no ink without Latin; or perhaps, as they thought, because no vulgar tongue was worthy to express the pure conceit of an Imprimatur; but rather, as I hope, for that our English, the language of men ever famous and foremost in the achievements of liberty, will not easily find servile letters enow to spell such a dictatory presumption [in] English.

And thus ye have the inventors and the original of book-licensing ripped up and drawn as lineally as any pedigree. We have it not, that can be heard of, from any ancient state, or polity or church; nor by any statute left us by our ancestors elder or later; nor from the modern custom of any reformed city or church abroad, but from the most anti-christian council and the most tyrannous inquisition that ever inquired.[8] Till then books were ever as freely admitted into the world as any other birth: the issue of the brain was no more stifled than the issue of the womb: no envious Juno sat cross-legged over the nativity of any man's intellectual offspring;[9] but if it proved a monster, who denies, but that it was justly burnt, or sunk

5. A proposed edict allowing the breaking of wind at table, recounted in Suetonius, Life of Claudius 32. Quoted in Latin in the margin of Areopagitica.
6. "Let it be printed" (Latin). See p. 349, n. 2.
7. The residence of the bishop of London, near St. Paul's Cathedral. Lambeth Palace, across the Thames from Westminster, is the London residence of the archbishop of Canterbury. In 1637 the Court of the Star Chamber decreed that before they were printed, all books had to be licensed by the bishop of London and the archbishop of Canterbury.
8. I.e., the oppressive Spanish Inquisition and the Council of Trent (see p. 356, n. 2). The Spanish Inquisition was established in 1478 in Seville, where the first auto-da-fé (act of faith) was held in 1481: six condemned men and women were burned at the stake. The Inquisition spread thereafter throughout Roman Catholic Europe (especially Italy, which Milton visited).
9. An allusion to the birth of the mythical hero Hercules, which Juno sought to prevent.

into the sea? But that a book, in worse condition than a peccant soul, should be to stand before a jury ere it be born to the world, and undergo yet in darkness the judgment of Radamanth and his colleagues ere it can pass the ferry backward into light, was never heard before,[1] till that mysterious iniquity, provoked and troubled at the first entrance of Reformation, sought out new limbos and new hells wherein they might include our books also within the number of their damned. And this was the rare morsel so officiously snatched up, and so ill-favouredly imitated by our inquisiturient[2] bishops, and the attendant minorites their chaplains. That ye like not now these most certain authors of this licensing order, and that all sinister intention was far distant from your thoughts, when ye were importuned the passing it, all men who know the integrity of your actions, and how ye honour truth, will clear ye readily.

But some will say, what though the inventors were bad, the thing for all that may be good? It may so; yet if that thing be no such deep invention but obvious and easy for any man to light on, and yet best and wisest commonwealths through all ages and occasions have forborne to use it, and falsest seducers and oppressors of men were the first who took it up, and to no other purpose but to obstruct and hinder the first approach of Reformation, I am of those who believe it will be a harder alchemy than Lullius[3] ever knew to sublimate any good use out of such an invention. Yet this only is what I request to gain from this reason, that it may be held a dangerous and suspicious fruit, as certainly it deserves for the tree that bore it, until I can dissect one by one the properties it has. But I have first to finish, as was propounded, what is to be thought in general of reading books, whatever sort they be, and whether be more the benefit or the harm that thence proceeds.

Not to insist upon the examples of Moses, Daniel, and Paul, who were skilful in all the learning of the Egyptians, Chaldeans, and Greeks, which could not probably be without reading their books of all sorts; in Paul especially, who thought it no defilement to insert into Holy Scripture the sentences of three Greek poets, and one of them a tragedian;[4] the question was notwithstanding sometimes

1. In Greek myth Rhadamanthus is a judge of the dead in the underworld. The point of this complicated jest is that licensing gets everything backward, causing books to be judged before they are born instead of after they have lived in the world, thus forcing them, preposterously, to cross the river Styx on Charon's "ferry" in the opposite direction from the souls of the dead.
2. Eager to play the inquisitor (Milton's coinage).
3. Ramon Llull (ca. 1232–ca. 1315), Catalan Franciscan monk, mystic, Arab linguist, and logician; he devised a mechanical system of great complexity (based on Arab models) for evaluating the truth of statements.
4. When addressing the Greeks on the Areopagus, Paul quotes the popular didactic poet Aratus (Acts 17:28). In Titus 1:12 he quotes the famous paradox of Epimenides the Cretan—"all Cretans are liars"—taking it at face value. In 1 Corinthians 15:33, Paul quotes a verse, possibly lifted from Euripides, from a lost play by the comic poet Menander—"evil communications (i.e., "evil company": ὁμιλίαι κακαί) corrupt good

controverted among the primitive doctors,[5] but with great odds on
that side which affirmed it both lawful and profitable; as was then
evidently perceived when Julian the apostate[6] and subtlest enemy to
our faith made a decree forbidding Christians the study of heathen
learning: for, said he, they wound us with our own weapons, and
with our own arts and sciences they overcome us. And indeed the
Christians were put so to their shifts by this crafty means, and so
much in danger to decline into all ignorance, that the two Apollina-
rii[7] were fain, as a man may say, to coin all the seven liberal sciences
out of the Bible, reducing it into divers forms of orations, poems,
dialogues, even to the calculating of a new Christian grammar.
But, saith the historian Socrates, the providence of God provided
better than the industry of Apollinarius and his son, by taking away
that illiterate law with the life of him who devised it.[8] So great an
injury they then held it to be deprived of Hellenic learning and
thought it a persecution more undermining, and secretly decaying
the Church, than the open cruelty of Decius or Diocletian.[9]

And perhaps it was the same politic drift that the devil whipped
St. Jerome in a Lenten dream for reading Cicero;[1] or else it was a
phantasm bred by the fever which had then seized him. For had an
angel been his discipliner, unless it were for dwelling too much
upon Ciceronianisms, and had chastised the reading, not the vanity, it had been plainly partial; first to correct him for grave Cicero,
and not for scurril Plautus, whom he confesses to have been reading not long before; next to correct him only, and let so many more
ancient fathers wax old in those pleasant and florid studies without
the lash of such a tutoring apparition; insomuch that Basil[2] teaches

---

manners"—which might be thought to go against Milton's argument. See p. 367: "who
shall forbid . . . all evil company?" The Byzantine church historian Socrates Scholasticus (ca. 380–450 C.E.) says the verse proves that Paul was conversant with the tragedies of Euripides (*Historia Ecclesiastica* 3.16), justifying Milton's phrase, "and one of
them a tragedian."
5. I.e., learned teachers of the early Christian church.
6. The emperor Julian (331–363 C.E.), called Julian the Apostate because he terminated
Christianity's status as the official religion of the empire and sought to restore worship
of the Olympian gods. Milton's interest in Julian is that he also forbade Christians to
receive a classical education or to teach in the schools.
7. Apollinarius of Alexandria (fourth century C.E.) and his son Apollinarius the Younger
(ca. 310–ca. 390), bishop of Laodicea, refashioned the Bible in the style of Greek literature to compensate for the effect of Julian the Apostate's edict against Christians
receiving a classical education.
8. Socrates Scholasticus observed that the death of the emperor Julian in battle (363 C.E.)
was more effective than the awkward attempt to Hellenize the Bible, for the emperor
Jovian lifted the edict against Christians receiving a classical education and restored
Christianity as the religion of the empire.
9. Two Roman emperors (249–251 and 284–304) under whom Christians suffered persecution, including martyrdom.
1. St. Jerome (347–420), the great translator of the Bible into Latin from Hebrew and
Greek sources, was taken in the spirit to heaven, accused of being a Ciceronian instead of
a Christian ("*Ciceronianus es, non Christianus*"), and scourged for it (*Epistiles* 22.30).
2. Basil the Great (ca. 330–379), bishop of Caesarea; he permitted and even encouraged
Christians to read pagan authors.

how some good use may be made of *Margites,* a sportful poem, not now extant, writ by Homer; and why not then of *Morgante,*[3] an Italian romance much to the same purpose?

But if it be agreed we shall be tried by visions, there is a vision recorded by Eusebius, far ancienter than this tale of Jerome, to the nun Eustochium and, besides, has nothing of a fever in it. Dionysius Alexandrinus was about the year 240 a person of great name in the Church for piety and learning, who had wont to avail himself much against heretics by being conversant in their books; until a certain presbyter laid it scrupulously to his conscience, how he durst venture himself among those defiling volumes. The worthy man, loath to give offence, fell into a new debate with himself what was to be thought; when suddenly a vision sent from God (it is his own epistle that so avers it) confirmed him in these words: *Read any books whatever come to thy hands, for thou art sufficient both to judge aright, and to examine each matter.*[4] To this revelation he assented the sooner, as he confesses, because it was answerable to that of the Apostle to the Thessalonians, *Prove all things, hold fast that which is good.*[5] And he might have added another remarkable saying of the same author: *To the pure, all things are pure;*[6] not only meats and drinks but all kind of knowledge whether of good or evil. The knowledge cannot defile, nor consequently the books, if the will and conscience be not defiled.

For books are as meats and viands are; some of good, some of evil substance; and yet God, in that unapocryphal vision, said without exception, *Rise, Peter, kill and eat,*[7] leaving the choice to each man's discretion. Wholesome meats to a vitiated stomach differ little or nothing from unwholesome; and best books to a naughty mind are not unappliable to occasions of evil. Bad meats will scarce breed good nourishment in the healthiest concoction; but herein the difference is of bad books, that they to a discreet and judicious reader serve in many respects to discover, to confute, to forewarn, and to illustrate. Whereof what better witness can ye expect I should produce, than one of your own now sitting in Parliament, the chief of learned men reputed in this land, Mr. Selden;[8] whose volume of natural and national laws proves, not only by great authorities brought together,

---

3. A parodic and coarse Italian chivalric romance by Luigi Pulci (1483). *Margites,* a burlesque ancient Greek poem, was in fact not written by Homer.
4. See Eusebius (fourth century C.E.), *Ecclesiastical History* 7.7.
5. "The Apostle" is Paul. See 1 Thessalonians 5:21. "Prove": put to the test.
6. Titus 1:15.
7. Acts 10:10–28. When he was hungry, Peter fell into a trance and saw a great sheet descending from heaven holding all kinds of meats forbidden by the Jewish law. The voice of the Lord urged him to rise, kill, and eat (13), to which he replied he would not eat anything unclean. The voice then said, "what God hath cleansed, that call not thou common" (15). By this vision Peter was instructed not to shun gentiles or hold himself superior to them. Milton applies the argument to non-Christian and immoral books.
8. John Selden (1584–1654), lawyer, scholar, member of the Long Parliament, among whose massively learned Latin works is *On the Law of Nature and of Nations According to the Teachings of the Hebrews* (1640).

but by exquisite reasons and theorems almost mathematically demonstrative, that all opinions, yea errors, known, read, and collated, are of main service and assistance toward the speedy attainment of what is truest. I conceive, therefore, that when God did enlarge the universal diet of man's body, saving ever the rules of temperance, he then also, as before, left arbitrary the dieting and repasting of our minds; as wherein every mature man might have to exercise his own leading capacity.

How great a virtue is temperance, how much of moment through the whole life of man! Yet God commits the managing so great a trust, without particular law or prescription, wholly to the demeanour of every grown man. And therefore when he himself tabled the Jews from heaven, that omer, which was every man's daily portion of manna,[9] is computed to have been more than might have well sufficed the heartiest feeder thrice as many meals. For those actions which enter into a man, rather than issue out of him, and therefore defile not, God uses not to captivate under a perpetual childhood of prescription, but trusts him with the gift of reason to be his own chooser. There were but little work left for preaching, if law and compulsion should grow so fast upon those things which heretofore were governed only by exhortation. Solomon informs us, that much reading is a weariness to the flesh;[1] but neither he nor other inspired author tells us that such or such reading is unlawful: yet certainly had God thought good to limit us herein, it had been much more expedient to have told us what was unlawful than what was wearisome. As for the burning of those Ephesian books by St. Paul's converts;[2] 'tis replied the books were magic, the Syriac so renders them. It was a private act, a voluntary act, and leaves us to a voluntary imitation: the men in remorse burnt those books which were their own; the magistrate by this example is not appointed; these men practiced the books,[3] another might perhaps have read them in some sort usefully.

Good and evil we know in the field of this world grow up together almost inseparably; and the knowledge of good is so involved and interwoven with the knowledge of evil, and in so many cunning resemblances hardly to be discerned, that those confused seeds which were imposed upon Psyche as an incessant labour to cull out and sort asunder[4] were not more intermixed. It was from out the rind of one apple tasted that the knowledge of good and evil, as two

9. See Exodus 16:13–23.
1. Ecclesiastes 12:12.
2. Acts 19:19.
3. I.e., did magic with books, rather than simply reading them to understand what magicians do, or think they do.
4. A reference to the story of Cupid and Psyche, as told by Apuleius in *The Golden Ass*. Cupid's angry mother, Venus, gave Psyche the seemingly hopeless task of sorting a great heap of different seeds before nightfall. Kindly ants sorted the seeds (6.10).

twins cleaving together, leaped forth into the world. And perhaps this is that doom which Adam fell into of knowing good and evil, that is to say, of knowing good by evil. As therefore the state of man now is what wisdom can there be to choose, what continence to forbear without the knowledge of evil? He that can apprehend and consider vice with all her baits and seeming pleasures and yet abstain, and yet distinguish, and yet prefer that which is truly better, he is the true warfaring Christian.

I cannot praise a fugitive and cloistered virtue, unexercised and unbreathed, that never sallies out and sees her adversary but slinks out of the race where that immortal garland is to be run for, not without dust and heat. Assuredly we bring not innocence into the world, we bring impurity much rather; that which purifies us is trial, and trial is by what is contrary. That virtue therefore which is but a youngling in the contemplation of evil, and knows not the utmost that vice promises to her followers, and rejects it, is but a blank virtue, not a pure; her whiteness is but an excremental whiteness. Which was the reason why our sage and serious poet Spenser, whom I dare be known to think a better teacher than Scotus or Aquinas,[5] describing true temperance under the person of Guion, brings him in with his palmer through the cave of Mammon, and the bower of earthly bliss, that he might see and know, and yet abstain.[6] Since therefore the knowledge and survey of vice is in this world so necessary to the constituting of human virtue, and the scanning of error to the confirmation of truth, how can we more safely, and with less danger, scout into the regions of sin and falsity than by reading all manner of tractates and hearing all manner of reason? And this is the benefit which may be had of books promiscuously read.

But of the harm that may result hence three kinds are usually reckoned. First, is feared the infection that may spread; but then all human learning and controversy in religious points must remove out of the world, yea the Bible itself; for that ofttimes relates blasphemy not nicely, it describes the carnal sense of wicked men not unelegantly; it brings in holiest men passionately murmuring against Providence through all the arguments of Epicurus; in other great disputes it answers dubiously and darkly to the common reader.

---

5. Great teachers and theologians of the thirteenth century. Milton's point is that whereas scholastic teaching is abstract and theoretical, Edmund Spenser (1552–1599), in his epic poem *The Faerie Queene*, is exemplary and inspiring. Milton would later acknowledge that Spenser was his "original"—i.e., Spenser's example awakened his own youthful poetic ambitions.

6. *The Faerie Queene* 2.7. The knight of Temperane, Guyon (*Guion* is an alternative but not Spenserian spelling), is willingly drawn into a vast, underground "delve," or artificial cave, by the demon Mammon, the giver of wealth and earthly power, and tempted for three days. See Matthew 6:24: "Ye cannot serve God and mammon." It slipped Milton's mind that Guyon's usual guide—the Palmer, who represents prudence—is absent during this trial. Compare *PL* 1.678–751.

And ask a Talmudist what ails the modesty of his marginal Keri, that Moses and all the prophets cannot persuade him to pronounce the textual Chetiv.[7] For these causes we all know the Bible itself put by the Papist into the first rank of prohibited books. The ancientest fathers must be next removed, as Clement of Alexandria, and that Eusebian book of Evangelic preparation,[8] transmitting our ears through a hoard of heathenish obscenities to receive the Gospel. Who finds not that Irenaeus, Epiphanius, Jerome,[9] and others discover more heresies than they well confute, and that oft for heresy which is the truer opinion?

Nor boots it to say for these, and all the heathen writers of greatest infection, if it must be thought so, with whom is bound up the life of human learning, that they writ in an unknown tongue, so long as we are sure those languages are known as well to the worst of men, who are both most able and most diligent to instil the poison they suck, first into the courts of princes, acquainting them with the choicest delights and criticisms of sin. As perhaps did that Petronius[1] whom Nero called his Arbiter, the master of his revels; and the notorious ribald of Arezzo,[2] dreaded and yet dear to the Italian courtiers. I name not him for posterity's sake whom Henry VIII named in merriment his vicar of hell.[3] By which compendious way all the contagion that foreign books can infuse will find a passage to the people far easier and shorter than an Indian voyage, though it could be sailed either by the north of Cataio[4] eastward, or of Canada westward, while our Spanish licensing gags the English press never so severely.

But on the other side that infection which is from books of controversy in religion is more doubtful and dangerous to the learned

---

7. Hebrew *kethiv*: what is written in the canonical Hebrew text ("Moses and all the prophets"). Where indecency appeared in the canonical text, an inoffensive substitute, the "Keri" (*qere*, "what is read") was placed in the margin for reading aloud. Milton's point is that the Bible is the word of God and nothing in it should be euphemized. "Talmudist": a scholar of the Talmud, a collection of commentaries on the Hebrew scriptures.

8. *Praeparatio evangelica* (*Preparation for the Gospel*), which contains materials collected from the pagan philosophers by Eusebius of Caesarea (fourth century C.E.), the father of church history and a favorite of Milton's. Clement of Alexandria (second century C.E.), himself a convert to Christianity, wrote extensively in his *Protrepticus* (*Exhortation*) on pagan rites, exposing their depravity and exhorting the Greeks to convert to Christianity. Both authors wrote in Greek.

9. Christian church fathers who sought with much zeal but little skill to refute all heresies. They brought to light more heresies than they could refute and often became entangled in the intricacies of their own arguments. Yet these books are very useful to the scholar.

1. Courtier to the emperor Nero (ca. 27–66 C.E.) and probable author of the obscene but sophisticated novel *Satyricon*.

2. Pietro Aretino of Arezzo (1492–1556), Italian Renaissance man of letters, notorious for his sonnets on sexual positions and feared for his satirical wit. He extorted payments to spare prospective victims.

3. Sir Francis Bryan (1490–1550), courtier, intriguer, rake, and facilitator of the English king's affairs and debauches.

4. Cathay (China).

than to the ignorant; and yet those books must be permitted untouched by the licenser. It will be hard to instance where any ignorant man hath been ever seduced by papistical book in English, unless it were commended and expounded to him by some of that clergy; and indeed all such tractates, whether false or true, are as the prophecy of Isaiah was to the eunuch, not to be *understood without a guide*.[5] But of our priests and doctors how many have been corrupted by studying the comments of Jesuits and Sorbonists,[6] and how fast they could transfuse that corruption into the people, our experience is both late and sad. It is not forgot since the acute and distinct Arminius was perverted merely by the perusing of a nameless[7] discourse written at Delft, which at first he took in hand to confute.

Seeing, therefore, that those books, and those in great abundance, which are likeliest to taint both life and doctrine, cannot be suppressed without the fall of learning and of all ability in disputation, and that these books of either sort are most and soonest catching to the learned, from whom to the common people whatever is heretical or dissolute may quickly be conveyed, and that evil manners are as perfectly learnt without books a thousand other ways which cannot be stopped, and evil doctrine not with books can propagate, except a teacher guide, which he might also do without writing, and so beyond prohibiting, I am not able to unfold, how this cautelous[8] enterprise of licensing can be exempted from the number of vain and impossible attempts. And he who were pleasantly disposed could not well avoid to liken it to the exploit of that gallant man who thought to pound up the crows by shutting his park gate.

Besides another inconvenience, if learned men be the first receivers out of books and dispreaders both of vice and error, how shall the licensers themselves be confided in, unless we can confer upon them, or they assume to themselves above all others in the land the grace of infallibility and uncorruptedness? And again, if it be true that a wise man, like a good refiner, can gather gold out of the drossiest volume, and that a fool will be a fool with the best book, yea or without book, there is no reason that we should deprive a wise man of any advantage to his wisdom while we seek to restrain from a fool that which being restrained will be no hindrance to his folly. For if there should be so much exactness always used to keep that from him which is unfit for his reading, we should in the judgment

---

5. Acts 8:30–31.
6. Scholars at the University of Paris, which grew from a theological college founded in 1257 by Robert de Sorbon.
7. Anonymous. The Dutch Protestant theologian Arminius (1560–1609) had his mind changed (on the subject of predestination) by a work that he took up with the original intention of refuting it. Milton's own theological position in *Paradise Lost*, Book Three, will become distinctly Arminian, emphasizing Christian liberty over predestination.
8. Over-wary.

of Aristotle not only, but of Solomon and of our Saviour,[9] not vouchsafe him good precepts, and by consequence not willingly admit
him to good books; as being certain that a wise man will make better use of an idle pamphlet than a fool will do of sacred Scripture.

'Tis next alleged we must not expose ourselves to temptations
without necessity, and next to that, not employ our time in vain
things. To both these objections one answer will serve, out of the
grounds already laid, that to all men such books are not temptations, nor vanities, but useful drugs and materials wherewith to
temper and compose effective and strong medicines, which man's
life cannot want. The rest, as children and childish men, who have
not the art to qualify and prepare these working minerals, well may
be exhorted to forbear, but hindered forcibly they cannot be by all
the licensing that Sainted Inquisition[1] could ever yet contrive.

Which is what I promised to deliver next: that this order of
licensing conduces nothing to the end for which it was framed; and
hath almost prevented me by being clear already while thus much
hath been explaining. See the ingenuity of Truth, who, when she
gets a free and willing hand, opens herself faster than the pace of
method and discourse can overtake her.

It was the task which I began with, to show that no nation, or
well-instituted state, if they valued books at all, did ever use this
way of licensing; and it might be answered, that this is a piece of
prudence lately discovered. To which I return, that as it was a thing
slight and obvious to think on, so if it had been difficult to find out,
there wanted not among them long since who suggested such a
course; which they not following, leave us a pattern of their judgment that it was not the not knowing but the not approving which
was the cause of their not using it.

Plato, a man of high authority, indeed, but least of all for his
Commonwealth, in the book of his Laws, which no city ever yet
received, fed his fancy by making many edicts to his airy burgomas-
ters, which they who otherwise admire him wish had been rather
buried and excused in the genial cups of an Academic night sitting.
By which laws he seems to tolerate no kind of learning but by unalter-
able decree, consisting most of practical traditions, to the attainment
whereof a library of smaller bulk than his own Dialogues would be
abundant. And there also enacts, that no poet should so much as

9. See Aristotle, *Nicomachean Ethics* 1.4, 1095b, quoting Hesiod, *Works and Days* 295–97,
to the effect that the true fool is the one who cannot hear wisdom. Proverbs (supposedly
authored by Solomon) 23:9: "Speak not in the ears of a fool: for he will despise the wisdom
of thy words." See also 17:24 and 26:4. In the Sermon on the Mount (Matthew 7:6) Jesus
says, "Give not that which is holy unto dogs, neither cast ye your pearls before swine."
1. The Spanish Inquisition, officially named the Tribunal del Santo Oficio de la Inquis-
ición (Tribunal of the Sacred Office of the Inquisition); Milton mocks this pretension
with the word "Sainted." See p. **357**, n. 8.

read to any private man what he had written until the judges and law-keepers had seen it, and allowed it.[2] But that Plato meant this law peculiarly to that commonwealth which he had imagined, and to no other, is evident. Why was he not else a lawgiver to himself, but a transgressor, and to be expelled by his own magistrates both for the wanton epigrams and dialogues which he made, and his perpetual reading of Sophron Mimus[3] and Aristophanes, books of grossest infamy, and also for commending the latter of them, though he were the malicious libeller of his chief friends, to be read by the tyrant Dionysius,[4] who had little need of such trash to spend his time on? But that he knew this licensing of poems had reference and dependence to many other provisos there set down in his fancied republic, which in this world could have no place: and so neither he himself, nor any magistrate or city, ever imitated that course, which, taken apart from those other collateral injunctions, must needs be vain and fruitless. For if they fell upon one kind of strictness, unless their care were equal to regulate all other things of like aptness to corrupt the mind, that single endeavour they knew would be but a fond labour; to shut and fortify one gate against corruption, and be necessitated to leave others round about wide open.

If we think to regulate printing, thereby to rectify manners, we must regulate all recreations and pastimes, all that is delightful to man. No music must be heard, no song be set or sung, but what is grave and Doric.[5] There must be licensing dancers, that no gesture, motion, or deportment be taught our youth but what by their allow-ance shall be thought honest; for such Plato was provided of. It will ask more than the work of twenty licensers to examine all the lutes, the violins, and the guitars in every house; they must not be suffered to prattle as they do, but must be licensed what they may say. And who shall silence all the airs and madrigals that whisper softness in chambers? The windows also, and the balconies must be thought on; there are shrewd books, with dangerous frontispieces, set to sale; who shall prohibit them, shall twenty licensers? The villages also must have their visitors[6] to inquire what lectures the bagpipe and the rebeck

---

2. Plato, *Laws* 7.801c–d; the poet must compose nothing except what the state approves and must not even show to another person any composition not approved by the judges and the protectors of the laws.
3. Sophron of Syracuse (flourished 430 B.C.E.), who wrote comic mimes. According to Diogenes Laertius (third century C.E.), Sophron's mimes were brought by Plato back from Sicily to Athens (*Lives and Opinions of the Eminent Philosophers* 3.18). Following the same source, Milton elsewhere says Plato read Sophron's mimes at night and "after made them his pillow." See *An Apology against a Pamphlet* (1642), in YP 1:879.
4. See p. 353, n. 5.
5. The Dorian mode, like the Phrygian, suits military discipline and is therefore favored by Plato over softer and more luxurious modes, such as the Lydian and Mixolydian, which make men effeminate (*Republic* 3.398e–399a). See *PL* 1.549–55 and n.
6. Official inspectors. The word is meant to recall Archbishop Laud's hated practice of requiring bishops to send "visitors" to every parish to report on any reluctance to imple-ment the new, more elaborate liturgy. For "officials," see p. 369, n. 4.

reads, even to the ballatry and the gamut[7] of every municipal fiddler, for these are the countryman's Arcadias, and his Monte Mayors.[8]

Next, what more national corruption, for which England hears ill abroad, than household gluttony: who shall be the rectors of our daily rioting? And what shall be done to inhibit the multitudes that frequent those houses where drunkenness is sold and harboured? Our garments also should be referred to the licensing of some more sober workmasters to see them cut into a less wanton garb. Who shall regulate all the mixed conversation of our youth, male and female together, as is the fashion of this country? Who shall still appoint what shall be discoursed, what presumed, and no further? Lastly, who shall forbid and separate all idle resort, all evil company? These things will be, and must be; but how they shall be least hurtful, how least enticing, herein consists the grave and governing wisdom of a state.

To sequester out of the world into Atlantic and Utopian polities,[9] which never can be drawn into use, will not mend our condition; but to ordain wisely as in this world of evil, in the midst whereof God hath placed us unavoidably. Nor is it Plato's licensing of books will do this, which necessarily pulls along with it so many other kinds of licensing as will make us all both ridiculous and weary, and yet frustrate; but those unwritten, or at least unconstraining, laws of virtuous education, religious and civil nurture, which Plato there mentions as the bonds and ligaments of the commonwealth, the pillars and the sustainers of every written statute: these they be which will bear chief sway in such matters as these, when all licensing will be easily eluded. Impunity and remissness, for certain, are the bane of a commonwealth; but here the great art lies, to discern in what the law is to bid restraint and punishment, and in what things persuasion only is to work.

If every action, which is good or evil in man at ripe years were to be under pittance and prescription and compulsion, what were virtue but a name, what praise could be then due to well-doing, what gramercy to be sober, just, or continent? Many there be that complain of divine Providence for suffering Adam to transgress. Foolish tongues! When God gave him reason, he gave him freedom to choose, for reason is but choosing: He had been else a mere artificial

---

7. I.e., the repertoire of ballads and the mastery of scales. "Rebeck": a three-string fiddle associated with the countryside. See "jocund rebecks" in the country scene of Milton's "L'Allegro," line 94.

8. Crude versions of Sir Philip Sidney's *Arcadia* (1590 and 1593) and the *Diana* (1559, with later versions) of Jorge de Montemayor (ca. 1520–1561), the latter a work much imitated and admired throughout Europe. Milton's point is that if licensing is required, it will be necessary to regulate popular entertainments, since the dangers these pose to the unlearned are the same as those posed by printed books to the literate. (He says nothing of the closing of the theaters two years earlier, in 1642.) The Puritan poet George Wither appealed for legal measures to be taken against "scurrilous and obscene songs" and "abominable gesticulations." See Ernest Sirluck, ed., *Areopagitica*, in *YP* 2:524 n. 138.

9. Two ideal commonwealths, described in Sir Francis Bacon's *The New Atlantis* (1626) and Sir Thomas More's *Utopia* (1516).

Adam, such an Adam as he is in the motions.[1] We ourselves esteem not of that obedience, or love, or gift, which is of force. God therefore left him free, set before him a provoking object, ever almost in his eyes; herein consisted his merit, herein the right of his reward, the praise of his abstinence. Wherefore did he create passions within us, pleasures round about us, but that these rightly tempered are the very ingredients of virtue?

They are not skilful considerers of human things who imagine to remove sin by removing the matter of sin; for, besides that it is a huge heap increasing under the very act of diminishing, though some part of it may for a time be withdrawn from some persons, it cannot from all, in such a universal thing as books are; and when this is done, yet the sin remains entire. Though ye take from a covetous man all his treasure, he has yet one jewel left, ye cannot bereave him of his covetousness. Banish all objects of lust, shut up all youth into the severest discipline that can be exercised in any hermitage, ye cannot make them chaste that came not thither so; such great care and wisdom is required to the right managing of this point. Suppose we could expel sin by this means; look how much we thus expel of sin, so much we expel of virtue: for the matter of them both is the same; remove that, and ye remove them both alike.

This justifies the high providence of God, who, though he command us temperance, justice, continence, yet pours out before us, even to a profuseness, all desirable things, and gives us minds that can wander beyond all limit and satiety. Why should we then affect a rigour contrary to the manner of God and of nature by abridging or scanting those means, which books freely permitted are, both to the trial of virtue and the exercise of truth? It would be better done to learn that the law must needs be frivolous which goes to restrain things, uncertainly and yet equally working to good and to evil. And were I the chooser, a dram of well-doing should be preferred before many times as much the forcible hindrance of evil-doing. For God sure esteems the growth and completing of one virtuous person more than the restraint of ten vicious.

And albeit whatever thing we hear or see, sitting, walking, travelling, or conversing, may be fitly called our book, and is of the same effect that writings are, yet grant the thing to be prohibited were only books, it appears that this Order hitherto is far insufficient to the end which it intends. Do we not see, not once or oftener, but weekly, that continued court-libel against the Parliament and City,[2]

---

1. Puppet shows.
2. *Mercurius Aulicus* (*The Court Mercury*), a weekly royalist news bulletin published in Oxford, where the king and court were. It was also printed secretly in London (the point of Milton's mentioning the "wet sheets") between 1642 to 1645, and occasionally after. It began publication in response to the parliamentary bulletin, *Mercurius Britannicus*; both are forerunners of the modern newspaper.

printed, as the wet sheets can witness, and dispersed among us, for all that licensing can do? Yet this is the prime service a man would think, wherein this Order should give proof of itself. If it were executed, you'll say. But certain, if execution be remiss or blindfold now, and in this particular, what will it be hereafter and in other books? If then the Order shall not be vain and frustrate, behold a new labour, Lords and Commons, ye must repeal and proscribe all scandalous and unlicensed books already printed and divulged after ye have drawn them up into a list, that all may know which are condemned, and which not; and ordain that no foreign books be delivered out of custody till they have been read over. This office will require the whole time of not a few overseers, and those no vulgar[3] men. There be also books which are partly useful and excellent, partly culpable and pernicious; this work will ask as many more officials,[4] to make expurgations and expunctions, that the commonwealth of learning be not damnified. In fine, when the multitude of books increase upon their hands, ye must be fain to catalogue all those printers who are found frequently offending, and forbid the importation of their whole suspected typography. In a word, that this your Order may be exact and not deficient, ye must reform it perfectly according to the model of Trent and Seville,[5] which I know ye abhor to do.

Yet though ye should condescend to this, which God forbid, the Order still would be but fruitless and defective to that end whereto ye meant it. If to prevent sects and schisms, who is so unread or so uncatechized in story that hath not heard of many sects refusing books as a hindrance and preserving their doctrine unmixed for many ages only by unwritten traditions? The Christian faith, for that was once a schism, is not unknown to have spread all over Asia ere any Gospel or Epistle was seen in writing. If the amendment of manners be aimed at, look into Italy and Spain, whether those places be one scruple the better, the honester, the wiser, the chaster, since all the inquisitional rigour that hath been executed upon books.

Another reason, whereby to make it plain that this Order will miss the end it seeks, consider by the quality which ought to be in every licenser. It cannot be denied but that he who is made judge to sit upon the birth or death of books, whether they may be wafted into this world or not, had need to be a man above the common measure, both studious, learned, and judicious; there may be else

3. Unlearned. The point is that only the most learned persons in the kingdom would be fit for licensing books. The huge task, depressing in itself, would also prevent the learned from doing their own more valuable work.
4. The term that in Milton's day denoted an officer of the ecclesiastical court charged with enforcing the will of the bishops. "[Archbishop] Laud let them loose over the country"; T. Holt White, ed., *Areopagitica* (London, 1819), cited in Sirluck, ed., *Areopagitica*, in *YP* 2:529 n. 155. In *Of Reformation*, in *YP* 1:543, Milton speaks of extortionate "rooking officials."
5. See p. 356, n. 2; p. 357, n. 8.

no mean mistakes in the censure of what is passable or not; which is also no mean injury. If he be of such worth as behooves him, there cannot be a more tedious and unpleasing journey-work,[6] a greater loss of time levied upon his head, than to be made the perpetual reader of unchosen books and pamphlets, ofttimes huge volumes. There is no book that is acceptable unless at certain seasons; but to be enjoined the reading of that at all times, and in a hand scarce legible, whereof three pages would not down at any time in the fairest print, is an imposition which I cannot believe how he that values time and his own studies, or is but of a sensible nostril,[7] should be able to endure. In this one thing I crave leave of the present licensers to be pardoned for so thinking; who doubtless took this office up, looking on it through their obedience to the Parliament, whose command perhaps made all things seem easy and unlaborious to them; but that this short trial hath wearied them out already, their own expressions and excuses to them who make so many journeys to solicit their licence are testimony enough. Seeing therefore those who now possess the employment by all evident signs wish themselves well rid of it; and that no man of worth, none that is not a plain unthrift of his own hours, is ever likely to succeed them, except he mean to put himself to the salary of a press corrector; we may easily foresee what kind of licensers we are to expect hereafter, either ignorant, imperious, and remiss, or basely pecuniary. This is what I had to show, wherein this Order cannot conduce to that end whereof it bears the intention.

I lastly proceed from the no good it can do, to the manifest hurt it causes, in being first the greatest discouragement and affront that can be offered to learning, and to learned men.

It was the complaint and lamentation of prelates, upon every least breath of a motion to remove pluralities,[8] and distribute more equally Church revenues, that then all learning would be for ever dashed and discouraged. But as for that opinion, I never found cause to think that the tenth part of learning stood or fell with the clergy: nor could I ever but hold it for a sordid and unworthy speech of any churchman who had a competency[9] left him. If therefore ye be loath to dishearten utterly and discontent, not the mercenary crew of false pretenders to learning, but the free and ingenuous sort of such as evidently were born to study, and love learning for

6. Daily labor for hourly wages, hence labor unbefitting a man of letters. See p. 369, n. 3.
7. Sensitive, elegant taste.
8. Two or more parish benefices, or ecclesiastical livings, held by one clergyman. In his poetic indictment of the Presbyterians, "On the New Forcers of Conscience under the Long Parliament" (1646?), Milton tasks them for hypocrisy in taking for themselves what they had taken away from the bishops: "To seize the widowed whore plurality / From those whose sin ye envied, not abhorred" (lines 3–4).
9. A sufficient income to live on.

itself, not for lucre or any other end but the service of God and of truth, and perhaps that lasting fame and perpetuity of praise which God and good men have consented shall be the reward of those whose published labours advance the good of mankind; then know that, so far to distrust the judgment and the honesty of one who hath but a common repute in learning, and never yet offended, as not to count him fit to print his mind without a tutor and examiner, lest he should drop a schism, or something of corruption, is the greatest displeasure and indignity to a free and knowing spirit that can be put upon him.

What advantage is it to be a man, over it is to be a boy at school, if we have only escaped the ferula to come under the fescue[1] of an Imprimatur; if serious and elaborate writings, as if they were no more than the theme of a grammar-lad under his pedagogue, must not be uttered without the cursory eyes of a temporizing and extemporizing licenser? He who is not trusted with his own actions, his drift not being known to be evil, and standing to the hazard of law and penalty, has no great argument to think himself reputed in the Commonwealth wherein he was born for other than a fool or a foreigner. When a man writes to the world, he summons up all his reason and deliberation to assist him; he searches, meditates, is industrious, and likely consults and confers with his judicious friends; after all which done he takes himself to be informed in what he writes, as well as any that writ before him. If, in this the most consummate act of his fidelity and ripeness, no years, no industry, no former proof of his abilities can bring him to that state of maturity as not to be still mistrusted and suspected, unless he carry all his considerate diligence, all his midnight watchings and expense of Palladian oil,[2] to the hasty view of an unleisured licenser, perhaps much his younger, perhaps far his inferior in judgment, perhaps one who never knew the labour of book-writing, and if he be not repulsed or slighted, must appear in print like a puny[3] with his guardian, and his censor's hand on the back of his title to be his bail and surety that he is no idiot or seducer, it cannot be but a dishonour and derogation to the author, to the book, to the privilege and dignity of learning.

And what if the author shall be one so copious of fancy as to have many things well worth the adding come into his mind after

---

1. A *fescue* is a small stick for pointing out letters to children learning to read. A *ferula* is a cane used to administer corporal punishment to young students for making errors. Milton's point is that coming under the fescue of licensing is even more degrading to an author than being under the ferula at school, which is degrading enough.
2. Pallas Athena is the goddess of wisdom and study. The olive tree is sacred to her, and fine, expensive olive oil was used in lamps for study at night.
3. A freshman or junior student in the schools (from the French *puis-né*, "born after"), but also, in the sense Milton intends, a student who is kept back in a junior grade despite his years.

licensing, while the book is yet under the press, which not seldom happens to the best and diligentest writers, and that perhaps a dozen times in one book? The printer dares not go beyond his licensed copy, so often then must the author trudge to his leave-giver that those his new insertions may be viewed; and many a jaunt will be made ere that licenser, for it must be the same man, can either be found, or found at leisure; meanwhile either the press must stand still, which is no small damage, or the author lose his accuratest thoughts, and send the book forth worse than he had made it, which to a diligent writer is the greatest melancholy and vexation that can befall.

And how can a man teach with authority, which is the life of teaching; how can he be a doctor in his book as he ought to be, or else had better be silent, whenas all he teaches, all he delivers, is but under the tuition, under the correction of his patriarchal licenser[4] to blot or alter what precisely accords not with the hidebound humour which he calls his judgment? When every acute reader, upon the first sight of a pedantic licence, will be ready with these like words to ding the book a quoit's distance[5] from him. I hate a pupil teacher, I endure not an instructor that comes to me under the wardship of an overseeing fist. I know nothing of the licenser, but that I have his own hand here for his arrogance; who shall warrant me his judgment? The State, sir, replies the stationer, but has a quick return: the State shall be my governors, but not my critics. They may be mistaken in the choice of a licenser, as easily as this licenser may be mistaken in an author: this is some common stuff; and he might add from Sir Francis Bacon, *That such authorized books are but the language of the times.*[6] For though a licenser should happen to be judicious more than ordinary, which will be a great jeopardy of the next succession, yet his very office and his commission enjoins him to let pass nothing but what is vulgarly received already.

Nay, which is more lamentable, if the work of any deceased author, though never so famous in his lifetime and even to this day, come to their hands for licence to be printed, or reprinted, if there be found in his book one sentence of a venturous edge, uttered in the height of zeal (and who knows whether it might not be the dictate of a divine spirit?) yet not suiting with every low decrepit humour of their own, though it were Knox[7] himself, the reformer of a kingdom, that spake

---

4. An allusion to Archbishop Laud, who at his trial was accused of aspiring to return England to the Roman Catholic Church and make himself its *patriarch*. The point is that the Parliament's order for licensing books will breed similar arrogance in unworthy persons appointed to the office of licenser.

5. To fling the book the distance of a discus throw.

6. *An Advertisement Touching the Controversies of the Church of England* (1589), in *Letters and Life of Francis Bacon*, ed. James Spedding, 3 vols. (London, 1861), 1:78; cited by Sirluck, ed., *Areopagitica*, in *YP* 2:534 n. 169.

7. John Knox (ca. 1514–1572), famous preacher and theologian, prolific author, leader of the Reformation in Scotland and founder of its Presbyterian church.

it, they will not pardon him their dash:[8] the sense of that great man shall to all posterity be lost, for the fearfulness or the presumptuous rashness of a perfunctory licenser. And to what an author this violence hath been lately done, and in what book of greatest consequence to be faithfully published, I could now instance, but shall forbear till a more convenient season.[9]

Yet if these things be not resented seriously and timely by them who have the remedy in their power, but that such iron-moulds as these shall have authority to gnaw out the choicest periods[1] of exquisitest books, and to commit such a treacherous fraud against the orphan remainders of worthiest men after death, the more sorrow will belong to that hapless race of men, whose misfortune it is to have understanding. Henceforth let no man care to learn, or care to be more than worldly-wise; for certainly in higher matters to be ignorant and slothful, to be a common steadfast dunce, will be the only pleasant life, and only in request.

And as it is a particular disesteem of every knowing person alive, and most injurious to the written labours and monuments of the dead, so to me it seems an undervaluing and vilifying of the whole nation. I cannot set so light by all the invention, the art, the wit, the grave and solid judgment which is in England, as that it can be comprehended in any twenty capacities how good soever, much less that it should not pass except their superintendence be over it, except it be sifted and strained with their strainers, that it should be uncurrent without their manual stamp. Truth and understanding are not such wares as to be monopolized and traded in by tickets and statutes and standards. We must not think to make a staple commodity of all the knowledge in the land, to mark and licence it like our broadcloth and our woolpacks. What is it but a servitude like that imposed by the Philistines, not to be allowed the sharpening of our own axes and coulters, but we must repair from all quarters to twenty licensing forges?[2] Had anyone written and divulged erroneous things and scandalous to honest life, misusing and forfeiting the esteem had of his reason among men, if after conviction this only censure were adjudged him that he should never henceforth write but what were

---

8. Mark indicating a deletion.
9. The identity of the violated book is uncertain. It may be the jurist Sir Edward Coke's *Institutes of the Laws of England* (1628), widely known to have been mutilated by censorship in the edition of 1641. Or it may be John Knox's *History of the Reformation in Scotland* (1584), from which passages were excised in the 1644 edition. Knox's book is "lately done," but at the time of *Areopagitica* Coke's is the better candidate for being judged of "greatest consequence."
1. Best sentences.
2. The ancient Israelites, forbidden by their Philistine overlords to have their own forges, which they could have used to make weapons, were compelled to go to the Philistines to have their farming implements sharpened (1 Samuel 13:19–22). "Coulter": the iron blade in front of the plowshare.

first examined by an appointed officer, whose hand should be annexed to pass his credit for him that now he might be safely read, it could not be apprehended less than a disgraceful punishment. Whence to include the whole nation, and those that never yet thus offended, under such a diffident and suspectful prohibition, may plainly be understood what a disparagement it is. So much the more, whenas debtors and delinquents may walk abroad without a keeper, but unoffensive books must not stir forth without a visible jailer in their title.

Nor is it to the common people less than a reproach; for if we be so jealous over them as that we dare not trust them with an English pamphlet, what do we but censure them for a giddy, vicious, and ungrounded people; in such a sick and weak state of faith and discretion as to be able to take nothing down but through the pipe[3] of a licenser? That this is care or love of them we cannot pretend whenas, in those popish places where the laity are most hated and despised, the same strictness is used over them. Wisdom we cannot call it because it stops but one breach of licence, nor that neither: whenas those corruptions, which it seeks to prevent, break in faster at other doors which cannot be shut.

And in conclusion it reflects to the disrepute of our ministers also, of whose labours we should hope better, and of the proficiency which their flock reaps by them, than that after all this light of the Gospel which is, and is to be, and all this continual preaching, they should still be frequented with such an unprincipled, unedified and laic rabble, as that the whiff of every new pamphlet should stagger them out of their catechism and Christian walking. This may have much reason to discourage the ministers when such a low conceit is had of all their exhortations, and the benefiting of their hearers, as that they are not thought fit to be turned loose to three sheets of paper without a licenser; that all the sermons, all the lectures preached, printed, vented in such numbers, and such volumes, as have now well nigh made all other books unsaleable, should not be armour enough against one single Enchiridion,[4] without the castle of St. Angelo[5] of an Imprimatur.

And lest some should persuade ye, Lords and Commons, that these arguments of learned men's discouragement at this your Order are mere flourishes, and not real, I could recount what I have seen and heard in other countries, where this kind of inquisition tyrannizes; when I have sat among their learned men, for that honour

---

3. Feeding tube for medicine.
4. Literally, "little thing in the hand" (Greek): usually a concise handbook but also a dagger.
5. The Castel Sant'Angelo in Rome: originally the mausoleum of the emperor Hadrian, in Milton's day it was the papal fortress and a prison.

I had, and been counted happy to be born in such a place of philosophic freedom as they supposed England was, while themselves
did nothing but bemoan the servile condition into which learning
amongst them was brought; that this was it which had damped the
glory of Italian wits; that nothing had been there written now these
many years but flattery and fustian. There it was that I found and
visited the famous Galileo, grown old, a prisoner to the Inquisition for thinking in astronomy otherwise than the Franciscan and
Dominican licensers thought.[6] And though I knew that England
then was groaning loudest under the prelatical yoke, nevertheless I
took it as a pledge of future happiness that other nations were so
persuaded of her liberty. Yet was it beyond my hope that those worthies were then breathing in her air, who should be her leaders to
such a deliverance, as shall never be forgotten by any revolution of
time that this world hath to finish. When that was once begun, it
was as little in my fear that what words of complaint I heard among
learned men of other parts uttered against the Inquisition, the
same I should hear by as learned men at home, uttered in time of
Parliament against an order of licensing; and that so generally that,
when I had disclosed myself a companion of their discontent, I
might say, if without envy, that he whom an honest quaestorship
had endeared to the Sicilians was not more by them importuned
against Verres,[7] than the favourable opinion which I had among
many who honour ye, and are known and respected by ye, loaded
me with entreaties and persuasions, that I would not despair to lay
together that which just reason should bring into my mind, toward
the removal of an undeserved thraldom upon learning. That this is
not therefore the disburdening of a particular fancy, but the common grievance of all those who had prepared their minds and studies above the vulgar pitch to advance truth in others, and from
others to entertain it, thus much may satisfy.

And in their name I shall for neither friend nor foe conceal what
the general murmur is; that if it come to inquisitioning again and
licensing, and that we are so timorous of ourselves, and so suspicious of all men, as to fear each book and the shaking of every leaf
before we know what the contents are; if some who but of late were
little better than silenced from preaching shall come now to silence

6. In 1633 the Inquisition placed the astronomer Galileo (1564–1642) under house arrest
   in Arcetri, in the hills south of Florence, where Milton visited him in 1638. Galileo was
   confined for defending, in his *Dialogue on the Two Chief World [i.e., Cosmic] Systems*
   (1632), the heliocentric system—Copernicus's purely theoretical proposal of 1543 that
   the earth orbits the sun and not the sun around the earth, as in the ancient Ptolemaic
   system. Galileo had first presented empirical evidence for the heliocentric system,
   based on his telescopic observations, in *Sidereus Nuncius* (1610, *The Starry Messenger*).
   See *PL* 1.288 and n. and 5.262.
7. Roman governor of Sicily, notorious for his corruption. Cicero, who was elected
   quaestor in 76 B.C.E., successfully prosecuted Verres in 70 B.C.E.

us from reading except what they please, it cannot be guessed what
is intended by some but a second tyranny over learning; and will
soon put it out of controversy, that bishops and presbyters are the
same to us, both name and thing.[8] That those evils of prelaty, which
before from five or six and twenty sees[9] were distributively charged
upon the whole people, will now light wholly upon learning, is not
obscure[1] to us: whenas now the pastor of a small unlearned parish
on the sudden shall be exalted archbishop[2] over a large diocese of
books, and yet not remove, but keep his other cure too, a mystical
pluralist.[3] He who but of late cried down the sole ordination of every
novice Bachelor of Art, and denied sole jurisdiction over the sim-
plest parishioner, shall now at home in his private chair assume
both these over worthiest and excellentest books and ablest authors
that write them.[4]

This is not, ye Covenants and Protestations, that we have made![5]
This is not to put down prelaty; this is but to chop[6] an episcopacy;
this is but to translate the Palace Metropolitan[7] from one kind of
dominion into another; this is but an old canonical sleight of com-
muting[8] our penance. To startle thus betimes at a mere unlicensed
pamphlet will after a while be afraid of every conventicle,[9] and a
while after will make a conventicle of every Christian meeting. But
I am certain that a State governed by the rules of justice and fortitude, or a Church built and founded upon the rock of faith and true
knowledge, cannot be so pusillanimous. While things are yet not

---

8. The Presbyterians were Milton's former allies in his writings against the bishops, the
most important of which was *The Reason of Church Government* (1642). But once in
power, as the Licensing Order concerning printed books proved, the Presbyterians
were no different from those they overthrew. See the final verse of "On the New Forcers of Conscience under the Long Parliament": "New *Presbyter* is but old *Priest* [i.e.,
bishop] writ large." See p. 370, n. 8.
9. Dioceses, territories under the jurisdiction of bishops.
1. Remote and subtle, removed from daily life. See *PL* 8.191–94.
2. I.e., as an official licenser.
3. *Mystical* because a single body cannot be in two places at once, except mysteriously; a
pluralist is one who occupies more than one ecclesiastical living, or one who defends
the practice. "His other cure": his original parish; i.e., he does not "remove" to the new
one but occupies two places at once.
4. Presbyterians strenuously opposed the exclusive right of bishops to ordain priests and
to exercise religious jurisdiction on all parishioners in their dioceses. Yet the power the
Presbyterians now arrogate to themselves is far greater. They want one of their licensers to judge, from a merely "private chair" (as opposed to a bishop's throne, which is at
least public), which books may be printed and what "ablest authors" must say.
5. The Solemn League and Covenant between England and Scotland, ratified by Parliament in 1643, undertook to abolish episcopacy and reform religion in England. Parliament's "Protestation" (1641) against King Charles's threats affirmed "the lawful rights
and liberties of the subjects." On Milton's interpretation, the Licensing Order is inconsistent with both revered documents.
6. Change for something else than in the end is no different.
7. Lambeth Palace, the archbishop of Canterbury's London residence. See p. 357, n. 7.
8. Diverting funds collected from fines for inappropriate purposes, as when Archbishop
Laud was charged with using such monies for the repair of the west end of Saint Paul's
cathedral, "making use of the method of *commutation*." See Sirluck, ed., *Areopagitica*,
in *YP* 2:541 n. 188.
9. A religious meeting not approved by the authorities.

constituted in religion, that freedom of writing should be restrained by a discipline imitated from the prelates and learnt by them from the Inquisition, to shut us up all again into the breast of a licenser, must needs give cause of doubt and discouragement to all learned and religious men.

Who cannot but discern the fineness of this politic drift, and who are the contrivers; that while bishops were to be baited down,[1] then all presses might be open; it was the people's birthright and privilege in time of Parliament; it was the breaking forth of light. But now, the bishops abrogated and voided out of the Church, as if our Reformation sought no more but to make room for others into their seats under another name, the episcopal arts begin to bud again, the cruse[2] of truth must run no more oil, liberty of printing must be enthralled again under a prelatical commission of twenty, the privilege of the people nullified and, which is worse, the freedom of learning must groan again, and to her old fetters: all this the Parliament yet sitting. Although their own late arguments and defences against the prelates might remember them[3] that this obstructing violence meets for the most part with an event utterly opposite to the end which it drives at: instead of suppressing sects and schisms, it raises them and invests them with a reputation. *The punishing of wits enhances their authority*, saith the Viscount St. Albans;[4] *and a forbidden writing is thought to be a certain spark of truth that flies up in the faces of them who seek to tread it out*. This Order, therefore, may prove a nursing-mother to sects, but I shall easily show how it will be a step-dame to Truth: and first by disenabling us to the maintenance of what is known already.

Well knows he who uses to consider, that our faith and knowledge thrives by exercise, as well as our limbs and complexion. Truth is compared in Scripture to a streaming fountain;[5] if her waters flow not in a perpetual progression, they sicken into a muddy pool of conformity and tradition. A man may be a heretic in the truth; and if he believe things only because his pastor says so, or the Assembly so determines, without knowing other reason, though his belief be true, yet the very truth he holds becomes his heresy.

There is not any burden that some would gladlier post off to another than the charge and care of their religion. There be—who knows not that there be?—of Protestants and Professors who live

---

1. The unpleasant comparison is to bearbaiting, an entertainment in which dogs were set on a bear chained to a stake.
2. Oil lamp. Milton is recalling 1 Kings 17:12–16: the prophet Elijah caused the lamp of a poor woman to burn at length, though it contained only a little oil.
3. Cause them to remember.
4. Sir Francis Bacon. Milton quotes from the same passage of *An Advertisement Touching the Controversies of the Church of England* that he cites above at p. **372**; see n. 6 there.
5. Psalm 85:11: "Truth shall spring out of the earth"; Song of Solomon 4:15: "a fountain of gardens, a well of living waters."

and die in as arrant an implicit faith as any lay papist of Loretto.[6] A wealthy man, addicted to his pleasure and to his profits, finds religion to be a traffic so entangled, and of so many piddling accounts, that of all mysteries he cannot skill[7] to keep a stock going upon that trade. What should he do? Fain he would have the name to be religious, fain he would bear up with his neighbours in that. What does he therefore, but resolves to give over toiling, and to find himself out some factor[8] to whose care and credit he may commit the whole managing of his religious affairs; some divine of note and estimation that must be. To him he adheres, resigns the whole warehouse of his religion, with all the locks and keys into his custody; and indeed makes the very person of that man his religion; esteems his associating with him a sufficient evidence and commendatory of his own piety. So that a man may say his religion is now no more within himself, but is become a dividual movable,[9] and goes and comes near him, according as that good man frequents the house. He entertains him, gives him gifts, feasts him, lodges him; his religion comes home at night, prays, is liberally supped, and sumptuously laid to sleep; rises, is saluted, and after the malmsey, or some well-spiced brewage, and better breakfasted than he whose morning appetite would have gladly fed on green figs between Bethany and Jerusalem,[1] his religion walks abroad at eight, and leaves his kind entertainer in the shop trading all day without his religion.

Another sort there be who, when they hear that all things shall be ordered, all things regulated and settled, nothing written but what passes through the custom-house of certain publicans[2] that have the tonnaging and poundaging[3] of all free-spoken truth, will straight give themselves up into your hands, make 'em and cut 'em out what religion ye please. There be delights, there be recreations and jolly pastimes that will fetch the day about from sun to sun, and rock the tedious year as in a delightful dream. What need they torture their heads with that which others have taken so strictly

---

6. Town in central Italy south of Ancona near the eastern (Adriatic) coast, a major Roman Catholic ("papist") pilgrimage site because of its Shrine of the Sacred House, said to be the house in which the Virgin Mary resided in Jerusalem (carried to Loretto by angels). For Milton's condemnation of Roman Catholic superstition, see the "limbo large and broad since called / The Paradise of Fools" in *PL* 3.490–96. "Professors": those who openly profess their religion.
7. Know how. "Mysteries": occupations.
8. Agent.
9. A movable possession, like furniture, which is distinct ("dividual") from land or buildings.
1. For Jesus hungering in the morning for figs, see Matthew 21:18–19 and Mark 11:12–14, 20.
2. Tax collectors.
3. Tonnage and poundage; a reference to a major import tax on barrels (tuns) of wine, and one shilling per pound of currency on the value of other goods. The right of the king to collect this tax without parliamentary approval was one of the contentious issues that led to the Civil War.

and so unalterably into their own purveying? These are the fruits
which a dull ease and cessation of our knowledge will bring forth
among the people. How goodly and how to be wished were such an
obedient unanimity as this, what a fine conformity would it starch
us all into! Doubtless a staunch and solid piece of framework as any
January could freeze together.

Nor much better will be the consequence even among the clergy
themselves. It is no new thing never heard of before, for a parochial
minister, who has his reward and is at his Hercules' pillars[4] in a
warm benefice, to be easily inclinable, if he have nothing else that
may rouse up his studies, to finish his circuit in an English Concordance and a topic folio, the gatherings and savings of a sober gradu-
ateship, a Harmony and a Catena;[5] treading the constant round of
certain common doctrinal heads, attended with their uses, motives,
marks, and means, out of which, as out of an alphabet, or sol-fa, by
forming and transforming, joining and disjoining variously, a little
bookcraft, and two hours' meditation, might furnish him unspeak-
ably to the performance of more than a weekly charge of sermon-
ing: not to reckon up the infinite helps of interlinearies, breviaries,
synopses, and other loitering gear. But as for the multitude of sermons ready printed and piled up, on every text that is not difficult,
our London trading St. Thomas in his vestry, and add to boot
St. Martin and St. Hugh,[6] have not within their hallowed limits
more vendible ware of all sorts ready made: so that penury he never
need fear of pulpit provision, having where so plenteously to refresh
his magazine.[7] But if his rear and flanks be not impaled,[8] if his back
door be not secured by the rigid licenser, but that a bold book may
now and then issue forth and give the assault to some of his old col-
lections in their trenches, it will concern him then to keep waking,
to stand in watch, to set good guards and sentinels about his
received opinions, to walk the round and counter-round with his
fellow inspectors, fearing lest any of his flock be seduced, who also

---

4. Ultimate goal. The pillars of Hercules (who is credited with placing them there) are the
   mountains on either side of the Strait of Gibraltar, once believed to be the western limit
   of the inhabited world.
5. A reference work consisting of a chain (Latin, *catena*) of extracts from the writings of the
   church fathers on organized topics, intended to enable its user to seem more learned
   than he or she is. A "Harmony," which coordinates passages from the four gospels, has a
   similar purpose. Such aids to sermonizing, comically catalogued, are summarized by the
   witty epithet "loitering gear": equipment for laziness.
6. London parishes—hence, "hallowed limits"—specializing in many kinds of merchandise. While some details of this passage are obscure, the meaning is that the "loitering
   gear" available to preachers, saving them the trouble of having to read and think for
   themselves, is as abundant in these parishes as the other trashy merchandize sold
   there. See Sirluck, ed., *Areopagitica*, in YP 2:547 n. 215.
7. Warehouse.
8. Defended by a fence. The defense is against any new thoughts that might depreciate
   the heaped merchandise of commonplaces in such reference works as those described
   earlier in the paragraph.

then would be better instructed, better exercised and disciplined. And God send[9] that the fear of this diligence, which must then be used, do not make us affect the laziness of a licensing Church.

For if we be sure we are in the right, and do not hold the truth guiltily, which becomes not, if we ourselves condemn not our own weak and frivolous teaching, and the people for an untaught and irreligious gadding rout,[1] what can be more fair than when a man judicious, learned, and of a conscience, for aught we know, as good as theirs that taught us what we know, shall not privily from house to house, which is more dangerous, but openly by writing publish to the world what his opinion is, what his reasons, and wherefore that which is now thought cannot be sound? Christ urged it as wherewith to justify himself, that he preached in public;[2] yet writing is more public than preaching; and more easy to refutation, if need be, there being so many whose business and profession merely it is to be the champions of truth; which if they neglect, what can be imputed but their sloth, or unability?

Thus much we are hindered and disinured[3] by this course of licensing toward the true knowledge of what we seem to know. For how much it hurts and hinders the licensers themselves in the calling of their ministry, more than any secular employment, if they will discharge that office as they ought, so that of necessity they must neglect either the one duty or the other, I insist not, because it is a particular,[4] but leave it to their own conscience how they will decide it there.

There is yet behind of what I purposed to lay open the incredible loss and detriment that this plot of licensing puts us to. More than if some enemy at sea should stop up all our havens and ports and creeks, it hinders and retards the importation of our richest merchandise, truth; nay, it was first established and put in practice by Antichristian malice and mystery on set purpose to extinguish, if it were possible, the light of Reformation, and to settle falsehood; little differing from that policy wherewith the Turk upholds his Alcoran by the prohibition of printing.[5] 'Tis not denied, but gladly confessed, we are to send our thanks and vows to Heaven louder than most of nations for that great measure of truth which we enjoy, especially

---

9. To grant as from a distant place; to cause to happen; to ordain (*OED*, "send" 7a). I.e., May God grant that our justified fear of such diligent guarding against new ideas will prevent us from desiring the laziness of life in a church that licenses books.
1. Aimless wandering crowd.
2. John 18:20: "I spake openly to the world . . . and in secret have I said nothing."
3. Made unable by lack of intellectual exercise.
4. A personal matter.
5. By prohibiting printing with movable type in 1515, the Turkish sultan and Islamic clerics upheld the authority of the Qur'an. The ban on printing in Turkey would last until 1784. By fostering the rapid dissemination of ideas the printing press was a major cause of the Protestant Reformation, as was widely recognized at the time.

in those main points between us and the Pope, with his appurte-
nances the prelates. But he who thinks we are to pitch our tent
here, and have attained the utmost prospect of reformation that the
mortal glass[6] wherein we contemplate can show us, till we come to
beatific vision, that man by this very opinion declares that he is yet
far short of truth.

Truth indeed came once into the world with her divine Master,
and was a perfect shape most glorious to look on: but when he
ascended, and his Apostles after him were laid asleep, then straight
arose a wicked race of deceivers who—as that story goes of the
Egyptian Typhon with his conspirators, how they dealt with the
good Osiris[7]—took the virgin Truth, hewed her lovely form into a
thousand pieces, and scattered them to the four winds. From that
time ever since the sad friends of Truth, such as durst appear, imitating the careful search that Isis made for the mangled body of
Osiris, went up and down gathering up limb by limb still as they
could find them. We have not yet found them all, Lords and Commons, nor ever shall do till her Master's second coming: he shall
bring together every joint and member and shall mould them into
an immortal feature of loveliness and perfection. Suffer not these
licensing prohibitions to stand at every place of opportunity, forbidding and disturbing them that continue seeking, that continue to
do our obsequies to the torn body of our martyred saint.

We boast our light; but if we look not wisely on the sun itself, it
smites us into darkness. Who can discern those planets that are oft
combust,[8] and those stars of brightest magnitude that rise and set
with the sun, until the opposite motion of their orbs bring them to
such a place in the firmament where they may be seen evening or
morning? The light which we have gained was given us not to be
ever staring on but by it to discover onward things more remote
from our knowledge. It is not the unfrocking of a priest, the un-
mitring of a bishop, and the removing him from off the presbyterian
shoulders, that will make us a happy nation. No, if other things as
great in the Church and in the rule of life both economical and

6. Mirror. 1 Corinthians 13:12: "For now we see as through a glass, darkly; but then face
   to face: now I know in part; but then shall I know even as I also am known." In ancient
   bronze mirrors, the image was a little obscure, or dark, although the Greek phrase Paul
   uses is "in an enigma or riddle" (ἐν αἰνίγματι).
7. Plutarch, On Isis and Osiris 13–18. The god Osiris, consort of Isis, was torn to pieces
   and scattered by his brother Set, whom Plutarch calls Typhon (see Glossary); Isis went
   over the earth seeking out the scattered pieces of Osiris. Plutarch himself interprets
   the tale as an allegory of the search for truth.
8. Burned up. The visibility of the planets Venus and Mars is "burned up" by the light of
   the sun, as is that of stars when close to the sun rising or setting. These bodies must be
   observed when they are opposite the sun in the sky, at evening or morning. "Their orbs"
   refers to the old belief that celestial bodies were fixed on transparent spheres that carry
   them around in their orbits. Milton will explicitly reject this notion, putting it in the
   Paradise of Fools. See PL 3.481–83 and n.

political be not looked into and reformed, we have looked so long upon the blaze that Zuinglius and Calvin[9] hath beaconed up to us that we are stark blind. There be who perpetually complain of schisms and sects, and make it such a calamity that any man dissents from their maxims. 'Tis their own pride and ignorance which causes the disturbing, who neither will hear with meekness, nor can convince; yet all must be suppressed which is not found in their Syntagma.[1] *They* are the troublers, *they* are the dividers of unity who neglect and permit not others to unite those dissevered pieces which are yet wanting to the body of Truth. To be still searching what we know not by what we know, still closing up truth to truth as we find it (for all her body is homogeneal and proportional), this is the golden rule in theology as well as in arithmetic[2] and makes up the best harmony in a Church; not the forced and outward union of cold, and neutral, and inwardly divided minds.

Lords and Commons of England! consider what nation it is whereof ye are, and whereof ye are the governors: a nation not slow and dull, but of a quick, ingenious and piercing spirit, acute to invent, subtle and sinewy to discourse, not beneath the reach of any point the highest that human capacity can soar to. Therefore the studies of learning in her deepest sciences have been so ancient and so eminent among us, that writers of good antiquity and ablest judgment have been persuaded that even the school of Pythagoras and the Persian wisdom took beginning from the old philosophy of this island. And that wise and civil Roman, Julius Agricola, who governed once here for Caesar, preferred the natural wits of Britain before the laboured studies of the French. Nor is it for nothing that the grave and frugal Transylvanian sends out yearly from as far as the mountainous borders of Russia, and beyond the Hercynian wilderness,[3] not their youth, but their staid men, to learn our language and our theologic arts.

Yet that which is above all this, the favour and the love of Heaven, we have great argument to think in a peculiar manner propitious and propending towards us. Why else was this nation chosen before any other, that out of her, as out of Sion,[4] should be proclaimed and

9. Two signal figures of the Protestant Reformation, Huldrych Zwingli (1484–1531), leader of the Reformation in Switzerland and pastor of Grossmünster church in Zürich, and John (Jean) Calvin (1509–1564), leader of the church at Geneva and major theologian, influential for his *Institutes of the Christian Religion* (definitive editions 1559, in Latin; 1560, in French).
1. A systematically arranged handbook: another example of "loitering gear." See p. 379, nn. 5 and 6.
2. The Golden Ratio, which governs many pleasing patterns in nature and in art (e.g., the spiral of the nautilus shell and the proportions of the Parthenon).
3. The ancient forest of southern Germany, of which the Black Forest is a relic.
4. See Glossary and *PL* 1.386: "Jehovah thund'ring out of Zion." The point of the reference is a large one: that the English are God's new Chosen People, as the Hebrews were of old.

sounded forth the first tidings and trumpet of Reformation to all Europe? And had it not been the obstinate perverseness of our prelates against the divine and admirable spirit of Wycliffe, to suppress him as a schismatic and innovator, perhaps neither the Bohemian Hus and Jerome, no nor the name of Luther[5] or of Calvin, had been ever known: the glory of reforming all our neighbours had been completely ours. But now, as our obdurate clergy have with violence demeaned[6] the matter, we are become hitherto the latest and the backwardest scholars, of whom God offered to have made us the teachers. Now once again by all concurrence of signs, and by the general instinct of holy and devout men, as they daily and solemnly express their thoughts, God is decreeing to begin some new and great period in his Church, even to the reforming of Reformation itself: what does he then but reveal himself to his servants, and as his manner is, first to his Englishmen? I say, as his manner is, first to us, though we mark not the method of his counsels, and are unworthy.

Behold now this vast city: a city of refuge,[7] the mansion house of liberty, encompassed and surrounded with His protection. The shop of war hath not there more anvils and hammers waking to fashion out the plates and instruments of armed justice in defence of beleaguered Truth than there be pens and heads there, sitting by their studious lamps, musing, searching, revolving new notions and ideas wherewith to present, as with their homage and their fealty, the approaching Reformation; others as fast reading, trying all things, assenting to the force of reason and convincement. What could a man require more from a nation so pliant and so prone to seek after knowledge? What wants there to such a towardly and pregnant soil, but wise and faithful labourers to make a knowing people, a nation of prophets, of sages, and of worthies? We reckon more than five months yet to harvest; there need not be five weeks; had we but eyes to lift up, the fields are white already.[8]

Where there is much desire to learn, there of necessity will be much arguing, much writing, many opinions; for opinion in good

5. Martin Luther (1483–1546), monk, theologian, Bible translator who, with his *Ninety-five Theses* of 1517, began the Protestant Reformation. Wycliffe was an important predecessor of Protestantism, and his followers in Prague, Jan Hus and Jerome of Prague (d. 1416), were both burned at the stake for heresy.
6. Conducted.
7. In Numbers 35:2–28, the Israelites who are about to conquer Canaan are instructed not to assign a separate territory to the tribe of the Levites but to give them forty-eight cities to dwell in, of which six are to be "cities for refuge" (6). Anyone who has committed manslaughter—not only Israelites, but also "the stranger" (15)—may flee to one of the six "for refuge from the avenger" (12). The comparison to London implies that the royalist armies besieging the city are vindictive and bloodthirsty, like "the revenger of blood" (19, 21, 24, 27).
8. John 4:35: "behold, I say unto you, Lift up your eyes, and look on the fields; for they are white already to harvest."

men is but knowledge in the making. Under these fantastic terrors of sect and schism we wrong the earnest and zealous thirst after knowledge and understanding which God hath stirred up in this city. What some lament of, we rather should rejoice at, should rather praise this pious forwardness among men to reassume the ill-deputed care of their religion into their own hands again. A little generous prudence, a little forbearance of one another, and some grain of charity might win all these diligences to join and unite in one general and brotherly search after truth; could we but forgo this prelatical tradition of crowding free consciences and Christian liberties into canons and precepts of men. I doubt not, if some great and worthy stranger should come among us, wise to discern the mould and temper of a people, and how to govern it, observing the high hopes and aims, the diligent alacrity of our extended thoughts and reasonings in the pursuance of truth and freedom, but that he would cry out as Pyrrhus[9] did, admiring the Roman docility and courage: If such were my Epirots, I would not despair the greatest design that could be attempted, to make a Church or kingdom happy.

Yet these are the men cried out against for schismatics and sectaries; as if, while the temple of the Lord was building, some cutting, some squaring the marble, others hewing the cedars, there should be a sort of irrational men who could not consider there must be many schisms and many dissections made in the quarry and in the timber, ere the house of God can be built.[1] And when every stone is laid artfully together, it cannot be united into a continuity, it can but be contiguous in this world; neither can every piece of the building be of one form. Nay rather the perfection consists in this, that out of many moderate varieties and brotherly dissimilitudes that are not vastly disproportional arises the goodly and the graceful symmetry that commends the whole pile and structure.

Let us therefore be more considerate builders, more wise in spiritual architecture, when great reformation is expected. For now the time seems come, wherein Moses the great prophet may sit in heaven rejoicing to see that memorable and glorious wish of his fulfilled, when not only our seventy elders, but all the Lord's people, are become prophets. No marvel then though some men, and some

---

9. Greek king of Epirus (313–372 B.C.E.) in the western Balkans, one of early Rome's most dangerous opponents. According to Lucius Annaeus Florus, Pyrrhus said, "O, how easy it would be for me to win the empire of the world if Roman soldiers were given to me or if I were given to the Romans as their king" (*Epitome rerum romanorum* 1.13.18).
1. Punning on *schisms* (from Greek *schizō*, "to split, cleave, rend"), Milton alludes to the verse at 1 Kings 6:7, which declares that the stone for Solomon's Temple "was made ready before it was brought thither: so that there was neither hammer nor axe nor any tool of iron heard in the house, while it was in building." This example had been used to argue *against* difference of opinion in the church. By focusing on the quarries where the stones were cut to size, Milton turns the earlier interpretation on its head, making the stones of the Temple an argument *in favor* of productive difference of opinion.

good men too perhaps, but young in goodness, as Joshua then was, envy them.[2] They fret, and out of their own weakness are in agony, lest these divisions and subdivisions will undo us. The adversary[3] again applauds, and waits the hour: when they have branched themselves out, saith he, small enough into parties and partitions, then will be our time. Fool![4] he sees not the firm root out of which we all grow, though into branches; nor will beware until he see our small divided maniples cutting through at every angle of his ill-united and unwieldy brigade. And that we are to hope better of all these supposed sects and schisms, and that we shall not need that solicitude, honest perhaps, though over-timorous, of them that vex in this behalf, but shall laugh in the end at those malicious applauders of our differences, I have these reasons to persuade me.

First, when a city shall be as it were besieged and blocked about, her navigable river infested, inroads and incursions round, defiance and battle oft rumoured to be marching up even to her walls and suburb trenches,[5] that then the people, or the greater part, more than at other times, wholly taken up with the study of highest and most important matters to be reformed, should be disputing, reasoning, reading, inventing, discoursing, even to a rarity and admiration, things not before discoursed or written of, argues first a singular goodwill, contentedness and confidence in your prudent foresight and safe government, Lords and Commons; and from thence derives itself to a gallant bravery and well-grounded contempt of their enemies, as if there were no small number of as great spirits among us, as his was, who when Rome was nigh besieged by Hannibal, being in the city, bought that piece of ground at no cheap rate whereon Hannibal himself encamped his own regiment.[6]

Next, it is a lively and cheerful presage of our happy success and victory. For as in a body, when the blood is fresh, the spirits pure

---

2. Numbers 11:27–29. When Joshua and others asked Moses to stop two men who were prophesying, Moses replied, "Would God that all the Lord's people were prophets, and that the Lord would put his spirit upon them!"

3. A double meaning: Satan (whose name in Hebrew means "adversary") and the party of the king at Oxford. The royalist bulletin *Mercurius Aulicus* gleefully reported increasing dissension among the parliamentary party in London.

4. I.e., the adversary, the royalist party, and the devil. "Over-timorous" (p. 385) proponents of licensing "fret" that these dissensions will undo them, not seeing that honest and open dissent indicates strength.

5. Since 1642 London had been under intermittent threat of siege and occupation by the royalist army, the prime reason for the increase in armaments manufacture in the city. A defensive circuit of trenches was built in 1643.

6. During the Second Punic War, after the disastrous Roman loss at the battle of Cannae, the victorious Carthaginian general Hannibal Barca (247–181 B.C.E.) marched to Rome (211 B.C.E.). He did not lay siege to the city, however. According to the Roman historian Livy (*Ab urbe condita* 26.11), he was deterred by tempests, by an unfavorable augury, by the confidence the Roman state showed in dispatching troops to Spain even as he was camped before the city, and lastly by the news that a citizen had purchased at full price the land on which the Carthaginian army was camped, thus showing a "well-grounded contempt" of the enemy.

and vigorous, not only to vital but to rational faculties, and those in the acutest and the pertest operations of wit and subtlety, it argues in what good plight and constitution the body is; so when the cheerfulness of the people is so sprightly up, as that it has not only wherewith to guard well its own freedom and safety, but to spare, and to bestow upon the solidest and sublimest points of controversy and new invention, it betokens us not degenerated, nor drooping to a fatal decay, but casting off the old and wrinkled skin of corruption to outlive these pangs and wax young again, entering the glorious ways of truth and prosperous virtue, destined to become great and honourable in these latter ages. Methinks I see in my mind a noble and puissant nation rousing herself like a strong man after sleep and shaking her invincible locks:[7] methinks I see her as an eagle mewing[8] her mighty youth and kindling her undazzled eyes at the full midday beam, purging and unscaling her long-abused sight at the fountain itself of heavenly radiance, while the whole noise of timorous and flocking birds, with those also that love the twilight, flutter about, amazed at what she means, and in their envious gabble would prognosticate a year of sects and schisms.[9]

What should ye do then? should ye suppress all this flowery crop of knowledge and new light sprung up and yet springing daily in this city? Should ye set an oligarchy of twenty engrossers[1] over it, to bring a famine upon our minds again, when we shall know nothing but what is measured to us by their bushel? Believe it, Lords and Commons, they who counsel ye to such a suppressing do as good as bid ye suppress yourselves; and I will soon show how. If it be desired to know the immediate cause of all this free writing and free speaking, there cannot be assigned a truer than your own mild and free and humane government. It is the liberty, Lords and Commons, which your own valorous and happy counsels have purchased us, liberty which is the nurse of all great wits; this is that which hath rarefied and enlightened our spirits like the influence of heaven; this is that which hath enfranchised, enlarged and lifted up our apprehensions degrees above themselves.

7. An allusion to Samson, whose strength was in his hair; it was shorn by his lover Delilah, who then betrayed him to his enemies, the Philistines. But after the hair grew back, Samson was able to tear down the temple of the Philistines (Judges 16:15–30). In Milton's drama, *Samson Agonistes*, "Dalilah" is herself a Philistine and Samson's wife.
8. Molting (casting off feathers): from Latin *muto*, "to change." The word suggests spiritual, intellectual, and political renewal. Other details are drawn from the medieval bestiary tradition, in particular the *Physiologus* of Theobaldus (eleventh century C.E.): the eagle molts its old feathers by burning them up as it flies close to the sun; it then renews them by plunging into a fountain.
9. The other, ignoble birds, loving the twilight of ignorance but amazed at the eagle, gabble enviously, like royalist geese, foretelling more dire sects and schisms among the parliamentary party.
1. Purchasers in bulk. Here, the twenty licensers ordained by the Order, who engross or collect all permitted knowledge into their own bushel—like speculators in grain—and starve us of the truth.

Ye cannot make us now less capable, less knowing, less eagerly pursuing of the truth, unless ye first make yourselves, that made us so, less the lovers, less the founders of our true liberty. We can grow ignorant again, brutish, formal and slavish, as ye found us; but you then must first become that which ye cannot be, oppressive, arbitrary and tyrannous, as they[2] were from whom ye have freed us. That our hearts are now more capacious, our thoughts more erected to the search and expectation of greatest and exactest things is the issue of your own virtue propagated in us. Ye cannot suppress that, unless ye reinforce an abrogated and merciless law, that fathers may dispatch at will their own children.[3] And who shall then stick closest to ye, and excite others? not he who takes up arms for coat and conduct, and his four nobles of Danegelt.[4] Although I dispraise not the defence of just immunities, yet love my peace better, if that were all. Give me the liberty to know, to utter, and to argue freely according to conscience, above all liberties.[5]

What would be best advised, then, if it be found so hurtful and so unequal to suppress opinions for the newness or the unsuitableness to a customary acceptance, will not be my task to say. I only shall repeat what I have learned from one of your own honourable number, a right noble and pious lord, who, had he not sacrificed his life and fortunes to the Church and Commonwealth, we had not now missed and bewailed a worthy and undoubted patron of this argument. Ye know him, I am sure; yet I for honour's sake, and may it be eternal to him, shall name him, the Lord Brook.[6] He writing of episcopacy, and by the way treating of sects and schisms, left ye his vote, or rather now the last words of his dying charge, which I know will ever be of dear and honoured regard with ye, so full of meekness

2. I.e., the bishops chiefly, plus the royalist party and the king.
3. The legal right of the Roman father, the *pater familias*, to power of life and death (*vitae necisque potestas*) over his children, his wife, and his slaves.
4. A tenth-century tax for defense against the Danes (Vikings), better known as the notorious Ship Money (a *noble* was an English gold coin). "Coat and conduct": a tax for clothing and transporting troops. During the Personal Rule these taxes were revived by King Charles, desperate for money, and imposed without parliamentary consent. His action aroused widespread indignation and was a vital point raised in the Grand Remonstrance of 1641. See p. 378, n. 3.
5. It is right to resist unjust taxation, and good to enjoy material privileges including "immunities" from such taxes. But we do not value these at the expense of peace, if money is all that's at stake. But it isn't: the principle of liberty is also at stake, especially the highest liberty, which is to argue according to one's conscience. As Milton said in an earlier pamphlet defending divorce as a private, family matter, it is abject to fight for money and not for more important freedoms: "What are all our public immunities and privileges worth . . . if we suffer ourselves in the meanwhile not to understand the most important freedom that God and Nature hath given us in the family" (*The Judgment of Martin Bucer Concerning Divorce* [London, 1644], in YP 2:438).
6. Robert Greville, second Baron Brooke (1607–1643), killed by sniper fire during the siege of Litchfield. His *Discourse Opening the Nature of That Episcopacy Which Is Exercised in England* (1641) drew from Milton's *Of Prelatical Episcopacy* (1641). In turn, Milton made use of the final section of Brook's *Discourse in Areopagitica*. Brook's open-mindedness is in the spirit of *Areopagitica*, hence this suitable tribute.

and breathing charity, that next to *his* last testament, who bequeathed love and peace to his disciples,[7] I cannot call to mind where I have read or heard words more mild and peaceful. He there exhorts us to hear with patience and humility those, however they be miscalled, that desire to live purely, in such a use of God's ordinances, as the best guidance of their conscience gives them, and to tolerate them, though in some disconformity to ourselves. The book itself will tell us more at large, being published to the world, and dedicated to the Parliament by him who, both for his life and for his death, deserves that what advice he left be not laid by without perusal.

And now the time in special is, by privilege to write and speak what may help to the further discussing of matters in agitation. The temple of Janus[8] with his two controversial faces might now not unsignificantly be set open. And though all the winds of doctrine[9] were let loose to play upon the earth, so Truth be in the field, we do injuriously, by licensing and prohibiting, to misdoubt her strength. Let her and Falsehood grapple; who ever knew Truth put to the worse in a free and open encounter? Her confuting is the best and surest suppressing. He who hears what praying there is for light and clearer knowledge to be sent down among us, would think of other matters to be constituted beyond the discipline of Geneva, framed and fabricked already to our hands.[1] Yet when the new light which we beg for shines in upon us, there be who envy and oppose if it come not first in at their casements.[2] What a collusion is this, whenas we are exhorted by the wise man to use diligence, *to seek for wisdom as for hidden treasures*[3] early and late, that another order shall enjoin us to know nothing but by statute? When a man hath been labouring the hardest labour in the deep mines of knowledge; hath furnished out his findings in all their equipage; drawn forth his reasons as it were a battle ranged; scattered and defeated all objections in his way; calls out his adversary into the plain, offers him the advantage of wind and sun, if he please, only that he may try the matter by dint of argument: for his opponents then to skulk,

---

7. John 14:27: "Peace I leave with you, my peace I give unto you: not as the world giveth, give I unto you. Let not your heart be troubled, neither let it be afraid."
8. The Roman god of doorways and beginnings. His shrine on the Roman Forum had double doors at each end, traditionally left open in time of war.
9. Ephesians 4:14–15: "That we henceforth be no more children, tossed to and fro, and carried about with every wind of doctrine . . . ; But speaking the truth in love, may grow up into him in all things, which is the head, even Christ."
1. Under John Calvin, the church of Geneva became the bulwark of Protestantism in the sixteenth century, when many English Protestants fled there during the Roman Catholic reign of Mary I (1553–58). Calvin's theology had been adapted and shaped, or "framed and fabricked," to Puritanism and Presbyterianism in England.
2. Windows.
3. Of several possible passages the italicized words point to, the closest and likeliest is Proverbs 2:2–5. The wise man is Solomon speaking of wisdom: "If thou seekest her as silver, and searchest for her as for hid treasures; Then shalt thou understand the fear of the Lord, and find the knowledge of God."

to lay ambushments, to keep a narrow bridge of licensing where the challenger should pass, though it be valour enough in soldiership, is but weakness and cowardice in the wars of Truth.

For who knows not that Truth is strong, next to the Almighty? She needs no policies, nor stratagems, nor licensings to make her victorious; those are the shifts and the defences that error uses against her power. Give her but room, and do not bind her when she sleeps, for then she speaks not true, as the old Proteus[4] did, who spake oracles only when he was caught and bound, but then rather she turns herself into all shapes, except her own, and perhaps tunes her voice according to the time, as Micaiah did before Ahab,[5] until she be adjured into her own likeness. Yet is it not impossible that she may have more shapes than one. What else is all that rank of things indifferent, wherein Truth may be on this side or on the other, without being unlike herself? What but a vain shadow else is the abolition of *those ordinances, that hand-writing nailed to the cross?*[6] What great purchase is this Christian liberty which Paul so often boasts of?[7] His doctrine is, that he who eats or eats not, regards a day or regards it not, may do either to the Lord.[8] How many other things might be tolerated in peace, and left to conscience, had we but charity, and were it not the chief stronghold of our hypocrisy to be ever judging one another?

I fear yet this iron yoke of outward conformity hath left a slavish print upon our necks; the ghost of a linen decency[9] yet haunts us. We stumble and are impatient at the least dividing of one visible congregation from another, though it be not in fundamentals; and through our forwardness to suppress, and our backwardness to recover any enthralled piece of truth out of the gripe of custom, we care not to keep truth separated from truth, which is the fiercest rent and disunion of

---

4. A Greek sea-god who could take any shape and had the power of prophecy. See Homer, *Odyssey* 4.384–93; Virgil, *Georgics* 4.387–52.
5. 1 Kings 22:15–23. The prophet Micaiah was brought before Ahab, wicked king of the separated northern kingdom (Israel), and Jehoshaphat, king of the southern kingdom (Judea). Micaiah was asked to lend his support to other prophets who were advising Ahab and Jehoshaphat to fight the king of Syria at Ramoth-gilead. At first, Micaiah complied, predicting victory. But when Ahab urged him to tell the truth, Micaiah prophesied defeat. Ahab then complained to Jehoshaphat that Micaiah prophesied nothing but evil. Provoked, Micaiah said he saw God enthroned among his host in heaven, calling for one to tempt Ahab to fight at Ramoth-gilead and die. A spirit stood before God and promised to do so, saying, "I will be a lying spirit in the mouth of all his prophets" (22). This figure is commonly interpreted as Satan. See *Paradise Regained* 1.371–76.
6. Colossians 2:14. Jesus Christ has forgiven us, "Blotting out the handwriting of ordinances that was against us . . . and took it out of the way, nailing it to his cross."
7. In Romans and Galatians, e.g., Galatians 5:1: "Stand fast therefore in the liberty wherewith Christ hath made us free."
8. Romans 14:6: "He that eateth, eateth to the Lord, for he giveth God thanks; and he that eateth not, to the Lord he eateth not, and giveth God thanks."
9. The linen vestments of the clergy, hated by the Puritans. They were insisted on by Archbishop Laud to lend greater dignity to the priestly office, and to elevate the priest above the people.

all. We do not see that, while we still affect by all means a rigid external formality, we may as soon fall again into a gross conforming stu-
pidity, a stark and dead congealment of *wood and hay and stubble*,[1]
forced and frozen together, which is more to the sudden degenerat-
ing of a Church than many subdichotomies of petty schisms.

Not that I can think well of every light separation, or that all in a
Church is to be expected *gold and silver and precious stones*:[2] it is
not possible for man to sever the wheat from the tares,[3] the good
fish from the other fry; that must be the Angels' ministry at the end
of mortal things. Yet if all cannot be of one mind—as who looks
they should be?—this doubtless is more wholesome, more prudent,
and more Christian, that many be tolerated, rather than all compelled. I mean not tolerated popery, and open superstition, which,
as it extirpates all religions and civil supremacies, so itself should
be extirpate,[4] provided first that all charitable and compassionate
means be used to win and regain the weak and the misled; that also
which is impious or evil absolutely either against faith or manners
no law can possibly permit that intends not to unlaw itself. But
those neighbouring differences, or rather indifferences, are what I
speak of, whether in some point of doctrine or of discipline, which,
though they may be many, yet need not interrupt *the unity of Spirit*,
if we could but find among us *the bond of peace*.[5]

In the meanwhile if any one would write, and bring his helpful
hand to the slow-moving Reformation which we labour under, if
Truth have spoken to him before others, or but seemed at least to

1. 1 Corinthians 3:10–13. The reference here and at the beginning of the next paragraph is
   to the various materials Christians may choose for building (by their deeds and faith)
   upon the immutable foundation of Christ: either "gold, silver, precious stones" or "wood,
   hay, stubble." But at the Last Judgment, "the fire shall try every man's work of what sort
   it is" (13).
2. See previous note.
3. Matthew 13:24–30 and 13:36–43: the parable of the householder who sows wheat.
   After his enemy comes and sows tares—here, harmful injurious weeds—among the
   wheat seed, he tells his servants to let the tares grow—but when harvest comes to
   gather the tares first, bind them, and burn them: "The field is the world; the good seed
   are the children of the kingdom; but the tares are the children of the wicked one; The
   enemy that sowed them is the devil; the harvest is the end of the world; and the reapers
   are the angels. . . . The Son of Man shall send forth his angels, and they shall gather
   out of his kingdom all things that offend . . . and shall cast them into a furnace of fire:
   there shall be wailing and gnashing of teeth. Then shall the righteous shine forth as the
   sun in the kingdom of their Father. Who hath ears to hear, let him hear" (38–43).
4. The argument against tolerating Roman Catholicism follows closely that expressed by
   leader of the Long Parliament, John Pym, on March 17, 1642: "The religion of the
   papists is a religion incomputable to any other religion, destructive to all others, and
   doth not endure anything that doth oppose it; . . . they bring them to ruin" (cited by
   Sirluck, ed., *Areopagitica*, in YP 2:565 n. 285). Milton's addition of "civil supremacies"
   anticipates his own argument in *Of True Religion, Heresy, Schism, Toleration, and
   What Best Means May be Used Against the Growth of Popery* (1673), and also the argument of John Locke in the *First Letter of Toleration* (1689), that to allow Roman Catholicism is to settle a foreign jurisdiction in the country. See Sirluck, ed., *Areopagitica*, in
   YP 2:565 n. 286. As for deliberate impiety and absolute evil, which are mentioned next,
   they deny all order and can't be tolerated without overthrowing law itself.
5. Ephesians 4:3: Paul exhorts the faithful to endeavor "to keep the unity of the Spirit in
   the bond of peace."

speak, who hath so bejesuited us that we should trouble that man
with asking licence to do so worthy a deed? and not consider this:
that if it come to prohibiting, there is not aught more likely to be
prohibited than truth itself; whose first appearance to our eyes,
bleared and dimmed with prejudice and custom, is more unsightly
and unplausible than many errors, even as the person is of many a
great man slight and contemptible to see to. And what do they tell
us vainly of new opinions, when this very opinion of theirs, that
none must be heard but whom they like, is the worst and newest
opinion of all others; and is the chief cause why sects and schisms
do so much abound and true knowledge is kept at distance from us;
besides yet a greater danger which is in it.

For when God shakes a kingdom[6] with strong and healthful com-
motions to a general reforming, 'tis not untrue that many sectaries
and false teachers are then busiest in seducing; but yet more true it
is, that God then raises to his own work men of rare abilities, and
more than common industry, not only to look back and revise what
hath been taught heretofore, but to gain further and go on some
new enlightened steps in the discovery of truth. For such is the
order of God's enlightening his Church, to dispense and deal out by
degrees his beam, so as our earthly eyes may best sustain it.

Neither is God appointed and confined, where and out of what
place these his chosen shall be first heard to speak; for he sees not
as man sees, chooses not as man chooses, lest we should devote
ourselves again to set places, and assemblies, and outward callings
of men; planting our faith one while in the old Convocation house,
and another while in the Chapel at Westminster;[7] when all the faith
and religion that shall be there canonized is not sufficient without
plain convincement, and the charity of patient instruction to supple
the least bruise of conscience, to edify the meanest Christian who
desires to walk in the Spirit and not in the letter of human trust, for
all the number of voices that can be there made; no, though Harry
VII himself there, with all his liege tombs about him, should lend
them voices from the dead to swell their number.[8]

6. Haggai 2:7: "And I will shake all nations, and the desire of all nations shall come: and I
   will fill this house with glory, saith the Lord of hosts."
7. The Convocation, an assembly of the clergy, met in the Chapter House of Westminster
   Abbey from the reign of Henry VIII (1509–47) to the fall of Archbishop Laud (1641).
   The Long Parliament transferred the Convocation's powers—which it increased—to
   the Westminster Assembly of Divines, which met from 1643 to 1652 in the Henry VII
   Chapel in Westminster Abbey, its purpose being to reform the Church of England. The
   Westminster Assembly of Divines, many of whom were Scottish Presbyterians, are sati-
   rized by Milton for their intolerance and hypocrisy, notably in the poem "On the New
   Forcers of Conscience Under the Long Parliament."
8. I.e., not all the voices of the members of the Westminster Assembly of Divines gathered
   in the Henry VII chapel, even if Henry VII himself were to cry out from his tomb in
   support, and even if the dead all about him (for numerous other monarchs are interred
   there) should add their voices, too, can sway the truly free conscience of the most

And if the men be erroneous who appear to be the leading schismatics, what withholds us but our sloth, our self-will, and distrust in the right cause, that we do not give them gentle meetings and gentle dismissions,[9] that we debate not and examine the matter thoroughly with liberal and frequent audience; if not for their sakes, yet for our own? seeing no man who hath tasted learning, but will confess the many ways of profiting by those who, not contented with stale receipts, are able to manage and set forth new positions to the world. And were they but as the dust and cinders of our feet, so long as in that notion they may yet serve to polish and brighten the armoury of Truth, even for that respect they were not utterly to be cast away. But if they be of those whom God hath fitted for the special use of these times with eminent and ample gifts, and those perhaps neither among the priests nor among the Pharisees,[1] and we in the haste of a precipitant zeal shall make no distinction, but resolve to stop their mouths because we fear they come with new and dangerous opinions, as we commonly forejudge them ere we understand them; no less than woe to us, while, thinking thus to defend the Gospel, we are found the persecutors.

There have been not a few since the beginning of this Parliament, both of the presbytery and others, who by their unlicensed books, to the contempt of an Imprimatur, first broke that triple ice clung about our hearts, and taught the people to see day: I hope that none of those were the persuaders to renew upon us this bondage which they themselves have wrought so much good by contemning. But if neither the check that Moses gave to young Joshua, nor the countermand which our Saviour gave to young John,[2] who was so ready to prohibit those whom he thought unlicensed, be not enough to admonish our elders how unacceptable to God their testy mood of prohibiting is; if neither their own remembrance what evil hath abounded in the Church by this let of licensing, and what good they themselves have begun by transgressing it be not enough, but that they will persuade and execute the most Dominican part of the Inquisition[3] over us, and are already with one foot in the stirrup so active at suppressing, it would be no unequal distribution in the first place to suppress the suppressors themselves: whom the change of their condition hath

---

humble Christian. Nor can legal threats and force do so. Only charitable persuasion, or "convincement," can sway a free conscience.
9. I.e., courteous greetings upon meeting and farewells upon parting.
1. A religious party within Judaism between the second century B.C.E. and New Testament times, in the first century C.E., which insisted on strict interpretation of and adherence to the Mosaic Law, often in conflict with Jesus. The Pharisees, to whom Milton is comparing the Westminster Divines, are traditional figures of self-righteousness and hypocrisy.
2. In Luke 9:49–50, Jesus tells John not to stop a stranger who was casting out devils in Jesus' name: "Forbid him not: for he that is not against us is for us" (50).
3. Book licensers under the Inquisition were usually Dominicans.

puffed up, more than their late experience of harder times hath made wise.

And as for regulating the press, let no man think to have the honour of advising ye better than yourselves have done in that Order published next before this, "that no book be printed, unless the printer's and the author's name, or at least the printer's, be registered."[4] Those which otherwise come forth, if they be found mischievous and libellous, the fire and the executioner[5] will be the timeliest and the most effectual remedy that man's prevention can use. For this authentic Spanish policy of licensing books, if I have said aught, will prove the most unlicensed book itself within a short while; and was the immediate image of a Star Chamber[6] decree to that purpose made in those very times when that Court did the rest of those her pious works, for which she is now fallen from the stars with Lucifer. Whereby ye may guess what kind of state prudence, what love of the people, what care of religion or good manners there was at the contriving, although with singular hypocrisy it pretended to bind books to their good behaviour. And how it got the upper hand of your precedent Order so well constituted before, if we may believe those men whose profession gives them cause to inquire most, it may be doubted there was in it the fraud of some old patentees and monopolizers in the trade of bookselling; who under pretence of the poor in their Company not to be defrauded, and the just retaining of each man his several copy, which God forbid should be gainsaid, brought divers glossing colours[7] to the House, which were indeed but colours, and serving to no end except

4. Order of January 29, 1642, making it illegal to publish anonymously.
5. Books condemned for libel were confiscated and burned by the public executioner, who administered any other punishments ordered, including mutilation. The most famous example at the time was the mutilation of the Puritan fanatic William Prynne, an adversary of Milton's, who had part of his ears cut off in 1634 for having written a learned, though verbose and vulgar, treatise against stage plays, *Histriomastix* (literally, "the player's scourge"; 1632), "wherein it is largely evidenced . . . that popular stage plays are sinful, heathenish, lewd, ungodly spectacles, and most pernicious corruptions" (title page). The work was thought to contain slander of the queen and the king, although it was written before the queen and her ladies performed in the masque to which his accusers claimed Prynne referred. For further publications, Prynne had the rest of his ears cut off in 1637 and was branded on both cheeks with the letters "S" and "L," standing for "seditious libeler." He wittily reinterpreted the letters as *stigmata laudis,* meaning both "sign of praise" and "mark of [Archbishop] Laud." In an early draft of the anti-Presbyterian poem "On the New Forcers of Conscience under the Long Parliament," Milton takes aim at the Westminster Assembly of Divines and hopes that Parliament, now equipped with "wholesome and preventive shears," will "Crop ye as close as marginal P——'s ears" (line 17). In the final version Milton removed the unmistakable reference to Prynne, changing the line to "Clip your phylacteries, though baulk your ears." Here Milton is not condemning the punishment, including mutilation, of authors of published books: he is objecting only to government censorship of books *before* publication. "The fire and the executioner" are still available as "the most effectual remedy" for published books deemed by the authorities to be "mischievous and libellous."
6. See p. 357, n. 7, and p. 338.
7. Specious reasons. Booksellers who hypocritically claim to support licensing, because it protects the copyrights of the poorer members of their trade, do so in truth only to oppress others, especially authors.

it be to exercise a superiority over their neighbours; men who do not therefore labour in an honest profession to which learning is indebted, that they should be made other men's vassals. Another end is thought was aimed at by some of them in procuring by petition this Order, that, having power in their hands, malignant books might the easier scape abroad, as the event shows.

But of these sophisms and elenchs[8] of merchandise I skill not. This I know, that errors in a good government and in a bad are equally almost incident; for what magistrate may not be misinformed, and much the sooner, if liberty of printing be reduced into the power of a few? But to redress willingly and speedily what hath been erred, and in highest authority to esteem a plain advertisement[9] more than others have done a sumptuous bribe, is a virtue (honoured Lords and Commons) answerable to your highest actions, and whereof none can participate but greatest and wisest men.

8. Sophistical proofs and refutations.
9. Notification.

CRITICISM

Classic Criticism of *Paradise Lost*

AEMILIA LANYER

A Digression in Defense of Eve
and for Women's Equality (1611)†

Aemilia Lanyer published her book of poems, *Salve Deus Rex Judaeo-rum* [Hail God, King of the Jews] in 1611. Milton was an infant at the time, not yet three years old. Although there is no apparent influence on Milton, Lanyer raises deep questions about the Bible that would also be tackled in *Paradise* Lost. But she does so very much from the woman's point of view.

Salve Deus Rex Iudaeorum was the first book of original English poems printed by a woman. In the title poem of the collection, Lanyer recounts the passion and death of Jesus, who is the God and King of her title. In a digression that was given the somewhat inaccurate title, "Eve's Apology [discourse]," Lanyer has come to the point in her narra-tive where Pontius Pilate sits in judgment on Jesus. Pilate has been warned by his wife (having herself been warned in a dream) not to condemn that "just man" (Matthew 27:19). "Hear the words of thy most worthy wife," Lanyer says to Pilate, "Who sends to thee to beg her Savior's life . . . Do not the thing that goes against thy heart." This is the point at which Lanyer opens a long digression on the traditional idea that Eve, and with Eve all women since, is solely responsible for original sin.

To defend against this calumny of women, and also to argue for the equality of women, Lanyer makes two points. The first point is that Eve's sin was not as great as Adam's because she was deceived into thinking that something good—knowledge—would be the result of eating the fruit. This point has obvious relevance to *Paradise Lost*: Milton emphasizes that Eve has been deceived by the serpent, Adam not; and when Eve is tempted by the serpent her desire for knowledge is the principal motivation for her fall.

Lanyer's second point is less immediately relevant to *Paradise Lost* but is well worth considering in connection with Milton's biblical sub-ject. Lanyer argues that if women are to be blamed for Eve's mere "fault," then how much more are men to be blamed for the crime of

---

† From *Salve Deus Rex Judæorum* (London: 1611).

397

Pontius Pilate, who unjustly condemned Jesus to death. Pilate's greater crime, says Lanyer, should free women of misogynist conclusions by men drawn from the example of Eve.

The following text is on signatures C4v to D2 of the unpaginated first edition of *Salve Deus Rex Iudaeorum, containing, 1, The Passion of Christ;* 2. *Eve's Apology in Defense of Women;* 3. *The Tears of the Daughters of Jerusalem;* 4. *The Salutation and Sorrow of the Virgin Mary. With Diverse Other Things not Unfit to be Read.* I have modernized spelling and punctuation and italicized a few words for emphasis.

Our mother Eve, who tasted of Tree,
Giving to Adam what she held most deare,
Was simply good and had no pow'r to see:
The after-coming harm did not appear:
   The subtle Serpent that our sex betrayed   5
   Before our Fall so sure a plot had laid.

That undiscerning ignorance perceived
No guile or craft that was by him [the Serpent] intended.
For had she known of what we were bereaved,
To his request she had not condescended.   10
But she (poor soul) by cunning was deceived:
No hurt therein her harmless heart intended.
   For she alleged God's word, which he [the Serpent] denies,
   That they [Eve and Adam] should die, but even as gods be wise.

But surely Adam cannot be excused!   15
Her fault, though great, yet he was most to blame:
What weakness offered [Eve's offer to Adam] strength [Adam's]
    might have refused:
Being lord of all, the greater was his shame.
Although the Serpent's craft had *her* abused
God's holy word ought all *his* actions frame: 20
   For he was lord and king of all the earth
   Before poor Eve had either life or breath. . . .

If Eve did err it was for *knowledge'* sake;
The fruit being *fair* persuaded him to fall:
   No subtle serpent's falsehood did betray him.   25
   If he would eat it, who had pow'r to stay [prevent] him?

Not Eve, whose only fault was too much love,
Which made her give this present to her dear,
That what she tasted he might likewise prove [try],
Whereby his knowledge might become more clear . . .   30
   Yet men will boast of knowledge, which he took
   From Eve's fair hand, as from a learnèd book. . . .

Her weakness did the Serpent's words obey,
But you [Pilate] in malice God's dear Son betray. . . .   35

Then let us have our liberty again
And challenge [claim] to yourselves no sov'reignty.
You came not in the world without our pain:
Make that a bar against your cruelty!
Your fault being greater, why should you disdain   40
Our being your equals, free from tyranny?
   If one weak woman simply did offend,
    This sin of yours [Pilate's, and by extension, all men's] hath no
      excuse nor end.

ANDREW MARVELL

On Mr. Milton's *Paradise Lost* (1674)†

When I beheld the poet blind, yet bold,
In slender book his vast design unfold,
Messiah crowned, God's reconciled decree,
Rebelling Angels, the Forbidden Tree,
Heaven, Hell, Earth, Chaos, all; the argument   5
Held me a while, misdoubting his intent
That he would ruin (for I saw him strong)
The sacred truths to fable and old song,
(So Sampson groped the temple's posts in spite)[1]
The world o'erwhelming to revenge his sight.   10
   Yet as I read, soon growing less severe,
I liked his project, the success did fear;
Through that wide field how he his way should find
O'er which lame faith leads understanding blind;
Lest he perplexed the things he would explain,   15
And what was easy he should render vain.
   Or if a work so infinite he spanned,
Jealous I was that some less skilful hand
(Such as disquiet always what is well,
And by ill imitating would excel)   20
Might hence presume the whole Creation's day
To change in scenes, and show it in a play.
   Pardon me, Mighty Poet, nor despise

---

† From *The Complete Poems*, ed. Elizabeth Story Donno (London: Penguin Books, 1996),
  pp. 192–93.
1. Judges 16:28–30.

My causeless, yet not impious, surmise.
But I am now convinced that none will dare   25
Within thy labours to pretend a share.
Thou hast not missed one thought that could be fit,
And all that was improper dost omit:
So that no room is here for writers left,
But to detect their ignorance or theft.   30
That majesty which through thy work doth reign
Draws the devout, deterring the profane.
And things divine thou treat'st of in such state
As them preserves, and thee, inviolate.
At once delight and horror on us seize,   35
Thou sing'st with so much gravity and ease;
And above human flight dost soar aloft,
With plume so strong, so equal, and so soft.
The bird named from that paradise you sing
So never flags, but always keeps on wing.   40
    Where couldst thou words of such a compass find?
Whence furnish such a vast expense of mind?
Just heaven thee, like Tiresias,[2] to requite,
Rewards with prophecy thy loss of sight.
    Well mightst thou scorn thy readers to allure   45
With tinkling rhyme, of thine own sense secure;
While the *Town-Bayes*[3] writes all the while and spells,
And like a pack-horse tires without his bells.
Their fancies like our bushy points appear,
The poets tag them; we for fashion wear.   50
I too, transported by the mode, offend,
And while I meant to *praise* thee must *commend*.
Thy verse created like thy theme sublime,
In number, weight, and measure, needs not rhyme.

JOHN DRYDEN

Epigram[†]

Three poets in three distant ages born,
Greece, Italy,[1] and England did adorn.
The first in loftiness of soul surpassed,

2. In Greek mythology, a Theban seer whom the gods made a prophet after they made him blind.
3. I.e., a hack poet.
† "Under Mr. Milton's Picture before His *Paradise Lost*," in *Poems and Fables*, ed. James Kinsley (London: Oxford University Press, 1962), p. 424.
1. The epic poets Homer and Virgil, respectively.

The next in majesty, in both the last.
The force of nature could no further go;
To make a third she joined the other two.

From Preface to Second Miscellany (1685)†

*   *   *

Imitation is a nice point, and there are few poets who deserve to be models in all they write. Milton's "Paradise Lost" is admirable; but am I therefore bound to maintain, that there are no flats amongst his elevations, when it is evident he creeps along sometimes for above an hundred lines together? Cannot I admire the height of his invention, and the strength of his expression, without defending his antiquated words, and the perpetual harshness of their sound? It is as much commendation as a man can hear, to own him excellent; all beyond it is idolatry.

*   *   *

JOSEPH ADDISON

From Spectator 297 (February 9, 1712)‡

*   *   *

There is another Objection against *Milton's* Fable, which is indeed almost the same with the former, tho' placed in a different Light, namely, That the Hero in the *Paradise Lost* is unsuccessful, and by no means a Match for his Enemies. This gave occasion to Mr. *Dryden's* Reflection, that the Devil was in reality *Milton's* Hero.[1] I think I have obviated this Objection in my first Paper. The *Paradise Lost* is an Epic, or a Narrative Poem, and he that looks for an Hero in it, searches for that which *Milton* never intended; but if he will needs fix the Name of an Hero upon any Person in it, 'tis certainly the *Messiah* who is the Hero, both in the Principal Action, and in the chief Episodes. Paganism could not furnish out a real Action for a Fable greater than that of the *Iliad* or *Æneid*, and therefore an Heathen could not form a higher Notion of a Poem than one of that kind, which they call an Heroic. Whether *Milton's* is not of a sublimer

---

† From *Works*, ed. Sir Walter Scott and George Saintsbury, vol. 12 (Edinburgh: William Paterson, 1885), pp. 300–1.
‡ From *Spectator*, ed. Donald Bond, vol. 3 (Oxford: Clarendon, 1965).
1. See *Dedication of the Æneis* (1697).

Nature I will not presume to determine: It is sufficient that I shew there is in the *Paradise Lost* all the Greatness of Plan, Regularity of Design, and masterly Beauties which we discover in *Homer* and *Virgil*.

*   *   *

Milton's Sentiments and Ideas were so wonderfully Sublime, that it would have been impossible for him to have represented them in their full Strength and Beauty, without having recourse to these Foreign Assistances. Our Language sunk under him, and was unequal to that greatness of Soul, which furnished him with such glorious Conceptions.

A second Fault in his Language is, that he often affects a kind of Jingle in his Words, as in the following Passages, and many others:

> *And brought into the* World *a* World *of woe.*
> *. . . Begirt th' Almighty throne*
> Beseeching *or* besieging *. . .*
> *This* tempted *our* attempt *. . .*
> *At one Slight* bound *high overleapt all* bound.[2]

I know there are Figures for this kind of Speech, that some of the greatest Ancients have been guilty of it, and that *Aristotle* himself has given it a place in his Rhetorick among the Beauties of that Art. But as it is in its self poor and trifling, it is I think at present universally exploded by all the Masters of Polite Writing.

The last Fault which I shall take notice of in *Milton's* Stile, is the frequent use of what the Learned call *Technical Words*, or Terms of Art. It is one of the great Beauties of Poetry, to make hard things intelligible, and to deliver what is abstruse of it self in such easy Language as may be understood by ordinary Readers: Besides that the Knowledge of a Poet should rather seem born with him, or inspired than drawn from Books and Systems. I have often wondered how Mr. *Dryden* could translate a Passage out of *Virgil* after the following manner.

> *Tack to the Larboard, and stand off to Sea.*
> *Veer Star-board Sea and Land . . .*[3]

Milton makes use of *Larboard* in the same manner. When he is upon Building he mentions *Doric Pillars, Pilasters, Cornice, Freeze, Architrave*. When he talks of Heavenly Bodies, you meet with *Eccliptick*, and *Eccentric*, the *trepidation, Stars dropping from the Zenith, Rays culminating from the Equator*. To which might be added many Instances of the like kind in several other Arts and Sciences.

---

2. *PL* 9.11, 5.868–69, 1.642, 4.181.
3. Dryden's translation of *Aeneid* 3.412–13.

I shall in my next Papers give an Account of the many particular Beauties in *Milton*, which would have been too long to insert under those general Heads I have already treated of, and with which I intend to conclude this Piece of Criticism.

From Spectator 303 (February 16, 1712)[†]

* * *

But there is no single Passage in the whole Poem worked up to a greater Sublimity, than that wherein his Person [the Devil] is described in those celebrated Lines:

> . . . *He, above the rest*
> *In shape and gesture proudly eminent*
> *Stood like a Tower, &c.*[1]

His Sentiments are every way answerable to his Character, and suitable to a created Being of the most exalted and most depraved Nature. Such is that in which he takes Possession of his Place of Torments.

> . . . *Hail Horrors, hail*
> *Infernal World, and thou profoundest Hell*
> *Receive thy new Possessor, one who brings*
> *A mind not to be changed by place or time.*[2]

And afterwards,

> . . . *Here at least*
> *We shall be free; th' Almighty hath not built*
> *Here for his envy, will not drive us hence:*
> *Here we may reign secure, and in my choice*
> *To reign is worth ambition, tho' in Hell:*
> *Better to reign in Hell, than serve in Heaven.*[3]

Amidst those Impieties which this Enraged Spirit utters in other places of the Poem, the Author has taken care to introduce none that is not big with absurdity, and incapable of shocking a Religious Reader; his Words, as the Poet describes them, bearing only a *Semblance of Worth, not Substance.* He is likewise with great Art described as owning his Adversary to be Almighty. Whatever perverse Interpretation he puts on the Justice, Mercy, and other Attributes of the

---

[†] From *Spectator*, ed. Donald Bond, vol. 3 (Oxford: Clarendon, 1965).
1. *PL* 1.589–91.
2. *PL* 1.250–53.
3. *PL* 1.258–63.

Supreme Being, he frequently confesses his Omnipotence, that being the Perfection he was forced to allow him, and the only Consideration which could support his Pride under the Shame of his Defeat.

Nor must I here omit that beautiful Circumstance of his bursting out in Tears, upon his Survey of those innumerable Spirits whom he had involved in the same Guilt and Ruin with himself.

> . . . He now prepared
> To speak; whereat their doubled ranks they bend
> From wing to wing, and half enclose him round
> With all his Peers: Attention held them mute.
> Thrice he assay'd, and thrice in spite of Scorn
> Tears, such as Angels weep, burst forth . . . [4]

* * *

VOLTAIRE

From Candide (1759)[†]

[Candide and his companion Martin visit the palace of Pococurante ("Cares for Little"), a Venetian nobleman. In the library, Pococurante delivers himself of negative opinions on many great authors. The last author to be entertainingly abused is Milton. But in the numerous inaccuracies of this attack Pococurante lives up to his name. Voltaire is satirizing literary criticism of the day. His own *Essay on Epic Poetry* (1728) praises Milton in the highest terms.]

Seeing a volume of Milton's *Paradise Lost*, Candide asked Pococurante if he did not regard at least this author as a great man. "Who?" said Pococurante, "that barbarian who made a long commentary in ten books of turgid verse on the first chapter of Genesis? That clumsy imitator of the Greeks who disfigured Creation, and who, while Moses showed the Eternal Being producing the world by his word, has the Messiah take a huge pair of compasses out of his heavenly cupboard and trace out his work in advance? Can I possibly esteem an author who spoils both the Hell and the devil of Tasso, who disguises Lucifer sometimes as a toad and sometimes as a pygmy? Who makes him go over a hundred times the same stale arguments and theological disputes? Who takes up in all seriousness a comic episode in Ariosto and makes devils fire off canons in Heaven? Neither I nor anyone else in Italy could take pleasure in

---

4. *PL* 1.615–20.
† From *Romans et contes*, ed. Henri Bénac (Paris: Garnier, 1960), p. 207. Translated by the editor for the first edition of this Norton Critical Edition.

such pathetic extravagances! The union of Sin and Death, and the snakes Sin gives birth to, would cause any man of sensibility to vomit. And the long description of a hospital is good for no one except a gravedigger, or a grave-robber! This poem, which is obscure, bizarre, and disgusting, was despised from its birth in its own country, and I concur."

From Essay upon the Civil Wars of France . . . And also upon the Epick Poetry of the European Nations from Homer to Milton (1727)[†]

*   *   *

What Milton so boldly undertook, he performed with superior strength of judgment, and with an imagination productive of beauties not dreamed of before him. The meanness (if there is any) of some parts of the subject is lost in the immensity of the poetical invention.

*   *   *

I have often admired how barren the subject appears and how fruitful it grows in his hands.

The *Paradise Lost* is the only poem wherein are to be found in a perfect degree that uniformity which satisfies the mind and that variety which pleases the imagination.

*   *   *

The heathens always, the Jews often, and our Christian Priests sometimes, represent God as a tyrant infinitely powerful. But the God of Milton is always a creator, a father, and a judge; nor is his vengeance jarring with his mercy, nor his predeterminations repugnant to the liberty of man. There are the pictures which lift up indeed the soul of the reader. Milton in that point as well as in many others is as far above the ancient poets as the Christian religion is above the heathen fables.

*   *   *

It is observable that in all other poems love is represented as a vice; in Milton only 'tis a virtue. The pictures he draws of it are naked as the persons he speaks of, and as venerable. He removes with a chaste hand the veil which covers everywhere else the enjoyments of that passion. There is softness, tenderness and warmth

† From *Le Bossu & Voltaire on the Epic*, ed. Stuart Curran (Gainesville, Fl.: Scholars' Fascimiles & Reprints, 1970), pp. 105, 107.

without lasciviousness; the poet transports himself and us into that state of innocent happiness in which Adam and Eve continued for a short time.

*   *   *

SAMUEL JOHNSON

From Lives of the English Poets (1779)[†]

From *Milton*

*   *   *

I am now to examine *Paradise Lost*, a poem which, considered with respect to design, may claim the first place, and with respect to performance the second, among the productions of the human mind.

By the general consent of criticks the first praise of genius is due to the writer of an epick poem, as it requires an assemblage of all the powers which are singly sufficient for other compositions. Poetry is the art of uniting pleasure with truth, by calling imagination to the help of reason. Epick poetry undertakes to teach the most important truths by the most pleasing precepts, and therefore relates some great event in the most affecting manner. History must supply the writer with the rudiments of narration, which he must improve and exalt by a nobler art, must animate by dramatick energy, and diversify by retrospection and anticipation; morality must teach him the exact bounds and different shades of vice and virtue; from policy and the practice of life he has to learn the discriminations of character and the tendency of the passions, either single or combined; and physiology must supply him with illustrations and images. To put these materials to poetical use is required an imagination capable of painting nature and realizing fiction. Nor is he yet a poet till he has attained the whole extension of his language, distinguished all the delicacies of phrase, and all the colours of words, and learned to adjust their different sounds to all the varieties of metrical modulation.

Bossu[1] is of opinion that the poet's first work is to find a *moral*, which his fable is afterwards to illustrate and establish. This seems

---

† From *Lives of the English Poets*, ed. George Birkbeck Hill (Oxford: Clarendon Press, 1905): 1:170–72, 174–75, 177–78, 183–86, 189–90, 194.
1. René Le Bossu (1631–1680), French critic and author of *Traité du poème épique* (1675, *Treatise of the Epic Poem*).

to have been the process only of Milton: the moral of other poems is incidental and consequent; in Milton's only it is essential and intrinsick. His purpose was the most useful and the most arduous: 'to vindicate the ways of God to man'; to shew the reasonableness of religion, and the necessity of obedience to the Divine Law.

*   *   *

The subject of an epick poem is naturally an event of great importance. That of Milton is not the destruction of a city, the conduct of a colony, or the foundation of an empire. His subject is the fate of worlds, the revolutions of heaven and of earth; rebellion against the Supreme King raised by the highest order of created beings; the overthrow of their host and the punishment of their crime; the creation of a new race of reasonable creatures; their original happiness and innocence, their forfeiture of immortality, and their restoration to hope and peace.

*   *   *

It is justly remarked by Addison that this poem has, by the nature of its subject, the advantage above all others, that it is universally and perpetually interesting.[2] All mankind will, through all ages, bear the same relation to Adam and to Eve, and must partake of that good and evil which extend to themselves.

*   *   *

The thoughts which are occasionally called forth in the progress are such as could only be produced by an imagination in the highest degree fervid and active, to which materials were supplied by incessant study and unlimited curiosity. The heat of Milton's mind might be said to sublimate his learning, to throw off into his work the spirit of science, unmingled with its grosser parts.

*   *   *The characteristick quality of his poem is sublimity. He sometimes descends to the elegant, but his element is the great. He can occasionally invest himself with grace; but his natural port is gigantick loftiness.[3] He can please when pleasure is required; but it is his peculiar power to astonish.

He seems to have been well acquainted with his own genius, and to know what it was that Nature had bestowed upon him more bountifully than upon others; the power of displaying the vast, illuminating the splendid, enforcing the awful, darkening the gloomy,

---

2. See Joseph Addison, *Spectator* 267 (January 5, 1712).
3. Algarotti terms it *gigantesca sublimità Miltoniana* [Johnson's note]. Francesco Algarotti (1712–1764), Italian art connoisseur; the quotation is from *Il Newtonianismo per le dame* (1737, *Newtonianism for Ladies*).

and aggravating the dreadful: he therefore chose a subject on which too much could not be said, on which he might tire his fancy without the censure of extravagance.

The appearances of nature and the occurrences of life did not satiate his appetite of greatness. To paint things as they are requires a minute attention, and employs the memory rather than the fancy. Milton's delight was to sport in the wide regions of possibility; reality was a scene too narrow for his mind. He sent his faculties out upon discovery, into worlds where only imagination can travel, and delighted to form new modes of existence, and furnish sentiment and action to superior beings, to trace the counsels of hell, or accompany the choirs of heaven.

But he could not be always in other worlds: he must sometimes revisit earth, and tell of things visible and known. When he cannot raise wonder by the sublimity of his mind he gives delight by its fertility.

*　　*　　*

But original deficience cannot be supplied. The want of human interest is always felt. *Paradise Lost* is one of the books which the reader admires and lays down, and forgets to take up again. None ever wished it longer than it is. Its perusal is a duty rather than a pleasure. We read Milton for instruction, retire harassed and overburdened, and look elsewhere for recreation; we desert our master, and seek for companions.

*　　*　　*

Milton's allegory of Sin and Death is undoubtedly faulty. Sin is indeed the mother of Death, and may be allowed to be the portress of hell; but when they stop the journey of Satan, a journey described as real, and when Death offers him battle, the allegory is broken. That Sin and Death should have shewn the way to hell might have been allowed; but they cannot facilitate the passage by building a bridge, because the difficulty of Satan's passage is described as real and sensible, and the bridge ought to be only figurative. The hell assigned to the rebellious spirits is described as not less local than the residence of man. It is placed in some distant part of space, separated from the regions of harmony and order by a chaotick waste and an unoccupied vacuity; but Sin and Death worked up a 'mole of aggregated soil,' cemented with asphaltus;[4] a work too bulky for ideal architects.

---

4. See *PL* 10.293–305.

This unskilful allegory appears to me one of the greatest faults of the poem; and to this there was no temptation, but the author's opinion of its beauty.

* * *

Through all his greater works there prevails an uniform peculiarity of *Diction*, a mode and cast of expression which bears little resemblance to that of any former writer, and which is so far removed from common use that an unlearned reader when he first opens his book finds himself surprised by a new language.

This novelty has been, by those who can find nothing wrong in Milton, imputed to his laborious endeavours after words suitable to the grandeur of his ideas. 'Our language,' says Addison, 'sunk under him.'[5] But the truth is, that both in prose and verse, he had formed his style by a perverse and pedantick principle. He was desirous to use English words with a foreign idiom. This in all his prose is discovered and condemned, for there judgment operates freely, neither softened by the beauty nor awed by the dignity of his thoughts; but such is the power of his poetry that his call is obeyed without resistance, the reader feels himself in captivity to a higher and nobler mind, and criticism sinks in admiration.

* * *

The highest praise of genius is original invention. Milton cannot be said to have contrived the structure of an epick poem, and therefore owes reverence to that vigour and amplitude of mind to which all generations must be indebted for the art of poetical narration, for the texture of the fable, the variation of incidents, the interposition of dialogue, and all the stratagems that surprise and enchain attention. But of all the borrowers from Homer Milton is perhaps the least indebted. He was naturally a thinker for himself, confident of his own abilities and disdainful of help or hindrance; he did not refuse admission to the thoughts or images of his predecessors, but he did not seek them. From his contemporaries he neither courted nor received support; there is in his writings nothing by which the pride of other authors might be gratified or favour gained, no exchange of praise nor solicitation of support. His great works were performed under discountenance and in blindness, but difficulties vanished at his touch; he was born for whatever is arduous; and his work is not the greatest of heroick poems, only because it is not the first.

5. Joseph Addison, *Spectator* 297 (February 9, 1712); see p. **401**, above.

FRANÇOIS-RENÉ, VICOMTE DE CHATEAUBRIAND

From Sketches of English Literature (1836)[†]

✳   ✳   ✳

Who ever wrote like this? What poet ever spoke such language? How miserable seem all modern compositions beside these strong and magnificent conceptions!

✳   ✳   ✳

There is, in the poem, something which at first sight appears unaccountable: the infernal republic attempts to overthrow the celestial monarchy; Milton, though his sentiments are wholly republican, invariably ascribes justice and victory to the Almighty! The reason of this is that the poet was swayed by his religious opinions. In accordance with the Independents, he desired a theocratic republic, a hierarchical liberty, subject only to the dominion of Heaven; he had represented Cromwell as the lieutenant-general of God and the protector of the republic:—

> Cromwell, our chief of men, who, through a cloud
> Not of war only, but detractions rude,
> Guided by faith and matchless fortitude,
> To peace and truth thy glorious way hast plough'd,
> And on the neck of crowned fortune proud
> Hast rear'd God's trophies, and his works pursued,
> While Darwen stream, with blood of Scots imbrued,
> And Dunbar field resounds thy praises loud,
> And Worcester's laureat wreath. Yet much remains
> To conquer still; peace hath her victories
> No less renown'd than war: new foes arise
> Threat'ning to bind our souls, with secular chains:
> Help us to save free conscience from the paw
> Of hireling wolves, whose gospel is their maw.[1]

Satan and his angels were pictured to Milton's imagination by the proud Presbyterians, who refused to submit to the *Saints*, Milton's own faction, of which he hailed the inspired Cromwell as the godly leader.

[†] From *Sketches of English Literature; with Considerations on the Spirit of the Times, Men, and Revolutions* (London: Henry Colburn, 1836), 2:130–31, 147–49.

[1]. Milton, Sonnet 16 (published 1694). Milton names sites of Cromwell's victories over the Scottish army (Darwen stream, August 1648; Dunbar field, September 1650) and Charles II (Worcester, September 1651).

We discern in Milton a man of troubled spirit; still under the influence of revolutionary scenes and passions, he stood erect after the downfall of the revolution which had fled to him for shelter, and palpitated in his bosom. But the earnestness of that revolution overpowers him; religious gravity forms the counterpoise to his political agitations. Stunned, however, at the overthrow of his fondest illusions, at the dissipation of his dreams of liberty, he knows not which way to turn, but remains in a state of perplexity, even respecting religious truth.

*   *   *

WILLIAM BLAKE

From The Marriage of Heaven and Hell (1793)†

From *The Voice of the Devil* (Plates 5–6)

*   *   *

Those who restrain desire, do so because theirs is weak enough to be restrained; and the restrainer or Reason usurps its place & governs the unwilling.

And being restrain'd, it by degrees becomes passive, till it is only the shadow of desire.

The history of this is written in Paradise Lost, & the Governor or Reason is call'd Messiah.

And the original Archangel, or possessor of the command of the heavenly host, is call'd the Devil or Satan, and his children are call'd Sin & Death.

But in the Book of Job, Milton's Messiah is call'd Satan.

For this history has been adopted by both parties.

It indeed appear'd to reason as if Desire was cast out, but the Devil's account is, that the Messiah fell, & formed a heaven of what he stole from the Abyss.

This is shewn in the Gospel, where he prays to the Father to send the comforter, or Desire, that Reason may have Ideas to build on, the Jehovah of the Bible being no other than [the Devil *del.*] he who dwells in flaming fire.

Know that after Christ's death, he became Jehovah.

But in Milton, the Father is Destiny, the Son, a Ratio of the five senses, & the Holy-ghost, Vacuum!

† From *William Blake's Writings*, ed. G. E. Bentley, Jr. (Oxford: Clarendon, 1978), 1:292.

Note: The reason Milton wrote in fetters when he wrote of Angels & God, and at liberty when of Devils & Hell, is because he was a true Poet and of the Devil's party without knowing it.

*   *   *

OLAUDAH EQUIANO

From The Interesting Narrative (1789)[†]

*   *   *

* * * [T]he next morning, the 30th of December, the wind being brisk and easterly, the Œolus frigate, which was to escort the convoy, made a signal for sailing. All the ships then got up their anchors; and, before any of my friends had an opportunity to come off to my relief, to my inexpressible anguish our ship had got under way. What tumultuous emotions agitated my soul when the convoy got under sail, and I a prisoner on board, now without hope! I kept my swimming eyes upon the land in a state of unutterable grief; not knowing what to do, and despairing how to help myself. While my mind was in this situation the fleet sailed on, and in one day's time I lost sight of the wished-for land. In the first expressions of my grief I reproached my fate, and wished I had never been born. I was ready to curse the tide that bore us, the gale that wafted my prison, and even the ship that conducted us; and I called on death to relieve me from the horrors I felt and dreaded, that I might be in that place

> Where slaves are free, and men oppress no more.
> Fool that I was, inur'd so long to pain,
> To trust to hope, or dream of joy again.[1]

*   *   *

The turbulence of my emotions however naturally gave way to calmer thoughts, and I soon perceived what fate had decreed no mortal on earth could prevent. The convoy sailed on without any accident, with a pleasant gale and smooth sea, for six weeks, till

---

[†] From *The Interesting Narrative of the Life of Olaudah Equiano, or Gustavus Vassa, The African, Written by Himself,* ed. Werner Sollors (New York: W. W. Norton, 2001), pp. 72–73. Copyright © 2001 by W. W. Norton & Company, Inc. Used by permission of W. W. Norton & Company, Inc.

1. From "The Dying Negro," a poem originally published in 1773. Perhaps it may not be deemed impertinent here to add that this elegant and pathetic little poem was occasioned, as appears by the advertisement prefixed to it, by the following incident. "A black, who, a few days before had run away from his master, and got himself christened, with intent to marry a white woman his fellow-servant, being taken and sent on board a ship in the Thames, took an opportunity of shooting himself through the head" [*Equiano's note*]. Only the first three lines of Thomas Day and John Bicknell's poem are included here.

February, when one morning the Œolus ran down a brig, one of the convoy, and she instantly went down and was ingulfed in the dark recesses of the ocean. The convoy was immediately thrown into great confusion till it was day-light; and the Œolus was illumined with lights to prevent any farther mischief. On the 13th of February 1763, from the mast-head, we descried our destined island Montserrat;[2] and soon after I beheld those

> Regions of sorrow, doleful shades, where peace
> And rest can rarely [never] dwell. Hope never comes
> That comes to all, but torture without end
> Still urges.[3]

At the sight of this land of bondage, a fresh horror ran through all my frame, and chilled me to the heart. My former slavery now rose in dreadful review to my mind, and displayed nothing but misery, stripes,[4] and chains; and, in the first paroxysm of my grief, I called upon God's thunder, and his avenging power, to direct the stroke of death to me, rather than permit me to become a slave, and be sold from lord to lord.

MARY WOLLSTONECRAFT

From A Vindication of the Rights of Woman (1792)[†]

*   *   *

If then women are not a swarm of ephemeron triflers, why should they be kept in ignorance under the specious name of innocence? Men complain, and with reason, of the follies and caprices of our sex, when they do not keenly satirize our headstrong passions and groveling vices.—Behold, I should answer, the natural effect of ignorance! The mind will ever be unstable that has only prejudices to rest on, and the current will run with destructive fury when there are no barriers to break its force. Women are told from their infancy, and taught by the example of their mothers, that a little knowledge of human weakness, justly termed cunning, softness of temper, *outward* obedience, and a scrupulous attention to a puerile kind of propriety, will obtain for them the protection of man; and should they be beautiful, every thing else is needless, for, at least, twenty years of their lives.

---

2. One of the Leeward Islands in the Lesser Antilles, West Indies.
3. From Milton, *PL* 1.65–68.
4. Flogging.
† From *A Vindication of the Rights of Woman*, ed. Deidre Shauna Lynch (New York: W. W. Norton, 2009), pp. 22–24, 36–38. Copyright © 2009, 1988, 1975, by W. W. Norton. Used by permission of W. W. Norton & Company, Inc.

Thus Milton describes our first frail mother; though when he tells us that women are formed for softness and sweet attractive grace,[1] I cannot comprehend his meaning, unless, in the true Mahometan strain, he meant to deprive us of souls,[2] and insinuate that we were beings only designed by sweet attractive grace, and docile blind obedience, to gratify the senses of man when he can no longer soar on the wing of contemplation.

How grossly do they insult us who thus advise us only to render ourselves gentle, domestic brutes! For instance, the winning softness so warmly, and frequently, recommended, that governs by obeying. What childish expressions, and how insignificant is the being—can it be an immortal one? who will condescend to govern by such sinister methods! 'Certainly,' says Lord Bacon, 'man is of kin to the beasts by his body; and if he be not of kin to God by his spirit, he is a base and ignoble creature!'[3] Men, indeed, appear to me to act in a very unphilosophical manner when they try to secure the good conduct of women by attempting to keep them always in a state of childhood. Rousseau was more consistent when he wished to stop the progress of reason in both sexes, for if men eat of the tree of knowledge, women will come in for a taste; but, from the imperfect cultivation which their understandings now receive, they only attain a knowledge of evil.

Children, I grant, should be innocent; but when the epithet is applied to men, or women, it is but a civil term for weakness. For if it be allowed that women were destined by Providence to acquire human virtues, and by the exercise of their understandings, that stability of character which is the firmest ground to rest our future hopes upon, they must be permitted to turn to the fountain of light, and not forced to shape their course by the twinkling of a mere satellite. Milton, I grant, was of a very different opinion; for he only bends to the indefeasible right of beauty, though it would be difficult to render two passages which I now mean to contrast, consistent. But into similar inconsistencies are great men often led by their senses.

> 'To whom thus Eve with *perfect beauty* adorn'd.
> 'My Author and Disposer, what thou bidst
> '*Unargued* I obey; So God ordains;
> 'God is *thy law, thou mine:* to know no more
> 'Is Woman's *happiest* knowledge and her *praise.*[4]

These are exactly the arguments that I have used to children; but I have added, your reason is now gaining strength, and, till it arrives

---

1. *PL* 4.297–99: "For contemplation he and valor formed, / For softness she and sweet attractive grace; / He for God only, she for God in him."
2. The Prophet Muhammad was commonly thought to have claimed that women lacked souls.
3. Francis Bacon, Essay XVI, "Of Atheism" (1612).
4. *PL* 4.634–38. The italics are Wollstonecraft's.

at some degree of maturity, you must look up to me for advice—
then you ought to *think,* and only rely on God.

Yet in the following lines Milton seems to coincide with me;
when he makes Adam thus expostulate with his Maker.

> 'Hast thou not made me here thy substitute,
> 'And these inferior far beneath me set?
> 'Among *unequals* what society
> 'Can sort, what harmony or true delight?
> 'Which must be mutual, in proportion due
> 'Giv'n and receiv'd; but in *disparity*
> 'The one intense, the other still remiss
> 'Cannot well suit with either, but soon prove
> 'Tedious alike: of *fellowship* I speak
> 'Such as I seek, fit to participate
> 'All rational delight[5]—

In treating, therefore, of the manners of women, let us, disregarding sensual arguments, trace what we should endeavour to
make them in order to co-operate, if the expression be not too bold,
with the supreme Being.

*   *   *

Gentleness of manners, forbearance and long-suffering, are such
amiable Godlike qualities, that in sublime poetic strains the Deity
has been invested with them; and, perhaps, no representation of his
goodness so strongly fastens on the human affections as those that
represent him abundant in mercy and willing to pardon.[6] Gentleness, considered in this point of view, bears on its front all the
characteristics of grandeur, combined with the winning graces of
condescension; but what a different aspect it assumes when it is the
submissive demeanour of dependence, the support of weakness that
loves, because it wants protection; and is forbearing, because it must
silently endure injuries; smiling under the lash at which it dare not
snarl. Abject as this picture appears, it is the portrait of an accomplished woman, according to the received opinion of female excellence, separated by specious reasoners from human excellence. Or,
they[7] kindly restore the rib, and make one moral being of a man and
woman; not forgetting to give her all the 'submissive charms.'[8]

---

5. *PL.* 8.381–92. The italics are Wollstonecraft's.
6. Isaiah 55:7: "And he will have mercy upon him; and to our God, for he will abundantly
   pardon."
7. "Vide Rousseau, and Swedenborg" [*Wollstonecraft's note*]. Later in her book, Wollstonecraft quotes a passage from Book 5 of *Émile* in which Rousseau denies independent moral agency to women. The Swedish mystic Emmanuel Swedenborg (1688–1772)
   believed that in the afterlife each married couple would form a single angel, with the
   wife contributing her capacity for love and the husband his wisdom.
8. *PL* 4.497–99: "he in delight / Both of her beauty and submissive charms / Smiled with
   superior love."

How women are to exist in that state where there is to be neither marrying nor giving in marriage, we are not told.[9] For though moralists have agreed that the tenor of life seems to prove that *man* is prepared by various circumstances for a future state, they constantly concur in advising *woman* only to provide for the present. Gentleness, docility, and a spaniel-like affection are, on this ground, consistently recommended as the cardinal virtues of the sex; and, disregarding the arbitrary economy of nature, one writer has declared that it is masculine for a woman to be melancholy.[1] She was created to be the toy of man, his rattle, and it must jingle in his ears whenever, dismissing reason, he chooses to be amused.

To recommend gentleness, indeed, on a broad basis is strictly philosophical. A frail being should labour to be gentle. But when forbearance confounds right and wrong, it ceases to be a virtue; and, however convenient it may be found in a companion—that companion will ever be considered as an inferior, and only inspire a vapid tenderness, which easily degenerates into contempt. Still, if advice could really make a being gentle, whose natural disposition admitted not of such a fine polish, something towards the advancement of order would be attained; but if, as might quickly be demonstrated, only affectation be produced by this indiscriminate counsel, which throws a stumbling-block in the way of gradual improvement, and true melioration of temper, the sex is not much benefited by sacrificing solid virtues to the attainment of superficial graces, though for a few years they may procure the individuals regal sway.

As a philosopher, I read with indignation the plausible epithets which men use to soften their insults; and, as a moralist, I ask what is meant by such heterogeneous associations, as fair defects, amiable weaknesses, &c.?[2] If there be but one criterion of morals, but one archetype for man, women appear to be suspended by destiny, according to the vulgar tale of Mahomet's coffin;[3] they have neither the unerring instinct of brutes, nor are allowed to fix the eye of reason on a perfect model. They were made to be loved, and must not aim at respect, lest they should be hunted out of society as masculine.

*   *   *

9. An echo of Jesus' account of the resurrection in Matthew 22:30.
1. Perhaps a recollection of Edmund Burke's *Philosophical Enquiry into the Origins of Our Ideas of the Sublime and the Beautiful* (1757). In attempting to distinguish the aesthetic category of "the beautiful" from that of "the sublime," Burke devotes many pages to outlining his notions of the distinctions that separate femininity from masculinity.
2. *PL* 10.891–92: "This fair defect / Of nature"; and Alexander Pope, "Of the Characters of Women" (1735), line 44: "Fine by defect, and delicately weak."
3. Wollstonecraft refers to a discredited European legend maintaining that at Muhammad's tomb in Medina giant magnets were used to suspend his coffin in midair.

WILLIAM WORDSWORTH

London, 1802[†]

Milton! thou should'st be living at this hour:
England hath need of thee: she is a fen
Of stagnant waters: altar, sword, and pen,
Fireside, the heroic wealth of hall and bower,
Have forfeited their ancient English dower   5
Of inward happiness. We are selfish men;
Oh! raise us up, return to us again;
And give us manners, virtue, freedom, power.
Thy soul was like a Star, and dwelt apart:
Thou hadst a voice whose sound was like the sea: 10
Pure as the naked heavens, majestic, free,
So didst thou travel on life's common way
In cheerful godliness; and yet thy heart
The lowliest duties on itself[1] did lay.

SAMUEL TAYLOR COLERIDGE

From Lecture 4 (March 4, 1819)[‡]

*   *   *

In the mind itself purity, piety, an imagination to which neither the
Past nor the Present were interesting except as far as they called
forth and embraced the great Ideal, in which and for which he
lived, a keen love of Truth which after many weary pursuits found
an harbour in a sublime listening to the low still voice in his own
spirit, and as keen a love of his Country which after disappointment, still more depressive at once expanded and sobered into a
love of Man as the Probationer of Immortality, these were, these
alone could be, the conditions under which such a work could be
conceived, and accomplished.

*   *   *

Compared with the Iliad, many of the books of which might
change places without any injury to the thread of the story—and

---

† From *William Wordsworth,* ed. Stephen Gill (Oxford: Oxford University Press, 1984),
    p. 136.
1. Wordsworth later changed *itself* to *herself.* I follow Nicholas Halmi in retaining the for-
    mer. See *Wordsworth's Poetry and Prose* (New York: W.W. Norton, 2014), p. 410 n. 1.
‡ From *The Collected Works of Samuel Taylor Coleridge,* vol. 5, *Lectures, 1808–1819: On Lit-
    erature,* ed. R. A. Foakes (Princeton, N.J.: Princeton University Press, 1987), 2:387–88.

2ndly—with both the Iliad and more or less in all epic Poems whose subjects are from History, they have no *rounded* conclusion—they remain after all but a single chapter from the volume of History tho' an ornamented Chapter—. In Homer too the importance of his subject, namely, as the first effort of confederated Greece, an after thought of the critics—& the interest, such as it is, derived from the event as distinguished from the manner of representing these, languid to all but Greeks—The superiority of the Paradise Lost is obvious, but not dwelt on because it may be attributed to Christianity itself, tho' in this instance it comprehends the whole Mahometan World as well as Xtndom[1]—and as the origin of evil, and the combat of Evil and Good, a matter of such interest to all mankind as to form the basis of all religions, and the true occasion of all Philosophy.

—Next the exquisite simplicity. It and it alone really possesses the Beginning, Middle, and End—the totality of a Poem or circle as distinguished from the *ab ovo* birth[2], parentage, &c or strait line of History.

* * *

From Unassigned Lecture Notes[†]

[*Milton and* Paradise Lost]

* * *

The character of Satan is pride and sensual indulgence, finding in self the sole motive of action. It is the character so often seen *in little* on the political stage. It exhibits all the restlessness, temerity, and cunning which have marked the mighty hunters of mankind from Nimrod to Napoleon. The common fascination of men is, that these great men, as they are called, must act from some great motive. Milton has carefully marked in his Satan the intense selfishness, the alcohol of egotism, which would rather reign in hell than serve in heaven. To place this lust of self in opposition to denial of self or duty, and to show what exertions it would make, and what pains endure to accomplish its end, is Milton's particular object in the character of Satan. But around this character he has thrown a

---

1. *Xtndom.* Christendom. The "X" is the Greek letter *chi*, the initial of "Christ": "*Christos*" the anointed—the title of a king.
2. See note to The Argument, p. 4.
† From *The Collected Works of Samuel Taylor Coleridge*, vol. 5, *Lectures, 1808–1819: On Literature.* ed. R. A. Foakes (Princeton, N.J.: Princeton University Press, 1987), 2:427–28.

singularity of daring, a grandeur of sufferance, and a ruined splendour, which constitute the very height of poetic sublimity.

*   *   *

   No one can rise from the perusal of this immortal poem without
a deep sense of the grandeur and the purity of Milton's soul, or
without feeling how susceptible of domestic enjoyments he really
was, notwithstanding the discomforts which actually resulted from
an apparently unhappy choice in marriage. He was, as every truly
great poet has ever been, a good man; but finding it impossible to
realize his own aspirations, either in religion, or politics, or society,
he gave up his heart to the living spirit and light within him, and
avenged himself on the world by enriching it with this record of his
own transcendent ideal.

From Table Talk[†]

[*Milton's Egotism, August 18, 1833*]

In the Paradise Lost—indeed in every one of his poems—it is Milton
himself whom you see; his Satan, his Adam, his Raphael, almost
his Eve—are all John Milton; and it is a sense of this intense egotism
that gives me the greatest pleasure in reading Milton's works. The
egotism of such a man is a revelation of spirit.

GEORGE GORDON, LORD BYRON

From Don Juan (1819–24)[‡]

From *Dedication*

X

If, fallen in evil days on evil tongues,
Milton appeal'd to the Avenger, Time,
If Time, the Avenger, execrates his wrongs,
And makes the word 'Miltonic' mean '*sublime*,'
He deign'd not to belie his soul in songs,
Nor turn his very talent to a crime;

---

† From *Table Talk,* ed. Carl Woodring (Princeton, N.J.: Princeton University Press,
1990), p. 636.
‡ From *Poetical Works*, ed. John Jump, 2nd ed. (Oxford: Oxford University Press, 1970).

He did not loathe the Sire to laud the Son,
But closed the tyrant-hater he begun.

XI

Think'st thou, could he—the blind Old Man—arise,
Like Samuel from the grave,[1] to freeze once more
The blood of monarchs with his prophecies,
Or be alive again—again all hoar
With time and trials, and those helpless eyes,
And heartless daughters—worn—and pale—and poor;
Would he adore a sultan? he obey
The intellectual eunuch Castlereagh?[2]

From *Canto III*

XCI

Milton's the prince of poets—so we say;
A little heavy, but no less divine:
An independent being in his day—
Learn'd, pious, temperate in love and wine;
But, his life falling into Johnson's way,[3]
We're told this great high priest of all the Nine
Was whipt at college—a harsh sire—odd spouse,
For the first Mrs. Milton left his house.

PERCY BYSSHE SHELLEY

From the preface to Prometheus Unbound (1820)[†]

*   *   *

The only imaginary being resembling in any degree Prometheus,
is Satan; and Prometheus is, in my judgement, a more poetical
character than Satan because, in addition to courage and majesty
and firm and patient opposition to omnipotent force, he is

---

1. For the summoning of the dead prophet Samuel at the behest of Saul, see 1 Samuel 28.
2. Robert Stewart, Viscount Castlereagh (1767–1822), British foreign secretary and leader of the House of Commons; he was attacked by Byron and others for his repressive domestic policies.
3. A reference to Samuel Johnson's *Life of Milton* (1779); see above.
† The following selections are from *Shelley's Poetry and Prose*, ed. Donald H. Reiman and Neil Fraistat, 2nd ed. (New York: Norton, 2002), pp. 206–7, 526–27.

susceptible of being described as exempt from the taints of ambition, envy, revenge, and a desire for personal aggrandisement, which in the Hero of *Paradise Lost,* interfere with the interest. The character of Satan engenders in the mind a pernicious casuistry which leads us to weigh his faults with his wrongs and to excuse the former because the latter exceed all measure. In the minds of those who consider that magnificent fiction with a religious feeling, it engenders something worse. But Prometheus is, as it were, the type of the highest perfection of moral and intellectual nature, impelled by the purest and the truest motives to the best and noblest ends.

From A Defence of Poetry (1821)

* * *

The poetry of Dante may be considered as the bridge thrown over the stream of time, which unites the modern and antient world. The distorted notions of invisible things which Dante and his rival Milton have idealized, are merely the mask and the mantle in which these great poets walk through eternity enveloped and disguised. It is a difficult question to determine how far they were conscious of the distinction which must have subsisted in their minds between their own creeds and that of the people. Dante at least appears to wish to mark the full extent of it by placing Riphæaus, whom Virgil calls *justissimus unus,*[1] in Paradise, and observing a most heretical caprice in his distribution of rewards and punishments. And Milton's poem contains within itself a philosophical refutation of that system of which, by a strange and natural antithesis, it has been a chief popular support. Nothing can exceed the energy and magnificence of the character of Satan as expressed in Paradise Lost. It is a mistake to suppose that he could ever have been intended for the popular personification of evil. Implacable hate, patient cunning, and a sleepless refinement of device to inflict the extremest anguish on an enemy, these things are evil; and although venial in a slave are not to be forgiven in a tyrant; although redeemed by much that ennobles his defeat in one subdued, are marked by all that dishonours his conquest in the victor. Milton's Devil as a moral being is as far superior to his God as one who perseveres in some purpose which he has conceived to be excellent in spite of adversity and torture, is to one who in the cold security of undoubted triumph inflicts the most horrible revenge upon his enemy, not from any

1. The very justest [among the Trojans]; Virgil, *Aeneid* 2.426–27. See Dante, *Paradiso* 20.68.

mistaken notion of inducing him to repent of a perseverance in enmity, but with the alleged design of exasperating him to deserve new torments. Milton has so far violated the popular creed (if this shall be judged to be a violation) as to have alleged no superiority of moral virtue to his God over his Devil. And this bold neglect of a direct moral purpose is the most decisive proof of the supremacy of Milton's genius. He mingled as it were the elements of human nature, as colours upon a single pallet, and arranged them into the composition of his great picture according to the laws of epic truth; that is, according to the laws of that principle by which a series of actions of the external universe and of intelligent and ethical beings is calculated to excite the sympathy of succeeding generations of mankind. The Divina Commedia and Paradise Lost have conferred upon modern mythology a systematic form; and when change and time shall have added one more superstition to the mass of those which have arisen and decayed upon the earth, commentators will be learnedly employed in elucidating the religion of ancestral Europe, only not utterly forgotten because it will have been stamped with the eternity of genius.

* * *

WALTER SAVAGE LANDOR

From Imaginary Conversations (1846)[†]

* * *

Southey. In the *Paradise Lost* no principal character seems to have been intended. There is neither truth nor wit however in saying that Satan is hero of the piece, unless, as is usually the case in human life, he is the greatest hero who gives the widest sway to the worst passions. It is Adam who acts and suffers most, and on whom the consequences have most influence. This constitutes him the main character; although Eve is the more interesting, Satan the more energetic, and on whom the greater force of poetry is displayed. The Creator and his angels are quite secondary.

Landor. Must we not confess that every epic hitherto has been defective in plan; and even that each, until the time of Tasso, was more so than its predecessors? Such stupendous genius, so much fancy, so much eloquence, so much vigor of intellect, never were

† From *The Works of Walter Savage Landor*, 2 vols. (London: Edward Moxon, 1846), 2:60, 64, 66, 72–73, 74.

united as in *Paradise Lost*. Yet it is neither so correct nor so varied as the *Iliad*, nor, however important the action, so interesting. The moral itself is the reason why it wearies even those who insist on the necessity of it. Founded on an event believed by nearly all nations, certainly by all who read the poem, it lays down a principle which concerns every man's welfare, and a fact which every man's experience confirms: that great and irremediable misery may arise from apparently small offences. But will any one say that, in a poetical view, our certainty of moral truth in this position is an equivalent for the uncertainty *which* of the agents is what critics call the hero of the piece?

*　*　*

> Yielded with coy submission, modest pride,
> And sweet, reluctant, amorous delay.[1]

I would rather have written these two lines than all the poetry that has been written since Milton's time in all the regions of the earth. We shall see again things equal in their way to the best of them; but here the sweetest of images and sentiments is seized and carried far away from all pursuers. Never tell me, what I think is already on your lips, that the golden tresses in their wanton ringlets implied nothing like subjection.

*　*　*

Southey. It appears then on record that the first overt crime of the refractory angels was *punning*:[2] they fell rapidly after that.

*　*　*

Landor. My ear, I confess it, is dissatisfied with everything for days and weeks after the harmony of *Paradise Lost*. Leaving this magnificent temple, I am hardly to be pacified by the fairy-built chambers, the rich cupboards of embossed plate, and the omnigenous images of Shakspeare.

*　*　*

After I have been reading the *Paradise Lost,* I can take up no other poet with satisfaction. I seem to have left the music of Handel for the music of the streets, or at best for drums and fifes. Although in Shakspeare there are occasional bursts of harmony no less sublime; yet, if there were many such in continuation, it would be

1. *PL* 4.310–11.
2. A reference to *PL* 5.869, "Beseeching or besieging"; and *PL* 6.559–67 n.

hurtful, not only in comedy, but also in tragedy. The greater part should be equable and conversational. For, if the excitement were the same at the beginning, the middle, and the end; if, consequently (as must be the case), the language and versification were equally elevated throughout,—any long poem would be a bad one, and, worst of all, a drama. In our English heroic verse, such as Milton has composed it, there is a much greater variety of feet, of movement, of musical notes and bars, than in the Greek heroic; and the final sounds are incomparably more diversified. My predilection in youth was on the side of Homer; for I had read the *Iliad* twice, and the *Odyssea* once, before the *Paradise Lost*. Averse as I am to everything relating to theology, and especially to the view of it thrown open by this poem, I recur to it incessantly as the noblest specimen in the world of eloquence, harmony, and genius.

*   *   *

A rib of Shakspeare would have made a Milton; the same portion of Milton, all poets born ever since.

*   *   *

VICTOR HUGO

From *Cromwell* (1827)[†]

From *Act 3, Scene 2*

MILTON, *speaking to himself.*

The future is my judge and will understand my Eve, falling, as in a sweet dream, into the night of Hell. The future will understand my Adam, who is guilty, yet good. And the future will understand my indomitable archangel, who is proud of reigning over his own eternity: magnificent in his despair and in his very madness profound. See! He rises from the lake of fire and with his immense wing beats down the flames! Milton shall live in his own thoughts and console himself there. As I silently brood over my audacious, unheard-of design, an ardent genius flames in my breast. Yes! I dare to emulate the Creator Supreme. Through the power of my own words I shall create a whole world: my own Heaven, my own Hell, my own Earth.

---

† From *Cromwell*, ed. Annie Ubersfeld (Paris: Garnier-Flammarion, 1968), pp. 262–63. Translated by the editor for the first edition of this Norton Critical Edition.

ALFRED, LORD TENNYSON

Milton (1863)†

O mighty-mouth'd inventor of harmonies,
O skill'd to sing of Time or Eternity,
    God-gifted organ-voice of England,
        Milton, a name to resound for ages;
Whose Titan angels, Gabriel, Abdiel,   5
Starr'd from Jehovah's gorgeous armouries,
    Tower, as the deep-domed empyrean
        Rings to the roar of an angel onset—
Me rather all that bowery loneliness,
The brooks of Eden mazily murmuring,   10
    And bloom profuse and cedar arches
        Charm, as a wanderer out in ocean,
Where some refulgent sunset of India
Streams o'er a rich ambrosial ocean isle,
    And crimson-hued the stately palm-woods   15
        Whisper in odorous heights of even.

MATTHEW ARNOLD

From Milton (1888)‡

*   *   *

Milton, from one end of *Paradise Lost* to the other, is in his diction and rhythm constantly a great artist in the great style.

*   *   *

That Milton, of all our English race, is by his diction and rhythm the one artist of the highest rank in the great style whom we have; this I take as requiring no discussion, this I take as certain.

The mighty power of poetry and art is generally admitted. But where the soul of this power, of this power at its best, chiefly resides, very many of us fail to see. It resides chiefly in the refining and elevation wrought in us by the high and rare excellence of the great style. We may feel the effect without being able to give ourselves clear account of its cause, but the thing is so. Now, no race needs the

---

† From *The Poems of Tennyson*, ed. Christopher Ricks (Harlow, Essex: Longman, 1987), p. 652.
‡ From *Essays in Criticism*, Second Series (London: Macmillan, 1888), pp. 62–66.

influences mentioned, the influences of refining and elevation, more than ours; and in poetry and art our grand source for them is Milton.

To what does he owe this supreme distinction? To nature first and foremost, to that bent of nature for inequality which to the worshippers of the average man is so unacceptable; to a gift, a divine favour. 'The older one grows,' says Goethe 'the more one prizes natural gifts, because by no possibility can they be procured and stuck on.' Nature formed Milton to be a great poet. But what other poet has shown so sincere a sense of the grandeur of his vocation, and a moral effort so constant and sublime to make and keep himself worthy of it? * * * Continually he lived in companionship with high and rare excellence, with the great Hebrew poets and prophets, with the great poets of Greece and Rome. The Hebrew compositions were not in verse, and can be not inadequately represented by the grand, measured prose of our English Bible. The verse of the poets of Greece and Rome no translation can adequately reproduce. Prose cannot have the power of verse; verse-translation may give whatever of charm is in the soul and talent of the translator himself, but never the specific charm of the verse and poet translated. In our race are thousands of readers, presently there will be millions, who know not a word of Greek and Latin, and will never learn those languages. If this host of readers are ever to gain any sense of the power and charm of the great poets of antiquity, their way to gain it is not through translations of the ancients, but through the original poetry of Milton, who has the like power and charm, because he has the like great style.

* * *

VIRGINIA WOOLF

From A Writer's Diary (1953)†

Tuesday, September 10th

Though I am not the only person in Sussex who reads Milton, I mean to write down my impressions of *Paradise Lost* while I am about it. Impressions fairly well describes the sort of thing left in my mind. I have left many riddles unread. I have slipped on too easily to taste the full flavour. However I see, and agree to some extent in believing, that this full flavour is the reward of highest scholarship. I am struck by the extreme difference between this poem and any

† From *A Writer's Diary*, ed. Leonard Woolf (New York: Harcourt Brace Jovanovich, 1953), pp. 5–6. Copyright © 1954 by Leonard Woolf, renewed 1982 by Quentin Bell and Angelica Garnett. Reprinted by permission of Houghton Mifflin Harcourt Publishing Company and The Society of Authors as the Literary Representative of the Estate of Virginia Woolf. All rights reserved.

other. It lies, I think, in the sublime aloofness and impersonality of the emotion. I have never read Cowper on the sofa, but I can imagine that the sofa is a degraded substitute for *Paradise Lost*.[1] The substance of Milton is all made of wonderful, beautiful and masterly descriptions of angels' bodies, battles, flights, dwelling places. He deals in horror and immensity and squalor and sublimity but never in the passions of the human heart. Has any great poem ever let in so little light upon one's own joys and sorrows? I get no help in judging life; I scarcely feel that Milton lived or knew men and women; except for the peevish personalities about marriage and the woman's duties. He was the first of the masculinists, but his disparagement rises from his own ill luck and seems even a spiteful last word in his domestic quarrels. But how smooth, strong and elaborate it all is! What poetry! I can conceive that even Shakespeare after this would seem a little troubled, personal, hot and imperfect. I can conceive that this is the essence, of which almost all other poetry is the dilution. The inexpressible fineness of the style, in which shade after shade is perceptible, would alone keep one gazing into it, long after the surface business in progress has been despatched. Deep down one catches still further combinations, rejections, felicities and masteries. Moreover, though there is nothing like Lady Macbeth's terror or Hamlet's cry, no pity or sympathy or intuition, the figures are majestic; in them is summed up much of what men thought of our place in the universe, of our duty to God, our religion.

A. E. HOUSMAN

From Terence,[1] this is stupid stuff (1896)[†]

*   *   *

O many a peer of England brews
Livelier liquor than the Muse,
And malt does more than Milton can
To justify God's ways to man.

*   *   *

1. A reference to William Cowper neo-Miltonic philosophical poem in six books, *The Task* (1785). The first book is entitled "The Sofa" because the poem arose from a lady's assigning the poet the task of writing an epic poem on that subject, in Milton's style. Cowper opens amusingly on the history of human seating, culminating in the sofa, but to his own surprise and ours grows serious and elevated, meditating on country scenes while condemning London and the rapacity of empire.
1. "Terence" is the persona of Housman himself. The original title of *A Shropshire Lad* was *The Poems of Terence Hearsay*.
† From *A Shropshire Lad* (Oxford: Woodstock Books, 1994), p. 91. Poem #LXII (62).

T. S. ELIOT

From Milton I (1936)†

While it must be admitted that Milton is a very great poet indeed, it is something of a puzzle to decide in what his greatness consists. On analysis, the marks against him appear both more numerous and more significant than the marks to his credit. As a man, he is antipathetic. Either from the moralist's point of view, or from the theologian's point of view, or from the psychologist's point of view, or from that of the political philosopher, or judging by the ordinary standards of likeableness in human beings, Milton is unsatisfactory. The doubts which I have to express about him are more serious than these. His greatness as a poet has been sufficiently celebrated, though I think largely for the wrong reasons, and without the proper reservations. His misdeeds as a poet have been called attention to, as by Mr. Ezra Pound, but usually in passing. What seems to me necessary is to assert at the same time his greatness—in that what he could do well he did better than anyone else has ever done—and the serious charges to be made against him, in respect of the deterioration—the peculiar kind of deterioration—to which he subjected the language.

Many people will agree that a man may be a great artist and yet have a bad influence. There is more of Milton's influence in the badness of the bad verse of the eighteenth century than of anybody's else: he certainly did more harm than Dryden and Pope, and perhaps a good deal of the obloquy which has fallen on these two poets, especially the latter, because of their influence, ought to be transferred to Milton. But to put the matter simply in terms of 'bad influence' is not necessarily to bring a serious charge: because a good deal of the responsibility, when we state the problem in these terms, may devolve on the eighteenth-century poets themselves for being such bad poets that they were incapable of being influenced except for ill. There is a good deal more to the charge against Milton than this; and it appears a good deal more serious if we affirm that Milton's poetry could *only* be an influence for the worse, upon any poet whatever. It is more serious, also, if we affirm that Milton's bad influence may be traced much farther than the eighteenth century, and much farther than upon bad poets if we say that it was an influence against which we still have to struggle.

*   *   *

† From *On Poetry and Poets* (London: Faber & Faber, 1957), pp. 156–57. Copyright © 1957 by T.S. Eliot. Copyright renewed © 1985 by Valerie Eliot. Reprinted by permission of Faber & Faber Ltd. and Farrar, Straus and Giroux.

From Milton II (1947)[†]

* * *

It seems to me also that Milton's verse is especially refractory to yielding up its secrets to examination of the single line. For his verse is not formed in this way. It is the period, the sentence and still more the paragraph, that is the unit of Milton's verse; and emphasis on the line structure is the minimum necessary to provide a counter-pattern to the period structure. It is only in the period[1] that the wave-length of Milton's verse is to be found: it is his ability to give a perfect and unique pattern to every paragraph, such that the full beauty of the line is found in its context, and his ability to work in larger musical units than any other poet—that is to me the most conclusive evidence of Milton's supreme mastery. The peculiar feeling, almost a physical sensation of a breathless leap, communicated by Milton's long periods, and by his alone, is impossible to procure from rhymed verse.

* * *

† From *On Poetry and Poets* (London: Faber & Faber, 1957), p. 179. Copyright © 1957 by T.S. Eliot. Copyright renewed © 1985 by Valerie Eliot. Reprinted by permission of Faber & Faber Ltd. and Farrar, Straus and Giroux.
1. In Latin, an entire, complex sentence (or a coordinated series of sentences) formed of balanced subordinate clauses, often building to a climax with the principal clause and main verb at the end. The sense of the word as only the termination of a sentence, or the mark of this termination, is post-classical. Eliot is using the word in the classical sense.

Modern Criticism of *Paradise Lost*

On Satan

C. S. LEWIS

From Satan[†]

* * *

* * * [I]t is a very old critical discovery that the imitation in art of unpleasing objects may be a pleasing imitation. In the same way, the proposition that Milton's Satan is a magnificent character may bear two senses. It may mean that Milton's presentation of him is a magnificent poetical achievement which engages the attention and excites the admiration of the reader. On the other hand, it may mean that the real being (if any) whom Milton is depicting, or any real being like Satan if there were one, or a real human being in so far as he resembles Milton's Satan, is or ought to be an object of admiration and sympathy, conscious or unconscious, on the part of the poet or his readers or both. The first, so far as I know, has never till modern times been denied; the second, never affirmed before the times of Blake and Shelley.

* * *

* * * [H]is revolt is entangled in contradictions from the very outset, and he cannot even raise the banner of liberty and equality without admitting in a tell-tale parenthesis that "Orders and Degrees Jarr not with liberty" (v, 789). He wants hierarchy and does not want hierarchy. Throughout the poem he is engaged in sawing off the branch he is sitting on, not only in the quasi-political sense already indicated, but in a deeper sense still, since a creature revolting against a creator is revolting against the source of his own powers—including even his power to revolt. Hence the strife is most accurately described as "Heav'n ruining from Heav'n" (vi,

† From *A Preface to* Paradise Lost (London: Oxford University Press, 1942), pp. 92, 94, 96–97. Reprinted by permission of Oxford University Press.

868), for only in so far as he also is "Heaven"—diseased, perverted, twisted, but still a native of Heaven—does Satan exist at all. It is like the scent of a flower trying to destroy the flower. As a consequence the same rebellion which means misery for the feelings and corruption for the will, means Nonsense for the intellect.

*　　*　　*

* * * He says "Evil be thou my good" (which includes "Nonsense be thou my sense") and his prayer is granted. It is by his own will that he revolts; but not by his own will that Revolt itself tears its way in agony out of his head and becomes a being separable from himself, capable of enchanting him (ii, 749–766) and bearing him unexpected and unwelcome progeny. By his own will he becomes a serpent in Book ix; in Book x he is a serpent whether he will or no. This progressive degradation, of which he himself is vividly aware, is carefully marked in the poem. He begins by fighting for "liberty," however misconceived; but almost at once sinks to fighting for "Honour, Dominion, glorie, and renoune" (vi, 422). Defeated in this, he sinks to that great design which makes the main subject of the poem—the design of ruining two creatures who had never done him any harm, no longer in the serious hope of victory, but only to annoy the Enemy whom he cannot directly attack. * * * From hero to general, from general to politician, from politician to secret service agent, and thence to a thing that peers in at bedroom or bathroom windows, and thence to a toad, and finally to a snake—such is the progress of Satan. This progress, misunderstood, has given rise to the belief that Milton began by making Satan more glorious than he intended and then, too late, attempted to rectify the error.

*　　*　　*

BALACHANDRA RAJAN

From The Problem of Satan†

* * * Satan became for [C. S. Lewis] "a personified self-contradiction", a being ultimately farcical, a creature who could not be brought into contact with the real without laughter arising "just as steam *must* when water meets fire". So challenging a formulation could naturally not pass unchallenged and Professor Stoll, backed by the resources of nineteenth century criticism, demanded at some length

---

† From Paradise Lost *and the Seventeenth Century Reader* (London: Chatto & Windus, 1947; rpt., Ann Arbor: University of Michigan Press, 1964), pp. 93–96, 101–2. Reprinted by permission of the Estate of Balachandra Rajan.

that the devil be given his due. Mr. Rostrevor Hamilton, using Raleigh's antithesis for a title, insisted that the poet had his reasons of which the Puritan knew nothing, and that the Satan created by Milton's imagination was nobler and more admirable than the devil conceived by his intellect. * * *

Now when a problem of this kind is presented to us the first thing we need to ask about is the adequacy of the vocabulary in which it is formulated. That "hero or fool?" is a leading question is not in itself regrettable. What is regrettable is that it is the sort of leading question which is bound to result in a misleading answer. Given certain ethical systems Satan is ultimately heroic and given others he is ultimately farcical. But what we are concerned with is poetry rather than ethics and Satan considered as a poetic force is different from Satan as a cosmic principle. For when that principle becomes dramatically real, when it comes alive in the radius of human experience, you cannot bring to its poetic deployment the simple emotions of mirth or admiration. Your response to it must not be unconditional. You have to see it as an element in a concerted whole, a single fact in a poetic process. Therefore to understand its nature and function you need to relate it to the pattern it fulfils and the background of belief against which it is presented.

It is when we undertake this reconsideration that critical differences of shading begin to emerge. Our response to Satan is, I imagine, one of cautious interest. We think of him either as an abstract conception or else, more immediately, as someone in whom evil is mixed with good but who is doomed to destruction by the flaw of self-love. But with Milton's contemporaries the response was predominantly one of fear. If like Calvin they thought of Satan as "an enemie that is in courage most hardie, in strength most mightie, in policies most subtle, in diligence and celeritie unweariable, with all sorts of engins plenteously furnished, in skill of warre most readie", that was only so that they could stand guard more vigilantly against their relentless opponent. If like Defoe they saw him as "a mighty, a terrible, an immortal Being; infinitely superior to man, as well in the dignity of his nature, as in the dreadful powers he retains still about him", the vision served to remind them inescapably that it was only by God's grace that they could hope to overcome the enormous forces against which they were contending. When Milton's great figure is silhouetted against this background the effect must be as Addison points out "to raise and terrify our imaginations".[1] So the heroic qualities which Satan brings to his mission, the

1. John Calvin, *Institution of the Christian Religion,* trans. Thomas Norton (London: 1561) I.xiv.13; Daniel Defoe, *Political History of the Devil* (London: 1726), ch. 4, "Bad Angels," p. 323; Joseph Addison, *Spectator* 303 (February 16, 1712).

fortitude, the steadfast hate, the implacable resolution which is founded on despair are qualities not to be imitated or admired. They are defiled by the evil to which they are consecrated. If Milton dwells upon them it is because he knows that you will put them in their context, that you will see Satan's virtues as perverted by their end and darkening therefore to their inevitable eclipse, corroded and eaten out by the nemesis beyond them. The moral condemnation is never explicitly, or even poetically, denied. Touched on repeatedly in parenthesis, it is also always there as an undertone to the imagery. Words like Memphis and Alcairo may be nothing more than brilliant names to us. To Milton's contemporaries they were darkened with contempt. When Satan was described to them as a "great Sultan" the phrase would have reminded them of tyranny rather than splendour. When the fallen angels were likened to the cavalry of Egypt, a plague of locusts and a barbarian invasion, they would have given full weight to the mounting disapproval which lies behind the simile. As for the great Satanic defiances, they would have admired them for their strength and deplored them for their perversity. To quote Addison once more, Satan's sentiments "are every way answerable to his Character, and suitable to a created Being of the most exalted and most depraved Nature. . . . Amidst the impieties which this enraged Spirit utters . . . the author has taken care to introduce none that is not big with absurdity and incapable of shocking a religious reader".[2] The sympathy for Satan which the poetry imposes, the admiration it compels for his Promethean qualities, are meant to be controlled by this sort of moral reaction. And the same sense of proportion should cover his intellectual argument. When Satan appeals to "just right and the fixt laws of Heav'n", when he grounds his mandate on the ultimate nature of things, and when, in betraying overtones, he couples God's "tyranny" with "the excess of joy", you are not supposed to take these statements at their face value. Other politicians have made claims somewhat similar, and Satan's assertions as the champion of liberty would amuse, rather than perplex, those who were brought up to think of him as the first liar.

But to set aside the problem at this point is to leave its most interesting elements unstated. It is right to insist that Milton's Satan is not presented in a moral vacuum, that there is a background of unremitting hostility against which his poetic presence must be built up. But though the system within which he exists is never questioned, though it is seldom ignored and frequently remembered, its immediate implications are progressively subdued. We know, and even Satan

2. See p. 403, above.

knows, that the God against whom he is contending is omnipotent. But against the settled strength of his heroism, against the desperate and deliberate valour of Hell, that fact dies down to an abstract and distant necessity. When the weight of the poetry is thus thrown in on Satan's side, the effect must be to equalize in our imaginations the relative magnitude of the contending forces. We see Satan so clearly that we can hardly see anything else, and though conscious, we are not always or inescapably conscious, of the strength and authority of the forces which control him. The conflict, then, is neither Promethean nor farcical. It is dramatically real in proportion as you assent to the illusion of equality which the poem communicates.

That illusion, however, is not intended to last.

*   *   *

In the fifth book we revert to a Satan who, chronologically, ought to be at his noblest. Instead, we find only a professional politician, a propagandist who, like all propagandists, is an ardent champion of the Rights of Man and is therefore able to be generously indignant about the despotic tendencies of government in Heaven. It is a Satan notably different from the Archangel of the first books . . . The intruder in Eden is not quite the explorer of Chaos.

*   *   *

WILLIAM EMPSON

From Satan†

*   *   *

I fully agree with the disgust felt by C. S. Lewis for Satan's character as it has now become, and could even agree that his doubts about God are now merely a means of deceiving himself. But surely one must also feel horror at the God who has deliberately reduced him to such a condition. Even now, he is still capable of being struck 'stupidly good' when first confronted with Eve alone (IX. 465). He is a less painful sight after the Fall, because totally corrupt and merely the Devil; as when he meets Sin and Death, on his way back to Hell, and urges them forward to enslave and destroy mankind (X. 400). His boastful speech on his return admits that God created the world, though still not that he created the angels. God

† From *Milton's God* (London: Chatto & Windus, 1961), pp. 70–71. Copyright © The Estate of William Empson. Reprinted by permission of Curtis Brown Ltd., London, on behalf of The William Empson Estate.

then turns all the rebels into snakes, thus proving to them that he was only playing cat and mouse all the time; and then of course turns them back, so that they may continue to work upon mankind.

Most critics are now agreed that there is a gradual calculated degradation of Satan, but this bit of understanding gets obscured by a hunger to argue that he is very bad from the start. The chief merit of the shape of the poem, I think, which has often been called magnificent architecture, is that it presents the change in Satan with such force. We first meet him certain of the righteousness of his cause though defeated, follow him into doubt and despair, switch back in the narrative of Raphael to find him confident that his cause will be victorious as well as just, then return to the story and find his character rapidly rotting away. As there is no slip-up anywhere in this involved programme, we can at least be sure that it was intended.

*   *   *

REGINA M. SCHWARTZ

From "Yet Once More": Re-creation, Repetition, and Return[†]

*   *   *

* * * Satan would not only avenge himself against his accusor, but against time itself, and he depicts his fall not as any wound, but specifically, as a *change*.

> how chang'd
> From him, who in the happy Realms of Light
> Cloth'd with transcendent brightness didst outshine
> Myriads though bright:
>
> (I.84–87)

And that change immediately inspires him to refuse any further change.

> yet not for those,
> nor what the Potent Victor in his rage
> Can else inflict, do I repent or change,
> Though chang'd in outward luster;
>
> (I.94–97)

† From *Remembering and Repeating: Biblical Creation in* Paradise Lost (New York: Cambridge University Press, 1988), pp. 94–95. Copyright © Cambridge University Press 1988. Reprinted by permission of Cambridge University Press.

The distinction he grasps for here, between outward and inward change, is obviously specious; he knows, as we know, that the inner reflects the outer, and amidst his verbal flailing between "change" and "no change," the simple truth emerges that he *has* changed and that he now stubbornly wills that change to be irrevocable. Indeed, his conjunction might well be more forcefully causal: Satan does not seize upon his resolve "though" changed in outward luster, but "because" of that diminishment. He will fix the will or "harden the heart" toward a single purpose. It is fixity, a "fixt mind / And high disdain," that emerges from the "sense of injur'd merit" he cannot recover (I.98–99).

Having suffered loss, Satan grasps for that which can brook no loss. If heaven cannot be his eternally, then at least hate can be immortal. In his frustration that he cannot recapture the past, to un-do and re-do it, he tries to seize control of change itself.

> What though the field be lost:
> All is not lost; the unconquerable Will,
> And study of revenge, immortal hate,
> And courage never to submit or yield:
> And what is else not to be overcome?
> (I.105–09)

These words are fraught with telling contradictions. "*Having lost,* I refuse to lose; *having been forced to yield,* I refuse to yield." And that last odd question, "what is else not to be overcome?" seductively suggests conflicting meanings. On the one hand, it suggests the tautology, "my will never to be overcome will never be overcome"; on the other, self-justification: "I must embrace revenge and hate for only they are of lasting consequence." But there is a more desperate underside to the sentiment: "We have been so thoroughly defeated that nothing is left us—'what is else?'—but defiance itself." The ostensibly heroic lines want to collapse into a plaintive "What have we left?" And the confusion we note here spills over into their sequel: "That Glory never shall his wrath or might / Extort from me" (I.110–11). What glory? The glory of revenge and hate, the glory of resolve itself? Is there a "glory" left for Satan that has not been "extorted" already? Satan answers that question himself, deflating his own posturing less than thirty lines later: all glory is "extinct" (I.141). The contradictions in these lines stem from a fundamental one: Satan's will to be unconquerable is born of the essential impotence of his will.

*   *   *

On God

C. S. LEWIS

From the conclusion to A Preface to Paradise Lost[†]

*   *   *

* * * Milton's presentation of God the Father has always been felt to be unsatisfactory. Here again it is easy to look too deep for the causes. I very much doubt whether the failure is due to Milton's religious defects or whether it chiefly consists in giving us a cold, merciless, or tyrannical Deity. Many of those who say they dislike Milton's God only mean that they dislike God: infinite sovereignty *de jure*, combined with infinite power *de facto*, and love which, by its very nature, includes wrath also—it is not only in poetry that these things offend. To be sure, better men than Milton have written better than Milton of God; but the offence of his conception is not wholly due to its defects. And furthermore, I think the offence of his presentation is not wholly, or even mainly, due to his conception. The theological flaws (however we assess them) would not be *poetically* disastrous if only Milton had shown more poetical prudence. A God, theologically speaking, much worse than Milton's, would escape criticism if only He had been made sufficiently awful, mysterious, and vague. When the poet is content to suggest, our theological scruples are cast to the winds. When we read

> About him all the Sanctities of Heaven
> Stood thick as Starrs, and from his sight receiv'd
> Beatitude past utterance.
> (III, 60),

or

> Dark with excessive bright thy skirts appear
> (III, 380),

we are silenced. It is when the Son bows over His sceptre or the Father entertains the angels with "rubied Nectar" served "in Pearl, in Diamond, and massie Gold" that we are displeased. Milton has failed to disentangle himself from the bad tradition (seen at its worst in Vida's *Christiad* and at its best in the *Gierusalemme*

[†] From *A Preface to* Paradise Lost (London: Oxford University Press, 1942), pp. 126–27. Reprinted by permission of Oxford University Press.

Liberata[1]) of trying to make Heaven too like Olympus. It is these anthropomorphic details that make the Divine laughter sound merely spiteful and the Divine rebukes querulous; that they need not have sounded like this, Dante and the Hebrew prophets show.

＊　＊　＊

WILLIAM EMPSON

From Critics[†]

The extremely thorough reconsideration of *Paradise Lost* during this century, beginning with Sir Walter Raleigh's splendid handbook (1900), has made the poem more interesting and beautiful by greatly advancing our understanding of it; but the general reader has not been much encouraged to regard the contestants in this cooperative light, and may well suppose that the fighting has merely died down out of exhaustion. In trying to bring the results together I am inherently offering to act as mediator, though the position may only invite brickbats from all sides. The opinions of both attackers and defenders of the poem have evidently corresponded to their various theologies or world-views; most of them have not cared to drive their argument to the point of saying so, but the subject cannot be viewed in a purely aesthetic manner, as Milton himself would be the first to claim. His God is somehow 'embarrassing'; indeed, almost all the contestants have used that coy word, with its comforting suggestion of a merely social blunder. Professor C. S. Lewis let in some needed fresh air (*A Preface to Paradise Lost*, 1942) by saying, "Many of those who say they dislike Milton's God only mean that they dislike God" (p. 126);[1] speaking as an Anglican, he decided that the poem merely uses beliefs which are central to any Christian theology, except for some minor and doubtful points; but even he was ready to grant that Milton might sometimes describe God 'imprudently' (p. 93). I am anxious to make my beliefs clear at the outset, because the revival of Christianity among literary critics has rather taken me by surprise. A number of young people nowadays, as one can readily understand, feel that 'modern' ideals and programmes, a very mixed bag of them, have worked out so badly that the traditional ones may be better; but how badly those used to

---

1. Two epic poems, Vida's (1535, in Latin) on the life of Christ and Tasso's (1581, in Italian) on the First Crusade.

† From *Milton's God* (London: Chatto & Windus, 1961), pp. 9–12. Copyright © The Estate of William Empson. Reprinted by permission of Curtis Brown Ltd., London, on behalf of The William Empson Estate.

1. See p. 438, above.

work out too seems to have been successfully kept hidden. Thus young people often join a Church because they think it is the only way to avoid becoming a Communist, without realizing that a Renaissance Christian State was itself usually a thorough-going police terror. 'Dislike' is a question-begging term here. I think the traditional God of Christianity very wicked, and have done since I was at school, where nearly all my little playmates thought the same. I did not say this in my earlier literary criticism because I thought it could be taken for granted, and that to fuss about it would do no good (like anyone else, I have sometimes expressed a solemn interest in the ancient craving for human sacrifice and its protean reappearances, but this does not imply Christian belief); and it seems that nowadays the gap often makes a reader find my position evasive or illogical. Having had ten years teaching in Japan and China, and having only been interested in propaganda during the war,[2] halfway through them, I am still rather ill-adjusted to the change of atmosphere. Lecturing at Government universities in the Far East, which means firmly nonmissionary ones, was not likely to prepare me for it; I gathered that those of my students who became interested in *Paradise Lost*, though too polite to express their opinion to me quite directly, thought "Well, if they worship such a monstrously wicked God as all that, no wonder that they themselves are so monstrously wicked as we have traditionally found them." Most Christians are so imprisoned by their own propaganda that they can scarcely imagine this reaction; though a missionary would have to agree that to worship a wicked God is morally bad for a man, so that he ought to be free to question whether his God is wicked. Such an approach does at least make Milton himself appear in a better light. He is struggling to make his God appear less wicked, as he tells us he will at the start (I.25), and does succeed in making him noticeably less wicked than the traditional Christian one; though, after all his efforts, owing to his loyalty to the sacred text and the penetration with which he makes its story real to us, his modern critics still feel, in a puzzled way, that there is something badly wrong about it all. That this searching goes on in *Paradise Lost*, I submit, is the chief source of its fascination and poignancy. * * *

The poem enlarges the experience of most readers in an important way; it is an impressive example of one of the more appalling things the human mind is liable to do.

The recent controversy about the poem, on the other hand, has largely been conducted between attackers who find it bad because it makes God bad and defenders who find it all right because it leaves God tolerable, even though Milton is tactless about him. Surely this is an absurd spectacle; the poem is not good in spite of but

2. I.e., World War II.

especially because of its moral confusions, which ought to be clear in your mind when you are feeling its power. I think it horrible and wonderful; I regard it as like Aztec or Benin sculpture, or to come nearer home the novels of Kafka, and am rather suspicious of any critic who claims not to feel anything so obvious. Hence I also expect that most of the attackers would find their minds at rest if they took one step further and adopted the manly and appreciative attitude of Blake and Shelley, who said that the reason why the poem is so good is that it makes God so bad.

*   *   *

NORTHROP FRYE

From The Garden Within[†]

*   *   *

*   *   * In Milton, God the Father, in flagrant defiance of Milton's own theology, which tells us that we can know nothing about the Father except through the human incarnation of the Son, does speak, and with disastrous consequences. *   *   * Further, he keeps on speaking at intervals, and whenever he opens his ambrosial mouth the sensitive reader shudders. Nowhere else in Milton is the contrast between the conceptual and the dramatic aspects of a situation *   *   * between recognizing that God is the source of all goodness and introducing God as a character saying: "I am the source of all goodness." The Father observes the improved behaviour of Adam after the fall and parenthetically remarks: "my motions in him." Theologically, nothing could be more correct: dramatically, nothing is better calculated to give the impression of a smirking hypocrite.

The speech the Father makes in Book Three has perhaps been modelled on the speech of Zeus at the opening of the *Odyssey*. But that speech is in perfect dramatic propriety. Zeus is merely saying that men often blame the gods for disasters they bring upon themselves, and gives an example, the death of Aegisthus, which has already occurred. What God does in Milton is to embark on a profoundly unconvincing argument purporting to show that Adam is responsible for his own fall, although God, being omniscient, foreknew it. But if God had foreknowledge he must have known in the instant of creating Adam that he was creating a being who would fall.

---

† From *The Return of Eden: Five Essays on Milton's Epics* (Toronto: University of Toronto Press, 1965), pp. 99–101. © University of Toronto Press 1965. Reprinted by permission of the publisher.

And even if the argument held together, the *qui s'excuse s'accuse*[1] tone in which it is delivered would still make it emotionally unconvincing.

Nor are the Father's other words and actions any more reassuring. They often do not seem very sharply distinguished from those of Satan. He professes a great concern for his creation ("thou knowest how dear to me are all my works," he says to the Son), yet when the news is brought him that one-third of his angelic creation has revolted against him he merely smiles. And although the Son is a considerably more attractive figure than the Father, he too has caught the contagion of unconcern: he is a "gracious Judge without revile," but there is nothing in him of Blake's Holy Word—

> Calling the lapsed Soul,
> And weeping in the evening dew[2]

—weeping such tears as even Satan has the grace to shed for his woebegone followers. Satan interprets his one-third as nearly half, and God the Father speaks of his two-thirds as "far the greater part," but there is little moral difference between the two communiqués. Satan is never shown sending his followers on pointless errands, though the Father, according to Raphael, frequently does so.

We understand Milton very well when he shows us Satan accommodating himself to his actions with "Necessity, the tyrant's plea," but the Father seems equally caught in the trap of his own pseudologic:

> I else must change
> Their nature, and revoke the high decree
> Unchangeable, eternal.[3]

* * * Why is everything rational in *Paradise Lost* so profoundly unreasonable?

*   *   *

ELEANOR COOK

From Melos Versus Logos, or, Why Doesn't God Sing? Some Thoughts on Milton's Wisdom[†]

*   *   *

The question may sound trivial. Yet if the human logos or word can have by analogy (or by whatever means, and the means are disputed

---

1. Who excuses himself, accuses himself (French).
2. William Blake, "Introduction" in *Songs of Experience* (1794).
3. *PL* 3.125–27.
† From *Against Coercion: Games Poets Play* (Stanford, Calif.: Stanford University Press, 1998), pp. 159–64. Cook's notes are omitted. Copyright © 1998 by the Board of Trustees of the Leland Stanford Junior University. Reproduced by arrangement with Taylor & Francis Books UK.

and important) some relation with a divine Word, then it has a significance that other terms, such as *melos* or *song*, lack in lacking this relation. And if one is a musician or a poet, and also a Christian in the Augustinian tradition, this matters a great deal. (Singing, by metonymy, may be poetry, as in Milton's "my advent'rous Song.") * * *

I began to think about this matter because of a coincidence in the rhetorical strategies of Milton and Karl Barth. These two powerful representatives of a logocentric tradition, separated by some 300 years, desire to find (and know the strategic importance of finding) a divine origin for music in Scripture. Both Milton in 1667 and Barth in 1947[1] take the Wisdom figure of Prov. 8:22–31, who is said to rejoice or play during or before creation, and both extend the word for "rejoice" or "play" to musical playing. The passage from Proverbs is well known:

> The Lord possessed me in the beginning of his way,
> Before his works of old . . .
> Then I was by him, as one brought up with him:
> And I was daily his delight,
> Rejoicing always before him;
> Rejoicing in the habitable part of his earth;
> And my delights were with the sons of men.
>
> (*King James Version*)

Here is Milton, in the invocation to book 7 of *Paradise Lost*, lines 1–12:

> Descend from Heav'n *Urania*, by that name
> If rightly thou art call'd, whose Voice divine
> Following, above th'*Olympian* Hill I soar,
> Above the flight of *Pegasean* wing.
> The meaning, not the Name I call: for thou
> Nor of the Muses nine, nor on the top
> Of old *Olympus* dwell'st, but Heav'nly born,
> Before the Hills appear'd, or Fountain flow'd,
> Thou with Eternal Wisdom didst converse,
> Wisdom thy Sister, and with her didst play
> In presence of th'Almighty Father, pleas'd
> With thy Celestial Song.

Milton's grammar in lines 9–12 does not say that the rejoicing or playing of Wisdom includes musical playing or Celestial Song. But his unobtrusive phrase "with her" merges Urania's song with Wisdom's rejoicing or playing. Whatever Wisdom may be—and it would be the height of folly to inquire into God's activities before Creation, as Milton says in the *Christian Doctrine* (I.7)—this

---

1. In a passage not included here, Cook discusses the first essay in Karl Barth's *Protestant Theology in the Nineteenth Century* (1947).

mysterious personification of the Godhead offers a way of associating music and poetry with the divine. ("Poetical personification"
is Milton's term for the Wisdom of Prov. 8.) Here at least, song is
not what it is elsewhere, almost without exception: a creaturely
activity—sometimes, to be sure, an activity of the highest creatures, but nonetheless creaturely. For Wisdom, if made, is not made
as angels or the universe are made. She is an agent of creation and
part of the Godhead. She is in Scripture. And she plays.

*   *   *

How strict Milton is about these matters, we may see by his diction for the activities of God in *Paradise Lost*. God speaks, beholds,
calls, says, sees, names, makes, and so on—all biblical verbs for his
activities. But some things God does not do. He does not "charm"
in either the magical or musical sense, although creatures, fallen
and unfallen, may do so. All the language of magic is kept away
from his activities. When Northrop Frye speaks of "the charm that
created order out of chaos" or "the Word of God itself, which pronounced the original spell to keep chaos away,"[2] it sounds a little
strange until we recognize a romance strategy of charm versus coun-
tercharm. So also Collins, when he makes Wisdom into a Fancy
figure, breathing "her *magic* Notes aloud" ("Ode on the Poetical
Character"; my emphasis). But this is not a strategy that Milton
allows himself in his later poetry.

Proverbs 8:22–31 is of great importance for Milton. It resounds
through his work more often and more profoundly than we have
realized.[3]

*   *   *

ON EVE AND ADAM

NORTHROP FRYE

From Children of God and Nature[†]

In the soul of man, as God originally created it, there is a hierarchy.
This hierarchy has three main levels: the reason, which is in control

---

2. Northrop Frye, "Charms and Riddles," in *Spiritus Mundi: Essays on Literature, Myth, and Society* (Bloomington: Indiana University Press, 1976), p. 129.
3. See, e.g., *PL* 7.8–10 n. and 225–27 n. [*Editor's note*]
† From *The Return of Eden: Five Essays on Milton's Epics* (Toronto: University of Toronto Press, 1965), pp. 60–63, 65, 67–68, 70. © University of Toronto Press 1965. Reprinted by permission of the publisher.

of the soul; the will, the agent carrying out the decrees of the reason, and the appetite. Reason and will, the decree and the act, are related in man much as the Father and the Son are related in the Godhead. The will is never free in the sense of being autonomous or detached from some other aspect of the soul, but when reason is in charge of the soul the will is free because it participates in the freedom of the reason. In one of his academic Prolusions Milton says, as an axiom generally accepted: "the human intellect, as head and ruler, surpasses in splendor the other faculties of the mind; it governs and illuminates with its splendor the will itself, otherwise blind and dark, that like the moon shines with another's light."

The appetite is subordinate to both, and is controlled by the will from the reason. Of the appetites two are of central importance: the appetite for food and the sexual appetite. Both of these are part of the divine creation, and are therefore good. Even so, it is curious how emphatic Milton is about food as an element of both paradisal and heavenly life. In the unfallen world eating has something sacramental about it: Raphael explains how it is part of the upward movement in nature back toward its Creator, and even the form in which food is provided indicates the "providence" behind it:

> The savoury pulp they chew, and in the rind,
> Still as they thirsted, scoop the brimming stream.[1]

The angels also eat and drink "in communion sweet,"[2] and Milton insists that, whatever the theologians may say, Raphael really ate the fruit salad provided for him by Eve. Not only does he eat it but he explains how he ate it. He appears to have no excretory organs except the pores of his skin—if angels have skin—but at any rate the upper end of his food pipe has been implanted in him by the Deity.

Milton also insists, again referring to objecting theologians, that sexual intercourse existed between Adam and Eve before the fall. There remains of course only the fourth question, the sexual life of angels, the subject of some curious speculations later on by Swedenborg.[3] We are told that spirits can assume either sex, which seems to imply that sex has some point even in a spiritual nature. Adam's natural curiosity, combined with other elements we shall look at in a moment, prompts him to ask Raphael a direct question on this point. The question, not unnaturally, is not directly answered, but when it is asked Raphael blushes, mutters something about having just remembered another appointment, and bustles off. He does not leave however until he has given Adam a very strong hint what the answer is:

1. *PL* 4.335–36.
2. *PL* 5.637.
3. Emanuel Swedenborg (1688–1772), Swedish scientist and Christian mystic.

> Let it suffice thee that thou know'st
> Us happy, and without Love no happiness.
> Whatever pure thou in the body enjoy'st
> (And pure thou wert created) we enjoy
> In eminence, and obstacle find none
> Of membrane, joint, or limb, exclusive bars.[4]

*　　*　　*

As far as the present world is concerned, we should remember something that many readers of Milton are apt to forget, that the authority of husband over wife is spiritual authority only. No man, except a man living entirely by the light of the gospel, would have the kind of integrity of which such an authority would be a by-product, nor could a woman who did not have a corresponding integrity be capable of responding to it. A bullying or dictatorial attitude toward one's wife would be merely one more example of what Milton calls man's effeminate slackness. Many theologians have asserted that the wife ought to be in subjection to her husband because woman brought sin into the world, but this is arguing directly from the unfallen to the fallen state, something Milton never does. Milton does say in *The Christian Doctrine* that the authority of the husband was increased after the fall, but this is an empirical observation on the patriarchal narratives in the Old Testament, not a deduction from the Eden story.

*　　*　　*

Milton's argument for divorce is really an argument for annulment, that is, an argument that if the relations between man and woman are intolerable, no marriage, in the gospel sense, has really taken place. The marriage Jesus describes as indissoluble is a lifetime companionship that can be consummated, or finished, only by the death of one of the partners. The union of Adam and Eve in Eden is the pattern of such a marriage, but not every legalized sex act in the fallen world achieves that pattern. But the argument for annulment really resolves itself into an argument against idolatry. The man has the right to divorce his wife (or the wife the husband) if she is a threat to his spiritual integrity, and she cannot be that without representing something of what idolatry means to Milton. When Eve, after her fall, comes to Adam and urges him to fall with her, that is the point at which Adam should have "divorced" Eve, hence the argument for divorce comes into the very act of the fall itself.

*　　*　　*

4. *PL* 8.620–25.

* * * When Raphael rebukes Adam, as Adam feels, unjustly, Adam makes a shrewd flanking attack by way of his question about Raphael's sex life, and on the way mentions in a parenthesis that he is sticking to his own views and is not allowing any angel to bully him out of them:

> Though higher of the genial bed by far,
> And with mysterious reverence, I deem.[5]

Let us return to the episode in Book Nine in which we are told that Eve has suddenly taken it into her head to go and do her pruning by herself. Adam makes a long speech, in impeccable blank verse, pointing out that, as they are about to be assailed by a clever and ruthless enemy, it might be better for them to stay together and not separate. Eve says that that is very true, and that she would like to go off and prune by herself. Adam makes another long speech, in equally impeccable blank verse, making the same point with elaborations. Eve says that all that is very true, and that she will now go off and prune by herself. At this point Adam attempts the manoeuvre which so many husbands have attempted, of trying to get the last word by telling her to go and do as she likes:

> Go in thy native innocence; rely.
> On what thou hast of virtue; summon all;
> For God towards thee hath done his part: do thine.
> So spake the Patriarch of Mankind; but Eve
> Persisted; yet submiss, though last, replied.[6]

*   *   *

After the fall, the hierarchy implanted by God in the human soul is not merely upset, but reversed. Appetite now moves into the top place in the human soul, and by doing so it ceases to be appetite and is transformed into passion, the drive toward death. The appetites are a part of the creation, and like every other part of the creation they are an energy which seeks its fulfilment in form. Hunger is specifically satisfied with food, and the sexual desire by sexual intercourse. When appetite is perverted into passion, the drives of sex and hunger are perverted into lust and greed. Passion operates in the mind as though it were an external force, compelling the soul to obey against its own best interests, and the passions of greed and lust have two qualities that the appetites do not have: excess and mechanical energy. Hunger can be satisfied by food, but greed cannot be satisfied by anything: it seeks an excess of food, and when it runs out of food,

5. *PL* 8.598–99.
6. *PL* 9.372–77.

it will seek to acquire other things out of mechanical habit. Eve is hungry before she eats the forbidden fruit, greedy immediately afterward, and her greed runs on into a desire to possess Adam.

*   *   *

What happens in the human individual happens by analogy in fallen human society. Passion acts as though it were an external force, a tyrant of the mind, and a society made up of passionate individuals becomes a tyranny, in which the tyrant is the embodiment of the self-enslavement of his victims, as Michael explains to Adam:

> Reason in Man obscured, or not obeyed,
> Immediately inordinate desires
> And upstart passions catch the government
> From reason, and to servitude reduce
> Man, till then free. Therefore, since he permits
> Within himself unworthy powers to reign
> Over free reason, God, in judgement just,
> Subjects him from without to violent lords,
> Who oft as undeservedly enthrall
> His outward freedom.[7]

Usually we have a secular tyrant and a spiritual tyrant or priest. The latter, in Christianity, is what Milton means by a prelate, a person who exerts temporal power in what ought to be the area of spiritual authority. Under the tyrant and the priest and their followers come the victims, the general public, and under them again come the few people equipped with enough reason to protest against what is happening and to try to rouse the conscience of the very small number who can be persuaded to agree and act with them.

*   *   *

DAVID QUINT

From Getting What You Wish For: A Reading of the Fall[†]

It takes two, Adam and Eve, to fall in book 9 of *Paradise Lost*, just as it takes both of them to reconcile with each other and accept the gift of God's grace in book 10. Eve falls deceived by the wiles of

---

7. *PL* 12.87–95.
† From *Inside* Paradise Lost: *Reading the Designs of Milton's Epic* (Princeton, N.J.: Princeton University Press, 2014), pp. 153, 156. Copyright © 2014 by Princeton University Press. Reprinted with permission of Princeton University Press. Quint's note is omitted.

Satan, failing the test she sets for herself to confront and withstand temptation as a lone individual. Adam knowingly falls with Eve, an act that combines marital love, human solidarity, and Adam's fear of repeating his earlier loneliness before Eve's creation: "To live again in these wild woods forlorn" (9.910). Adam's choice—the choice of death—aligns him with the second Adam, the Son, who will die for and in the place of humanity, and might seem to place Adam on a higher ground, heroic and moral, than his wife, "much *deceived,* much failing, hapless Eve" (9.404). Milton provides a version of the Genesis story that accords with 1 Timothy 2:14: "And Adam was not deceived, but the woman being deceived was in the transgression." Paul glosses the divine judgment of Genesis 3:16—"thy desire shall be subiect to thy husband, and he shall rule over thee"—and notoriously uses the deceived and transgressing Eve to subordinate not only wives to husbands but women to male authority, and to ordain their silence. "Deceived," a word used sparingly in *Paradise Lost* in any case, reappears in the second of its only two uses in book 9 at the moment when Adam falls, an explicit echo of the Pauline passage: "he scrupled not to eat / Against his better knowledge, *not deceived,* / But fondly overcome with female charm" (9.997–99).

*   *   *

* * * Eve's fall stages and, of necessity, criticizes the first wish of spiritual self-sufficiency and quest for recognition; Adam's fall does the same for the second of human love and codependency. They each seem to tip, to one side or the other, the equilibrium that *Paradise Lost* explores between the vertical relationship of proving oneself in the sight of God and the collateral relationship of love and community, between going it alone and going it together. Each wish maps out a sphere for the exercise of human freedom and will that is initially divinely sanctioned—to make a trial of oneself, to choose a loving relationship with another. In each case disobedience would make that sphere autonomous from God. But, at the same time, these wishes lend heroic dignity to the tragedy of the Fall: their respective impulses—to affirm faith, to share charity—are good and already proto-Christian, and thus can still be understood as expressions of prelapsarian innocence, up to the very point of the Fall. And they will be vindicated after the Fall, when human beings, particularly in the affective realms of marriage and love, appear, in fact, to have gained an increased Christian liberty and independence: they have outgrown the divine tutelage in Eden for whose loss the poem simultaneously mourns. In the formal resolution of the epic, Adam and Eve appear to have exchanged the two wishes, he now to obey the only God, she now to stay at his side; it implies a new sense of the relationship between male and female roles. How

the poem makes us *feel* about this realignment is another question.
Eve gets the last word in *Paradise Lost*.

                    *   *   *

JOANNA PICCIOTTO

From Labors of Innocence in Early Modern England[†]

                    *   *   *

We are poorly prepared for *Paradise Lost* by the tradition of paradisal representation that precedes it, but it is this tradition that has
shaped the poem's critical legacy.

                    *   *   *

Milton's restorative project inevitably has some purely construc-
tive aspects. In order to "score out" to epic length the handful of
sentences with which Genesis describes the first state of creation—
and to extend that length across the life of humanity—Milton had
to make things up. In assuming narrative responsibility for innocent existence, he engaged not in fiction but experimentation: an
ongoing effort of rational reconstruction. The distinction was lost
on many of his contemporaries. Lucy Hutchinson's hexameral[1] epic
Order and Disorder, clearly written as a corrective to *Paradise Lost,*
is prefaced by the disclaimer, "I tremble to think of turning Scripture into a romance"; the poem consists largely of pious refusals to
fill in gaps in the Genesis account. The experimental speculation
that Hutchinson strives at all costs to avoid was for Milton a necessary condition of regenerate art and the regenerate life. While
Hutchinson lards her margins with biblical citations, Milton's epic
interposes itself between scripture and the reader as an instrument
of magnification, to help us see further into the world Genesis
describes. It could be regarded as even more dangerous than
"romance" for this very reason. * * *
    * * * Rather than petrified idols for the mind's eye to stare at, the
poem provides materials for the mind's eye to see with; instead of
colonizing the reader's mind with fictions about paradise, it exercises

---

† From *Labors of Innocence in Early Modern England* (Cambridge, Mass.: Harvard Univer-
    sity Press, 2010), pp. 402–5. Copyright © 2010 by the President and Fellows of Harvard
    College. Reprinted with permission of the publisher. Picciotta's notes are omitted.
1. Describing the six days of creation.

her ability to see through fictions into paradise—and, ultimately, I will argue, through it. Experimentalist practitioners cultivated innocence as a method; aligning himself with Galileo, the only named contemporary in the poem, Milton recovers it for us as a perspective. Turning paradise itself into a perceptual medium, the poem becomes an instrument with which the reader works to cultivate a vision adequate to creation.

* * *

N. K. SUGIMURA

From Milton's Metaphysic and Linguistic Practice in *Paradise Lost*†

From *Adam's Naming of the Animals*

In book VIII of *Paradise Lost,* where Adam gives his own "naming narrative," Milton hints that there are two possible ways of understanding Adam's act of naming. In the lines "I nam'd them, as they pass'd, and understood / Thir Nature, with such knowledg God endu'd / My *sudden apprehension*" (VIII.352–54; italics added), the experience, as in Pareus, is revelatory and resists Pererius's[1] claim that Adam had perfect knowledge *ab ovo*.[2] Milton's choice of the word "endu'd"—which is applied to the application of forms to matter in Raphael's "one first matter all" speech (V.473)—reinforces the notion that Adam's apprehension of the animals and "Thir Nature" (VIII.353) occurs simultaneously with his act of naming them. The emphasis is on the process itself: "I nam'd them, *as they pass'd*" (352; italics added). The fact that this movement of the animals before Adam in humble subjection (VIII.349–51) takes place concurrently with his act of naming implies that Adam possesses a fully natural, or Cratylian,[3] language in Eden as a result of divine illumination.

Still the line "I nam'd them, as they pass'd, and understood" (VIII.352) must give us pause. If the "as" does not carry over for the

† From *"Matter of Glorious Trial": Spiritual and Material Substance in* Paradise Lost (New Haven, Conn.: Yale University Press, 2009), pp. 65–68. Reprinted with permission of Yale University Press. Sugimura's notes are omitted.
1. Spanish Jesuit philosopher and theologian (1535–1610). David Pareus (1548–1622), German Protestant theologian.
2. I.e., from the beginning. See p. 4.
3. Holding the view of Cratylus, a main interlocutor in Plato's dialogue of that name; he argues that the connection between names and things is natural, not arbitrary. The other main interlocutor, Hermogenes, argues that only convention determines which words designate which objects.

entire line, then a split-second temporal divide—between the naming and understanding—occurs. The name will first exist as an indication that something exists; then, as we move toward an understanding of its *quidditas* (or "thisness"), it is followed by knowledge of what this thing is. The process of work and the shift from "as" to "and" thus invokes the idea of sequence. Names mark out the process of the mind's movement toward differentiation and knowledge. The "whatness" (as opposed to the "thisness") of the thing ends up yielding a general concept.

This account coincides with Hermogenes' view of language, in which naming is arbitrary, fixed by a kind of cultural fiat. * * *

* * * At VIII.270, we encounter the first act of naming that is done outside Eden. Recounting his birth to Raphael, Adam tells us that while he wondered "who I was, or where, or from what cause, / Knew not" (270–71), he found himself able to name the sun and much more: "to speak I tri'd, and forthwith spake, / My Tongue obey'd and readily could name / What e're I saw" (VIII.271–73).

This account is a significant improvement on the Lucretian account that Milton echoes: in Lucretius, various sounds are associated and then acquire meaning ("leap into form") by fortuitous circumstance;[4] in *Paradise Lost,* the process is divinely guided. . . .

The creation of Adam and his consciousness does not blaze forth in *Paradise Lost* in a moment of divine revelation; rather, it unfolds as an exciting story or narrative sequence (though it takes place at great speed). The names which are later said to match nature and are ascribed to the assistance of divine revelation are here imposed by Adam alone. The phrase "speak I tri'd" (VIII.271) thus hints that Adam's experiment with naming outside Paradise has furnished him with conceptual knowledge (God transplants Adam to the "Garden of Bliss" at VIII.299–304). In drawing attention to the sequence—to the idea of a trial—Milton places concepts as prior to knowledge of things themselves. . . .

Language appears to be built from preconceptions that, so running ahead, are not only true, but also necessary to the art of naming. Adamic language reflects not things but conceptions of things.

                              *   *   *

---

4. The Roman poet and Epicurean philosopher Lucretius (ca. 94–55 B.C.E.) discusses the origins of language in *On the Nature of Things* 5.1028–90.

STEPHEN GREENBLATT

From The Rise and Fall of Adam and Eve[†]

* * *

In order to invent a compelling Satan, Milton carefully studied how Shakespeare had done it. The depiction of Macbeth's murderous ambition and despair provided a psychological and rhetorical template for the Prince of Darkness, and Milton added notes he took from Richard III and from Iago. He was almost too brilliant a student, for the result was a character so vivid that he threatened to take over the poem, particularly in its early books. In the later books Milton chose deliberately to diminish Satan in order to make room for the characters who were at the center of his lifelong obsession, Adam and Eve.

But Adam and Eve posed a challenge much greater than any that bedeviled his depiction of heaven or hell. There were almost no precedents, literary or otherwise, for the sustained depiction of a marriage. Shakespeare had almost nothing to offer Milton, nor did Homer or Virgil, Dante or Petrarch. Marriage figured in their works, when it figured at all, as a goal to be pursued or as a simple fact, not as a sustained partnership of intimate companions. A significant exception in Shakespeare was the marriage of the Macbeths, but that would hardly serve as a model for an Edenic couple. Milton believed deeply that at the center of marriage was intimate conversation between husband and wife, but to imagine and depict such intimacy was largely uncharted territory, not for him alone but for all of the literary culture in which he had steeped himself.

* * *

Milton did not want to depict Adam and Eve through a kind of mystical haze or delicately hidden from view by strategically placed fig leaves. He wanted to see them—and to have his readers see them—in all the vigor of robust youth. There was nothing ethereal about them. Deeply in love, Milton thought, they must have walked hand in hand through their delicious garden, stopping often to chat and kiss and indulge in "youthful dalliance" (4:338). When hungry, they sat down on a soft bank by a stream and ate the fruit that grew abundantly around them. "The savory pulp they chew," as the poem pictures the scene, "and in the rind/Still as they thirsted scoop the brimming stream" (4:335–36).

† From *The Rise and Fall of Adam and Eve* (New York: W. W. Norton, 2017), pp. 210, 212–14. Copyright © 2017 by Stephen Greenblatt. Used by permission of W. W. Norton & Company, Inc., and by Kneerim & Williams on behalf of the author.

Milton was in part going out of his way to make a theological point. Adam and Eve were not allegorical emblems; they were flesh-and-blood people, better than we are, to be sure, but not different in kind and not philosophical abstractions. Even the angels, he proposed, should be understood in human terms, for our material nature does not cut us off from higher forms of life. Thus when the poem depicts a friendly visit to Eden by the angel Raphael, sent by God to warn Adam and Eve about Satan, it imagines the heavenly guest sitting down with the humans for a meal and eating not "in a mist, the common gloss/Of theologians, but with keen dispatch/Of real hunger" (5:435–37). Spiritual beings are made of matter, just as humans are. Milton went still further. He insisted that, if angels actually ate real food, then they must also, like humans, have digested it and eliminated whatever "redounded." But, he added, with a sidelong glance at his own lifelong digestive problems, at least angels did not suffer from any gastric discomfort: "what redounds, transpires/Through Spirits with ease."

But it was not only bodily existence that Milton had to represent vividly in order to ground in reality the literal truth of the first humans. That was the easy part, thanks to the Renaissance art that helped to shape his vision. It was their inner lives and the substance of their relationship that posed the far greater challenge. The most difficult question was how to make Adam and Eve's marriage come alive. If Shakespeare could not help him here, still less could Augustine or Luther or Calvin. Milton's years of public service, writing angry polemics and educational treatises and diplomatic correspondence, were of no use. He found the way forward in his most private experiences, in his passionate friendship with Charles Diodati, in the fantasies he cherished during the long years he struggled to preserve his chastity, and above all in the feelings aroused in him around the time of his first marriage and disastrous honeymoon. Only by tapping into these recesses, courageously and relentlessly, did he begin to discover what he needed. As a poet, he aspired to make his creation real—that was, he knew, not only Augustine's theological imperative but also the secret of the greatest literature. And he succeeded. In *Paradise Lost,* Adam and Eve took on a more intense life—the life both of fully realized individuals and of a married couple—than they had ever possessed in the thousands of years since they were first conceived.

※   ※   ※

On Style and Versification

DOUGLAS BUSH

From *Milton*†

XII

MILTON

Whoever the third of English poets may be, Milton's place has been next to the throne, and for most of us he still stands there, 'Like Teneriff or Atlas unremov'd'. But to the defeatism of the 'Armistice' period, 1918–39, the naturalistic passion and irresponsibility of Donne appealed much more than a passion for order and righteousness, and devotion to one kind of writing necessitated a zealous dislike of all other kinds. The supreme English artist, the only one to be matched with Virgil and Dante in what Arnold called 'the sure and flawless perfection of his rhythm and diction', became the rhetorician who had crushed the fruitful metaphysical movement, divorced thought and feeling, and imposed an artificial style and prosody upon English poetry for over two hundred years, until it was freed from bondage by the 'metaphysical' poets of our time. In addition to such recent detractors Milton has always had dubious friends. The admiration for the great rebel felt by men like Blake and Shelley was mixed with antipathy for the theological system to which he was supposedly committed, and nineteenth-century critics in general were inclined to save his 'poetry' by casting his ideas overboard. In our day, while a few critics were reacting violently against him, Milton's thought began to be seriously explored and appreciated by scholars; they invoked a broader formula to unify and save the artist and thinker, and the rigid son of the Reformation became the bold son of the Renaissance. This conception, however, gained ground just as its ideological parent, Burckhardt's popular theory of the Renaissance, was being abandoned, and the new Milton, though he embodied some significant and amiable features which had been lacking in the grim Puritan, looked decidedly too much like a nineteenth-century liberal. This brief and unqualified summary indicates at least that Milton's poetic and philosophic character is less simple and obvious than friends as well as foes have often assumed it to be. Our present

† From *English Literature in the Earlier Seventeenth Century, 1600–1660* (Oxford: Clarendon Press, 1946), pp. 159–60 and 388. See also T. S. Eliot, From "Milton II" p. 429 and n. Reprinted with permission of Oxford University Press.

view of Milton is not unanimous or final but, with a better understanding of his background, roots, and evolution, we have perhaps
struck a juster balance between the Renaissance humanist and the
Puritan. Milton may be called the last great exponent of Christian
humanism in its historical continuity, the tradition of classical reason and culture fused with Christian faith which had been the
main line of European development.

The use of blank verse for an heroic poem was a great innovation,
and Milton's handling of it added, not a new province, but a new
world, to English prosody. But we cannot touch upon technicalities
or even go very far into generalities. Milton's versification is of
course inseparable from his diction and tone, and in recent years
the organ-voice of England has been charged with an inorganically
monotonous elevation of style and movement remote from the language and rhythms of common speech. There are always people
who complain that Poussin is not Picasso or that Bach is not Proko-
fiev. Milton's poetic and critical heritage and his own purpose prescribed a long poem, and in a long poem the reader must be made
to feel the continuity, 'the enormous onward pressure of the great
stream' on which he is embarked.[1] It is rather idle to compare bits of
Paradise Lost with the short pieces of the metaphysical poets or
with the dramatic texture of Shakespeare, or with such a totally
different kind of epic as Dante's. Standing before the altar, as Milton habitually stood, he would have been profane if he had not
worn his singing robes. A ritualistic elevation of style and movement may be as essential to an heroic subject as colloquial realism
to realistic subjects and, on the Miltonic level, is a much rarer phenomenon. We can hardly imagine the gap there would be in English
poetry, or in our own experience, if *Paradise Lost* were not there.

*   *   *

LEAH WHITTINGTON

From Vergil's Nisus and the Language of Self-Sacrifice in *Paradise Lost*†

When the Son of God offers to die for mankind in book 3 of *Paradise Lost* (1667), readers who have been tempted to join the devil's
party for the first two books of the poem confront an unsettling

---

1. C.S. Lewis, *A Preface to "Paradise Lost."* (1942; rpt. Oxford: Oxford UP, 1962), p. 46.
† From *Modern Philology* 107.4 (May 2010): 588–91, 606. Copyright © 2010 by the Uni-
versity of Chicago Press. Reprinted with permission of the publisher. All notes are
Whittington's; some have been edited or omitted.

dramatic scene: the assembly in heaven is staged as a mirror image of the demonic council at Pandemonium. The listening host suddenly grows quiet, and a solitary hero figure emerges out of the silence to take on the burden of raising the collective fortune. Placed beside the Son's promise to atone for man's sin with his death, Satan's exploratory mission to earth comes into focus as a fallen reflection of self-sacrifice, a self-aggrandizing perversion of the poem's heroic ideal now articulated in the Son.

This moment of internal self-reference has often been identified as part of Milton's didactic strategy to confront the reader with proof of his own fallenness, but it is less often recognized that the Son's speech to the angelic host makes use of an allusion that gives it a central place in the story of Milton's engagement with classical epic. When the Son supplicates God on man's behalf and offers to exchange his life for man's, he echoes the language of Vergil's Nisus, the Trojan youth who tries to save his friend Euryalus from the Rutulians in book 9 of the *Aeneid* by begging them to kill him instead:

> Behold me then, me for him, life for life
> I offer, on me let thine anger fall;
> Account me man; I for his sake will leave
> Thy bosom, and this glory next to thee
> Freely put off, and for him lastly die
> Well pleased, on me let Death wreck all his rage;[1]

> "me, me, adsum qui feci, in me conuertite ferrum,
> o Rutuli! mea fraus omnis, nihil iste nec ausus
> nec potuit; caelum hoc et conscia sidera testor;
> tantum infelicem nimium dilexit amicum."[2]

> ["Me—here I am, I did it! Turn your blades on me,
> Rutulians! The crime's all mine, he never dared,
> could never do it! I swear by the skies up there,
> the stars, they know it all! All he did was love
> his unlucky friend too well!"][3]

The Son's allusion to Nisus's desperate repetition of "me, me" has appeared among the classical echoes listed in commentaries on *Paradise Lost* since the early eighteenth century, but interpretation has been slow to follow because the parallel seems so unlikely. Milton invites us to read the Son's voluntary self-sacrifice, the poem's central act of heroism, in conjunction with an episode of the *Aeneid*

1. John Milton, *Paradise Lost*, ed. Alastair Fowler, 2nd ed. (London: Longman, 1998), 3.236–41, hereafter cited parenthetically as *PL*.
2. Vergil, *Aeneid*, ed. R. A. B. Mynors (Oxford: Clarendon, 1969), 9.427–30. [The Rutulians are led by Volcens, who kills Euryalus—*editor's note*.]
3. Translations are from Vergil, *The Aeneid*, trans. Robert Fagles (New York: Viking, 2006).

often described as a digression or epyllion. The story of Nisus and Euryalus does not appear to advance the cause of Aeneas and Rome and even puts pressure on the *Aeneid*'s governing ethical principles of *pietas* and the subordination of personal desire to the service of the community. But if Milton's allusion to the story of Nisus and Euryalus at this crucial moment in book 3 is surprising in itself, the issue is further complicated by the fact that the same Vergilian language resurfaces in two key passages of book 10, when Adam and Eve, struggling to make sense of life after the Fall, both invoke Nisus's repetition of "me, me" in their successive attempts to take on all the blame for the sin that now shrouds them in shame, resentment, and despair. Adam recalls the language first in a lyrical complaint delivered at the height of his dejection:

> All my evasions vain
> And reasonings, though through Mazes, lead me still
> But to my own conviction: first and last
> On me, me only, as the source and spring
> Of all corruption, all the blame lights due;
> So might the wrath.
>
> (*PL* 10.829–34)

Shortly after Adam's lament, Eve returns to the same Vergilian vocabulary of self-sacrifice when she attempts to placate Adam's anger by insisting that the responsibility for the Fall should lie entirely with her:

> On me exercise not
> Thy hatred for this misery befallen,
> On me already lost, me than thyself
> More miserable; both have sinned but thou
> Against God only, I against God and thee,
> And to the place of judgment will return,
> There with my cries importune Heaven, that all
> The sentence from thy head removed may light
> On me, sole cause to thee of all this woe,
> Me me only just object of his ire.
>
> (*PL* 10.927–36)

*   *   *

This shift from a heroic posture of self-sufficiency to mutual compassion and love offers the poem's final reading of the story of Nisus and Euryalus. In Adam's pity for Eve, Milton activates the sympathy of Vergil's apostrophe to the two Trojan lovers but displaces Vergil's passionate outburst on their behalf onto Adam, transferring the sympathetic response of the external poet to an internal character who has the power to act in the narrative of the poem. In Vergil's story the pity that could have saved Euryalus if placed in the hands of Volcens is deflected onto the poet, whose expression of sympathy is heartfelt but powerless to change the tragic course of events. Milton brings together the disparate pieces of Vergil's narrative and unites the two most powerful emotional moments—Nisus's offer of self-sacrifice and the poet's apostrophe—into one intimate scene between the two characters who will become history's new heroes as they venture out of Eden. In recombining elements that were separated in the *Aeneid*, Milton constructs a Vergil who is not so much a rival as a peer and friend. The recurrence of Nisus as a key figure shows that the new definition of Christian heroism comes to be articulated not in opposition to the ancient tradition but precisely through it, even if Milton will ultimately offer something new. And finally, Eve's echo of Nisus, followed by Adam's transformation of that echo into the language of mutuality, invites the reader to reflect on the idea that in the earthly context of marriage, self-sacrifice by itself is not enough. It requires the pity and sympathy that Nisus and Euryalus tragically receive only after their deaths, but that Adam and Eve offer each other as they prepare to face the world after paradise has been lost.

ANN BAYNES COIRO

[Verse Paragraphs in *Paradise Lost*]†

This essay approaches the longstanding argument about the nature and efficacy of *Paradise Lost*'s form by focusing on its innovative verse paragraphs. In the blank verse paragraph, Milton found a form that had roots in English conceptions of classical epic and that significantly contributed to the extraordinary power of the early modern English stage. He found a form that was musical, thus honoring his own father, and also new, part of a European-wide musical revolution. Above all, in the blank verse paragraph Milton found a form that revivified the ancient connection of poetry and performance by making print readers the actors of his poem.

*   *   *

† From "Sufficient and Free: The Poetry of *Paradise Lost*," in *Milton Now: Alternative Approaches and Contexts*, ed. Catharine Gray and Erin Murphy (New York: Palgrave Macmillan, 2014), pp. 85–86, 89–90, 107. Copyright © Catharine Gray and Erin Murphy, 2014. Reprinted with permission of SNCSC. Coiro refers to paragraph breaks as they appear in the 1674 edition of *Paradise Lost*. See p. xxxii.

Performing Paragraphs

On the printed pages of this poem narrated by a blind man, we literally *see* a powerfully innovative engine of our experience: *Paradise Lost* works in 363 verse paragraphs of widely varying lengths, paragraphs that shape the blank verse in sweeping waves or psychologically complex eddies or brief narrative cues.[1] Modeled on new print conventions for prose and drama, the verse paragraphs shape each reader's response.

As a formal structure, the verse paragraph gives Milton amazing creative freedom. At the same time, the varying paragraphs make the reading experience feel organic and unpredictable. *Paradise Lost's* verse paragraphs range in length from one line to 416 lines; Book 1 has only 14 paragraphs, whereas Book 9 has 48. The variety of uses the verse paragraph can serve is similarly capacious: invocation, exposition, song, brief narrative link, and speeches of all varieties, including lessons, lectures, arguments, seductions, dialogues, and monologues. Across this wide range, however, the working principle of the organization of *Paradise Lost's* paragraphs is dramatic coherence. Almost always, a paragraph is spoken by one speaker; it is knit by assonance and alliteration; and, long or short, the paragraph is determined by the speaker's purposes and emotions. Readers thus move through the poem unmoored by set forms: the fluid, variable paragraphs guide us, shaping our voices continuously and surprisingly.

The shortest paragraph in *Paradise Lost*, for example, is Eve's simple statement: "The Serpent me beguil'd, and I did eate" (10.162).[2] Its humility and brevity demonstrate Eve's acceptance of responsibility, an act of heroism. Even as we read it, however, the one-line paragraph portends Eve's gradual silencing.

Only a few of the poem's paragraphs are very long (over 150 lines); when they occur, their length is similarly expressive and meaningful. The four longest verse paragraphs in *Paradise Lost* demonstrate a range of possible effects. Book 1's paragraph naming fallen angels

---

1. I am using Bradford's graphireading, albeit in a very different way than he proposed [see Richard Bradford, "Milton's Graphic Poetics," in *Re-membering Milton: Essays on the Texts and Traditions*, ed. Mary Nyquist and Margaret W. Ferguson (New York: Methuen, 1988), pp. 179–96]. Verse paragraphs are discussed by Sprott in 1953 [S. E. Sprott, *Milton's Art of Prosody* (Oxford: Blackwell, 1953)], Sypher in 1955 [Wylie Sypher, *Four Stages of Renaissance Style: Transformations in Art and Literature, 1400–1700* (Garden City, N.Y.: Doubleday, 1955)] and, in particular, Whaler in 1956 [James Whaler, *Counterpoint and Symbol: An Inquiry into the Rhythms of Milton's Epic Style* (Copenhagen: Rosenkilde and Bagger, 1956)]. Critics working on numerological readings of *Paradise Lost* have used verse paragraphs as formal units. See Maren-Sofie Røstvig, *The Hidden Sense* (Oslo: Universitetsforlaget; New York: Humanities Press, 1963), Gunnar Qvarnström, *The Enchanted Palace: Some Structural Aspects of* Paradise Lost (Stockholm: Almquist and Wiksell, 1967), and Dennis Danielson, *Milton's Good God: A Study in Literary Theodicy* (Cambridge: Cambridge University Press, 1982).
2. There is one other one-line paragraph: "Thus Adam his illustrious Guest besought" (7.109).

"Innumerable" (1.338) rolls out, in 291 imposing and terrifying lines, a "multitude" (1.351) "all the while / Sonorous metal blowing Martial sounds" (1.539–40) until the paragraph culminates in Satan "proudly eminent" (1.590) struggling to speak through tears (1.331–621). *Paradise Lost's* longest paragraph provides a second example: Satan's lonely exploration in search of earth in Book 3 moves from the emptiness that will become the Limbo of Vanities to the Sun where Satan sees Uriel and disguises himself; its chronicle of Satan's peregrinations feels exploratory rather than military (3.416–653). Third, Michael relentlessly compresses human history in a 191-line verse paragraph in Book 12, as arid a stretch of instruction as *Paradise Lost* contains (12.79–269).

The fourth example is one of the most memorable and controversial long paragraphs in *Paradise Lost*; it begins: "Now to th' ascent of that steep savage Hill / Satan had journey'd on, pensive and slow" (4.172–73). Within this paragraph, Satan leaps into paradise, the narrator breaks in, opining that "little knows / Any, but God alone, to value right / The good before him" (4.201–03), Satan sees the plenitude and beauty of paradise, and then sees Adam and Eve and their "happy nuptial League" (4.339), until evening rises "When Satan still in gaze, as first he stood, / Scarce thus at length fail'd speech recover'd sad" (4.356–57). So much of our interpretation of the rest of *Paradise Lost* rests on this paragraph, with its lushly sexual representation of Paradise and its overdetermined description of Adam and Eve, "Hee for God only, shee for God in him" (4.299). Its pivotal importance rests upon the difficulty each reader goes through to determine point of view: are we seeing Adam and Eve through Satan's perverted eyes or is the description of the first man and woman the narrator's and thus to be taken as licensed by inspiration? The conventions established for the poem's verse paragraphs suggest to the reader that the point of view is Satan's. Yet the narrator's perspective bleeds in with his intrusion. Unsettlingly, we realize, in the end, Satan has been staring all this time in a trance. In other words, the experience of reading this long paragraph stanza is treacherously complicated, a thrilling but destabilizing introduction to perfection.

Although there is no pattern for the length of verse paragraphs, at the end of the poem our initial expectation bends back upon itself. The last verse paragraph of *Paradise Lost* is 26 lines, as long as the splendid invocation of Book I that begins "Of Man's First Disobedience" (1.1). The narrator speaks both, but in the first he is imploring a muse, asking for her help to enable his voice. In the last, he is not addressing inspiration but begins by reporting a woman's speech: "So spake our Mother Eve, and Adam heard" (12.624). The first verse paragraph is Biblical and momentous; the last is ordinary and yet unforgettable. The Cherubim become, by a grammatical slippage, mist gathering "ground fast at the Laborer's heel / Homeward return-ing" (12.631–32). The narrator is disappearing, turning the poem to Adam and Eve and to us. Thus begins the final act of the reader's choice; alone and together, at the end of *Paradise Lost* we must embrace our role as performers in the mortal world.

*   *   *

MARY ANN RADZINOWICZ

From How Milton Read the Book of Psalms: His Formal, Stylistic, and Thematic Analysis[†]

Milton read the Book of Psalms as the record of a journey through life traversing all the tempers, moods, passions, and uneven reac-tions that mark the psalmist's search for an adequate faith.

*   *   *

A consequence of interweaving diverse psalm genres in both *Par-adise Regained* and *Paradise Lost* is what we may call multivocality, and that multivocality plays an important role in the architecture of each epic. Each is received by the reader not just as one speaker's continuous delivery of a transcendent mimesis drawn either from Luke or from Genesis and its aftermath, but also as a blending of many voices, rhetorically as well as psychologically and intellectu-ally distinctive. Thus each epic reveals both a powerful, unifying, personal impulse urging Milton to express in poetry a lyrical act of worship and an equally powerful, comprehensive, impersonal impulse urging him to express in poetry a fullness of knowledge. Milton nowhere claimed to have seen in the unified diversity of the Book of Psalms a comprehensive formal pattern for epic; other books of the Bible performed that function for him, when he looked to scriptural authority to strengthen classical models for epic— Genesis for *Paradise Lost*, Job for *Paradise Regained*. Rather his atten-tiveness to the psalms taught him something not learnt elsewhere about the generation of a long heroic poem out of the impassioned speech of brief poems. The distinctive psalmic genres act as choral voices creating multivocality for the epic, as arcs uniting the work

† From *Milton's Epics and the Book of Psalms* (Princeton: Princeton University Press, 1989), pp. 3–6. Copyright © 1989 Princeton University Press. Reprinted by permission of Princeton University Press.

while spacing the process of change and variety within it. To some of the genres or kinds, Milton adds his own voice. He too laments, warns, hymns, expostulates, and teaches upon occasions anticipated by the groups of psalms, in decorum anticipated by their intentions. But he is not limited to them, nor obliged to give his own voice to all. When, for example, in *Paradise Lost*, the proems draw on prophetic psalms or the angelic songs imitate hymns, Milton capably unites his voice to that of bard or angel. To some of Adam's laments he adds his personal voice, while from others he withholds it to encourage our ironic awareness of original, ordinary self-pity. As the Book of Psalms in Milton's reading is more than the sum of its lyrical parts in representing a journey of wisdom learned through suffering, so the multi-vocality of *Paradise Lost* draws all speakers and the audience as well into *paideia* [education]. Similarly, in the briefer narrated dialogues of *Paradise Regained*, Milton constructs from psalms the two angelic hymns and the laments of Mary and of the disciples, now more rarely but pointedly merging his voice with those of his speakers. His epics are not univocal but multivocal; the vatic voice is not composed of short self-reflexive songs but takes its color from alterations in mood and occasion; the unity of the heroic intellectual enterprise not only controls, but is qualified by, a diversity of lyric energies.

Milton's recognition of psalm genres coexisted with his reading of the unity of the Book of Psalms as an encyclopedic representation of the heroic idea that human suffering is purposive and educative. The limitations of lyric from Milton's point of view drove him to write the heroic poem; the lyrical effects of intensity and unity checked for him the potential endlessness of epic. The heroic poem confronts for a whole society those threats to high achievement posed by its own experience of chaos. The narrative of that confrontation glorifies the active virtues its society must attain as alone sufficient to perfect its culture. The epic poet undertakes to narrate the deeds of heroic figures best suited to exemplify the actual or potential achievements of his civilization in that confrontation. * * * Psalm reading was of enormous value to Milton in showing him models both of intense lyricism and of comprehensive heroism, just as it was of value in showing him models of generic multivocality and of an intellectually unified journey toward abstract comprehensive knowledge.

* * *

IAN BALFOUR

Figures in Excess and the Matter of Inversion in the Discourse of the Sublime[†]

* * *

The first great reflection on the sublime, Longinus's *On the Sublime* (*Peri hypsous*), is in large measure a rhetorical treatise, aimed at what the author calls "political men" [andres politikoi]. It defines and gives examples of any number of figures and tropes that characterize and can be enlisted for the sublime, the lofty sort of discourse said to transport and overwhelm like, in Longinus's glosses, a thunderbolt *à la* Demosthenes or a conflagration *à la* Cicero (see S, 12.4).[1] One is rendered beside oneself: *"ek-stasis"* (S, 1.4). Figures are a prime mechanism for the generation of these effects. Longinus contends that figures [σχήματα] are "natural allies" of the sublime, and one glimpses already in the term "allies" something of Longinus's figural nexus of power and violence: the sublime as *agon*[2] (S, 17.1). The sublime is variously conjured as a domain of great force, danger, and near-death experiences, whose attendant discourse is elaborated in charged figures of speech that both participate in and reflect such danger. * * *

Of the many figures defined and exemplified, Longinus reserves the most space not for metaphor, Aristotle's exemplary figure, but the seemingly less central one of hyperbaton or inversion. . . . [which] arises naturally from powerful, urgent emotion resulting in a wrenching of what might have been a natural sequence of words into a de-natured one. * * *

The figure of inversion rears its head again, though less overtly, in another of the canonical works of theory of the sublime: Edmund Burke's *Philosophical Enquiry into the Origins of our Ideas of the Sublime and Beautiful*, separated from Longinus by a millennium and a half. * * * Virtually all of Burke's examples of the sublime come from poetry, strictly speaking, or poetic parts of the Bible, with the two most quoted poets being John Milton and Homer, who were legendarily—and it seems not coincidentally—blind.

† From *ELH* 84.2(2017): 315–23. Copyright © 2017 Johns Hopkins University Press. Reprinted with permission of Johns Hopkins University Press. Balfour's notes are omitted.

1. Parenthetical references with S refer to Longinus' treatise by standard section and subsection numbers in the Greek text and in modern translations. Balfour cites from Longinus, *On the Sublime*, ed. and trans. W. H. Fyfe, revised by Donald A. Russell, in *Aristotle, Longinus, Demetrius* (1995; rpt. Cambridge, MA: Harvard University Press, 1999).
2. "contest, struggle."

From Burke, consider the following extreme, highly figured passage:

> The ideas of eternity and infinity are among the most affecting we have; and yet perhaps there is nothing of which we really understand so little, as of infinity and eternity. We do not anywhere meet a more sublime description than this justly celebrated one of Milton, wherein he gives the portrait of Satan with a dignity so suitable to the subject:
>
>> —He above the rest
>> In shape and gesture proudly eminent
>> Stood like a tower; his form had yet not lost
>> All her original brightness, nor appeared
>> Less than archangel ruined, and th' excess
>> Of glory obscured: as when the sun new risen
>> Looks through the horizontal misty air
>> Shorn of his beams; or from behind the moon
>> In dim eclipse disastrous twilight sheds
>> On half the nations; and with fear of change
>> Perplexes monarchs.—
>>
>>   (E, 61–62)[3]

Burke comments:

> Here is a very noble picture; and in what does this poetical picture consist? In images of a tower, an archangel, the sun rising through mists, or in an eclipse, the ruin of monarchs, and the revolutions of kingdoms. The mind is hurried out of itself by a crowd of great and confused images, which affect because they are crowded and confused. For, separate them, and you lose much of the greatness; and join them, and you infallibly lose the clearness. The images raised by poetry are always of this obscure kind[.]   (E, 62)

. . . It is striking that Burke considers these ideas among the most affecting there are: we are moved, he contends, by these impossible-to-represent ideas, not just puzzled intellectually. Sublime in themselves, these concepts become all the more so for the precise mode of their presentation, whereby "a croud of great and confused images" hurries the mind "out of itself," in an echo of Longinus's *ekstasis* . . .

I am interested in an aspect of Milton's language here that Burke leaves unremarked, though one for which he provides a framework later on in the *Enquiry*, namely, his emphasis on how words are put

---

3. Parenthetical references with *E* refer to Edmund Burke's 1757 treatise, *A Philosophical Enquiry into the Origin of Our Ideas of the Sublime and the Beautiful*, ed. James T. Boulton (Notre Dame: University of Notre Dame Press, 1958). Burke's quotation is from *Paradise Lost* 1.589–599.

together, what he calls "assemblage" (E, 171). Surely part of this passage's effect lies in its charged word order, its departures from the
ordinary, which is how Quintilian in general characterizes the figurative. Milton's lines are replete with textbook instances of inversion.
We read of Satan as an "archangel ruin'd" not a "ruined archangel"
and of his "glory obscur'd," not "obscured glory": nouns before adjectives. First we have the positive image of an archangel only to have it
"ruined" in the next, belated breath. Then we first imagine glory in
all its glory, only to learn one world later that it has been "obscur'd."
This is all the more pointed in that such sequences rehearse the
grand transition from good to bad organizing the poem, as most
spectacularly in the fall of man. Just the same sequence is writ large
in the very title of *Paradise Lost*. The logic of the poem all but forbids
one calling the poem by some prosaic alternative such as "lost paradise." Inversion might be to syntax what peripeteia[4] is to plot, a
change that renders the simple complex, which Aristotle seems to
prefer for intellectual or logical reasons as much as dramatic ones.
One recalls that *Paradise Lost* was conceived as a tragedy before being
realized as an epic.

A possible final instance of inversion in the passage occurs in the
phrase "dim eclipse disastrous" that sheds twilight, prompting
the fear of change that "perplexes monarchs." In this passage, we can
be lulled into thinking we are in the presence of normal word order,
since "dim eclipse" conforms to type but that does not prevent Milton from adding another adjective afterwards, one that is syntacti-
cally ambiguous: "disastrous" could modify "eclipse" just before it or
"twilight" just after it. It's a rhetorical twilight zone. Often in Milton
one is temporarily uncertain about the relative status of parts of a
sentence, as in the great phrase "human face divine." One could
be forgiven for thinking there would be no inversion here, since we
have adjective preceding a noun but the unexpected post-hoc adjective makes its poignant point, in a turn of phrase that William Blake
would transform into a matter of belief in what he calls the "human
form divine." * * *

This sort of inversion, which some see as one kind of hyperbaton,
is part of a larger complex in Milton of what one might call retroactive
qualification that has much of the same force. "[L]et us consider,"
Burke says, "those lines of Milton, where he describes the travels of
the fallen angels through their dismal habitation:

    —O'er many a dark and dreary vale
    They passed, and many a region dolorous;
    O'er many a frozen, many a fiery Alp;

---

4. "Reversal, sudden change of fortune," especially in tragedy [*Editor's note*].

> Rocks, caves, lakes, fens, bogs, dens, and shades of death,
> A universe of death.   (*E*, 174)[5]

Burke then comments:

> Here is displayed the force of union in
> *Rocks, caves, lakes, dens, bogs, fens, and shades*;
> which yet would lose the greatest part of their effect, if they
> were not the
> *Rocks, caves, lakes, dens, bogs, fens, and shades—of* Death.

> This idea or this affection caused by a word, which nothing but
> a word could annex to the others, raises a very great degree of
> the sublime; and this sublime is raised yet higher by what fol-
> lows, a "*universe of Death.*"   (*E*, 174–5)

Burke's fine analysis points to what is so often powerfully the case
in Milton: that one moves abruptly from what one sees or without
much trouble imagines to something difficult or impossible to
picture . . . "a universe of death." Who could possibly visualize
that? * * *

I have long thought, following G. W. F. Hegel and Georg Lukàcs,
that high epic in the line of Homer, Virgil, and Milton had become
impossible for the Romantics largely because of a preponderance of
lyric subjectivity and the concomitant difficulty in rendering socio-
political totalities. There were other obstacles in the way too, such
as Harold Bloom's anxiety of (Miltonic) influence, but it is remarkable how Keats finds inversion to be the signature figure of Miltonic epic, a figure he felt compelled to repeat but could not sustain
or abide. One can see, with Keats, how inversion in its Miltonic
guise could come across as mannered, dated, or artificial, though
Longinus had posited the figure in general as a mark of real emotion,
Keats's "true voice of feeling." When the Bay Area poet Jasper Ber-
nes, in a poem ending his recent collection *We Are Nothing And So
Can You*, uses the phrase "the seat perilous of the party historical,"
it comes across as outdated and outré, as pastiche of another era,
and this in a poem otherwise about riots now and the police now
and poetry of the future. Its topic and ethos could hardly be more
contemporary. Hardly anyone, as a rule, writes in Miltonic inver-
sions anymore, some contortions for the sake of rhyme notwithstanding, including in pop songs. Use of the figure is a delicate
matter, as it risks being an anachronous provocation.

* * *

5. Burke quotes *Paradise Lost* 2.618–22. The initial word is not "O'er" but "Through."
["O'er" begins line 220. The slip suggests Burke is quoting by heart.' —*Editor's note.*]

ON CHRISTIAN IDEOLOGY

A. S. P. WOODHOUSE

From Paradise Lost, I: Theme and Pattern[†]

* * *

Paradise Lost is the outcome of Milton's deliberate effort to write a classical epic on a Christian theme, and specifically on the fall of man. Any attempt to isolate and explain the effect of the poem must seek to draw out the implications of this truism, and essay once more some comparison of *Paradise Lost* with its two great models, the *Iliad* and the *Aeneid*. It must watch the poet imposing an analogous pattern upon very different materials, and be alert to detect the modifications and extensions of the pattern which his Christian theme, outlook, and purpose demand or permit.

When full allowance is made for Milton's heresies, *Paradise Lost* remains unequivocally a Christian poem. It assumes the two orders of nature and grace and the priority of the order of grace. Its theme is man's fall from grace and it adumbrates the terms on which, by divine intervention, he will be restored. *Paradise Lost* cannot be adequately described as an epic which substitutes Christian machinery for Olympian, or even Christian legend for pagan, though it does both: it is an epic which finds its subject at the heart of Christian revelation. Implicit in the difference between *Paradise Lost* and its classical models is the whole difference between Christianity and the Graeco-Roman religions and philosophies which it replaced. The points, relevant to our discussion, at which the Christian view of things and the classical most sharply diverge must be set down, at whatever risk of oversimplification.

The classical recognizes only one order of existence, the natural, though it acknowledges gradations within this order, whereas Christianity adds to the order of nature the superior order of grace, which alone holds the key to the enigma of life. And this addition of a second order which, in man, intersects with the first may serve to remind us that the Christian view of existence, like every great system of thought, is itself a pattern, and consequently contains elements which can be readily incorporated in the aesthetic patterns

† From *The Heavenly Muse: A Preface to Milton* (Toronto: University of Toronto Press, 1972), pp. 177–80, 188–90. Copyright © 1972 University of Toronto Press. Reprinted by permission of the publisher.

of the poet, as Dante would illustrate and as Milton will. But let us pursue for a moment the more obvious results of the single order in the classical systems and the twofold order in the Christian. The essential naturalism of the classical systems permeates any conceptions of the supernatural they may entertain, whether in the pantheon of Homer or in the religion of Virgil, who saw 'Universal Nature moved by Universal Mind.'[1] In Christianity, on the contrary, the supernatural dominates the natural. Though it ratifies many of the natural virtues before transcending them, Christianity will not rest content therewith, but adds its own special virtues of piety, humility, and love; and the Christian virtues combine to produce an ideal of heroism, realized in Christ, and very different from classical conceptions of the heroic, a fact which impinges directly upon epic poetry. Nor may we ignore the way in which Christianity extends what I will call the vertical range of human experience: in the classical view man may rise to the specifically human or sink to the level of the barbarian or the beast; in the Christian vision he is confronted by the dizzy alternatives of rising to heaven or plunging to the bottomless pit. I am the more insistent on this fact since Christianity is often thought merely to restrict the poet's outlook. It does not, I think, at all restrict him in his treatment of evil, but it does afford him a new orientation in several ways and with important results. Thus providence replaces the classical fate. 'Necessitie and Chance Approach not mee,' says Milton's God, 'and what I will is Fate' (7:172–3). This is something very different from fate in Homer, or even from the fate which in Virgil plays providence to the Roman race. One result is that on a total view there can be no such thing as divine tragedy, but only a divine comedy. We do not, however, always take total views, and in the divine comedy there is ample provision for tragic episodes. To prove it, one need not invoke the most moving spectacle in all history, Christ on the Cross: it will suffice to remember that as he turns to the story of man's actual fall, Milton, as he says, 'now must change Those notes to Tragic' (9.5–6). And well he may; for this tragic episode, 'with loss of *Eden*' brings 'Death into the World, and all our woe' (1.3–4). But on a total view the episode takes its place in the divine comedy as the *felix culpa*, the fortunate fall, and the lost Eden is replaced by 'a paradise within thee, happier farr' (12.587). Christianity does not eliminate the tragic from human life: it may even accentuate the tragic; but it places the tragic episode in the divine comedy, and thus invites us to take of it a double view. . . .

---

1. Alfred, Lord Tennyson, "To Virgil" (1882).

In Homer the hero is by no means the master of his fate, but he is the captain of his soul.[2] In Milton he is in some degree the master of his individual destiny, but Christ is the captain of his soul.

* * *

Despite the strong inclination of Christian humanism to approximate the Virgilian and the Christian ideals, there was a point, as Dante saw, beyond which Virgil could not go.[3] And in the particular matter of the heroic Milton is equally categorical. For him the ideal of heroism is realized once and for all in Christ. Long ago he had described Christ as 'most perfect *Heroe*' (*The Passion* 13), and significantly it was in connection with the heroic martyrdom of the crucifixion and the seeming defeat. The experience of the intervening years had brought home to Milton with a new urgency the idea of heroism in defeat, and this accounts for his exclusive emphasis upon it in the prologue to Book 9. But the idea does not subsist alone: the temporary defeat is part of the divine purpose which cannot fail of victory in the end, and Christian piety, yet more definitely than the Roman *pietas*, means complete submission to, and cooperation with, the divine purpose. Christ, then, is the real hero of *Paradise Lost* in the sense that, like Achilles and Aeneas, he sets the standard of heroism. It is not Christ the heroic martyr, however, that actually figures in the poem, though he is clearly adumbrated there. It is Christ the victor, clad with the Father's irresistible might, who drives Satan out of heaven, and thus performs, like Achilles, what a lesser hero could not achieve. In the successive stages of the heroic, and as it is brought under the control of morality and religion, the element of power, represented by the strength, prowess, and courage of Achilles, is not eliminated, but, by its alliance with the divine purpose, sustained and exalted. . . .

But the strong impression that Satan, though not the hero of the poem, is still in some sense heroic will not be easily relinquished and need not be. In epic protagonist and antagonist must meet as mighty opposites, and this demands in the antagonist certain marks of heroism. . . . [Milton] bestows upon Satan, in the beginning, all the qualities of the Homeric hero. Satan has the strength, prowess, and daring of Achilles, the same irresponsibility and recklessness, the same egoistic desire for glory and impatience of constraint, and like Achilles, though for a different reason, the pathos of the doomed. The intended dilemma of Raleigh's question about Satan, 'Hero or fool?'[4] is no dilemma at all. He is both—like Achilles and Turnus. . . .

2. An echo of the concluding lines of William Ernest Henley's "Invictus" (1875).
3. Virgil is Dante's guide in *Inferno* and *Purgatorio*, but because he is a pagan he gives way to Beatrice in *Paradiso*.
4. Sir Walter Raleigh, in *Milton* (London: E. Arnold, 1900), declares that Satan's situation "makes him either a fool or a hero, and Milton is far indeed from permitting us to think him a fool" (p. 133).

We see now that it is because Satan is pitted against Christ, not because he is pitted against Adam, that Milton is obliged to bestow upon him marks of the heroic. But it must be a heroism compatible with folly and wickedness, that is, a pagan heroism; and for this Milton looks in the ancient epics. Such heroism Satan has in abundance at the beginning; but, as the story proceeds, and Satan sinks deeper into wickedness, he is gradually divested even of this, as if Milton were saying that without virtue, without Christian heroism, all heroism is an illusion.

*   *   *

STANLEY FISH

From With Mortal Voice: Milton Defends against the Muse[†]

*   *   *

* * * It is only when Milton creates a character more or less out of whole cloth that he can even imagine what it would be like not to feel the stirrings he describes as "that last infirmity of Noble mind."[1] That character is Abdiel, the zealous loyalist, whose finest moment is not seen by anyone, including himself. It is a moment that follows upon something more visibly heroic, his rising to affirm his fidelity to the Father even in the midst of the Satanic host. Now he is on the way back to his friends, but the surprise that awaits him when he arrives is anticipated in the syntax of book 6's opening lines:

> All night the dreadless Angel unpursu'd
> Through Heav'n's wide Champaign held his way, till Morn,
> Wak't by the circling Hours, with rosy hand
> Unbarr'd the gates of Light.   (6.1–4)

"Unpursu'd" is an early clue as to what will soon happen—or, rather, not happen: Abdiel's flight is without the temporal pressure, at least in one direction, that usually gives such actions point. The significant shift, however, occurs at the end of the second line. When we first read it, "till Morn" seems an adverbial phrase modifying "held his way" and therefore a gloss on *Abdiel's* action; but line 3 reveals that in the fuller syntax "till Morn" is the object of the participle "Wak't" (the morn is waked) and then the subject of

† From *ELH* 62.3 (1995): 524–26. Copyright © 1995 The Johns Hopkins University Press. Reprinted with permission of The Johns Hopkins University Press.
1. "Lycidas," in *John Milton*, ed. Stephen Orgel and Jonathan Goldberg (New York: Oxford University Press, 1990), 41, line 71 [*Fish's note*].

"unbarr'd." What this means is that in the course of these lines the
agency is taken away from Abdiel and given to the Morn, who now
has the forward initiative. It is *her* way, not his, and moreover it is a
way that will proceed independently of anything Abdiel does or
doesn't do. The hours circle—that is, they don't go in a straight line
but describe motions that return always to the same appointed
place. The effect of this image is to further undercut the urgency
and point of Abdiel's linear flight; and that effect is itself redoubled
when that flight is interrupted by a leisurely explanation of the
subordinate and indeed decorative role of time in the realm of the
heavens:

> There is a Cave
> Within the Mount of God, fast by his Throne,
> Where light and darkness in perpetual round
> Lodge and dislodge by turns, which makes through Heav'n
> Grateful vicissitude, like Day and Night.   (6.4–8)

That is, for the sake of variety (here a purely aesthetic category)
there is a light show in heaven that *simulates* day and night, that
simulates the "Diurnal Sphere" in which the passing of time is
attended by crisis, choice, and unpredictable consequences. In
Heaven time's passing is devoid of such risks because everything is
always and already centered on the central and informing value of
the universe; so that when in line 12 Raphael tells us that "now went
forth the Morn," we are meant to understand that "now" merely
marks a turn-taking and not a moment of poised urgency; and if we
miss the point, the verse quickly reminds us of it: "Such as in highest
Heav'n" (6.13). "Shot through with orient Beams" (6.15) further dis-
sipates the already attenuated energy of Abdiel's flight, and for all
intents and purposes Abdiel disappears from the passage, reemerg-
ing only as the *object* of the effect he had hoped to cause:

> when all the plain
> Cover'd with thick embattl'd Squadrons bright,
> Chariots and flaming Arms, and fiery Steeds
> Reflecting blaze on blaze, first met his view.
> (6.15–18)

The "first" in line 18 is very precise: the view *precedes* his "taking it
in"; it is before him in two senses of the word; it is in front of him,
and it was there before he saw it; in relation to it, he is superfluous;
it doesn't need him, and the extent of his inefficacy is given a slow
deliberate gloss: "War he perceiv'd, war in procinct, and found /
Already known what he for news had thought / To have reported"
(6.19–21). That is, Abdiel had thought that there was something he
could *do*, something he could *say*, words that only he could

produce, words that would make a difference because they would *be* different, not already spoken in the eternal present; but that thought, and the vision of self and identity of which it is an extension, are countermanded by a reality that has no place for them—the reality of the "omnific Word."

At this moment Abdiel is exactly in the position the epic narrator occupies in the opening of book 7, confronted by the suffocating omnipresence of the deity he serves. What distinguishes the two is their reaction, or, rather, the fact that Abdiel doesn't have a reaction. The hinge between what he has just "met"—the castrating sight of his undeniable impotence—and what he now does is the word "gladly": "Already known what he for news had thought / To have reported: gladly then he mixt" (6.20–21).

The extraordinary thing about "gladly" is that it participates in both actions (because it participates in two syntactic structures) and thereby acknowledges no difference between them: Abdiel would have been glad to report and he just as gladly mixes, that is, loses himself in a host already composed without his reportorial aid. I don't mean that he says to himself, "Well, that was a disappointment (not to have reported), but I can still enjoy the fellowship of my peers"; he doesn't say *anything* to himself. The two possible modes of action which for us would be seen as active and passive respectively are for him absolutely continuous, of a piece, alternative forms of service. He can take no credit for not feeling aggrieved at having his great moment snatched from him, because it never occurs to him to be aggrieved, and therefore he deserves credit precisely in the measure he would not think to claim it. As far as he is concerned, he just does what he does, or is what he is, and as he is named, the servant of God.

* * *

VICTORIA SILVER

From Milton's God[†]

* * *

* * * [T]his distinctiveness of the poem's justifying can be elucidated by John Rawls's "veil of ignorance" and some possible implications of that similarly instrumental fiction, which serves to exclude all particular knowledge that might keep two parties from distinterestedly

† From *Imperfect Sense: The Predicament of Milton's Irony* (Princeton, NJ: Princeton University Press, 2001), pp. 47–59, 354. Copyright © 2001 by Princeton University Press. Reprinted by permission of Princeton University Press.

and mutually pursuing justice.[1] The excluded knowledge in a case of inequity must be reciprocal, encompassing the personal or corporate circumstances of both parties at once, since the intent behind such a "veil of ignorance" is to create a position of artificial parity between disputants, and thus to remove from consideration those real differences in status and interest which might hamper even the hypothetical pursuit of justice. * * *

* * * Because Milton too, as a Christian of the reformed or Protestant persuasion, must argue a "veil of ignorance" that has to do simply and absolutely with the hidden God whose ways he sets out to make right with humanity. He must talk about God as though he knew deity in some sufficient shape or form, like Rawls's negotiating parties—as though there were some clear and determinate correlation between God's intent and Milton's account of it, when theologically there can be neither in his view. Indeed, the relative status of divine expressions is so profoundly, inexpressibly different from deity itself that their distinction can only sever relationship, in which case the speaker of *Paradise Lost* and humanity with him would be forced to suffer the sense of God's injustice without possibility of redress or relief—as Job fears in his own case.

* * * Milton must propose a purely functional parity in his representation between things human and divine that would allow for our experience and understanding of deity, even as this representation must somehow acknowledge the incalculable difference between what it says about God and what deity is in itself. When Calvin defines "the fear of God," he has in mind something like this predicament. * * * In other words, the "fear of God" acknowledges the abysmal difference between what deity is and what we know of it, thus restricting our ability to anticipate what its purposes are or to say how its expressions mean: the picture we have of God is thus peculiarly groundless and inutile as it applies to our knowledge of the divine nature. At the same time, it is entirely viable insofar as that picture, articulated by faith, permits and sustains a relationship between two absolutely disparate parties. As Rawls hopes for his version of the same device, a religious "veil of ignorance" is not invalidating but instead instrumental to Milton's work of justification, because it alone sets up the mutuality between divine and human worlds that must exist for any communication, much less justice to be pursued between them. But that mutuality depends on an artificial likeness or parity of persons that must constantly be exposed as such, unless we are to behave like idolaters and take God's expressions as though they said everything about God and nothing about ourselves, who are their ironical subject even as Job, not the creator God, was the subject of

---

1. *A Theory of Justice* (Cambridge, Mass.: Belknap Press, 1971), pp. 136–42.

the Lord's theophany from the whirlwind. "The ways of God" describe deity only in its relative character as *our* God in those "acts he presents to our eyes" and in the "riddle" of our experience.

*   *   *

MICHAEL LIEB

From The Theopathetic Deity[†]

* * * [T]he poetic representation of God must be understood on its own terms, which may or may not be in accord with the treatise through which deity emerges as a distinctly "theological" entity. I am not talking about formal or unyielding structures here. My fundamental point is to allow the God of the theological treatise and the God of the poetry to "breathe," that is, to enjoy distinct identities without being hemmed in or manacled by a determination to view them as one and the same. Approaching Milton's God in this manner should help to ensure the integrity of the texts (theological and poetic) through which deity is imbued with life and meaning. * * *

I do not, however, intend to focus on all aspects of Milton's delineation of God in the poetry. In fact, I make a point here of limiting my focus drastically. I do so in order to unearth what might be called the subterranean aspects of deity, aspects that suggest the "dark side" of God, the "other" God, one who exhibits emotional fervor in a manner that can be construed as threatening and even unstable in the extreme. * * * What is true of the theological treatise is no less true of the poetry: Milton's God is in many respects the hidden God come to life, come to haunt both the prose and the poetry. * * * I am not claiming that Milton's God is not good. He is a very good God indeed (at least in most respects). But there is a side or "face" to him that is decidedly dark, decidedly disturbing. That disturbing quality emerges in the revelation of his hiddenness. With that revelation comes the release of emotional energy, anger, and even hate. The faces of God we behold in the revelation of the dark side may be troublesome and unsettling, but they are as much a part of the God of Milton as any other aspects one can imagine. If the God of the theological treatise and the God of the poetry do not necessarily correspond in all respects, they do nonetheless represent the means by which much of what is disturbing about Milton's deity assumes both a discursive and a poetic bearing.

[†] From *Theological Milton: Deity, Discourse and Heresy in the Miltonic Canon* (Pittsburgh: Duquesne University Press, 2006), pp. 127–29, 162. Reprinted by permission of Pennsylvania State University Press. Lieb's notes are omitted.

                              *   *   *

    Paradise Lost is not the Bible, and Milton's God does not possess
the same authorized presence as he does in the Bible. As far as
Milton is concerned, however, his poem is the most authoritative
reenactment of what happens in the Bible as one can possibly imagine. In the process of that reenactment, the passibility [1] of God is
accorded a new and distinctly compelling status, one in which a sub-
limely feeling, indeed, passionate deity becomes the focal point of all
the creative energies that Milton's poem is able to marshal. * * *

                      ON RACE AND RELIGION

                      FEISAL G. MOHAMED

                From Milton's Enmity towards Islam
                  and the *Intellectus Agens*†

The most prominent Muslim in Milton's writings, of course, is
Satan. Among other things his barbarous rule is Eastern rule, with
its combination of luxury and absolutism. He is a "great Sultan"
whose "great consulting Peers" sit in a "dark *Divan*".[1] For Milton
the association of the Ottomans with autocracy was long-standing.
Eikonoklastes[2] brands Charles I's monarchy a "Turkish tyranny" for
its refusal to be restrained by law. That catchy alliterative phrase
apparently held appeal, turning up as well in the *Observations on
the Articles of Peace* and in the *Commonplace Book*. Each time it
serves as a polar opposite to Christian monarchy mindful of Christian liberty, making Milton's views on the political order of the
Turks clear enough.
    But there are reasons to inquire further. Much as he consistently
despised Turkish rule, Milton recognized as early as his seventh
Prolusion that its Arabic predecessor did unite political authority
with the advancement of learning. And some of the references in
Paradise Lost to the Islamic world of the present day, as Gordon
Campbell has shown with respect to "Arabia" and "Ormuz", were not
necessarily associated with Islam in the seventeenth century,

---

1. In theology, God's capacity for feeling and suffering.
† From *English Studies* 96.1 (2015): 65–68, 72–74, 76–77. Reprinted by permission of
  the publisher Taylor & Francis Ltd. Unless otherwise indicated, notes are by the editor
  of this Norton Critical Edition.
1. *PL* 1.348, 10.457 and n.
2. Literally, "Image Breaker," written by Milton in 1649 to answer *Eikon Basilike* (*Image
  of the King*), a defense of the recently executed Charles I.

making the East more ambiguous and multifaceted in Milton's imagination than we might first suppose.[3] If, as his licensing of the *Racovian Catechism* implies and as John Dennis proclaimed, Milton was "a little tainted with Socinianism",[4] then by the standards of the time he was also a little tainted with Mahometanism. It did not escape the notice of seventeenth-century polemicists that Socinian scepticism on the divinity of Jesus looked rather like the Muslim view of him as a prophet. And pursuing the English Arabists of the seventeenth century places us very much in Milton's orbit. Milton clearly admired John Selden, who receives a glowing mention in *Areopagitica* and whose *De diis Syriis* [On the Gods of the Syrians] strongly informs the catalogue of fallen angels in *Paradise Lost*.[5] The manuscript of Ibn Tufayl's *Hayy Ibn'Yaqzan* translated by Edward Pococke the younger generated interest in the Hartlib circle and amongst Restoration Quakers. The first English writer to attempt a balanced life of Mohammed was Henry Stubbe, who defended Milton in print and was chaplain to the younger Sir Henry Vane, the martyred English republican and proponent of liberty of conscience for whom Milton had long-standing, enormous admiration. Looking beyond England, we might wonder if Milton's interest in the work of Hugo Grotius might lead him to reconsider the Islamic tradition, given the Dutch jurist's composition of an apology in the spirit of Juan Luis Vives' *De veritate fidei Christianae* [*On the Truth of the Christian Faith*] (1543). We might also wonder if Milton's considerable investment in cosmology would lead him to Arabic sources, as it did Joseph Scaliger. Milton's intellectual milieu offered numerous invitations to inquire into the Islamic tradition. And yet, frustratingly, we have no real evidence that he ever entertained the possibility.

* * * Milton was clearly aware of the power, political and economic, wielded by the sultan in his time, and of the ways in which England's commercial aspirations faced challenges, diplomatic and piratical, from the Maghreb countries holding the keys to the Strait of Gibraltar.

This aspect of the period is becoming increasingly familiar, thanks in no small measure to the scholarship of Nabil Matar.[6] But even as it applies just limits to Europe's perceived influence in the period, it does very little to challenge "the West" as a cultural

---

3. See Gordon Campbell, "'To the Shore of Tripoli': Milton, Islam, and the Attacks on America and Spain," in *Fundamentalism and Literature*, ed. Catherine Pesso-Miquel and Klaus Stierstorfer (Basingstoke: Palgrave Macmillan, 2007), pp. 14–16 [*Mohamed's note*].
4. John Dennis, *The Grounds of Criticism in Poetry* (London, 1704) [*Mohamed's note*].
5. For Selden, see above p. 360 and n. 8.
6. Author of numerous books on cultural and political relations between Islam and Europe, especially England and the Magreb, i.e., Gibraltar and the North African or Barbary Coast. See *Britain and Barbary, 1589–1689* (Gainesville: University Press of Florida, 2005).

construct circumscribing a set of traditions. Our second branch of inquiry unsettles this assumption more fully in focusing on Milton's investment in an intellectual category of largely Islamic provenance: the *intellectus agens*, or agent[7] intellect. Having roots in Aristotle's *De anima* [On the Soul], it is developed significantly in the thought of al-Farabi,[8] whence it comes to have a strong presence amongst philosophical writings in all three Abrahamic religions.

*   *   *

Milton's invocation to light has already been associated with Christian mysticism rooted in the Pseudo-Dionysian treatise *De divinis nominibus* [On the Divine Names]: "the Good . . . generously reveals a firm, transcendent beam, granting enlightenments proportionate to each being, and thereby draws sacred minds upward to its permitted contemplation".[9] This figuring of divine radiance as light is equally common amongst Islamic mystics and philosophers, we should expect, given the densely metaphorical "light verse" of The Qur'an, quoted above, itself drawn from a Sura devoted to light.[1] The 1649 English Qur'an only hints at this verse's complexities: "God illuminateth the heaven and the Earth, as the Lamp that is in the Lanthorn of Chrystall, fed with oyl of the blessed Olive. It seemeth to be a Star full of light, which goeth neither to the West, nor the East, and yeildeth [sic] brightness upon brightness."[2] To provide an early modern example of Islamic thought figuring divine wisdom as light, we might turn to Ismail Ankaravi's *Illuminative Philosophy*. A sixteenth-century member of the Bayrami Sufi order, Ankaravi, his early biographers tell us, focused his attention on "spiritual illuminations" after going blind. His sight was miraculously cleared when he left Ankara and became a disciple of the Sufi sheikh Bostan Celebi I, whose death in 1630 lamentably made it impossible for Milton to have sought this cure.

*   *   *

Had Milton come upon the writings of al-Farabi, he would have appreciated its closely interwoven logic, epistemology, cosmology and political philosophy. Even as one of his most famous works is a

---

7. *intellectus agens*: "the intellect acting" implies an active, grasping faculty, in contrast with the theocentric idea of the mind as the passive recipient of divine illumination.
8. Great tenth-century Islamic scholar and philosopher, who wrote on all areas of philosophy and whose commentaries preserved much of the Greek texts of Aristotle.
9. Pseudo-Dionysius, *Pseudo-Dionysius: The Complete Works (Classics of Western Spirituality)*, trans. Colm Luibhéid and Paul Rorem (New York: Paulist Press, 1987), p. 50 [*Mohamed's note*].
1. Qur'an, Sura 24, verse 35 (not included here): it begins, "God is the light of the heavens and the earth."
2. Alexander Ross, trans., *The Alcoran of Mahomet* (London, 1649), pp. 216–17 [*Mohamed's note*].

taxonomy of the spheres of knowledge, in his most developed
thought al-Farabi does not separate these branches of study. Rather,
his two parallel treatises, *The Principles of Beings* and *On the Perfect State*, move from the nature of human intellect and the universe to political order, flawed and ideal.

*   *   *

The passage of Milton's poetry toward which we have been moving
is the invocation to light in book 3 of *Paradise Lost*. The "holy Light"
with which the invocation begins is a "sovran vital Lamp" pointedly
defined against physical light.[3] . . . That immediate sense of divine
illumination inflects the distinction in book 3 between inner and
physical sight:

> cloud in stead, and ever-during dark
> Surrounds me, from the chearful ways of men
> Cut off, and for the Book of knowledg fair
> Presented with a Universal blanc
> Of Natures works to mee expung'd and ras'd,
> And wisdom at one entrance quite shut out.
> So much the rather thou Celestial light
> Shine inward, and the mind through all her powers
> Irradiate, there plant eyes, all mist from thence
> Purge and disperse, that I may see and tell
> Of things invisible to mortal sight.[4]

Much as the language reminds us of the Aristotelian and Neoplatonic traditions in which al-Farabi participates, Milton seems anxious to draw key distinctions. There does seem to be a portion of
the mind most capable of intellection, and the passage points to it
emphatically—"*there* plant eyes, all mist *from thence* / Purge and
disperse"—suggesting a physical location for what Raphael describes
in his dialogue with Adam, the small share of *noûs* [Mind] available
to humanity.[5] . . .

But we ought not to downplay the significance of Milton describing a portion of the mind as the seat of intellection. The point is a
significant addition to the treatise on faculty psychology with which
Adam regales Eve at the beginning of book 5, where the representations of the senses feed "fancy", which "forms imaginations"
weighed by a reason residing above fancy.[6] As in al-Farabi, the imaginative will in and of itself does not engage in moral choice. Also like
al-Farabi, Milton wants to show that Adam's view of reason and

3. *PL* 3.1, 22.
4. *PL* 3.45–55.
5. See *PL* 5.470–90.
6. *PL* 5.100–109.

moral choice does not take sufficient account of that spiritual knowledge residing above discursive reason, the intellection that Raphael
describes later in this book as our greatest resemblance to angelic
thought. In a way setting Milton apart from the rational religion taking shape in the late seventeenth century, the seat of intellection must
be receptive to illumination from the realm of invisibles. In Milton
and in al-Farabi, the will thus formed has a moral dimension, for the
highest portion of the mind described in the invocation to light looks
very much as though it is equivalent to the "Umpire *Conscience*" to
which God the Father later refers in book 3.[7] For Milton the light conscience receives is much more theocentric than it is for al-Farabi and
others in the *intellectus agens* tradition: the "light after light" leading
us to safe arrival is clearly and emphatically divine grace.[8]

Milton is in dialogue with a tradition of strongly Islamic provenance, but in his disputatious way. He might find congenial the
remarks of that other parliamentarian immortalized in *Areopagitica*, Lord Brooke, who observes that though many volumes have
been written on the *intellectus agens*, the "wiser sort" perceive the
"thinnesse, aërialnesse and crazinesse of this Spiders web", and
"have with greater probability made *God* to be *intellectus agens*, by
his influence upon the understanding".[9]

*   *   *

ISLAM ISSA

From Milton's Presence: Texts and Translations[†]

In the Arab-Muslim world, John Milton is not a household name
like William Shakespeare or, perhaps surprisingly, Agatha Christie.
Where Milton is known in the region, it is chiefly as the blind poet
who wrote *Paradise Lost*. Many views on Milton are derived primar-
ily from some Arab critics from the first half of the twentieth
century, some of which have been influenced by Romantic responses.
Moreover . . . there are major misconceptions and generalisations
about Milton. Recurring themes and perceptions that characterize
the reception of Milton in the Arab-Muslim world include a strong

7. *PL* 3.195.
8. *PL* 3.196–97.
9. Robert Greville, Baron Brooke, *The Nature of Truth, Its Union and Unity with the Soule*
   (London, 1641), pp. 19–21. For Milton's reference to Lord Brooke in *Areopagitica*, see
   p. 387 and n. 6 above. For his reference to Selden in the same tract, see p. 360 and n. 8.
† From *Milton in the Arab-Muslim World* (New York: Routledge, 2017), pp. 28, 41–42, 47.
   Copyright © 2017 Islam Issa. Reproduced by arrangement with Taylor & Francis Books
   UK. Unless otherwise indicated notes are by the editor of this Norton Critical
   Edition.

emphasis on biography, particularly his religious views and his blindness, as well as a focus on the character of Satan in *Paradise Lost*. Milton's biography has been used in the region to support various Islamic viewpoints, while Milton's seventeenth-century context and construction of Satan have been particularly important in the unexpected utilization of Milton in issues of Middle Eastern politics. Furthermore, the accessibility and translation of Milton's works shed light on the revival of Arab culture and literature, this culture's relationship with its Western counterparts, and the intricacies of religio-cultural issues in the inconsistent political and social climate of the region.

*   *   *

*** In fact, both personal and political events are explored through direct reference to the poet. While [John] Carey's journalistic alignment of *Samson Agonistes* with a political maelstrom—in that case, 11 September 2001—is well known,[1] such a manoeuvre to connect Milton with politics, through the press, is not unprecedented and is perhaps more common in non-Western media. ***

It is clear that Milton is used in the political debates of the Arab world—and in differing ways. Muhammad El-Sharqawi's 1999 column in *Al-Ahram* newspaper, entitled 'A political story', and subtitled 'Adam and Eve—and the route to Paradise', praises Milton's revolutionary character and works. El-Sharqawi asserts that 'liberty, at the time of the magnificent British poet John Milton, was trying to escape from its chains and its captivity'. Giving brief historical context from seventeenth-century England, El-Sharqawi argues that Milton struggled in order to win political and personal freedoms, both of which were epitomised by the subject matter of the 'wonderful epic *Paradise Lost*'. The column refers to Boris Yeltsin, the first president of the Russian Federation (1991–1999), who had recently stormed out of an August 1999 conference after U.S. President Bill Clinton criticized him for the war on Chechnya—a war that Arab populations opposed strongly. According to El-Sharqawi, Yeltsin initially 'played Cromwell's game', for he 'started as a defender of liberty, then fired his canons at parliament, the symbol of democracy', and 'now wears the sash of Charles II'. El-Sharqawi hints that there are positives in Yeltsin's rise to power as an anti-establishment figure, as well as the initial economic reforms in his first term of presidency. However, the columnist sees that Yeltsin's confrontations with Parliament and the military invasion of Chechnya in which tens of thousands of civilians were

---

1. John Carey, "A Work in Praise of Terrorism?," *Times Literary Supplement*, September 6, 2002, 15–16.

killed—here compared to Charles II's conflict with Parliament and instigation of the Second Anglo-Dutch War—made the Russian turn into an unpopular, oppressive figure. El-Sharqawi concludes that as 'the grandchildren of Adam and Eve', we have a stark reminder in *Paradise Lost* of how our actions can change destiny for the worse, and how after being 'sent down to the earth and its blaze', we should search for 'the Paradise of justice and liberty'. Yeltsin would resign on the final day of that millennium.

*   *   *

Milton has a certain but overlooked presence in the Arab world. He may even have influenced Arab-Muslim culture beyond literature, academia, and the press. One example is the term *'al-firdaws al-mafqūd'*, or 'the lost Paradise', the common Arabic translation of the phrase *Paradise Lost* and the translated title of Milton's epic. Like the English, the syntax of the term places 'Paradise' before 'lost'; literally 'the Paradise the lost'. In historical studies, this Arabic term has been used very commonly to refer to the fall of the Islamic empire of Andalusia (*c.* 700–1600 A.D.). Accordingly, the term has found its way into recent histories, anthologies, media, and educational courses about Andalusia. For Muslims in Europe, too, many relate Andalusia to the English term 'the lost paradise'. Recently, the term has also been used to refer to the occupation of Palestine. It is possible, though scarcely provable, that Milton's epic played a part in the creation of this term among present-day Muslims. What can be proven is that Milton does hold a place in the academic, literary, and popular culture of the region.

*   *   *

PEGGY SAMUELS

From Riding the Hebrew Word Web[†]

As a result of the explosion of Hebrew learning in the sixteenth century, seventeenth-century readers of Hebrew were able to draw readily on the use of lexicons, concordances, and polyglots as they negotiated the Hebrew Bible. These aids to reading record particular ways of thinking about and handling the language. In looking both at the prefatory material that describes the Hebrew language

---

[†] From *Living Texts: Interpreting Milton*, ed. Kristin A. Pruitt and Charles W. Durham (Cranbury, N.J.: Associated University Presses), pp. 162–63, 165–67. Reprinted with permission of Associated University Presses. Unless otherwise indicated notes are by the editor of this Norton Critical Edition.

and at the treatment of individual words, we can gather a sense of
how readers were working with the language. Written while modern philology was in its formative years, early modern dictionaries
of Hebrew sometimes reveal a motivated shaping of the knowledge
that was being gathered and transmitted via the dictionaries.
Edward Leigh's dictionary, *Critica Sacra. Observations on all the
Radices, or Primitive Hebrew words of the Old Testament,* and the
more scholarly *Lexicon Hebraicum* of Johannes Buxtorf, demonstrate the labile nature of the meanings of individual Hebrew words
and illuminate the ways in which Milton and other seventeenth-
century readers widened the meanings of Hebrew words.

     * * *We can glimpse the emotional force behind these beliefs
[concerning the divinity of the Hebrew language] in Brian Walton's
preface to the polyglot of 1656.[1] Walton states that God's goodness,
so manifest in the world, was demonstrated vividly in his having
"poured out on the first men" this divine language. Walton thinks
of divine wisdom as having been scattered in other languages
because "certain remnants of [Hebrew] are found in all languages."
He claims that those long centuries "when the whole earth ha[d]
been buried in deep shadows of error" can only be reversed by trying to grasp at these scattered, tiny shards of light located in
Hebrew. Walton studied Hebrew lexicons, biblical translations and
Targums, hoping to be able to gain access to those "divine mysteries concerning the eternal well-being of humanity, which were
established and first passed on in this language." When Walton
imagines the reader gaining entrance to the Hebrew language, he
says that it is as if one who had always had to view sacred things
from a distance was now "admitted into the sanctuary with priests[;]
he himself [the one who knows Hebrew] is a witness and a judge of
all those things which are going on in the inner rooms." *Areopagitica*'s imagery of gathering the scattered body of truth, like the frag-
mented pieces of Osiris [see p. 381 and n. 7], is also the image that
occurs in the preface to Walton's polyglot, between the covers of
which the fragments of Hebrew and of other languages that revealed
its meanings were collected.

✻   ✻   ✻

     * * *The working out of, or dilation of, the theme of overly curi-
ous searching may be thought of as Milton's bringing into the view
of his English-reading public—that is, "translating" as fully as possible—the multiple meanings contained in a single Hebrew word.
The lexicographers use the phrase "to open a word" when they are
elucidating its meanings. To "open" a word is to gain entrance to its

---

1. Brian Walton, ed., *Biblia sacra polyglotta*, 6 vols. (London, 1653–57).

meanings, as if each word is a door, leading to a new conceptual stream. This view of the Hebrew language can contribute to Milton's sense that he is "opening" rather than adding to Scripture. A full, complete reading or rendering of Scripture would have to include these links between "serpent," "overly curious searching," and "searching by augury."

Some of these multiple meanings, particularly the ones that are based on etymological (often false etymological) connections, are familiar to us because the Bible mentions them when speaking about the name of a child or a place. For example, Renaissance dictionaries follow the biblical text in making an etymological connection between Moses (in Hebrew, *Mosheh*) and the verb "to draw out" [*mashah*]. Of the many ways that Milton conceptualized himself as a kind of Moses, one of the most powerful nodes of identification many have been through this false etymology of the one who "draws out"—not just the one who was drawn out of the water but the one who draws out water from the rock.[2]

Often, the occurrence of two meanings within a single Hebrew root arises from the feature that Walton calls "the modulation through various conjugations." He uses the phrase to describe what he is watching as he is studying the meaning of Hebrew words. He is referring to the way that the verbal system in Hebrew depends on varying the form of a verb in order to convey sometimes intensified, sometimes additional meanings. To give a simple example, the word *naga* [to touch] has also the intensified meaning of "to strike" when it moves through what Walton calls another "conjugation." And, in the passive, *naga* denotes "to be stricken," as in defeated in battle, or struck (by the plague), or (of fate) to befall. "Touch," "harm," "strike," "to be defeated," "to be stricken (with the plague or fate)": the language feels like a series of palimpsests in which one word has other words above and below it. Or, as an alternative image, one can think of it as overtones on a flute in which one can hear the meanings hovering over (or under) the meaning that is invoked.

To turn to an example that also occurs as a thematic strand in *Paradise Lost*, the verbs "to place" and "to rest" are actually different forms of the same root (*noach*). In *Paradise Lost*, Satan cannot have found a true place for himself because he is unable to rest. Adam and Eve lose their place as they lose their ability to find repose. Certainly these thematic links have a long history in Christian tradition and literature. They also have an elemental

---

2. In Exodus 2:5 the baby Moses is drawn out of the water by Pharaoh's daughter. In Numbers 20:10–11 Moses draws water out of the rock by striking it with his staff. Cf. Exodus 17:6.

relationship to one another in the verbal system of the Hebrew language. It would be difficult for someone learning Hebrew (not necessarily a native speaker of Hebrew) to forget "rest" [*noach*] as he/she reads "and he placed him" [*yanichahu*]. So as God "places" man in the Garden of Eden to work it [*avdah*] and watch over it [*shamarah*], the idea of "rest" is inside, or resonates within, the verb "to place," intensifying the sense that one can be at work (placed there to serve and to watch over) while simultaneously being at rest. Milton's construction of an Eden in which human labor never seems to counteract the feeling of repose surely has cultural causes, yet the Hebrew language provides a grounding from which such a cultural construction can both find confirmation and unfold.

* * * Each use of a word recalls its former use, in another verse, and sets up a comparison between the two contexts. For example, the word "send" [*shalach*] is used for "to send a messenger" or, with an increased sense of honor, "to send on a mission" or "to send off" as in escorting part way; in the next conjugation, however, the meaning alters, becoming "send away," "dismiss," "cast out." In *Paradise Lost,* Milton uses the full range of meanings for the verb. He deploys its forms when describing the satanic crew "sent" (cast out) from Heaven (1.750), angels "sent" (as messengers) to the garden (7.72), Christ "sent" as Judge and Savior (10.209), and Adam and Eve "sent" out of the garden (11.261). Milton needs to have one English word bear this range of oppositional meanings (even if he sometimes also uses the words "cast out") in order to create a correlative to the way the Hebrew word holds within itself a comparison of different kinds of "sending." By repeating the word in different contexts, Milton can lead his reader simultaneously to hold onto the different contexts for the word's use. To hold in one's mind the extremes of this range ("to cast out," "to send on a divine mission") has an impact on the resonance of Milton's final use of the word as Adam and Eve are sent out of the garden. That moment of leave-taking, then, hovers between the sense of "expelled" and "sent out as if destined[.]" * * * Adam and Eve's experience of being sent out of the garden is held in tension between all of the meanings "sent" has acquired during the poem.

*   *   *

486

REGINALD A. WILBURN

From Making "Darkness Visible":
Milton and Early African American Literature[†]

Ever since Phillis Wheatley published *Poems on Various Subjects, Religious and Moral* in 1773, there has been a need for theorizing the Word that governs African Americans' receptions of John Milton.[1] That need has intensified for more than two and a half centuries as subsequent African American writers and orators continued to follow Wheatley's Miltonic lead by making darkness visible in reception studies devoted to England's epic poet of liberty. Through the art of poetic intertextuality, writers from Olaudah Equiano,[2] David Walker, and Frederick Douglass to Frances Ellen Watkins Harper, Anna Julia Cooper, and Sutton Griggs have evidenced their remastery of the English language by completing and complicating Milton in ways that have yet to be examined in literary criticism.

* * * Literary criticism has yet to theorize on the hermeneutic practices deployed by this unseen collective of black authors. This void in scholarship proves increasingly detrimental to critics in Milton and African American literary studies as contemporary writers in the African American tradition continue to extend these intertextual ties to England's epic poet of liberty. For instance, Toni Morrison's novel *A Mercy* is a recent text that tropes with Milton, yet no theoretical examination exists to account for her relation to her predecessors within this neglected literary tradition. * * *

* * * Miltonic appropriations in early African American tradition reveal this distinct interpretive community as caught up in similar struggles due to their marginalized status in Western civilization. One of the routes members of this community charted in order to elevate themselves from spheres of abject darkness drew upon cultivating a subversive fluency with Milton. * * * Within this tradition, early African American authors remastered the English language, completing and complicating Milton on demonic grounds of contention. While occupying these grounds, they preached satanic gospels of black revolt but for messianic purposes of racial uplift in the cause of liberty and pursuit of freedom.

† From *Preaching the Gospel of Black Revolt: Appropriating Milton in Early African American Literature* (Pittsburgh: Duquesne University Press, 2014), pp. 1–6. Reprinted with permission of Pennsylvania State University Press.
1. Phillis Wheatley (c. 1753–December 1784), the first African American poet, was born in West Africa and enslaved as a child. She was purchased by the wealthy John Wheatley of Boston and educated in the family. She read classical authors and was strongly influenced by Milton's style.
2. For Equiano, see pp. 412–413.

As a rebellious methodology, demonic grounds represent a surveying of racial-sexual sites of spatial unrepresentability and the geographical contestations that transform these violent landscapes through indeterminable processes or outcomes.

*   *   *

* * * Early African American authors transform this interpretive landscape considerably when they forge rhetorical affiliations with Milton through the infernal hero of *Paradise Lost* and his tradition of poetic fallenness. As a result, they make darkness visible in Africanist receptions of Milton.

*   *   *

At the same time, their engagements with Milton throw intertextual shades of meaning on the epic poet's canon, illumining the after-effects of his presence across the literary color line. This phenomenon in intertextual engagement likewise points to a demonic grounds of contention, for these practices encourage hermeneutic activities that will lead to a charting of new cartographies in literary study. Such an enterprise enlarges the interpretive terrain with the end goal of cultivating a greater appreciation for Milton's afterlife in the Western canon. Charting these explorations embodies aspects of the demonic as well, for the endeavor frustrates the problems of intertextuality along the literary color line that until now have kept both areas of study segregated from one another for more than three centuries of criticism.

The reason why no reception history of African Americans' intertextual engagements with Milton has been conducted prior to now most likely stems from problems along the color line in literary studies. Students are not likely to encounter discussions of race or works by African American authors in courses devoted to Milton. Similarly, discussions of Milton are not apt to occur in African American literature courses. Furthermore, bringing both traditions into dialogue with each other requires levels of expertise in at least two comprehensive areas of literary study. Because these traditions are often segregated from each other in teaching practices, their estrangement sustains the phenomena of an absented racial presence in reception studies devoted to Milton. Hence, the epic writer's (in)visibililty in studies of African American literature often mirrors the absented presence of race in scholarly examinations of Milton.

*   *   *

On Politics

FREDRIC JAMESON

From Religion and Ideology: A Political Reading of *Paradise Lost*†

Nothing is more appropriate, in the second year of the Iranian Revolution and the first of the Islamic Republic,[1] than a return to 1642
and a meditation on the work of the greatest English political poet.
The renewed vitality of a religious politics—and in particular the
will to abolish the split between the public and the private, between
state and church—can be expected to impose new ways of reading
Milton; while the theological coding of the first great bourgeois revolution in the west—an experience which may be called a properly
English cultural revolution—ought to place the Iranian situation in
a more comprehensible, or at least less alien, light. It should at any
rate be clear that Marxists can no longer afford the luxury of assigning the problem of religion to the ashcan of history. An impulse that
turned out the largest urban demonstrations ever recorded in the
history of the human race, and that overturned a regime that was the
model and showcase for high technological repression in the Third
World, certainly has something to teach us about how theory 'grips
the masses'. Nor should the vital role played by radical religion in
the American anti-war movement of the 1960s be forgotten, nor the
crucial and strategic one currently being played by the theology of
liberation in revolutionary struggles in Central and South America.

I would not want to be understood as claiming that religion is not
also often reactionary: indeed, I am afraid that at a certain moment
in the revolutionary process it must always become that, and Milton
will be no exception * * *. Nor am I suggesting even a primary role for
religion in the initiation of revolutions: indeed, it would be the worst
kind of historical error, and an affront to the dead, to attribute to the
Iranian mullahs a revolution which was in fact begun by armed left
guerrillas in winter 1971, and in which the left played a major role.

What I would like to do in the following remarks is twofold: to make
at least a beginning in the historically actual and indispensable

---

† From *Literature, Politics and Theory: Papers from the Essex Conference 1976–84,* ed.
Francis Barker, Peter Hulme, Margaret Iversen, and Diana Loxley (London: Methuen,
1986), pp. 35–39. Reprinted by permission of the publisher Taylor & Francis Ltd. Jameson's
notes are omitted.
1. The Iranian Revolution began with demonstrations against Mohammad Reza Shah in
January 1978. The shah left the country in January 1979, and the Islamic Republic of
Iran was established by referendum on April 1, 1979.

task of understanding the relations between religion and politics; and to do this by way of a more specifically literary or interpretive problem, namely that of proposing a political reading of *Paradise Lost*, or better still, of deconcealing the political content of *Paradise Lost*. The difficulties of this second project should not be underestimated: not merely must such an interpretation impose itself as unavoidable, so that anti-political readers and interpreters are forced to waste precious energies in conjuring it away; it must also open up a perspective on something like a line-by-line or paragraph-by-paragraph rereading or rewriting of the poem.

This means that the political focus generally proposed for Milton is insufficient: to be sure, in a general way, there is no great problem in understanding the relationship between the global impulse of *Paradise Lost* and the political situation itself: the moment of the failure of revolution, the dissipation of the revolutionary ethos, the reappearance of the old institutions and business as usual (or in other words, in the language of the time, of sin). * * * Still, the stronger analogy would probably be the sense of frustration and bitterness, the self-criticisms and guilty introspection, the fatigue and depoliticization, that followed May 1968. This inward turn—a displacement from politics to psychology and ethics—is marked not merely by the revival of the Calvinist meditation on original sin and the Fall, but very explicitly by the emphasis on personal, private salvation and the repudiation of millenarianism in *Paradise Regained* and the last two books of *Paradise Lost*.

* * *

I propose that we retrace our steps, and begin again with the seemingly more abstract problem of religion. But first an initial qualification: if you believe in the theory of modes of production, that is, if you are committed to the idea that capitalism is a qualitatively and structurally distinct type of social formation from the various other kinds that have preceded it upon the earth, then you will want to make room for the possibility that religion in its strong form in pre-capitalist societies is functionally and substantively distinct from what it is today, which is to say a mere private hobby and one ideological subcode among many others. In a pre-secular and pre-scientific world, one in which commerce is itself a limited and interstitial phenomenon, religion is the cultural dominant; it is the master-code in which issues are conceived and debated; it is then—religion, the sacred, the centred body of the despot, the centred space of the Forbidden City and the four cardinal points—the form taken by ideology in precapitalist societies, except that since ideology is a modern term and a modern phenomenon, there is something anachronistic and misleading about putting it this way.

But perhaps this point should also be made in existential terms. We are accustomed, whatever our positions on the matter, to think of religion in terms of belief. But belief is a very privatized and subjective phenomenon. * * * In our own society it seems clear that belief in this privatized sense is an accompaniment of social fragmentation and atomization, of *anomie*, of the construction of equivalent monads within the market system, each one of which is endowed with freedom to sell its labour power. Belief in that sense is thus a by-product of that very dissolution and destruction of the older organic social groups of which religion, in the older strong sense, was precisely the organizing ideology and the cement. So we will find ourselves pursuing a mirage if we conceive of an earlier religious position, an object of theological debate, such as Milton's Arianism, in terms of a belief[.] * * *

To conceive of a social formation for which subjectivity in this modern sense does not exist means, however, to attempt to grasp religion not as a private language or a unique incommunicable form of consciousness, but rather as the sign of group praxis and group membership, as a badge of collective adherence, as something like a set of pseudo-concepts whose concrete function is to organize this or that form of communal relationship and structure. I am sorry to say so, but I am afraid that here we still must come to terms with Durkheim's fundamental insight (in *The Elementary Forms of Religious Life*) into religion as the privileged mode in which a pre-capitalist collectivity comes to consciousness of itself and affirms its unity as a group. What follows, however, is a consequence that Durkheim did not draw, namely that religious and theological debate is the form, in pre-capitalist societies, in which groups become aware of their political differences and fight them out.

*   *   *

MARY NYQUIST

From Genesis, Dominion, and Servitude in *Paradise Lost*[†]

A ruler's wrongful claim to "dominion," loss of fraternal rule, and the fraught relations among natural, penal, and political slaveries come together when Milton introduces Nimrod into *Paradise Lost* (1667). Milton's Nimrod is an early modern royalist *avant la lettre* in

† From *Arbitrary Rule: Slavery, Tyranny, and the Power of Life and Death* (Chicago: University Press of Chicago, 2013), pp. 137–39. Copyright © 2013 by the University of Chicago Press. Reprinted by permission of the publisher. Nyquist's notes are omitted.

that he purports to rule by divine right ("claiming second Sovran-tie"). Equally important to the anti-tyranny discourse Nimrod's entry inspires is the phrase "arrogate Dominion undeserv'd / Over his brethren," an allusion to the Deuteronomic "law" of fraternal rule:

> till one shall rise
> Of proud ambitious heart, who not content
> With fair equalitie, fraternal state,
> Will arrogate Dominion undeserv'd
> Over his brethren, and quite dispossess
> Concord and law of Nature from the Earth,
> Hunting (and Men not Beasts shall be his game)
> With Warr and hostile snare such as refuse
> Subjection to his Empire tyrannous[.]   (12.24–32)[1]

Milton's Nimrod not only hunts "Men not Beasts," but in turning them into enemies by "Warr," he hunts men *as* beasts, as "game." So unmistakably does Nimrod reduce human to nonhuman that the adjective *tyrannous* is nearly redundant.

Like other political theorists exploring the origins of tyranny and slavery, Milton must contend with Aristotle's doctrine of natural slavery, which he does here. In book I of *Politics*, Aristotle discusses the slave-by-nature in connection with nature's provision of non-human animals for human use. Whether tame or wild, Aristotle says, animals can be used for labor, for food, and in the form of the vari-ous products made from them. Acquisition, Aristotle has argued, is an "art," which, being employed for the acquisition of slaves in a just war, indicates slavery's naturalness: "[T]he art of war is a natu-ral art of acquisition, for the art of acquisition includes hunting, an art which we ought to practice against wild beasts, and against men who, though intended by nature to be governed, will not submit; for war of such a kind is naturally just". Possibly with this text in mind, *Paradise Lost* revisions Aristotle's declaration by emphasizing human resistance to subjection in the face of an unjust, tyrannous war. For Aristotle, war-as-hunting has as its object the submission of those whom nature intends for enslavement but who refuse to submit. Likewise, in *Paradise Lost* Nimrod uses his art ("hostile snare") to capture "such as refuse / Subjection to his Empire tyran-nous." Milton's emphasis on a collective refusal of subjection springs from his passionate, never-extinguished commitment to a natural, divinely sanctioned right of resistance.

*   *   *

1. Nyquist also includes lines 33–37.

MELISSA E. SANCHEZ

From "My Self/Before Me": The Erotics of Republicanism in *Paradise Lost*†

* * * For Milton, the best form of government will not attempt to ignore or abolish the passions. It will make them part of the formula for building a godly state. . . . In *Paradise Lost*, Milton's conception of godly rule rests on a nuanced view of the place of sexual desire and cross-gendered identification in legal and political structures. *Paradise Lost* attests to the dangers of treating human reason and perception as though they are separate from human desire and fantasy and therefore infallibly stable and objective. A central concern for Milton is the ease with which the idealization of individual virtue can lead to the destruction of the republican order such virtue is supposed to support. While Milton had initially seen individual rectitude as a source of public justice, his experience of its failure during the Protectorate and Restoration encouraged a skepticism that colors his prose and poetry in the 1650s and 1660s. In these writings, Milton suggests that the perverse pride and ambition he had earlier identified as the hallmarks of tyranny are ineradicable aspects of the human condition as such.

*   *   *

In *Paradise Lost*, Milton's analysis of the desires that undermine republican liberty finds its fullest articulation not in Satanic machinations, but in Edenic marriage.

*   *   *

Critics have long noticed the conflicted relationship between desire and dependence in *Paradise Lost*, where Eve's very existence threatens Adam's identity as God's preeminent creation. Such analyses of Edenic marriage have tended to focus exclusively on determining Milton's conception of women, but a feminist attention to the problem of gender relations can also make available a more complex view of Milton's political theory. * * * As Milton's divorce tracts intimate, and as the interactions of Adam and Eve illustrate, the need for others may really express a narcissistic desire for mastery and coherence, so that any expression of difference or autonomy on the part of the beloved also inspires aggression and hate.

---

† From *Erotic Subjects: The Sexuality of Politics in Early Modern English Literature* (New York: Oxford University Press, 2011), pp. 207–08, 210–12. Reprinted by permission of Oxford University Press. Sanchez's notes are omitted.

This need for dominance threatens to dissolve not only marital bonds but also republican ideals of public service, debate, and compromise.

However, Milton's recognition of the universality of human imperfection does not lead to an argument against self-rule. Instead, it proves the necessity of a republican system in which all members accept that they need aid and opposition if they are to keep their inner tyrants at bay.

* * *

As Adam and Eve's relationship in *Paradise Lost* attests, the "joyning . . . in conjugall fellowship" that Milton celebrates thus threatens the compromise, counsel, and debate that upholds republican rule—for the tyrant's wish to dominate and devour is but the flip side of the yearning for ecstatic dissolution into an other. Indeed, much as Milton's defense of divorce emerged from his acknowledgment that he was himself subject to the same affective delusion and misplaced allegiance as the "common lump of men," so *Paradise Lost* acknowledges that even our unfallen parents, and therefore the most virtuous of postlapsarian political actors, are vulnerable to the pathologies that haunt eros.

* * *

If Eve is to avoid the self-destructive pursuit of pleasure and power to which she is instinctively drawn, she must conform to the godly republican values of sacrifice and compromise. Such a choice requires that she admit the insufficiency of her solitary self. Eve signifies her reluctant acceptance of the need for relation with an other in her marriage to Adam, with whom she shares her creaturely status. Adam's imperfection figures her own. Eve has to recognize as her true image one that is "less fair / Less winning soft, less amiably mild / than that smooth wat'ry image" with which she was initially smitten (4.478–480). Before she actually sees Adam, Eve has been told that, in contrast to the image in the pool, Adam is "hee / Whose image thou art," an other whom Eve "shalt enjoy / Inseparably thine" (4.471–473). Eve's acceptance of Adam as her image is also her acceptance of the humility on which republican government depends and which royal absolutism denies.

* * *

SHARON ACHINSTEIN

From Milton's Political Ontology of the Human[†]

* * *

How does Milton's representation of his first humans give evidence of the situation and capability prior to political institutions, and give rise to what Hannah Arendt would call a "right to have rights"?[1] Writing of stateless persons after the Second World War, Arendt detached political rights from the history of statehood. Her notion, of the right to have rights, combines the moral and political aspects of human experience in a common world, "to live in a framework where one is judged by one's actions and opinions" and "a right to belong to some kind of organized community."[2] For Milton, writing before human rights, I am going to ask, what originary constitution— of the body, of sociality through speech and comportment with others (in Adam's case, Eve, Angels, animals, and God)—serves as ground for the political that will, after the Fall, take the form of contracts for self-protection and alliance?

* * *

In the Eden of *Paradise Lost,* as we shall see, there is an extended thought experiment about the nature, purpose, and activity of each member of the couple, and that Milton spends as much time as he does on this first pair is not simply a paean to romantic love, or a prelude to the disastrous Fall that will undo their bliss, though of course it is both those things. Before politics, before the public/private split, we have the garden and the bower: and in these spaces there are representations of forms of equality, difference, hierarchy, and most important for the work here, a lot of talk. The couple in *Paradise Lost* is, indeed, a constitutive plurality, and this, I suggest, may be considered a significant ground of the political in Milton.

* * *

In *Paradise Lost,* Milton offers accounts of human creation from several speaking positions. Reworking Genesis, with its double-tellings, Milton fashions the autobiographical

---

† From *ELH* 84 (2017): 592–600, 602–35, 610–11. © 2017 by Johns Hopkins University Press. Reprinted with permission of The Johns Hopkins University Press. Unless otherwise indicated, notes are by the author; some notes are shortened or omitted.

1. Hannah Arendt, *The Origins of Totalitarianism* (New York: Harcourt, 1976), 296.
2. Arendt, *Origins,* pp. 296–97. On the many meanings of "the right to have rights," see Seyla Benhabib, *The Rights of Others: Aliens, Residents and Citizens* (Cambridge: Cambridge University Press, 2004), 56–60.

remembrances of the key protagonists.[3] We learn of Adam and Eve's creations through their tellings of their life stories: Eve's first, then Adam's. It is not, as in Aristotle, that humans are political animals, with politics inherent in human nature, but that the humans' humanity is constituted through the actions of their speech, their inquiry into their natures, and their expression of these natures through the utterances that narrate that self-awareness. Both stories of creation show the newly-made humans desiring companionship, each craving sociality and relation with another like to themselves, and their speech constitutes their sociality and their pleasure.

*   *   *

Adam also seems to arrive ready-made with the desire to converse with others, and reveals himself in mutual relationship not with an image in a pool but with the rest of creation. Reciprocality is there as the sun is itself "fed" by his birth-sweat (8.256). Adam's original disposition in the world is into a situation eliciting and producing his utterance ("thus I call'd" [8.283]). As Adam calls out, he begins to discover his relative inequality to nature through this encounter, his relative difference from the rest of creation. It occurs when he first experiences himself as not simply biological life. His is not yet divinely-commanded life; he has yet to meet his maker. He has not, as yet, been put in relation to Eve. Michel Foucault has defined biopolitics as that moment in the transformation in the idea of politics where politics came to be seen as power over life, a change that took place in early modernity.[4] But in Adam's (though not in Eve's) retelling of his awakening to himself amidst the bounty of creation, natality is not simply mere biological life, nor has it (yet) transformed into politics.

The world was given to Adam: but only Adam could call its worldness into being by drawing himself as a separate being in relation to it. Instead, he is becoming free through self-initiated action, specifically, the action of speech. While in the Christian orientation, free action is a function of will, in *Paradise Lost* it is a function of speech, of recognition through address with another. Indeed, in his first awareness of the world, he places the Sun into a relationship with himself:

3. For an analysis of the ways Milton uses the Jahwist and Priestly accounts in Genesis, see Mary Nyquist, "Gynesis, Genesis, and the Formation of Milton's Eve," in *Cannibals, Witches, and Divorce: Estranging the Renaissance*, ed. Marjorie Garber (Baltimore: Johns Hopkins University Press, 1987), 147–208, and "The Genesis of Gendered Subjectivity," *Re-Membering Milton: Essays on the Texts and Traditions*, eds. Nyquist and Margaret W. Ferguson (New York: Methuen, 1987), 99–127.
4. Michel Foucault, *The History of Sexuality, Vol. 1: An Introduction*, trans. Robert Hurley (New York: Vintage, 1980), 135.

> As new wak't from soundest sleep
> Soft on the flow'ry herb I found me laid
> In Balmy Sweat, which with his Beams the Sun
> Soon dri'd, and on the reeking moisture fed.
> (8.253–56).

Adam's own humanity is derived from his own comparison with the sensed, external objects around him and with whom he is in tender relation. Yet, as Adam challenges his maker, it is because he perceives these other creations are not equal to him. This desire for a mate arises indeed out of Adam's awareness of his distinctiveness within creation. His search for a likeness is not simply a narcissism but a gesture towards the characteristic of an equality of species-relation, that which can be called human. While Adam can conceive the benefit to "man" of the creation—"all this good to man"—what he seeks is something more particular (8.361). He desires a plurality:

> In solitude
> What happiness, who can enjoy alone,
> Or all enjoying, what contentment find?
> (8.364–67)

That plurality is, furthermore, to be one of equals:

> Among unequals what society
> Can sort, what harmony or true delight?
> Which must be mutual, in proportion due
> Giv'n and received [. . .]
> In unity defective, which requires
> Collateral love, and dearest amity.
> (8.383–426)

Adam's calling for an equal, his demand for reciprocity, may represent his first articulation of an entitlement, and thus this moment may be taken as his political self-constitution as human. Although in a different way, and in the poem's misogynistic fashioning it is something taken awry, Eve has a like search too, a yearning for collateral love, "answering looks / Of sympathy and love."[5]

※   ※   ※

The political ground of "the human" was changing radically in the seventeenth century. This happened over a long time, and in a number of different domains of knowledge; one account is given by Foucault in his prehistory of the concept of Man in his story of the emergence of biopolitics.[6] For our purposes, conceptions of the human in

5. *PL* 4.464–65 [*Editor's note*].
6. For the emergence of the concept of "Man" as an object of speculative knowledge in the Early Modern period extending through the Enlightenment, see Michel Foucault, *The*

the Renaissance were not simply the result of a new emphasis on the individual; or of the dialectical relations with a newly consolidated States as nations or within an international economic system of different peoples. Indeed, the political category of the human was undergoing intense torquing, with respect to the new economic relations not only within capitalizing societies but also in economic relations between Christians and non-Christians; in the reworking of the human-property relation arising out of the European conquest of natives and creation of enslaved populations; in a geopolitical situation of contact with diverse peoples with its development of the anthropologies of the human; in the geological interest in the fossil record. It is my view that all these components bear on the newly contested theological constitutions of freedom and the will, matter, the body, sexuality, and the family wrought by Reformed and Counter-Reformed political theologies. Indeed, Milton hurtles towards a secularism which he is also at pains attempting to dismantle. In his theology he is unafraid to venture into an investigation of the meaning of earthliness not as simply creatureliness, createdness, but through an investigation of human actors within the given world. For him, early modern worries that produced various theological solutions (for example free-will, voluntarist or Arminian) were not simply salvational problems addressing the end of human time, but rather debates over what could be the ground of political life—that is, over the capacities and agencies of humans in their dwelling together on earth.

*　*　*

ON GENDER AND SEXUALITY

ELIZABETH CADY STANTON

From The Woman's Bible[†]

From *Comments on Genesis*

*　*　*

Adam Clarke,[1] in his commentaries, asks the question, "is this an allegory?" He finds it beset with so many difficulties as an historical

---

Order of Things, trans. Alan Sheridan (1973; rpt. New York: Vintage, 1994), pp. 339–42. For *biopolitics* and its broader category, *biopower*, see 495 n. 4 above [*Editor's note*].

† From *The Woman's Bible* (New York: European Publishing, 1895), pp. 23–27.
1. British Methodist theologian (1762–1832), author of *Commentary on the Bible* (8 vols., 1810–26). The passage discussed is Genesis 3:1–24. See pp. 316–17.

fact, that he inclines at first to regard it as a fable, a mere symbol, of some hidden truth. His mind seems more troubled about the serpent than any other personage in the drama. As snakes cannot walk upright, and have never been known to speak, he thinks this beguiling creature must have been an ourang-outang, or some species of ape. However, after expressing all his doubts, he rests in the assumption that it must be taken literally, and that with higher knowledge of the possibilities of all living things, many seeming improbabilities will be fully realized.

A learned professor in Yale College,[2] before a large class of students, expressed serious doubts as to the forbidden fruit being an apple, as none grew in that latitude. He said it must have been a quince. If the serpent and the apple are to be withdrawn thus recklessly from the tableaux, it is feared that with advancing civilization the whole drama may fall into discredit. Scientists tell us that "the missing link" between the ape and man, has recently been discovered,[3] so that we can now trace back an unbroken line of ancestors to the dawn of creation.

As out of this allegory grows the doctrines of original sin, the fall of man, and woman the author of all our woes, and the curses on the serpent, the woman, and the man; the Darwinian theory of the gradual growth of the race from a lower to a higher type of animal life, is more hopeful and encouraging. However, as our chief interest is in woman's part in the drama, we are equally pleased with her attitude, whether as a myth in an allegory, or as the heroine of an historical occurrence. . . .

The unprejudiced reader must be impressed with the courage, the dignity, and the lofty ambition of the woman. The tempter evidently had a profound knowledge of human nature, and saw at a glance the high character of the person he met by chance in his walks in the garden. He did not try to tempt her from the path of duty by brilliant jewels, rich dresses, worldly luxuries or pleasures, but with the promise of knowledge, with the wisdom of the Gods. Like Socrates or Plato, his powers of conversation and asking puzzling questions, were no doubt marvellous, and he roused in the woman that intense thirst for knowledge that the simple pleasures of picking flowers and talking with Adam did not satisfy. Compared with Adam she appears to great advantage through the entire drama.

The curse pronounced on woman is inserted in an unfriendly spirit to justify her degradation and subjection to man. With

2. Daniel Cady Eaton, Professor of Botany [*Stanton's note*].
3. "Missing link" is a now-discredited term for a transitional fossil in a supposedly linear chain of development. The reference is probably to Java Man fossil discovered in 1891 and 1892.

obedience to the laws of health, diet, dress, and exercise, the period of maternity should be one of added vigor in both body and mind, a perfectly natural operation should not be attended with suffering. By the observance of physical and psychical laws the supposed curse can be easily transformed into a blessing. Some churchmen speak of maternity as a disability, and then chant the Magnificat[4] in all their cathedrals round the globe. Through all life's shifting scenes, the mother of the race has been the greatest factor in civilization.

We hear the opinion often expressed, that woman always has, and always will be in subjection. Neither assertion is true. She enjoyed unlimited individual freedom for many centuries, and the events of the present day all point to her speedy emancipation. Scientists now give 85,000 years for the growth of the race. They assign 60,000 to savagism, 20,000 to barbarism, and 5,000 to civilization. Recent historians tell us that for centuries woman reigned supreme. That period was called the Matriarchate. Then man seized the reins of government, and we are now under the Patriarchate. But we see on all sides new forces gathering, and woman is already abreast with man in art, science, literature, and government. The next dynasty, in which both will reign as equals, will be the Amphiarchate,[5] which is close at hand.

✳   ✳   ✳

BARBARA K. LEWALSKI

From "Higher Argument": Completing and Publishing *Paradise Lost*†

✳   ✳   ✳

At the center of his epic, Milton set a richly imagined representation of prelapsarian love, marriage, and domestic society. It is a brilliant though sometimes conflicted representation, in which Milton's internalization of contemporary assumptions about gender hierarchy, his idealistic view of companionate marriage, his own life experiences, and his deeply felt emotional needs sometimes strain against each other. Most profoundly, he explores through Adam and Eve the fundamental challenge of any love relationship: the uneasy,

---

4. The traditional hymn of praise by Mary in Luke 1:46–55, which she sings after the angel has told her she shall conceive and bring forth a son, Jesus.
5. *amphi* "on both sides" + *archia* "rule," i.e. rule by both genders.
† From *The Life of John Milton: A Critical Biography* (Oxford: Blackwell, 2000), pp. 479–84. Reprinted by permission of John Wiley and Sons. Lewalski's notes are omitted.

inevitable, and ultimately creative tension between autonomy and interdependence.

In a sublime epithalamion, Milton celebrates marriage as the foundation of human society, and also gives his representation of Edenic marriage political resonance as he contrasts Adam and Eve's joyous and fulfilled marital love with the sterility and licentious indulgence of "Court Amours"—Charles I's cavaliers and the Bacchic "revelers" of Charles II's Restoration court:

> Haile wedded Love, mysterious Law, true source
> Of human ofspring, sole proprietie
> In Paradise of all things common else.
> By thee adulterous lust was driv'n from men
> Among the bestial herds to raunge, by thee
> Founded in Reason, Loyal, Just, and Pure,
> Relations dear, and all the Charities
> Of Father, Son, and Brother first were known . . .
>
> Here Love his golden shafts imploies, here lights
> His constant Lamp, and waves his purple wings,
> Reigns here and revels; not in the bought smile
> Of Harlots, loveless, joyless, unindeard,
> Casual fruition, nor in Court Amours
> Mixt Dance, or wanton Mask, or Midnight Bal.   (4.750–68)

This paean elides female relationships: no mention is made of mothers and sisters, though the Bard implies, with modern anthropologists, that these social bonds are forged through women. He also imagines Adam and Eve's archetypal marriage according to the forms of the Early Modern institution, as an arrangement between the father and the husband which the woman is to accept or (in rare cases) decline. After brief resistance Eve accepts the husband offered by God the Father and the role prescribed for her: to produce "multitudes like thy self," and to be for Adam "an individual solace dear" (4.449–91).

Milton's epic inscribes gender hierarchy, though in a complex and nuanced version. Adam and Eve are described first in terms of their shared nobility, majesty, and authority over all other creatures; their moral and spiritual equality is based on their creation as God's images, exhibiting "Truth, wisdome, Sanctitude severe and pure" (4.287–95). Then their different physical qualities are interpreted as emblems of their unequal natures and roles: "For contemplation hee and valour formd, / For softness shee and sweet attractive Grace, / Hee for God only, shee for God in him" (4.297–9). Later Adam, after admitting to Raphael his unsettling passion for Eve, says that he knows she is inferior to himself in qualities both of mind and body:

> For well I understand in the prime end
> Of Nature her th'inferiour, in the mind
> And inward Faculties, which most excell,
> In outward also her resembling less
> His image who made both, and less expressing
> The character of that Dominion giv'n
> O'er other Creatures.   (8.540–6)

Raphael confirms this judgment, urging Adam not to attribute "overmuch to things / Less excellent," to cultivate proper self-esteem so that Eve will "acknowledge thee her Head," to eschew passion, and to love Eve's higher qualities as a means to make a Neoplatonic ascent to heavenly love (8.565–75). More authoritative still, the Son, judging Adam after the Fall, confirms that Adam's proper role is to act as Eve's head and governor, not make an idol of her to set in place of God:

> Was shee thy God, that her thou didst obey
> Before his voice, or was shee made thy guide,
> Superior, or but equal, that to her
> Thou did'st resigne thy Manhood, and the Place
> Wherein God set thee above her made of thee,
> And for thee, whose perfection far excell'd
> Hers in all real dignitie: Adornd
> Shee was indeed, and lovely to attract
> Thy Love, not thy Subjection, and her Gifts
> Were such as under Government well seem'd,
> Unseemly to beare rule, which was thy part
> And person, had'st thou known thy self aright.
>   (10.145–56)

Yet this conventional view of gender is destabilized by elements of Milton's imaginative vision that invite a more egalitarian conception: if Milton could not fully work through such conflicts, he did provide liberalizing perspectives upon which some later feminists could and did build. One such is the poem's unusually fluid concept of hierarchy, the concomitant of Milton's monist ontology: if humans and angels differ only in degree and humans can expect the gradual refinement of their natures to angelic status, the distance between male and female on the hierarchical scale must be minimal. Moreover, Raphael's comment that creatures hold their place on that scale "as neerer to him [God] plac't or neerer tending" (5.476) allows that if Adam is at first "plac't" marginally higher than Eve, their final places will depend on how they develop, whither they "tend." In line with this, in Milton's unique representation of the state of innocence, Adam and Eve are both expected to grow, change, and develop in virtue by properly pruning and directing their erroneous apprehensions and perilous impulses, as well as their burgeoning garden.

*   *   *

Milton also accords Eve important areas of initiative and autonomy that further qualify patriarchal assumptions. Both before and after the Fall Eve often proposes issues for discussion, initiates action, and leads in some new direction. She first raises questions about the order of the cosmos; she proposes the proto-capitalist idea of the division of labor to help meet the problem of the garden's burgeoning growth; she first responds to "prevenient grace" and makes the first motion to repentance; she proposes suicide or sexual abstinence to prevent visitation of the Fall's effects on all humankind. When their dialogic interchanges are working properly, Adam responds to, develops, and where necessary corrects Eve's initiatives, as Raphael does Adam's, to advance their common understanding. In the realm of literary creativity, Eve constructs the first autobiographical narrative as she recounts her earliest recollections—with the implications autobiography carries of coming to self-awareness, probing one's own subjectivity, interpreting one's own experience, and so becoming an author (4.449–91). She is as much a lyric poet as Adam, perhaps more so. Their hymns and prayers are joint expressions, but Eve creates the first love lyric in Eden—the delicate, rhetorically artful, sonnet-like pastoral that begins "Sweet is the breath of Morn" (4.641–56). And if Adam brought this lyric form to higher perfection in his *aubade* echoing the Song of Songs (5.17–25), Eve after the Fall perfects the tragic lyric. Adam's agonized complaint, "O miserable of happy" (10.720–862), ends in despair, while Eve's moving lament, "Forsake me not thus, *Adam*" (10.914–36), opens the way to repentance, forgiveness, and reconciliation.

Also, Milton brings the ideology of gender hierarchy up against the characters' different experiences and psychology. Eve and Adam offer very different autobiographical accounts of their creation, first encounter, and marriage, accounts that evidently reflect Milton's reading of female and male psychology. Eve tells of constructing herself first through pleasurable self-contemplation, which she mistakes as a response to another female "shape," and then by freely accepting a marriage relationship; but she does not express any need for completion by another. She recounts as an episode "oft remembered" (4.449–91) how she woke on a flowery bank in some wonderment about herself, and how she then followed a murmur of waters to a pool that reflected a female image bending toward her as she to it "with answering looks / Of sympathie and love" (4.464–5). As a version of the Narcissus myth, Eve's story suggests her potential for self-love, but in most respects she is defined against the Narcissus story. * * *

Adam's narrative (8.355–99), by contrast, testifies to a psychological and emotional neediness that in some ways undercuts gender hierarchy and recalls Milton's similar testimony in the divorce tracts. Adam reports his initial attempts to discover who he is by contemplating nature and his immediate inference that "some great Maker" created both it and him. Then he recounts his eloquent pleas with God for a mate, emphasizing his keen sense of incompleteness and loneliness without an "equal" companion. Recounting the courtship event he explains Eve's hesitation not as she herself did but by projecting onto her a serene consciousness of self-worth, "That would be woo'd, and not unsought be won," and a demeanor of "obsequious Majestie" in accepting his suit (8.500–10). He underscores the conflict between ideology and experience by emphasizing the disconnect between what he "knows" of Eve's inferiority to him and what he experiences when he is with her:

> when I approach
> Her loveliness, so absolute she seems
> And in herself compleat, so well to know
> Her own, that what she wills to do or say,
> Seems wisest, vertuousest, discreetest, best, . . .
>
> Authority and Reason on her waite,
> As one intended first, not after made
> Occasionally, and to consummate all,
> Greatness of mind, and nobleness thir seat
> Build in her loveliest, and create an awe
> About her, as a guard Angelic plac't.   (8.546–59)

Though Raphael rightly rebukes Adam for such potentially dangerous sentiments Milton allows Adam to qualify the angel's apparently rigid Neoplatonism from the perspective of his (and our) experience of something beyond Raphael's ken, the "mysterious reverence" due the marriage bed and marriage itself, an institution angels do not have (8.598–9).

*   *   *

JULIA M. WALKER

From Eve: The First Reflection[†]

* * *

Engender in and by the Pool

In books 4 and 5, Eden is gendered feminine and given an identity inextricably linked with Eve's. As Eve's face is bounded by the edge of the mirroring lake, so is the question of gender identity and self-knowledge framed by the gendered geography of Eden. Eve neither recognizes nor names herself. Eve's ultimate act in her book 4 creation narrative is to yield, not to learn. She submits to the arbitrary gender displacement, coming to see Adam as at once the generative image of and better than herself, but thus learning—or accepting—that she can know herself only in herself only in relation to Adam. There is no place for interiority in this construction of selfhood. Milton presents Eve to herself and to the reader only in relation to Adam and to the gendered universe of which she and Eden are each a part. As the relationships among the valley and the river and the lake are not perfectly separable, neither can the identities of Eden, Eve, and Adam be neatly categorized, although the latter will be given an interior self. Milton reiterates at many points his gendering of the Earth as feminine, but Adam seems to have no sense that it is from this feminine Earth that he was formed. He draws his self-identity solely from his maker and not from matter, but expects Eve to privilege his absent rib above any other aspect of her being.

At what point does Eve cease to be a part of Adam, becoming not his rib but her self?

Never.

At what point does Eve cease to seek for self-knowledge from her reflection?

Never.

Can a narrative act of gender displacement generate a representation of self-knowledge—even in its most simple form, physical self-recognition—sufficient to stand as self-identity, the sort of simple self-identity Adam exhibits when he peruses his own body, calling it *Myself* (8.267)?

No.

† From *Medusa's Mirrors: Spenser, Shakespeare, Milton, and the Metamorphosis of the Female Self* (Newark: University of Delaware Press, 1998), pp. 166–67, 169. Reprinted by permission of Associated University Presses. Walker's notes are omitted.

Does she ever see Adam, "hee whose image thou art," as her own image?

She does not.

Literally, then, Eve never recognizes anything; she does not "know again"; she simply accepts the cognition given to her by the voice and hand of God and by the voice and hand of Adam. In the gendered geography of Eden—the geography of the river, the valley, and the lake—Milton presents his readers with a pattern of displacement, a paradigm of arbitrarily gendered causality, which he immediately repeats in human terms in Eve's cognition scene. Milton does not here rely on mere conjunction. By using the first displacement as the generative locus for the second, by having Eve turn without recognition of her identity in the re-gendered mirror of the lake's water, Milton emphasizes the necessity of reading one reinscription through and by the other, thus calling attention to the arbitrary nature of both types of gendering and to their inextricable relation.

*   *   *

Not only is Eve's initial encounter with Eden rendered problematic by Milton's invocation of the Narcissus story, but as a narrative it lacks the specificity of Adam's in many ways. Not the least important is her omission of any gendered pronouns. Even though this narrative is presented as memory, memory that we might expect to be embellished by subsequent knowledge, Eve's speech does not gender. She quotes the "voice" who will take her to "hee / Whose image thou art, him thou shalt enjoy."[1] That voice gives her two names, Eve and Mother, but these names are not gendered by the voice of God or by Eve, only by our fallen knowledge. Eve also quotes Adam's odd third-person identification of himself, "whom thou fli'st, of him thou art, / His flesh, his bone,"[2] but she uses no other gendered pronouns in this narrative. Neither Eve nor God's voice nor Adam genders her. She is drawn to the feminine lake; the mirror of that lake gives her the first vision she has of another human form; but she is not allowed to identify herself with that vision, nor indeed does she identify by gender anything that she sees. She speaks of "it"; she is first told of and then shown "he," and she quotes God and Adam's use of the masculine pronoun; but there are no feminine pronouns in this narrative. Only the reader's knowledge of the feminine lake and of fallen sexuality gender Eve's identity. Eve herself genders nothing and the voices she hears speak only of maleness, leaving her otherness unnamed. How, then, can she identify herself as physically different and individual from either Adam or her surroundings? She cannot

1. *PL* 4.471–72.
2. *PL* 4.482–83.

know herself as separate and particular, as an individual entity unique in the cosmos, as Adam knows himself. As she is allowed to know her image only in relation to Adam, so can she know her function only in relation to the fruitful earth with which she is associated, not seeing herself as a unique Other—which explains why, in book 9, she worries that Adam might enjoy "another Eve" (9.827).

*   *   *

JONATHAN GOLDBERG

From Milton's Angels[†]

*   *   *

* * * [I]t will be my aim in what follows to track signs of male desirability and of male-male desire in Milton. Especially by locating it in the angels of *Paradise Lost,* who, in their ability to eat and make love, are embodiments of Milton's monism, I mean to show that sexual desire is not incompatible with philosophical monism.

*   *   *

Milton's materialism, the "one first matter all" (5.472) that Raphael explicates for Adam, is a principle of sameness and difference, of hierarchy and degree within a same that involves ultimately a form of matter that is incorporeal. This hierarchy is, undeniably, one in which Eve is placed lower and further away from God than is Adam. This system bears enough similarity to the physics of Milton's time to ensure that it is not a static grid but a dynamic principle. And although Milton envisions it as a dynamic vectored up and down—where love leads man to aspire to angelic status and oneness with God—Michael's revelation that God is everywhere and that distance makes no difference is cognate with the decentered universe that follows from Lucretian atomism and is foundational to Galileo's physics.

*   *   *

Exactly parallel to his explanation of why and how angels eat is Raphael's answer to Adam's question:[1]

love thou say'st
Leads up to heaven, is both the way and guide;

---

† From *The Seeds of Things: Theorizing Sexuality and Materiality in Renaissance Representations* (New York: Fordham University Press, 2009), pp. 181, 192–98, 207–9, 243–45. Reprinted with permission of Fordham University Press. Unless otherwise indicated, notes are by the author.
1. I.e., whether angels make love physically [*Editor's note*].

> Bear with me then, if lawful what I ask;
> Love not the heavenly spirits, and how their love
> Express they, by looks only, or do they mix
> Irradiance, virtual or immediate touch?   (8.612–17)

The sex that Raphael describes is, like the eating process, one that makes angelic copulation the fulfillment of human aspiration. It is fitting that the four-book seduction that is the conversation between Adam and Raphael should end with this moment, in which Raphael not only insists that Adam's love for Eve should lead him upward but also holds out for Adam the kind of sex life that angels have with each other: "Whatever pure thou in the body enjoy'st / . . . we enjoy / In eminence" (8.622–24). The body that impedes is replaced by the possibility of total oneness, total interpenetration possible to the pure body—the body that has attained the materiality meant by spirit, the body as sheer vitality, life.

Raphael's description of angelic sex—"easier than air with air, if spirits embrace, / Total they mix, union of pure with pure / Desiring" (8.626–28)—is one where likeness is sameness, a coupling that is undeniably homo. And yet what is striking in this account and makes it very unlike every other depiction of heavenly life that he has offered Adam is that the hierarchies that rank angels, and that divides them when a Son as a new form of creation takes precedence, are completely absent. This coupling, where no "membrane, joint, or limb" functions as impediment to coition, is also one devoid of "exclusive bars" (8.625); just as earlier Raphael had explained to Adam that the angelic body cannot be harmed because it is "vital in every part" (6.345) and hence is "all heart . . . , all head, all eye, all eye, all ear, / All intellect, all sense" and entirely freed from any determinate form of limbing (6.350–53), there is no hierarchy in his description of angelic sex. Indeed there is also, it seems, no monogamy, just as there is also no sense of correct "position" in angelic sex acts. * * * Gender difference may be a form of impediment to angelic realization but, at the same time, the sexual intercourse of the first couple is on a continuum with what Raphael describes, much as human and angelic appetite are, much as human and angelic embodiment are as well.

Raphael's offer of angelic sex, like his promise of angelic being to Adam, looks forward to that time when all will be all and differences will no longer obtain. That forward thrust temporalizes the physics of a thinker like Lucretius, who insists on the eternal matter that subtends all forms of life, the indestructible atoms from which everything is made and that survive the undoing of particular configurations. Milton shares with Lucretius, at the very least, a recognition of sameness that should dispel invidious difference; he also insists upon the present state as one constituted by difference, while committed to making difference a matter of degree rather than kind. Hence, even Raphael's account to Adam of angelic sex, in dispelling all forms of hierarchy and difference and dispensing with the couple form, goes beyond what we actually do see in the poem. For there is undoubtedly one angelic couple in the poem, Lucifer and Beelzebub. After the very moment when God exalts the Son, Satan finds it impossible to fall asleep. If it is worth noting that angels need sleep, it is worth even further notice that Satan has a bedfellow, a form of same-sex intimacy utterly unremarkable as a phenomenon of early modern life:

> Sleep'st thou companion dear, what sleep can close
> Thy eyelids? and rememb'rest what decree
> Of yesterday, so late hath passed the lips
> Of heaven's almighty. Thou to me thy thoughts
> Wast wont, I mine to thee was wont to impart;
> Both waking we were one; how then can now
> Thy sleep dissent?   (5.673–79)

Unable to sleep, Satan rouses Beelzebub with these words, infusing him with his "bad influence" (5.695). The words spoken are extraordinary insofar as they suggest that the two angels share a normative form of friendship and intimacy, a sharing of thoughts that translates into sharing a bed. "Thou to me . . . / Wast wont, I to thee was wont": a mirror scene of mutuality and oneness, this past may even be the present of angelic sex that Raphael describes to Adam. But the union of Satan and his partner is broken by the divine decree, which appears not to trouble Beelzebub until Satan reminds him of their lost unanimity. At the moment that imparting becomes "bad influence," normative same-sex intimacy, registered in "companion dear," acquires the taint of sodomy.[2] This moment in the poem is a demonstration of Bray's thesis that only a hair's breadth separates the two.[3] It would be wrong to suspect in the reported companionship, the intimacy of shared thoughts and shared beds, anything other than the kind of relationships that angels have with each other and that Raphael celebrates in the complete oneness of bodily interpenetration available to them.

Throughout the poem, these forms of coupling and pairing are hierarchized. The Beelzebub that we see as the poem opens, "next" to Satan (1.79), is likely to be where he was when he and Lucifer were

---

2. This moment is presumably coincident with Satan's self-generation of Sin and his coupling with her to produce the figure of Death, whose shapelessness and insatiable desire are a dark version of angelic existence, a point I owe to Karma deGruy.
3. See Alan Bray, "Homosexuality and the Signs of Male Friendship in Elizabethan England," in *Queering the Renaissance*, ed. Jonathan Goldberg (Durham: Duke University Press, 1994), pp. 40–61 [Editor's note].

in heaven and joined as bedfellows. Often the differences between
angels are marked as degrees and kinds of beauty, which eroticize
them. Satan, flying to earth, stops for directions from Uriel, whom
he sees, "a glorious angel":

> His back was turned, but not his brightness hid;
> Of beaming sunny rays, a golden tiar
> Circled his head, nor less his locks behind
> Illustrious on his shoulders fledge with wings
> Lay waving round.   (3.624–28)

Uriel is deep in thought, oblivious to Satan. His distance and self-
absorption are represented by his turned back and by the dazzling
light that he casts. He is unapproachable and, at the same time,
mesmerizing, and his unavailability is registered precisely by the
turning of his back, which makes him all the more desirable for
being impossible to have. The allure lies in his hair (to which attention also is paid in the descriptions of Adam and Eve), drawing the
viewer's eyes to his shoulders, to his wings, signs of his power. To
this figure, Satan accommodates himself in the form that would
seem to correspond erotically. He appears to Uriel as a "stripling
cherub" (3.636), and the palpability of his looks is immediately
apprehended; he is younger than Uriel, the very embodiment of the
condition that "cherubic" comes to name: "yet such as in his face /
Youth smiled celestial, and to every limb / Suitable grace diffused"
(3.637–39). Uriel falls for him and gives him everything he wants.

   What he wants is information, and Uriel supplies it, complimenting the glowing cherub, the "fair angel" for his "desire . . . to know"
(3.694). This is but one of the numerous scenes of pederastic
instruction in the poem, the incitement to know that is mobilized
as well in the fall. Adam and Raphael, or Adam and Michael, or
Adam and God are paralleled in this scene, just as the difference in
status and beauty marks the scene that follows, when Satan is discovered by Zephon, another figure of cherubic beauty. "Know ye
not me?" Satan snarls, "Ye knew me once no mate / For you . . . /
The lowest of your throng" (4.828, 831). Even in heaven, we recall,
Mammon had been "the least erected spirit . . . / his looks and
thoughts / Were always downward bent" (1.679–81), while none
"fairer" (2.110) than Belial fell, Belial, the very epitome of sodomitical sex (1.500–506). Indeed, it appears that had this lowly Zephon
been Satan's "mate" in heaven, something like sodomy would have
been the name for the untowardness of a coupling of figures so
disparate, a coupling akin to what happened when angelic lust
flares for human women. The ability of angels to assume whatever
form they choose (1.423–31) seems realized only in couplings across
kind, transformations across gender. Hence, as Raphael and Adam

enjoy Eve's naked ministrations to them, providing them food, we are reminded that "if ever, then, / Then had the sons of God excuse to have been / Enamoured at that sight" (5.446–48), even as we are assured that no sodomitical cross-species sex is about to occur. But something like that occurs in the reversal of hierarchy that Satan experiences with Zephon when his bravura is answered by abashment, feeling "how awful goodness is," seeing it "in her shape so lovely" in the cherub who once would not have been a fit bed companion but who now defies him (4.846–48).

In *A Preface to Paradise Lost*, C. S. Lewis confessed to "a certain amount of critical prudery" that Milton's angels had once aroused in him, thanks to what Lewis had seen (not incorrectly, as I have been suggesting, though he proceeds to deny it), "a life of homosexual promiscuity."[4] Convinced that Milton's "real meaning is certainly not filthy" (113; and, of course, certain that homosexuality is), Lewis chose to believe that whatever form of sex life the angels have, it is not human sex. Angels don't "breed," and they don't die, and that makes them enough not like us to guarantee that their sex lives are not like ours. Lewis assimilated Milton's angels to those of Henry More, a Cambridge Platonist, and his solution to the question of angelic sex—that is, his regarding it as a problem that needed to be dispelled—is not unlike the sexlessness that Luxon extends to Adam and Eve, who live for the possibility of an eros devoid of the need for copulation and breeding. Even Gregerson, in defining Milton's erotic system as Neoplatonic, tends in this direction, and of

---

4. C. S. Lewis, *A Preface to Paradise Lost* (Oxford: Oxford University Press, 1942), pp. 112–13. Gregory Bredbeck opens his discussion "Milton's Sodomite," chap. 5 of *Sodomy and Interpretation: Marlowe to Milton* (Ithaca, N.Y.: Cornell University Press, 1991), by demurring from this point in Lewis. Denise Albanese, *New Science, New World* (Durham: Duke University Press, 1996), like Lewis, thinks that angelic sex and human sex are distinct. Whereas Lewis solves what he sees as the problem of angelic sex by drawing this distinction, Albanese stresses how human sex is "materially different" from, even if "metaphysically analogous" (135) to the angelic variety; this makes human/angel difference parallel to female/male gendered difference, and for Albanese, as for Guillory [John Guillory, "From the Superfluous to the Supernumerary: Reading Gender into Paradise Lost," in *Soliciting Interpretation*, ed. Elizabeth D. Harvey and Katharine Eisaman Maus (Chicago: University of Chicago Press, 1990)], this difference appears to be insuperable, dividing "spiritual and material" (36). Albanese does not connect Milton's monism to the science she studies.

The earliest response to Lewis can be found in the characteristically brilliant and perverse comments of William Empson in *Milton's God* (Cambridge: Cambridge University Press, 1981). Empson regards angelic sex as showing the "happiness of having an understanding partner who need not be continually snubbed" (106), as Eve must be. Angelic sex is egalitarian, the only happiness for angels, who are routinely humiliated by a God who imposes meaningless tasks at which they invariably fail: "Apart from this private act of love, which Raphael blushes even to mention, the good angels never have any fulfillment at all" (108). For a recent similar celebration of angelic sex, see Clayton Delery, "John Milton's Unusual Angels or 'How Many Wings Does Raphael Have?'" *James White Review* 19, no. 2–3 (Spring/Summer 2002): 5–12. My thanks to Michael Moon for bringing this essay to my attention.

course her theologizing heads there as well.[5] Elsewhere in his book, Lewis claims a deep affinity between Milton and St. Augustine, and he is undoubtedly correct to do so. But precisely in the matter of Edenic sex, Milton and Augustine depart from the Platonizing and pathologizing that Lewis bequeaths to literary criticism.[6]

*   *   *

* * * [W]ithin the Lucretian framework that Milton uses to depict this realm of originary matter, Night is most readily associated with the void that is to be found in Lucretius, the empty space through which atomic substance moves. This, of course, is not a condition of material ruination but allows for the other feature of Lucretian physics, movement, the condition of chance couplings and decouplings that permit all things to be as they arise from an initial state of confusion to the regularities that follow. We have seen that Milton's universe is dynamic, and not one simply registering the *horror vacui* that Leonard genders invidiously.[7] (He does usefully suggest that Milton's coining of the terms *void* and *space* may well be indebted to Lucretius; 203.) But it is also important to register the fact that Rumrich is not in error when he associates a womb with chaos;[8] that is, the qualities of the place so named partake in a quite indeterminate fashion of the particulars attached to the figures who preside over it (and besides Chaos and Night, there also are Orcus and Ades, Demogorgon, Rumour, Chance, Tumult, Confusion, and Discord; 2.964–67). In other words, there is no very direct correlation between the allegorical figures and the nature of the place. The place is a "wild abyss, / The womb of nature and perhaps her grave" (2.910–11), while its ruler Chaos, a monarch—or rather, Anarch—and consort, "sable-vested Night, eldest of things" (962), can be only loosely attached to particular features of the place (even the darkness of Night is represented as a mantle that covers her, rather than what she is). In this abyss, an abyssal logic is at work

5. See Thomas H. Luxon, *Single Imperfection: Milton, Marriage and Friendship* (Pittsburgh: Duquesne University Press, 2005); Linda Gregerson, *The Reformation of the Subject: Spenser, Milton, and the English Protestant Epic* (Cambridge: Cambridge University Press, 1995) [*Editor's note*].

6. Stephen Fallon, *Milton among the Philosophers* (Ithaca, N.Y.: Cornell University Press, 1991), shows how More's angels are not the embodied creatures that Milton depicts, thereby countering Lewis as well as Robert H. West, *Milton and the Angels* (Athens, Ga. University of Georgia Press, 1955), who also drew Milton into More's orbit, although to argue that Milton exceeds him in his belief in the goodness of matter (173). However extreme Milton's views are, West is sure that they are nonetheless congruent with what he terms Puritanism.

7. See John Leonard, "Milton, Lucretius, and 'the Void Profound of unessential Night,'" in *Living Texts: Interpreting Milton*, ed. Kristin A. Pruitt and Charles W. Durham (Selinsgrove, Pa.: Susquehanna University Press, 2000), pp. 198–217 [*Editor's note*].

8. See John Rumrich, "Milton's God and the Matter of Chaos," *PMLA* 110 (1995): 1035–446; Rumrich, "Of Chaos and Nightingales," in Pruitt and Durham, eds., *Living Texts*, pp. 218–29 [*Editor's note*].

in "the dark unbottomed infinite abyss" (2.405), for however much "abyss" would seem to name a place, it names a place without bottom, the condition of placelessness. (This is perhaps the deep into which Lycidas also descends.) When rulership is anarchy, it is not exactly rule, and yet, as Rumrich has suggested, it is nonetheless the condition that precedes and houses a rule, an *archē*. The antiquity of Night has particularly vexed commentators; might she represent an ur-condition that precedes even the existence of God? She is, after all, "unoriginal Night" (10.476). Raphael's speech, which equates the "almighty is" (5.469) with "one first matter" (5.471), would seem to make impossible anything before being and matter, which are coincident. But the void troubles this and perhaps does so even more as originary "thing," which seems to materialize a state otherwise insistently without matter, "the wide womb of uncreated night" (2.150). Is this night Night? Can what is without origin be before origin? Rumrich usefully notes in his 1995 *PMLA* essay that the transcendent negatives applied to this realm are cognate with those applied to God ("Milton's God," 1043), and, as Harinder Singh Marjara has commented, the situation seems to be akin to the speculations that fueled the thought of Nicholas Cusanus, intent on the state of being in which opposites, in their most extreme forms, coincide.[9] Cusa's parsing of the paradoxes of a deity like a circle whose center is everywhere and circumference nowhere anticipates the decentered universe of post-Galilean physics; it can be found, of course, in Lucretius as well. Eternity and infinity are the very absence of time and space. Both God and the originary matter of Chaos and Night are in the same unspeakable condition.

The attempts to think gender in this originary state are, of course, prompted by Milton, by his placing a king and his consort to rule over a realm without rule or dimension, one that does not exist (if to exist means to be in time and space). A realm that is God and is Not. Not surprisingly, therefore, how critics see gender in this locus seems to tell us more about how they view gender, whether politically correct or socially conservative, deeply and darkly misogynist or not so much so. Rumrich seems, in his most recent attempt, to have silently withdrawn claims to God's feminine part. Now he dwells on the womb of chaos as a site of God's "potency" rather than privation ("Of Chaos and Nightingales," 222); God has been rephallicized. He also is in Marshall Grossman's attempts to think "the genders of God" by considering, among

---

9. Harinder Singh Marjara, *Contemplation of Created Things: Science in* Paradise Lost (Toronto: University of Toronto Press, 1992), p. 98. [Nicholas of Cusa (1401–1464), German cardinal, scholar, and philosopher—*Editor's note.*]

other instances, Chaos and Night.[1] Grossman arrives once again at
the scene by the pool in its hetero rewriting, in which Eve can only
be the mirror in which Adam is bolstered, made erect, "the womb
of meaning that exceeds the masculine will of its author so that he
may enjoy and regain himself" (110–11), the female made from and
for the male. Gordon Teskey, on the other hand, grotesquely picks
up on Rumrich, pronouncing Chaos "a menstruation issuing from
the body of God," likening it to the blood that drips from Adam's rib
as Eve is shaped from it.[2] Criticism founders at this locus precisely
because, whatever the status of human gender in Milton's poem (and
it is not one thing), it applies to this ur-condition only insofar as it is
also a site of contradiction. "Good" Chaos and Night fold into God in
a manner in which gender difference is subsumed into the masculine,
indiviously or not in the commentators' parsing of this; "Bad" Chaos
and Night exhibit the rebellion or even sheer negation of the feminine, or violation of gender difference that should attach itself to gendered bodies that know their place. (Night, like Eve, never speaks to
the spaceman that has entered her realm.) The lurking horror of this
bottomless bottom is perhaps glimpsed when Schwartz names it
"unclean," matter out of place or, worse, "unkind," unnatural in its
couplings.[3]

   Did someone ask, is the rectum a grave?[4] Did someone answer
and say that the fundament is foundational?[5] Milton takes his place
in line with the masculine bias of the inquiries launched by Bersani
and Masten, but in his most overtly Lucretian investigation of the
beginning of things, he posits a place that, in its gendering, and
indeed in its darkness, may acknowledge as foundational forms of
difference that are nonetheless within his monist same, a "first
matter" that is "one" even as it is not.

1. Marshall Grossman, "The Genders of God and the Redemption of the Flesh in *Paradise Lost*," in *Milton and Gender*, ed. Catherine Gimelli Martin (Cambridge: Cambridge University Press, 2004), pp. 95–114.
2. Gordon Teskey, *Delirious Milton* (Cambridge: Harvard University Press, 2006), p. 121.
3. Regina Schwartz, *Remembering and Repeating: Biblical Creation in Paradise Lost* (Cambridge: Cambridge University Press, 1988), p. 17.
4. Leo Bersani, "Is the Rectum a Grave?" *October* 43 (Winter 1987): 197–222.
5. Jeffrey Masten, "Is the Fundament a Grave?" in *The Body in Parts*, ed. David Hillman and Carla Mazzio (New York: Routledge, 1997), pp. 129–45.

514

GENERAL CRITICISM

HELEN VENDLER
From Milton's Epic Poem[†]

* * *

The enlargement of the mind by time and space, seen from afar or up close, conveyed sometimes in the decrees of God, sometimes in the account of an angel, sometimes through the eye of the human narrator, is only a material reflection of the true enlargement of the mind at which the epic aims: the expansion of our thinking about human experience. Since God looks on from His privileged vantage-point in eternity, to Him the whole story is ever-present. Stationed at any point in the story, He can see both backward and forward. At the moment of Christ's birth, for instance, Noah's Flood belongs to the past, and would be presented in a flash-back; but at the moment of the Creation the Flood is yet to come, and would have to be voiced as a flash-forward. This omniscient position proper to God is adopted by the narrator of the poem, who is both the blind and aging seventeenth-century John Milton ("On evil days . . . fall'n, and evil tongues") and the all-seeing tale-teller, who knows, by the divine inspiration of his Muse, what is happening on earth, in Heaven, and in Hell; now, in the past, and in the future. It is Milton's Godlike ambition to know all of space and span all of time: no other Western poet has taken on, and successfully carried out, such a task. Only from God's point of view, Milton realizes, can he "justify the ways of God to men".

To conceive of that justification, Milton had to begin to think of himself not as a just man, but as a sinner. Of course he had always believed that he, like every other person since Adam's fall, had suffered the consequences of that "original sin"—the darkening of the intellect and the weakening of the will that make human beings susceptible to actual present sin. Yet he had—or thought he had—sternly fortified himself against those consequences, training his intellect vigorously in all its faculties, disciplining his will to diligence in the service of God. In his earlier writings Milton never represented himself as someone who had fallen into actual sin in his active life. No concession, then, could have been more humbling

[†] From Paradise Lost: A *Poem in Twelve Books*, John T. Shawcross, ed. (San Francisco: Arion, 2002), pp. xv–xxi, xxvi–xxviii. Unless otherwise indicated notes are by the author. Reprinted by permission of the publisher.

to a man of Milton's temperament—proud, competitive, unyielding, and aggressive—than to admit that he had been deeply mistaken in his political conviction that the cause of good must succeed in this life. He had fallen unawares into the deadly sins of pride and ambition, Satan's own vices.

When Milton was in his thirties, hatred of his enemies, and the certainty of his own righteousness, had reached a point of unbridled violence visibly unleashed in his prose: in one tract he imagined his enemies finally consigned to Hell, where they would be tortured in the most savage manner, and made the slaves, the "negroes" of the other damned souls:

> But they . . . after a shameful end in this life (which God grant them), shall be thrown down eternally into the darkest and deepest gulf of hell, where, under the despiteful control, the trample and spurn of all the other damned, that in the anguish of their torture, shall have no other ease than to exercise a raving and bestial tyranny over them as their slaves and negroes, they shall remain in that plight forever, the basest, the lower-most, the most dejected, most underfoot, and downtrodden vassals of perdition.
>
> (*Of Reformation*, 1641)

Now in the catastrophe of his fifties, Milton could echo Job: "If I justify myself, mine own mouth shall condemn me: if I say, I am perfect, it shall also prove me perverse" (9.20). God's providence was a darker force than he had realized: "He destroyeth the perfect and the wicked," Job declared (9.22). The thoughts of the fallen angels mirror Milton's own tortured meditations on fate, God's foreknowledge, and free will:

> Others apart sat on a hill retir'd,
> In thoughts more elevate, and reason'd high
> Of providence, foreknowledge, will, and fate,
> Fix'd fate, free will, foreknowledge absolute,
> And found no end, in wand'ring mazes lost.
> Of good and evil much they argu'd then,
> Of happiness and final misery,
> Passion and apathy, and glory and shame.
>
> (ii, 557–64)

As Milton revolved within himself his own bafflement, pain, misery, and shame, he saw his former erring judgments as ones that, stemming from pride, had drawn him into his present blighted state. To find archetypes of his own post-calamity suffering, Milton began to investigate Aftermath in all its forms: we can say that *Paradise Lost* is in its entirety a meditation on Aftermath.

The poem opens in the sulfurous aftermath of the angels' fall, as we see Satan tormented by "the thought / Both of lost happiness and lasting pain". He finds himself in a region "where peace / And rest can never dwell, hope never comes / That comes to all; but torture without end / Still urges". When Satan arrives in Eden to tempt Eve, the angels themselves are shadowed over by the pall of aftermath: "Dim sadness did not spare / That time celestial visages". The Fall of Man brings about a bitter aftermath in the relations of Adam and Eve: one of mutual shame, accusation, blame, and passionate repudiation. While these psychological aftermaths occur within the "realistically drawn" characters of the poem, Milton adds a hideous allegorical story of aftermath as well. From Satan's head, at his Fall, there sprang forth (in a parody of the birth of Athena) a daughter, Sin; Satan copulates incestuously with his daughter, who brings forth a son, Death; Death in turn copulates incestuously with his mother Sin, whereupon she gives birth to the barking hellhounds of mortal vice. This philosophically motivated chain of personified consequences sexualizes aftermath into generational perpetuity, as though evil becomes unstoppable once the Tempter knows Sin and Sin knows Death.

There are recurrent historical aftermaths, too, throughout *Paradise Lost,* many of them drawn from the first books of the Bible: the Flood comes to destroy the sinful population of the world; mutually incomprehensible speech follows on the building of Babel; fire incinerates Sodom and Gomorrah. All of these aftermaths are shown to be caused by human sin. If Milton then finds himself in aftermath, has he too not sinned by yielding to the same worldly ambition that built the vain tower of Babel? And is not his fate the fate of the whole human race? Milton's encyclopedic internalizing of history documents for him, as one aftermath of the Fall, the endless suffering of the human tribe. Within the poem, however, Milton turns his knowledge of the past into prophecies of the future, as the angel Michael shows Adam a pageant of human time in which every sort of historically recorded evil—war, genocide, murder, theft, and rape, as well as the bodily and mental suffering that would so appall Keats—pass before his eyes. "What else should I have expected?" Milton must have asked himself as he contemplated his ruined state in 1660: "Who was I that I thought myself exempt from the common human fate displayed in every history I have read?" "In what sort of pride did I imagine I could help establish the kingdom of God on earth in a material government?"

The gravest aftermath of the Fall is of course the death of the Son of God. It is also the hinge on which aftermath turns into something else. After the Atonement, aftermath is transformed into its second and unexpected phase, which can be called by many names. The

theological name for it is Resurrection; Milton's psychological name
for it is "a paradise within thee, happier far"; the literary name for it
is symbol, in which intractable fact is projected on to an aesthetic
plane where it finds resolution. Milton had reflected on the achievement of a paradise within (though not in those terms) in 1644 in
Areopagitica, his prose-poem on liberty and faith:

> It was from out of the rind of one apple tasted that the knowl-
> edge of good and evil, as two twins cleaving together, leaped
> forth into the world. And perhaps this is that doom which
> Adam fell into of knowing good and evil, that is to say, of
> knowing good by evil. . . .
>   I cannot praise a fugitive and cloistered virtue, unexercised
> and unbreathed, that never sallies out and sees her adversary,
> but slinks out of the race where that immortal garland is to be
> run for, not without dust and heat. Assuredly we bring not
> innocence into the world, we bring impurity much rather; that
> which purifies us is trial, and trial is by what is contrary.[1]

"That which purifies us is trial, and trial is by what is contrary."
Milton lived to see this truth cruelly proved on his own person, and
he was chastened by it, and purified. *Paradise Lost* is the poem of that
chastening. But the chastened sometimes forget the emotions that
attended them in their earlier passion of pride and vaunting desire.
Milton's genius is that he forgets nothing—not his resentment, not
his fear, not his envy, not his anger, nor his sense of being unjustly
treated, nor his earlier conviction of superiority to others. He pours
all these emotions, in unquestionably authentic form, into his Satan
stretched on the burning marl, plotting with his fellow rebels, defy-
ing God, and deviously seeking revenge as he crosses the turbulent
realm of Chaos on his way to seduce Eve into disobedience.

Because Satan is the first dramatic figure in the epic, his emotions
have uncorrected power over us at the beginning (Blake's judgment
testifies to that power). Because Adam and Eve stand at the human
center of the poem, their recriminations and mourning after the Fall
strike us as if they were our own. Because we, like Milton, have read
history, we can ratify the grief attending on Michael's pageant of
human evil and interminable suffering. But what are the emotions we
are to feel about the other half of the poem's aftermath-testimony—
the paradise within?

That positive, or "comic," aftermath has proved harder for many
readers to credit, because Milton's language framing it comes from
theological formulations of the mercy of God mediated by the
atonement of Christ. The redeeming aftermath is announced in the

1. See p. 361–62, above.

most abstract passages of the poem, those spoken by God enthroned in heaven and replied to by the Son of God sitting at his right hand. Blake was right in saying that Milton's imagination was "in fetters" here, because almost every statement that God utters is drawn from his speeches in the Bible. To invent imaginative digressions for God was in Milton's eyes blasphemous; and so in these passages he subjected his powerful pen to the voice of biblical revelation, confining his imagination as he did not feel obliged to do when writing of the fallen angels or of Adam and Eve.

But Milton was not mechanically rephrasing Christian doctrine. The redeeming aftermath—following on the rage of failure—had certainly been experienced by him, or he could not have written his epic. He firmly believed that ultimately truth, mercy, and justice will be seen to be truth, mercy, and justice, and that lies and vices will be unveiled as lies and vices. Although such exposure can sometimes occur within historical time, Christian faith puts this revelation in its ultimate form at the Last Judgment; in this life, as recorded history witnesses, the wicked flourish as the bay tree.[2] Although human confidence may be shaken by the victories of sinners, in God's view, since all is ever-present, there is no need to wait for apocalypse: truth and justice and mercy are always in sight, here and now. By seeing through God's eyes, one can possess that happier paradise, finding oneself always in the presence of the real, the just, and the true no matter how compassed round by evil one might be. It was by imagining what it would be to see through God's eyes that Milton found his own second paradise (and decided on the perspective of his narrator). How does the poet represent God, and God's speech, so as to convey to us what it would be like to speak always from that interior faith in which all is as it should be—redeemed, justified, at peace?

In the epic, God is not shaken, God is not afraid, God is not vengeful; he is serene, secure, and (usually) unswayed by temporary emotions. He repudiates special pleading; he cannot, seeing all, see without judging. Another name for his judgment is the anthropomorphized "wrath," but God's wrath is a self-evident decree, not anger in the human sense. Transgression, in the mathematics of justice, requires punishment; but in the compassion of mercy, transgression requires alleviation. In the long loop of God's foreknowledge, the seed of the woman will bruise the heel of the serpent, and mankind will be brought into a new and closer relation to the divine because the Son of God will become man. When God speaks of these things in *Paradise Lost,* his tone is one of veracity and serene acknowledgment.

2. Psalm 37:35 [*Editor's note*].

Milton is convinced that the entity he names God embodies the most authentic justice, the truest estimation of events, the best providential intent, and the wisest and most merciful disposition. We perhaps find it hard to imagine the Good, the True, and the Radiant in one uncreated Being—"Bright effluence of bright essence increate"—but Milton did not. God, he intimates, speaks as we would speak if we ourselves were virtuous and saw clearly and without personal bias. Nonetheless, the anthropomorphizing of deity is the most difficult for us of the poem's strategies, biblical though it is. (And it is true that Milton's God sometimes—as in his anger in Book x at Satan, Sin, and Death—speaks with passion and derision, as Milton's sardonic irony grimly escapes its divine "fetters".)

* * *

Milton was lucky in inheriting, from the antecedent biblical script, such grand phenomena as stimuli to his imagination. But he inherited, too, one large stumbling-block which he needed to explore and understand: the command laid by God on the newly created pair that they shall not eat of the fruit of one tree in the garden. It is a purely arbitrary rule; there is nothing intrinsically sinful in eating fruit. It is not as though God had commanded Adam not to be cruel to Eve, or commanded Eve not to kill her children. Such commands would introduce ordinary moral evil, and obscure the intrinsic moral fable of Genesis, in which God makes a single rule: his creatures are to obey his command. As long as they grant him wisdom and goodness superior to their own, they are safe. As soon as they believe their own judgment to be the equal of his—or superior to his—they have disturbed the hierarchy of goodness and flouted the conclusions of reason. How can God *not* be superior to them in wisdom and goodness, since he created them and established them in supreme happiness? When Adam and Eve sin, their sin is one of disobedience (not one of carnal appetite) and of pride (estimating themselves as creatures above their creator). By God's explicit command, the angel Raphael has already alerted them to the tempter and his malice; and in disregarding God's forewarning, Adam and Eve rank their own judgment superior to his. When they lose their faith in God's wisdom, they will fall. Raphael bids farewell to Adam with a single injunction:

> Stand fast; to stand or fall
> Free in thine own arbitrament it lies.
> Perfect within, no outward aid require;
> And all temptation to transgress repel.
> (VIII, 640–43)

Because for Milton the indispensable condition for happiness is liberty, liberty was for him the essential quality of Paradise, and liberty requires the availability of choice. By this reasoning he could ratify God's establishing of a single test, giving his creatures the power to choose for or against the good. Milton too had had liberty to act as he thought best: to make common cause with the Puritans, to take part in their government and their pamphlet-wars, to serve Cromwell as Cromwell took up arms against his enemies. He perceived that like Adam, he had forgotten the warnings of God distinguishing between material and spiritual success, and had fallen. His sin was putting his trust in earthly gains and believing himself to be God's appointed messenger. In his anger against his enemies, he had betrayed love and charity, on which all other virtues depend. Milton's poem traces his own choices, made through pride and moral blindness, back to their archetypes in the pride of Satan and the heedless disobedience of Adam and Eve.

By the end of the poem, Adam has learned "that suff'ring for truth's sake / Is fortitude to highest victory". The Archangel Michael reminds him, however, that knowledge by itself is not virtue: Adam must add "deeds to thy knowledge answerable". As Michael enumerates those "deeds", we see that they are not the warlike ones of the Puritan "saints" raising an army to establish God's kingdom on earth. Rather, they are deeds of Christian forbearance, patience, and faithful love:

> . . . only add
> Deeds to thy knowledge answerable, add faith,
> Add virtue, patience, temperance, add love,
> By name to come call'd charity, the soul
> Of all the rest: then wilt thou not be loath
> To leave this Paradise, but shall possess
> A paradise within thee, happier far.
>   (XII, 581–87)

When we compare the tone of this passage with the virulent rage of the early Milton imagining with unleashed glee the fate of his enemies in Hell, we can understand how much his character was deepened by undergoing, and then meditating on, his own fate, experienced first as tragedy but subsequently as a redemptive chastening and a source of deeper self-understanding.

✻   ✻   ✻

NIGEL SMITH

From Is Milton Better than Shakespeare?†

*   *   *

To use Milton to think through our contemporary dilemmas means to go back to appreciate the nature of his achievement. In summary form, that achievement sounds stupendous. He set out from an early age to become the complete poet: to master the art of poetry and then to write the greatest heroic poem in his own language, in a conscious dialogue with the best precepts of poetry and poetic achievement in ancient and more recent European languages. While he did this, programmatically and determinedly, it was also an interrupted process, and along the way he theorized religious, political, and civil liberty, including divorce and a theology of free will. He analyzed the nature of tyranny, he explored the ways in which republican liberty might be known to English people, and he defended the English republic to a European readership. * * * All of these fine achievements were then recast during his later years (when he lived in modest retirement, officially shunned for his Puritanism and republicanism) in his three great poetic works, *Paradise Lost, Paradise Regained,* and *Samson Agonistes,* albeit more pessimistically, but no less thoughtfully, and in many ways more so. Soon after its publication, *Paradise Lost* was recognized as the greatest poem in the language, despite the repugnance for Milton's political and religious views felt by some of his most eminent admirers. * * *

* * *The majesty of his writing embodies that sense of rebellion, even as it honestly admits to the energy required by such a struggle against custom and the contradictions that such an enterprise necessarily involves. Even now, I believe that the nature and complexity of that contradictory energy is not appreciated, even by Milton specialists, and it is largely my purpose to set that record straight. In this way, the reach of Milton's achievements is far greater than Shakespeare's. However much we celebrate Shakespeare's grasp of humanity or poetry, his troubling displays of power, and his wonderful and delightful exposure of sexual identity, however much great acting companies, actors, and actresses produce staggering performances of his plays, Milton's interrogations of free will, liberty, and the threat to it are more riveting. No student of Milton has left *Paradise Lost* without feeling such an admiration, indeed an ardor of admiration.

*   *   *

MARJORIE B. GARBER

Fallen Landscape: The Art of Milton and Poussin[†]

In the spring of 1638, John Milton, then twenty-nine years of age, set out upon what was to be his only visit to the European continent. The voyage was for him an "Italian journey" in the sense in which the phrase is usually applied to painters—a pilgrimage to the birthplace of Western civilization, the source of Western literature, philosophy, and art. Painters, of course, are obliged to make such pilgrimages if they are to see the works of their predecessors; poets might reasonably stay at home and read printed copies of works written in distant lands. But for Milton this journey was, at least in part, a conscious voyage into the past, an attempt to inhabit the ancient, animate worlds of the *Georgics*, *Eclogues*, and *Metamorphoses*, as well as the modern Arcadian landscape of Sannazaro and the epic countryside of Tasso and Ariosto. Modern Italy had much to offer the young poet in the way of intellectual excitement. He traveled to Naples to visit Manso, the famous patron of Tasso and Marino. In Florence he "contracted an intimacy with many persons of rank and learning, and was a constant attendant at their literary parties; a practice which prevails there, and tends so much to the diffusion of knowledge and the preservation of friendship"; and in Rome he "experienced the most friendly attentions from Lucas Holstein, and other learned and ingenious men."[1] The only difficulty he seems to have encountered was in matters of religion, in which he was outspoken, despite warnings from Manso and others that such freedom of expression was both unwelcome and unsafe.

On his way to Italy Milton had passed briefly through the France of Louis XIII and Cardinal Richelieu, "despising," as he later wrote to a friend, "the luxuries of Paris," and eager "to enjoy the pleasures of literature and the conversations of the learned" in Italy. Some fourteen years earlier, moved by a similar distaste for Parisian ways, and also by a desire to see at first hand the paintings and sculpture of Italy, a young French painter had arrived in Rome, and was to remain there, with one brief exception, for the rest of his life. Nicolas Poussin had come to Italy at the instigation, and perhaps at the expense, of the fashionable Italian poet and connoisseur Gian Battista Marino,

---

† From *English Literary Renaissance* 5.1 (1975): 96–101, 104–5, 109. Reprinted by permission of the publisher. Some of Garber's notes have been omitted [*Editor's note*].

1. *Second Defense of the English People*, in John Milton, *Complete Poems and Major Prose*, ed. Merritt Y. Hughes (New York: Odyssey Press, 1957), p. 829. Quotations from Milton's poetry and prose, including translations of his work in Latin, are taken from this edition unless there are indications otherwise.

the celebrated pupil and protégé of Manso. He had attracted the poet's favor by executing for him a series of mythological drawings, probably in illustration of Ovid's *Metamorphoses*, and when he arrived, Marino, though ill, was instrumental in introducing him to important Roman intellectuals and patrons. Through the art collector Sacchetti, a friend of Marino, he made the acquaintance of the even more influential patron Cardinal Francesco Barberini, chief statesman for his uncle Pope Urban VIII, and the same cleric who was to show unusual favor and honor to Milton. There is good reason to believe that he also visited Naples, where his friendship with Marino and his admiration for the writings of Tasso would have no doubt made him a welcome guest.

Quite naturally the interests of both Milton and Poussin were drawn to the productive cluster of poets and writers lately situated in Naples. In his tract *Of Education* and elsewhere, Milton explicitly praises Tasso's essay *On Heroic Poetry* as a guide to "what the laws are of a good epic poem," linking him in skill and correctness with the epic poets of antiquity. He seems also to have favored Tasso's dictum on landscape, in the same essay, that "the sight of deserts and the horrifying severity of the Alps please us after the agreeableness of lakes and gardens." His admiration for *Gerusalemme Liberata* is evident not only from the many echoes in his own poetry, but also in the poem *Mansus*, presented to Manso in gratitude for his hospitality. In view of this evident respect on Milton's part for Tasso's power as teacher and example, it is interesting to find Poussin in the 1630s not only undertaking a series of paintings in illustration of love themes from the *Gerusalemme Liberata*, but also borrowing directly from *On Heroic Poetry* in his own theoretical writings, at times merely substituting the word "painting" for Tasso's "poetry." Thus he writes, for example, that "Painting is simply the imitation of human actions," and modifies another phrase to assert that "Colors in painting are a snare to persuade the eye, like the charm of the verse in poetry." It seems safe to conclude that the French painter and the English poet found common instructive ground in a treatise on the Italian epic.

Milton's *Mansus*, however, goes further in its praise of Neapolitan poets, lauding not only "magno . . . Tasso" (l. 7) but also "dulciloquum . . . Marinum" (l. 9), the "sweet-tongued" Marino, Poussin's particular patron and friend. Marino had combined his interest in painting and poetry by compiling a volume called *La Galeria*, a series of short poems each describing a single painting, most of them mythological in nature, but his most celebrated work was the extremely lengthy *Adone*, a version of the story of Venus and Adonis, which has been suggested as a direct model for *Comus*. Whatever the merits of this claim, it is clear that Milton knew the *Adone*, and drew upon it directly in *Paradise Lost*, where the image of Eve with her hair half-hiding her breast (*PL* IV.304–08, 494–97) is closely patterned after Marino's Venus. But the argument of *Mansus* does not rest with praise of Manso and his distinguished protégés. Instead, alluding gracefully to his disadvantageous "Hyperborean" or northern origins in a land thought too cold for true poetry, Milton asserts his own candidacy as a third great pupil of the master, and seeks, rhetorically, for a friend to celebrate him after death, as he here celebrates Manso, Tasso, and Marino. The language in which he phrases this elegant plea is the "southern" language of pagan mythology: "we also worship Phoebus" (l. 38), he proclaims, and, of Manso himself, "it shall be said that of his own free will Apollo dwelt in your house, and that the Muses were familiar attendants at your doors" (ll. 54–55). The object he seeks for himself is tacitly that which he predicts for all three Neapolitans, to "mount the way of immortality" (l. 53) through the fame of their poetry.

What is of special interest here is the decorous way in which the poet blends classical and modern, Christian and pagan intimations. *Mansus* is an occasional poem, and therefore in a sense analogous to a commissioned painting: the fundamental design and subject matter are established from the start. Yet Milton transmutes this conventional form by establishing an imaginative world in which dwell both Phoebus and King Arthur, a pagan and a Christian Olympus, an Ovidian Marino and a Vergilian Tasso. And this natural skill in blending Christian and pagan to produce not only a synthesis but also a commentary on the present is a talent he demonstrably shares with Poussin.

*   *   *

Discernibly, Milton and Poussin alike endowed their mythological creations with a quasi-allegorical quality intended to incorporate into the present day rich visions of the past, viewed almost as a literary Golden Age and surely as a lost aspect of imperial Rome. There is a certain striking similarity between Marino's "a thousand other falsehoods are applicable to the truth" and Milton's method.[2] In *Paradise Lost*, for example, Raphael is asked by Adam and Eve to explain the War in Heaven, and replies that he can only describe it by "Lik'ning spiritual to corporeal forms" (V.573) and by "measuring things in Heav'n by things on Earth" (VI.893). The fall of Mulciber is similarly described by the poetic speaker as a distillation of deliberate falsehood: "how he fell / From heav'n, they fabl'd, thrown by angry Jove. . . . thus they relate, / Erring" (I.739–46). The poet here stands in approximately the same relation to his audience as Raphael

---

2. I.e., the falsehoods of classical myth reflect Christian truth. The quotation is from the famous poet Giovanni Battista Marino's *Sacred Discourses*, as quoted in Gerald Ackerman, "Gian Battista Marino's Contribution to Seicento Art Theory," *Art Bulletin* 43 (1961), 333. [Cited elsewhere by Garber—*Editor's note.*]

stood to Adam and Eve, and myth is asserted as a fallen or intermediary means of communicating hidden Christian truth. The number
of such instances in Milton's poetry is almost beyond reckoning. We
may consider one or two more well-known examples.

> In shadier Bower
> More sacred and sequester'd, though but feign'd,
> Pan or Sylvanus never slept, nor Nymph,
> Nor Faunus hunted.   (*PL* iv.704–07)
>
> .   .   .   .   .
>
> Spot more delicious than those Gardens feign'd
> Or of reviv'd Adonis, or renown'd
> Alcinous, host of old Laertes' Son,
> Or that, not Mystic, where the Sapient King
> Held dalliance with his fair Egyptian Spouse.   (*PL* ix.439–43)

Likewise Proserpina (iv.268ff.), Pandora (iv.714ff.), and Pomona
(ix.394ff.) in *Paradise Lost* are all "feign'd" foreshadowings of Eve,
just as Eve herself foretokens the coming of the Virgin, "blest
Mary, second Eve" (v.387). We recognize this as a key aspect of
Milton's poetical design, very different from the allegorical method
of Spenser, his predecessor in the English epic. The strong presence of the Christian Ovid, and particularly of the *Metamorphoses*
as a "feign'd" or half-truth, provides a kind of pivot point from
which the poet can look simultaneously backward to the Golden
Age of myth and forward to the redeemed future of the risen
Christ. * * *

Italy as seen through the eyes of the traveler Milton and the resi-
dent Poussin was clearly a rarefied atmosphere, a very small sub-
sector of the larger world. Milton refers to the "private Academies of
Italy," to "literary parties" and "learned and ingenious men." He met
Cardinal Barberini, he almost surely met Rospigliosi, he visited the
patron of Tasso and Marino—in short, he inhabited, for the brief
period of his visit, the cultural salons of the day, the places of literary
and philosophical ferment. Did he meet Poussin? It is impossible to
say. But in so small and intense a cultural circle they knew many of
the same people. Milton, like Poussin, spent months "viewing the
antiquities of that renowned city" of Rome. Their works show similarities in the treatment of mythological and allegorical subjects
which are often striking. At the very least, we can infer that these
similarities may well have been affected in an important way by common experiences, and common ideas.

II

It has been objected that Milton was indifferent to the pictorial arts. Jonathan Richardson, an early biographer and himself a painter, chose a conventional metaphor of the time—1734—to praise the poet's imagination: "No Man ever Painted like Him in That Way,"—but quickly adds, "though (which I have Often wonder'd at), He does not appear to have Much Regarded what was done with the Pencil; no not even when in *Italy*, in *Rome*, in the *Vatican*. Neither does it seem Sculpture was Much Esteem'd by him."[3] Likewise Coleridge, a hundred years later, finds it "very remarkable that in no part of his writings does Milton take any notice of the great painters of Italy, nor, indeed, of painting as an art." Yet a few lines later he reverses himself to observe that "in one passage in the *Paradise Lost* Milton has certainly copied the fresco of the Creation in the Sistine Chapel at Rome," and a modern critic has convincingly stated the case for the influence of pictorial art, basing his argument on internal evidence: "Milton nowhere alludes to the work of the great painters which must have confronted him everywhere. But *Paradise Lost* is best illustrated by comparison with these analogous expressions, and its fusion of Christian and pagan imagery, its visualizations of biblical legend and of classical mythology, its rich perspectives and its profusion of detail, are probably more indebted than Milton himself realized to what his eyes took in on the ceilings of the Sistine Chapel or the walls of the Doge's Palace."[4]

*   *   *

In short, both Milton and Poussin were Renaissance humanist intellectuals, which meant that they sought authority in their works from the Bible and from antiquity, while at the same time drawing upon contemporaries—in each case mostly Italian—whose artistic or philosophical contributions seemed natural outgrowths of the classical tradition.

*   *   *

3. Jonathan Richardson, "The Life of Milton, and a Discourse on *Paradise Lost*" (1734), *Early Lives of Milton*, ed. Helen Darbishire (London, 1932), p. 212.
4. James Holly Hanford, *John Milton, Englishman* (New York, 1949), p. 97.

DENISE GIGANTE

From Mortal Taste: Milton[†]

* * *

* * * [I]n *Paradise Lost* Raphael describes a symbolic economy of con-sumption in which all of creation participates. In a luncheon collo-quy with Adam, having been invited to "sit and taste" (5.369), he explicates this monist world in which all eating leads back up to God:

> food alike those pure
> Intelligential substances require
> As doth your Rational; and both contain
> Within them every lower faculty
> Of sense, whereby they hear, see, smell, touch,
> Tasting concoct, digest, assimilate,
> And corporeal to incorporeal turn.
> For know, whatever was created, needs
> To be sustain'd and fed. . . .   (*PL* 5.407–15)

Scholars have studied this meal as a symbolic event: John E. Parish compares it to other biblical scenes of eating and to classical meals shared between gods and mortals; John F. Huntley finds reference to the meal Sin prepares for Death in *Paradise Lost* and the one Satan offers Christ in *Paradise Regained*; Marshall Grossman inter-prets it as a prelapsarian communion associated with a Protestant understanding of the sacrament; Anthony Low focuses on the vege-tarian nature of the meal as a typological prefiguration for the Puri-tan communion service; and Jack Goldman, also reading the meal for its sacramental significance, questions the distinction between prelapsarian vegetarianism and postlapsarian carnivorousness.[1]

* * *

Raphael's description of angelic eating in *Paradise Lost* thus invests all meals—all eating whatsoever—with new significance. One no longer need limit oneself to bread, for the Word opens up to include a world of edible matter that is all part of one divine

† From *Taste: A Literary History* (New Haven, Conn.: Yale University Press, 2005), pp. 32–34, 190–91. Reprinted with permission of Yale University Press. All notes are Gigante's.
1. John E. Parish, "Milton and the Well-Fed Angel," *English Miscellany* 18 (1967): 87–109; John F. Huntley, "Gourmet Cooking and the Vision of Paradise in *Paradise Lost*," *Xavier University Studies* 8:2 (1969): 44–54; Marshall Grossman, "Milton's 'Transubstantiate': Interpreting the Sacrament in *Paradise Lost*," *Milton Quarterly* 16:2 (May 1982): 42–47; Anthony Low, "Angels and Food in *Paradise Lost*," *Milton Studies* 1 (1969): 135–45; Jack Goldman, "Perspectives of Raphael's Meal in *Paradise Lost*, Book V," *Milton Quar-terly* 11:2 (1977): 31–37.

substance. In this sense, the Protestant problem of ingesting a vacuity in a purely symbolic version of communion is solved, since now one
can really eat God, displayed in a manifest world of unified taste
objects. Raphael makes clear that in addition to virtue and knowledge,
such eating provides *pleasure*. He explains that angels (here simply a
higher form of humans) enjoy eating with all five senses, "whereby
they hear, see, smell, touch, taste, / Tasting concoct, digest, assimilate"
(5.411–12), a pleasurable process that knowingly controverts a scholastic tradition accustomed to viewing angels as purely spiritual, "the
common gloss / Of Theologians" (*PL* 5.435–36). But Raphael challenges tradition not only in asserting *that* angels eat: he also describes
how they eat in a manner certain readers have found discomforting.
C. S. Lewis, for instance, protests that the physiological detail was
poetically necessary because *true* (emphasis his): "It is inconceivable
that Milton should have so emphasized the reality of angelic nourishment (and even angelic excretion) if the bodies he attributed to his
angels were merely a poetical device . . . Milton put it there simply
because he thought it *true*."[2] Despite Lewis's insistence on the veracity of the scene, Milton has nothing specific to say about how or
what angels eat in *Christian Doctrine,* and one might conclude
against him that Milton's silence on this matter in his lengthy theological treatise suggests he had no particular investment in the
"truth" of angelic eating. But it is important not to miss the accent
of Lewis's defense: his readerly distaste with the passage stems from
the *gust* of it, the fact that having been invited to "sit and taste,"
Raphael does not hesitate to indulge in epicurean pleasure.

Milton's relatives inform us that the poet was a bit of an epicure
himself and that "what he had, he always loved to have of the best."[3]
The picture of the poet that emerges is one of a temperate but fine
connoisseur, not afraid of sensual delight. (Temperance is stressed
by all modern gastronomers as a means to prolong and heighten the
pleasures of the palate.) Shortly before his death, Milton recalled
his marriage vows to his third wife, Elizabeth, in culinary terms:
"God have mercy, Betty, I see thou wilt perform according to thy
promise in providing me such dishes as I think fit whilst I live; and,
when I die, thou knowest that I have left thee all."[4] When Raphael
falls to his food in *Paradise Lost* "with keen dispatch / Of real hunger, and concoctive heat / To transubstantiate," his lower faculties
are put to work tasting, concocting, digesting, assimilating, and

2. C. S. Lewis, *A Preface to "Paradise Lost"* (London: Oxford University Press, 1942), p. 106.
3. William Riley Parker, *Milton: A Biography,* ed. Gordon Campbell, 2d ed., 2 vols.
(Oxford: Clarendon Press, 1966), 1:584.
4. Quoted from Milton's maid, Elizabeth Fisher, in David Masson, *The Life of John Milton:
Narrated in Connexion with the Political, Ecclesiastical, and Literary History of His Time,* 7
vols. (reprint of 1877–96 ed. by Macmillan; Gloucester, Mass.: Peter Smith, 1965), 6:728.

corporeal to incorporeal turning in a systematic process whose ultimate end is the Almighty, but whose immediate end is pleasure (5.436–38): "O *Adam*," exclaims the happily feasting angel, "one Almighty is, from whom / All things proceed, and up to him return" (5.469–70). Of course, Raphael intends "transubstantiate" in a sense opposite from that of the author of *Christian Doctrine,* since here it means turning the corporeal into the incorporeal.

In *Paradise Lost* God's substance is not "downward purged" [*PL* 7.37] so much as sublimated upward as spirit in a symbolic economy of circulation that comes to define aesthetic taste. Leigh Hunt, one of the poem's most acute Romantic critics, was quick to recognize the importance of the pleasures of eating to Milton: "the great poet shewed so deep a sense of the attention worth bestowing upon his diet, and of the possible dignity, nay, divineness of the pleasure of feeding, that, during the above blissful dinners in the fifth book of *Paradise Lost,* he enters into an elaborate argument to shew the probability of there being eating and drinking in heaven itself; which is what few persons, we suspect, ever cared to think about, when they hoped to go there."[5] By calling attention to the divine "pleasure of feeding," Hunt emphasizes that Raphael joins a symbolic economy *of pleasure*. It is certainly pleasure that is at stake later in the poem when the archangel Michael warns Adam: "Judge not what is best / By pleasure" (*PL* 11.603–04). He might have stepped in several books earlier, and he might have said, "judge not what is best by pleasure *alone*," for in Milton's world pleasure is tied to knowledge, as it is to virtue, and Raphael does not attempt to disguise his pleasure when he judges it best to accept Adam's invitation to "sit and taste."

❊   ❊   ❊

ANGELICA DURAN

From John Milton and Disability Studies in Literature Courses[†]

❊   ❊   ❊

There is one especially ripe opportunity in literature courses for including disability studies: when teaching the works of John

---

5. Leigh Hunt, *Leigh Hunt's Literary Criticism,* ed. Lawrence Huston Houtchens and Carolyn Washburn Houtchens (New York: Columbia University Press, 1956), p. 557.

† From "Comment from the Field: John Milton and Disability Studies in Literature Courses," *Journal of Literary & Cultural Disability Studies* 6.3 (2012): 327–30, 336, 338–39. Reprinted with permission of Liverpool University Press. Unless otherwise indicated, all notes are Duran's.

Milton (1607–74), an author who includes blind narrators in a number of his works and who became completely blind when he was 43 years old. Because he is such a mainstay in major-author, world literature, and early British survey literature courses, I am especially keen on sharing some of the ways I integrate the important (inter-) disciplines of disability studies and Milton Studies in my undergraduate and graduate courses. Because those courses usually fulfill either area requirements for English majors and minors, and graduate students in English and comparative literature, this combination exposes a good number of future leaders in literary studies to this vibrant research area. Fortuitously, these same courses often fulfill general breadth requirements, like the "Western heritage" category, for non-English majors, so the combination will also reach students with other specializations.

Integrating literary depictions of blindness into these courses positions disability studies as one of many valuable theoretical perspectives that I also bring into the conversation about how to approach literary texts: * * * hence my current interest in addressing as many students in literature courses as possible.

* * *

Many artists have reflected and perpetuated a deep interest in the blind Milton's ability of getting all 10,565 lines of *Paradise Lost*, and the combined 3,828 lines of his other later works *Paradise Regained* and *Samson Agonistes*, down on paper by dictating orally to amanuenses. (Here already we come to a linguistic conjunction of disability studies and Milton Studies. Miltonists are familiar with the term *amanuenses* as referring to Milton's friends and family members who converted his spoken word to written script. The term is also familiar to current users and administrators of disability resource centers: it is the term for the specifically trained employees who take notes in class and aid disabled persons in written examinations.) The onus is on instructors to hone this general interest into critical interpretation of such issues as physical impairment, the social construction of disability, visual culture, access, dependence, and other major topics that disability studies has been a vanguard in investigating.

The most well-known among the "Milton dictating" illustrations are those by Swiss-Briton Henry Fuseli (1741–1825), Frenchman Eugene Delacroix (1798–1863), and Hungarian Mihály Munkácsy (1844–1900), all of which represent Milton's daughters as his amanuenses. Not as widely circulated are illustrations that represent male amanuenses, as the ones by Irishman James Barry (1741–1806) and Briton John Calcott Horsley (1817–1903) depicting Quaker Thomas Ellwood in the role. Depending on copyright and institutional guidelines, these can be projected in class or included in course readers and web-based course content sites (e.g. Blackboard).

* * * I electronically project and read aloud the following description from an excerpt from an anonymous article, "Milton and London" (1898), written in immediate response to J. C. Horsley's "Milton dictating" illustration * * *:

> An interesting attempt to portray Milton in the act of dictating *Samson Agonistes* to the young and faithful wife [Elizabeth Minshull] who cheered him in the last years of his life was made by the late Mr. J. C. Horsley, R. A. In this picture Milton's friend, Thomas Ellwood, is seated by the open window, through which there is a view of the tower of St. Giles's, Cripplegate, framed by a creeper that has mounted the wall from the pleasant garden below. *Samson Agonistes* was written in 1667 while London was rebuilding after the Great Fire; Mr. Horsley has indicated that fact by introducing in the far distance a spire surrounded by scaffolding.[1]

* * *

This exercise has multiple pedagogical benefits. Students gain a great respect for the kind of clear, descriptive prose I seek to aid them in developing. They recognize the cognitive processes they must inculcate when unable to rely on the visual representation, which in turn gives them some understanding and respect for the processes that individuals with visual and cognitive disabilities must hone. Additionally, the students' attentiveness to detail enables them to appreciate the diversity of the society of three that is represented in the illustration—diverse in religion, age, gender, and physical abilities—rather than focusing on only one trait. Finally, the article situates this moment of collaboration that resulted in one of the greatest artistic works within the imagined context of recovery from a devastating historic event, the Great Fire.[2]

* * *

* * * Most eighteenth- and nineteenth-century editions of *Paradise Lost* include author portraits of Milton that depict him alone and that give no visual indicators of blindness. The "Milton dictating" illustrations, on the other hand, focalize the social network in the production of Milton's late, great works. These matters are of interest of course to disability studies and are of concentric interest in religious studies, reception studies, and translation studies, since we

1. John Calcott Horsley, *Milton Dictating "Samson Agonistes,"* in *The Outline of Literature,* ed. John Drinkwater, 3 vols. (New York: Putnam, 1923–24), 1:202.
2. The fire of 1666 that destroyed much of the City of London. See Introduction, p. xxx. [*Editor's note*].

are discussing a Spanish translation by a Catholic cleric, Juan de
Escoiquiz, of a work by a British Puritan listed in the Spanish Catholic Inquisition's list of prohibited books and authors, the *Index Libro-
rum Prohibitorum*. Of special significance in assessing the differing
and similar meanings ascribed to Milton across time and geographic
borders is Escoiquiz's preface, which represents Milton's blindness as
a component of his artistic acumen: "All attribute to the loss of his
sight his facility for concentration and his elevation of spirit, which
so radiates in the astonishing creation of his sublime imaginings and
elevated sentiments, of which his Paradise is full."[3] This closing
statement to the preface is not indicative but rather generative. In
contrast to this Hispano-Catholic translation, many of Milton's
detractors—including his compatriots—often and ferociously wielded
the trope of physical blindness as an expression of God's wrath or
as an external manifestation of Milton's moral blindness.

                         ❋   ❋   ❋

    ❋ ❋ ❋ Medical and legal studies deserve much credit for situating
disability as a category that eradicates euphemistic categories such
as *blind bard*; and disability studies [deserve credit] for recapturing
the Renaissance assumption that the norm was for individuals to
possess both externally apprehensible and invisible disabilities. The
onus is now on new literary researchers to build upon that work to
contribute equally profound and productive findings related in literary studies. ❋ ❋ ❋

DIANE KELSEY McCOLLEY

From "Sole, or responsive": voices in Milton's choirs[†]

Milton's imagination is essentially musical. Visual contexts help us
perceive his innovations and distinctions, but music enters inti-
mately into the workings of his thought. He has the ability to think
in sound and in precise diction simultaneously. The sound does not
choose the words, nor the diction sacrifice the sound. Like Herbert, he draws words from that mysterious source of both music
and language whence precision, relation of sound to signification,
and resonance among parts spring forth inseparable. His architec-
tonics combine massiveness, unity, balance, and symmetry with
beauty of detail and sublime flights, like the figural diversity within

---

3. Juan de Escoiquiz, prólogo to *El Paraíso Perdido* (Barcelona: Nueva San Francisco,
   1883), p. viii. Translation mine.
† From *Poetry and Music in Seventeenth-Century England* (Cambridge: Cambridge University Press, 1997), p. 175. Copyright © Diane Kelsey McColley 1997. Reprinted with
   permission of Cambridge University Press.

structural unity of the works of Taverner, Tallis, or Byrd. His early poems incorporate his musical experience at home, at Cambridge, and in collaboration with Lawes. The textures of his epic, like the English verse anthem and the Italian *stile concertante*, combine solo and choral voices, and the polyphonic church music, madrigals, consort songs, and keyboard music he knew pattern forth the richness of multiple relations in his language. His prosody is both mimetic and expressive. As in monody, his characters express powerful feelings through sound as well as signification; as in part-music, each line of thought has its linear energy and goal and at the same time forms consonances and dissonances with other simultaneous lines of thought. Though Milton scoffs at the music of the prelates and praises Henry Lawes for subordinating music to words, *Paradise Lost* is full of polyphony, and the way we hear it affects our response to his representation of goodness, of the politics of heaven, and of a God who shall be "All in All."

*   *   *

AYESHA RAMACHANDRAN

From "This Pendant World": Creating Miltonic Modernity[†]

"Thus thou hast seen one world begin and end," the archangel Michael tells Adam, at the beginning of the final book of *Paradise Lost,* pausing momentously "betwixt the world destroyed and world restored."[1] Awestruck and appalled, the first man is silenced by the grand spectacle of creation and destruction. Until this point, he has restlessly questioned what he sees, transforming the middle books of the epic into an extended dialogue on the nature of the universe. In this silence, in the long pause that opens the final book poised between old and new worlds, Milton reveals not only an unfolding biblical drama but also a historical transition of global, and yet deeply personal, dimensions.

Milton himself must have felt both the dumb-struck wonder of Adam as well as the triumphant revelatory power of Michael. His life spanned the better part of a century that historians repeatedly identify as the bridge to a recognizably modern world, defined variously in terms of scientific advancement, socio-economic upheaval,

† From *The Worldmakers: Global Imagining in Early Modern Europe* (Chicago: University of Chicago Press, 2015), pp. 182–86. Copyright © 2015 by the University of Chicago Press. Reprinted by permission of the publisher. Unless otherwise indicated notes are by the editor of this Norton Critical Edition.
1. *PL* 12.1–6.

and political revolution. And his long career, from the early poetry of the 1640s and the notorious regicidal pamphlets of the 1650s to the fallen, "evil days" of the Restoration, was entwined politically and intellectually with many of those changes. This proximity to major historical events of his time gives Milton's writings—particularly the retrospective later works—a unique doubleness, a Janus-like quality that balances a belated, nostalgic humanism that would not have been out of place in the sixteenth century with an early intellectual liberalism that would have been at home in the eighteenth. Poets before Milton had described the world, but it had been a finite and perfectly crafted entity, comfortably limited in scope. The sublime sweep of the narrator's gaze across the created universe in *Paradise Lost,* from the "dark Abyss," the realm of Chaos and eternal Night, to the empyreal heaven, the plurality of planetary systems and "this pendant world," now carries a thrilling, double power: a new humbling apprehension of the uncontrollable vastness of space and time, but also the individual poet's triumphant ability to contain it all within his imaginative grasp.

*

Milton's universe teems with worlds. Raphael sails through "worlds and worlds" when he glides down from Heaven on a sunbeam; Satan sees "innumerable stars, that shone / Stars distant, but nigh hand seemed other worlds / Or other worlds they seemed . . ."; Uriel reminds us that God "hath bestowed / Worlds" on Adam and Eve.[2] If empirical investigation alone could establish the subject of a poem with any certainty, *Paradise Lost* would be a poem about the world: the word "world" appears one hundred and thirty times in the epic, more often than either Adam or Eve, and cedes place in terms of frequency only to God and Earth.[3] The adjectives most frequently applied to the world in Milton's poem are familiar ones—"new," "new created," "other," or "another"—calculated to recall Europe's encounter with America.[4] And like the new geographic discoveries of the early modern period, the worlds of *Paradise Lost* are novel and unfamiliar. They lurk at the edges of the known in the vast sea of infinite cosmic space, like the Hesperian isles "famed of old"; and

2. *PL* 5.268, 3.565–66, 3.673–74.
3. "Adam" appears 119 times, "Eve" 118 times, "God" 271 times, and "Earth" 213 times. "Universe" appears only seven times, while "cosmos" is never used. These searches were conducted electronically using the Chadwyck-Healey Literature Online database and cross-checked against Celia Florén, *John Milton: A Concordance of* Paradise Lost (New York: Olms-Weidmann, 1992) [*Ramachandran's note*].
4. Despite several uses of the phrase "new world" or "new created world," direct allusion to America occurs only once in Paradise Lost, in the first simile after the Fall (9.1115–18). For detailed analysis of the poem through the lens of American expansion and imperial conquest, see J. Martin Evans, *Milton's Imperial Epic: Paradise Lost and the Discourse of Colonialism* (Ithaca: Cornell University Press, 1996) [*Ramachandran's note*].

like the islands of the Mediterranean or the Americas, they invite travelers and theorists to make sense of their origin and order.

Profuse and multiple, the worlds of *Paradise Lost* thus map a new cosmic and intellectual consciousness where knowledge of "the world" is never complete, never finite. As the scope of "world" blurs into the boundless universe, there are always new worlds being created, new knowledge to be discovered. Writing in the wake of Montaigne, Galileo, and Descartes, who struggled variously with the skeptical problem posed by this rapidly changing world-picture, Milton inherits the challenge of comprehending the whole, of seeing "things invisible to mortal sight."[5] His acute awareness of this epistemological limitation—the need to capture the world's totality despite the fundamental impossibility of the task—fuels his epic quest to explore the implications of worldmaking.

Milton goes beyond his literary predecessors, Camões and Spenser, who had tested the worldmaking potentials of the epic through allegory and classical myth. *Paradise Lost,* by contrast, reimagines the *urtext* of European worldmaking itself as Milton defiantly takes on the subject of Genesis—the topic that even Descartes had abandoned with *Le monde.* Genesis presented a dangerous invitation to would-be worldmakers, for it promised cosmic renovation on an unprecedented scale. Like the cosmos whose creation it described, the status of Genesis as the ideal, unshakeable union of scientific knowledge and salvation history was increasingly under assault in the seventeenth century. To shore up the subject of Genesis was effectively to reinvent the world. Milton was thus not merely drawing on scripture to buttress the claims of his epic and his own poetic fame; rather, his epic sought to remake the world and reimagine its sacred origins for a post-Cartesian era.

*   *   *

* * * How did a post-Columbian and post-Galilean perspective on the world, with its skeptical investigation into the nature and order of things, its acknowledgement of cultural heterogeneity and difference, affect the ancient tale of the divine making of the world?

*   *   *

Paradise Lost stages this dilemma[6] as a clash of worldmaking narratives, from Satan's colonizing assault on Eden to various characters' retellings of the Genesis story in their quest to understand how the world was crafted. This preoccupation with the literal act of making the world—the entire cosmos, but also the many "worlds"

5. *PL* 3.55.
6. I.e., that of reconciling a Biblical world view with a scientific one. [*Editor's note*]

within it—marks Milton's sharp rejection of the epic's favorite theme of imperial desire, which now literally becomes a Satanic practice. In its place, the poet fully embraces the cosmological turn initiated by Camões and Spenser. The poem repeatedly juxtaposes competing creation accounts: the opening invocation in book 1, Uriel's and Raphael's strikingly different descriptions in books 3 and 7, Satan's shocking denial of divine creation in favor of self-begetting and Abdiel's furious insistence on created being in book 5. These culminate in a speculative dialogue on world systems that Milton dramatizes in book 8 between Adam and Raphael. Taken together, these narratives produce a strongly skeptical approach to the matter of creation itself—and thus to the question of God's relation to the world—as they point to a fundamental mystery at the world's origin. For Milton, even more than for Descartes, skepticism about our ability to understand the world empirically through the senses—"the unspeakable desire to see, and know" (3.662)—leads to a powerful affirmation of faith in the divine, in "the things invisible to mortal sight." At the same time, such epistemic uncertainty heightens the importance of humanly made fictions of the world—fictions, like *Paradise Lost* itself, which give the decentered, amorphous "new world" of early modernity a renewed coherence, order, and harmony. The poem thus revels in a newfound understanding of world order as humanly and poetically created, even as it longs to defend belief in an absolute, divinely established order of things. Caught between human and divine makers, *Paradise Lost* becomes a powerful investigation of *how* new world-systems are produced, where they originate, and why we need such narratives of overarching order when faced with a transition to modernity.

* * *

Glossary of Names in *Paradise Lost*

Aaron *3.598*   Older brother of Moses. The first high priest of Israel. The jewels in his breastplate had beneficent magical powers. Exodus 29:9. See MOSES, URIM.

Abarim *1.408*   A ridge of mountains east of the Jordan, in Moab, including Nebo and Pisgah. Contemporary sources suggested to Milton that they were in the "wilds" to the south. Numbers 21:11.

Abássin kings *4.280*   Abyssinian, or Ethiopian. See AMARA.

Abbana *1.469*   See DAMASCUS.

Abdiel *5.805*   A seraph, whose name means "Servant of God." He confronts and rebukes Satan.

Abraham *12.152*   Father, or patriarch, of the Hebrews and the Arabs. His name was changed from "Abram" so as to mean "Father of many nations." Genesis 17:5. See CANAAN and UR.

Accaron *1.466*   Later "Ekron," the northernmost of the five Philistine cities associated with the worship of Beëlzebub. 2 Kings 1:2 and Zephaniah 2:4.

Acheron *2.578*   One of the traditional four rivers of Hell; its name means "without joy." Mentioned by Virgil, Dante, and Spenser. The other rivers are Lethe ("oblivion"), Phlegethon ("fiery"), and Styx ("horror").

Achilles *9.15*   Hero of the *Iliad* who pursued Hector around the walls of the city and killed him. See TROY.

Adam *3.285*   The first man, formed from dust and given life when God breathes into him: "And the LORD God formed man of the dust of the ground, and breathed into his nostrils the breath of life; and man became a living soul" (Genesis 2:7). In Hebrew, Adam's name means "dust" or "earth," and God plays on this meaning when he judges Adam: "For dust thou art, and unto dust shalt thou return" (Genesis 3:19). In the account of creation that was added to the Bible at a later date but placed at the beginning (Genesis 1–2:3), Adam and Eve are made in the *image* of God without reference to dust, bone, or breath: "So God created man in his own image, in the image of God created he him; male and female created he them" (Genesis 1:27). See EVE.

Ades *2.964*   A personification of darkness and uncertainty associated with the classical underworld.

Adonis *1.450*   River in Lebanon named after the boy who was beloved of Aphrodite and fatally wounded by a boar. Aphrodite turned him into a flower so that he would be annually reborn. The river runs red annually, supposedly discolored with Adonis's blood. See Shakespeare's "Venus and Adonis" and Spenser's *Faerie Queene* 3.6.29–47. See THAMMUZ.

Adramelech *6.365*   "Splendid king," an idol worshipped in Samaria, to whom children were sacrificed by being burned alive. 2 Kings 17:31. See MOLOCH.

Adria *1.520*   Adriatic Sea, which washes Italy's east coast.

Aegean *1.746*   The sea of Greece and its islands in the eastern Mediterranean.

Afer *10.702*   A southwest wind.

Agra *11.391*   Great Mogul capital in northwestern India.

Ahaz *1.472*   Wicked king of Judah. 2 Kings 16. See 1.471 n.

Aialon *12.266*   Broad valley west of Jerusalem over which the moon stood still at Joshua's prayer. Joshua 10:12. See GIBEON.

Aladule *10.435*   King of the mountainous country of Armenia. He trained assassins in a paradisal garden.

Alcairo *1.718*   Ancient Memphis, capital of Egypt, where Osiris, Serapis, and other gods were worshipped. Famous for its magnificence, identified by Milton with nearby Cairo.

Alcides *2.542*   Hercules' patronymic ("son of Alcaeus").

Alcinous *5.341*   King of the Phaeacians on the island of Scheria who welcomed Odysseus at his court, which had an orchard paradise Milton associated with Eden. *Odyssey* 7.112–32.

Aleian field *7.19*   The wide plain onto which Bellerophon fell from Pegasus. See BELLEROPHON.

Algiers *11.404*   A country in North Africa, and its chief city of the same name.

Almansor *11.403*   Muslim ruler in Spain and northern Africa.

Amalthea *4.278*   In older tradition, the nymph who raised the infant Zeus (Jove) on Mount Ida, in Crete, concealing the young god from his father, Cronos, who wished to devour him. She is sometimes identified with the goat who supplied the infant with milk and whose horn, when broken off by the infant, became the horn of plenty, which is magically replenished with fruit and flowers. Milton alludes to a later tradition in which Amalthea is the mother of Bacchus, the wine god (hence "florid son," 4.278), by Ammonian Jove. See AMMON.

Amara *4.281*   A fabulous paradise on a high rock where the younger sons of the emperor of Ethiopia were kept so that they could not overthrow their father. Another false, pagan version of Eden.

Amazonian targe *9.1111*   The shield of an Amazon. The Amazons, better known for their bows and arrows, are mythical female warriors.

Ammon *4.277*   Son of Zeus (Jove) by a daughter of Atlas, and king of Libya, or North Africa generally. See BARCA and CYRENÈ. Identified with Jove—Milton's "Libyan Jove" and "Ammonian Jove" (9.508)—and said to be the father of the wine god Bacchus, the "florid son" of Amalthea. Milton identifies Ammon with "old Cham" (4.276), that is, Ham, the son of Noah and patriarch of the African peoples. Typically for Milton, the fabulous, pagan myth is a distortion of biblical truth, which is historical. In the Bible, it is Noah who first cultivates wine. Rather than being the father of the wine god, Ham merely sees his father drunk (Genesis 9:20–27). See AMALTHEA, CHAM, NYSEAN ISLE, and OLYMPIAS.

Ammonite(s) *1.396*   Semitic people, often at war with the Israelites. See MOLOCH.

Amphisbaena *10.524*   Mythical serpent with a head at each end. Greek for "going both ways."

Amram *1.339*   Father of Moses.

Andromeda *3.559*   In Greek mythology, a princess chained to a rock to be devoured by a monster. A constellation next to Aries.

Angels *1.38*   Immortal beings created by God before human beings. Most of the angels' names are derived from Hebrew words ending with *El* ("of God"). See, e.g., GABRIEL. The angels serve God in various ways, according to their orders, or degrees. The Greek word *angelos* means "messenger." In *Paradise Lost*, Raphael and Michael perform the most important angelic missions. Other missions are Uriel's steering the sun (3.645–53) and warning Gabriel of Satan's approach (4.124–30, 549–75), Gabriel's guarding the Garden (4.543–54), and Zephon and Ithuriel's mission (assigned them by Gabriel) to find and arrest the intruder in the Garden (4.788–96). See CHERUBIM, MICHAEL, and RAPHAEL.

Angola *11.401*   A rich African kingdom, comparable in power to the kingdom of the Congo.

Aonian mount *1.15*   Mount Helicon in Greece, sacred to the Muses and Apollo. Site of the Hippocrene spring. Helicon is near Mount Parnassus, the site of Delphi, also sacred to Apollo and the Muses. Both mountains are just north of the Gulf of Corinth and visible from it. See PEGASEAN WING.

Apostate *5.852*   One who stands apart, a rebel.

Arabian shore *3.537*   The shore of the Arabian Peninsula, on the Red Sea.

Arcadian pipe *11.132*   Arcadia is a remote, mountainous province of Greece in the central Peloponnesian peninsula, where pastoral poetry, sung to the accompaniment of the pipe, is said to have begun.

Archangel *1.243*   An angel of the highest rank.

Argestas *10.699*   A west-northwest wind.

Argo *2.1017*   Ship of Jason and the Argonauts on their quest for the Golden Fleece.

Argob *1.398*   Pagan kingdom of Og. Deuteronomy 3:4. See BASAN.

Argus *11.131*   Many-eyed herdsman who was set to guard Io and was lulled to sleep and beheaded by Hermes. After his death, Juno put his eyes in the tail of the peacock. Ovid, *Metamorphoses* 1.624–28, 717–22; 2.531–33.

Ariel *6.371*   "Lion of God" or "divine light," one of the rebel angels.

Aries *10.329*   Constellation of the Ram.

Arimaspian *2.945*   Fabulous one-eyed people who steal gold from gryphons. Herodotus 3.116, 4.27; Pliny 7.2; Lucan 3.280.

Arioch *6.371*   "Lion-like," one of the rebel angels.

Armoric knights *1.581*   Knights of Brittany.

Arnon *1.399*   A river that flows from the east into the Dead Sea near its southern end. Deuteronomy 3:8. An important boundary in biblical times. Numbers 21:13.

Aroer *1.407*   Northern Moabite town.

Ascalon *1.465*   One of the five cities of the Philistines, on the Mediterranean Sea. Judges 14:19; 2 Samuel 1:20; Zephaniah 2:4.

Ashtaroth *1.422*   Plural of the goddess Astoreth and, in her Phoenician form, Astartè, a fertility goddess worshipped throughout Palestine and associated with the moon, whence the "crescent horns" (1.439) with which she was often depicted. She is also associated with the Greek goddess of love, Aphrodite. See ADONIS.

Asmadai *6.365*   A rebel angel. See ASMODEUS.

Asmodeus *4.168*   A jealous spirit who killed a young woman's seven husbands before being driven off by the eighth, Tobias, aided by the angel Raphael, who instructed Tobias to burn the entrails of a fish, the smell of which drove Asmodeus into upper Egypt, where Raphael bound him. Tobit 7:11–8:3. See RAPHAEL and TOBIAS.

Asphaltic Pool *1.411*   The Dead Sea, so called for its oily scum or bitumen. Called "the Asphaltic Sea" in the Septuagint (the Greek translation of the Hebrew scriptures).

Asphaltic slime *10.298*   Binding agent used by Sin and Death to hold together the substance of chaos for the bridge across Hell. Greek *asphaltos* is mentioned in the Septuagint as the substance used to build the Tower of Babel. Genesis 11:3. Also the tarry remains of the cities of Sodom and Gomorrah. Naphtha (1.729) is its liquid form.

Aspramont *1.583*. A resonant name in chivalric epics from the twelfth to the sixteenth centuries. *Aspromonte* is mountainous region in southernmost Calabria across the Strait of Messina from Sicily, famous for Charlemagne's victory over an army led by the African Saracen king Agolante, when the young and unarmed Orlando defeated the king's son Almonte. Orlando acquired Almonte's enchanted armor, his horn, his horse Brigliadoro, and his sword Durindana, originally wielded by Hector. Numerous references in *Orlando Furioso*, esp. 1.28, 30; 12.43; 14.43; 17.14; 24.48, 40.54.

Assyria *1.721* A great kingdom in upper Mesopotamia, with its capital, Nineveh, on the Tigris river. At one time its power extended over the entire Near East and into Egypt.

Assyrian mount *4.126* See MOUNT NIPHATES.

Astartè *1.439* See ASHTAROTH.

Astoreth *1.438* See ASHTAROTH.

Astracan *10.432* Astrakhan. A city near the mouth of the Volga River, which empties into the Caspian Sea.

Astraea *4.998* The constellation Virgo. Goddess of justice who lived on the earth in the Golden Age but fled to heaven when humanity became wicked.

Atabálipa *11.409* Inca ruler, whose kingdom, Cusco, in Peru, was plundered by Pizarro.

Athens *9.671* The most famous ancient Greek city, the birthplace of the classical arts, of democracy, and of political oratory, famed also for its leadership in the war against the tyranny of the Persians.

Atlantic sisters *10.674* See PLEIADES.

Atlas *4.987* Mount Atlas in the extreme west of northern Africa. Atlas was a Titan who for rebelling against Zeus was compelled to hold up the sky. He was changed to a mountain by Perseus. See GORGON.

Auran *4.211* The western boundary of the large country of Eden (of which the garden, Paradise, is but a small part).

Ausonian land *1.739* *Ausonia* is an ancient name for Italy.

Azazel *1.534* A rebel angel, Satan's standard-bearer, and a chief devil in the book of Enoch.

Azores *4.592* A group of islands in the Atlantic, eight hundred miles west of Portugal, representing the extreme west where the sun sets.

Azotus *1.464* Ashdod, one of the five Philistine cities and a center of Dagon worship. The ark of the covenant, after its capture by the Philistines, was taken to Ashdod and put in the temple of Dagon where the idol was mysteriously knocked down and mutilated. 1 Samuel 5:1–7. See DAGON.

Baälim *1.422*   A plural form of Hebrew *Baal,* which means "lord."
See BEËLZEBUB, BELIAL, and BELUS.

Babel *1.694*   The tower intended to reach to Heaven. God frus-
trated the project by causing the builders to speak different
languages. Genesis 11:1–9. Milton supposed Nimrod to be the
builder and associated the tower with Babylon. Cf. 12.24–62.

Babylon *1.717*   The great city on the lower Euphrates near the Persian Gulf, famous for its brick buildings, associated with the
Tower of Babel. The Israelites were taken into captivity there
after the conquest of Jerusalem in 586 B.C.E. Thus Babylon, like
Egypt, is a place of captivity and a symbol of bondage.

Bacchus *4.279*   The Roman name for Dionysus, the god of wine.

Bactrian Sophy *10.433*   Persian ruler.

Barca *2.904*   North African or Tunisian desert region called Cyre-
naica. See CYRENÈ. *Aeneid* 4.42–43.

Basan *1.398*   Bashan, a country east of the Jordan ruled by Og,
an enemy of Israel; also associated with the Ammonites, enemies of Israel. Deuteronomy 3:1.

Beëlzebub *1.81*   *Baal-Zebub,* "Lord of Flies." In Matthew 12:24 he
is called "the prince of the devils." Perhaps originally a god with
the power to deliver a city from an infestation of flies. See ACCA-
RON. 2 Kings 1:1–3.

Beërsaba *3.536*   Beersheba, in southern Palestine.

Belial *1.490*   Hebrew for "worthlessness." Belial is named as a devil
in the New Testament (2 Corinthians 6:15). In the Old Testament, however, the phrase "sons of Belial" means men given over
to shameless, dissolute, and murderous lives. See GIBEAH and
SODOM.

Bellerophon *7.18*   The hero who tried to reach the home of the
gods by riding the winged horse Pegasus up Mount Olympus.
Zeus sent a gadfly to sting Pegasus, who threw Bellerophon.
See PEGASEAN WING and ALEIAN FIELD.

Bellona *2.922*   Roman goddess of war.

Belus *1.720*   A version of *Bel, Baal,* a Babylonian god whose name
means "lord."

Bengala *2.638*   A great Indian kingdom.

Bethel *1.485*   "House of the Lord." In the idolatrous northern kingdom of Israel, King Jeroboam set up two places in which golden
calves were worshipped, Bethel and Dan: Bethel in the extreme
south of the northern kingdom, Dan in the extreme north.
1 Kings 12:28–29. This act repeats and doubles the crime of the
worship of the golden calf in Exodus 32:1–6. See JACOB.

Biserta *1.585*   A Mediterranean seaport in Tunisia, North Africa,
from which a Saracen army prepares to sail for France.
Boiardo, *Orlando Innamorato* 2.29.1–22.

Bizance *11.395*   Byzantium or Constantinople, modern Istanbul, conquered by the Turks in 1453 and so in Milton's day ruled by a sultan. It guards the Bosphorus, the narrow strait that forms part of the boundary between Asia and Europe.

Book of knowledge *3.47*   The Book of Nature, God's revelation in his creatures.

Books of life *1.363*   Records of the angels' now blotted out, glorious titles. Cf. Revelation 3:5, "I will not blot out his name out of the book of life."

Boreas *10.699*   A north wind.

Bosphorus *2.1018*   Narrow strait between Asia and Europe where the clashing rocks, the Symplegades, threatened the ship of Jason and the Argonauts. Apollonius of Rhodes, *Argonautica* 2.317–23, 552–67.

Briareos *1.199*   The hundred-handed monster who aided Zeus against the other gods when they sought to bind him. Briareos fought with the gods against the Titans. *Iliad* 1.396–406.

Busiris *1.307*   Legendary Egyptian tyrant identified with Pharaoh of the book of Exodus.

Cacias *10.699*   An east-northeast wind.

Cadmus *9.506*   Legendary founder and king of Thebes. Zeus turned him and his wife, Hermione, into snakes. Ovid, *Metamorphoses* 4.563–601.

Calabria *2.661*   The southern part of mainland Italy across the strait of Messina from Sicily. See ASPRAMONT, PELORUS, TRINACRIAN SHORE, and TYPHON.

Cambalu *11.388*   Peking (Beijing), capital of China.

Canaan *12.135*   The Promised Land of the Hebrews, corresponding (roughly) with modern Israel and the West Bank. Bounded on the north by the mountains of Lebanon, on the south by the desert and the borders of Egypt, on the east by the Jordan River and the Dead Sea, and on the west by the "Great Sea," or Mediterranean. Canaan is promised first to Abraham and his descendants and again to the Israelites when they leave Egypt. Canaan is named after Noah's grandson, whose father was Ham. Enraged by Ham's disrespect, Noah cursed Canaan's descendants, justifying the conquest of the Promised Land under Joshua and the subjection of the Canaanites. For Abraham, see Genesis 12:1–7. For Noah, see Genesis 9:18–27. For the division of the land under Joshua, see Joshua 15–21. See CHAM.

Cape [of Good Hope] *2.641*   The southern tip of Africa, which had to be rounded on the sea route to India.

Capitoline [Jove] *9.508*   An epithet of Jove referring to his temple on the Capitoline hill in Rome. See SCIPIO.

Capricorn *10.677*   The constellation of the Goat, and the southern tropic, or "turning place" from which the sun begins its journey north across the equator to the Tropic of Cancer. See CRAB.

Carmel, Mount *12.144*   A high promontory on the Mediterranean coast marking the westernmost point of the Promised Land, scene of the contest between Elijah and the prophets of Baal (1 Kings 18).

Casbeen *10.436*   Kazvin in northern Persia, a former capital.

Casius, Mount *2.593*   A mountain in northern Syria near Aleppo and the Orontes River, visible from the Mediterranean Sea. See ORONTES.

Caspian [Sea] *2.716*   Largest enclosed body of water on earth (i.e., not connected to an ocean). Situated between Europe and Asia.

Castalian spring *4.274*   A spring at the Oracle of Delphi, on Mount Parnassus, sacred to Apollo. Its waters inspired those who drank them with the gift of poetry. See AONIAN MOUNT and DELPHIAN CLIFF.

Cathaian Khan *11.388*   Ruler of Cathay, descendant of Genghis Khan.

Cathayan coast *10.293*   Cathay, an ancient kingdom occupying the northern half of China. Often identified with China.

Celtic [fields] *1.521*   British Isles, plus Brittany in northwest France. See 1.520–21 n.

Centaur *10.328*   The constellation Sagittarius, the archer.

Cerberus *2.655*   The monstrous barking hound guarding the entrance to Hell, mentioned by many classical authors. He is represented with at least two and as many as one hundred heads, although three is the usual number.

Ceres *4.271*   Latin name for Greek Demeter, goddess of crops, especially grain. Ceres was mother of Proserpina (Persephone), who was seized by the god of the underworld, Pluto (or Hades), while she was gathering flowers in the field of Enna, in Sicily. Mourning her daughter, Ceres refused to let crops grow, whereupon Proserpina was allowed to return to the earth for two-thirds of the year. For the remaining third of the year, winter, the earth is barren.

Chaldea *12.130*   See UR.

Cham *4.276*   Ammon, father of Bacchus, identified with Jove and with the constellation Aries, the Ram. Also identified with Noah's son Ham. See AMMON and CANAAN.

Chaos *1.10*   Chaos is three things: a cosmological concept, a narrative scene (although not, strictly speaking, a place), and a personification. Only in this last sense should *Chaos* be capitalized. As a cosmological concept, chaos is the region surrounding the three created systems of Milton's cosmos:

Heaven, Hell, and the universe. Chaos is infinitely extended and utterly disorganized. There is no limit to chaos and no measure within it: no time, no space. Chaos is not a vacuum, however. It is filled with "materials" in a wildly turbulent state that is often compared to the ocean, the most turbulent system visible on Earth. These materials were originally in God the Father, who extended to infinity. When the Father withdraws from infinity and situates himself in Heaven (which he creates), the materials of chaos are left behind. Being now entirely distinct from the Father, the materials of chaos are neither evil nor good. But of these materials the Son, assisted by the Spirit, forms the created universe, which *is* good. See 2.890–92 and 7.210–33. As a narrative scene, chaos does have distance, time, and direction, an "up" and a "down" (2.75–81). This chaos is the "wasteful deep" (6.862) through which the rebel angels can fall for nine days (6.871); it is the "unvoyageable gulf" (10.366) across which Satan does voyage from Hell to the universe (2.917–50); and it is the "gulf / Impassable" (10.253–54) across which Sin and Death nevertheless form a "stupendious bridge" (10.351). Finally, as a personification, Chaos is the king of chaos, "the power of that place" (2. Argument), enthroned beside his queen, "sable-vested Night" (2.959–62). Milton confers on him the inspired title *anarch* (2.988), from Greek *a* ("without") + *archē* ("origin, rule"). As a king, Chaos is indignant at divine incursions into his realm (2.999–1002). In Book Six, Chaos is still a fairly close personification when he "roar[s]" at the fall of the rebel angels "Through his wild anarchy" (6.871–73). By Book Ten, Chaos has become a vestigial personification, "vexed" (10.314) at the bridge built by Sin and Death and exclaiming against it: "On either side / Disparted Chaos overbuilt exclaimed / And with rebounding surge the bars assailed" (10.415–17).

Charlemagne *1.586* "Charles the Great." King of the Franks in the eighth to ninth century C.E. Holy Roman emperor and defender of Christendom against Saracen aggression, particularly from Spain. His rear guard, commanded by the great hero Roland (Orlando), was obliterated by a Saracen army at Roncesvalles, a pass in the Pyrenees near Fontarabbia (Fuenterrabia). In the Old French epic poem *The Song of Roland*, neither Charlemagne nor his peerage fell.

Charybdis *2.1020* A monster in Homer's *Odyssey* 12.55–126, 222–59, a giant whirlpool or sucking gulf on one side of the narrow strait between Sicily and Italy. Charybdis sucks ships down into her gulf and vomits them out. On the other side of the strait, on a cliff, is the monster Scylla, who has six fierce dog heads. One monster seizes from below, the other from above (Ovid, *Metamorphoses* 7.62–65 and 13.730–32).

Chemos *1.406*   Chemosh, "Subduer." National deity of the Moabites, long-standing enemies of Israel. Yet Chemosh was idolatrously worshipped in Israel from the reign of Solomon to Josiah, who purged the worship of foreign gods. Numbers 21:29; Jeremiah 48:4–7, 13, 46; 1 Kings 11:7; 2 Kings 23:13–14. See PEOR.

Chersonese *11.392*   Remotely derived from a Greek word for "dry land." Milton means the peninsula of Malacca in Malaysia, east of India across the Bay of Bengal. The ancient Jewish historian Josephus (*Antiquities* 8.6) says that Solomon sent a fleet to the Chersonese to obtain gold.

Cherubim *1.387*   Hebrew plural of cherub, the second of the nine orders of angels: seraphim, cherubim, thrones, dominations, virtues, powers, principalities, archangels, and angels. Only archangels and angels function as intermediaries between God and Man. Cherubim were responsible for guarding the presence of God from profanity. In Genesis 3:24, a cherub guards the tree of life after the expulsion of Adam and Eve. In Exodus 25:18, two golden figures of the cherubim guard the ark. Later, sculptures of the cherubim overshadow the ark of the covenant in Solomon's temple. 1 Kings 6:27. Milton audaciously represents cherubim among the fallen angels in Hell.

Chimera *2.628*   Fire-breathing monster with a lion's head, a goat's body, and a serpent's tail.

Circean call *9.522*   Circe, a witch-goddess in Homer's *Odyssey*, transforms men into obedient beasts (10.210–43).

Cleombrotus *3.473*   A Greek youth who, wanting to enjoy sooner the afterlife promised in Plato's *Phaedo*, leaped from a high wall into the sea. Callimachus, *Epigram* 23.

Cocytus *2.579*   A river of Hell whose name comes from a Greek word meaning "to shriek and wail over the dead." See ACHERON.

Columbus *9.1116*   Great Genoese navigator and explorer, also guilty of enslavement, torture, mutilation, and genocide of native peoples in the Caribbean. In 1492, under the patronage of the Spanish crown, Christopher Columbus made the first of several of his voyages to the Americas in search of a western sailing route to India. His was the first known voyage to the Americas resulting in settlement since that of Leif Erikson five centuries before. (Portuguese fishermen on the Grand Banks probably landed regularly to dry and salt their catches.) The point is uncertain, but Columbus may never have realized he had come upon a new continent, a discovery made by Amerigo Vespucci, after whom the Americas are named. Hoping that he was in India, Columbus called the native peoples of the Caribbean islands "Indians." See 9.1102–3 and 1116 n.

Congo *11.401*   In Milton's day, a region covering most of West Africa south of the Sahara.

Crab *10.675*   The constellation Cancer, which marks the farthest point north that the sun travels away from the equator before turning south. These movements of the sun belong to the astronomical system in which everything moves around a stationary Earth. See CAPRICORN; see also PLEIADES, SPARTAN TWINS, TAURUS, VIRGIN, and ZODIAC.

Cronian Sea *10.290*   The Arctic Ocean, frequently a barrier of ice. Named after Cronos, often identified with Saturn, who was driven by his son Zeus from Olympus and into the northern regions of the earth.

Cusco *11.408*   See ATABÁLIPA.

Cycladës *5.264*   A group of islands forming a circle in the southern Aegean Sea.

Cyrenè *2.904*   Ancient North African city in the region of Barca.

Cytherea's son *9.19*   Aeneas, the hero of Virgil's *Aeneid*; Cytherea is the goddess Venus.

Dagon *1.462*   Philistine fish-god. When the Philistines captured the ark of the covenant and set it beside the idol of Dagon, the idol fell on its face. When they repeated the experiment on a second night, they found in the morning that the head and hands of Dagon were cut off: "only the stump of Dagon was left to him" (1 Samuel 5:4).

Dalilah *9.1061*   Lover of Samson who betrayed him to the Philistines while he was sleeping by having a man cut off his hair, the source of his strength (Judges 16:19).

Damasco *1.584*   See DAMASCUS.

Damascus *1.468*   Capital of Syria, where Naaman, a leper, was captain of the army. When told by the prophet Elisha that he would be cured by bathing seven times in the Jordan River, he compared the Jordan unfavorably with Abbana and Pharphar, the rivers of Damascus. But when he bathed in the Jordan he was cured (2 Kings 5.1–14). In Ariosto's *Orlando Furioso* 17.80–105, Muslim and Christian knights joust at "Damasco." See 1.584. An urban paradise, Damascus has two crystalline rivers that are described by Ariosto as flowing in many courses throughout the city, watering its infinite gardens and filling the streets with their scent (17.19). Cf. the waterworks of Milton's Paradise, 4.237–41.

Damiata *2.593*   An ancient city on the delta of the Nile.

Dan *1.485*   A city in the extreme north of Palestine at the headwaters of the Jordan (1 Kings 12:28–33). See BETHEL.

Danaw *1.353* The Danube River, forming, with the Rhine, the northern boundary of the Roman Empire. It flows east through central Europe into the Black Sea. In the fifth century C.E. it was crossed by the barbarian hordes that destroyed the Empire. See RHENE.

Danite *9.1059* One who is of the tribe of Dan.

Daphne *4.273* A nymph, daughter of the river-god Peneus, beloved of Apollo. When fleeing Apollo, she prayed to her father to save her, whereupon she was transformed into a laurel tree, thence sacred to Apollo. Ovid, *Metamorphoses* 1.452– 567. See ORONTES for the grove named after her.

Darien *9.81* The isthmus of Panama, barring the ocean from flowing between the Atlantic and the Pacific. For this image, see Job 38:8–11.

David *12.326* The second king of Israel. He captured Jerusalem, made it his capital city, and transferred the ark of the covenant there. David is the type of man who is a sinner but has a passionate faith. He was traditionally supposed to be the author of the Psalms and is often portrayed with a harp. The prophets said that the Messiah would be of the royal line of David (Psalm 89:34–37; Isaiah 11:10). Jesus' kingship rests on his being a descendant of David: "the Lord God shall give unto him the throne of his father David" (Luke 1: 32).

Death *2.787* The son of Sin and Satan, Death is described as dark and shapeless but with the appearance of a crown on his head. He is armed with a javelin and a whip of scorpions (1.672 and 701). His body is later described as a vast, loose-skinned corpse that cannot be filled even by all the prey that waits for him on Earth (10.599–601). Death is described in Hell smelling the flesh of living creatures by raising "His nostril wide into the murky air" (10.280). Death is born to Sin soon after she is placed at the gates of Hell. Once out of her, he rapes her, whereupon she gives birth to the hellhounds that torment her at his urging (2.778–809). At the end of time, the Son will defeat Sin and Death and "fix their stings" in Satan's head (12.431–33). The Son will then hurl Sin and Death back through chaos to Hell, where their bodies will seal up the gates. Until then, Sin resides in all of mankind and prepares them as a meal for her son: "Till I in Man residing . . . season him thy last and sweetest prey" (10.607–9). See SIN.

Deccan *9.1103* In Milton's day, the region of India lying inland from the port of Goa on the northwest coast. See MALABAR.

Delia *9.387* A name for Diana (Artemis), so called for her birthplace on the island of Delos.

Delos 5.265 The smallest of the Greek islands in the Cyclades. It is sacred to Apollo and Artemis, who were born there. It once floated freely but when Leto arrived to bear her twins, Apollo and Artemis, stone pillars rose from the seafloor to fix it in place. The gods called it Asteria, the star, because from the point of view of the gods in heaven it appears as a star on the dark-blue earth. Pindar "Prosodion to Delos" lines 4–5 and 6–11; Callimachus *Hymns* 4 "To Delos" lines 36 and 53–54.

Delphian cliff 1.517 High on Mount Parnassus, overlooking the Gulf of Corinth, Delphi is one of the holiest sites of ancient Greece. It is home to the oracle of Apollo and the Pythian games in honor of Apollo, the most important games after those held at Olympia in honor of Zeus. Because of its height, Milton would associate the worship of the pagan gods that took place at Delphi with the devils who would occupy the "middle air." Delphi is analogous to the "high places" of pagan worship which are often mentioned in the Bible, 1 and 2 Kings. See PYTHIAN FIELDS, PYTHIAN VALE, and PYTHON.

Demogorgon 2.965 In medieval (but not classical) mythography, the most ancient and terrible of the gods, whose name is dreadful to utter or to hear. Demogorgon is given prominence by Boccaccio in his *Genealogy of the Pagan Gods* and is mentioned by Spenser in *The Faerie Queene* 1.1.37: "Great *Gorgon*, Prince of darknesse and dead night, / At which *Cocytus* quakes, and *Styx* is put to flight."

Deucalion 11.12 Greek king who with his wife, Pyrrha, was saved from the flood with which Zeus destroyed the men of the Bronze Age. For Milton, their story is a pagan version of the true story of Noah's Flood. After praying at the shrine of Themis, goddess of law, they restored the human race by throwing stones over their shoulders. The stones Deucalion threw became men; those Pyrrha threw became women.

Dictaean 10.584 Epithet of Jove (Zeus), born in a cave of the mountain range of Dicte, in Crete.

Dipsas 10.526 Monster whose bite causes overpowering thirst.

Dis 4.270 Pluto, or Hades, king of the underworld. See CERES.

Dodona 1.518 The site of a very ancient oracle of Zeus, where Zeus's instructions were uttered by the rustling leaves of a sacred oak tree. Homer, *Odyssey* 19.296–97.

Dominic 3.479 Founder of an order of monks (Dominicans) known for their white robes.

Dominions 2.11 Fourth of the nine orders of angels. Colossians 1:16. See CHERUBIM.

Dorian mood *1.550*   An ancient musical mode associated with military discipline. Plato, *Republic* 3.398e–399a.

Doric land *1.519*   Greece.

Dothan *11.217*   A town in northern Palestine that was besieged by a Syrian king attempting to capture Elisha (2 Kings 6:13–18). At Elisha's request, God struck the armies of the Syrian king blind.

Dryad *9.387*   A tree nymph. Greek *drus*, "tree."

Ecbátan *11.393*   Hamadan, ancient summer capital of Persian kings. *Paradise Regained* 3.286: "Ecbatana her structure vast there shows."

Eden *1.4*   The large country between the upper Tigris and Euphrates Rivers in which the garden of Paradise, where Adam and Eve live, is situated. Since the Tigris forms the eastern boundary of Eden and, in *Paradise Lost*, flows under the mount of Paradise, the garden is in the easternmost place possible in the land of Eden. Genesis 2:8: "And the LORD God planted a Garden eastward in Eden; and there he put the man whom he had formed." See 4.208–14 and 9.71–73. In the final line of *Paradise Lost*, Adam and Eve have been expelled from the Garden but are still in the vast territory of Eden, through which they pass: "Through Eden took their solitary way." See PARADISE.

Egyptian Thebes *5.274*   See THEBES, EGYPTIAN.

El Dorado *11.411*   "The Golden." Fabled capital of Guiana sought by the Spanish and later by Sir Walter Raleigh in the expeditions of 1595 and 1616.

Elealè *1.411*   One of the towns in Moab that the tribes of Reuben and Gad wished to occupy with their cattle. These tribes asked Moses not to bring them across the Jordan River into the Promised Land but to let them settle in Elealè and the surrounding towns, a request that contributed to God's decision to allow none of the men who left Egypt to enter the Promised Land, except Caleb and Joshua (Numbers 32:1–12). See HESEBON.

Eli's sons *1.495*   The wicked sons of the aged high priest: "They lay with the women that assembled at the door of the tabernacle of the congregation" (1 Samuel 2:22). Eli's sons are, for Milton, types of the wicked priests in the established church.

Ellops *10.525*   A kind of serpent-fish, like the lamprey eel.

Elysium *3.472*   The classical paradise, often referred to as fields or meadows, which is located in the underworld, as in Virgil, or among the isles of the blessed in the far western ocean. The location of "Plato's Elysium" is various, but in the *Phaedo* it is situated on islands in the region of the sky, on the true surface of the earth, which is far above where we live. These islands, surrounded by air as the land is by sea, are visible when the earth is seen from above. The *Elysian flow'rs* (3.359) of Milton's Heaven are for him the true location of what Plato, in his account, was struggling to grasp.

Empedocles *3.471* Pre-Socratic philosopher-poet who was fabled to have leaped into the volcanic vent of Mount Etna to ensure his fame and be deemed a god. See Horace, *Art of Poetry* 464–66.

Enna *4.269* The meadow in Sicily where Persephone (Proserpina) was abducted by Hades (Pluto), king of the underworld. See CERES.

Epidaurus *9.507* Greek town on the eastern coast of the Peloponnesus and home of Asclepius (Latin, Aesculapius), the god of healing. The god took the form of a holy serpent. The symbol of Asclepius is two snakes entwined around a staff.

Ercoco *11.398* Modern Arkiko, Eritrea, port on the west, or African, coast of the Red Sea. In Milton's day, the only port of the empire of Negus.

Erebus *2.883* A place of darkness between Earth and Hades, the classical underworld.

Esau *3.512* The elder of Isaac's two sons, and the hairier, tricked out of his inheritance by his smooth brother Jacob, who wore "skins of the kids of the goats" on his hands and neck to deceive the blind Isaac on his deathbed (Genesis 27). See JACOB.

Estótiland *10.686* A fabled, utopian island off the northeast coast of North America. Milton means only an extremely cold northern region.

Ethiopian (sea) *2.641* The Indian Ocean off the east coast of Africa.

Etna *1.233* An active volcano in Sicily, visible from the strait of Messina: the prison of the giant Enceladus and also of the monster Typhon, both of whom Jove struck down with his thunderbolt and pinned beneath the mountain. Etna is also the subterranean forge where the Cyclopes made Jove's thunderbolts (Virgil, *Georgics*, 4.170–75; *Aeneid* 3.568–82, 8.424–53). See TYPHON.

Etrurian shades *1.303* Etruria, the ancient name of Tuscany, in north central Italy. Mountainous and heavily wooded. See VALLOMBROSA.

Euboic Sea *2.546* The strait between Thessaly, in northern Greece, and the large island of Euboea. The strait is overlooked by Mount Oeta, in Thessaly. See LICHAS.

Euphrates *1.420* One of the two rivers of Mesopotamia ("land between the rivers")—the other being the Tigris, to the east— and one of the four rivers of Paradise (Genesis 2:14). Spenser calls the Euphrates "immortal" (*Faerie Queene* 4.11.21). The Euphrates rises in the mountains of Anatolia, in Turkey, and flows south-southeast for seventeen hundred miles to join the

Tigris near the Persian Gulf. The upper Euphrates forms the northeastern boundary of the land promised to the Jews: "Unto thy seed have I given this land, from the river of Egypt [not the Nile, but a stream south of Gaza] unto . . . the river Euphrates" (Genesis 15:18).

Eurus *10.705* East-southeast wind.

Eurynome *10.581* Milton interprets her name to mean "wide-encroaching." With her husband, Ophion, a serpent-god sometimes identified with the serpent who tempted Eve in Eden, she ruled Olympus until expelled by Cronos and Rhea.

Eve *1.364* The first woman, formed from a rib taken from the side of the first man, Adam. Eve's name is taken to mean "life" in Hebrew, which it does when said with a harsh aspiration, an *H*: "And Adam called his wife's name Eve; because she was the mother of all living" (Genesis 3:20). In the Greek Septuagint Bible, Eve's name is *Zoē*, "life." See ADAM.

Ezekiel *1.455* The prophet who went into exile in Babylon with the Israelites in the sixth century B.C.E. Famous for his vision of God in the opening chapter of his book.

Father *3.56* See GOD.

Faunus *4.708* Benevolent Roman god of shepherds and woods identified with the Greek Pan. See PAN and SILVANUS.

Fesolè *1.289* Fiesole, celebrated hill town high above Florence to the northeast. Galileo lived under house arrest in Arcetri, across the Arno River to the south of Florence, where he had an observatory. He might well have made observations from Fiesole, which is at nearly twice the altitude of Arcetri, before his confinement in 1633. See TUSCAN ARTIST, GALILEO, and VALDARNO.

Fez *11.403* A walled desert city inland in Morocco, north Africa, famous for its marble palaces and temples and its pink stone. In his *Commonplace Book*, Milton notes the great honor in which poets were held there.

Flora *5.16* Roman goddess of flowers. In Ovid's *Fasti* 5.193–206, Flora is beloved of Zephyr, the god of the west wind. Milton draws on Zephyr's pursuit of Flora for his account of the first meeting of Adam and Eve.

Fontarábbia *1.587* See CHARLEMAGNE.

Fount of life *3.357* Milton takes the idea of a paradisal fountain of life from the last chapter of Revelation 22:1: "And he shewed me a pure river of water of life, clear as crystal, proceeding out of the throne of God and of the Lamb." The phrase "fountain of life" is from Psalm 36:9. See TREE OF LIFE.

Furies *2.596* The Greek female spirits of vengeance, the Erinyes, are in Latin called the Dirae or Furiae. Milton recalls the

Erinyes' first intelligible utterance in Aeschylus's *Eumenides* (130), when they cry "seize!" repeatedly. For the Furies in Latin literature, see Cicero, *On the Nature of the Gods* 3.18.46; Virgil, *Aeneid* 6.570–72, 7.323–571, 12.845–68; Ovid, *Metamorphoses* 4.451–54. See also *Iliad* 9.454; *Odyssey* 2:135. See HARPY-FOOTED FURIES.

Gabriel *4.549*   "Strength of God," one of the four archangels; he commands the troop of angels set to guard the Garden of Eden and confronts Satan there (4.866–1015).

Galileo *5.262*   Great Italian scientist and astronomer, the first to look into the heavens with a telescope, disproving the time-honored, geocentric, Ptolemaic system and proving the Copernican hypothesis: that the earth revolves around the sun. He also noted erosion on the moon. See TUSCAN ARTIST.

Ganges *3.436*   One of the two great rivers of northern India, sacred to the Hindus; it flows into the Bay of Bengal, on the east side of the Indian subcontinent. Identified with the first of the four rivers of Eden, the Pison (Genesis 2:11). See HYDASPES.

Gath *1.465*   One of the five Philistine cities. See AZOTUS.

Gaza *1.466*   The southernmost of the five Philistine cities. See AZOTUS.

Gehenna *1.405*   The word for Hell in the Greek text of the New Testament. Matthew 5:22 and 10:28: "fear him which is able to destroy both soul and body in hell [*geennē*]." It is derived from Hebrew *gê-hinnom*, literally the valley Hinnom, also called "Tophet" ("drum"), to the southwest of Jerusalem. A grove in this valley was sacred to Moloch, to whom children were sacrificed by being burned alive.

Gentiles *4.277*   People who are not Jews. Milton uses the term twice in *Paradise Lost* to refer specifically to Greek-speaking peoples. See 12.310: "Joshua, whom the gentiles 'Jesus' call."

Geryon *11.410*   A red, winged, three-headed, cattle-hoarding monster killed by Hercules. He is associated by Spenser with Spanish tyranny and aggression: "He that whylome in Spaine so sore was dred, / For his huge powre and great oppression" (*The Faerie Queene* 5.10.9). Milton therefore refers to the Spanish conquistadors in the New World as "Geryon's sons."

Giant brood *1.576* In classical mythology, the giants are incited to war against the Olympian gods to avenge the Titans. See 7.605 n. and TITAN.

Gibeah *1.504*   A city near Jerusalem in the territory of Benjamin where a Levite and his concubine (improved by Milton to "matron") were, during a journey, hospitably received for the night by an old man. "Certain sons of Belial" (Judges 19:22) beat at the door demanding that the Levite be sent out to them to be raped. The concubine was sent out instead and was raped to death. This crime was the occasion of the civil war in Israel against the tribe of Benjamin.

Gibeon 12.265   The place over which Joshua prays to the sun to stand still so that he can complete his slaughter of the Amorites (Joshua 10:12–13). See AIALON.

Gibraltar 1.355   The promontory on the south coast of Spain at its closest point to Africa, separating the Atlantic from the Mediterranean. The barbarian hordes passed through Spain, crossed the Strait of Gibraltar, and spread across North Africa, or Libya.

Goblin 2.688   Ugly demon.

God 1.12   The infinite, all-knowing, all-powerful being who withdraws from infinity to occupy Heaven, which he creates. God is called the Father of all things because he is their creator and ruler. But in some special sense God is father of the Son, who participates in God's being and is God's creative Word. Milton wishes us to understand that God is not only all-powerful but also good, just, merciful, and loving. He leaves these last two attributes to be shown by the Son. God sees all times at once and therefore knows, well in advance of the event, that Adam and Eve will fall (3.92). But God adds that because Adam and Eve are free, his foreknowledge is not a cause of their fall, even though his foreknowledge makes it certain (3.117–19). Despite this certainty, God says he made mankind "Sufficient to have stood though free to fall" (3.99). Because God is just, mankind must be punished (3.210). Because God is merciful, mankind must be redeemed from punishment, which would otherwise be eternal. The Son achieves this redemption by becoming incarnate, as Jesus, and dying for mankind: "On Me let thine anger fall" (3.237). See CHAOS, MESSIAH, SON, SPIRIT, and WORD.

Golgotha 3.477   "Place of the skull," also called Calvary. Latin *calva*, "skull." The hill of execution outside Jerusalem on which Jesus was crucified.

Gordian twine 4.348   Referring to the Gordian knot in Asia. Legend said that whoever untied it would rule Asia. Alexander the Great cut it with his sword.

Gorgon(s) 2.628   Three female monsters with snakes for hair, the sight of whom turned viewers to stone. One of them was Medusa, who was killed by the hero Perseus and her head mounted on Athena's shield. Numerous references in Ovid's *Metamorphoses*. For example, at 4.655–62, Perseus uses the head of Medusa to turn the Titan Atlas into the mountain of that name in northern Africa, across from Gibraltar. See OPHIUSA.

Gorgonian terror *2.611*   Having the power to turn to stone. E.g., the "Gorgonian rigor" of Death's "look" (10.296–97).

Goshen *1.309*   District where the captive Israelites lived in Egypt (Genesis 47:6).

Graces *4.267*   The Charites, attendants of Aphrodite, commonly represented in art as three naked young women, their arms interlocked, two facing toward us and one away. Aglaia ("splendor"), Euphrosyne ("mirth"), and Thalia ("blossoming").

Great Mogul *11.391*   The Mogul emperor in India.

Guiana *11.410*   Region of northern South America, much larger than the present country of that name. It is "yet unspoiled" (11.409) because the Spaniards had not yet found and sacked it. Sir Walter Raleigh failed in his two attempts to do so.

Hamath *12.139*   In Syria on the river Orontes.

Haran *12.131*   A city, far up the Euphrates valley, on the Belikh, a south-flowing tributary of the Euphrates, to which Abraham's father, Terah, traveled with his family when he left Ur on the lower Euphrates. From Haran, at God's command, Abraham would journey south into Canaan (Palestine).

Harpy-footed furies *2.596*   Harpies are female winged demons with eagle-clawed feet who carry off children and souls. Their name is derived from a Greek verb meaning "to seize." Hesiod says that they are as swift as winds, birds, and time (*Theogony* 267–69). In Virgil, they carry food off or defile it and are also among the monsters at the doors of Hell (*Aeneid* 3.211–18, 6.289). See FURIES.

Heaven *1.27*   The place of God's presence, populated by the angels whom he created and who serve and praise him. First described in Book Three of *Paradise Lost*, especially 3.344–71, modeled on the heavenly Jerusalem of Revelation 21–22. Milton situates Heaven outside the created universe, which is suspended from it by a golden chain. Seen by Satan from far off, it has jeweled towers and battlements, which are alive. In Book Six, when the war in Heaven is recounted, Heaven appears as a vast country, much more extensive than the lands on Earth.

Hell *1.28*   Not situated in the earth but far off in chaos, at a great distance from Heaven and the created universe. As a place of eternal punishment, Hell was created to receive the rebel angels as they fell. Also the place of punishment at the end of time for reprobate men and women. Milton's Hell seems to be circular, like a furnace. See 1.542, 2.635. Yet it is also like a vast continent, with four infernal rivers—Styx, Acheron, Cocytus, and Phlegethon—and a landscape that the angels explore. See 2.570–628. There is a burning lake on which the angels lie unconscious for nine days before being wakened by Satan and going to the shore, which also burns under their feet. See 1.50–74, 227–37. The rebel angels build a palace in Hell, Pandemonium. See 1.700–30. The gates of Hell, guarded by Sin and Death, are made of brass, iron, and adamantine rock and are encircled with fire. When opened, fire and smoke belch through them into chaos. See 2.645–48, 876–89. See GEHENNA.

Hellespont *10.309*   Now called the Dardenelles, the strait between Asia and Europe. When invading Greece, the Persian emperor Xerxes commanded a bridge to be made across the Hellespont. When the bridge was destroyed by a storm, Xerxes ordered that the bridge makers be beheaded, that the waves of the Hellespont be scourged with three hundred strokes of the lash, and that the men with the whips utter barbarous insults while doing so. This act of hubris brought disaster on Xerxes' campaign (Herodotus 7.33–35).

Herculean *9.1060*   Similar to Hercules, a hero and demigod who performed twelve great labors and, like Samson, was undone in the end by a woman. His wife, Deianeira, hoping to regain his love, sent him a robe dyed in what she supposed to be a love potion but was actually poison. In his agony, Hercules climbed Mount Oeta, raised his own funeral pyre, and burned away his mortal part, ascending to heaven as a god. In the madness caused by his agony, Hercules threw his companion Lichas into the Euboic sea. See LICHAS.

Hermes *3.603*   Winged-footed messenger of the gods, himself a god. Mercury to the Romans. Milton uses the name with its technical sense in alchemy, where mercury was supposed to be "bound" in the process of obtaining gold from baser metals.

Hermione *9.506*   See CADMUS.

Hermon *12.141*   Mount Hermon, snowcapped peak in Palestine, northeast of the Sea of Galilee. The headwaters of the Jordan are at its feet. Mount Hermon was regarded by the Israelites as their northern border, but Milton follows contemporary cartographers in supposing it to be the eastern boundary.

Hesebon *1.408*   A Moabite, later an Amorite, town to the east of the Jordan River, northeast of Mount Nebo. It is included in the towns mentioned in Isaiah's prophecy of the destruction of Moab. Isaiah 15:4: "And Heshbon shall cry, and Elealeh; . . . therefore the armed soldiers of Moab shall cry out." See ELEALÈ.

Hesperian fields *1.520*   In this context, Italy, the western land, from the perspective of Greece. See n.

Hesperian gardens *3.568*   A fabled paradisal garden located in the far west of the world on the border of the ocean, where the sun sets. See 8.631–32. A tree planted there by Jove grew golden apples that were guarded by the Hesperides, daughters of Night and Darkness. In this office they were assisted by a multiheaded dragon. Because the apples recall the fruit in the Garden of Eden and the dragon recalls the serpent, Milton regards the Hesperides as being, like other Greek fables, a deformation of biblical truth. See 4.250–51: "Hesperian fables true, / If true, here only."

Hesperus *4.605*   The first star to appear in the evening, and the brightest. Actually the planet Venus.

Hinnom *1.404*   See GEHENNA.

Hispahan *11.394*   Ispahan, a Persian capital city.

Horonaim *1.409*   A city of Moab mentioned in Isaiah's prophecy against Moab: "My heart shall cry out for Moab; . . . for in the way of Horonaim they shall raise up a cry of destruction" (Isaiah 15:5). See also HESEBON.

Hours *4.267*   Female deities, Horae, responsible for changes of season.

Hydaspes *3.436*   A river in India, rising in the Himalayas, and a tributary of the Indus. The limit of Alexander's conquest. Milton's reference to it probably is intended to take in the Indus. See INDUS.

Hydra *2.628*   A venomous serpent with nine heads; one of the offspring of Echidna, Typhon's mate. Killed by Hercules.

Hymen *11.591*   The Greek god of marriage.

Ida *1.515*   Mountain on the island of Crete that is the birthplace of Zeus. See AMALTHEA.

Ilium *1.578*   The city of Troy, where the action of Homer's *Iliad* unfolds. For Milton, the men of the "heroic race" that fought at Ilium are midway in stature between men and giants.

Illyria *9.505*   Ancient kingdom to the northwest of Greece, across the Adriatic from southern Italy. Cadmus and his wife Hermione fled to Illyria from Thebes, the city he founded. There, they are changed into benevolent serpents. See Ovid, *Metamorphoses* 4.563–603.

Imaüs *3.431*   Mountains extending north from the Himalayas through central Asia, around which lived the Tartars and the Scythians. The name was supposed by Pliny to mean "full of snow."

Ind *2.2*   India.

India *5.339*   In Milton's day, India was known for spices and as a source of wealth. In his readings on India, especially Samuel Purchas's *Pilgrimage* (1625), Milton seems to have been excited by Indian fruits and shocked by Hindu religious rites.

Indian mount *1.781*   The Himalayas.

Indus *9.82*   One of the two great rivers of northern India (see GANGES); it rises in the Himalayas, in Tibet, and flows into the Arabian Sea on India's west coast. See HYDASPES.

Ionian gods *1.508*   Ionia is that part of the shore and islands of Asia Minor that was inhabited by Greeks. Homer and the early Greek philosophers came from Ionia. The "Ionian gods" are therefore the Greek gods, whom Milton supposes to have been men of "Javan's issue." Javan is the son of Japhet, one of the three sons of Noah, who are the patriarchs of the Semitic, African, and Indo-European (Greek and Hittite) peoples. Milton suggests that the Greek gods, like the gods of Syria, Palestine, and Egypt, are fallen angels disguised as gods. But he also speculates (following ancient euhemeristic tradition) that the Greek gods are remote ancestors of the Greeks elevated to the status of gods.

Iris *11.244*   A messenger of the gods, herself a goddess, personified as the rainbow.

Isaac *12.268*   Hebrew patriarch, father of Esau and Jacob. See ESAU and JACOB.

Isis *1.478*   Egyptian goddess with a cow's horns, wife to Osiris.

Israel *1.413*   Not the geographical country (see CANAAN) but the nation of the Hebrews.

Ithuriel *4.788*   Angel whose name means "discovery of God."

Jacob *3.510*   After cheating his brother, Esau, out of their father's blessing, Jacob fled to Bethel (near Padan-Aran) in Syria, where he dreamed of angels ascending and descending on a ladder between Earth and Heaven (Genesis 28). See ESAU.

Janus *11.129*   Double-faced Roman god of gateways.

Japhet *4.717*   Noah's son, patriarch of the Greeks (see IONIAN GODS), identified with Epimetheus ("afterthought"), son of the titan Iapetus and brother of Prometheus ("forethought"). Pandora ("all gifts") was given to Epimetheus as punishment for Prometheus's having stolen fire from heaven. The large wine jar Pandora brought with her, when opened, released into the world all the ills that afflict mankind (Hesiod, *Works and Days* 54–105).

Javan *1.508*   See IONIAN GODS.

Jehovah *1.386*   God the Father, Yahweh.

Jesus *10.183*   The Latin form of Greek *Iesous* and Hebrew *Yeshua*, which Englished is *Joshua*. See 12.310. See JOSHUA.

John *3.623*   The author of the book of Revelation. In Milton's day identified with the author of the fourth gospel.

Jordan *3.535*   The holy river of Israel and the eastern boundary of Israel above the Dead Sea, into which the Jordan flows from the north (see HERMON). The name *Jordan* is from the Hebrew *Yarad*, "to go down." When the Israelites crossed the Jordan to enter the Promised Land, the river stood back to let them pass, just as the Red Sea had parted when they fled from Pharaoh (Joshua 3; Exodus 14).

Joshua *12.310*   Joshua is the severe leader of the Hebrews who after Moses' death conquers the Promised Land. Greek *Iesous* (Latin *Jesus*) is the translation of the Hebrew *Joshua*, or *Yeshua*. In medieval biblical exegesis, Joshua is a *type*, or symbolic anticipation, of Jesus: as Joshua led the Israelites across the Jordan into the Promised Land, so Jesus will lead all mankind through death to eternal life. Milton follows Christian tradition in seeing Moses as a symbol of the Law, and so incapable of leading the people into the Promised Land. Joshua therefore bears the "name and office" of Jesus, who will lead humanity "Through the world's wilderness . . . Safe to eternal Paradise of rest" (12.313–14).

Josiah *1.418*   King of Judah 637–608 B.C.E., a religious reformer who violently purged the nation of the worship of false gods. 2 Kings 23:25: "And like unto him was there no king before him, that turned to the Lord with all his heart, and with all his soul, and with all his might, according to all the law of Moses; neither after him arose there any like him." A figure much admired by Milton, who saw Cromwell as a figure like Josiah. Josiah died at Megiddo in battle against Necho, king of Egypt (2 Chronicles 35:20–24).

Jove *1.198*   See JUPITER.

Judah *1.457*   The southern kingdom remaining after the division of Israel into two kingdoms following Solomon's death. The northern kingdom retained the name "Israel." Although the kingdom of Judah had Jerusalem as its capital, and the temple with the ark of the covenant, it was much smaller than the northern kingdom, made up of only two small tribes, as opposed to the ten in the north. Judah is "alienated" because its leaders are in captivity in Babylon. Milton is referring to Ezekiel's vision (Ezekiel 8) of the idolatrous worship practiced in and near the temple in Jerusalem.

Juno *4.500*   The Roman equivalent of Hera, the wife of Zeus.

Jupiter *4.499*   The Roman equivalent of the Greek king of the gods, Zeus.

Laertes' son *9.441*   Odysseus. See ULYSSES.

Lahore *11.391*   Mogul capital in northern India.

Lapland *2.665*   The extreme north of Scandinavia, associated with storm-causing wizards and witches.

Lavinia *9.17*   Turnus's promised bride, given to Aeneas instead. See TURNUS.

Lazar-house *11.479*   A place of confinement for sufferers of leprosy.

Lebanon *1.447*   The mountainous country to the north of Israel where the Adonis River runs, discolored each summer with reddish mud, or the petals of the anemone, supposedly the blood of Thammuz. See ADONIS.

Lemnos *1.746*   Large island in the northern Aegean Sea to which Hephaistos fell when Zeus threw him from Olympus (*Iliad* 1.590–93).

Leo *10.676*   Constellation of the Lion.

Lethe *2.583*   See ACHERON.

Leucothea *11.135*   "White goddess," associated with dawn and with sea spray.

Leviathan *1.201*   The whale or sea monster, associated with Satan.

Libecchio *10.706*   Italy's southwest wind.

Libra *3.558*   Constellation of the Scales.

Libya *1.355*   In Milton's day, most of North Africa, including the Sahara Desert. See GIBRALTAR.

Libyan Jove *4.277*   See AMMON.

Lichas *2.545*   Hercules companion and the innocent bearer of the poisoned cloak. See HERCULES.

Living Strength *1.433*   Jehovah, God the Father.

Lucifer *5.760*   "Light bearer," the morning star, perhaps the name of Satan before his fall: "Satan (so call him now, his former name / Is heard no more in Heav'n)" (5.658–59). Milton uses the name *Lucifer* to recall the prophecy of Isaiah (14:12–14) against Babylon, a figure of Satanic pride: "How art thou fallen from Heaven, O Lucifer, son of the morning! . . . For thou hast said in thine heart, I will ascend into Heaven, I will exalt my throne above the stars of God: I will sit also upon the mount of the congregation, in the sides of the north: I will ascend above the heights of the clouds; I will be like the most High."

Luz *3.513*   The earlier name of Bethel. See also JACOB.

Maeonides *3.35*   Homer's patronymic, "son of Maon."

Maeotis *9.78*   The Sea of Azov, north of the Black Sea and connected to it by a narrow channel. Shallow, reedy, semifresh water. Milton calls it "the *pool* Maeotis" from the Latin *palus Maeotis*, where *palus* can mean "a marsh."

Magellan *10.687*   Strait of Magellan, at the southern tip of South America. Named after the Portugese navigator Magellan.

Mahanaïm *11.214*   The place east of the Jordan River where Jacob met the angels of God (the name literally means "two hosts/camps"). Genesis 32:1–2.

Maia's son *5.285*   Hermes, messenger of the gods.

Malabar *9.1103*   Region on the western coast of Hindustan in India, famous in Milton's day for fig trees, the extended branches of which take root in the ground, forming an extensive system of arches.

Mammon *1.678*   One of the devils, his name a Semitic word meaning "wealth" that became personified; in Matthew 6:24 Jesus says, "Ye cannot serve God and mammon." See MULCIBER.

Mary *5.387*   Virgin mother of Jesus, called the "second Eve" because, being innocent of all sin, she is able to bear Christ, who will restore humanity to the state from which Eve fell. Milton emphasizes that it is through Eve too that what was lost shall be restored: "though all by me is lost, . . . By me the promised Seed shall all restore" (12.621–23).

Media *4.171*   Persia.

Medusa *2.611*   See GORGON.

Megaera *10.560*   One of the three Furies, the others being Alecto and Tisiphone, depicted in ancient literature and art with serpents for hair and with serpents in their hands. See FURIES.

Meliboean purple *11.242*   A famous, rare purple dye produced in Meliboea, on the coast of Thessaly. This is the best and brightest purple there is, yet Michael's cloak is "Livelier." See SARRA.

Melind *11.399*   Malindi, on the coast of Africa, in modern Kenya, the port from which Vasco da Gama crossed the Indian Ocean to Goa, in India.

Memnonian palace *10.308*   Persian winter palace (also called Susa), named after its builder Memnon, the son of Tithonus and Eos (Dawn).

Memphian chivalry *1.307*   Cavalry of Memphis, ancient capital of Egypt.

Messiah *5.664*   "The anointed one" in Hebrew, the general term for a king. The first king, Saul, was anointed by the prophet Samuel (1 Samuel 10:1), as was the great king David (1 Samuel 16:1–13). In Psalm 89:20, God says, "I have found David my servant; with my holy oil have I anointed him." In the prophetic books of the Bible, a messiah is prophesied who will sit on David's throne and govern all the nations of the earth in a time of universal peace: Isaiah 11:1–12, 32:1–2; Jeremiah 33:14–16; Ezekiel 37:24–28; Zechariah 12:6–8; Malachi 4. The Christian gospels would apply these prophecies to Jesus, whose name "Christ" (Greek *ho christos*, "the anointed one") means "messiah": "We have found the Messias, which is, being interpreted, the Christ" (John 1:41; cf. 4:25). In Milton's Heaven, before the Creation of the World, the Son is proclaimed Messiah.

Michael *2.294*   The name means "who is like El (the Lord)." The chief of the archangels, Michael contends with Satan at the apocalypse (Jude 9; Revelation 12:7). Although he appears seldom in the Bible, Michael is an important figure in later Christian literature and art, notably in Milton. In the war in Heaven,

Michael is commander of the celestial armies (6.44, 202–3, 411–13, 686–87, 777–78) and is the greatest of the angelic warriors (6.320–23, 250–61). Abdiel knocks Satan backward (6.193–95), but Michael alone wounds him (6.320–27; see 2.293–95). As executor of divine justice, Michael is sent with a troop of cherubim at his command to expel Adam and Eve from Paradise.

Moab *1.406*   The kingdom to the east of Israel on the other side of the Dead Sea, its people closely related to the Israelites. (In some periods, Moab extended far enough north to border on the Jordan River as well.) Israel and Moab often fought (Numbers 22–24; Judges 3:12–30, 11:17; 1 Samuel 14:47–48; 2 Samuel 8:2). Moses, the most sacred of Israel's leaders, was buried by God in an unknown location in Moab: "And the children of Israel wept for Moses in the plains of Moab thirty days" (Deuteronomy 34:8). Despised for their idolatry, which was associated with sexual license, the Moabites (and the Ammonites) were said to be descended from Lot's incestuous union with his daughters, after the destruction of Sodom and Gomorrah (Genesis 19:30–38). Ruth, the great-grandmother of David, came from Moab (Ruth 1:22, 4:13–22). See HORONAIM.

Moloch *1.392*   "King"; cf. Hebrew *Melech*, "king." God of the Ammonites, who were said to be descendants of the incestuous union of Lot with his daughters. See MOAB. Moloch was worshipped in Rabba, the capital city of the Ammonites, and his worship spread to Israel. See GEHENNA. Moloch's idol was a large brass figure, enthroned and crowned, with arms extended and with the head of a bull, into which infants were thrown through its mouth to be incinerated. As Milton's friend John Selden reports in his treatise on the gods of Syria, drums and other instruments were sounded to drown out the screams. Leviticus 18:21: "And thou shalt not let any of thy seed pass through the fire to Molech."

Mombaza *11.399*   Mombasa in modern Kenya, in East Africa.

Montalban *1.583*   Rinaldo's castle (Ariosto, *Orlando Furioso* 30.93). In Boiardo's *Orlando Innamorato* 2.23, 3.4, there is a large battle around Montalban between Charlemagne and the Saracens. See CHARLEMAGNE.

Montezume *11.407*   Probably Moctezuma II, because he was emperor of the Aztec empire at the time of European contact. His empire, like that of Peru (11.408), was destroyed by the Spanish.

Moreh *12.137*   The site of Sichem (Shechem; modern Nablus), the first place in the land of Canaan where Abraham made camp (Genesis 12:6).

Morocco 11.404   Kingdom in northwest Africa with coastline on both the Mediterranean Sea and Atlantic Ocean and facing Spain on the southern side of the Strait of Gibraltar.

Moses 12.170   The most sacred of Israel's leaders, Moses led the Hebrews out of Egypt and through the wilderness to the borders of the Promised Land, Canaan. While in the wilderness, at Mount Sinai, Moses received from God the covenant of the Law, the basis of Jewish ritual. Moses was led by God to the top of Mount Pisgah and shown the Promised Land, which he was not allowed to enter. First named in *Paradise Lost* as "That shepherd who first taught the chosen seed . . . how the heav'ns and earth / Rose out of chaos" (1.8–10), Moses is the supposed author of the Pentateuch, the first five books of the Bible, including the first, Genesis (Deuteronomy 31:24). It was supposed that the Pentateuch was dictated to Moses by God on Mount Sinai (Exodus 24:3–15). Milton gives more space to the Hebrews' Exodus from Egypt and journey to the Promised Land under Moses' leadership than to any other event recounted in the historical books (11 and 12) of *Paradise Lost* (12.169–260). This emphasis is due in part to Milton's seeing the Israelites' journey in the wilderness, from bondage in Egypt to freedom in Canaan, as a type of the English Revolution. See JOSHUA and AARON.

Mount of God 5.643   In *Paradise Lost,* the place of the presence of God in Heaven and the site of God's throne. Based on the two most sacred mountains in the Bible, Mount Sinai, where Moses received the Law, and Mount Sion (Zion) in Jerusalem. See 6.5 and 7.584–86.

Mozambique 4.161   In Milton's day, district of East Africa that had been settled by Arab traders and colonized by the Portuguese. See SABEAN.

Mulciber 1.740   The devil Mammon. Along with Vulcan, a Latin name of the Greek god Hephaistos, famous for elaborate metalwork. In the *Iliad* he fashions the shield of Achilles and in the *Aeneid* he fashions the shield of Aeneas. At the end of the first book of the *Iliad* (590–94), he describes being thrown from heaven by Zeus and falling onto the Greek isle of Lemnos. Typically, Milton regards the Greek story as a deformation of the truth, which is his own account of the fall of the rebel angels into Hell. See MAMMON.

Muse 1.6   See also 7.1 n. The Muses are the daughters of Zeus and Mnemosyne ("Memory"). Milton follows the great epic poets, chiefly Homer, in invoking the muse at the outset of his epic. Classical tradition names nine muses, who were patrons of the various arts and sciences, including Clio, the muse of history, and Calliope, the muse of epic poetry. Since his poem

is both an epic and an account of the origin of history, Milton
would intend both these muses to be suggested in his invocation. However, the only classical muse Milton names is Urania (7.1), whose name is from the Greek *Ourania*, "the
heavenly one." Hesiod, *Theogony* 78; Ovid, *Fasti* 5.55. Urania
is the muse of astronomy and, for Christian poets, of Christian poetry, notably the French poet Guillaume de Salluste,
seigneur du Bartas (1544–1590) and his English follower
Joshua Sylvester (1563–1618), whom Milton read as a boy. For
Milton, the muses of classical antiquity are a distorted memory
of divine wisdom (7.1–7); the Word of God as he gave the Law
to Moses on Mount Sinai (Exodus 34:28) and to David, for the
Psalms, on Mount Sion; the Spirit or inner light associated with
reason and conscience; and the Spirit of God that moves on the
face of the waters (Genesis 1:2). See SINAI and SION. At 1.376,
Milton reinvokes the muse before his catalog of the leaders of the
rebel angels who in the future will be the pagan gods of
Egypt, Palestine, Greece, and Rome. In this Milton imitates
Homer's catalog of the ships and their commanders who went
to Troy (*Iliad* 2.484–877). Because the Muses are the
daughters of Memory, these epic catalogs function as guaran-
tees of the factual truth of what the poet sings. See Lily B. Campbell, "The Christian Muse," *Huntington Library Bulletin* 8 (1935):
29–70.

Nebo *1.407*   A headland of the northern plateau of Moab, east of
the Jordan River. From one part of it, Mount Pisgah, Moses was
shown the Promised Land (Deuteronomy 32:49, 34:1). Milton's
phrase is from 1 Chronicles 5:8: "who dwelt in Aroer, even unto
Nebo."

Negus *11.397*   Title of the emperor of Abyssinia, in East Africa.
See ERCOCO.

Neptune *9.18*   Roman god of the sea and of earthquakes. His
Greek name was Poseidon. Milton is referring to the Greek
god, who was angry with Odysseus.

Niger *11.402*   Great river in West Africa flowing eastward and
then south into the Atlantic, in the Gulf of Guinea. Adam's
gaze sweeps northward from the Niger across the Sahara to
Mount Atlas on the Mediterranean.

Night *1.543*   The consort of Chaos, whom Milton calls "eldest of
things" (2.962). See Spenser, *The Faerie Queene* 1.5.20–28,
where the chariot of Night is drawn by coal-black steeds from
Hell whose mouths foam with tar.

Nile *1.344*   The great river of Egypt, longest river in the world,
flowing 4,160 miles from the Abyssinian highlands through
the desert to the Mediterranean Sea.

Nilus *4.283* The Nile River.

Niphates, [Mount] *3.742* An Armenian mountain, from which the Tigris River was supposed to spring. Strabo *Geography* Book 11.522. The name, from Greek *niphoeis*, means snow-capped.

Nisroch *6.447* One of the rebel angels, who will become the Assyrian idol worshipped by Sennacherib (2 Kings 19:36–37).

Norumbega *10.696* A town vaguely situated in Maine or farther north, perhaps on the Penobscot River.

Notus *10.702* The south wind.

Nyseian isle *4.275* The isle of Nysa in the Triton River in North Africa, an earthly paradise, birthplace of Dionysus (Diodorus Siculus 3.67). See AMMON.

Ob *9.78* A river in Siberia, Milton's Muscovy, flowing north to the Arctic Ocean.

Ocean *4.165* Oceanus, the eldest of the Titans, the father of rivers and a personification of the ocean that surrounds the terrestrial world.

Oechalia *2.542* A town in Euboea, in northern Greece, conquered by Hercules, from which he was returning when he put on a poisoned robe sent him by his wife, Deianeira. He burned his mortal part on top of Mount Oeta. See HERCULEAN and OECHALIA.

Oeta *2.545* Mountain in southern Thessaly by the Euboic Sea. See HERCULES.

Olympias *9.509* Wife of Philip II of Macedon, impregnated by Ammonian Jove in the form of a serpent. The child born of this union was Alexander the Great. A similar story accompanies the birth of Scipio. See SCIPIO.

Olympus *1.516* A snowcapped mountain in the far north of mainland Greece, on the border of Macedonia; home of the Greek gods, especially of Zeus after his departure from Mount Ida on the island of Crete.

Ophion *10.581* A serpent-god who ruled with his consort Eurynome before Cronos and Rhea, the parents of Zeus. The name means "serpent." See EURYNOME.

Ophir *11.400* Fabulous land where Solomon was thought to have obtained gold of exceptional purity for his temple. It was sometimes identified with Sofala, a wealthy port on the east coast of Africa.

Ophiuchus *2.709* Northern constellation, the "serpent bearer."

Ophiusa *10.528* Perhaps one of the Balearic Islands, which are off the coast of Spain in the western Mediterranean. The name means "full of serpents." These sprang from drops of Medusa's blood when Perseus flew over the islands. See GORGON.

Ops *10.584* Rhea, or Cybele, wife to Cronos, or Saturn. She became the Roman goddess of plenty.

Orcus *2.964*   Roman god of death, closely identified with Pluto, or Hades.

Oread *9.387*   A mountain nymph. Greek *oros*, "mountain." See DRYAD.

Oreb *1.7*   Horeb, Sinai in Exodus 3:1, where Moses met God, who appeared to him as a burning bush. See Deuteronomy 1:6 and SINAI.

Orion *1.305*   A constellation, represented as a hunter or an armed giant, the rising of which is associated with the season of storms. See *Aeneid* 1.535.

Ormus *2.2*   City of great wealth on an island in the Persian Gulf. The name survives in the Strait of Hormuz.

Orontes *4.273*   A Syrian river that flows into the Mediterranean. A grove of Daphne stood beside it. See 9.80.

Orphean lyre *3.17*   Orpheus was the legendary shamanistic poet who descended to the underworld to retrieve his wife, Eurydice, and, because of the beauty of the music he made, was allowed to return to the upper world with her, on condition that he not look back. He did look back, and Eurydice was lost. Milton says he sings with "other notes" than those that Orpheus used because he is inspired by the true God. Orpheus's music, which caused rocks, animals, and trees to listen spellbound, became a symbol of the power of poetry over the natural world. A troop of maenads, female worshippers of Bacchus, tore Orpheus to pieces and threw his head into the Hebrus River. The head floated to the island of Lesbos, where it was buried with full honors by the inhabitants of that island (Ovid, *Metamorphoses* 10.1–60). For this act of piety, the people of Lesbos would always have fine poets among them. The greatest of these poets was Sappho, a woman who wrote love poems to women. At 7.32–38 Milton compares the danger in which he stands—that of being drawn and quartered—to the fate actually suffered by Orpheus, the "Thracian bard" (34).

Orus *1.478*   Horus, Egyptian sky god, son of Osiris and Isis. He has a hawk's head. The pharaoh is a human incarnation of Horus.

Osiris *1.478*   Egyptian god of fertility and of the dead, dismembered by his brother, Seth. The scattered parts were collected by his wife, Isis, who gave them life, making him god of the underworld.

Oxus *11.389*   A large river in Asia that flows into the Aral Sea in Kazakhstan. Maps in Milton's day show it flowing into the Caspian Sea.

Padan-Aram *3.513*   Plain in Syria, north of Palestine, adjacent to the upper Euphrates, in which Jacob had his vision of the ladder ascending from the earth to heaven (Genesis 28:2, 10–17).

Pales 9.393   Roman goddess of flocks and pastures.

Pan 4.266   Greek god of nature, shepherds, and flocks. He is depicted as a goat-god who is mostly human from the waist up (though with horns and goatlike features including large ears) and a goat from the waist down. See FAUNUS and SILVANUS.

Pandemonium 1.756   Literally, "assembly place of all demons."

Pandora 4.714   See JAPHET.

Paneas 3.535   A city near Mount Hermon in northern Palestine at a spring of the Jordan, now Banias. Identified with Dan.

Paquin 11.390   Peking (Beijing), capital of China, which was thought to be a kingdom distinct from Cathay.

Paradise 3.354   The Greek word *paradeisos*, "garden," used for the garden of Eden in the Septuagint, the Greek translation of the Hebrew scriptures. Paradise is situated in the northeastern-most part of a large country, Eden, on the top of a high mountain. Milton's paradise is unusual in including work and sexual intercourse. For Milton, the ideal natural state must include having children. The unfallen state, therefore, is an open system in which humans are to spread throughout the earth: "Hail Mother of Mankind whose fruitful womb / Shall fill the world more numerous with thy sons / Than with these various fruits the trees of God / Have heaped this table!" (5.388–91). Unlike Dante, Milton does not enclose human innocence within the confines of the garden. Innocence and happiness are destined to spread over the earth (11.339–46). Politically, the garden is the "capital seat" (11.343; cf. "high seat," 4.371) of Adam, who is intended to be a benevolent, yet august, ruler over all his descendants. In paradise, Adam and Eve represent not only the perfect human marriage but also the ideal polity, with Adam as the ruler and Eve as its only citizen. (But Eve contains all future citizens of that polity.) When Adam and Eve fall, they lose not only their ideal relation to the natural world but also the ideal political state, leaving humanity to suffer all the political evils to be manifested in history, especially tyranny. See EDEN, EVE.

Pegasean wing 7.4   The winged horse Pegasus created the source of the Hippocrene spring on Mount Helicon by striking the rock with his hoof. The Hippocrene spring is identified with poetry, especially epic poetry, in dactylic meter, which can sound like hoofbeats. See AONIAN MOUNT, BELLEROPHON.

Pelorus 1.232   The promontory on the northeast corner of the island of Sicily (Trinacria), on the Strait of Messina, exposed to the blast of the north wind (Ovid, *Metamorphoses* 13.726–27). Pelorus faces the rock of Scylla on the Italian mainland. The whirling waters of Charybdis are just off its shore. Looming behind Pelorus is the volcanic Mount Etna. In Greek the words *pelōr* and *pelōrios* describe creatures that are huge and monstrous, such the Python, defeated by Apollo ("Homeric Hymn to Apollo," 374), the Cyclops (*Odyssey* 9.428), and Typhon (Hesiod, *Theogony* 820–68; Ovid, *Metamorphoses* 5.346–58). Zeus pinned the monstrous Typhon's head under Etna and his right hand under Pelorus. Eruptions of Etna were connected by the above authors (except Hesiod) with the monster's continuing struggles and torments, vomiting fire. Scylla, the *pelōr kakon* (evil monster) of *Odyssey* 12.87, resembles Milton's Sin. See CALABRIA, PYTHON, TRINACRIAN SHORE, TYPHON, SCYLLA, CHARYBDIS, PHLEGRA, and SIN.

Peor *1.412*   Alternate name for CHEMOS. Canaanite god associated with sexual orgies on Mount Peor in Moab. In Numbers 25, many of the Israelites, during their journey in the wilderness, "commit whoredom with the daughters of Moab" and make sacrifices to Baal-peor (Numbers 25:1–3), whereupon God commands Moses to have the offenders killed and brings on a plague that kills twenty-four thousand people.

Peter, Saint *3.484*   The disciple Jesus names as the rock (Greek *petra*) upon whom he will found his church (Matthew 16:18–19). Peter was the first bishop of Rome, and in Roman Catholic eyes the popes are his successors as heads of the Church. In postbiblical tradition, Peter is stationed at the gates of Heaven where, before the Last Judgment, he admits or refuses to admit each human soul. Those not admitted go to Hell or to Purgatory. Milton thinks that the text of the Bible warrants belief only in the Last Judgment.

Petsora *10.292*   The river Pechora in Siberia, which flows from the Urals to the Arctic Ocean.

Pharphar *1.469*   See DAMASCUS.

Phineus *3.36*   Thracian king and blind prophet.

Phlegethon *2.580*   See ACHERON.

Phlegra *1.577*   The plain on which the gods and giants fought (a *gigantomachia*, "war against the giants"), located by classical authors in various places; Milton may have favored the volcanic and sulfurous Campi Flegrei northwest of Naples, near ancient Cuma, having probably been taken there by Giovanni Manso.

Plato *3.472*   Greek philosopher. See CLEOMBROTUS.

Plebeian *10.442*   A Roman term for a person of the lowest class.

Pleiades *7.374*   A dense cluster of stars, known as the Seven Sisters and the Atlantic Sisters, that rises in the spring when it is time to plow the earth. They are thought to pour, by benign *influence* ("flowing-in"), fertility into the earth (Job 38:31). See CRAB and TAURUS.

Plutonian hall *10.444*   Hall of Pluto, Roman god of the underworld. See DIS.

Pomona *5.378*   Roman goddess of fruit.

Pontus *5.340*   The Black Sea.

Potentates *5.749*   See CHERUBIM.

Powers *2.11*   See CHERUBIM.

Proserpine *4.269*   Roman name of Persephone. See CERES.

Proteus *3.604*   A sea-god under Neptune, or Poseidon. He is the "shepherd" of all the creatures in the ocean, especially seals. Proteus can change his form into any shape. He also has the power of prophecy. See *Odyssey* 4.365–570. Alchemists took the god Proteus to be a symbol of the many forms of matter, yet they also thought that matter has one true, essential form, as the god Proteus does. Alchemists attempted to isolate this true essential form of matter in their alembics, or retorts, in the vain attempt to turn base matter into gold. See HERMES.

Punic coast *5.340*   The south coast of the Mediterranean sea at Carthage, in North Africa. The Romans called the Carthaginians the Poeni (Greek *Phoinix*) from their Phoenician origin, and referred to their own wars with the Carthaginians as the "Punic wars," *Punica bella*.

Pygméan race *1.780–81*   Not an African but a Southeast Asian people, rainforest hunter-gatherers.

Pyrrha *11.12*   See DEUCALION.

Pythian fields *2.530*   At Delphi, the site of the Pythian games, sacred to Apollo. See DELPHIAN CLIFF.

Pythian vale *10.530*   The mountain valley at Delphi, where Apollo slew Python. See DELPHIAN CLIFF and PYTHON.

Python *10.531*   A monstrous serpent born from the slime deposited by Deucalion's flood. Python was slain by Apollo.

Quiloa *11.399*   Kilwa-Kisiwani, an island port off the east coast of Africa.

Rabba *1.397*   Principal city of the Ammonites, worshippers of Moloch. It is situated east of the Jordan, to the north. In 2 Samuel 12:27, Rabbah is called "the city of waters." See Jeremiah 49.

Ramiel *6.372*   His name means "one who exalts himself against God." In the pseudepigraphical book 1 Enoch (6:7), Ramiel is among the angels who take a vow to fornicate with women. They do so and bring forth a race of cannibalistic giants. The episode is based on the tamer account given in Genesis 6:1–4. Ramiel's violence recalls Virgil's phrase "the violence of Turnus," *violentia Turni* (*Aeneid* 11.376).

Raphael *5.221*   "Health of God." In Tobit 3:17, the angel Raphael is a healer and an exorcist, driving out and binding the evil spirit Asmodeus. See ASMODEUS and TOBIAS.

Red Sea *1.306*   The sea whose waters, at Moses' command, divide so that the Israelites may pass. When the army of Pharaoh pursues, the sea closes over it. Exodus 14.

Rhea *1.513*   Wife of Cronos. Because her husband ate their children as soon as they were born, Rhea hid the infant Zeus in a cave on Mount Ida in Crete, deceiving Cronos by throwing into his gullet a stone wrapped in swaddling bands. See AMALTHEA.

Rhene *1.353*   The Rhine River, major waterway of western Europe, which, with the Danube, formed the northern boundary of the Roman Empire. It flows northwest into the North Sea. In the fifth century C.E., barbarian tribes crossed the Rhine, sweeping away all opposition in their path, sacking Rome, deposing the last emperor, and establishing their own kingdoms in the territories of the former empire. See DANAW.

Rhodopè *7.35*   A mountain range in northern Thrace, sacred to Dionysus, where Orpheus made music and was torn apart by the maenads (Ovid, *Metamorphoses* 10.77). See ORPHEAN LYRE.

Rimmon *1.467*   Syrian god, worshipped in Damascus. See DAMASCUS.

River-dragon *12.191*   The pharaoh. Ezekiel (29:3–4) speaks a tremendous prophecy against the pharaoh: "Behold, I am against thee, Pharaoh king of Egypt, the great dragon that lieth in the midst of his rivers, which hath said, My river is mine own, and I have made it for myself. But I will put hooks in thy jaws, and I will cause the fish of thy rivers to stick unto thy scales, and I will bring thee up out of the midst of thy rivers."

Rome, free *9.671*   The state of Rome under the Republic, before the emperors. Political oratory flourished under the Republic.

Sabean *4.162*   The Kingdom of Saba is at the southern end of the Arabian peninsula. Famous for myrrh, an aromatic resin.

Samarkand *11.389*   The capital city of Tamburlaine's vast Asian empire. A city of the same name is in Uzbekistan. In Marlowe's *The Second Part of Tamburlaine the Great*, Tamburlaine describes his city: "Then shall my native city Samarcanda, / And crystal waves of fresh Jaertis' stream, / The pride and beauty of her princely seat, / Be famous through the furthest continents; / For there my palace royal shall be plac'd, / Whose shining turrets shall dismay the heavens" (4.3.107–12). See TEMIR.

Samoed shore *10.696*   Samoedia, northeastern Siberia.

Samos *5.265*   An island in the Aegean, not one of the Cyclades but one of the Sporades; it is the birthplace of Hera. The two islands, Delos and Samos, are associated by Ovid in *Metamophoses* 8.221 and by Milton because they are both places of sacred birth. See DELOS.

Samson *9.1060*   Hebrew hero from the book of Judges whose divine strength depended on his hair not being cut. See DALILAH.

Sarra *11.243*   Tyre, a Phoenician seaport on an island just off the Mediterranean's eastern shore. It was famous for, and wealthy because of, its rich, purple dye, obtained from the murex sea snail. See MELIBOEAN PURPLE.

Satan *1.82*   The Hebrew *ha-satan* (used also in the Greek New Testament) means "the adversary."

Saturn *1.512*   Roman counterpart of the Greek Cronos, ruler of the gods until deposed by his son Jupiter (the Greek Zeus). See RHEA.

Scales *10.676*   The constellation Libra.

Scipio *9.510*   Scipio the Great, or Scipio Africanus, so named because of his victory over Hannibal in North Africa, which ended the Second Punic War. Considered the greatest Roman military hero, he was said to have been conceived in the same way as Alexander the Great, whose mother was impregnated by Ammonian Jove in the form of a serpent. The serpent with which Scipio's mother dallied was Capitoline Jove. See OLYMPIAS.

Scorpion *4.998*   The constellation Scorpio.

Scylla *2.660*   In Homer's *Odyssey*, 12.55–126, 222–59, a monster on a cliff on the strait between Italy and Sicily. Opposite her is the monster Charybdis. See CHARYBDIS. In Ovid's *Metamorphoses*, 13.730–34 and 14.40–67, Scylla is a maiden who is beloved of Glaucus and resented for that reason by the enchantress Circe, who transforms Scylla's lower body into heads of barking dogs.

Seleucia *4.212*   The city that marks the eastern limit of the large country of Eden. For Milton, the more recent name of Telassar, built by the Macedonians ("Grecian kings") in the wake of Alexander the Great's conquest of Palestine. Seleucia is situated on the Tigris River (the great river to the east of the Euphrates) below Baghdad. Under the name *Thelasar* or *Telassar*, Seleucia is twice mentioned in the Bible as the place where the "children of Eden" lived. See 2 Kings 19:12 and Isaiah 37:12. See AURAN and EDEN.

Senir *12.146*   The ridge of mountains of which Mount Hermon is a part. The northern limit of the Promised Land (Deuteronomy 3:8–9).

Sennaär *3.467*   Shinar, in Babylonia, the plain on which the Tower of Babel was built.

Seon *1.409*   Sihon, king of the Amorites who refused the Israelites passage through his land when they were traveling to the Promised Land. He was therefore destroyed and his land taken. Among the cities occupied was his capital, Heshbon, which was named after him (Numbers 21:23–28).

Seraphim *1.129*   The highest order of angels. Unlike the cherubim, who guard God, and therefore turn their attention away from Him, the seraphim are forever gazing upon and praising God. They are seen only once in the Bible, in Isaiah 6:1–3, where they have six wings, two covering the face, two covering the feet, and two used for flight. They chant, "Holy, holy, holy, is the Lord of hosts: the whole earth is full of his glory." In Milton's more active vision they are, at least once, in the war in Heaven, "fighting Seraphim." One of the most impressive characters in *Paradise Lost*, and one of the most militantly active of the angels, is Abdiel, "than whom none with more zeal adored / The Deity" (5.805–6). See ABDIEL and CHERUBIM.

Serapis *1.720* A combination of Osiris and Apis, the bull-god. The worship of Serapis was introduced into Greece by the first Ptolemy to establish a common worship for the Egyptians and the Greeks.

Serbonian bog *2.592* A vast region of quicksands in Egypt that devoured whole armies (Diodorus Siculus 1.30). See also Lucan, *Pharsalia* 8.540. Herodotus (Herodotus 3.5) says that Lake Serbonis is where Typhon is supposed to be buried. See TYPHON and SYRTIS.

Sericana *3.438* Serica. The longer form is used by Boiardo and Ariosto. Broad, arid plains to the south of the mountains of Imaus, in Scythia. Milton imagines the plains of Sericana north of the Himalayas. Maps in Milton's day depicted sailing wagons on Sericana.

Serraliona *10.703* Sierra Leone, a cape on the west coast of Africa.

Shechem *12.136* See MOREH.

Sibma *1.410* A Moabite town, noted for vines and fruits. The "vine of Sibmah" is mentioned in Isaiah's (16:8–9) prophecy of the destruction of Moab.

Sidon *1.441* A wealthy Phoenician seaport where the moon goddess Astarte (identified with Aphrodite) was worshipped. She may have been worshipped by "virgins," but virginity was not required of all her priestesses. Temple prostitution, where priestesses engaged with worshippers in sexual practices regarded as religious rites, was common in Palestine and is one reason why idolatry is so often described in the Bible as a kind of prostitution. Solomon himself is "Beguiled by fair idolatresses" (1.445).

Siloa *1.11* Siloam, a spring (Gihon) in the Kidron Valley immediately to the east of Jerusalem. The waters of Gihon pass through a passage cut in the rock to the Pool of Siloam, the overflow from which waters the king's garden (Nehemiah 3:15). Jesus cures a blind man with the waters of Siloam (John 9:1–11). Because Siloam is associated with David, the supposed author of the psalms, Milton sees it as the true form of the Heliconian springs that inspire Greek poetry. See PEGASEAN WING.

Silvanus 4.707   A Roman divinity of woods, not clearly distinct from Faunus and often identified with Pan. He is represented as an old man with the strength of youth, living in sacred groves removed, but not remote, from human habitation. See FAUNUS and PAN.

Sin 2.760   Satan's consort in Heaven, born from the left side of Satan's head and impregnated by him with their son Death. Sin falls with the rebel angels but is given a key and charged to keep the gates of Hell. There, her son Death is born and immediately rapes her. From this union the hellhounds are born and are ranged about her middle, barking ceaselessly. Periodically they reenter her womb and gnaw her insides. Below Sin's loins her body becomes that of a serpent with a "mortal sting" (2.653). The image of Sin as a beautiful woman above and a serpent below is traditional; but Milton may be drawing more particularly on Spenser's monster Error, who is a woman above and a serpent below, armed with a mortal sting. Error's brood of eyeless frogs, toads, and small serpents creep in and out of her mouth (not her womb) until the Redcross knight cuts her head off. They then drink her blood, swell up, and burst. See *The Faerie Queene* 1.1.14–26. The hellhounds barking about Sin's middle are derived, as Milton indicates (2.659–61), from Ovid's Scylla, whose lower body is composed of the heads of barking hounds. See SCYLLA. When Satan and Death confront each other at Hell's gates, Sin reconciles them, reveals that Death is Satan's son by her, and opens the gates of Hell, allowing Satan to pass through them into chaos. After Adam and Eve fall, Sin and Death build a bridge across chaos from Hell to the created universe, thus making it easy for devils to come into the world. When Satan meets Sin and Death at the head of their completed bridge, he tells them what to do with mankind: "Him first make sure your thrall and lastly kill" (10.402). The killing is Death's business; the enthralling is Sin's. See DEATH.

Sinaean kings 11.390   Chinese kings. See PAQUIN.

Sinai 1.7   The holy mountain in the desert of the Sinai. The Israelites encamp there at the beginning of their journey to the Promised Land. Sinai is the same mountain as *Oreb* ("Horeb," Deuteronomy 1:6), but they are different peaks, Sinai being the higher of the two. It was on the top of Sinai that Moses received from God the Hebrew Law inscribed on tablets of stone (Exodus 19–20). In addition to being a symbol of the Hebrew Law, Mount Sinai is for Milton a site of divine inspiration. Its "top" is "secret" in the Latin sense of being removed from common sight, for Moses ascended the mountain alone (12.227–30). Its summit is hidden in dark clouds and smoke. See OREB.

Sion *1.10*   Zion. The low mountain on which Jerusalem is situated. The site of the Temple and, more important for Milton, the place where King David was inspired to compose sacred songs, the Psalms.

Sirocco *10.706*   The Italian name (Scirocco) for the southeast wind. It is warm, moist, and dusty, and is thought to bring disease.

Sittim *1.413*   Shittim, the place where the Israelites were encamped on the east side of the Jordan River, across from Jericho. There, the Israelites committed "whoredom with the daughters of Moab." The sexual crime was compounded by idolatry (Numbers 25:1–3, 33:49; Joshua 2:1, 3:1; Micah 6:5). See PEOR.

Sodom *1.503*   One of the two wicked cities on the plain at the southeast end of the Dead Sea, the other being Gomorrah. While living in Sodom, Abraham's nephew Lot hospitably receives in his house two visiting angels. The men of Sodom surround the house and call to Lot to deliver the visitors over to them to be sexually abused (Genesis 19:5). Lot offers to send out his two daughters instead and is refused. The angels then strike the men in the street blind "so that they wearied themselves to find the door" (19:11). After Lot escapes the city with his daughters, God rains fire and brimstone on Sodom and Gomorrah so that nothing is left living there (Genesis 19:12–28). Against instructions, Lot's wife looks back at the burning city and is changed to a pillar of salt (19:26).

Sofala *11.400*   See OPHIR.

Solomon *1.401*   Son of King David by Bathsheba, and king of Israel after David's death. Unlike his father, Solomon was permitted to build the temple at Jerusalem, where the ark of the covenant would be housed. Solomon was legendary for his wealth and wisdom. He was also known for his 700 wives and 300 concubines, the former of whom led him into idolatry (1 Kings 11:1–10), hence Milton's phrase for him, "that uxorious king" (*PL* 1.444–46).

Son *3.79*   Milton's Son is not inseparable from God the Father (and the Holy Ghost), as in the orthodox Christian view of the Trinity: "On [God's] right / The radiant image of His glory sat, / His only Son" (3.62–64). The Son is begotten by God, as a true son, but he is also the first being created by God: "of all Creation first, / Begotten Son, divine similitude" (3.383–84). He is the agent of all the Father's actions, but he is also the wisdom, or forethought, behind those actions. The Father calls him "My Word, my wisdom, and effectual might" (3.170). In these capacities the Son defeats the rebel angels, creates the world (and Adam and Eve), goes to Earth as the man Jesus, teaches humans, and dies to redeem them. At the end of time it is the Son who executes judgment.

Some of Milton's terms suggest that the Son is subordinate to the Father, as when the Father calls the Son "Effulgence of my glory" (6.680), an echo of Hebrews 1:3: "the brightness of [God's] glory, and the express image of his person." But the Son is also the "Filial Godhead" (7.175), participating in the being of Father as God. The supposed heresy of Milton's subordinationist view of the Son is not so important for the poem as it has been made to seem. The Son is certainly God's equal and is himself God, notably in the Creation narrative of Book 7. While Milton cannot see how the Son can be anything other than a creation of the Father, the Father confers on the Son the dignity of a son, as in Roman adoption. This dignity, because it has been earned by the Son's merit ("By merit more than birthright Son of God," 3.309), is a higher dignity than being simply "begotten." As the Father explains at 3.305–12, the Son rises to the dignity of oneness with the Father's glory because of his willingness to sacrifice himself "to save / A world from utter loss" (3.307–8). Finally, as the Father himself declares, the Son's love of humanity outshines the Father's glory: "Love hath abounded more than glory abounds" (3.312). See GOD, MESSIAH, SPIRIT, and WORD.

Spartan twins *10.674* The constellation of the Twins, Gemini, through which the sun is here imagined to pass as it moves north toward the Tropic of Cancer. See CRAB.

Spirit *1.17* In traditional Christianity, the Spirit, or Holy Ghost, is the third person of the Trinity and one of the three equal parts of God. In Milton, the Spirit represents God's creative power and is subordinate to the Father and to the Son. When the Father sends the Son into chaos to create the world, he says, "My overshadowing Spirit and might with Thee / I send along" (7.165–66). Milton identifies this Spirit with his own creative power, too. The power that assists in creating the world is also the power that assists Milton in writing his poem. See 1.17–22. See GOD, SON, and WORD.

Stygian flood *1.239* Waters of the infernal river *Styx*: "horror." See ACHERON.

Styx *2.577* See ACHERON.

Sus *11.403* A North African Muslim kingdom, in southwest Morocco, stretching from the coast inland through the desert. See FEZ.

Susa *10.308* See MEMNONIAN PALACE.

Synod 2.391 A council of potentates, officials, or clergymen, and the like, gathered to consider some important question. *Synod* can also refer to a conjunction of stars. The word *consider* (*con*, "with," + *sider*, "star": to study the position of the stars before taking some action) also carries an astrological metaphor.

Syrian king 11.218 See DOTHAN.

Syrtis 2.939 A region of huge sandbanks and quicksands off the North African shore in which ships are lost. The region appeared to be neither water nor land, being impossible either to sail in or to walk on. The Roman poet Lucan mentions the quicksands as an image of matter in its chaotic state before nature gave it form (*Pharsalia* 9.303–4). See SERBONIAN BOG.

Tantalus 2.614 The son of Zeus and the nymph Plouto, daughter of Cronos. Among other crimes, Tantalus offered the gods a stew containing the dismembered body of his son Pelops, after whom the Peloponnesian peninsula, in Greece, is named. The gods discerned the ruse and restored Pelops to life. Tantalus was condemned in the underworld to a punishment from which we take the word *tantalize*: while he suffered intense thirst and hunger, water and food remained eternally just out of his reach (Homer, *Odyssey* 11.582–92).

Tarsus 1.200 An important biblical city on the south coast of modern Turkey, ancient Cilicia, the birthplace of Saint Paul. Milton mentions Tarsus in connection with the hundred-headed monster Typhon, who, according to Pindar (*Pythian Odes* 1.15–17), formerly resided in his "worshipped-under-many-names cave" in Cilicia. See TYPHON.

Tartar(s) 3.432 Nomadic Mongols of Central Asia.

Tartarus 6.54 The deepest region of the world, beneath Hades, it is as far beneath Hades as Earth is beneath Heaven. The gods stowed their divine enemies in Tartarus, not in Hades, which is for human souls. See Pindar, *Pythian Odes* 1.15.

Tauris 10.436 Tebriz, in northwestern Persia (modern Iran).

Taurus 1.769 The constellation of the Bull, containing the Pleiades, through which the sun passes as it returns north from the Tropic of Capricorn in the spring. See CRAB and PLEIADES.

Telassar 4.214 See SELEUCIA.

Temir 11.389 Tamburlaine. See SAMARKAND.

Teneriffe 4.987 A high peak in the Canary Islands, visible from a great distance at sea.

Ternate 2.639 With Tidore, one of the "spice islands" in the Moluccas.

Thammuz 1.446 Syrian dying god associated with Adonis and idolatrously worshipped by women before the temple (Ezekiel 8:14).

Thamyris *3.35*   A Thracian poet blinded by the Muses (Homer, *Iliad* 2.594–600).

Thebes *1.578*   After Ilium (Troy), the most famous besieged city of antiquity, where great heroes fought. It was the subject of a tragedy by Aeschylus and an epic by the late Roman poet Statius. In Boeotia, Greece, not Egypt. See THEBES, EGYPTIAN.

Thebes, Egyptian *5.274*   Ancient political and religious center of Egypt in the Middle and Late Kingdoms (modern Luxor). Situated far up the Nile River, some eight hundred miles from the Mediterranean and more than three hundred miles from ancient Heliopolis, which was near modern Cairo.

Themis *11.14*   The goddess of law, in the lineage of the Titans, daughter of Ouranos (Sky) and Ge (Earth). See DEUCALION.

Thracian *7.34*   Of Thrace, mountainous semi-wild region of northern Greece, associated with the worship of Dionysus and with the poet Orpheus. See ORPHEUS.

Thrascias *10.700*   A north-northwest wind from Thrace.

Thyestean banquet *10.688*   Atreus killed the sons of his brother Thyestes and served them to him in a stew, a crime that began the curse on the house of Atreus (Aeschylus, *Agamemnon* 1591–1602). Seneca (*Thyestes* 776–77, 784–884) says the sun went dark at the crime.

Tidore *2.639*   See TERNATE.

Tigris *9.71*   See EUPHRATES.

Tiresias *3.36*   Prophet of Thebes whose prophetic powers were divine compensation for the loss of his sight.

Titan *1.510*   The oldest son of the sky, Ouranos, and brother of Zeus, who fought with the other Titans against the Olympians.

Tobias *5.222*   In the apocryphal book of Tobit, Tobias, the son of Tobit, is sent on a long journey by his father. Tobias is accompanied on this journey by a benevolent friend, later revealed to be the angel Raphael. With Raphael's help, Tobias rescues his kinswoman Sarah from the power of the demon Asmodeus and marries her (Tobit 5–9). See ASMODEUS and RAPHAEL.

Tobit's son *4.170*   Tobias.

Tophet *1.404*   In the valley of Hinnom, southwest of Jerusalem, where children were sacrificed to Moloch. The practice was stopped by the religious reformer King Josiah: "And he defiled Topheth, which is in the valley of the children of Hinnom, that no man might make his son or his daughter to pass through the fire to Molech" (2 Kings 23:10). See GEHENNA, JOSIAH, and MOLOCH.

Trebizond *1.584*   A rich Byzantine city on the Black Sea.

Tree of Knowledge [of Good and Evil] *4.221*   The tree on which the forbidden fruit grows. After he creates Adam, God says, "But of the tree of the knowledge of good and evil, thou shalt not eat of it: for in the day that thou eatest thereof thou shalt surely die" (Genesis 2:17). Eve repeats this to the serpent when he tempts her (Genesis 3:2–3), to which the serpent replies that God has forbidden the fruit to prevent Adam and Eve from becoming gods themselves: "For God doth know that in the day ye eat thereof, then your eyes shall be opened, and ye shall be as gods, knowing good and evil" (Genesis 3:5). Eve then sees that the fruit of the tree is attractive to eat, that it is beautiful to look at, and that it is desirable for the wisdom it affords. Milton carefully follows these three phases of attraction. His Eve calls the fruit "this fruit divine, / Fair to the eye, inviting to the taste, / Of virtue to make wise" (9.776–78). In the Bible, the knowledge the fruit gives is closely tied to sexual shame: "And the eyes of them both were opened, and they knew that they were naked; and they sewed fig leaves together, and made themselves aprons" (Genesis 3:7). Although Milton's account of the knowledge of good and evil includes sexual shame and its related but opposite feeling, lust, he understands knowledge of good and evil in the larger, ethical sense of those words. His interpretation, which he had developed in *Areopagitica*, is that to know a thing is to take it into oneself, to taste it (Latin *sapio* means "to taste, to know," whence our *sapience*). For Adam and Eve to know good and evil (good being already in them) is to lose the absolute goodness that they had before: "We know / Both good and evil: good lost, and evil got" (9.1071–72).

Tree of Life 3.354   One of the more mysterious elements of the Genesis story, the Tree of Life seems to come from older folk-loric legends of a magical tree, the fruit of which has the power to confer eternal life. The Tree of Life is mentioned alongside the Tree of the Knowledge of Good and Evil: "And out of the ground made the Lord God to grow every tree that is pleasant to the sight, and good for food; the tree of life also in the midst of the garden, and the tree of knowledge of good and evil" (Genesis 2:9). The two trees are mentioned again when Adam and Eve are expelled from the garden: "And the Lord God said, Behold, the man is become as one of us, to know good and evil: and now, lest he put forth his hand, and take also of the tree of life, and eat, and live for ever: Therefore the Lord God sent him forth from the garden of Eden, to till the ground from whence he was taken" (Genesis 3:22–23). To protect the Tree of Life, God places at the east gate of the garden a guard of cherubim and also a magic flaming sword (Genesis 3:24). The Tree of Life reappears in the final chapter of the Bible, Revelation 22:2, where it grows on both sides of the river of water of life, bearing twelve kinds of fruit through the entire year, and healing the nations—the gentiles—with its leaves. This image blends the tree in the garden of Eden with those trees seen by Ezekiel in his vision of the holy waters flowing from the sanctuary: "And by the river upon the bank thereof, on this side and on that side, shall grow all trees for meat, whose leaf shall not fade, neither shall the fruit thereof be consumed: . . . and the fruit thereof shall be for meat, and the leaf thereof for medicine" (Ezekiel 47:12). See FOUNT OF LIFE.

Tremisen *11.404* A North African city in Nubia, noted, like Fez, for the honor it confers on poets. For sites in North Africa, Milton draws on Ariosto, *Orlando Furioso* 33.98–107; "Tremisenne" appears in stanza 101. See FEZ.

Trinacrian shore *2.661* Sicilian shore, opposite Calabria on the straits separating Sicily from the Italian mainland. *Trinacria* means "three promontories" (Gr. *akros* "high point," "extremity"), which mark the island of Sicily's triangular shape. Ovid, *Metamorphoses* 5.346–53, refers to Sicily (when it is thrown on top of Typhon) as the "vast Trinacrian isle." See CALABRIA and PELORUS.

Triton *4.276* See NYSEIAN ISLE.

Troy *9.16* The great city in Asia Minor besieged by a confederacy of Greek (Achaean) kingdoms in Homer's *Iliad*. Also called "Ilium." The fate of the city is sealed when the Greek hero Achilles pursues and kills Troy's chief defender, Hector.

Turnus *9.17* In the second half of Virgil's *Aeneid*, Turnus, incensed by the loss of his promised bride, Lavinia, leads a confederacy of native Italian (Ausonian) kingdoms against the Trojans, led by Aeneas.

Tuscan artist *1.288* Galileo, who was from Tuscany and was confined by the Inquisition in a villa in Arcetri, above Florence. He is called *artist* in the sense of "artificer" for his invention of scientific instruments and mechanical devices. See FESOLÈ and GALILEO.

Typhoean rage *2.539* See TYPHON.

Typhon *1.199* Born of the union of Earth with Tartarus after the defeat of the Titans, Typhon is the most dangerous opponent of the Olympian gods and the only one who is a continuing threat. He has one hundred bellowing, fire-breathing dragon heads, and his vast body terminates in vipers, which is how Milton describes him in "On the Morning of Christ's Nativity": "Typhon huge, ending in snaky twine" (line 226). A symbol of arrogant pride and open violence, Typhon alone puts the Olympians to flight—all except Zeus and Athene, who for Milton are the types of the Father and the Son. The other gods flee to Egypt, where they disguise themselves as animals and are worshipped in that form, an event alluded to by Milton when he calls the Egyptian gods "wand'ring gods disguised in brutish forms" (1.481). Zeus at last pins Typhon under the volcano Etna, in Sicily, or under the entire island of Sicily and the volcanic region of southern Italy. In the passage on Typhon in Aeschylus's *Prometheus Bound* (351–72), many elements of Milton's Hell and Milton's Satan appear, e.g., the "gorgonian gleam" of Typhon's eyes (see GORGONIAN TERROR); the continuing effect of Zeus's lightning not only on Typhon's body but also on his mind (see *Paradise Lost* 1.94 and 1.126); the prostration of Typhon's huge body, not on a lake of fire but beneath the "roots" of Mount Etna; Typhon's boast, spoken in high language, that he will overthrow "the tyranny of Zeus" (*Prometheus Bound* 357; cf. *Paradise Lost* 1.124); and Prometheus's prophecy that Typhon's continuing inner torment will one day cause him to vomit fire that will destroy the fruitful fields of Sicily. Numerous references in ancient poetry to the fruitfulness of Sicily made it for Milton a type of Eden. Hesiod, *Theogony* 820–68; Pindar, *Pythian Odes* 1.15–29 and 8.16–18; *Olympian Odes* 4.6–7; and Ovid, *Metamorphoses* 5.346–53. See PELORUS.

Ulysses 2.1019 Latin name for the hero of the *Odyssey*, Odysseus, who suffers much and passes through many dangers returning from Troy to his kingdom on the island of Ithaca. See CHARYBDIS and SCYLLA.

Ur 12.130 An ancient city of Chaldea on the west bank of the lower Euphrates River, near the Persian Gulf. The original home of Terah, father of Abraham, and a place where idolatry and polytheism were practiced. The Chaldeans were also famous for astronomy. Terah and his family left Ur and traveled up the Euphrates valley to Haran, to the northeast of Palestine. From Haran, Abraham was called by God to enter the Promised Land. See ABRAHAM and CANAAN.

Urania 7.1 See MUSE.

Uriel 3.648 Angel whose name means "light (or fire) of God" (2 Esdras 4:1).

Urim 6.761 Together with the Thummim, mysterious, symbolic, and magical objects (Milton imagines them as jewels) on the breastplate of the high priest: "and thou shalt put in the breastplate of judgment the Urim and the Thummim; and they shall be upon Aaron's heart, when he goeth in before the Lord" (Exodus 28:30). They were used for divination and casting lots, and had some role to play when people wished to seek counsel of God (Numbers 27:21). See AARON.

Uther's son 1.580 Arthur, later King Arthur, who defended Britain against Saxon invasions and is a patriotic symbol for the

English. At an early stage, Milton considered writing an epic poem on Arthur.

Uzziel 4.782 Angel whose name means "strength of God." He is Gabriel's lieutenant in the troop guarding the garden.

Valdarno 1.290 Valley of the Arno River, which flows through Florence. The Arno descends from the Apennine Mountains in a deep valley surrounded by high hills. The entire region, with its spectacular heights, is called *Val d'Arno.*

Vallombrosa 1.303 "Shadowy valley." A remote monastery on a mountain in Tuscany overlooking the valley of the Arno. Milton means the whole valley.

Vertumnus 9.395 Roman god of gardens who pursues Pomona, goddess of fruit.

Virgin 10.676 The constellation Virgo, through which (in the earth-centered, Ptolemaic system) the sun passes on its way south from the Tropic of Cancer, which is north of the equator, to the Tropic of Capricorn, which is south of the equator. See CRAB.

Virtue, angelic 5.371 An expression in Greek and Latin epic poetry, where a character is referred to as a "strength" or "force," as when Homer speaks of "the strength of Priam," the "force of Hector," and "the force of Alcinous" (*Iliad* 3.105, 14.418; *Odyssey* 7.167), or when Virgil speaks of the "smelling-strength of dogs," *odora canum vis* (*Aeneid* 4.132).

Well of Life 11.416 See FOUNT OF LIFE and TREE OF LIFE.

Word 3.170 When *Word* is capitalized it refers to the Son of God (Greek *logos,* "word" and "reason principle"). When he is incarnate in the world, the Son of God is Jesus. When the Father addresses the Son as "My Word," he goes on to define what this title means: "my wisdom, and effectual might" (3.170). The Christian belief that the Son is both the Word of God and the power that created the world by spoken command (Genesis 1:3) is based on the opening verses of the Gospel according to John (1:1–5): "In the beginning was the Word (*logos*), and the Word was with God, and the Word was God. The same was in the beginning with God. All things were made by him; and without him was not any thing made that was made. In him was life; and the life was the light of men. And the light shineth in the darkness; and the darkness comprehended it not." In Book 7 Milton shows the actual creation of the world as acts of the Son. At two moments, however—when mankind is created and when the Son returns to heaven—Milton asserts that the Father is really present with the Son when the Son creates (7.516–19 and 7.588–90). By doing so, Milton makes his own account of creation consistent with that of Genesis. See MESSIAH, SPIRIT, and SON.

World 2.347   The entire created universe, formed by the Son from chaos, provided with an outer, protective shell, on the outside of which Satan lands (3.418–22), and containing the sun, the stars, the planets, and the earth. This world is attached to Heaven by a golden chain (2.1005 and 2.1051). Although the world contains the entire universe observable from earth, when it is first spotted by Satan from chaos it appears extremely small: "in bigness as a star / Of smallest magnitude" (2.1052–53). The world appears in its true, vast proportions, however, when the Son uses his huge golden compasses to draw its circumference: "One foot He centered and the other turned / Round through the vast profundity obscure" (7.228–29).

Xerxes 10.307   The Persian king who invaded Greece in 480 B.C.E. See HELLESPONT.

Zephon 4.788   Angel whose name means "searcher of secrets."

Zephyr 4.329   See FLORA.

Zodiac 11.247   A band of stars marking the apparent paths of the sun, moon, and planets about the earth, assuming the earth to be the center of the astronomical system. This band is divided into twelve constellations resembling (when lines are drawn between the stars) certain mythological animals and persons. For the movement of the sun through the zodiacal signs to either side of the equator, see CRAB.

Zophiel 6.535   Angel whose name means "spy of God." During the war in Heaven, Zophiel, "of cherubim the swiftest wing," discerns the approach of the rebel angels and in brilliant language urges the loyal angels to prepare to fight.

Suggestions for Further Reading

• indicates a work excerpted in this Norton Critical Edition.

Achinstein, Sharon. *Milton and the Revolutionary Reader*. Princeton, N.J., 1994.

• ———. "Milton's Political Ontology of the Human." *English Literary History* 84 (2017): 591–616.

Adams, Robert Martin. *Ikon: John Milton and the Modern Critics*. Ithaca, N.Y., 1955.

Allen, Don Cameron. *The Harmonious Vision: Studies in Milton's Poetry*. Baltimore, 1954.

• Balfour, Ian. Figures in Excess and the Matter of Inversion in the Discourse of the Subline. *ELH* 84.2 (2017): 315–23.

Barker, Arthur E. *Milton and the Puritan Dilemma, 1641–1660*. Toronto, 1942.

Beer, Anna. *Milton: Poet, Pamphleteer, and Patriot*. London: 2009.

Belsey, Catherine. *John Milton: Language, Gender, Power*. Oxford, 1988.

Bennett, Joan S. *Reviving Liberty: Radical Christian Humanism in Milton's Great Poems*. Cambridge, Mass., 1989.

Broadbent, John B. *Some Graver Subject: An Essay on* Paradise Lost. London, 1960.

Burnett, Archie. "'Sense Variously Drawn Out': The Line in *Paradise Lost*." *Literary Imagination* 5.1 (2003): 69–92.

Burrow, Colin. *Epic Romance: Homer to Milton*. Oxford, 1993.

Bush, Douglas. *John Milton: A Sketch of His Life and Writings*. London, 1964.

Campbell, Gordon. *A Milton Chronology*. London, 1977.

Campbell, Gordon, and Thomas N. Corns. *John Milton: Life, Work, and Thought*. Oxford, 2008.

Campbell, Lily B. "The Christian Muse," *Huntington Library Bulletin* 8 (1935): 29–70.

Cavanagh, Michael. *Paradise Lost: A Primer*. Ed. Scott Newstock. Washington, D. C.: Catholic University of America Press, 2020.

• Coiro, Ann Baynes. "Sufficient and Free: The Poetry of *Paradise Lost*." In *Milton Now: Alternative Approaches and Contexts*, ed. Catharine Gray and Erin Murphy. New York, 2014.

Coiro, Ann Baynes, and Blair Hoxby, eds. *Milton in the Long Restoration*. Oxford, 2016

• Cook, Eleanor. *Against Coercion: Games Poets Play*. Stanford, Calif., 1998.

Corns, Thomas N. *The Milton Encyclopedia*. New Haven, Conn. 2012.

———. *Milton's Language*. Oxford, 1990.

• Cummings, Brian. *The Literary Culture of the Reformation: Grammar and Grace*. Oxford, 2002.

Daiches, David. *Milton*. London, 1957.

Danielson, Dennis. *The Cambridge Companion to Milton*. 2nd ed. Cambridge, 1999.

———. *Milton's Good God: A Study in Literary Theodicy*. Cambridge, 1982.

Demaray, John G. *Cosmos and Epic Representation: Dante, Spenser, Milton, and the Transformation of Renaissance Heroic Poetry*. Pittsburgh, 1991.

Diekhoff, John S. *Milton on Himself*. London, 1965.

Duran, Angelica. *The Age of Milton and the Scientific Revolution*. Pittsburgh, 2007.

• ———. "Comment from the Field: John Milton and Disability Studies in Literature Courses." *Journal of Literary & Cultural Disability Studies* 6 (2012): 327–40.

———. *Milton Among the Spaniards*. Charlottesville, VA, 2020.

DuRocher, Richard J. *Milton and Ovid*. Ithaca, N.Y., 1985.

• Empson, William. *Milton's God*. London, 1961.

• Equiano, Olaudah. *The Interesting Narrative of the Life of Olaudah Equiano, or Gustavus Vassa, The African, Written by Himself*. 1789. Ed. Werner Sollors. New York, 2001.

Evans, J. Martin. *Milton's Imperial Epic:* Paradise Lost *and the Discourse of Colonialism*. Ithaca, N.Y., 1996.

Fallon, Robert Thomas. *Divided Empire: Milton's Political Imagery*. University Park, Pa., 1996.

Fallon, Stephen M. *Milton among the Philosophers: Poetry and Materialism in Seventeenth-Century England*. Ithaca, N.Y., 1991.

Ferry, Anne D. *Milton's Epic Voice: The Narrator in* Paradise Lost. Cambridge, Mass., 1963.

Fish, Stanley E. *Versions of Antihumanism: Milton and Others*. Cambridge, 2012.

———. *How Milton Works*. Cambridge, Mass., 2001.

———. *Surprised by Sin: The Reader in* Paradise Lost. 2nd ed. Cambridge, Mass., 1997.

• ———. "With Mortal Voice: Milton Defends against the Muse." *English Literary History* 62.3 (1995): 522–25.

Flesch, William. *Generosity and the Limits of Authority: Shakespeare, Herbert, Milton.* Ithaca, N.Y., 1992.

Fresch, Cheryl H., and P. J. Klemp. *A Variorum Commentary on the Poems of John Milton.* Vol. 5, part 4, Paradise Lost, *Book 4.* Pittsburgh, 2011.

• Frye, Northrop. *The Return of Eden: Five Essays on Milton's Epics.* Toronto, 1965.

• Garber, Marjorie B. "Fallen Landscape: The Art of Milton and Poussin." *English Literary Renaissance* 5.1 (1975): 96–124.

Gardner, Helen. *A Reading of* Paradise Lost. Oxford, 1965.

• Gigante, Denise. "Mortal Taste: Milton." In *Taste: A Literary History.* New Haven, Conn., 2005.

Gilbert, Allan H. *A Geographical Dictionary of Milton.* New Haven, Conn., 1914.

• Goldberg, Jonathan. *The Seeds of Things: Theorizing Sexuality and Materiality in Renaissance Representations.* New York, 2009.

———"What Dost Thou in This World?" In *Milton Now: Alternative Approaches and Contexts,* ed. Catharine Gray and Erin Murphy. New York, 2014.

Gray, Catherine, and Erin Murphy, eds. *Milton Now: Alternative Approaches and Contexts.* London, 2014.

• Greenblatt, Stephen. *The Rise and Fall of Adam and Eve.* New York, 2017.

Gregerson, Linda. *The Reformation of the Subject: Spenser, Milton, and the English Protestant Epic.* Cambridge, 1995.

Grose, Christopher. *Milton and the Sense of Tradition.* New Haven, Conn., 1988.

Gross, Kenneth. "Satan and the Romantic Satan: A Notebook." In *Re-Membering Milton: Essays on the Texts and Traditions,* ed. Mary Nyquist and Margaret W. Ferguson. New York, 1987.

Grossman, Marshall. *The Story of All Things: Writing the Self in English Renaissance Narrative Poetry.* Durham, N.C., 1998.

Guillory, John. *Poetic Authority: Spenser, Milton, and Literary History.* New York, 1983.

Hanford, James Holly. *John Milton: Englishman.* New York, 1949.

Haskin, Dayton. *Milton's Burden of Interpretation.* Philadelphia, 1994.

• Herbst, Seth. "Milton and Music." *Essays in Criticism* 66 (2016): 96–116.

Hill, Christopher. *The Experience of Defeat: Milton and Some Contemporaries.* London, 1977.

———. *Milton and the English Revolution.* London, 1984.

Hollander, John. *The Figure of Echo: A Mode of Allusion in Milton and After.* Berkeley, 1981.

• Issa, Islam. *Milton in the Arab-Muslim World*. Abingdon, Oxon., 2017.

• Jameson, Fredric. "Religion and Ideology: A Political Reading of *Paradise Lost*." In *Literature, Politics and Theory: Papers from the Essex Conference 1976–84*, ed. Francis Barker et al. London, 1986.

Jones, Edward. *Milton: The Emerging Author, 1620–1642*. Oxford: 2012.

Kahn, Victoria. "Allegory and the Sublime in *Paradise Lost*." In *John Milton*, ed. Annabel Patterson. London, 1992.

Kendrick, Christopher. *Milton: A Study in Ideology and Form*. London, 1986.

Kermode, Frank. "Milton in Old Age." In *An Appetite for Poetry*. Cambridge, Mass., 1989.

Kerrigan, William. *The Sacred Complex: On the Psychogenesis of Paradise Lost*. Cambridge, Mass., 1983.

• Kilgour, Maggie. *Milton and the Metamorphosis of Ovid*. Oxford, 2012.

Knoppers, Laura Lunger. *Historicizing Milton: Spectacle, Power, and Poetry in Restoration England*. Athens, Ga., 1994.

Kolbrener, William. *Milton's Warring Angels: A Study of Critical Engagements*. Cambridge, 1997.

Leonard, John. *Faithful Labourers: A Reception History of* Paradise Lost, *1667–1970*. 2 vols. Oxford, 2013.

———. *Naming in Paradise: Milton and the Language of Adam and Eve*. Oxford, 1990.

• Lewalski, Barbara Kiefer. *The Life of John Milton: A Critical Biography*. Cambridge, Mass., 2000.

———. *Paradise Lost and the Rhetoric of Literary Forms*. Princeton, N.J., 1985.

• Lewis, C. S. *A Preface to* Paradise Lost. London, 1942.

• Lieb, Michael. *Theological Milton: Deity, Discourse and Heresy in the Miltonic Canon*. Pittsburgh, 2006.

———. *Milton and the Culture of Violence*. Ithaca, N.Y., 1994.

Loewenstein, David. *Milton and the Drama of History*. Cambridge, 1990.

MacCaffrey, Isabel. Paradise Lost *as Myth*. Cambridge, Mass., 1959.

MacCallum, Hugh. *Milton and the Sons of God: The Divine Image in Milton's Epic Poetry*. Toronto, 1986.

Machacek, Gregory. *Milton and Homer: "Written to Aftertimes."* Pittsburgh, 2011.

Martin, Catherine Gimelli. *Milton's Italy: Anglo-Italian Literature, Travel, and Religion in Seventeenth-Century England*. New York, 2017.

———. *The Ruins of Allegory:* Paradise Lost *and the Metamorphosis of Epic Convention*. Durham, N.C., 1998.

Martz, Louis L. *Poet of Exile: A Study of Milton's Poetry.* New Haven, Conn., 1980.

McColley, Diane Kelsey. *Milton's Eve.* Urbana, Ill., 1983.

McDowell, Nicholas, and Nigel Smith, eds. *The Oxford Handbook of Milton.* Oxford, 2009.

Milton, John. *The Complete Poetry and Essential Prose.* Ed. William Kerrigan, John Rumrich, and Stephen M. Fallon, New York: 2007.

———. *Paradise Lost.* Ed. David Scott Kastan. Indianapolis, 2005.

———. *Paradise Lost.* Ed. Barbara K. Lewalski. Malden, Mass., 2007.

———. *Paradise Lost: The Biblically Annotated Edition.* Ed. Matthew Stallard. Macon, Ga., 2011

———. *Prose: Major Writings on Liberty, Politics, Religion, and Education.* Ed. David Loewenstein. Malden, Mass., 2013.

Miner, Earl, William Moeck, and Stephen Jablonsky, eds. *Paradise Lost, 1668–1968: Three Centuries of Commentary.* Lewisburg, Pa., 2004.

Mohamed, Feisal G. *Milton and the Post-Secular Present: Ethics, Politics, Terrorism.* Stanford, Calif., 2011.

• ———. "Milton's Enmity towards Islam and the *Intellectus Agens.*" *English Studies* 96 (2015): 65–81.

Mohamed, Feisal G., and Patrick Fadely, eds. *Milton's Modernities: Poetry, Philosophy, and History from the Seventeenth Century to the Present.* Evanston, Ill., 2017.

———. *Sovereignty: Seventeenth-Century England and the Making of the Modern Political Imaginary.* Oxford: 2020.

Moyles, R. G. *The Text of* Paradise Lost: *A Study in Editorial Procedure.* Toronto, 1985.

Mulryan, John. *"Through a Glass Darkly": Milton's Reinvention of the Mythological Tradition.* Pittsburgh, 1996.

Murrin, Michael. *History and Warfare in Renaissance Epic.* Chicago, 1994.

Newlyn, Lucy. Paradise Lost *and the Romantic Reader.* Oxford, 1992.

Norbook, David. *Writing the English Republic: Poetry, Rhetoric, and Politics, 1627–1660.* Cambridge, 1999.

• Nyquist, Mary. *Arbitrary Rule: Slavery, Tyranny, and the Power of Life and Death.* Chicago, 2013.

———. "The Genesis of Gendered Subjectivity in the Divorce Tracts and in *Paradise Lost.*" In *Re-Membering Milton: Essays on the Texts and Traditions,* ed. Mary Nyquist and Margaret W. Ferguson. New York, 1987.

Nyquist, Mary, and Margaret W. Ferguson, eds. *Re-Membering Milton: Essays on the Texts and Traditions.* New York, 1987.

Patrides, C. A. *Milton and the Christian Tradition.* Oxford, 1986.

Pattison, Mark. *Milton.* Cambridge, 1879.

• Picciotto, Joanna. *Labors of Innocence in Early Modern England.* Cambridge, Mass., 2010.

Poole, William. *Milton and the Making of* Paradise Lost. Cambridge, Mass., 2017.

Quilligan, Maureen. *Milton's Spenser: The Politics of Reading.* Ithaca, N.Y., 1983.

• Quint, David. *Inside* Paradise Lost: *Reading the Designs of Milton's Epic.* Princeton, N.J., 2014.

• Radzinowicz, Mary Ann. *Milton's Epics and the Book of Psalms.* Princeton, N.J., 1989.

———. *Towards* Samson Agonistes: *The Growth of Milton's Mind.* Princeton, N.J., 1972.

• Rajan, Balachandra. *Milton and the Climates of Reading: Essays.* Toronto, 2006.

———. *The Lofty Rhyme: A Study of Milton's Major Poetry.* Miami, 1970.

———. Paradise Lost *and the Seventeenth-Century Reader.* 2nd ed. London, 1962.

Raleigh, Walter Alexander. *Milton.* Cambridge, 1900.

• Ramachandran, Ayesha. *The Worldmakers: Global Imagining in Early Modern Europe.* Chicago, 2015.

Rappaport, Herman. *Milton and the Postmodern.* Lincoln, Neb., 1983.

Redman, Harry, Jr. *Major French Milton Critics of the Nineteenth Century.* Pittsburgh, 1994.

Ricks, Christopher. *Milton's Grand Style.* Oxford, 1963.

Rogers, John. "Transported Touch: The Fruit of Marriage in *Paradise Lost.*" In *Milton and Gender,* ed. Catherine Gimelli Martin. Cambridge, 2004.

———. *The Matter of Revolution: Science, Poetry, and Politics in the Age of Milton.* Ithaca, N.Y., 1996.

Rosenblatt, Jason P. *Torah and Law in* Paradise Lost. Princeton, N.J., 1994.

Rumrich, John. *Milton Unbound: Controversy and Reinterpretation.* Cambridge, 1996.

• Samuels, Peggy. "Riding the Hebrew Word Web." In *Living Texts: Interpreting Milton,* ed. Kristin A. Pruitt and Charles W. Durham. Selingsgrove, Pa., 2000.

• Sanchez, Melissa E. *Erotic Subjects: The Sexuality of Politics in Early Modern English Literature.* Oxford, 2011.

Sánchez, Reuben. *Typology and Iconography in Donne, Herbert, and Milton: Fashioning the Self after Jeremiah.* New York, 2014.

Sauer, Elizabeth. *Milton, Toleration, and Nationhood.* New York, 2014.

———. *Barbarous Dissonance and Images of Voice in Milton's Epics.* Montreal and Kingston, 1996.

• Schwartz, Regina M. *Remembering and Repeating: On Milton's Theology and Poetics.* 2nd ed. Chicago, 1993.

Shawcross, John T. *John Milton and Influence: Presence in Literature, History and Culture:* Pittsburgh, 1991.

———. "A Note on the Text." In Paradise Lost: *A Poem in Twelve Books* by John Milton. Ed. John T. Shawcross. San Francisco, 2002.

Shoulson, Jeffrey S. *Milton and the Rabbis: Hebraism, Hellenism, & Christianity.* New York, 2001.

• Silver, Victoria. *Imperfect Sense: The Predicament of Milton's Irony.* Princeton, N.J., 2001.

• Smith, Nigel. *Is Milton Better than Shakespeare?* Cambridge, Mass., 2008.

———. *Literature and Revolution in England, 1640–1660.* New Haven, Conn., 1994.

Song, Eric. *Dominion Undeserved: Milton and the Perils of Creation.* Ithaca, NY, 2013.

Sprott, Ernest S. *Milton's Art of Prosody.* Oxford, 1953.

St. Hilaire, Danielle A. *Satan's Poetry: Fallenness and Poetic Tradition in* Paradise Lost. Pittsburgh, 2012.

• Stanton, Elizabeth Cady. *The Woman's Bible*, Mineola, N.Y., 2002.

• Sugimura, N. K. *"Matter of Glorious Trial": Spiritual and Material Substance in* Paradise Lost. New Haven, Conn., 2009.

Summers, Joseph. *The Muse's Method: An Introduction to* Paradise Lost. London, 1962.

Taylor, Edward W. *Milton's Poetry: Its Development in Time.* Pittsburgh, 1979.

Teskey, Gordon. *Delirious Milton: The Fate of the Poet in Modernity.* Cambridge, Mass., 2006.

———. *The Poetry of John Milton.* Cambridge, Mass., 2015.

———. "Prophecy Meets History: Frye's Blake and Frye's Milton." In *Educating the Imagination: Northrop Frye Past, Present, and Future*, ed. Alan Bewell, Neil ten Kortenaar, and Germaine Warkentin. Montreal, 2015.

Tillyard, E. M. W. *Milton.* 2nd ed. New York, 1966.

Trubowitz, Rachel. *Nation and Nurture in Seventeenth-Century English Literature.* Oxford, 2012.

Turner, James G. *One Flesh: Paradisal Marriage and Sexual Relations in the Age of Milton.* Oxford, 1987.

• Vendler, Helen. "Introduction." In Paradise Lost: *A Poem in Twelve Books*, by John Milton. Ed. John T. Shawcross. San Francisco, 2002.

von Maltzahn, Nicholas. "The First Reception of *Paradise Lost (1667)*." *Review of English Studies* 47.188: 479–99.

———. *Milton's History of Britain: Republican Historiography in the English Revolution*. Oxford: Clarendon Press, 1992.

Waldock, A. J. A. Paradise Lost *and Its Critics*. Cambridge, Mass., 1947.

• Walker, Julia M. *Medusa's Mirrors: Spenser, Shakespeare, Milton, and the Metamorphosis of the Female Self*. Newark, Del., 1998.

———. *Milton and the Idea of Woman*. Urbana Ill., 1988.

Webber, Joan. *Milton and His Epic Tradition*. Seattle, 1979.

Whittington, Leah. *Renaissance Suppliants: Poetry, Antiquity, Reconciliation*. Oxford, 2016.

• ———. "Vergil's Nisus and the Language of Self-Sacrifice in *Paradise Lost*." *Modern Philology* 107 (2010): 588–606.

• Wilburn, Reginald A. *Preaching the Gospel of Black Revolt: Appropriating Milton in Early African American Literature*. Pittsburgh, 2014.

Wittreich, Joseph A., Jr. *Feminist Milton*. Ithaca, N.Y., 1987.

———. *Milton and the Line of Vision*. Madison, Wis., 1975.

• Wollstonecraft, Mary. *A Vindication of the Rights of Woman*. 1792. Ed. Deidre Shauna Lynch. New York, 2009.

• Woodhouse, A. S. P. *The Heavenly Muse: A Preface to Milton*. Toronto, 1972.

• Woolf, Virginia. *A Writer's Diary: Being Extracts from the Diary of Virginia Woolf*. Ed. Leonard Woolf. New York, 1954.